BRYCE F. RYAN, Ph.D., Harvard University, is Professor and Chairman of the Department of Sociology and Anthropology at the University of Miami. He has also taught at Rutgers—The State University and Iowa State University. Dr. Ryan has served as President of the Southern Sociological Society.

SOCIAL AND CULTURAL CHANGE

BRYCE F. RYAN
UNIVERSITY OF MIAMI

THE RONALD PRESS COMPANY · NEW YORK

Library of Congress Catalog Card Number: 79–84081
PRINTED IN THE UNITED STATES OF AMERICA

And in this staggering disproportion between man and no-man there is no place for purely human boasts of grandeur, or for forgetting that men build their cultures by huddling together, nervously loquacious, at the edge of an abyss.

Permanence and Change, by Kenneth Burke. Revised edition, 1954. Hermes Publications, Los Altos, California.

Preface

This text is for courses dealing with the diverse forces and processes through which socio-cultural systems undergo modification or transformation. It was begun several years ago when the author was organizing his own course in this field. In an area that is so central to sociology it was disheartening to find a dearth of up-to-date general books on the sociology of change. The lack seemed particularly acute in light of the advances that had been made in our understanding of historical causation, processes of innovation and diffusion, and a number of other areas that fall conceptually and historically within the realm of sociology.

This book also endeavors to reflect the extraordinary recent growth of structural and functional theory and associated research on change, together with the dramatic reawakening of concern in evolutionary processes and sequences as the transformations in underdeveloped countries have restimulated interests in problems of linear societal trends. Further, the directions of change in American society have perhaps never been more fervently debated. A comprehensive text, which this book aims to be, seems more necessary than ever before.

The approach here is eclectic: the very diversity of sociological orientations to problems of change practically precludes the adoption of any particular theoretical premise. It is unlikely that even such major contemporary approaches as those of technological diffusion, social movements, and stress–strain models, let alone theories of dynamics, can be brought into a single comprehensive theoretical scheme. Yet these are but a few of the approaches to change which are a living part of the discipline of sociology. This book therefore attempts to show how various sociological theories, concepts, and research findings are applied to understanding the phenomena of change. The basic assumption of this book is that undergraduates who are consistently exposed to the more adequately developed structural approaches to society also deserve systematic introductory exposure to theories and research as these relate to the dynamics and temporally processual phases of social life.

I am deeply grateful to various professors who attempted to teach me something about social change, particularly Carle C. Zimmerman,

Pitirim Sorokin, Warner E. Gettys, T. Lynn Smith, and Clarence E. Ayres. To many colleagues with whom the problems of change have been discussed, my sincere thanks. Outstanding among these persons are C. Arnold Anderson and Aaron Lipman, to each of whom my appreciation and debt is great indeed. Both Professor Anderson and Professor Lipman read the entire manuscript at various stages and offered cogent criticisms and suggestions. I am most grateful also to John W. Milstead and Marlene Stefanow Milstead for their valued suggestions, particularly in reference to social and demographic trends. To the staff of the University of Miami's Otto G. Richter Library, my sincere thanks for their excellent services and inexhaustible patience.

BRYCE F. RYAN

Coral Gables, Florida
August, 1969

Contents

SOCIAL AND
CULTURAL CHANGE

1

Introduction

For man, the die was cast for change when that ultimate ancestor opted for life on the ground as an erect, walking animal. Man, the self-builder of his group structures, the self-domesticator, and the creator of his own technologies, contrasts most sharply with all other animals in this capacity to modify his patterns of life through mindful effort. Change is a permanent feature of man's social life. This is perhaps the most pervasive and universal of all possible generalizations regarding society. Human beings cannot be termites with a millennially stable social structure identically replaced by each generation, nor can human beings retain the distinctive meaning of *human* and simply mill through life in trance or in robot-like, will-less regimentation. Whether produced as a Utopia or as a *Nineteen Eighty-Four*, a condition of changelessness would make man something less than human. The whole weight of knowledge in modern social science pushes toward the conclusion that social change is one thing that is here to stay.

TOWARD A DEFINITION OF SOCIAL CHANGE

Social change arises when the relationships among persons or groups are modified. Alvin Boskoff stated this as a definition when he wrote that: "Social change refers to the intelligible process in which we can discover significant alterations in the structure and functioning of determinate social systems" (p. 263).*

* Published works which are referred to in the text, or are closely relevant to the topic discussed, are listed at the end of the book. The citation in parentheses shows the author, if this is not specified in the preceding sentence, and the page or chapter of the reference if required. Where several works by the same author are cited, the date of publication will identify the particular one to which reference is made. If further identification is necessary, the date is followed by a letter, e.g., 1965a.

3

A key term here, as Boskoff points out, is *significant alterations*. By this is meant variations that have novel consequences for the social system being studied. Novelty alone, whether in thought, action, or material, does not constitute social change. Change occurs only when novelty alters the patterned system through which a group functions, either in its internal life or in reference to external realities.

This conception of social change includes matters of great and small public significance. If we are dealing with the interpersonal relations of two individuals and find that their interaction once described as one of emotional warmth and sharing must now be described in terms of impersonality, then social change has occurred in that system of relationships. Also within our conception would be the rise of capitalism, the achievement of civil rights for Negroes, and the reduction of family functions in modern city life. We cannot deal fruitfully with such a vast range of realities without setting boundaries to the areas under discussion and establishing concepts to express common elements in seemingly unlike series of events. The larger part of this book is devoted to the analysis of the processes of change which in varying combinations and contexts operate in any and all concrete cases. Our concern is with processes more than with the specific content of change.

Having accepted a conception of social change broad enough to include the rise of a once meek housewife to dominance over her husband as well as the vast shifts associated with urbanism, we must distinguish changing social relationships as such from *social change*. Social change always arises in reference to some established pattern in social relationships. Many continuing relationships have patterned modifications in behavior built in as part of their established plan for operating. When a boy and a girl meet, fall in love, and get married this sequence of events entails substantial change in their social relationships from the stage of boy-meets-girl to that of a householding husband and wife. However, from the standpoint of one seeking evidence of change in the American marriage system, this whole sequence of events becomes a datum without necessary significance. We would have to find out if the particular sequence of events fits into an established pattern. As described here it would seem to imply social stability in the American marriage system rather than change. Yet the changes in interpersonal relations for the young people concerned are very real.

There is also the question of how persisting a modification must be in order to qualify as a change. Permanence is as relative a matter as is the degree to which the novel is truly new. However, in so far as new qualities arise in patterned relationships, or novel patterns of relationships are established, these represent social change whether they are long-lasting or short. An analyst of change would overlook short-range changes at considerable peril. Temporary changes may have relevance for the group's future even though the particular change at hand does not persist.

Of the short-range transitory changes there is one type—collective behavior—which is border-line but of importance to social and cultural change. Collective behavior is social behavior occurring in situations which are not firmly structured or patterned. Since the situation is not clearly prepatterned in terms of behavioral expectations and organizational structure, spontaneous actions are likely to arise. Some of the familiar forms of collective behavior include crowd behavior, panics, fads, crazes, and mass hallucinations. These may or may not be social change. The fad of the long-haired adolescent male is not social change in itself. But if it is associated with a modified relationship of adults and teenagers, or modified concepts of sex statuses and sex roles, it then becomes part of the data manifesting new sorts of patterned relationships. Similarly, the bank "runs" in the 1930's were not in themselves social change, but in historic fact these panics were part of the process through which the structure of the American banking system was revised. Frequently however, such immediate events have only transitory significance, the groups soon returning to something like the old equilibrium.

Our most serious concern with collective behavior in social change is as it manifests unrest and dissatisfactions to support or to resist change in the structure of the group. Out of such collective behavior social movements may arise which persist as organized pressures for or against change in structured social relationships. Collective behavior is not social change unless it results in new kinds of social relationships. In subsequent chapters attention will be given collective behavior primarily as it arises in the kind of social change pressed by social movements.

THE CONCEPT OF THE SOCIAL SYSTEM

Social change occurs within or with reference to systems of interaction (Parsons; Loomis, Essay 1). In other words, "something novel" arises in the manner through which members of a group function together, or in the way one group functions in relation to another group. In the latter instance we have considered the two different groups *in their relationships* as forming a single, articulated, complex system. The term "social system" is frequently used in reference to a group to connote the presence of structure or organization and persistence in the patterned inter-relationships of the persons involved. There is, of course, no reason why the term cannot be expanded to include systems composed of systems. Such complex or associational type systems may range from the social structure of an orchestra with its precisely organized sections brought into high level, coordinate functioning, to the total community, or to the nation as a social system with a multitude of constituent social systems integrated in ways which are often vague and imprecise.

All social systems are held together by a generally agreed upon structure in which group goals, norms of conduct, statuses and roles, and other matters essential to group persistence are understood. When a sociologist describes the structure of a group, he is attempting to give an accurate cross-sectional view of what is actually a living and on-going system of relationships. To describe structure, one acts as if the group were frozen in the time dimension. Spontaneous actions which arise in the relationships of members are taken into account through statements of the general pattern expressed by these relationships. Daily fluctuations in behavior, as well as infrequent but recurrent events which are part of the group's stable, and continuing, organized life, must also be recognized in generalizations. Thus, from the standpoint of students in a university, an examination or a holiday may seem a change from attending lectures, but from the standpoint of the university as a social structure, examinations and holidays are stable and recurring facts. These activities are inherent to the structure of the university as an on-going social system.

When we speak of the American family system, or of a feudal or of a parliamentary system, we are no longer referring to specific groups of individuals operating in a bounded network of interaction. Yet we do not hesitate to refer to entities like these, often calling them institutions and offering generalizations about their structures and their changes. Reference to *the* American family system would imply that there are generalizable features about American families conceived as a whole. The American family is an abstraction derived from the analysis of the real family life of some 200 million Americans. We can and do discuss *the* American family on the basis of census material, court records, vital statistics, and innumerable research inquiries. Out of these diverse data are drawn carefully qualified conclusions regarding the structure and functioning of the American family. Constructs like the American family might be called *analytical systems,* in contrast to concrete, living groups which are *real systems.*

Whereas the structure of a real system is determined by repeated observations, we determine the structure of an analytical system by the observation of many different constituent real systems. If we were to generalize as to the structure of the Nixon family who live on Pennsylvania Avenue we would make numerous observations of that family and then, following some plan of structural analysis, describe that family in terms of its authority patterns, role structure, norms, etc. (We may gain some view of change in that family by a subsequent series of life observations which are comparable to the first series, e.g., changes in the role relationships after moving from the Pennsylvania Avenue address.)

When we generalize as to the structure of *the* American family we use a telescopic view rather than repeated microscopic observations. Now the Nixon family is seen as one out of many which, we suggest, belong to the same general type—once we strip them of idiosyncrasies and the effects of different stages in the family cycle, etc. When we deal with change in such analytical systems, commonly called social institutions, *social trends* are discernible insofar as a significant number of real social groups have modified their structure. When we refer to the "emancipation of women" or the "small family pattern" or the shift of the family from "institution to companionship," we are referring to coherent change patterns created by numerous real groups responding similarly to similar pressures. The search for institutional and societal patterns in change is considerably more complex and hazardous than is the determination of difference between two descriptive accounts of a real group at different points in time. Of course the analysis of social change processes involves much more than the comparison of "structural snapshots" taken at different points in time.

SOCIAL CHANGE AND CULTURAL CHANGE

"Group," "society," and "social" are all terms pertaining to inter-relationships among people. All denote man interacting with other men. *Culture* on the other hand has no such meaning. Culture refers to the *creations* of interacting men. Societies are large, reproducing social units composed of a variety of sub-groups such as families, work groups, play groups, communities, religious groups, etc. Cultures do not have groups as their component parts. A culture is composed of "things" not interacting people. The "things" which compose culture would include norms, symbolic meanings as in language, technologies and artifacts, concepts of good and evil, the meaning of life, and the understandings of science. The concept of culture relates to the body of knowledge and technique and values through which a society directs and expresses its life as an interacting, functioning group entity.

It seems clear that a great number of changes frequently discussed are cultural rather than social. The development of nuclear fission is in the realm of new knowledge and new technology. It is not a development within the realm of social relationships, hence it exemplifies cultural rather than social change. So also does the development and use of computers, space ships, underarm deodorants, and atomic war-heads. One may insist, however, that each of these sets of changes has significance for modified social relations. That may well be so. But the significance of each of these cultural changes for social life is something to be demonstrated; it is not intrinsic to the trait under discussion. These are all changes in man's creations, and in these particular instances, in the implements through which he meets nature and through which he meets other men. Automation, atomic war-heads, and spray-on deodorants all have potential impact upon the relationships of individuals, or groups, to each other. This is to say that cultural changes may be an impelling force toward social change, an idea which is evident, for example, in contemporary concern over the adjustment of developing nations to the impact of factories and machines.

Cultural change may lead to social change by more subtle processes as well. Values, laws, customs, and moral precepts are no less cultural creations than is technology. Where people are converted to novel values, or develop novel precepts of moral conduct, recognized inconsistencies between social behavior and avowed cultural standards may also impel adjustive reaction. Civil rights legislation, for example, is to be viewed as a cultural phenomenon. However, it is a creation produced for the explicit purpose of affecting the way in which members of a society actually relate to one another. While the new bill may or may not influence psychological realities like prejudice, it certainly has modified social realities such as racially discriminatory behavior in restaurants and in universities.

It is apparent that members of a society must interact with reference to the tools, knowledge, and precepts present in their culture. Neither society nor culture can exist without the other. Out of society comes culture. Out of culture comes the plan and the knowledge whereby the society functions, orders, and maintains itself. When in illustrating the impact of culture on society we show how a new set of legal norms changes social relations, we must not forget that those legal norms were forged through the long and often painful interaction of people. New norms arise when old norms no longer yield orderly or palatable guides to conduct. Society is not a passive body responding to the impositions of its culture. Society holds the creative forces but these are forces restrained, guided, and facilitated by the society's cultural environment.

We shall refer to change as *cultural* when an emphasis is desired upon change as a modification of the body of knowledge of a people or their tools, or their idealized patterns in contrast to the actuality of their behavior. The term *social change* will be applied when emphasis is upon modifications in interaction, as in novel response to role expectations, or in the formation of social movements. In a good many instances the two concepts will be fused into the term *socio-cultural change* when nothing is to be gained by distinguishing the social from the cultural. When we speak of established patterns in social interaction, we are discussing a matter which is *cultural* if emphasis is to be placed on the normative precepts governing the conduct and *social* if emphasis is on the fact that human personalities are responding each to the stimuli of the various others.

SOCIOLOGICAL APPROACHES TO THE STUDY OF CHANGE

The field of social change has lacked a cohesive body of concepts and theory since the collapse of the grandiose but sadly deficient social and cultural evolutionary theories which bloomed in the later years of the nineteenth century (Martindale, Chap. 1). To some extent the immature state of contemporary theory in reference to change has been due to a greater interest in persistence than in change of social structures. But it is also true that among scholars concerned with change, the field has been so variously defined, and conceived upon such vastly different scales, as to make a common ground difficult to achieve. Broadly the scholarly interests of sociologists in the phenomena of change can be grouped in three categories: (1) analysis of dynamic and causal forces giving rise to social and cultural change, (2) analysis of the processes of change within social systems, and (3) analysis of the transformation or evolution of social systems, especially in regard to historical stages and trends in institutions and in society generally. In modern times, by far the greatest research interest has been shown in the second category although there is today a reawakening of interest in problems of historical direction and evolution.

This book is organized with reference to these three orientations. Part I deals with problems of causation and dynamic forces underlying change; Part II analyzes the various processes through which change proceeds in social systems; Part III is devoted to social trends and evolutionary processes. The remainder of this present chapter introduces briefly each of these major sociological orientations to the study of change.

Dynamic and Causal Forces

The problem of causation of change has frequently been posed in large-scale theories addressed to the "reasons" behind the rise and fall of civilizations. Many theories of this type posit "prime movers" behind institutional and societal changes. For some years the study of change dynamics was dominated by an evolutionary theory in which "progress" in civilization occurred as the natural product of competitive struggle and the "survival of the fittest." Others have sought the prime mover of the historical process in forces of the natural environment, particularly climate, and still others in biological factors of innate genius or in racially founded creativity.

Few contemporary sociologists pay serious attention to theories which attribute change in society to the extrinsic forces of nature, either biological or environmental. However, the search for societal prime movers is not dead. During the past generation substantial attention has been given theories of change assigning priority and dynamic power to various elements in culture. Most influential of these theories have been those crediting "material culture"—especially technology or energy and its utilization—with determinate power. In these, it is generally accepted that man's social life is modified in adaptation to the demands and potentials inherent in his productive cultural equipment and related techniques. Frequently this orientation has also been followed in small-scale researches attempting to show the social impact of particular inventions.

In contrast to the materialist, technological, and energy theories of dynamics are the teleological and the ideological. Social teleology assumes that through the power of mind man can establish societal goals and approach them through willful planning and action. Ideological theories of change causation attempt to show how specific belief systems have led to changes in social structure and culture. Many of these theories do not claim universality in their application. That is, they are intended to apply only to a particular civilization or some specific institution which, it is argued, has been produced through the introduction of a specific belief system. Additionally, there are theories, some implied and some highly systematized, which would credit social change to special categories of people, such as a distinctive type of elite, or the "socially disenchanted." In some manifestations these theories also seek to explain "social progress" generally, while in others they are applied on a small scale toward understanding a limited historical period in a particular society.

Testing universal theories of historical dynamics has proved an extremely difficult and unsatisfactory undertaking. Modern sociology has largely abandoned a quest for *the* cause of all great changes in institutions or total societies. It has, furthermore, largely avoided the assumption that simple cause and effect sequences are to be found. This does not mean that prediction in the realm of change has ceased to be an ultimate goal, but rather that we are now better sensitized to the complexities of social dynamics. Also, in the past generation, sociologists have, for various reasons, expended more effort on understanding how social systems "hold together" and function than upon how their structures undergo change.

In recent years, the problems of causation and dynamics have received renewed attention. There is, however, no tendency to revert to older conceptions of universal "prime movers," i.e., singular causal forces. The question once posed as, "What causes change in society?" is rarely asked today. Better questions, questions more consistent with the real complexities of social life, have been substituted. Instead of "What causes change?" contemporary sociologists are more likely to ask, "What are the structured *conditions* under which certain types of innovations arise? Through what processes is novelty communicated and spread? What are the qualities of social systems which facilitate or retard changes of particular types?" In responding to questions such as these, there is no assumption made regarding causation in the sense of a final or of a universal cause. If cause is to be sought for change, it is to be found through the analysis of the conditions and processes giving rise to the particular sequence of events. A science of social change must be built upon the foundations of innumerable and varied inductive studies.

Processes of Change Within the Social System

Innovation. Social systems are to be conceived not only as organizational structures but as fields of tension in which dissatisfactions are perceived, and amelioration or improvement is contemplated. Social and cultural change occurs when novel patterns of thought or action arise in the organization of a group or its culture. The appearance of novelty *is* innovation.

Innovation comes into being through two different processes. It may come about through inventing, or it may arise through the very interaction of people as they respond to each other's stimuli and expectations. Inventing involves the rearrangement of existing ideas into a novel and meaningful pattern. An *invention* is an *emergent*, a novelty created through a convergence of separate items of knowledge. The emerging novelty is thence an object for response by people. Inventive configurations of ideas may be represented in physical contrivances such as harpoons, sling shots, and space capsules. They may also take form in works of art, mathematical formulae, in social inventions like the United Nations Organization, or in purely ideational constructs such as a concept of sin. All of these arise as products of the manipulation of ideas. All are inventions.

Quite different is the genesis of novelty through social interaction. This innovative process is sometimes referred to as *immanent change* implying that the change is generated within the relationship itself rather than in response to some outside stimulus such as an invention. Social change through interaction is an unfolding, as interacting persons create a sequence of stimulus-response relationships which deviate from established patterns to culminate in a modified structure for their relationship. Of course, if we were all perfectly regimented robots our responses to every social stimulus would conform narrowly and rigidly to some overall design. In fact, no human society is so rigidified, and human beings respond to each other with some degree of spontaneity and individuality. They vary within the limits prescribed for them as proper or normative behavior, and they also deviate beyond those prescribed limits. When such spontaneity or deviance is unique and was not to have been expected through a knowledge of the cultural prescriptions set up to guide the individual, such behavior is innovative. (People may value it in terms ranging from "heroic" to "way out" to "immoral" or "criminal"—the social significance of the deviation is another matter.) Probably most innovations arising in interaction are of no serious significance for social change. They involve sporadic idiosyncratic or "offbeat" responses. In this, no doubt, they are like inventions since most novel idea configurations are probably "bright ideas" of no great social significance.

The Spread of Innovation. Diffusion is the process through which inventions are communicated from the originating source to a recipient. Although diffusion is sometimes called "cultural borrowing," it is more precisely the communicating or "spreading abroad" of novelty. It may occur within a single group as knowledge of a new invention spreads or it may occur between groups as a cultural item possessed by one is communicated to another. From the standpoint of the donor group, the item may be a traditional one but from the standpoint of the recipient, diffusion always involves innovation. Ordinarily some classes of communication of novel ideas are set outside the diffusion process. We do not ordinarily consider the transmission of knowledge from one generation to the next as being diffusion.

Robert MacIver has drawn a distinction between innovations which are spread through *distributive* process and those spread through *collective action* (pp. 302 ff.). The distributive process is implicit in our concept of diffusion, as separate individuals in pursuit of personal ends respond approvingly to an invention. Examples of such separate but similar "responses" are evident in the spread of television sets, jet planes, lawn mowers, and sewing machines. In collective action, people as a group act toward the innovation. Change is pursued as a common goal rather than as a set of similar but private objectives. Social movements frequently arise where innovations are seen in collective terms, e.g., movements for civil rights legislation, movements to "ban the bomb," etc. It is evident that distributive diffusions are sometimes supported or retarded by associated collective actions. For example, the spread of contraceptive devices is largely a matter of distributive diffusion. However, this diffusion is supported and facilitated through the planned parenthood movement, whose collective goal can be attained only through the individual decisions of millions of persons not members of that movement.

Whether or not a novel design or action develops toward social change rests in the reception given it by potential adopters or respondents. This is true whether one acts as an acceptor or rejector of an invention or whether one responds in an aggressive, withdrawing, or other manner to someone's deviant behavior. The respondent must assess the novelty and act in reference to it if innovation is to move on toward social change. Robert MacIver viewed this evaluation process as the very starting point of social change, and to emphasize its action significance he coined for it the phrase *dynamic assessment* (pp. 293–294).

The Integration of Innovations.   Whether a novel design is created by invention or through interaction, it constitutes socio-cultural change only as it is fitted into the on-going life of the group. No social system is a mere dumping ground holding unrelated persons and disparate cultural ideas and implements. Every living group requires some integration in the behavior of its members and some consistencies among its cultural elements. The analogy of the group with the organism is commonly drawn to illustrate how parts are coordinated with other parts and all function together through continuing life processes. Much as the organism is not static but is undergoing constant modification while maintaining its identity, so, it is said, does society maintain an identity while functioning through time. In terms of contemporary sociological theory, the elements of the social system persist in a state of dynamic equilibrium. At a crude level this may be illustrated by the fact that technological skills must be integrated with the structure of the artifacts in use, if the group is to function and persist effectively. If the plow replaces the hoe, the farmer must accordingly change his patterned skills, if the land is to be cultivated. The modification of either skill or artifact sets up stress which is evidenced in malfunctioning. Presumably a group seeking perpetuation would be concerned with maintaining a moving balance between changes in artifacts and in the skills whereby they are used.

There are various routes whereby the group can merge an innovation into their persisting way of life, but no invention is ever adopted without some further adjustive innovations being touched off. If a diffusing trait were a perfect substitute for an existing one, it would require no adjustments, but as a *perfect* substitute it would be merely a replication of the other. Novelties invariably have functional significance not present in established cultural traits. Substitute traits are never simply substitutes and nothing more, although some (like the introduction of a new brand of cigarettes) may have very little adjustive consequence. The processes through which novelties are digested so that they become part of a smoothly working system are varied. They may entail simple mechanical adjustments as in the illustration of the artifact and the skill or they may involve subtle re-definitions of value systems toward a logical consistency, or perhaps combinations of these and still more complex integrative processes.

Sequential Patterns in Change Processes. To list various processes of change in social systems does violence to the complex inter-relationships and feedbacks among these processes. Neil Smelser has presented what amounts to a "natural history" of social change in his work *Social Change in the Industrial Revolution* (pp. 32–40). Although he claimed no extension of this scheme beyond his own research findings, it clearly has wide applicability. In the following pages, his seven-stage paradigm has been telescoped into five stages. It should be remembered that these stages are not separate and discrete. Nonetheless, Smelser's scheme plunges us into the realization that change within social systems proceeds through time by means of specific complexes of inter-related processes.

Stage 1. Dissatisfaction. Arising from the operation of the established social system is a feeling that all is not well or is not as well as it might be. That someone has such a feeling would seem to be *sine qua non* for social change. If an existing system were visualized by its members as being perfect, change then could arise only as the direct result of forces beyond the control of the members. Thus a people's level of living might deteriorate due to loss of natural resources, but if the legend of societal perfection remained intact the society would presumably prefer to perish than to switch. Such states of affairs do not arise, since the value of societal survival, when threat is fully perceived, usually takes precedence at some point. Normally the roots of dissatisfaction are vaguely understood, and often the dissatisfactions are little more than a sense of uneasiness in a present patterning, a latent receptiveness to change. Disquieting perceptions may even arise only after something novel is presented for evaluation, perhaps through diffusion. It may well have been that no one had previously shown dissatisfaction since before this time no sense of potential improvability existed.

Stage 2. Manifest Unrest. Following upon Stage 1 in which improvement of a situation is desired, Stage 2 is one of overt unrest in regard to that persisting situation. Such unrest can stimulate emotional contagion and possibly concerted action or it may remain at the level of distributed manifestations of anxiety, and of aspirations inharmonious with the status quo. Smelser has used the terms "unjustified" and "unrealistic" to describe behavior at this stage. By this he means that behavior aimed toward correcting or toward changing institutions is at this point likely to be either misdirected or undirected in its efforts (p. 39).

The rioting which followed the introduction of textile machinery in the English Midlands during the early decades of the nineteenth century is a classic example of this stage in social change (pp. 254–264). Already impoverished hand workers perceived textile manufacturing devices such as the fly-shuttle and mule as dire threats to their jobs and to the continued existence of the family as a work unit as well. Response to these acute dissatisfactions took many, and often unrealistic, forms. There were pleas for programs of direct financial aid, utopian schemes were proposed, and movements arose to destroy machines. During the depressed period 1825–26, frightened and angry handloom weavers joined in bands which roamed the countryside destroying some 1,000 power looms and at times clashing with the military.

Stage 3. The Search for and Assessment of Solutions. Anxieties and disturbances are at once threats to the established order and stimulative of modification. The forces of the status quo impose controls upon disturbances which threaten orderliness but find it expedient to consider ways and means of preserving social values and structural continuity in the face of threat. At this point there are stimuli to inventors, "trial balloons" are sent up, meetings are called to hammer out innovative compromises, and even revolutionary plots may be hatched. Frequently it is a stage of trial and error in search of new patterns which are both acceptable and workable. These can range from retreatism to drastic redefinitions of group or institutional structure. On a large scale entrance to this stage is currently evidenced in regard to the indecision and the plethora of proposed schemes which would abate the blight, misery, and crime in America's central cities. Although disturbances continue, innovations are rife, but we are not yet sure just which ones will prove useful and acceptable.

Stage 4. Formalization of Patterns. The schemes and inventions arising in Stage 3, working toward the resolution of dissatisfaction have to undergo the tests of practical application. Novel plans are subjected to critical revision through the test of consequences. Certain of them fall by the wayside and others are generally accepted, refined, and diffused. The surviving patterns may or may not be the most effective of all those which have arisen in the earlier exploratory stage, but they are the patterns which were capable of achieving public acceptance. At this point specialized agencies operate with regard to the proposals, working toward their refinement and their spread.

The stage of formalization is illustrated in the United States by the status of programs for the welfare of aged persons. Although many alternative schemes for handling the problems of retired individuals in an individualistic society began to be proposed a few decades ago, the United States now seems to be building a consistent core of viable programs. While many of the current innovations are still challenged by a vocal minority, the federal pension system and medical care, low cost housing, and other public and private welfare programs are either in existence or in process of formation. The right of the elderly to a decent life is close to becoming part of the American creed, and specialized agencies both official and unofficial work vigorously toward stronger and more diversified programs. Public responsibility for the welfare of the aged has now almost passed into Stage 5.

Stage 5. Legitimation and Institutionalization. As novel patterns gain a place of established acceptance they become legitimate parts of the social order—the final stage. It might be said that the variant novelty has now become institutionalized within the "cake of custom." Harry M. Johnson has observed that "institutionalized expectations are rights (p. 638)." To say that novelty is "legitimated" is to emphasize its acceptance by society within the normative order. To say that novelty is "institutionalized" is to emphasize its solidification within the normative order and the growth of supporting organizations, rituals, and ideologies, all of which render it the more impermeable to subsequent change. This does not mean that controversy ends but rather that it changes its character. Proposed modifications no longer challenge the very existence of the novelty.

Examples of innovations which have achieved institutionalization abound. The movement toward the emancipation and equality of women carried with it many innovations which are now firm parts of our social order. The fully respected rights of women to vote and to pursue professional careers culminated a change process which had hardly begun by the middle of the last century. The Women's Suffrage Movement in the United States did not gain its objective until 1920. Yet the emancipation of women from a traditional subservient status has now reached such a stage that Russell Lynes can entitle his delightful essay on husbands, "The New Servant Class."

Evolution of Social Systems

Many roots of sociology as a discipline lie in the effort to unravel the "meaning" of history and to establish laws regarding the growth of civilization. Such grand conceptions of the task of sociology were evident in nineteenth-century evolutionary theory and related doctrines of social progress. Auguste Comte, who gave sociology its name, saw a progression in society from an early stage of superstition toward the heights of a civilization to be guided by the scientific laws of change. A few years later Herbert Spencer asserted his famous formula of evolutionary process, i.e., progression from a stage of homogeneity and instability toward increasing heterogeneity and stability, and posited "the struggle for existence" as the dynamic force behind progression. The later nineteenth century was sociologically dominated by pretentious theories, many of which combined change dynamics with ideas on the nature of historical trends and the direction in which civilization is moving.

Antedating linear theories, but eclipsed by them in the evolutionary zeal of the nineteenth century, have been numerous cyclical schemes showing that history is a repetition of the cycles of birth, youth, maturity, and death, in successive societies or civilizations. These cyclical theories have usually visualized historical development as analogous to the life cycle of an organism. Elements of linear theory are frequently combined with cyclical ideas as the birth of a new civilization is found in the graveyard of its predecessor.

Although nineteenth-century change theory in sociology was not strictly limited to theories of the grand sweep of history, the problems of social change were generally conceived in this manner. Such grandiose theorizing largely circumvented middle-range research and generalizing, placing, as it did, little emphasis on direct, inductive studies of change in specific groups. Reactions from the insufficiencies and errors in evolutionary theories stimulated a retreat from grand theories of evolutionary process and, indeed, a movement away from historical perspective generally. The inductive study of relationships within social systems at a given point in time superseded concern with sequential and temporal relationships in the transformation of social systems. In the general shift of sociology and anthropology toward structural and functional interests, there remained a few scholars continuing the theoretical traditions of the evolutionists and the cyclists. Professor Leslie White at the University of Michigan remained at the core of a small group keeping alive the evolutionary orientations of the American anthropologist Lewis Henry Morgan. Pitirim Sorokin in sociology, much as historian Arnold Toynbee, developed cyclical theories of the grand panorama of history. More numerous contemporaries continued to build upon theories of historical direction associated with earlier scholars, particularly Ferdinand Tönnies, Emile Durkheim, and Henry Sumner Maine.

In the past decade, there has been a crescendo of self-criticism in sociology and in anthropology for failure of these disciplines to address themselves more vigorously to the historical processes and patterns of change in society. The term "social evolution," so recently a virtual synonym for grandiose and biased viewpoints, is creeping back into use. Historical sociologists long interested in the transformation and institutionalization of patterns of interaction, have become more articulate. Even some of those who derided evolutionary perspectives thirty years earlier are confessing need for a return to the study of directional patterning in change and the processes of transformation of social systems. This renewed focus has gained substantially from the interests of social scientists in newly developing nations which appear to follow patterns similar to, but far from identical with, those once followed in Western Europe in the rise of Western, urban, and industrial civilization.

CONCLUSION

Every social system persists through a balance of forces toward stability and forces toward innovation. Social change occurs when social systems are significantly altered in regard to their structure and functioning. Social systems are of two types: real systems and analytical systems. Real systems are structured, interacting groups. Analytical systems are generalizations or models based upon the analysis of constituent real systems. In the study of institutional and societal changes modifications in constituent real systems provide data for conclusions regarding changes at the institutional and societal levels.

Social change is distinguished from cultural change as the interactions of men are distinguished from the crystallized designs in reference to which their interaction is patterned. Frequently, in this book the term *socio-cultural* will be used when no distinction or emphasis is useful.

Sociology approaches the study of change at several different levels or orientations. These are the study of change in terms of: (1) dynamics or causation, (2) the constituent processes in change within social systems from innovation to the institutionalization of novelty, (3) the historical patterning, or evolutionary processes, through which institutions and societies go.

This book is organized so that Part I deals with change causation, Part II deals with processes of change within the social system, and Part III deals with evolutionary trends and social development.

1

CAUSES AND CONDITIONS OF CHANGE

2

Theories of Causation in Socio-Cultural Change

A perennial question haunting historians and social thinkers through the ages has been why some times and places have known rapid change and others have been close to static. (For diffusionist theories see Chap. 6.) The question is posed in many dimensions: What caused the "fall" of Rome? What forces yield modernization in underdeveloped regions? Why did an industrial civilization arise in Europe rather than in Asia or Africa? Thoughtful answers to such problems range in dynamics from a mystic and inscrutable destiny to causally indeterminate analyses.

In this chapter we will first consider several theoretic points of view which assign dynamic force to certain prime movers. Such theories are *deterministic* in that they assume the existence of direct cause and effect relationships in historic sequences and they are *particularistic* in assigning dynamic or causal significance to a single variable or to some closely related set of variables. As will be noted, some of these theories have been intended to explain all major societal changes on the basis of a single set of variables, while others have more limited scope seeking to explain changes within a specific institution or in some limited historical period. Where causal ideas form parts of larger theories of social change, that fact will be noted but no attempt will be made at this point to present those theories as they extend into the problems of sequence and relationships in continuing social evolution or development. The second part of this chapter will deal with the movement of modern sociology away from particularistic and deterministic views of change causation. Here attention will be given the functional approach to social change and the inter-

21

actionist approach, especially in the revival of a conflict theory of social dynamics.

DETERMINISTIC AND PARTICULARISTIC THEORIES

Theories Emphasizing Natural Forces

The interaction between the human being and the natural environment has been a familiar starting point for theories over many centuries. For some scholars the dynamic force is placed upon man's insatiable inborn quest to know and to do, while in others the dynamic force rests in natural, environmental conditions such as climate. From each of these basic positions a vast range of theorizing grew, to include on the one hand "racial determinism," and "climatic determinism" on the other. Contemporary scholars, however, rarely view the "rise of civilization," or any social changes for that matter, as due to some particular universal causal force. Mainly these naturalistic theories have historic interest except that they are supported in some brands of popular thinking.

Geographic Environment as a Force in Change. As any good text on the history of sociological or ethnological theory will demonstrate, geographical explanations of change can be traced from the writings of the ancient Greeks, or earlier, on into the twentieth century. Jean Bodin (1530–1596) probably set the base for modern writers in this vein. He minutely characterized the various peoples of whom he knew, relating their qualities, abilities, and vices to geographic forces, especially climatic ones (p. 356). Peoples of the South he found to be destined for philosophical accomplishment and those of the North for manual arts and war. Those of mid-latitudes, Bodin believed, have been the founders of great nations and empires and expanders of trade.

From the sixteenth century onward it was popular to link various geographic conditions with styles of life and differences in temperament. Such enterprise was almost inevitably transformed into geographic theories of social change. These range from the simple emphasis upon geographic factors as they *influence* and limit the growth of cultures to outright deterministic theories rooted upon one or more variables in the natural environment.

In the earlier years of this century, two related theories of climate and the rise of civilization vied. On the one hand, history was so read as to support the "equatorial drift" of civilization and on the other to support the "northward trend of civilization" (Gilfillan 1920). This evident contradiction was reconciled in the view that while progress occurs under the stimulation of reasonably cold climate, ultimately the hardy creators of the high civilization suffer disenchantment and drift southward carrying along their cultural vigor. Although the "equatorial drift" theory succeeded in plugging up some serious holes in the "northward trend" theory, its supporters never quite got around to explaining how the climatically stirred leaders of the North permitted their high cultures to get out of hand nor how such leadership retained its vigor under the benign southern influences.

A zenith in climatic theories of social change was reached in the works of Ellsworth Huntington, especially in his *Civilization and Climate* published in 1924. For a generation Huntington led a vocal school of social change theorists which sought clues to the rise and fall of civilizations through the study of climatic distributions and changes. These theories were founded on the premise that climate is decisive for human health and mental vigor. Since the growth of a civilization is said to rest directly upon the energy and mental efficiency of a population, pulsations in climate are the decisive forces in the progress or regress of civilizations.

Myriad variations have been given geographically deterministic theories, one now emphasizing natural resources and another climate or some other factor of man's ecological milieu. In general the determinative claims of such theories are disrupted by the historic fact that in identical geographical circumstances some ages have witnessed the preservation of "primitive cultures" and others the rise of great civilizations. Centers of civilizational dominance have shifted bewilderingly from a strict geographic standpoint.

By the mid-twentieth century it is improbable that climatic or other geographically deterministic theories have much more than antiquarian value among social scientists. The grievous errors in logic and in statistical method, as well as the highly selective choice of historical data, have long since reduced the "drift" theories along with "climatic pulsations" to the status of historical curiosities. The misuse of historical data in such theories becomes apparent if we consider for a moment the plausibility that the shift in world power from Spain to England took place because England was north of Spain or that the dominance of the Baganda in contrast to the Hottentots occurred because they too were northerners albeit closer to the equator.

Despite the overwhelming rejection of these monistic theories among historians and social scientists alike, some of the essential ideas in them have had great persistence. In Arnold Toynbee's theory of history, the central principle in the rise of civilizations is close to one argued frequently and inconclusively by geographic determinists. Toynbee finds civilizations rising when reasonable challenges are placed upon them by their environment—natural and social. He pursues the quest for that same well-spring of change which has dominated the geographic determinists for generations. Like them he discovered that "moderate adversity" is "just right" for the growth of cultures; "too little" or "too much" adversity cannot give proper stimulation. With vague concepts of what constitutes a civilization and an elastic definition and measurement of "challenge," the thesis is more or less true—and almost totally unhelpful in its imprecision. Why did the Indus Valley provide optimum challenges to man in 2000 B.C. or the Peruvian Andes in the fifteenth century A.D.—but not, apparently, a few thousand years later in the case of the Indus Valley and a few hundred years later in the case of Peru? And what utterly different challenges man has encountered and responded to in the arid plains of the Indus and in the alpine heights of South America. Toynbee's more fertile ideas arise in regard to development processes in history rather than in the vague "challenge and response" theory.

Biological Nature of Man as a Force for Change. The search for the source of change in the nature of man himself has at least as long a history as the search for prime movers in natural forces external to him. Such explanations have ranged from the nature of "man's indomitable soul" to racial interpretations of history. Broadly biological theories of change dynamics are divided into four groups: (1) those in which change is referred to some instinctive attribute of man in general, (2) theories which refer change to individual natural genius, (3) theories which attribute dynamic force to the nature of particular categories of mankind, especially racial categories, and (4) demographic theories of fecundity emphasizing reproductive vitality and degeneration.

INSTINCTS. Instinctivist theories of change are scarcely to be taken seriously in modern social science. Such ideas are inherited from a period in social psychology—more than in historiography—in which values, aspirations, and motivations which we today understand to be derived through learning processes were commonly attributed to inborn and organic sources. When one attributes all social activities and motivations to "instinctive" roots, obviously the forces of change will be found in those self-same roots. Some writers specified instincts which were really instincts of change, e.g., the instinct of curiosity, "instinct of workmanship," instinct for construction, etc. (Bernard).

Such mysterious biological forces appear in the explanations for the rise of capitalism given by economic historian Jacob Streider:

It was something at work in the background, often behind the threshold of consciousness—the need that the strong personality felt for activity, the restless mysterious lust to create, that drives its bearer to activity in the sphere in which he is placed. [P. 4.]

Practically all social scientists agree that individuals acquire workman-like traits and aspirations through socialization and similarly derive their interests in things which stimulate exploration, construction, etc. However, the fact remains that instinctivism, like environmental determinism, has left some residue in popular if not scientific thinking. A Committee of the American Association for the Advancement of Science, reports in regard to the project for exploration of the moon:

> In the scientific considerations of the Apollo program, we have found several instances in which scientific advisory groups assert, in their reports, that the Apollo program is justified by such nonscientific motivations as "man's innate drive to explore unknown regions. . . ." [AAAS, p. 184.]

While it goes without saying that the scientific advisory groups referred to above were not composed of *social scientists,* there is some lingering thought that man is by nature "curious," "dissatisfied with things as they are," "inherently at war with nature," "ever striving to improve his lot." It is no part of the present work to engage in the discussion of the organic and induced aspects of socialization. It is perhaps sufficient to recall that Christians were once but not today curious as to how many angels could stand on the end of a pin; that many peoples possess world views in which man is part of nature not an enemy of it; that things which may satisfy you may well frustrate me; and at the very least there is some substantial disagreement in the world over what constitutes "improvement." The vague dismissal of the complex forces which drive people toward change or which inhibit them, as being some "innate drive to explore," is today a vulgar retreat from the realities of social science.

GENIUS. The idea of genius as a source of change emphasizes the heroic and unique elements in innovation often with biological implications. It also implies the inscrutability of the sources of change. The very word "genius" derives from roots denoting magical power, and as Abbot Payson Usher (p. 160) has pointed out, is a term placing inventiveness in the realm of transcendental and unanalyzable power. When genius has not been explained through recourse to the voice of God through man, it has frequently been attributed to roots in genetic processes.

Cesare Lombroso, the "discoverer" of the born criminal, also did much to consolidate the idea of the born innovator. Not satisfied with finding that the criminal is an atavism, a biological throwback born into civilized society, Lombroso argued that genius as well has a biological base. He gave some systematic expression to the idea that great innovative minds are "sick," a myth which has virility in Sunday magazine sections but not in scientific research.

More seriously the biologic basis of genius is sought in assessments of individual heredity, a practice still prevalent among biographers and others. As A. M. Tozzer shows, the idea of natural genius is not supported so much by deliberate argument as in subtle reflection from the literary sources with which we are deluged from childhood. Tozzer observes that:

In eight out of ten of all biographical or autobiographical works, from Plutarch almost to Arthur Schlesinger, Jr., the author, in his first chapter, feels impelled to find something on his subject's parentage on which to hang characteristics and aptitudes. . . . [Pp. 145–146.]

This search for potential chromosomes takes many forms; they may be minutely catalogued through several and sometimes distant generations from the immediate maternal or paternal ancestor, from the race or races of the parents, from their nationalities, from the father's occupation, from the parents' religious faith, or from some other "carrier." . . . [P. 148.]

A difficulty is encountered when there are several children and only one is of outstanding position. A second wife sometimes comes in to help. . . . [P. 149.]

The ridiculous methodologies used in studies purporting to demonstrate hereditary genius is soundly and pointedly derided by Professor Tozzer. The relationship between genetic background and intelligence is extremely complex and when this is confounded with the relationship of each to creativity and to achievement, the arguments become very slippery indeed.

RACE. Racial theories of change have also virtually passed out of serious consideration by social scientists, but they are still prevalent in popular mythology and in certain political writings, especially in the United States and South Africa. Unlike geographic and familiar genetic factors, the idea of racial determination of culture is without even the saving grace of partial truth. The earliest self-conscious racial interpretation of history was that of Count Arthur de Gobineau, a Frenchman who developed his thesis fundamentally as a support of the French aristocracy. Since de Gobineau's *Essay on the Inequality of Human Races* in 1853–1855, the heroes and villains in the story have shifted from group to group, many of which were no more truly racial than de Gobineau's aristocrats (Hankins; Sorokin, pp. 222–234). The usual thesis maintained in such works is that Europeans generally, or a particular branch of that race, have the inherent capacity for building civilizations while other racial groups are devoid or lacking in this capacity. De Gobineau saw the rise of all world civilizations in terms of the actions of such a special body of men. The downfall of those civilizations occurred because of miscegenation of the civilization builders with inferior peoples.

This doctrine, which many persons of European ancestry have found pleasing, received crucial literary support particularly in the United

States and Germany. As is well known today, there is no reasonable evidence of inborn racial differences in intelligence, creativity, or temperamental qualities. Nor has miscegenation any deleterious effect on man either mentally or physically as assumed by racial determinists (Klineberg). Nonetheless, the emotional climate of the United States in the 1960's is such that the tradition of de Gobineau is being given renewed support in slick publications as well as in more obvious propaganda.

FECUNDITY. A still different variety of biologic determinism in the rise and fall of civilizations has been offered by the Italian demographer, Corrado Gini (Barnes and Becker, II, pp. 1025–1026; Sorokin, pp. 422–427). Gini, as part of a larger theory of social change, seeks to interpret the rise and fall of civilizations as due to changes in fecundity. In this view society is treated as an organism literally enjoying seminal vitality in youth and a loss of virility in old age. Gini contends that the primary cause of the evolution of nations must be sought in biological factors and more specifically in their changing reproductive capacity. Disregarding Gini's ingenious reasoning to account for the declining reproductive faculty in old societies, there is no shred of factual evidence to support, for example, the view that the biological capacity to reproduce is less in long-historied England than it is in "youthful" Israel.

A variant form of the fecundity theory of social change has been presented recently by S. C. Gilfillan. Gilfillan is reported to have discovered evidence that the fall of Rome arose from the utilization of lead dishes, which in turn produced arsenic poisoning and hence sterility in the Roman population, especially the elite [*Time Magazine*, Sept. 23, 1966]. This theory will no doubt take its place among many other explanations for the collapse of Rome, including one that finds the decline due to a depleted hay supply (Simkovitch).

Theories Emphasizing Cultural Forces

In earlier generations, many scholars seeking to explain social change could see no alternative to explanations resting upon man's organic nature or the forces of the natural environment. Modern social science has persistently shifted toward explaining socio-cultural facts by recourse to socio-cultural facts. Cultural determinism in change has arisen in two main streams. On one hand are scholars who find dynamic forces in man's "material culture" and on the other are those who see ideologies as the driving forces for change.

"Material Culture" as the Force for Change.   MARX'S CONCEPTION OF CHANGE CAUSATION.   Sociology and anthropology during the past century have been generally more sympathetic to materialistic interpretations of history than to ideological ones. While Marx was influential in setting this tone, of greater importance has been the immense actual concern with technical achievement and material welfare in Western society.

Marx's theory of history is based upon the principle that the organization of society must be congruent with its modes of production (Bober, pp. 26–28; Gray). The institutional "superstructure" must be functionally integrated with its economic base, i.e., the modes of production. The changing nature of that material base is the determinative force for change. Throughout his writings, Marx, with Engels, reiterates that his is a *materialistic* interpretation of history. The economic facts of life are the prime movers of history.

It is much debated how narrow was Marx's conception of what constituted the "modes of production." It is clear that he was giving no simple technological theory of historical change. Broadly "materialistic," Marx saw the determinative foundations of society in the relationships among labor, technology, and the objects of labor, i.e., natural resources. At points in Marxian writings, it seems possible that the system of economic exchange was to be included in this broad conception and at still other points one might gain the impression that the growth of science is fundamental to changing technology (Bober, pp. 26–28). The emphasis given by Marx varies widely in different writings depending upon his intended audience and the context of the discussion. Engels even argues that in primitive society, the family system, more than the modes of production, stimulated change (Bober, pp. 49–50). Consistency is difficult to find; hence our difficulty in knowing just what Marx really meant by his ideas of the material base and the institutional superstructure. Nor does he always pay strict attention to any division of this sort when he deals in concrete cases. Yet for all of this, we know that Marx saw the superstructure of feudalism arising upon the base of small local peasant agriculture and domestic handicrafts. The capitalist era is introduced not by technological inventions but by enlargement of the workshop group and a shifting ownership of the implements of production from the worker to the bourgeois employer-supervisor. For each economic base there is presumably a distinctive form of family life, religious system, etc. Change is introduced through variation in one or another of the factors of production. In different times and places variations spring up in numerous different ways. Significant force for change is credited by Marx to various sources including technological invention and the introduction of slavery into a free labor market (Bober, pp. 49–50).

The dynamism of technology for social change was subsequently given special emphasis by the American economist Thorstein Veblen. Veblen was possibly more directly influential upon recent American "material culture" theories of change dynamics than was Marx. The technological interpretations of history also was supported in the theories of the great American anthropologist Lewis Henry Morgan (Lowie, Chap. 6). Morgan visualized the evolution of culture through a series of rather fixed states. Each of these stages arose around a particular technology. For savages at a level prior to the discovery of pottery, Morgan believed that a particular set of institutions prevailed. With the introduction of pottery this institutional system shifted to another form. Although Morgan had total disinterest in communism, his theories of history and his researches on primitive society in pursuance of his theory were seized upon enthusiastically by Marxian writers, including Engels.

Morgan's brand of evolution is also significant as a source for a modern school of anthropology centering around Professor Leslie White and the sociologist Fred Cottrell. White and his associates have found inspiration in Morgan toward the understanding of social dynamics. White sees the crucial force driving historical change in the source of energy and the efficiency with which energy is harnessed by man. The dynamism of energy sources is incorporated into a broader theory of cultural evolution through sequential stages. In the work of Cottrell, the energy theory of history is given explicit analysis and support. Cottrell finds that the source of energy and the efficiency of its conversion are the forces giving rise to moral codes and systems of social relationship. Shorn of the labyrinthian economic and social analyses of Marx, and without communist bias, it becomes a narrowed version of the materialist interpretation of history.

W. F. OGBURN AND TECHNOLOGICAL EMPHASIS. The most influential work on social change ever published by an American sociologist was that by William F. Ogburn. His *Social Change,* first published in 1922, quickly achieved fame and lasting remembrance through the concept of "cultural lag" which it introduced. Professor Ogburn was less interested in writing the history of human culture than he was in promoting the cultural viewpoint regarding the forces underlying change and the idea that social problems arise in the very nature of change processes.

Ogburn's argument was that "material culture," or artifacts, change by a process which is fundamentally different from changes in norms and social organization. "Material culture," he says, represents new combinations of existing culture traits. Hence the larger the culture base, i.e., the bigger the technical knowledge of the society, the greater is the possibility of new combinations. Material culture tends to grow exponentially, i.e., at increasing rates of increase. On the other hand, nonmaterial culture is adaptive to the material culture. Rules of the game depend upon the instruments of the game, and the instruments undergo more rapid and prior modification. One cannot devise methods for controlling and utilizing new technology prior to the acceptance of the

technique. Hence culture lags appear in that controls and social relationships cannot keep pace with the new conditions established by new
material instruments. It is improbable that Ogburn really intended to
present a theory of material culture as a prime mover in all historic
processes. However, as he viewed the rise of civilization it appeared
unequivocal that technological advances had preceded and stimulated
developments in "non-material" culture. Priority and dynamic force was
attributed to the technical, material, inventive processes.

A position similar to that of Ogburn's was taken by S. C. Gilfillan
(1935). Gilfillan also emphasized the accumulative aspects of material
culture and by implication at least assigned it a dynamic role in regard
to social organization. Gilfillan's view of technological change is almost
that of an inevitable evolutionary process of increasing knowledge and
technical efficiency. Although in some writings he proposed climatic
determinants to stimulate such processes, elsewhere he has suggested
organic factors. In his major work, *The Sociology of Invention,* he treated
invention in processual, cultural terms without specifying a prime mover
behind its process or within it. In both Ogburn and Gilfillan there is an
acceptance of the idea that social change arises in adaptation to technical
inventions and that technical inventions arise through what is practically
a natural law of inevitability. When the time is ripe, believes Gilfillan,
the invention *will* appear. The prime moving force, then, lies in the
principle of material cultural accumulation and in the principle of combination and recombination of cultural items to form new inventions.

While critical of the Ogburn-Gilfillan approach, Hornell Hart over a
period of more than thirty-five years has developed a theory of cultural
growth in similar terms (1931; 1937, Chap. 3; 1959). Hart asserts that
the basic cause of cultural acceleration lies in the increasing number of
culture elements from which novel combinations can be made. Leaving
Hart's more precise researches aside, his basic position in regard to prime
movers is identical with that of Ogburn.

Other than those who have erected general theories of socio-cultural
growth on material cultural invention, there are almost countless scholars
who have in fact, if not in theory, attributed to some particular invention
the dynamic power of change. Lewis Mumford, no narrow materialist
in his view of history, is willing to single out the clock as "the key-
machine of the modern industrial age" (pp. 12–14). Carleton Coon, the
anthropologist, has offered an even more far reaching particularizing conclusion when he contends that fire is the key to man's mastery of nature
and to his contemporary problems (p. 63).

In the research tradition particularly associated with Ogburn and Hart,
numerous scholars have sought to show that particular inventions have
had permeating effects upon society. Most of these are implicitly material-

cultural deterministic approaches. They have been sufficiently numerous to give the writing about change of the last generation a decidedly cultural and technologically determinative slant. Under the influence of Ogburn, S. McKee Rosen and Laura Rosen wrote an introductory text on social change in 1941 with its emphasis clear in its title, *Technology and Social Change*. Ogburn produced his *Social Effects of Aviation* in 1946 and later, with Meyer F. Nimkoff, *Technology and the Changing Family* (1955). In various symposia the viewpoint of technology as the source of societal change was supported. From the side of anthropology is the work edited by Edward Spicer, *Human Problems in Technological Change* and more recently one to which Hart, Ogburn, and Nimkoff are contributors, *Technology and Social Change* (Allen *et al.*).

It would be unfair to these writers to claim that they see all social change arising in response to man's successful search for efficiency in tools. Professors Ogburn and Nimkoff would, for example, have objected strongly to the allegation that they saw no dynamic power in ideologies or in social movements. Nonetheless, the cumulative impact of so many and such articulate scholars *emphasizing* technological forces in change has served to perpetuate a materialistic bias in contemporary thought on historical processes.

The criticisms of technological interpretations of change have been voluminous, although less so than the literature supporting them. The thesis of Marxian materialism was not, in honest fact, invariably utilized even in the historic writings of Marx and Engels themselves. Modifications in family organization seem to be credited with priority in their analysis of early society in change, and some Marxists, like Sorel, have emphasized the power of ideological factors. In regard to non-Marxian "material culture" determinists it is notable that Ogburn in his later writings revised and modified his early rather deterministic statements. Gilfillan has apparently shifted his interests to biologic-demographic forces for change. Leslie White and the "energy school" remain essentially consistent with the basic premise of technological dynamism in cultural growth. In general it seems fair to say that technological interpretations of change are less wrong than they are insufficient. Man is not a plaything of his machines though it is evident that he persistently responds to them in the course of his cultural development. Perhaps the most direct criticism of such theories lies in the equally valid and equally limited claims that the course of history is driven by ideologies.

Ideas as the Sources of Change. Contrasting with those who emphasize the dynamic force of material conditions and tools are change scholars who see the ideas and beliefs of men as fundamental to social change. Philosophic idealism has deep historical roots in Western scholarship. Philosophers such as Kant and Hegel laid the groundwork for its introduction to social science. As such theories came into the realm of developing social science they divided into the two main types: (1) teleological theories which emphasize man's willful power to control his own destiny, and (2) deterministic theories wherein specific belief systems are assigned dynamic power.

THE TELEOLOGICAL CONCEPTION. The idea that man can wilfully control historical process and mold its direction by his own planning exists in the very roots of sociology. Early in the nineteenth century Count Henri de Saint-Simon, an enthusiastic believer in the idea of human progress, wrote influentially on the need for a science of social action (*la science politique*). Saint-Simon advocated the utilization of Christianity as a dynamic emotional force toward progressive change and placing control of the destiny of society in the hands of social technologists who would discover and apply the new social science. Comte took up Saint-Simon's theory of change, termed it *sociology*, and developed the plan of its application in minute detail.

In the United States the Comtian version of social evolution was supported most strongly by Lester Ward. Ward believed that social evolution had hitherto been naturalistic in its determination but that the day of "social telesis" must be at hand. Contrasting with Herbert Spencer who saw social evolution as part of a natural cosmic process, Ward insisted upon the power of man to control his destiny.

The power of man's self-determination of society's future has, of course, been implicit in the writings of utopian socialists who set up ideal constructs of society as goals toward which mankind should strive. However, within the Marxian tradition of thought, the role of ideology has also been given stronger emphasis as a force in change than Marx himself professed for it. Notably, Georges Sorel, in the early years of this century, concerned himself with the power of ideological constructs in the proletarian revolution. In no way renouncing Marxian materialism, Sorel qualified it to give dynamic force to the significance of *the myth*—a statement of the expected ideal state regardless of the accuracy of its delineation, to drive men toward positive action.

Experience shows that the *framing of a future, in some indeterminate time,* may, when it is done in a certain way, be very effective and have few inconveniences; this happens when the anticipations of the future take the form of those myths which enclose with them all the strongest inclinations of a people, of a party, or of a class . . . [Sorel, pp. 124–125.] *

* From *Reflections on Violence* by Georges Sorel, translated by T. E. Hulme and J. Roth with an Introduction by Edward A. Shils. Copyright 1950 by The Free Press. By permission The Macmillan Company.

Although the impetus in social science during the past generation has been toward the emphasis of materialistic forces for change, teleological theory has retained vitality. Implicitly it is accepted in our increasing dependence upon economic and social planning and in the new community development programs. The theory of self-guidance as a positive force in change has been given strong expression by Kenneth Boulding, the American economist, and by Fred L. Polak. Polak has presented the essence of his minutely documented work in these terms:

The prevailing positive images of the future, perpetually breaking through the frontiers of time, have formed powerful—often the most powerful—long-range dynamic force pushing history through time. The pounding beat of historical dynamics, ever moving from past through present to a future which is again becoming past, is for a large part explicable only through the idealistic driving force, inspiring spiritual power and rousing faith of positive and progressive images of the future. They operate through the spirit of men, regardless of whether one might wish to define this more closely as the magnetic force of ideal goals, as fiery enthusiasm, radiating myth, or as a glowing, sparkling ethos and pathos. They operate, in short, through the pulsating dynamic of ideas.

So powerful was the impact of these images that they can even hold the non-captive observer of far later times spell-bound and lay him open to the charges of exaggeration and overvaluing of his material. Although the author is well aware of the danger of being led astray by a favourite idea which has been intensely experienced so that it becomes an idee-fixe and is magnified out of all proportion, he does not see any reason for toning down or modifying the above proposition. Rather he would intensify and sharpen it still further by adding: *the history of culture is the history of its images of the future.*

These images of the future, in their non-fulfilment as well as in their partial fulfilment and continuous renewal that they may yet achieve ultimate fulfilment, have provided a more or less accurate foreshadowing of the future, and thus have caused this same not-yet-existent future to affect current thought and aspirational action as though it were already here—especially that expectational activity which is purposefully directed towards future goals. [Vol. II, pp. 115–116.]

SPECIFIC BELIEF SYSTEMS. Determinative power for change has been claimed for a wide range of specific ideologies. Indeed, no one can question the influence upon social structures of such diverse systems of belief as Christianity, "Free Enterprise," "Marxism," and German Nazism. It is understandable that most writers on the consequences of ideologies and their associated movements have not sought to give universal generalizations regarding "prime movers" in historic process. Attention here will be given to a limited group of theories related to the rise of the "modern" Western-type, scientific, achieving, industrial social order.

One of the most influential theories in modern times has been that of

Max Weber's analysis of the rise of capitalism, a theory which has had permutations in accounting for the development of modern science and other aspects of contemporary life. Weber, in his widely known work, *The Protestant Ethic and the Spirit of Capitalism* argued brilliantly that the ethos of Puritanism provided an essential ethical climate and driving power behind the rise of capitalism in Western Europe.

While ideological forces are emphasized, this theory is not propounded as a universal theory comparable to Marx's historical materialism. Weber shows that the capitalism of the West was unique in world history and that the drive toward its formation lay in the equally unique juxta-position of various doctrines in Puritan religious ideology. In essence his argument is that "ascetic Protestantism" gave men a burning desire to know whether they were damned or saved in their future life. Salvation rested not in the works of the man himself, but was predestined by God. However, this divine judgment could be revealed to the extent that God smiled upon one in his life and gave worldly success to his efforts. Worldly, secular achievement becomes a test of a predestined status. With an agonizing fear of hell the devout Puritan worked diligently that God's blessing might be known. At the same time the Protestant ethic removed odium from making money out of money and shop-keeping. It enjoined one to restraint in matters of sensory gratification and concom-mitantly encouraged thrift. In contrast to the more passive conceptions of the ideal man expressed through Roman Catholic, Hindu, and Buddhist thought, Protestantism yielded an ideal of self-reliance, energy, and dis-ciplined secular life to carry out God's work on earth. The Protestant ethic would thus drive toward economic enterprise, trade, and the forma-tion and use of capital. Weber painstakingly shows how these ideological forces created the moral and intellectual climate required for the develop-ment of modern capitalism.

Weber suggested but did not develop the idea that Protestantism may have served a similar function for the rapid growth of science and tech-nology in the West, and hence industrialism as well as capitalism. This hypothesis was explored notably by Robert K. Merton (1938). Merton's study of scientific development in seventeenth-century England supports the extension of Weber's theory into scientific and industrial spheres. The seventeenth century was a period of critical growth in science, and a dis-proportionate number of scientists in this century appear to have been Protestant. Further, as Merton shows, the ideas of Protestantism inte-grated with concepts of progress arising from secular sources and in a qualified way, with utilitarianism. More basically, however, the Reforma-tion was based upon the principles of the "rightful duty of free inquiry" and the "priesthood of all believers" (Merton, 1938, p. 537). Weber's view of Protestantism has been extended in recent decades to account for, at lease partially, rising personal anxieties and man's flight to the "security" of authoritarian political structures (Fromm).

The critical literature of the Weberian argument is immense, but his work will stand as a model study of the integration of institutional systems regardless of its fate in terms of causal analysis (Green; Samuelsson). Recently Merton's evidence on the relationship between Protestantism and science has been challenged by Lewis S. Feuer, who replaced the Weberian thesis by another. Feuer assesses the scientific intellectuals in the Copernican Revolution, the medieval nominalists, the eighteenth-century Scots, and various other groups renowned for scientific achievement. He finds the relationship between any form of Protestant thought and scientific achievement to be nebulous and fortuitous. In dismissing one ideology as a social force, Feuer argues the case for another:

> . . . The scientific intellectual was born from the hedonist-libertarian spirit which, spreading through Europe in the sixteenth and seventeenth centuries, directly nurtured the liberation of human curiosity. Not asceticism, but satisfaction; not guilt, but joy in the human status; not self-abnegation, but self-affirmation; not original sin, but original merit and worth; not gloom but merriment; not contempt for one's body and one's senses, but delight in one's physical being; not the exaltation of pain but the hymn to pleasure—this was the emotional basis of the scientific movement of the seventeenth century. Herbert Butterfield has spoken of "a certain dynamic quality" which entered into Europe's "secularization of thought" in the seventeenth century. What I shall try to show is how the hedonist-libertarian ethic provided the momentum for the scientific revolution, and was in fact the creed of the emerging movements of scientific intellectuals everywhere. [Pp. 7–8.] *

Since World War II there has been reawakening interest in the forces which make nations "get up and go," a question which in earlier years had often arisen in reference to the Reformation and the Industrial Revolution in the West. With the sudden movements toward modernization in Asia, Africa, and Latin America, the problem of accounting for spurts here and lags there is extended to a world-wide scope. Some of the recent analyses place crucial significance upon belief systems or ideologies. David C. McClelland, author of *The Achieving Society*, argues that the driving force beyond the rise of Western civilization lies in its high individual achievement motivation. He is insistent that we understand the rise of underdeveloped countries not as dependent upon political freedom and hardware but upon the intensity of their achievement drive.

What, asks McClelland, accounts for the rise of civilization? And he replies firmly that the answer does not lie in such material conditions as natural resources, factories, or markets, but in the entrepreneurial spirit which utilizes and exploits such factors (1962). This enterprising and

* From *The Scientific Intellectual* by Lewis S. Feuer, Basic Books, Inc., Publishers, New York, 1963. By permission.

dynamic spirit, McClelland believes, is most often prevalent among businessmen. Unlike some economists like Streider who have similarly posed spiritual forces which drive men on, but who have been negligent in fixing the source of such dynamic emotions, McClelland finds the roots of achievement motivation in the values and ideologies current in a society. He notes that these not only fluctuate in intensity but in the direction of their achievement orientation. He recognizes that Protestantism and the secular religions of nationalism and communism have all provided dynamic emphasis upon achievement, with consequences for economic growth. However, in the last analysis, McClelland offers little more than a variant restatement of Max Weber's basic thesis set in the more secular context of the mid-twentieth century.

The matter of achievement motivation is one to which we will return later in this chapter. Not all writers find it clearly rooted in some specific set of value premises howsoever dynamic. It would seem obvious that entrepreneurial achievement is most probable when people behave like entrepreneurs. The question remains whether this arises from "secular" or "sacred" religious ideologies or elsewhere in the socio-cultural structure. Within the same historic circumstances which concern McClelland quite different ideological forces may be suggested that also have dynamic power. The world historian Ralph Turner chose to emphasize the potency of an ideology of freedom and a new sense of human dignity in the contemporary transformation of Asian peoples (pp. 16 ff.). Turner epitomized this force as an awakening of long suppressed Asian peasantry to the realization that "We are people too." To accept the power of one ideological force does not require one to negate the power of the other. Nor should we be constrained, as McClelland appears to think we should, from recognizing the significance of "hardware," capital resources, etc. also as crucial ingredients in the change situation.

Specific Social Categories as Forces for Change

Speculation and research has frequently been directed toward the location of categories or classes of individuals in society which are significant for social change. At times such inquiries have resulted in deterministic theories crediting certain types or groups of persons with dynamism toward change. We are concerned here with *social categories* which have been singled out as special movers in historic process. In this connection two main types of theories will be considered: (1) theories in which elites and their replacements mold historical process, and (2) socio-psychological theories attributing dynamic power to certain social or psychological types.

The Elite as a Force.   Posed now in terms of an intellectual elite and again in terms of a political or economic oligarchy, the power of the dominant few to determine the course of history is a recurrent theme in sociological writings.   Mosca in the late nineteenth century made much of the role of power cliques in overthrowing monarchies and hence to rule toward their own interests.   Somewhat similarly Michels wrote of the tendency of democratic institutions toward oligarchy and of the interest of the oligarchs in the preservation of a status quo, i.e., the change inhibiting aspects of oligarchic power.   From other sides the actions of a powerful minority to inhibit change have been emphasized among many Marxian writers as well as non-Marxists impressed by the inhibiting pressures of "vested interests" toward the preservation of their power.

Perhaps the most sophisticated theory of the elite in its historic determining role is that of Vilfredo Pareto (pp. 1421–1432, 1515).   Pareto writing early in this century developed his theory of "circulation of elites" as a cyclical conception of change in the economic and political institutions.   Pareto postulated two basic social or personality types in society. On one hand there are the persons strong in the "residue of persistence of aggregates."   These are types who are stable, disciplined, and forceful. In contrast is another basic type characterized by the "residue of combinations."   These are the wily schemers and imaginative tacticians. Pareto, finding little democratic power in society in fact, sees political and economic rule by factions composed of one type or the other.   As one type finds itself secure in power it tends to relax its hold on the population.   At the same time it becomes ingrown and dominated strictly by persons of the same type.   This, of course, means that increasing numbers of able and power-seeking individuals of opposite type are prevented from gaining access to the elite.   With this explosive situation created, Pareto (p. 1430) concludes with reasonable accuracy that "history is the graveyard of aristocracies."

Another cyclical and "elite" theorist, utterly different from Pareto, is the Christian idealist and world historian Arnold Toynbee (Boskoff, pp. 146–149).   The "creative minority" seems in Toynbee's thought to be a sort of specialized omniscient group which withdraws from workday life to think out its creative responses to social challenges and returns into the workday world to apply these innovations.   Toynbee believes that in time such creative minorities lapse in their functions and attempt to preserve their elite position by force.   A critical social stimulus behind historical "progress" and "regress" is the creative minority and its natural life cycle.

A recent emphasis upon the elite as a force for social change, is that of C. Wright Mills in his concept of the "power elite" (1957; 1959).   Mills, concerned with contemporary world events, characterizes his power elite as an "often uneasy coincidence of economic, military and political power." He finds scant separation in the composition of the elites of arms, of industry-finance, and of politics and government. This multiplication of powers in somewhat overlapping hands is, in Mills' analysis, vastly more significant today than it would have been in times past. The contemporary elite has not only power over multiple spheres of life but it has unparalleled intensity of power as well. This is due to numerous factors chief of which is the high degree of centralization existing today in government and in industry (both, according to Mills, infiltrated by the military) and the unprecedented power of the implements of coercion brought forth through nuclear and other branches of science. Like Mosca and Pareto, Mills derogates and bypasses the force of democratic planning and control and seems to be reaffirming the idea that historic directions are to be understood as the self-interested decisions made by the power cliques.

Socio-Psychological Theories. In one sense the "great man theory of history" might be construed as a psychological approach since it seeks the well-springs of change in human personalities. Rarely, however, have such biographical accounts resorted to truly psychological theories of history. We have had occasion here to relate such ideas now to biologic determinism and at other points to transcendentalism. In recent years, however, sophisticated psychological explanations for change have been presented which call for more mature consideration. Certain of these have been set forth as determinative and causal theories, while others have been more directed at ascertaining personality types which under given circumstances are favorable to the introduction of innovation.

Two recurring themes in the personality approach to change causation are to be found in the ideas that (1) persons who are marginal to or unenchanted with the social order, alienated, or anomic are the sources of change and the persons most susceptible to proposed change, and (2) persons who have been frustrated become instruments of change through aggressive leadership. Each of these positions has been developed in a variety of forms and fitted into an extremely wide range of contexts. Basic to all, however, is the premise that certain personality types arise in society through their similarities in socialization experiences and that certain of them, depending upon the theorist, have dynamic impetus toward change.

Some writers would refuse to assign causal primacy to psychological types but nonetheless view them as crucial points for beginning study of the interminably complex forces for change. It is this that we find in the personality constructs set up by Howard W. Becker (pp. 182 ff.; Boskoff, 1964, pp. 144–146). Becker outlined various personality types having relevance for change, his logical scheme resting upon the mode with which individuals are integrated with the established social order. Examples of these are the "desocialized or demoralized" type, who have "unlearned" the traditional values often through the effects of extreme personal crisis situations and whose behavior tends to be unpredictable, violent, and aimless; the "decadent or sophisticated type" which engages in an insatiable search for variety—such individuals seek change for change's sake; and the "liberated stable" type, a rather idealistic "constructive" change seeker. It should be remembered that Becker is not a psychological determinist. His change-prone types are established to indicate the weak links in the force of tradition to perpetuate itself through socialization.

From a different standpoint, Homer Barnett (Chap. 14) also attaches great significance to imperfectly integrated individuals. Barnett develops his personality type theory in the context of susceptibility to proffered innovation. Robert K. Merton (1949) has similarly emphasized the significance of the "deviant" for innovation and change, but no more than Becker was he attempting a psychologically deterministic theory.

A theory of social change developed by economist Everett Hagen is, however, a psychologically determinative one (1962; 1963). Hagen's theory is rooted in a mixture of the concepts of anomie, frustration-aggression, and the "authoritarian personality." Since Hagen has written a recent and elaborate theory of social change and economic development, it is important to recount here the causal roots of growth that he postulates. Hagen argues that the personality type which arises from child-training practices in traditional societies is an authoritarian one. This personality structure is rigid and uncreative. It is from authoritarian child-training practices that we are to understand the traditionalist's compulsive clinging to the ways of the past. Fortunately for progress, inadvertent circumstances arise which interfere with the production of simple authoritarians. Hagen speculates that such a circumstance arises when a strong mother and a weak-charactered father get together. Under such conditions there is, he thinks, an almost ideal environment for the development of a child with an anxious, driving sort of creativity. Gradually there emerges in the society a group of individuals who are alienated from traditional values and driven by a gnawing urge to prove themselves. Dynamic, creative anxieties are translated into forces for economic growth through a series of typical social events.

Hagen seems to find that everywhere the enterpriser in the midst of traditional society is so created, although not merely by this socialization process that went awry. He is further driven through frustration in his status needs. Enterprisers arise from sectors of the population who have suffered "status withdrawal," i.e., having once known prestige, have had it subsequently withdrawn. Such status deprivation turns the anxious, creative personality toward non-traditional means of status acquisition, that is, business enterprise. Hagen adduces several societies which he thinks demonstrate the action of such processes in the formation of an entrepreneurial class.

Granting the significance of motivations for cultural change, and for economic growth especially, there is little firm support for Hagen's thesis. Historical and anthropological data are given selective treatment to support a thesis born of psycho-analytical inferences. Further, as Wilbert Moore (1963, p. 296) has observed, the odds on developing productive understanding of change forces lie less in exploring psychological mechanisms than in the direct study of changing social structures.

Particular Social Processes as Forces for Change

Struggle for Existence. Nineteenth-century social evolutionary thought stemming from Herbert Spencer saw all social change arising through the outworkings of a natural law of progress. The dynamic force in progress was, like that in biological evolution, the competitive struggle for existence in which the fit survive and the unfit perish (Hofstadter). This theory of dynamic force in progress was especially seized upon by those scholars today referred to as social Darwinists—though Darwin himself was no social Darwinist. In the hands of William Graham Sumner, famed author of *The Folkways*, the struggle for survival was equated with economic competition. In Sumner, and in Spencer for that matter, free and untrammeled competition is essential for society's continued thrust toward progress. (The teleological theories of Lester Ward were aimed against Sumner's assumption of this natural law in the society of thinking men.) In its narrowest sense, the dynamic force of struggle was a "war for survival." By some writers the process was viewed as intersocietal and by others as an intrasocietal one, as in Marx's concept of class struggle. Few writers, however have held that outright warfare is the basis of progress although many have noted its stimulation to various types of innovation (Sorokin, Chap. 6). Most evolutionary scholars have viewed war as a primitive form of struggle for survival but one that with continued social evolution passes away in favor of milder and less inhumane forms, e.g., intellectual, political, and economic rivalries.

A critical response to the conflict school of evolution was made not only in the humane welfare "sociologies" of the early twentieth century but also among others who were evolutionists as well (Rauschenbush, 1907; 1957; Hofstadter; Kropotkin; Ward). Lester Ward rejected such an order of nature in human affairs and the ideas were rejected as well by socialist writers. Prince Peter Kropotkin, a philosopher-anarchist, took pains to emphasize cooperation as a dynamic force in social evolution. He correctly argued that even a complete analogy between organic and social evolution must accept cooperation as a basic principle of survival *within* the species. On this basis he developed the thesis that social evolution has proceeded through cooperation among men rather than through their contraventions.

Shorn of its determinism and status as natural law, conflict is still viewed by some modern sociologists as the process most basic to change. In recent years the conflict theory of change has been revived notably by Lewis Coser and Ralf Dahrendorf. This revival, however, has not been to provide us with a deterministic "prime mover" in history. Rather, modern conflict theory is non-deterministic in that it establishes that process as basic to an interactional approach to change, not as a particularistic explanation of it.

Moral Density. A different form of evolutionary thought was expressed by Emile Durkheim who was also one of the leading critics of those who applied Darwinian concepts to social processes (Parsons, 1949; Bellah). However, Durkheim accepted one of the tenets of Spencerian evolution while rejecting the theory of survival and "natural law" which underlay it. Durkheim agreed that the trend of history lies in the increasing differentiation of society (increasing division of labor) which stimulates crucial social change. He sought to ascertain the ultimate cause of the trend toward differentiation and found the answer in increasing density of population. He did not, however, leave the argument as a crude bio-demographic principle. He introduced the concept of "dynamic or moral density" as the evolutionary force. This is to say, differentiation is the central process of change and it is stimulated by the dynamism of the group's intensified struggle for life. Increasing physical density can be accomplished feasibly only by increasing specialization in functions with new specialized inter-dependencies. It is to this intensified interaction speeding men toward specialized and inter-dependent roles, that Durkheim sought to rest his search for a dynamic force in history. This is an hypothesis also developed by Ferdinand Tönnies and by others in the same generation as Durkheim, and continues in the present day, reflected in the work of Godfrey and Monica Wilson.

Rooted rather directly in Durkheim's theory of change, the Wilsons have proposed the concept of "increasing scale" in social relationships as the fundamental process in the modernization of today's tribal peoples in Africa. This theory of undergoing "increasing scale" is a stimulative one which has relevance to many underdeveloped societies in the throes of modernization. The theory of scale rests upon the assumption that increasing size and density in a society requires correlative changes in its constituent social relationships. By scale the Wilsons mean "the number of people in relation and the intensity of those relations" (p. 25). The total interdependence of persons upon others is the same in all societies regardless of size. With increasing size, the scale or extensity of the individual's dependencies increases. The Bushman is as dependent upon his fellows as is the urbanized Westerner. But his fellows are fewer in number; his dependencies intensely circumscribed within a small body of neighbors. Increasing density offers pressure toward specialization in relationships and their expansion beyond local horizons. While the Wilsons recognize that it is the increase of scale that is the determining factor in change, they find population growth a dynamic force toward increasing scale, and war a force toward its contraction.

More clearly demographic are the studies which, stimulated by the rapid expansion of population in underdeveloped regions, view increasing crude physical density as a force toward change (vander Kroef).

The Catastrophic Theory of Change

Related to both demographic and conflict origins for change are theories which attribute human progress to catastrophic events and crisis, especially mass migrations and conquests. In recent times, this theory has been advanced by Robert E. Park who found support for his ideas in the writings of Karl Bucher, the economic historian, and Gumplowicz, and Oppenheimer, who were "conflict sociologists" (Ponsioen, pp. 100–103).

Park believed that great cultural changes were due to confrontations of peoples and their cultures in which a revolution of society came about through the impact of the outsiders upon the society in question. Such invasions disorganize the society under attack, necessitating its reorganization by the conquering force, often a minority. Park believed that this theory applied more closely to societies of the past than to those of modern times, and he is scarcely to be viewed as a "catastrophic" determinist. He found historic basis for concluding that major social changes have arisen out of invasion and critical culture contacts. He did not intend this emphasis to serve as an exclusive source of major social change.

NON-DETERMINISTIC THEORIES

Retreat from Deterministic Theories

One of the early firm retreats in American sociology from simple cause and effect analysis in social phenomena was that stated by P. Sorokin in his discussion of Vilfredo Pareto's contributions to sociology.

The concept of a "cause" and "effect" supposes a relationship of one-sided dependence between two or more phenomena. Factually, such a relationship is almost never given in the relationship of various social phenomena. As a rule they are mutually dependent. If, for instance, the qualities of the members of a society influence its social organization, the latter also influences the former. For this reason, the conception of a one-sided relationship of a cause and effect could not be applied to a scientific study of social phenomena. . . . By the fallacy of a "simplicist theory" I mean the following: Let us take a society. Its character and equilibrium are composed of, and are dependent on, geographical environment; (A) economic situation; (B) political constitution; (C) religion; (D) ethics and knowledge; (E) and so on. All these variables mutually depend on, and mutually influence, one another. Through this interaction they permanently change the character of a society and its equilibrium. We have then a mutual dependence of these "variables," and a dynamic equilibrium of a society which may pass permanently from one state:

A, B, C, D, E, .to another
A', B', C', D', E', ...
A", B", C", D", E" . . . . .and so on

Now a "simplicist" theorizer takes an element A, as a cause, and tries to view B, or C, D and E, as its "effects." Some other simplicists may take B, or C, or D, as a "cause" and try to view the other elements as effects. In this way we receive, and we indeed have, plenty of various contradictory theories which all represent a simplicist type of sociological theory (all of them being one-sided theories which try to explain the whole social life through a geographic, racial, economic, political, or any other factor). As a result of such a procedure, the theory is inevitably one-sided; its generalization, inadequate; its diagnoses, false; and its formulas, fallacious; to say nothing of the useless fights between various simplicist theories which are caused. [Sorokin, pp. 42–43.]

The denial of "simplicist" or particularistic theories of change causation was associated with new and non-deterministic approaches. In general these involved declining interest in the historical antecedents to a particular situation and a focus on an existing structure and how it responds to some innovative trait or action. Although he may not have meant it literally, Malinowski contended that the origins of cultural phenomena lie in the relation of man's biological endowment to the natural environment (Bidney, pp. 223–236). Malinowski made the logic of relationships a substitute for cause and effect sequences. In this extreme form of functionalism, understanding the history of a culture trait would tell us nothing about its *cause* . . . its *cause* would be found in the functions that it serves.

The position of Malinowski was extreme and in fact was not consistently held by him, but it serves to illustrate the retreat from both historical interests in social science and from the conventional idea of cause and effect sequences. There was a general reticence regarding the use of the word "cause" and the word "effect." Kluckhohn studying Navaho witchcraft insisted upon substituting the term "functional" for "causal," because the relationship between the variables was interdependent (p. 124).

"Cause," if we may use the word rejected by Kluckhohn, was found to work to its effect through the mutual interdependence of many situational forces. At about the same date, the late Robert M. MacIver (1942), also weary of simple, deterministic theories of causation, reached much the same conclusion as Kluckhohn. MacIver, however, saw no need to give up the concept of causation. Rather, he emphasized the perceiving, assessing, and valuing individual as the key point in social causation. MacIver proposed the concept of "dynamic assessment" as the central point in the process of causation. By dynamic assessment he meant the actor's balanced judgment of the ingredients in a situation requiring action. It is at this point of dynamic assessment that we must begin if we are to pursue successfully the quest for the causes of change. Beginning at the point of the dynamic assessment of a situation by actors ". . . the phenomena of change . . . are the differences that occur in things in the endless reciprocity of their acting and being acted upon" (MacIver, pp. 28–29).

By the early 1940's sociologists were facing up to the fact that causation in social change is multiple and reciprocal, not particularistic, simple, and direct. In MacIver's terms, change originates at the point of the dynamic assessment.

Functionalism and Causes of Change

If "school" it has been, the dominant school of sociology in North America for the past thirty years has been functionalism. The breadth of the idea of functionalism is so great, however, it may be misleading to call it a "school" or even a theory (Davis). More accurately it is an orientation to study of social life within which there is room for numerous varieties of theory. The basic position of functionalism is that social phenomena are to be studied in terms of "what they do." The meaning of a social fact arises from understanding it in its positive or negative effect upon other social facts. The early anthropological "functionalist" Radcliffe-Brown would have said it somewhat differently but with the same essence—i.e., the study of the contribution a part makes to the ongoingness of the whole. In the United States, functionalism was particularly redefined and developed by Talcott Parsons (1951) and by Robert K. Merton (1949). Parson's works have emphasized the structural variables in a bounded social system and have laid a groundwork for analysts seeking to study the inter-relationships among the various parts of a social structure.

The functional orientation to change rests upon the concept of social equilibrium. Following an organic analogy the social group lives in a state of ongoing dynamic equilibrium. Upsetting forces introject themselves into this equilibriated system. These, in functional terms, would be construed as innovation stimulii. The equilibriated social system responds adjustively (re-equilibration) to these disturbances and accommodates them into the functioning structure. Functional theory has been particularly useful in the analysis of "small" changes occurring within well-defined groups of moderate size. Charles P. Loomis and Alvin Bertrand, respectively, have given generalized statements of such a theory of change. Bertrand refers to this as a theory of "micro-change." He outlines the procedure used in the analysis of the effects of innovation toward disequilibration with consequent strain upon the functioning of the group with resultant efforts toward achievement of new equilibrium so that the group may again function effectively.

Weaknesses of Functionalism and Attempts To Overcome Them. Critics charge that functionalism is an essentially static view of society in which the question of change is evaded in favor of a process which is really that of digesting a potentially upsetting idea or culture trait. Wayne Hield has claimed that functionalism makes the study of change into a study of social problems and society's efforts to overcome them. This is widely denied by functionalists, although it is generally admitted that most change studies by functionalists are in fact oriented toward a structural, equilibrium—disequilibrium—re-equilibrium approach.

Wilbert Moore (1960), while recognizing that one must understand how social structures operate before one can analyze their dynamics and changes, does not accept this as sufficient reason to delay the search for valid theories of dynamics. Moore believes that it is too soon to develop a "pure" theory of social change. Instead, he suggests that structuralists (or functionalists) ask additional questions rather than different questions from the ones they have been asking. He would extend structural and functional theory into the realm of dynamics by insisting on some fundamental questions involving temporal sequences and forces. To the conventional problem of contemporary structural and functional sociology, he would add questions as to trend and dynamic forces for change within the structure. To some extent Moore and Arnold S. Feldman have in fact expanded functional theory to the analysis of developing nations (1960). However, theory of this type indicates the kinds of questions to be asked rather than the kinds of causal hypothesis to be tested.

Particularly open to methodological criticism are functional studies which fix upon some specific technological innovation and proceed to find linkages of chain effects emanating from that innovation. Complex and revolutionary sequences of change in primitive society have been traced back to the introduction of a new type of axe, or again, a change student starts with the elevator as an innovation and follows its functional implications into myriad byways, e.g., erection of skyscraper, increasing density of population, traffic problems, etc. From a causal standpoint these studies are as weak as the climatic simplistic ones criticized by Sorokin. But it should be recalled that many functionalists have not claimed causal analysis as a purpose. Insofar as functionalism has brought increased awareness of the integration and interdependent relationships of different elements of culture, objection must be over-ruled. This is not, however, moving toward causal and predictive generalization in the field of change.

The most serious criticism of the functional approach is, as Wayne Hield and others have claimed, that it has usually provided a static model of a social system in reference to which change analysis is made. According to Hield, change in the functionalist theory, is caused by an "infection which upsets equilibrium." Unquestionably, there is much left out in the literal application of this approach. It does not help much in regard to causal theory nor does it lead toward understanding long-range patterns of social change such as are found in institutional trends over periods of time. Functionalists have been highly successful in studies of change in small social systems insofar as change is to be understood through an equilibrium model. Change in the very structure of social systems is another matter and turns us to problems of the forces, sequences, and directions through which groups and institutions are transformed through time. The analogy of biological science is useful here. Functionalism in sociology has been analogous to functionalism in biology. It studies how the "organism's" constituent parts work together and the effect of change in one part upon the organism generally. As in biology, this point of view is exceedingly useful, but it does not tell us how the "organism" *evolves* either in sociology or in biology. The concepts needed for an understanding of evolutionary or trend processes are beyond those needed for an understanding of "functional" processes.

Adamant critics like Hield would probably insist that there can be no marriage between the theory of functional analysis and theories pertaining to temporal evolutionary sequences. However, such pessimism regarding a general theory of change is not entirely justified. Apparently recognizing the issue, Talcott Parsons opened up the problem of "systems change" in 1961, suggesting that an evolutionary orientation could be compatible with functional analysis, and others have attempted to apply functional theory to evolutionary dynamics as well.

Smelser's Change Causation Theory.   Neil Smelser's analysis of social change during the Industrial Revolution in England is a constructive extension of functionalism toward understanding the transformation of social systems.

Reminiscent of MacIver, Smelser finds the starting point for the socio-logical analysis of change in the tensions, dissatisfactions, unrest, and consequent "definitions" or assessments which are made toward action and change. Selecting a historic period during which extensive institu-tional transformations were stimulated, Smelser utilizes functional con-cepts in reference to an evolutionary process, i.e., the differentiation of roles and institutions associated with industrialization. Much as Spencer and Durkheim, he treats increasing social differentiation (specialization and segmentalization of social relationships) as the central direction of social change. As increasing specialization permeated weaving and spin-ning mills, on the heels of technological advances, these created pressures upon family division of labor with consequent increased differentiation within the family structure itself. Similarly, pressures extended toward differentiation in other social systems. As to a theory of causation of change, Smelser writes:

The subject of the "causes," "conditions," "determinants," or "underlying factors" leading to the industrial revolution in cotton (or the entire industrial revolution) is seldom neglected by historians and others; yet the highest con-fusion reigns both in the definition of these terms and in the search for appro-priate empirical conditions to fit the definitions. . . .

One cannot deny the place of coal, steam, water, and climate; nor can one eliminate commercial and technological features; and enough is known of values and ideology to admit their importance in industrial development. In addition, however, these factors do not constitute a simple list of conditions, each logically co-ordinate as a "cause" or "determinant." The significance of each appears *at different stages of development.* For this reason the notion of simple cause or determination may be misleading because it implies a "be-fore-after" relationship. In fact industrial development involves an interplay of qualitatively different factors which "add their value" to growth at different stages and in different weights. [Smelser, pp. 60–62.]

Multiple causation has long been suggested as a realistic substitute for simple cause-effect analysis in social phenomena. The recognition that multiple precipitating causes operate sequentially rather than in a single temporally defined situation is possibly the greatest advance that Smelser has given to the functional theory of change. Like MacIver he has also reinforced that often neglected fact that causation is always mediated through the assessments and the judgments of willful human beings.

Conflict Theory

In recent years there has been a revival of the idea that social conflict is a basic process stimulating social change (Coser, 1956, 1957; Dahren-dorf). Conflict theorists have typically been critical of the structural and functional approach to change but the two approaches can be reconciled. Modern conflict theory emphasizes the dynamic, fluid, temporal-processual aspects of social life which structural and functional analysts have often overlooked. Conflict theory accepts the functional approach as a valid one for *structural studies* but asks the additional question of what drives society on? Dahrendorf, an advocate of conflict theory in change analysis writes:

If we extrapolate the analytical approaches of the structural-functional theory somewhat beyond their boundaries and investigate their implicit postulates, we can construct a model of society which lies at the base of this theory and determines its perspectives. The essential elements of this societal model are these:

    1. Every society is a relatively persisting configuration of elements.
    2. Every society is a well-integrated configuration of elements.
    3. Every element in a society contributes to its functioning.
    4. Every society rests on the consensus of its members.

It should be clear that a theory based on this model does not lend itself to the explanation, not even the description, of the phenomena of social conflict and change. For this purpose, one needs a model which takes the diametrically opposite position on all the four points above:

    1. Every society is subjected at every moment to change: social change is ubiquitous.
    2. Every society experiences at every moment social conflict: social conflict is ubiquitous.
    3. Every element in a society contributes to its change.
    4. Every society rests on constraint of some of its members by others.

The remarkable nature of our vantage point becomes evident when we examine the two groups of postulates with respect to their truth content, that is, if we ask ourselves which of the two models promises greater utility for cognition of reality. It appears that the juxtaposed pairs of postulates are in no way mutually exclusive with respect to social reality. It is impossible to decide by an empirical investigation which of the two models is more nearly correct; the postulates are not hypotheses. Moreover, it seems meaningful to say that both models are in a certain sense valid and analytically fruitful. Stability and change, integration and conflict, function and "dysfunction," consensus and constraint are, it would seem, two equally valid aspects of every imaginable society. They are dialectically separated and are exhaustive only in combination as a description of the social problems. Possibly a more general theory of society may be thought of which lifts the equivalidity of both models, the coexistence of the uncombinable, onto a higher level of generality. As long as we do not have such a theory, we must content ourselves with the finding that society presents a double aspect to the sociological understanding, each no better, no more valid, than the other. It follows that the criticism of the unapplicability of the structural-functional theory for the analysis of conflict is directed only against a claim of generality of this theory but leaves untouched its competence with respect to the problem of integration. It follows, on the other hand, also that the theory of conflict and change is not a general theory. Comparisons between natural and social sciences always carry the danger of misunderstanding. However, it may be maintained, without attributing to this analogy more than a logical meaning, that the situation of the sociologists is not unlike that of the physicists with respect to the theory of light. Just as the physicists can solve certain problems only by assuming the wave character of light and others, on the contrary, only by assuming a corpuscular or quantum theory, so there are problems of sociology which can be adequately attacked only with an integration theory and others which require a conflict theory for a meaningful analysis. Both theories can work extensively with the same categories, but they emphasize different aspects. While the integration theory likens a society to an ellipse, a rounded entity which incloses all of its elements, conflict theory sees society rather as a hyperbola which, it is true, has the same foci but is open in many directions and appears as a tension field of the determining forces. [Dahrendorf, pp. 174–175.]

CONCLUSION

Many nineteenth- and early twentieth-century theories of change sought to establish a universal "prime mover" which, as a causal and determining force, gave rise to the great sweeps or trends of history. Often such causal theories were associated with still grander conceptions of "progress" or social evolution. These theories, in their causal aspects, were usually particularistic and deterministic. They sought to attribute change to a particular variable or set of variables as direct cause-and-effect relationship. Many of them attributed change to forces extrinsic to social life, e.g., climate, race, or instinct. In "social Darwinism," "progress" was attributed to the natural outworking of the evolutionary principles of "struggle for existence" and "survival of the fittest." Countering such naturalistic theories, were teleological ones viewing social evolution as purposeful striving among men. In the works of still other scholars, specific aspects of culture or specific sectors or processes in society were given causal status. In America, great attention was paid "material culture" and its accelerating development as a force requiring adjustment and change in social organization. Other sociologies have attributed special dynamic significance to particular segments of society, e.g., an elite, "marginal social types," and others.

Modern sociology has almost fully abandoned the search for the elusive well-spring of social evolution. There has further been consistent retreat from any assumption of simple, direct, and unilinear causal sequences in social phenomena. Particularly under the impact of functionalism, analytical emphases have shifted from attempts to find the causation of a given condition in a prior event to an analysis of reciprocating relationships in the elements of a social system. The concept of cause in the older, deterministic sense has given way to a recognition that social events arise out of multiple processes which operate reciprocally rather than determinatively.

It has often been alleged that functionalism retarded the study of social change because of the structural, equilibrium model of a social system from which it proceeds. In recent years, however, functionalists have attempted to move beyond the equilibrium model into the realm of evolutionary process through which social systems are transformed—not merely re-equilibrated. At the same time, a revival of conflict theory has emphasized a tension-conflict model for the analysis of processes culminating in change. The interactional conflict approach associated with functionalist developments gives promise of new advances toward a theory of social change causation. At the point at which causal analysis begins, both approaches posit the mindful individual who assesses a situation and acts toward preserving the status quo or toward change. In the next chapter, the conditions are laid out under which such innovative assessments are stimulated or are inhibited.

3

Conditions Conducive
to Change

If we had knowledge of a truly static human society it might serve
as a contrasting model to help us understand the conditions which give
rise to change. But our only models of societal stasis are those derived
from the study of the social insects. Where social organization rests
in biological and chemical processes it can persist unchanged for thousands and even millions of years. Where social organization is built by
designing, symbolizing, and interacting men, stasis in any literal sense is
inconceivable. There are conditions inherent to the society of men which
necessitate or require change. This is true howsoever highly valued the
ways of the past, and however unchanging a society may appear when
viewed over any short span of years. Obviously, societies differ greatly
in their capabilities for rapid change as well as in their capacities to
stimulate particular kinds of changes.

Underlying most social change is the fact of prior change. Any given
innovation usually arises in a social situation which is already dynamic.
Many innovations appear in response to prior innovations. Real societies
rarely "hold still" while a single novelty is introduced and responded to.
Social systems possess enduring structures but typically these structures
are in process of continuous modification. When we begin the study
of change with the introduction of innovation, it must be remembered
that innovation usually enters into a stream of social life which is already
dynamic.

Anthropologists have persistently reported upon societies which were
so slow to change that they appeared, at a given time, to approximate

stasis (Holmberg; Piggott, pp. 138ff.). For a better understanding of the conditions conducive to change, it is instructive first to review the conditions of minimal change. Typically these societies (1) have been small in size, (2) isolated to a high degree from contact with differing cultures, (3) have had a small store of technical equipment, (4) have lacked means of storing and transmitting knowledge through writing. It is generally observed that such societies also have (5) venerated or "moralized" a wide range of traditional patterns of action, (6) held a relatively homogeneous and consistent value system and (7) possessed a socio-cultural system which was closely integrated and internally consistent.

Even where the above characteristics are found in extreme degree, the development of a perfectly equilibrated social order persisting in a perfectly equilibrated relationship to other groups and to the ecological milieu is beyond (or below) human capabilities. The present chapter is devoted to the conditions which make this so or, stated in other terms, the conditions which give rise to innovative behavior in distinctively human societies.[1]

HOW SOCIAL ORGANIZATION STIMULATES CHANGE

Imperfect Integration of the Internal Social System

A society and its culture is not a junk heap of unrelated traits and individuals. Technologies hold functionally integrated relationships to tools; norms have some consistency with social values; individual aspirations also bear relationship to societal values; the mechanisms of social mobility are related to the worthy goals set out in value systems; etc. Sub-groups and individuals also operate with patterned reciprocities and related accommodation channels. In the perfectly integrated system, each existing part would give support to the retention of each other part. The introduction of any novelty at any point in such a system implies adjustive change in every other part, much as the shift in the size of a cog in a clock mechanism would have dynamic significance for the entire mechanism—if it is to continue functioning. When the elements of a system are closely integrated there are few tension points to be perceived and hence to stimulate unrest (Sharpe).

Human societies must be sufficiently integrated that they can function toward individual and group goal achievement. But the full analogy

---

[1] Implicit in this emphasis upon the conditions favoring change is the recognition of converse conditions unfavorable to change. For a sophisticated analysis of obstacles to change with particular reference to developing societies, see Wilbert E. Moore (1951, especially Chap. 2). See also Chapters 8 and 14 below.

of clockwork perfection would not apply even to a social insect society much less to societies composed of biologically human materials. Ralph Linton expressed this many years ago when he wrote:

No culture, of course, will ever be in a perfect state of integration, i.e., have all its elements in a condition of complete mutual adjustment, as long as change of any sort is under way. Since change of some sort, whether due to invention or diffusion, is always going on, this means that no culture is ever perfectly integrated at any point in its history. Integration thus becomes a matter of degree and presumably there is a point below which it cannot sink without the paralysis of the culture and the consequent destruction of the society as a functioning entity. However, this point is rarely if ever reached. . . .

In this the fact that culture is a socio-psychological and not a physical phenomenon once more comes to the fore. The degree of integration which is required for its successful functioning is in no way comparable to that necessary to the successful functioning of an organism. Cultures, like personalities, are perfectly capable of including conflicting elements and logical inconsistencies. [Linton, pp. 357–358.] *

The preservation of inconsistencies appears to be a universal feature of human society. Partly this is possible because activities in one sector of life are not bound up with all others, e.g., how one cares for his garden may or may not affect how one worships his God and vice versa (Sorokin, Chap. 1). Partly, these inconsistencies arise because of the diverse functional potentials of any given behavior or belief. Faith in divine revelation can be functionally consistent with a particular social authority system while being functionally inconsistent with maximizing one's crops. Familiar incongruities also arise when conflicting demands exist within a single role or when legitimate effort is frustrated in the achievement of its legitimate rewards, or where established reciprocities are imbalanced in their rewards to each party. Such inconsistencies establish stresses which, when perceived by individuals, become sources of unrest and strain. Individuals frequently respond to such strains with innovations toward more satisfying, integrative relationships which will purportedly resolve the strains. However, such basic stresses are not necessarily responded to by innovation and modification in social organization. Instead of modifying the social organization, a new ideology can be introduced which can provide a satisfying acceptance of an inherently stressful status quo. White supremacists, for example, have attempted to preserve a system of inequality on grounds of "God's will" and Biblical injunction. "Pie in the sky" is a familiar alternative to changes in the social order. In sum, imperfect integration offers a stressful condition which may be perceived by members and stimulate them to think of ways of modifying either the organizational structure itself or the ideology which supports it.

Imperfect Integration of the External Social System

Not only do outside groups offer stimulus to change by proffering cultural novelty either advertently or inadvertently through diffusion; they also stimulate change in a given group or society simply by modifying their own patterns so that linked groups must make some adjustments to the changes. Rarely if ever is a social system without patterned relationships integrating it to other systems. These patterns reflect some degree of accommodation, e.g., mutually accepted boundaries, accepted prerogatives, and trade reciprocities. When the exterior group behaves in a manner which appears to reject these understandings, or even threatens to contravene them, reciprocal changes are stimulated in the other social system.

The integration developed between groups is essentially of the same type as that developed among interlocked individuals within a social system. Frequently threats to intergroup equilibrium are met through innovative devices modeled upon those which exist for mediating and controlling tensions within social systems. Insofar as every social system is in relationship with external ones, change within either set stresses for change in the other. Internal structure is in part determined by the kinds of relationships existing with other groups. When the external group shifts its position, account must be taken of this shift no matter how perfect is the established internal equilibrium. This is decisively illustrated in the case of boundary expansion by one of several complementing groups within a community and by the internal consequences of military attack by one political state upon another.

Imperfect Integration of the Ecological System

Every persisting society has a body of knowledge and technology sufficiently effective to preserve its ongoingness in the natural environment. Tensions arise as behavior patterns toward the environment fail adequately to fulfill the requirements for group survival or the standards of expectation within the group. Where methods of relating to natural forces were actually dysfunctional, those societies would not long have survived.

The environmental adaptations of the Eskimo and northern Amerindians to Arctic conditions in contrast to the environmental technology of the eighteenth- and nineteenth-century European travelers makes the point. The Eskimos had built a specialized system of organization and technology for dealing with their environmental forces. The technology of the European did not permit him to cope successfully in the new environment. Functional devices such as sod-houses, snow-houses, parkas, and seal-skin boots were quickly assessed and adopted by the outsiders.

Since human life is ultimately dependent upon the effectiveness of patterned relationships to natural forces, people tend to be highly sensitive to modifications perceived in their bio-physical environment. Sometimes natural forces are so catastrophic and dramatic in their effects that traditional patterns are abandoned temporarily in massive unrest and the search for a panacea. The exhaustion of critical resources is an ultimate force for cultural change, if life itself is not to be extinguished. There is, however, no way of predicting just what kind of changes will be made except by recourse to an understanding of the particular social forces which guide decision making. The natural environment may thrust change upon a people, but it is indeterminative as to what direction or type of change is stimulated.

In the Eastern jungles of Ceylon, slash and burn cultivation has been sufficiently functional that community life has been preserved for many centuries (Ryan et al., 1955). In recent years jungle ecology has changed. In this system of shifting cultivation, the bush is burned and crops planted for a single season. Land is then permitted to revert to jungle and given time to re-establish fertility before it is again burned and planted. For whatever reason, in this particular locale normal jungle growth is not returning to the burned-over land. Instead, a rhizome grass is replacing it which cannot be successfully burned off. Disequilibrium has arisen between the socio-cultural system and the natural environment so that life itself is threatened. Peasants perceive the force for change in this new ecology and they correctly foresee the demise of a way of jungle life which is dear to them. If we would know just what kind of external system will replace the old one, we would have to take into account government conservation and resettlement policies, alternative resources, introduction of superior technical equipment, the possibilities of urban migration—and central to all of these, the assessments made by the peasants themselves as responsive action is charted. But the basic choice is between starvation and innovation.

Despite the complex technological buffer which Western societies have built between them and the natural environment, the United States has been pushed to adjustive response in regard to resource changes. Dust storms and erosion which became critical in the 1930's awoke America to the realization that soils are not a permanent gift of God. It has been claimed that unless drastic changes are made in land-use practices, the vast and fertile Mississippi Valley will be a wasteland before the end of the next century (Vogt). Social change becomes an imperative either before or after the fact. Innovations may be directed toward preservation of the soil through modifications in technology, governmental controls, etc. They may also be directed toward finding functional equivalents for the rich farmlands of the Midwest in the form of synthetic foods, hydroponic farming, etc. Actually, both types of response are being followed—certain of them, such as experimentation with synthetic foods, in response also to more complex incentives than those provided in soil erosion, e.g., space travel, population growth, threat of war, profit through chemistry.

A more immediate instance of shift in a natural resource is that of the water supply in the United States (Morcell). Lowering water tables and depletion of reserves were dramatized in New York City in 1965 when strict rationing was required even to the matter of the conventional glass of water served in the restaurant. Conservationists in Florida are considering ways of preventing the Everglades from shifting to virtual desert through a lowered water table. Elsewhere de-salinization plants are being constructed against the day when the oceans must serve as a regular supply source for industrial and residential purposes.

In the area of energy sources, the threat of depletion in coal supplies and increasing costs of production provided a stimulus to oil as a coal replacement (Cottrell; Isard and Whitney, 1952; Landsdell; Whitney, 1950). Coal, a fossil fuel laid down thousands of years ago and wholly unreplenishable by man, must be replaced if high energy societies are to survive. The equilibrium established in relationship to coal is partially maintained through a partial shift in industrial uses to petroleum. This newer fossil fuel is also limited, and perception of this stimulates innovative effort in adapting to nuclear energy and possibly to sun and tidal energy for power needs.

Loose and Rigid Social Structure

The theory of loose and rigid structure has been advanced as a special way of looking at socio-cultural integration in relationship to innovation (Embree; Ryan and Straus). Societies appear to differ in the precision with which groups are organized and norms defined and imposed. This is not a matter of lacking integration but rather one involving degrees of rigidity in structure. A loosely structured society is one marked by the presence of numerous normative alternative patterns of behavior, tolerance to deviance, latitude in role prescriptions, and vagueness in the boundaries of its constituent groups. Members of loosely integrated societies are enjoined to stay within the main streams of normative expectation but are not given precise precepts of conduct. For example, the precept to "Remember the Sabbath and keep it holy" has more closely defined behavioral significance for the orthodox Jew than for the Unitarian, although both of them would accept the validity of the injunction. Similarly in role behavior, the specific precepts of Confucius in regard to behavior toward one's father contrast sharply with injunctions of a society which demands that one honors one's father, without ritualizing or circumscribing the modes by which this is to be done.

While definitive comparisons of various societies in regard to looseness and rigidity have never been undertaken, several studies support its significance for social change (Angell, pp. 140–142). Thus, loose integration has been utilized as a condition explaining the smoothness with which modern innovations in values and attitudes have been introduced into Ceylon.

Permissiveness of individual behavior in the sense of many alternative norms, imprecisely defined role patterning, and tolerance even to non-normative deviation combine with weak norms of group solidarity to yield the condition of "loose structure." As Embree has pointed out for Thailand, 'The permissiveness of individual behavior variation in the culture does not mean that the society is poorly integrated. On the contrary, the loose integration is a functional one, allowing not only variation in individual behavior but also in national behavior. It has survival value . . . that is, a loosely integrated structure such as the Thai may adjust to external cultural influences with less drastic over-all changes than a more rigid structure such as the Japanese or Vietnamese.' Thus, for the Sinhalese, it has been argued that colonial rule had immediate organizing effects upon Sinhalese institutions rather than degenerative or disorganizing effects. While this observation requires qualification in reference to the caste system, for the familial institution European influence was never disorganizing in spite of deliberate statutory restriction upon customary marriage practices. There is every indication that European influence had a formalizing and rigidifying effect through the partial limitation of old alternatives rather than the demolition of old norms in favor of new. The fact that the norms of Sinhalese life . . . are matters of principle rather than specifications of conduct offers wide latitude for change so long as it is consistent with the non-specific normative principles. [Ryan et al., 1958, p. 193.]

The limited evidence suggests that ambiguity and latitude in structure offers innovative opportunity through both tolerance for normative deviance and misunderstandings of both norms and role expectations. There is also reason to believe that "loosely structured" societies are more amenable to innovation through their tolerance to a variety of alternative behavior patterns within any given situation.

Social Replacement and Succession

Every group with persistence in time must undergo the replacement of members and, almost as inevitably, the shifting of members from one position to another. Theodore Caplow (pp. 85 ff.) has pointed out that for the continuity of an organized group it must be possible to determine which members occupy which positions at any given moment; to add or subtract members; to add or subtract positions; and to move members from one position to another. Organizational persistence requires continuity in the positions within the group and acceptance of associated role expectations as members shift from one position to another.

However firmly a group attempts to groove the individual into a continuing role slot, individuals remain individuals. Variations arise in the ways in which role responsibilities are accepted or understood or acted upon. The problem of "strategic replacement" is critical for stability in group operations. Many investigators have shown how the replacement of one individual by another in a leadership role has brought re-definition of group goals with consequent changes in organization (Gouldner, 1954; Caplow, pp. 155 ff.). Alvin Gouldner found such a circumstance in a gypsum plant to which he gave close study. Upon the replacement of a plant manager by a new man with differing values, lower supervisory staff at first impeded the new procedures. As the uncooperative supervisors were replaced by the new manager's trusted aides, the new ideas of the new manager were activated, along with new attitudes which permeated the plant. Alexander Leighton in his study of internment camps during World War II and Richard H. McCleery studying prison structure have both shown significant changes in group structure occurring because of "imperfect" replacements in the respective organizational bureaucracies.

Even the physiological aging process alone requires shifting of the individual's positions in the social system and, with shifts, replacement. When replacement follows a patterned rhythm, the social organization remaining the same, we may not say that social change has taken place. However, processes of replacement represent points of tension in the status quo since the recruit is not in fact identical to the predecessor. As a new personality takes on the old office, modifications in the informal relationships within the group are certain—and even structural changes may, or may not, follow. Raymond Firth has expressed this in discussing such origins of change in Tikopia. He has pointed out that with the succession of a new chief to office, the *structure* of social relationships is not altered, but that social change arises through the fact that relations between specific persons and groups are modified. A new chief brings a new kin group into dominance, requiring the reorientation of various other kin groups to the new seat of power as well as to each other.

The theory of change through social replacement has been particularly well developed in the field commonly termed "circulation of elites." In such theories, replacement is generally presumed to be by different social types than those previously in the roles of power. Pareto (p. 1515), for example, shows cycles of replacement in the political and economic institutions. Such a cyclical conception relies upon the tendency of elites once in power to recruit regular replacements of their own type. However, while the iron-willed "lions" seek to maintain themselves in power, the wily "foxes" down below are plotting their downfall. Pareto does not extrapolate his theory of societal change, but it is clear that the rule of "foxes" is a different rule from that of "lions." Without accepting literally the cycle of elites as portrayed by Pareto, the replacement process in political upheavals is frequently of this order.

Succession and Bureaucracy. In Max Weber's theory of historical change, societies are viewed as alternating between charismatic and either bureaucratic or traditional (e.g., patriarchal) modes of authority (Gouldner, 1950, pp. 644–659). Charismatic authority rests upon the unique personal attributes of the leader. It is hence unstable and ephemeral as such a leader's methods of operation cease to conform to the needs set by changing conditions. The problem of succession is consequently a crucial one since the qualities of charismatic leadership are unique and hence not readily replaceable by another individual. The problems inherent in succession are forces toward bureaucratization since through the elaboration and rigidification of norms and procedures the scope of individuality is restricted. This is especially important where a high rate of succession occurs. As Gouldner observes, "authority becomes something of a commodity handed back and forth under certain general conditions" (p. 657). Bureaucracy makes explicit the expectations attached to an authority position and sets close limits to personal definitions of rights, duties, responsibilities, and procedures. It renders a particular authority legitimate on the basis of the office held rather than upon personal leadership qualities.

Quantitative Differences in Membership

When the number of persons involved in a set of relationships increases or decreases, innovation in the interactional system is imminent. Such innovations may take the form of simple multiplication or subtraction of sub-units within the established group structure. They may take the form of increasing or decreasing differentiation into specialized sub-groups. They may involve the unique differences between two-person and three-person groups as indicated below. Whatever the case, the simple fact of number shift absolutely requires revision, or contraction or expansion, in the group's interactional system.

Dyads and Triads. The classic contrasts of dyadic and triadic groups were those of G. Simmel upon whose ideas numerous inductive studies have been reared (Wolff). In the dyad, each of the two feels himself confronted only by the other, and the participant must recognize that the very group itself is dependent upon his continued participation. By the same token a majority can be found only through unanimity. Further, since the participants are undistracted, pure and intense reciprocity with jealous cohesion is stimulated. The triad, however, is a particularly unstable group. Subsequent research has demonstrated Simmel's point, that the threesome tends to break up into a pair and a third party (Mills). Caplow has observed that the introduction of a third party serves a catalytic function and that "the mere presence of a superior or inferior on the scene modifies a pair relationship in predictable ways" (p. 112). Even in larger groups the presence of even and odd numbers of persons change certain of the terms of interaction. On a moot issue the group with ten members can split into two equal parts, precluding a majority opinion (Bales, Borgatta). Add one member and the organization's potential is different.

Size, Density, and Social Change. Increasing density of population has long been viewed as a condition yielding tensions in a society. Howsoever far one follows Durkheim's position regarding "moral density," it is clear that many social relationships among persons in metropolitan communities are of a different order from those found in small, immobile communities, and that higher levels of technical efficiency are required. While it is not our purpose to investigate these contrasting community types, it is safe to say that a modern metropolis can not function governmentally through a town meeting nor exert adequate social control through gossip and ostracism, nor can it provide economic production and services through primary groups and traditional reciprocities. Under some circumstances population increase may add on as "segmental additions," i.e., new sub-groups no different from existing ones. Firth (p. 341) has described this process in Tikopia when a decision to split up sub-lineage land simply created new sub-lineage segments in the society. However, as *density* increases in a given area, there is substantial pressure toward the efficiencies of specialization, exchange, and "associational" structures. New sub-lineages might provide a solution in Tikopia, but New York City could never have grown as a multiplication of adjacent villages.

The large, dense, modern community absolutely requires that a high proportion of social relationships be impersonal, contractual, and formal in their quality, and that a large proportion of social groups be formally structured in their rules and relationships with specificity in role demands and in the nature of role reciprocities (Warner and Hilander: Indik). If high density does not *require* the contractual *gesellschaftlich* social structure, it at least makes mathematically impossible a life spent exclusively in primary relationships. To the depersonalizing and formalizing consequences of massiveness in groups, there is usually the further force of mobility in large complex societies to enhance impersonality and touch-and-go relationships.

Intense population concentration and related trends have been associated with numerous functional consequences as the nineteenth-century industrial city grew inwardly and produced its universal design of blight and overcrowding. Given humanitarian and rising socialistic values, such concentrations ultimately yielded innovations such as building codes, sanitation laws, settlement houses, and eventually zoning ordinances and renewal programs. Decentralization in urban growth sets the stage for new consequences, especially as separate municipalities are linked to form sprawling metropolitan regions. Novel concepts of governmental autonomy, as in Miami and Toronto, are virtually dictated by the new ecological patterns.

In any particular ecological layout, there are stringent limits to the kind of governmental structuring which can maintain order. As a society or community approaches these limits, disorder must increase and the social system face disruption, although within the limits, alternatives are possible.

Demographic Transition. In the modern world there have been two or three major demographic conditions each of which has produced identifiable response patterns (Hauser). During the 1930's natural increase fell to such a low point in most Western nations that there was consternation over the potential effects of a transition to stable and even declining populations. Predicting certain adverse consequences of these trends for military security and economic growth, Western governments began to explore varying alternative means to stimulate their birth rates. The rapid move toward socialism in the Scandinavian countries was substantially stimulated by the capacity of such systems to reduce the burdens of parenthood. Some nations found differing alternatives, e.g., Hitler sought to induce births through strict abortion laws and by honoring mothers as well as by offering financial subsidy.

An ironic twist occurred at the end of the 1930's, when, with continued drops in death rates, birth rates shifted from their downward course and rose substantially in many Western countries. This new era of more rapid population growth is having profound effect upon national economies and institutions. With such fixed values as the "American level of living" and "full employment," there is an almost ominous pressure toward increasing our national product and toward greater rationality in its distribution. In other spheres it is evident that schools feel the pressures of the "baby boom," and the plight of the aged becomes more dramatic as a larger share of our population lives into the years of retirement.

In the many regions of the world which have long been in relative stasis economically and have suffered from conditions so aptly described by Malthus nearly two hundred years ago, the 1940's saw even more dramatic stimuli to change through demographic pressures. Where Malthusian conditions of high fertility and high mortality had long been true, the 1940's brought significant declines in the death rates. In some regions of virtually uncontrolled fertility, death rates were nearly halved in two or three years through modern insecticides, improved nutrition, and to a lesser degree by "miracle drugs."

In a society which combines primitive technology with a high birth rate and a low death rate, something must give. Either productive power must be increased to support a rapidly enlarging population, or the rate of population growth is to be cut either by a drop in the birth rate or a rise in the death rate or by some combination of these. To be sure, there are other alternatives also entailing specific innovative patterns. Emigration may become general or economic aid may be secured in ever-increasing amounts from outside the region. The latter, however, are not realistic long-range solutions. That major changes *must* occur in these regions as a result of demographic factors is clear (see below, Chap. 14).

Response to demographic conditions is like responses to all other situational forces in that it is mediated by other factors such as social values and technical capacities. The contemporary dilemma of countries like India, Ceylon, and Puerto Rico has arisen through the interplay of social values and recent technological diffusions in medicine and health. Specifically the dilemma entails the basic values of health and life confronted for the first time with the technical means of good health and longevity.

Population Composition. Any shift in age or sex structure requires adjustive actions in the society. For example, increased proportions of children or of aged means decreased proportions of able-bodied working adults. Changes in proportion of men to women requires that some account be given in institutions associated with mating and family life and probably in occupational and other roles. An outstanding example of stress toward change through shifting population composition is that offered by the aged sector of the American population.

The aged in American society constitute about double the proportion of total population that they did a century ago. This has been due to a long-range reduction in the fertility rate and somewhat reduced death rates for persons in the middle and later years of life. Many of the consequences of this shift were predictable. Stimulation was given to medical problems of chronic nature and to distinctive services required by the elderly. In a society in which "retirement" had been a rather haphazard affair, it was to become a more formally recognized stage of life.

The "roleless role" of the aged was increasingly pronounced not only by virtue of increased numbers but by shifts in the welfare values of Americans, increasing demand for the dexterities of youth in production, the shift from rural to city living, and many other related trends. Adjustive efforts to "find a place" for the aged have ranged from the initiation of Senior Citizens organizations to hobby clubs and retirement villages. Economically a smaller proportion of the population must support a larger proportion of the population than before. Furthermore, novel mechanisms must be developed for routing the services and goods the elderly require but are incapable of acquiring through their own immediate effort.

Catastrophes and Disasters

Some catastrophes such as economic depression arise through the functioning of the internal social system. However, natural forces or actions of other societies can create catastrophic conditions for societies normally well and efficiently integrated internally, ecologically, and to outside groups as well. It is unlikely that the force of a natural versus a socially generated catastrophe has in itself any differential significance for the stimulation of change. More important than the source of tension are such variables as pre-disaster preparation, duration of the catastrophic force, its intensity, and extensity and its particular selectivity of victims. Some catastrophes are typically of short duration, e.g., tornadoes and hurricanes, while others like plagues and floods may persist for long periods (Carr). Some, like plagues and hurricanes, are widespread in impact; others, like explosions, are concentrated. Plagues are long lasting, hurricanes are not—and both are probably selective of the poor in their most violent effects.

The very terms "catastrophe" and "disaster" connote crisis—a situation which cannot be effectively dealt with by conventional or usual methods. The significance of critical events has led some scholars to view them as the key factors in social change generally (Washburne; Herman). Overwhelming events must indeed be faced, but this does not signify that crises necessarily have critical change effect upon the society enduring them.

Charles P. Loomis and others have emphasized the frequency with which communities meet their disasters through substantial retention of their normal patterns of action (Loomis, Essay 3; Bates et al.). "It generally is not true," writes Loomis, "as is so widely believed, that collective and individual actions immediately become unstructured and unpredictable" (p. 132). Pre-existing patterns are especially prone to reassert themselves in the recovery and post-disaster stages. Disaster research indicates a high degree of return of pre-disaster norms and continued acceptance of historic role responsibilities throughout the period of crisis and beyond. In addition many disasters arise as calculated risks for which a community is more or less prepared in the organizational sense. Key West and Miami, for example, with the recurrent hurricanes, "have the situation pretty well in hand" to the limit of technical knowledge and capacity to control. Change has already been evoked in the sense of preparatory innovations, novel role allocations for emergency, strict building codes, etc. The community may not be much different six months after the hurricane than it was before.

In the study of one natural disaster in Louisiana, the hurricane Audrey, it would seem that the major effects on the community were in the rearrangement of short-term social relationships (Bates *et al.*). However, certain innovations stemmed directly out of the situation immediately caused by Audrey. In the aftermath, disaster relief teams moved in with highly organized facilities and left behind them certain of these structures and some stimulus toward further formal civil and protective organization. The cautious words of the authors of the Audrey study regarding innovative response to threatened catastrophe are worth quoting:

If Hurricane Audrey had struck in 1947 instead of 1957, its social change consequences might have been quite different—perhaps more radical and drastic than they were in 1957. What changes occur after such a disaster depend on the point in the change cycle or life arc at which a community or society is caught. If there are many potential changes stored up in the system, a flood of change is likely to occur, but if a flood is already ebbing, the chances of a disaster releasing a new torrent of change are small. Furthermore, the changes that do occur at such a time will fit into the pre-existing pattern of change and represent expressions of it rather than completely new and different trends. One must also consider the possibility that disaster might retard change. This might be particularly true of economic change, for example. A disaster might destroy the resources—human, financial, or natural—upon which economic growth and change might have been based, and thereby inhibit changes which were already underway. [Bates *et al.*, pp. 112–113.] *

The changes noted in the Audrey study, however, cannot by any stretch of the imagination be described as overwhelming. It is concluded that the observed changes represented an acceleration of already operating processes rather than the introduction of completely new directions into the normal change process. It is probable that older theories on the place of crisis in social change exaggerated the climactic significance of "overpowering events." Discontinuity with the pre-disaster social system is maximized by catastrophes which permanently destroy the ecological balance of the society, e.g., intrusion of salt water into the soils of an agriculturally based community.

* Reprinted from *The Social and Psychological Consequences of A Natural Disaster: A Longitudinal Study of Hurricane Audrey*, National Academy of Sciences—National Research Council, Washington, D.C., 1963.

HOW CULTURE STIMULATES CHANGE

Qualities of the Culture Base Limit Innovation

Inventions are contrivances put together with material available to the inventor. They involve new designs or new configurations of ideas which are already known. Hence, invention is always limited by the society's body of knowledge at any given time. This is as true for inventions in the realm of social organization, like the corporation or the Supreme Court, as it is for mechanical devices. No stone-age society can produce a mechanical clock since the culture base does not include such knowledge as the malleability of metal or the techniques of casting, let alone the use of gears. No society without organized production and trade could devise the concepts of the corporate individual and limited liability. The limits of inventing lie in what is available for the inventor to work with. The nature of the available material defines the ultimate range of things that can be created through inventive effort.

Size of the Culture Base

No single invention ever relies upon a society's entire body of knowledge, nor upon any large share of it. For example, in inventing an atom bomb it is improbable that existing knowledge of genetics came to bear upon the problem in any remote way. However, scores of other lines of discovery and invention were required to form the groundwork upon which the inventors built. Since invention is the new combination of previously known ingredients, it follows that the larger the stock of potential ingredients the greater is the number of possible combinations. It does not follow that *all* possible combinations, nor even the majority, would constitute culturally useful innovations. Yet substantial evidence has been amassed that "culture accumulates at an increasing rate of growth." Ogburn called this the exponential principle of cultural accumulation. Such a principle is not to be construed as "natural law." There is nothing inherent in culture which *makes* it grow in such a manner. The more modest truth is that the more knowledge and cultural traits that exist, the greater is the likelihood of a manipulating animal—man—turning up some new arrangement of cultural interest. The craftsmen limited to a piece of wood and a knife cannot fabricate as many different objects as those possessing more elaborate materials. There is nothing which says that either group of craftsmen will in fact ever and always increase the rate of their inventing or, for that matter, even continue to increase the absolute size of the body knowledge and equipment, though the latter is highly probable.

With passing time the body of knowledge and techniques seems to grow larger and larger both in general and in specific societies. This is dramatized in Western society in which today no single individual understands more than a tiny part of an immense cultural heritage. The sum total of ideas and contrivances has grown larger and larger. No doubt the same process takes place in practically all societies, it being more apparent under modern conditions of rapid innovating. This growth suggests that new knowledge and new tools do not merely replace old knowledge and old tools but also that the new is added to the old. Not only do old techniques come to be absorbed into new inventions but few useful arts are completely lost from the body of knowledge even though more efficient substitutes are discovered. Fish hooks and nets are very old, yet they are used by modern refrigerator ships. Wind-jammers give way to steam and nuclear powered ships, but the skills of sailing, tacking, and rigging are carried on. Modern techniques of house building cannot do without the ancient invention of the lintel. While much specific knowledge gained by Paleolithic men is no longer functional, much of his general knowledge is still vitally incorporated in our instruments. And in matters of non-material innovation such as concepts of God, new theologies do not replace old theologies so much as they provide growing and alternative systems of belief. The late Alexander Goldenweiser expressed these ideas very clearly:

Let us not forget, then, in connexion with invention, that persistence is an equally ubiquitous and no less significant phenomenon. The basic primitive inventions are not dead—they live on among us, either as constituent parts of later inventions, or side by side with them. The lever, though not understood theoretically, was used as an empirical device among many primitives, and it still constitutes one of the pillars of modern mechanics. The sapling, bent out of its natural position to provide the dynamic factor in a primitive trap, is the remote forerunner of the spring which runs untold millions of watches and performs numerous other tasks in modern technology. The achievement of Alexander the Great in cutting the Gordian Knot, though dramatic, did not equal that other achievement—the tying of the first knot. And this knot, in the midst of an ever growing family of knots, is still with us. [Goldenweiser, p. 134.]

Though the rate of invention tends to increase over time, many old inventions continue usefully and also form a basis for newer, more efficient, or at least more desired, items which do the same job.

Value-Norm Systems

Every society holds certain fundamental truths to be sacred and not to be defiled. These form a matrix of values in reference to which man views nature, the supernatural, and his fellow man (Kluckhohn and

Strodtbeck). More or less consistent with these ultimate verities are the moral norms, those precepts for the guidance of action which share in the sacredness of the values which they support and manifest. In sum these determine the ethos of a people—their characteristic way of looking at things, their style of life—and, in terms commonly used by anthropologists, their "world view."

In the value-norm system of every society are implicit concepts specifying which of man's achievements are worthy and what orientations are to be used as fixed points in testing the rightness and wrongness of all actions. These fundamental orientations of life are reflected in concrete institutions; in the behaviors which are sanctioned or condemned, and in the kinds of sacrifices which men will and will not make. It is, for example, from such broad concepts that we may approach a summary understanding of what it was that occurred in Western Europe to give rise to the greatest spurt of innovation and social and cultural change the world has yet seen—barring the dependent, contemporary transitions in Asia and Africa.

A powerful force working toward discovery and invention in Western society was the conviction that man's proper sphere lay in the conquest of nature. This view of man, pitting himself against natural forces, was supported by the nineteenth-century theory of progress to yield powerful stimulants to science and technology. At the same time Protestantism dignified work and profit and supported movements which would yield knowledge of the natural world through observation rather than through revelation. If Protestant movements valued life after death as much as did medieval churchmen, their differing views as to its attainment also worked to stimulate secular labor, science, and increasing productivity. Man should achieve in a secular sense, man should produce, man should use his talents to their greatest secular "good." In this movement the non-religious assertors of humanism, the secular gospel of man striving ever for knowledge and control for human ends, worked toward the same transformation.

Truth through faith was toppled by a new truth through sensory experience. Passive man in a God-ordered universe yielded to active man building his own destiny. The national political state rose as a structure within which men could exercise their newly created "natural rights" of individuality and achievement. In this emancipation of the individual and deification of individual striving, humane goals were frequently lost sight of, in the zeal with which productive achievement by individuals was pursued (Nisbet). The enterpriser acted to the glory of God, and the industrial inventor was God's hand servant.

The role of the inventor in this new world order was illustrated by Charles Goodyear, the inventor of vulcanized rubber. Goodyear was sure that he had been called by God that He might have His bidding done on earth. Goodyear himself wrote:

He who directs the operation of the mind can turn it to development of the properties of Nature in his own way, and at the time when they are specially needed. The creature imagines he is executing some plan of his own, while he is simply an instrument in the hands of his Maker for executing the divine purposes of beneficence to the race. [Thompson, pp. 160–165.]

We might question if Goodyear could have persevered through his years of disappointment had he not been imbued with inspirations more powerful than those of craftsmanship or wealth.

One may consider also a world view which contrasts with both the medieval and with the modern Western, but is similar in innovative consequence to that of the former. Primitive societies frequently accept man as part of nature, visualizing him as part of the balanced natural order. Man's aim is not set toward mastery of his environment. Nor is he properly an exploiter of the natural order, nor an instrument of the supernatural. He copes with and uses nature, never defying it. He does not force it and make demands upon it. Dorothy D. Lee has described the Hopi in such terms (Lee; Redfield, pp. 105-106). The Hopi, in making a living from the natural environment, have no thought of "conquering" nature. Rather, food is produced through a harmonic state of mutual dependence between man and natural forces. Man works *with* the elements, not *against* them. While there is dependence upon the crops, this is understood as a mutual interdependence with nature rather than as exploitation and control. It is obvious that such a world view is not likely to motivate men toward inventions calculated to wring the most from a niggardly natural environment. Whatever may be true of other spheres of life, this orientation yields a passivity in regard to technological inventing that Goodyear would have found an unintelligible miscarriage of God's plan. In a different context Lyle Saunders has described the world view of Spanish-speaking peoples in the Southwestern United States. Here the background of peasant villages has yielded time concepts in which man sees no purpose in hurry or in precision, a cultural view which similarly lacks dynamism for technological change.

Theories of nature, physiology, and the sacred status of traditional truths may all operate against dynamism toward change. It is less that the traditional societies fear the new than that they place high values upon the world as they know it and upon the truths which have served their forefathers in the same milieu. While all such societies have spheres of activity in which more productive innovations may be welcome, they have not felt the driving forces which entered Western Europe with the rise of modern cities and the revolutionary outlooks of those who built concepts making progress a living philosophy.

Every society varies in the personal achievements and goals to which individuals are led to aspire. Where such values are associated with the traditional social and technical order, innovative behavior is inhibited. Thus, a prerequisite for mechanical invention is tinkering with existing gadgets and the handling of tools. No societies would view such behavior as morally wrong. Many, however, make it socially unacceptable and even degrading. In the traditionally caste-structured society of Ceylon, persons of education or high social position associate mechanical tinkering with low status responsibilities. Education here has implied manipulation of symbols, but not of artifacts. Business enterprise, a tremendous stimulant to utilitarian invention in the West, is also degraded. The kind of achievement motivations which drive these people do not stir the feeling of "progress" (Ryan, 1961).

Social values and norms are not always clearly distinguishable but analytically norms are behavior patterns, while values and world views are the basic viewpoints from which behavioral precepts or norms are derived, or to which they are rationalized. When norms are protected by effective legal sanctions or strong moral tones, they merge with values. Persons who depart from them are usually termed deviants rather than innovators. Much "deviant" behavior is not innovative since innumerable deviant patterns already exist to be learned by budding criminals, bohemians, or hippies. Yet novel deviant behavior patterns must be considered innovative whether they arise in reference to moral precepts, etiquette, or role definitions. Since all societies have a sacred attachment to at least part of the normative order, innovating in these fields is treated with greater discouragement than is usually encountered by innovative, mechanical technologists. That customary and legal norms do in fact undergo innovative processes is attested by fairly recent redefinitions of the propriety of bikinis, lipstick, divorce, and the legality of segregated schools. Nonetheless, the strength of moral tone which a society grants a pattern of behavior is, other matters being equal, a measure of the degree to which innovators are warned off the premises. Since "other matters" do not remain equal, we find, for example, the new urban milieu accepting innovative deviant behavior which the surrounding countryside holds to be immoral and unacceptable.

Changing times and circumstance, if nothing else, inspire innovators to act in regard to norms. Frequently, such actions are unself-conscious, or perhaps reluctant, adjustments to new situations. As a caste-conscious Hindu villager observed, "A man just can't keep his religion in the city," implying in this context that the moral precepts of caste untouchability simply wouldn't work there in a physical sense.

In the United States an outstanding innovator in normative social relationships was the eminent Judge Ben Lindsey (Lindsey and Evans).

Judge Lindsey, already beloved and famous as a proponent of the Family Court, proposed that we adopt a plan of trial or companionate marriage as a means of cutting down marital mismatches with their consequent unhappiness and divorce. Judge Lindsey had a rational device and it was well worked out in plan. It was a true social invention. Of course, the idea did not arise full-blown in the Judge's mind; other reformers had similar ideas and the Judge was well aware that deviant "innovators" were already practicing along the lines he detailed. Yet he formulated a clear social plan and showed how it could be put into operation. The response to Judge Lindsey by the public is sufficient to tell us why innovative plans in the "moral" sphere are so infrequently attempted on a self-conscious level. Judge Lindsey, who at the point of this proposal was one of America's most honored jurists, came overnight to be described as a public villain and betrayer of youth. Textbooks used in courses on Marriage and Family usually side-step the issues raised by Lindsey and almost never overtly support innovations in sexual matters—until uncoordinated deviations from tradition have reached the status of relative respectability. Forward planning in moral inventions is not a value in our society and few persons are brave enough to assign themselves to such innovative tasks.

These behavior patterns which a society moralizes are hence less fertile fields for innovation than those which are "cold" from the standpoint of sentiments. Nonetheless, even non-moral patterns become institutionalized so that thoughtful tampering is discouraged. Vested interests have been known to discourage inventions which might reduce profits (Stern). Innovative suggestions are not developed rapidly in regard to classroom procedures in universities. In a nation which annually spends billions of dollars on research, that part which goes into research on behavioral innovation of any type is small. But the application of scientific attitudes and research to social change is nonetheless rapidly gaining. Many of the inventive and modifying plans in some fields come as responses to technological "advance." They arise as men grope for patterns which will permit institutional life to go forward with minimum deviation from the older norms and precepts. The rapidity of change in Western societies arises in no small part from the fact that it has so thoroughly emancipated wide spheres of behavior from the realm of the sacred.

Systems of Truth and Knowledge

Alfred North Whitehead once observed that the most staggering invention of all time was the invention of the method of invention. The rise of science as a means of acquiring truth regarding nature introduced a revolutionary potential from the standpoint of change. For cultural and social dynamics, it matters greatly whether or not a society finds the ultimate source of truth in revelation and tradition or in the verification of hypotheses through pragmatic, sensory observation. When the methods of sensory observation become systematized into the institution of science, the potential for technological change is explosive. The rapidity of change in modern society is outstanding not only because of the high valuation of technical progress but also because of the systematization and institutionalization of the means for attaining verifiably functional knowledge. While technological change is not social change, it is evident that some equilibrium must exist between the technological and the normative and organizational structures. The crucial differences between the truth of science and that resting upon other grounds is that scientific truth can be verified and improved by the same methods that produced it. It is never absolute or final truth.

Particularly in modern times, groups have been formed with the express purpose of innovating. The solitary inventor in his armchair and his private laboratory is not a thing of the past, but increasingly social and mechanical innovations are worked out by teams and teams of teams (Jewkes *et al.*, Chaps. 6, 7). Division of labor in the innovative process is one reason for the immense rapidity of the technical and social change in our era. In this connection, the National Resources Planning Board, seeking ways and means of protecting America's resources, was as much an inventive body as is the research branch of a chemical corporation. Virtually every government bureau contains "program analysis" sections to assess organizational plans and procedures and with eyes toward innovation. In the U.S. Department of Agriculture sub-organizations of economists, sociologists, and psychologists do team research on scores of projects calculated to modify existing rural programs and even the structure of the Department of Agriculture itself so that it can meet changing conditions set by international affairs, new political interests, and changing American values in regard to government and its functions. Large sums are spent by government, universities, research foundations, and private industry on "basic" research, from which it is presumed ultimate inventing will rely. Vaster sums are spent upon direct organized innovative effort in practical technology in the well-advertised laboratories of Bell Telephone, duPont, and scores of other corporations and universities. According to the National Science Foundation, the United States spent some $24 billion on research and development in 1967. The federal government has been the largest contributor throughout. By 1965 over half a billion persons were employed as full time scientists in research and development programs. Although basic research receives much less support ($3.2 billion in 1966) outlays here have been increasing at an even more rapid rate than money devoted to more immediately practical research and development. Never before has inventing been as deliberately fostered as through immensely supported networks wherein the research findings of one may be built upon by another.

HOW SOCIAL CONTACT STIMULATES CHANGE

Isolation has a retarding effect upon innovation and change. This is true whether the isolation arises from ecological factors or as a purely social, segregative process. Any barrier to communication has negative effects upon change. This is true for three reasons. (1) Isolation in the social sense denotes lack of communication and only through communicative contacts are novel ideas diffused from one society to another or from a given sector of a society to others. Even awareness that an existing state can be improved upon often depends upon knowledge of how outsiders do things. (2) When novelty is diffused it stimulates further innovating in the very process of being integrated into the new sociocultural system. (3) The body of culture being enlarged through this diffusion, a larger cultural base is provided upon which inventors can work.

It is doubtful if anywhere in the voluminous literature of anthropology there is reported any society which has lived in complete isolation from all other differing ones. There is evidence of extensive migrations of man even in the Lower Paleolithic period. Where strict territorial boundaries are maintained among primitive peoples, a stray arrow shot into forbidden territory can provide innovative stimulus, and boundaries are rarely if ever so firmly fixed for long. Through the histories of all civilized societies, there are persistent records from the earliest times of migrations, invasions, and cultural emissaries. In modern times, physical barriers are surpassed without the need of personal contact between communicators.

Neither physical contact nor radio transmission guarantees that innovative ideas will be accepted across cultural boundaries. In response to intense outside cultural contact, peoples frequently become strongly defensive of their traditional ways. Yet it is difficult to find societies which have lived side by side for long periods of time either as autonomous peoples or as conqueror and conquered who have not exchanged ideas and had long-lasting influences on each other. Often such exchanges are imbalanced, in the sense that one party accepts more than the other, but exchange almost invariably occurs. With mass communication media the trans-cultural flow of ideas is immensely extended and intensified. Even where diffusion does not occur in the sense of adoption of new cultural traits, mere awareness of previously unsensed possibilities can stir action toward change in the status quo.

Within a social system the isolation of various sectors from each other similarly serves to inhibit the interplay of ideas essential for inventing.

This has been a factor, for example, in the retardation of change in traditional India where the relative communicative isolation of castes within the same region or village has been systematically supported in ritual and structure. Any invention which required the combining of technological elements involved in one occupational craft with those of another would be inhibited by the stringent restrictions on intercaste communication and common work. It is improbable that any qualifying case can be found in which barriers to, or distortions of, communicative processes do not retard socio-cultural change.

CONCLUSION

The idea of a static society is presented for its heuristic value in pointing up the conditions of man which make true social stasis impossible. No human society is perfectly integrated so that its constituent parts mesh in complete working harmony. Tension leading to dissatisfactions and innovative actions arises from structural ambiguities, malfunctionings, and inconsistencies. Briefly, we may say that "the way a society is put together" sets conditions for change. These conditions arise not only in the internal workings of the society but also in the systematic relationships established with other groups and with the ecological milieu. Shifts in the posture of external groups, as well as changes in the natural environment, force adjustive innovations upon societies if they are to survive. The fact of succession and replacement in leadership and functional roles further assures imperfect preservation of a given social structure through several generations. In addition to strictly social and ecological conditions making for innovation, shifts in population size and density are also conditions requiring innovative change in social organization. Malintegration (*dysfunctions* among integrated elements of the social structure) sets up tensions to which men respond innovatively toward resolution. These responses are manifest in new spontaneous pathways in interaction and in deliberately contrived inventive designs.

In addition to the structural features which give rise to tension and innovation, societies respond to their own cultural characteristics. Creative men contrive novel designs from the materials provided by their culture. The size and the qualities of culture are significant for what is contrived. Societies possessing a small cultural base are limited in their potential constructions. Significant too are the values and norms which stimulate or retard inventing or direct it toward or away from particular innovations.

Communicative relationships between and within societies are also crucial for innovation and change. The bombardment of novel ideas from beyond the boundaries of the culture not only adds to the body of knowledge and equipment, it stimulates tensions toward further innovation.

Although all societies undergo change, it is evident that some change more rapidly than others. Change is most rapid in complex societies wherein structural tensions are common and communication systems highly developed and cultural values favor the manipulation of a large cultural base.

II

PROCESSES OF CHANGE
IN SOCIAL SYSTEMS

4

Invention

THE NATURE OF INVENTION

Invention as a Constellation of Ideas

An invention is a novel design which has meaning or function (Barnett, pp. 7–8). It is a *novel design* in that it is a new configuration of ideas. It possesses *meaning* in that it can be appreciated or valued as in the case of a work of art, or *function* in that it "does something" as in a tool or machine. Some inventions such as works of art and machines have tangible, physical manifestation; others, like moral concepts, or devised group structures, such as the corporation, are no less real but are not manifested in physical materials.

Nor does *inventing* require the actual construction of some novel device (Kneale, pp. 89–90). Leonardo da Vinci invented a submarine though he neither built one nor induced another person to build one. Leonardo worked out an operable design. He coupled the idea of underwater travel with an original arrangement of additional ideas as to how this might be done. Later, men who further rearranged these ideas were also inventors. We cannot grant, however, that the man who assembled parts or who put in the rivets or even the one who drew up the architectural specifications was an inventor. Invention takes place in the creation of an ideational design. If one quibbles that to be an invention such a design must be "successful" or "workable," let us recall that there are infinite degrees of "workability." Many an invention has become practical or economically successful through rather minor changes in an earlier inventor's "less practical" device. Invention is involved at each stage, insofar as the improver made an original re-arrangement of the

77

design. For the sake of clarity and brevity, generally, we will omit from our discussion innovations which are neither socially meaningful nor operable. It should be understood that this distinction is based on pragmatic rather than theoretical grounds. On a theoretical level, for example, if a painting is not meaningful as art in one generation but is so defined in another, is it less than an innovation in the unappreciative generation?

Inventions Which Do Not Result in Social Change

Inventions are significant for social change only when people utilize or respond to them. The U.S. patent office contains numerous inventive designs which have had no impact on society. The mechanical hat-tipper is a classic case in point. Although not patentable, a similar unproductive fate has been known for novel group structures presented to the public hopefully for diffusion and adoption. When Judge Ben Lindsey devised a system of companionate marriage which he thought would be beneficial if adopted by American youth, he invented something. His invention was assessed but the response was negative. His plan did not have much effect on social behavior or values.[1] It did not constitute social change just because it was a social invention. On the other hand, the idea of limited liability, equally an inventive design, had immense significance when combined with the joint stock company to found the concept of the modern corporation.

Invention and Discovery

Popularly, invention is distinguished from discovery in that inventing is "making" and discovering is "finding." A tractor is called an invention because it is something contrived or created by man, whereas a law regarding the expansion of gases is a statement regarding something which has always existed but was previously unknown. This distinction is not one which is easy to live with. There are more points of identity between invention and discovery than meet the eye. We will, of course, reject out of hand the idea that an invention is a deliberate conscious development whereas discovery is something developed unconsciously or accidentally. The utility of a new design can be recognized after that design's creation as well as before it is actually contrived.

W. C. Kneale (pp. 101 ff.) has observed that the word "invention" came to hold its present meaning of "novel contrivance" or "device" in

---

[1] It should be noted, however, that while Judge Lindsey's proposal was being received with consternation by the defenders of public morality, there seems to have been a trend in interaction going on in the United States in somewhat the same direction that Lindsey proposed as a formulated, systematic design.

almost modern times. Cicero's book titled *Invention* was not related to the development of novel contrivances but dealt with the finding of arguments. In the seventeenth century the "logic of invention" meant the process of *discovery*. English, as well as other languages, has developed from a point at which there was no vocabulary distinction between "discovering" or "finding" and "inventing" or "contriving." Indeed, our modern distinction becomes less clear the more we consider it. Is the creation of a new mathematical system an invention or a discovery? No doubt it conforms more closely to the popular idea of discovery, although the mathematician Jacques Hadamard deliberately titled his work on this subject *The Psychology of Invention in the Mathematical Field*.

The process whereby a truth is *discovered* is basically the same process as that whereby an invention is "thought up" or conceived. Though one is the establishment of new knowledge and the other an application of knowledge, both are rooted in mental constructions involving novel rearrangement of data. The submarine which Leonardo invented was a mental construct as truly as is a system of mathematics. Leonardo *discovered* a process and a structure whereby man could sail underwater.

We may conclude that invention is a special form of discovery. *It is a discovery which works directly toward some end or purpose of man.* Thus mathematical novelties may or may not be harnessed into, say, a "practical" electronic computer. Similarly, knowledge of the way people behave in the time of stress and crisis may or may not be embodied in an innovative program to prevent panic. In each instance the development of knowledge is pure discovery, while the electronic computer and the panic prevention program arise as mental constructs which are goal-oriented discoveries and hence inventions.

Strategic, Basic, and Improving Inventions

Some inventions or discoveries are more important than others in that they stimulate a series, or perhaps many different series, of further inventions and discoveries. This is a different matter from assessing the importance of an invention on the basis of its own consequences or effects on society, a problem which will be taken up much later. Certain discoveries and certain inventions are of significance in stimulating "chain reactions" of further discovery and invention, while others are not. The discovery of the blood circulation system in the body permitted numerous new developments in physiological and medical knowledge. The invention of the cathode tube, likewise, was a crucial factor in the development of radio and innumerable other electronic devices. We will here follow Usher (Chap. 4) in calling such inventions *strategic*. The strategicness of any innovation is strictly a matter of degree.

No invention is *basic* in the sense that it is constructed without the use of previous innovations. The cathode tube, for example, rested upon numerous components which Mr. de Forest hitched together in a novel and particularly significant and strategic way. No matter how significant an invention is in stimulating further development, still earlier inventions are always essential to its existence. The terms *basic* and *improving* will be limited respectively to an original design and its subsequent modifications (Linton, Chap. 18), Leonardo's submarine was in this sense the basic invention. Modifying or improving inventions have occurred making the design operable and increasingly efficient.

Any line drawn between basic design and developmental or improving modifications is an arbitrary one. One might contend that since the submarine is a water-borne carrier, it is a modification of the sailing ship, which in turn is a modification of a "canoe," *ad infinitum*. Such chains in the evolution of invention are quite real, but they go beyond the present meaning. There are usually improving developments upon every invention which changes its design slightly, but are most significant from the standpoint of use or marketability. Jewkes, Sawers, and Stillerman have illustrated the developmental inventions associated with a "basic" invention, nylon:

. . . in 1935, after seven years' work of varying fortune and many disappointments, work which might have led anywhere or nowhere, W. H. Carothers, in the laboratories of the duPont Company, produced the first nylon fibre and duPont undertook to translate it into a marketable product. By 1939 large-scale production of nylon hosiery had commenced. Thus, in a matter of four years of development, duPont had reached its appointed goal. Estimates put the total cost of the early stages of research and development at about $6 million; at that time 230 technical experts were engaged in the work. What precisely was involved in the development undertaken after Carothers' initial discovery?

First it was necessary to find ways of producing on a large scale the intermediate constituents of nylon which, up to that time, had been made only on a small scale. The two important materials were adipic acid and hexamethylenediamine. Adipic acid had been manufactured in Germany for some time but there had been no commercial exploitation of it in the United States. The German processes were not readily adaptable to the plants of DuPont and it became imperative to develop a new catalytic technique for this purpose. Hexamethylenediamine posed even greater difficulties; it was merely a laboratory curiosity and had never been manufactured on a commercial scale before. Success here required the discovery of new catalysts and the proper handling of heat transfer problems. Next, a great deal of work had to be done at the stage where the materials react to form the long chain molecules of the nylon polymer. The first polymers were made in glass equipment in Carothers' laboratory, but glass equipment was completely unsuitable for commercial manufacture and metal equipment had to be designed. Methods of controlling the degree of polymerization had to be evolved, since a failure to stop the reaction at precisely the right time resulted in the production of different and far less useful polymers than nylon. The technologist had to learn how to make one batch of the product exactly like another.

At the next stage of manufacture the flakes of the polymer had to be melted and some means found to transfer the molten mass to the spinning machines. Only pumping gave the filaments adequate uniformity, but unfortunately there were no existing pumps suitable for the task. A new type of pump was required embodying new alloys capable of withstanding the heat of the molten polymer. At the next stage of spinning, the machinery had to be specially designed for the task, since nylon could not be spun in the same manner as cotton, wool, viscose, or cellulose acetate. The winding and the cold drawing processes also confronted the developers with problems which were novel and for which specially designed machines were required. Thus at each one of these stages—the mass production of what had formerly been made only on a small scale, the maintenance of unusual degrees of purity, the flexible controlling of the chemical processes and the devising of mechanical aids for handling materials with novel properties, the developers were confronted by one hurdle after another. It was only when the process reached the stage of knitting and weaving that existing and familiar techniques could be called in to help. But at every stage workers knew what they were looking for, and, with varying degrees of certainty, they knew it could be found. [Jewkes *et al.*, pp. 21–23]. *

Let us reiterate, however, that when we use the term "basic design" we do not mean that one invention compared to some different one is more or less "important." Indeed it can hardly be said that a basic invention like nylon *per se* is more *important* than a subsequent improving invention, if without the latter nylon is unusable. If the terms "basic" and "improving" or "developing" are to be used, they always apply to a relatively small cluster of closely related inventions, i.e., forming a single configuration.

The Prevalence of Invention

Innovative ideas have been achieved by every individual of normal intelligence (Barnett, Chap. 1). Who has not thought of some rearrangement which gives new brilliance to scrambled eggs, or a short-cut method of doing some common daily chore? These are all inventive innovations. Each embodies discoveries. Whether or not any of these "bright ideas" take the form of devices which are diffused, they are nonetheless novel configurations. Inventing is far more common than

---

* From *The Sources of Invention*, by John Jewkes, David Sawers, and Richard Stillerman, published by Macmillan & Company Ltd., London; St. Martin's Press, New York; and The Macmillan Company of Canada Ltd. By permission of the publishers.

is generally realized. While a small proportion of novelties are patented, there were over 65,000 patents issued in the United States alone during the single year 1967. Invention is not rare. Nor is it confined to any particular society, race, or time. Unquestionably, some societies are more innovative than others and societies differ in the kinds of things they invent. However, members of Western type society exaggerate their own innovative prowess as compared with that of other and differing peoples. Actually, if we were to take a very rigorous criterion for strategic inventions, it might be argued that *most* strategic inventions have origins outside western Europe or modern North America.

Weapons utilizing propulsion and hence extending the physical power of man beyond arm's reach, date back to man's early beginnings. The discovery and use of fire far predate Homo sapiens himself. Methods of making fire have been discovered and systematized into inventions by practically all primitive people. Neolithic men in Southwestern Asia were prodigious innovators. Wheeled vehicles, domestic animals, territorial states, city life, agriculture, and writing, all appeared in or just after the Neolithic period and each involved numerous related inventions. Except for those derived from the American Indians, few food crops have been discovered since Neolithic times and these were discovered in Southwestern Asia. Weaving, pottery making, fishing by nets and hooks, harpooning, and trapping are all inventions by primitives which are basic to countless modern developments. The alphabet, arithmetic, and calendrical systems predate Greek civilization and none was European in origin. And the Greeks were familiar with the "five simple machines" which are still basic principles: the axle and wheel, the lever, the pulley, the wedge, and the screw. Usher (Chap. 6) suggests that possibly even in the sixteenth century there was little heavy-duty machinery that involved anything beyond these principles. The Greeks were surely not their discoverers although these were matters of theoretic concern to the Byzantine and Alexandrian Greeks.

All peoples of the world have built, borrowed, or both, the equipment and the knowledge essential for orderly survival in their natural environments. None has stopped with just this. A truly immense range of inventions may be found in any primitive people's culture. Consider the ingenuity of a blow-gun, an outrigger canoe, boomerang, and harpoon with detachable point. Consider also the discovery that roots like manioc can be good eating—once the prussic acid is removed. In statecraft, Zulus and Dahomey in Africa, the Iroquois tribes in North America, and the Incas in South America built the intricate governmental devices needed to maintain order over vast territories and diverse peoples. Barnett (pp. 26–27) believes that if one insists upon a rigorous distinction between basic and improving inventions, a good case could be made for primitive man as the *inventor* and modern man as simply the *elaborator*.

Does Necessity Mother Invention?

No amount of need can yield an invention where the technical culture base does not provide the component ideas required for the contrivance. The Japanese *needed* an atom bomb as much as did the Americans, but the technical cultural base had been extended further in supporting directions in America. More basically we might ask if an atom bomb was *needed* by either nation. Innumerable alternative pathways could have been pursued and in fact were being pursued in both nations. No single device was necessarily indispensable. It is also conceivable that the "need" for greater destructive power could have been dissolved if one or both nations had sought more innovations in the devices of peace. "Necessity" is highly elastic. Need can be redirected into various channels or resolved by alternative devices. What a society sees as "need" is determined by the values and goals of that society. Response may come in a modification of these values and goals. Or the "need" may be simply unfulfilled, and perhaps forgotten.

Vast numbers of inventions appear that have virtually nothing to do with the idea of "necessity" or even "need" as these terms are usually construed. While economic competition is a spur to industrial inventive effort, a considerable part of this is expended upon devices which duplicate older ones insofar as their satisfaction of human need is concerned. In regard to competitive races to get new products on the market, *Time Magazine* reported (March 29, 1963, p. 83) that a small company successfully marketing a novel product cannot hold its favorable position long before it is overwhelmed by more powerful firms with rival products. *Time* referred to this as "the Lestoil syndrome," so named from the rapid rise of the household cleaner by that name and its abrupt fall as the major soap companies hit the market with rival products.

But competition also stimulates improved designs in an original invention, and as importantly it stimulates alternative solutions to the given problem. As Gilfillan has observed, once a need for an invention is perceived, numerous solutions arise which would perform the same function through differing means (1935a, p. 12). Thus communication with early California could soon be accomplished by clipper, steamer, pony express, or telegraph. Gilfillan was undoubtedly correct in observing that inventions tend to arrive in functional groups.

Gilfillan has suggested further that the adage of "necessity" might well be reversed, to say that "invention is the mother of necessity . . . ," i.e., necessity of further invention. As we have observed, innovation begets innovation. As a new device appears, the possibilities of its fusion with existing culture traits and freshly innovated ones appear. Readjustments are generally required as an invention is incorporated into a going society. Most inventions require further inventing as they create stresses and are fitted into the social or cultural order.

In a further sense also, invention "mothers" necessity. In a gadget-conscious, progress-oriented, profit-seeking society like ours there is a proliferation of new devices for which "need" is induced. "Planned obsolescence" is well known in our economy. "Teflon," a substance which refuses to let other material cling to it, was inadvertently discovered in 1938 (*Time Magazine*, March 13, 1964, p. 95). Having the product in hand, duPont spent a reported $100 million in developing it and in finding uses for it. Not until 1964 did the "Teflon" frying pan become a household necessity and the invention show promise of major industrial significance. Only in the vaguest sense does a feeling of need give rise to a paste underarm deodorant, which is then superseded by a roll-on, which in turn bows to a spray-on. Some cynics might suggest that the real "need" is for men and women to smell like men and women. At best we may conclude that a feeling of need is promoted by actual or potential dissatisfaction with established patterns. "Felt dissatisfaction" with an established pattern is a crucial element in change. It is not always present in the public prior to the appearance of the innovation. When we conclude that inventions arise through a feeling by *someone* that *something* is to be gained for *somebody* through novel rearrangement, we have thoroughly watered-down the *necessity* element in invention. Additionally many inventions are less stimulated by their functional ability to satisfy utilitarian wants than by aesthetic or by spiritual values.

THEORIES OF INVENTION

Scholars have long sought to explain how inventions arise. Theories in this realm have tended to polarize around two contrasting approaches. On the one hand are those theories which emphasize the psychological processes culminating in an invention; on the other hand are the theories which emphasize cultural processes. Psychological theories focus upon the individual inventor while cultural theories find the particular individual inventor unimportant in comparison with the social and cultural forces to which he responds.

In a broad sense the psychological orientation to invention is consistent with the "great man" theory of history in that sources of change are sought in individuals rather than in "circumstances." It is also related to efforts to interpret great social movements in terms of the personalities of their leaders. In most extreme form such theories fall back upon the unanalyzable presence of "genius." In less extreme forms they represent substantial efforts to examine psychic processes of creativity through inductive as well as introspective methods. Gestalt psychologists have pioneered in this area.

Cultural theories of inventing came into prominence in the 1920's, partly in reaction to individualistic and biological theories of social change generally. In their extreme positions the psychologically oriented scholars focused on the great man of genius, while the cultural approach at times viewed the inventor as a pawn in the grand sweep of social evolution. In one approach the significance of the cultural base as a source of the inventor's ideas was neglected, and in the other the role of creative thought was passed by. Both approaches generally accepted the importance of demand for the particular invention in the society wherein it appeared and was applied. The cultural approach was more awake to the significance of diffusion in stimulating invention.

Out of these conflicting research orientations it is today possible to reach a reconciliation in which psychic and cultural processes are each brought into complementary focus upon the problem of inventing. The economic historian Abbot Payson Usher pioneered in this theory building, which, for lack of a better term, might be called "creative evolution."

Psychological Theories of Invention

The Innovative Act. The act of inventing occurs in the imaginative recombination of existing ideas. If by random physical manipulation one builds a new relationship between objects, and then "sees" that this tangible creation has meaning and function, the creative fact lies in this mental construction placed upon the physical reality. A rearrangement of leaves on the grass may take place by action of the wind. This is not an act of innovation. However, if an artist derives from it a novel artistic patterning, his is an innovative or creative act. This novel pattern may then be translated to canvas or into a fabric or it may remain a concept without material referent. A new configuration of elements has been made, which, as a totality, possesses meaning. This is invention![2] It arises in the novel and meaningful *configuration of constituent parts.* Homer Barnett (p. 181) has called such imaginative reconstruction a "complex conmingling of perception, cognition, recall and affect." Barnett believes psychic mechanisms are utilized to yield

---

[2] H. Poincaré, writing in the late nineteenth century, emphasized the view that invention *is* making choices from among alternatives so that the result is a useful combination. See especially his essay on mathematical creation (pp. 383–447).

innovative design through the intimately related processes of *identification, substitution,* and *discrimination* (p. 188).

Through the processes of *identification,* one finds equivalences in different, and even dissimilar, objects, events, or constructs. This is the type of analytical abstraction through which one locates elements of sameness in apparently dissimilar things. A hammer, for example, is used to drive a nail, but lacking a hammer, one searches the tool chest for some different implement which may serve the same purpose. A pipe wrench and a hammer are quite different in concrete "reality" but the searcher may find aspects, e.g., hardness and weight, in which they are identical.

Close upon the recognition of equivalence comes *substitution,* in which a partial equivalent is replaced in a configuration. The pipe wrench has been identified as serving the hammer's function and is placed in a configuration wherein it substitutes for the hammer. Obviously no substitution of perfectly identical elements, if they existed, would be meaningful. The dramatic contrast between the old device and the new arises from those aspects of the new which differ from the old. The pipe wrench is like the hammer in terms of hardness and weight, but it is unlike the hammer in terms of shape and balance. While its introduction into the hammering sequence is innovative, *discrimination* reveals that it is not an "efficient" innovation. On the other hand, the metal hammer had been an "efficient" substitute for the stone hammer. Metal has advantages over brittle stone in such a configuration. The original transference required abstract abilities in which certain qualities of stone were recognized to exist in particular metals treated in particular ways and certain other qualities were recognized as absent. While like stone, the processed metal has hardness, its dissimilarities give it immense utilitarian advantages which inventors came to recognize through processes of *discrimination.*

Past experience and the social milieu influence the discriminations, as well as the types of analytical abstractions or identities, which individuals perceive. Given the mental abilities and experience background for perception and the pool of ideas (or culture traits), the stage is set for creative thought. The perception of a new, meaningful configuration has been called the "act of insight" by Gestalt psychologists and "creativity" by others.

Köhler's studies with chimpanzees provided basic experimental evidence regarding "creativity." He was the pioneer in such research and his experiments with apes at Tenerife in 1913–1917 are still classics in this field. Köhler determined that apes are capable of achieving innovative configurations, and he attempted to explain the processes involved. In his interpretations it may be that Köhler over-stressed the importance of the immediate visual field of perception in the formation of a novel pattern. Also it is likely that man is capable of more imaginary constructions based upon memory and recall, although these processes were undoubtedly present in ape behavior as well.

Nueva was tested three days after her arrival (11th March 1914). She had not yet made the acquaintance of the other animals but remained isolated in a cage. A little stick is introduced into her cage; she scrapes the ground with it, pushes the banana skins together into a heap, and then carelessly drops the stick at a distance of about three-quarters of a meter from the bars. Ten minutes later, fruit is placed outside the cage beyond her reach. She grasps at it, vainly of course, and then begins the characteristic complaint of the chimpanzee: she thrusts both lips—especially the lower—forward, for a couple of inches, gazes imploringly at the observer, utters whimpering sounds, and finally flings herself on to the ground on her back—a gesture most eloquent of despair, which may be observed on other occasions as well. Thus, between lamentations and entreaties, some time passes, until—about seven minutes after the fruit has been exhibited to her—she suddenly casts a look at the stick, ceases her moaning, seizes the stick, stretches it out of the cage, and succeeds, though somewhat clumsily, in drawing the bananas within arm's length. Moreover, Nueva at once put the end of her stick behind and beyond the objective, holding it in this test, as in later experiments, in her left hand by preference. The test is repeated after an hour's interval; on this second occasion, the animal has recourse to the stick much sooner, and uses it with more skill; and, at a third repetition, the stick is used immediately, as on all subsequent occasions. Nueva's skill in using it was fully developed after very few repetitions. . . . [Köhler, pp. 32–33.]

In one of the experiments described previously, Sultan came very near putting one box on the top of another, when he found the one insufficient; but instead of placing the second box, which he had already lifted, upon the first, he made uncertain movements with it in the air around and above the other; then other methods replaced these confused movements. The test is repeated; the objective is placed very high up, the two boxes are not very far away from each other and about four meters away from the objective; all other means of reaching it have been taken away. Sultan drags the bigger of the two boxes towards the objective, puts it just underneath, gets up on it, and looking upwards, makes ready to jump, but does not jump; gets down, seizes the other box, and, pulling it behind him, gallops about the room, making his usual noise, kicking against the walls and showing his uneasiness in every other possible way. He certainly did not seize the second box to put it on the first; it merely helps him to give vent to his temper. But all of a sudden his behavior changes completely; he stops making a noise, pulls his box from quite a distance right up to the other one, and stands it upright on it. He mounts the somewhat shaky construction, several times gets ready to jump, but again does not jump; the objective is still too high for this bad jumper. But he has achieved his task.

The objective hangs still higher up; Sultan has fasted all the forenoon and, therefore, goes at his task with great zeal. He lays the heavy box flat underneath the objective, puts the second one upright upon it, and, standing on the top, tries to seize the objective. As he does not reach it, he looks down and round about, and his glance is caught by the third box, which may have seemed useless to him at first, because of its smallness. He climbs down very carefully, seizes the box, climbs up with it, and completes the construction. [Köhler, pp. 139–142.] *

There is no doubt but that the chimpanzees engaged in innovative substitution. What "went on in their minds" is, of course, Professor Köhler's inference. Even human inventors are rarely capable of articulating their own thought processes and these are subject to the uncertainties of introspection. However, the following extract from the autobiography of Frederick L. Fuller, a professional business machine inventor, provides a retrospective account of the sequences through which he invented a machine for sorting checks. We can only wonder, were they capable of articulate speech, how similarly Nueva or Sultan might have thought back on their achievements.

Mr. McKennett (the employer) worked very closely with me. In order that I might be familiar with the condition I was seeking to improve, he took me to a few banks where we watched the operation of sorting and classifying foreign checks. Every one we talked with agreed that it was one of the most laborious operations in banking, and of course it was of first importance that there should be no errors either in classifying the checks or totaling the amounts they represented.

The proposition was especially fascinating because there was no machine in existence which could be used. It was virgin territory. I sat at my desk for hours thinking out ways and means. Every time I looked up I would see a sign that bore the magic word THINK. As I walked about the laboratory, or went down to the main office, that THINK sign kept presenting itself to my vision. And THINK I did.

At first I had tried to visualize a mechanism that would take the checks to their proper pocket. One objection after another bobbed up. It could be done, but not in any simple way. The thing was rapidly becoming one of the most difficult problems I had ever encountered.

"By George," I said to myself, "this is almost as hard as that old hyperbolic paraboloid." [The solution of a previous problem.] While I was letting my mind rest I would frequently muse over past experiences in invention, and the instant that this hyperbolic paraboloid came into my thoughts I was on the track of the solution I sought for the bank machine. I didn't recognize it instantly, but when I finally recalled how I had simplified that old scale device by rolling it up on the outer edge of a cylinder I found that on the desk tablet in front of me I had absent-mindedly sketched a wheel. Something about the wheel arrested my attention and I began to put a series of pockets around the inside of the circumference. Check pockets! I would stop trying to take the checks to the pockets. Instead I would use a wheel to bring the pockets to the checks.

After a few more rough sketches I called in an artist and had him make a finished drawing of the machine itself. Not any of the necessary mechanism,

* From *The Mentality of Apes* by Wolfgang Köhler, New York, Humanities Press Inc., 1926. By permission.

of course. Just a picture of a machine, as if it had all been completed. This was the way I imagined it would look when it was complete. All I had to do now was put in the works.

Having found the correct starting point for the proof machine in July, 1928, I worked along, step by step, until on October 21, 1930 . . . it required only a little more than two years to start from nothing but an idea and arrive at a complete machine in which were embodied many new applications of ancient mechanical principles. [Fuller, pp. 53–56.]

A. P. Usher and the Stages of Inventing. Usher has described the emergence of novelty or innovative thought and action as a genetic sequence of four steps (p. 65). These appear to apply equally well to the stages reflected through Köhler's ape studies and to such introspections as those of Fuller, and many others. The first step lies in the *perception of the problem,* typically an unfulfilled want. This does not imply that all invention arises through foresight or through intent. Rather, the stimulus for manipulation must be present, whatever the motivation. The second step is that of bringing into thought the data essential to solution. This Usher refers to as the *setting of the stage.* In the case of Köhler's apes the stage was set by the experimenter. Fuller articulately emphasizes this second stage. His perceptual field was broadened by selective recall, in which analogies and substitutions were sought and tested.

Usher (p. 65) believes that this second step in inventing is dependent upon either pure chance ("fortuitous configuration") or some degree of systematic effort to find a solution. Effort toward a meaningful configuration is often at the level of aimless fumbling, although at higher levels of scientific activity, trial and error is guided and controlled through systematic experimentation. With the "stage set," the third step is the *act of insight,* innovative configuration per se. A solution of the problem is now accomplished. A reconfiguration with meaning has taken place. Working particularly from the analogous hyperbolic paraboloid, Fuller visualized his solution in an innovative configuration (stage 3) through redintegrative imagery. Presumably like the chimpanzees, the culmination of the process appears to him as having been a momentary and exultant "act of insight." Of course, for both, lifetimes of experience and learning were behind them. The redintegrative culmination is even more acutely expressed by Watt in an experience occurring two years after his first work on the steam engine and six years after his first studies of heat.

I had gone to take a walk on a fine Sabbath afternoon. I had entered the Green by the gate at the foot of Charlotte Street, and passed the old washinghouse. I was thinking upon the engine at the time, and had gone as far as the herd's house, when the idea came into my mind that, as steam was an elastic body, it would rush into a vacuum, and, if a communication were made between the cylinder and an exhausted vessel, it would rush into it, and might be there condensed without cooling the cylinder. I then saw that I must get rid of the condensed steam and injection-water if I used a jet, as in New-comen's engine. Two ways of doing this occurred to me: First, the water might be run off by a descending pipe, if an offlet could be got at the depth of 35 or 36 feet, and any air might be extracted by a small pump. The second was, to make the pump large enough to extract both water and air . . . I had not walked farther than the Golf-house, when the whole thing was arranged in my mind.[3]

There were, of course, many difficult engineering problems to be resolved in the course of constructing a model reflecting Watt's break-through.

The final stage is that of *critical revision* in which the newly per-ceived relationships are mastered and worked into their broader context. Thus Fuller states that after getting his big idea, "all I had now to do was put in the works"; "putting in the works" was a two years' task of critical revision. After his insight of the "born criminal," Lombroso spent the rest of his lifetime in critical revision, only to culminate in an eclectic position which made this original "insight" all but meaningless. His is a grand example of creative thought in which meaning was at-tached to an innovative configuration through misunderstanding of the ingredients and fallacies regarding their relationships. It was nonethe-less an innovative discovery—though a fallacious one. Mechanical in-ventors who have "solved" perpetual motion have faced similarly the unbearable problem of critical revision.

It is not to be supposed that these stages are necessarily neatly followed in inventive design. They are at best an attempt to articulate an ideal set of sequences which can be discerned analytically. Be-tween these stages there may be years of groping and a return by the potential innovator to a preceding level for further study or manipula-tion. His act of insight may prove unrealistic in terms of his ability to operationalize existing materials. Hence, he either may have to modify his original configuration or establish a separate innovative process in regard to some subordinate piece of the overall design he has imagina-tively established.

J. HADAMARD AND THE "INCUBATION PERIOD." Hadamard is particularly impressed by what might be called a "period of incubation" prior to the seemingly sudden creative insight. It is possible that a parallel exists in the quiescence of Köhler's apes prior to their problem solutions. How-ever this may be, the idea of a period following study and manipulation during which attention is not focused upon the problem seems present in

---

[3] From "Reminiscences of James Watt," by Robert Hart in *Transactions of the Glasgow Archeological Society*, 1859 as cited by Robert H. Thurston (pp. 87–88).

many modern strategic innovations. This "dormant" period had been noted nearly a century ago by Henri Poincaré. Poincaré's introspective data are supported by similar recollections among numerous eminent mathematicians, scientists, and artists. Following a stage which Poincaré described as that of "preparation" (setting the stage), comes a "rest period" when, as must often happen, the thinker caught in an unproductive groove gets rid of his false leads and hampering assumptions to approach the problem with an 'open mind.'" This Hadamard calls the "rest hypothesis," equating the psychic state involved with the "firing consciousness" of William James. Here ideas are entertained in somewhat the way one focuses on an irrelevant object while peripherally seeing much else besides.

Poincaré illustrates the "rest period" in an anecdote regarding one stage in his solution of a mathematical problem on which he was working in 1881.

Just at this time, I left Caen, where I was living, to go on a geologic excursion under the auspices of the school of mines. The changes of the travel made me forget my mathematical work. Having reached Coutances, we entered an omnibus to go some place or other. At the moment when I put my foot on the step the idea came to me, without anything in my former thoughts seeming to have paved the way for it, that the transformations I had used to define the Fuchsian functions were identical with those of non-Euclidian geometry. I did not verify the idea; I should not have had time, as, upon taking my seat in the omnibus, I went on with a conversation already commenced, but I felt a perfect certainty. On my return to Caen, for conscience's sake, I verified the result at my leisure. [Pp. 387–388.]

Unquestionably, innovative design is developed under conditions other than those described by Poincaré, but the incubation period is reported with sufficient frequency to give credence. The "peripheral look" at the problem when not focusing upon it may have a psychological parallel in what occurs when a "new" or "sideways" look at a pyramid of squares offers a sudden rearrangement.

The Inventor as a Genius

The very word "genius," in its etymological roots, denotes supernatural guidance. Throughout the ages strategic innovators have been viewed as possessing unique and inexplicable gifts. While the capacities and abilities and processes which are exercised in innovation are indeed little understood, they are only mysterious to the extent that scientific tools have not been sufficiently applied to their analysis. As we have seen, chimpanzees are capable of inventive behavior, or, if one prefers, of "creative insight" in that they can form novel and meaningful configurations. If the voice of God speaks in the innovative behavior of apes and men, it surely speaks through knowable mechanisms and through analyzable processes. These mechanisms, organic and cultural, appear to be present in all mankind. They are exercised more fruitfully by some individuals than by others, in some cultural contexts more than in others, and in regard to certain types of innovation more than others. Our limited knowledge of creative thought suggests that the capacities upon which it rests are not equally distributed among all individuals.

Whatever else, innovativeness is not some unitary trait. While individuals may well vary in their innovative capacity, the variance is of degree and direction. Little is known as to the extent to which creative ability is generalized or specific. Is the creative artist also a potential inventor? Certain outstanding personalities, such as Leonardo da Vinci, suggest that all-around innovators may exist. Commonly, however, most inventors are more closely bound, if not by their capacities and motivations, then by their competence within limited areas of subject matter and the specialized skills required to manipulate that particular body of knowledge. Eminent technological innovators have proved frequently to be naive philosophers. "Gifted minds" usually arise in close affiliation with the subject areas of their contribution. Hart's study of 171 inventors indicated that 60 percent were closely familiar with the particular field in which they invented and 20 percent were professional inventors (1931). Hart also concluded that most were motivated by the joy of manipulation rather than any sense of need for their contrivance or even for financial gain. It is not coincidental that tool-making apes have had experience in manipulating sticks, jumping, and other skills upon which their new configurations depended. We should recall that Watt was a tool maker by profession; Hargreaves a worker in a cotton mill; Charles Darwin a student of medicine and later sufficiently concerned with natural processes as to take a job as an unpaid naturalist on the *Beagle* (Butler). Alexander Graham Bell was a professor of vocal physiology. Novel configurations with *meaning* do not spring from the minds of the uninformed. It may be reasonably surmised that the unknown who first stuck an axle between two wooden discs knew well the functioning of a log roller and the use of some wood-working tools. Fanciful dreams occur to all, but even these are fashioned from the materials provided through experience. The "dream" which can be made operative is possible only when the "dreamer" has a grasp of available materials and of their potential relationships.

No genius can transcend the limits imposed by his cultural base in terms of the raw materials available for manipulation. Furthermore he must know or find out the nature of these raw materials insofar as they are required by his design. Here and there, vague dreams of the uninformed have operational potential when placed in the hands of an informed person. But proposed patents for perpetual motion devices do not arise from university physics, mathematics, or engineering departments.[4] They are typically the dreams of the poorly informed. "Let us learn to dream, gentlemen," said the distinguished chemist August Kekulé in 1890, "then, perhaps, we shall find the truth . . . but let us beware of publishing our dreams before they have been put to the proof by the waking understanding" (Japp, p. 100). Kekulé was, it should be noted, speaking before his peers. It is not inconceivable that the great dream, the insight, can occur before the assemblage of data is present in any very complete way. The dreamer must, however, assemble such data and reformulate his dream with reference to them if his imaginary configuration is to be meaningful. Hornell Hart (1931, p. 569) recounts the tale of a retired U.S. Army captain, John Symes, who lectured widely on his novel insight during the early part of the nineteenth century. Symes contended that the earth is hollow and habitable within. He proposed to explore this inner earth by entering at either the north or south pole, where according to his theory, openings occurred. He pleaded for the world's support of his venture. The emotional attachment Captain Symes expressed for the details of his configuration suggests the unlikelihood of critical revisions to come.

The mathematician Hadamard observes, "Good mathematicians, when they make them [errors], which is not infrequent, soon perceive and correct them. As for me (and mine is the case of many mathematicians), I make many more of them than my students do; only I always correct them so that no trace of them remains in the final result" (p. 49). Hadamard, nonetheless, continues to recount his personal errors which arose through almost stubborn unwillingness to shift the grounds in which he sought relationships among his data. But there are important distinctions between Captain Symes' and Hadamard's innovative processes. As Getzels and Jackson (Chap. 3) observe, we must distinguish between independence and unruliness; between individuality and rebelliousness; between ambiguity and irresolution; between judging and forejudging. Nor can genius be conceived simply as the capacity to take infinite pains. Genius entails the capabilities to perceive patterned relationships which in sum have meaning beyond the separate parts. Hadamard suggests that mathematical insights are rooted in aesthetic standards, and he does not hesitate to use such words as "beauty" and "elegant" in reference to his solutions. In the introspective accounts of artists and mathematicians alike, Hadamard finds persistent reference to

[4] Nearly 600 applications for patents on such machines were filed in the British Patent Office between 1854 and 1903 and numerous others have been filed in the U.S. Patent Office. No one has ever submitted a working model (Hering, pp. 75–80; Hart, p. 569).

a culmination process which none of the great innovators could analyze but which seemed in the words of Gauss, "like a sudden flash of lightning, the riddle happened to be solved. I myself cannot say what was the conducting thread which connected what I previously knew with what made my success possible" (Hadamard, p. 15).

What is true in Gauss's account is precisely what he says, and no more. The masterful design *seemed* to dawn like a flash of lightning. Who better than Gauss realized that the "dawning" was a culmination of years of study applied to this mathematical theorem. Why had not the lightning struck months earlier? Why did it strike now? What were the neural sequences through which it struck? Could it have struck if Gauss had lacked even one datum which he held in memory? If we cannot provide all of the correct answers, let us at least ask ourselves some correct questions regarding genius.

THE CREATIVE PERSONALITY.   In recent years psychological researchers have been providing new inductive insights into the nature of creative thought. Largely these relate to the kinds of background and personality traits correlated with creativity in individuals. However, these offer hints as to principles and processes of creativity. One thing seems virtually certain, neither knowledge nor intelligence separately or combined, and howsoever measured, are sufficient to account for creativity. Drevdahl and Cattell found that eminent writers and artists differed significantly from the general population in a wide range of personality factors. In their sample, creative individuals, compared with a normal population, were more intelligent, dominant, and self-sufficient. They had high ergic tension and emotional sensitivity. They were less cyclothymic, less surgent, and less subject to group standards. The results of this study are fairly typical of many researches seeking out the personal background features and personality attributes of creative individuals (Drevdahl; Van Zelst and Kerr; Luchins; Porterfield; Hart; Getzels and Jackson).

Donald W. MacKinnon has reported upon researches undertaken by himself and others mainly on studies of creativity among architects, in a manner which very nearly sums up present knowledge in this field (MacKinnon, 1962a, b; Gough). These findings are largely consistent with those of Drevdahl and Cattell as well as the studies of children by Getzels and Jackson, and other researches. MacKinnon finds that highly creative persons are inclined to have a good opinion of themselves while at the same time are frank in expressing self-criticism. Whereas less creative persons frequently described themselves as "reliable," "sincere," and "understanding," the highly creative used terms like "determined," "independent," and "enthusiastic." One striking conclusion in the studies reported upon by MacKinnon, is that highly creative men show very high scores on measures of "femininity" in personality. "The evidence is clear," says Professor MacKinnon, "the more creative a person is the more he reveals an openness to his own feelings and emotions, a sensitive intellect, an understanding self-awareness, and wide-ranging interests including many which in American culture are thought of as feminine."

Studies of inventive or creative persons frequently evidence quite low but positive relationship between measures of intelligence and measures of creativity. Among the groups reported upon by both MacKinnon and by Wallach and Kogan, intelligence held no relationship whatever to creativeness. Apparently what we think of as intelligence is unrelated to creativeness provided the individual has a reasonably normal mental capacity. This very significant finding is strikingly supported by Getzels and Jackson in their research on children.

The highly creative groups reported on by MacKinnon showed strong preference for complex and asymmetrical designs, appearing to prefer a richly disordered situation to a simple but barren one. Related to this and of close importance for the understanding of inventive process is the preference found among the highly creative for "intuitive" over "sensory" perceptions. Most of the normal population prefers to deal with problems in which the solution is directly presented to the senses. In sharp contrast, the highly creative prefer problems in which solutions are not apparent through immediate sensory evidence but must be sought out in as-yet-not-realized solutions. And for the truly creative, "it is not sufficient that problems be solved, there is a further demand that the solutions be elegant. He seeks both truth and beauty" (MacKinnon, 1962a, p. 490).

The inductive studies appear to support the more introspective analysis of Hadamard in regard to the aesthetic quality in inventiveness as well as the general Gestalt view that invention is a configurational learning process rather than an associational one. We have here something reminiscent of Pareto's "residue or combinations." It is an ability to "shake things up" and come out with a novel re-patterning. L. S. Kubie has emphasized this when he uses the terms "cogita" for creative thought, meaning literally "to shake together," in contrast with "intelligo" meaning literally "to select from among" (Kubie; Getzels and Jackson, pp. 128–129; Wertheimer; Lowenfeld, Chap. 8).

Cultural Theories of Invention

Cultural Accumulation and Acceleration. William F. Ogburn's work, *Social Change,* published in 1922 was a clear and influential statement of the deterministic force of culture itself in the processes of social evolution. Recognizing that invention, as well as social movements, proceed though the personal media of individual leaders, he viewed such leaders or inventors as arising almost inevitably as social and cultural conditions generated them (Ogburn, 1926; Ogburn and Thomas, 1922). Similar ideas were being expressed in anthropology, notably by Alfred L. Kroeber (1917, 1919).

Ogburn's theory of invention rested basically on two postulates: (1) the principle of cultural accumulation, and (2) the principle of cultural trait combination as the mechanism of inventing. He applied these principles to change particularly in material culture, i.e., utilitarian instruments rather than norms, values, etc. The accumulation of "material" culture "lies not in the life of the particular object but in the perpetuation of the knowledge of the method of making the object, which is passed on from generation to generation" (Ogburn, 1922, p. 74). Along with such persistence of cultural forms, novelties are added through the principle of new combinations among existing forms or traits. In this connection Ogburn amassed substantial evidence to show that inventions appear with something like the rapidity with which the existing culture offers potential recombinations. The larger the material culture base the greater is the possibility of novel combination of forms within the culture, and accordingly, the greater is the potential rate of technological change. With the increasing size of the cultural base, the increased possibility of novel combinations rises at a staggering rate. Ogburn indeed finds that material culture tends to increase at increasing rates of speed and compares cultural growth to a compound interest curve. In subsequent works by members of the Ogburn group, this idea of growth was given systematic expression in what has been called the "exponential principle" of growth. The works of two of Ogburn's outstanding colleagues, S. C. Gilfillan, and Hornell Hart, notably expanded the basic theory.

Gilfillan, in addition to writing a superb technological history of the ship, applied himself particularly to the demonstration of cultural determinism. Impressed by Ogburn's and his own findings in the simultaneous appearance of notable inventions in differing places at about the same time, Gilfillan (1936) argued that inventions were highly predictable. Assuming some utility in an invention, Gilfillan contended that when the culture base can support its construction, the invention cannot long remain uncreated.

Hornell Hart, over many years, has produced voluminously toward the refinement of predictive generalizations as to the rate of invention in particular cultural fields of change (Hart, 1931; 1946; 1957). Beginning with *The Technique of Social Progress,* published in 1931, Hart studied acceleration in the rates of invention in such areas as efficiency in cutting tools, world speed records, and the power of man to kill and destroy. With certain qualifications, Hart has found change to follow growth curve patterns in these and other fields. In a recent work he concludes:

It is as natural for culture to accelerate as it is for a baby to grow into an adult. We have seen that this is true for four reasons: (1) the elements ready to be combined into new inventions become more and more numerous, faster and faster, because inventions breed inventions; (2) the inventions of all the world are more and more pooled, as the barriers of communication progressively break down; (3) the elements being combined are becoming not only more and more numerous but also more and more powerful; and (4) the methods of defining the problems to be solved, collecting the elements to be combined, and working out the most effective combinations of those elements, are all being improved more and more swiftly as our methods of invention become more and more scientific. [1957; p. 53.] *

CRITICISMS OF THE ACCUMULATION-ACCELERATION SCHOOL. The accumulation-acceleration theories of Ogburn, Hart, and Gilfillan have been most seriously and basically challenged in a recent provocative work in the sociology of science by Jewkes, Sawers, and Stillerman.[5] In this work it is argued on the basis of convincing evidence that today (1) individual inventive temperaments are still crucial for continuing technological advance; (2) the prediction of inventions is hazardous at best; (3) the very organizational devices through which we would accelerate technical invention may work toward its retardation.

These writers argue that the sociological trend which viewed the inventor as but a creature of deep cultural forces is more plausible than supportable by the evidence. That many simultaneous inventions have occurred is probably true—evidencing cultural forces—but that still more non-simultaneous inventions have occurred is also true. Further, those like Gilfillan and Ogburn who have argued the predictability of invention have overlooked the bulk of specific inventions which have *not* been predicted. Jewkes and his associates contend that most of the main technical features of modern life not only were not predicted but crept upon us almost without our awareness. Furthermore, vast numbers of erroneous predictions have been made by men who should have known better.

From close study of inventors and invention in the nineteenth and twentieth centuries, these authors conclude that the newly recognized productive power of organized, team inventing is exaggerated both

* From "Acceleration in Social Change," by Hornell Hart in *Technology and Social Change,* by Francis R. Allen, *et al.* Copyright © 1957 by Meredith Corporation. Reprinted by permission of Appleton-Century-Crofts.

[5] Many earlier criticisms have also been made, particularly of the "cultural lag" concept (cf. Merton; Boskoff).

in its newness and in its efficiency. They contend that the inventive drive continues to be found in the kind of people who are temperamentally difficult to organize. Furthermore, much inventing still requires fairly superficial exploration with a few technical tools but with acute observation and imagination. Without denying the importance of the growth of science for technological inventing, Jewkes and his collaborators correctly point out that only part of the progress in basic scientific knowledge is channelable into technological achievement, while much technological achievement arises in work with existing technology without recourse to new scientific advances.

In the institutionalization of modern research and development, there are serious dangers to the preservation of independent, innovative minds. As the scales are tipped toward participation in massive organizational research, room for the independent inventor is narrowed down. Present trends suggest the possibility that technical progress may be endangered by the very practices commonly used to stimulate it.

The work of Jewkes and his colleagues is not one of despair. It is one of warning to those who accept at full face value theories of inevitability in technical progress and neglect the creative significance of the individual scientist and inventor. Sociological thought which reacted so strongly against the early bias of individualism in invention is now being modulated.

It is human beings after all who provide the dynamism in change, manipulating as they do the particular and limited body of knowledge and devices available to them. The culture base limits invention by providing limited materials. It does not determine that an invention shall in fact be made. Frequently creative thought runs ahead of provisions already existing in the culture base. Having planned an ultimate device, the inventor, or some branch of the inventive team, must direct himself to a line of research calculated to overcome some tangential problem which must be resolved before the design can be produced. The superbomb, for example, could be designed in detail, but until metallurgical skills could produce its required "shell" or "skin," the invention remained incomplete. The ultimate inventive design stimulated deliberate extensions of the culture base to meet predictable problems. When a new design departs widely from the culture base in its constituent requirements, we would better term it an innovative phantasy than an invention. The border between the two is an inexact one.

Invention as an Evolutionary Process.   It may seem strange to insist that invention is a set of processes rather than a fact. The *World Almanac*—and many other reference works—will unhesitatingly tell one the date upon which a particular invention occurred and the precise person who created it. Why then is invention process rather than "event"? From the historical, genetic, or evolutionary point of view, relatively few inventions can in actual fact be pinpointed to a particular inventor on a particular date. When we are told that Fulton invented the steamboat or Watt invented the steam engine, we are being given a partial truth . . . for Fulton somewhat less than a half truth (Gilfillan, 1935b; Singer *et al.*, Vol. 5, Pt. 2, Chap. 7). Each of these men made contributions to the harnessing of steam for man's uses. Others before them had done likewise and others after them as well. It is a matter of argument if we are even justified in picking out Watt or Fulton as persons who made the "most crucial" of these contributions.

In dealing with the genetic aspects of invention we are concerned with process in two related senses. In the first place the particular artifact or machine practically always goes through a time period of improvement once the basic idea is given. Neither Watt nor Fulton contributed the basic ideas with which their names are associated, i.e., harnessing steam to drive machines and adapting it to the ship, respectively. Both Watt and Fulton must be seen as contributing members in a long sequence of steam harnessers and adapters. In a second sense the evolutionary aspect of invention is a process in that various and frequently unrelated innovations are drawn in to form a particular, specific invention. Watt could not build his steam engine except insofar as metallurgical techniques permitted, and Fulton required a previously developed invention, the ship, before his adaption was possible. We must then view any particular invention as an outgrowth of events in fields which come to be related.

Gilfillan (1935a) has observed that an invention is like an organic process of evolution. It has neither a definable beginning nor a definable end. It may be viewed at any particular moment as something fixed and stable, but this is really but one momentary cross-section in the flow of continual modifications. Through time "an" invention is to be seen as a perpetual accretion of detail. This idea of invention as a continuous process of evolutionary change is easier to grasp when we think of something which is continually being modified before our very eyes. Thus during one lifetime almost countless inventions and discoveries have made immense changes in the automobile. There is no tangible sign that this evolution of the car is approaching an end. Similar continuity is characteristic of all times and places. Although the time span of the Paleolithic period was much spread out, the stone axe, as well as the stone blade, were persistently refined through modifying inventions.

EXAMPLES OF EVOLUTIONARY SEQUENCES: STEAM ENGINE AND AUTOMOBILE. If we construe the most basic idea in the steam engine as the harnessing of inanimate power, its origins are lost in the mist of prehistory. Sails, dead fall traps, and even cooking all testify to men's early discovery and application of innovative knowledge in utilizing energy from natural phenomena. The power of steam applied to mechanical contrivances definitely was recognized by Greeks before the Christian Era (Usher, p. 392). Hero of Alexandria described steam driven gadgets in his work *Pneumatics* written in 130 B.C. Steam power was confined to toys and mystifying devices until the sixteenth century. In that century Cardan and Porta made studies of steam and its effects. Solomon de Caus (1576–1630) discovered that steam differed from air and developed a series of propositions basic to understanding the expansion of gases. He realized that the potential of steam was greater than that of air pressure. The actual harnessing of steam to do a prosaic job was probably accomplished by Edward Somerset (the Second Marquis of Worcester) in the first half of the seventeenth century. His engine is believed to have been installed in Raglan Castle for the purpose of pumping water (Usher, p. 345). Quite a stir was caused by the Raglan Castle engine, but it seems to have been forgotten after 1670. (Its actual existence has been questioned since neither the engine nor its particular drawings have survived. However, that another similar engine appeared in 1698, there is no doubt.) Savery in 1698 sought patents on "The Miner's Friend." Several such engines were built, one for pumping water from a mine and others for water pumps in country houses. Pressure failures were common and poor metallurgy made explosions a constant hazard.

In the years that followed, many inventors worked on steam engines. Usher has hailed Newcomen's "atmospheric engine" as the greatest single act of synthesis in the history of the steam engine. This useful engine was widely used in mines by 1752 and was without equal for 75 years. Its greatest asset was that low steam pressure could be used, since the amount of pressure did not determine the amount of power in the pumps as had been the case with Savery's. Newcomen's engine was greatly improved by John Smeaten in 1770, several years after Watt began working on his own improvements upon the Newcomen engine. While Watt's revisions required high steam pressure, he devised a method of saving much power previously wasted. His great achievement was in finding a method of keeping the cylinder hot as the steam entered it. From this time on, the steam engine rapidly developed and was adapted to multiplicities of uses.

We may now well ask, "Who *invented* the steam engine?" Since innovation is at core a novel idea we might credit Hero—though his idea was not readily adapted to practical uses. Or perhaps it was the theorist De Caus who may first have seen the potentials of steam power. Or should we say, Somerset—who likely built the first working engine. Or perhaps Newcomen who finally designed a steam engine of great practicality, or scores of others who worked along with these. Watt, we must conclude, was the improving inventor who hit the jack pot. In the last analysis every one of the men mentioned, with the possible exception of Hero, was no doubt an *improving* inventor in that he added to the effectiveness of using steam energy.

The more one studies the history of technology, the more one is impressed with Gilfillan's analogy with organic evolution. In regard to relatively few inventions can we point to some year and place and say, "Here is the creation." The development of the steam engine was in no way unique when we consider the whole panoply of modern contrivances, social as well as mechanical. On the mechanical side the automobile is a case in point. If by automobile we mean the use of inanimate power for driving a land vehicle, its inventor is an eighteenth-century Frenchman, Cugnot, although Newton almost a century earlier had foreseen the possibility of a steam driven car (Chapin, pp. 314–337; Kettering). In 1770, Cugnot drove his three-wheeled carriage using the power of steam. It was slow and had to stop frequently to build up pressure, but it went. Before 1860 there were a dozen or more steam cars operating, constructed by various inventors. Gurney, an Englishman who built such a car in 1828, established a bus route near London. The modern type of automobile powered by an internal combustion engine was first designed by Krebs in 1894. It was called the Panhard and was a modern car in its chassis, in its front and hooded engine, clutch, brake pedals, and gear transmission. But let us not jump to the conclusion that Krebs was *the* inventor. Cugnot at least had the basic idea long before. Gottlieb Daimler had patented an internal combustion engine in 1885, and Narkus in Austria had an operating four-wheel vehicle powered by internal combustion engine in 1875. Benz, in Germany had also built an internal combustion engine and had successfully powered a tricycle with it at about the same time.

Many texts seem to imply that an American named Selden synthesized the group of inventions necessary for the modern car. Selden did in fact acquire such a series of patents (he was an attorney) in 1903, in the United States, but they were largely based upon the earlier European inventions. Americans were, however, crucially involved in the early explorations of automotive travel. R. E. Olds, whose name was perpetuated for many years in the car called Reo and still is known through the Oldsmobile, was one of these, as was Henry Ford, who in no sense can be considered *the* inventor of the automobile, contrary to much popular impression. But he was an *improving* inventor in a sequence that places many before and many after him. Ford brought mass production to a high point, but no doubt his greatest contribution to the automotive industry was in breaking the stranglehold in car production which the Seldon patents gave their owners (Greenleaf). Ford openly violated the patent restrictions and then won the case at law which resulted. He broke the restrictive monopoly and went on to develop the large-scale production methods for which he is famous. Lest it be thought that he single-handedly created the assembly-line principle, one of the first three patents granted by the United States government, in 1790, was to Oliver Evans, a Delaware millwright who proposed to carry grain and flour about a mill by means of steam-powered belt and screw conveyors (Berle and DeCamp, pp. 2–3).

Our business here is not to give the historical development of steam, nor of vehicular travel. These cases serve to illustrate the idea that invention is a series of accretions, some significant and some minor. An invention is a single step in a staircase of continuous events. Paraphrasing Gilfillan, we may say an invention is one level in a perpetual accretion of details. Inventions are cumulative. Having once been made, they rarely pass from the fund of knowledge, and once an invention shows practical use there is set off a chain of related, improving inventions. The consequences of any invention or improvement may indeed be revolutionary and without precedent. The invention itself is one stage of rearrangement of the body of knowledge relevant to the central course of events.

All inventions rest upon the culture base, and few have really short lines of central evolutionary history. The cotton gin is one of the rare and practically important mechanical inventions which lacks recognizable direct ancestors. Joseph Wickham Roe (p. 14) has pointed out that this is one of a very few great inventions that can be attributed wholly to one man. There was no gin of any type before Whitney's and all the elements in his design are still used in modern gins. Finished inventions of this type are uncommon, and correspondingly rare are major inventions which can indisputably be assigned to a single inventor.

AN EXAMPLE OF EVOLUTIONARY SEQUENCE IN SOCIAL INVENTION—THE LAW OF THEFT. Social norms, whether formalized in law or abiding in the folk tradition of the community, are also the devisements of creative men. They differ in that their modifications, taking no physical form, are more difficult to distinguish and document. However, where norms have the status of law, their re-arrangements, extensions, and accretions through time can be documented in tangible "stages" much as the evolution of the steam engine can be documented from the form given it by Somerset through those of Savery, Newcomen, and by Watt.

An eminent scholar of sociological jurisprudence, Jerome Hall, has painstakingly documented the historic sequences in the law of theft, as this body of law was modified by the search for social order in the rapidly changing milieu of England from the late fifteenth century into modern times. As Hall remarks,

Related immediately to the development of property interests and characterized by its concern with relatively refined methods of illegal acquisition, this
body of law has a long and well-marked history which can be definitely and
significantly traced. For each ultimate link in the chain of its history is a
specific case or statute. [P. 3.]

The English law of theft to the mid-fifteenth century was directed
to the protection of movable property, such as cattle, farm products, and
furniture. Since theft of cattle was the most important crime against
property, the definition of the law was explicitly framed toward this
offense. It was inevitable that growing industry and commerce should
stimulate men to wrongfully—though perhaps legally—appropriate commercial products by necessarily new methods—circumstances quite beyond the going concept of the law of theft.

In the Carrier's Case of 1473, the defendant who had been hired to
carry certain bales of cloth or wool to Southampton, took the goods to
another place, broke open the bales and took the contents. The case
was discussed at length before the most illustrious judges of the period.
One of the ablest of these contended throughout the case that no felony
had been committed, i.e., in terms of existing law. Modern scholars agree
that prior to this case larceny (more precisely "trespass") meant a direct,
simple, overt taking from another's possession. Had not this defendant
himself been "in possession" when he "broke bulk"? This being agreed,
how then could he have committed a larcenous act? Yet, we must sym-
pathize with a prosecutor who observes: "he cannot take them feloniously,
being in possession; but still it seems here that it is felony . . ." (Hall,
p. 9). In the upshot of the case, the defendant was found guilty through
a circuitous line of reasoning which distinguished the separable contents
of the bales from the bales themselves, to which he had been given
possession. Hall points out:

Modern legal scholars agree that the Carrier's Case was an important innovation in the law of larceny. The difficulty of formulating an objective
standard to determine the existence and extent of departure from precedent
which any case represents, arises from the fact that is impossible to fix the
meanings of many decisions with a high degree of precision. Moreover, for
various reasons, but chiefly because of a felt-need to perpetuate traditional
theories of the judicial function, the courts almost invariably assume, if their
opinions are to be taken at face value, that their decisions necessarily result
from the logical application of prior rules. [Pp. 11–12.]

It is apparent that the Carrier's Case created new law, but the new law
was built creatively upon the foundations of the long developing concepts
of "felony," "trespass," "bailment," (holding goods in trust), "larceny by
a servant," etc. These concepts were not invented by the Carrier's Case
judges but they were so re-contrived as to form a revolutionary precedent,
to be built upon in following centuries.

The law of theft, like other bodies of law, does not stand still. Old legal concepts may not achieve order or justice in novel circumstances, but the new concepts which presumably do are derived through manipulations, revisions, extensions, and limitations of older concepts and principles. Like technology, the cultural base provides the conceptual materials out of which functional inventions are contrived. And, like technology, the law too becomes increasingly complicated as the body of knowledge expands and the problems to be solved become increasingly complex.

Invention as Cultural Recombination. When invention is defined as a novel design or reconfiguration it as much as says that it is a combination of culture traits set into new relationships with each other. A device is not an invention unless it differs from existing ones in the materials or ideas composing it or in the relationships between the constituent materials or ideas. As has been observed earlier, unless such a reconfiguration of cultural materials has taken place, the presumed invention would be nothing but a replication of an existing device. On the other hand, no inventor can throw into his novel configuration materials which do not exist.

At the most elementary level, an invention involves mere *variation* in the pattern of an existing device. Variation is close to the borderline of what can be properly termed an invention (Barnett, Chap. 1). However, at least some variations represent significant creative achievements, although they remain borderline cases from the standpoint of any recombination of ingredients. We would here hail as an invention a variation such as occurred when the digging stick (dibble) used in primitive gardening was flattened at one end to give it a spade-like quality and function. We would also construe as innovative or inventive the decrease in the size of Paleolithic fist axes, or the increase in the number of spokes in early cart-wheels.

Involving somewhat more clear-cut novelty in the combination of culture traits are inventions created by *substitution* of materials. In material substitution an ingredient of an existing design is replaced by a new ingredient. An outstanding example of this type of invention is in the transformation of household utensils. The old designs, originally formed in pottery, remained constant while metal replaced clay as the major ingredient and, ultimately, as plastics came to replace metal in some cases. Both of these substitutions were inventions.

Inventions which are simply variants or substitutes are usually fairly simple ones and in any case do not represent any large share of technological growth. Most inventions are clearly novel combinations of materials. Harrison has termed such inventions *mutations.* Mutations are the novel designs which culminate through the innovative fusion of diverse cultural elements. They include the most complex inventions and are central to the evolution of culture generally. In mutation, a familiar implement at a certain point of development is combined with some feature which had its own development in a distinct and separate course of events.

At its simplest level, mutations involve the combination of diverse objects existing in nature to form a single implement, as a piece of bark or animal's skin is appropriated to cover the hand in grasping a sharp object. Of greatest concern to modern technology, however, is the fusion of developed separate inventions to form a novel design. The automobile, for example, utilizes rubber for tires, latex having been brought to European notice after its discovery and use by American Indians. Inventions in rubber processing and utilization had their own course of events, which in one facet was ultimately merged with vehicular transport. The wheel has misty origins in Asia and had its own course of development in application to potting and water lifting, as well as wagons, carriages, and ultimately steam- and gasoline-powered vehicles.

The internal combustion engine developed within the course of inanimate power explorations and has its own history quite apart from that of the automobile in the vehicular sense. Both the modern automobile engine and the developed steam engine required pistons. Von Guericke's research with pistons was known in England by 1657 (Usher, p. 340).

Metallurgy, needed for engine construction, has its course of growth from the end of the Neolithic period. Inadequate metallurgical knowledge stringently limited the early English developments of the steam engine. High pressures could not be safely used until metal strength had been increased. The handling of such metal required in turn machine tool development. A boring machine invented by John Wilkinson in 1766 enabled Watt and Boulton to bring their engine to the point of practicality. Working without this tooling invention, Watt had found it impossible to bore his cylinders with the necessary degree of accuracy (Thompson, p. 184).

Any given invention arises in the context of a particular stream of utilitarian, aesthetic, or ideological interests, as wagon follows cart, which is followed by automobile. At the same time other parts of the culture base do not remain static. Varied and seemingly unrelated branches of knowledge and technology also grow. Here and there these are fused by imaginative men, as the carriage and wagon are fused with an engine; or indeed as centuries earlier the sledge was associated with the wheel.

PRINTING: AN EXAMPLE OF CULTURAL MUTATIONS. The printing press which was a fifteenth-century culmination in the shops of Gutenberg in Germany and Coster in Holland was preceded by the development of many previously unrelated courses of inventive efforts: rubbings and block printing, paper, ink, metal casting, presses, and others (Carter; Singer *et al.,* Vols. I, III; Usher, Chap. 10). Many of these constituent requirements for the ultimate culmination were diffused out of Asia; others represented courses of events largely of European origin. Paper, and later the idea of block printing on paper, travelled to Europe in the form of playing cards and printed money from the Mongol Empire. Playing cards apparently stimulated printing activity in Europe whereas primitive block impressions already known to Europeans had been given little interest. Factories for the production of playing cards appeared in Germany and Italy early in the fifteenth century. The press itself was not borrowed from Asia but rather from the wine and linen industries of Italy, Spain, and France. Its use may have been suggested by the technical impression problems arising from the type of paper used with the available ink. The development of metallurgy in Europe in the thirteenth, fourteenth, and fifteenth centuries led to the knowledge of making punches, matrices, and alloys necessary for the growth of efficient typecasting. The discovery of antimony in the fifteenth century was eagerly seized upon by metallurgists concerned with printing, since for the first time a lead alloy of sufficient hardness could be made. From the Flemish school of art came the development of oil-base ink by the borrowing of linseed oil to replace water. This was ultimately essential for metal type printing. And fundamental to this entire jigsaw puzzle was the long development of the alphabet from its origins in Southwest Asia. The few symbols it required and their shape in the Latin form were fortuitously ideal for the printer's purpose. In the shop of Gutenberg in Mainz, of Lauren Coster in Haarlem, and probably others in France these exotic ingredients were creatively stirred up together and modern printing emerged.

EVOLUTION AND MUTATION IN SOCIAL INVENTIONS. Histories of technology adduce on practically every page the evidence of continuity, mutation, and the other processes of invention. The excellence of technological history, coupled with the feeling that the facts of social life are more discontinuous and adaptive to material technology, has obstructed our view of evolution in social values, forms, and norms.

Forms of government, distinctive types of educational institutions, religious structures, and even magical practices all develop and change through the processes of innovation. While modifications in social structures and modes of conduct (norms) may differ in some respects from the processes of technical "material" culture, social structures also arise by mutations in some evolving central course of events. The adaptive character of "social" inventions has often been stressed as a unique feature, e.g., modern traffic laws have their origin in problems created by the auto-

mobile. This is a part-truth. Norms must indeed be developed which
"fit" a situation, and in our society technical achievements are quite obviously requiring us to create new controls, new social structures, new
roles, and new norms. Associated with motor traffic has been a wealth
of new road laws, new control bodies, new commissions, etc. However,
each of these adaptive innovations has its own roots. Today's rules of
the road enjoy some descent from earlier practices regarding right-of-way,
safety, and order in carriage, wagon, and earlier automobile travel. Highway patrols are innovations in a long stream of organized policing systems. An Interstate Commerce Commission might have a seemingly
sudden birth, but its roots in governing theory, constitutional law, experience in bureaucratization, and developing control mechanisms go far
back. The quite obvious maladjustments in our society ("culture lags")
should not overshadow the universality of evolutionary and mutation
principles in innovation. "Social" inventions are more complicated in
that they must bring order into constantly changing circumstances, these
changes frequently but certainly not always being due to technical inventions and their use. We must remember also that technical inventions
may be modified to fit into certain social structures and normative systems
as in a search for *normatively* acceptable birth control devices.

Both the unilinear growth and the variations and mutations involved
in social invention were recognized and documented many years ago by
F. Stuart Chapin. Chapin's studies of the development of the commission
form of municipal government and the city manager plan show in concrete detail how the system came into being. The mutation processes are
fundamentally the same as in the evolution of printing or other complex
machines.

A great hurricane followed by a tidal wave and flood devastated the city
of Galveston, Texas, on September 8, 1900. The city government was immediately faced with a most urgent need of preserving order, relieving those
in want and planning wise rehabilitation measures. Under the pressure of this
catastrophe the existing bicameral system of city government, with its mayor,
common council and board of aldermen, broke down and failed to function.
It was at this juncture that a committee of substantial business men of the
city took up the matter and attempted to meet the desperate situation. A
sub-committee of three men set to work to gather information about the government of other cities in which the principle of corporate business enterprise
of concentration of power and responsibility had been tried out in the management of municipal affairs. They secured the charters of several cities including Baltimore, Md., and the legislation covering the city of Washington,
D. C., and the Taxing Commission of Memphis after the yellow fever epidemic
of 1878. Their study and deliberations led to the proposal that a commission
of five persons be appointed to govern the city. Concentration of both power
and responsibility in a small group of five men set up a form of city government as nearly as possible like the board of directors of a business corporation.

The original plan called for commissioners as part-time civilian and advisory heads of departments rather than as expert professional heads. This latter principle came into effect later. The committee which devised the plan did not at the time realize that they were inventing any new form of political structure. They felt that they were merely meeting an acute problem.

The success of this new plan of municipal government influenced the neighboring city of Houston to obtain a new charter embodying the commission form of government. It went into effect in 1905. Houston retained the five commissioner arrangement of Galveston but in other ways changed the plan. The commissioners were not elected by wards but at large. The mayor was given greater power. There were other differences, but the outstanding addition to the pattern was a referendum on the franchises and bond issues.

The fame of the Galveston plan spread to Des Moines. Here a meeting of citizens listened with interest to the city attorney's account of his visit to Galveston and what he there observed. Other meetings and discussion followed. As a result a commission was appointed to prepare a bill for submission to the Iowa legislature. From Galveston came the five commissioner arrangement and from Houston the referendum. To these elements the following new ones were added: the recall of unsatisfactory officials was borrowed from Los Angeles (1903); the initiative in combination with the referendum was probably suggested by Dallas (although a right possessed by Iowa's cities since 1898); the non-partisan ballot suggested by the earlier experience of Massachusetts where in 1888 party designations were dropped (also Boston Charter of 1909); and finally, a civil service commission (the Federal Law was passed in 1883). The new pattern was thus made up of political practices already known and tried out. The attribute of "newness" consisted, therefore, as in the case of other inventions, only in the fact that the Des Moines plan represented a combination of political traits (culture traits) never made before. The cultural threshold for the new political integration was ripe, and popular dissatisfaction with the conventional bicameral system was crystallized by glowing reports of new experiments in Galveston and Indianapolis. [Chapin, pp. 337–341.]

CONCLUSION

Inventions are ideational constructs. They are designs composed of ideas juxtaposed in a new configuration. This view of invention denotes that it is always a rearrangement of existing knowledge toward an emergent pattern which is new. Many inventions can be constructed in tangible physical form; others can be composed out of socio-cultural "materials" but the manifestation of novelty into some physical or social form is not crucial for the idea of invention.

Inventions do not necessarily bring social change. As a new design, an invention stimulates change only insofar as it is taken into account, utilized, or responded to. Some inventions, when they deal with social organization itself, will yield social change just by virtue of their adoption, as one social form replaces another. Other inventions, like mechanical devices, yield social change as they are responded to adjustively in the social system.

Theories of invention are of two major types—those emphasizing psychological processes in creativity and those emphasizing cultural accumulation and evolution. In contemporary research both in creativity and in technological history, these two approaches complement each other in producing an approach to inventing in terms of creative evolution. Inventions come into being as problem-solving men manipulate and re-configurate ideas which are present in the cultural heritage. The fact that most inventions are to be understood as small steps in a long evolutionary sequence does not mean that these steps can be taken without the creative perceptions of specific individuals. Psychologically, inventing takes place through processes as yet only vaguely understood but rooted in man's capacity for abstractions, i.e., to perceive likenesses in unlike things. Gestalt psychologists have made special contributions in the distinction between problem solving or configurational learning and associational type learning. From the standpoint of cultural accumulation, the creative acts of man are given substance in the mutation or fusion of ideas and of instruments so that, though composed of old constituent elements, new designs with novel meaning and function are added to the cultural heritage to become part of the culture base upon which succeeding inventors operate.

5

Innovation Through Social Interaction

THE IDEA OF IMMANENT CHANGE

Change in the life-ways of social groups can and does arise spontaneously or immanently as social relationships persist over time. Immanent change develops out of interaction itself as an unfolding process rather than as a devisement or invention. Pitirim Sorokin has expressed this idea in the following words:

Any system, especially a sociocultural system, being a "going concern," incessantly functioning, inevitably changes as long as it continues to exist and function, even if it is placed in a wholly static environment. Change is an inherent property of all functioning systems. The most efficient automobile engine is bound to change if it is left running, even under the best conditions. Likewise any biological organism or system inevitably changes as long as it lives, even if the external conditions are static. . . .

Whether the system is scientific or religious, aesthetic or philosophical, whether it is represented by a family, a business firm, an occupational union, or a state, it bears within itself the seeds of incessant change, which mark every action and reaction even in a fixed environment. . . .

Through this incessant generation of consequences attending each of its changes a system perceptibly determines the character and course of its own future career. The whole series of changes it undergoes throughout its existence is to a large extent *an unfolding of its inherent potentialities.* [Sorokin, pp. 696–697; cf. Eisenstadt.] *

* From *Society, Culture, and Personality* by Pitirim Sorokin. Copyright 1947 by Pitirim A. Sorokin. Reprinted by permission of Harper & Row, Publishers.

To descend from the sublime affirmations of sociological science to plebeian realities, let us consider a fairly commonplace situation by way of general illustration. A nagging wife produces responses in her husband. These responses, almost regardless of the particular form they may take, in turn stimulate responsive behavior in the mate. Wherever we go from here, the honeymoon is over! Two personalities have risen above the normative expectations of the situation to achieve a set of cumulative interactions which may in the long run yield a unique adjustment or may yield chaos and group disruption. That this dyadic group is to undergo change is clear. That this change arose from interacting personalities is equally clear. While their culture may have provided some patterning for their cycle of inter-stimulating, the particular sequence was home-spun and spontaneous. It did not descend upon them as does the culturally derived pattern of retirement in old age or "Sunday in the Park." Although the two as a total group may well have been responding to cultural pressures, they themselves built the shifting world of interaction which was their own. With great sophistication, William Foote Whyte has documented the shifting social positions of members of a street corner "gang." Here out of the very interaction of the group itself, the status of a member is created and reduced and re-created. It is this realm of innovation with which we are dealing here, as a route, a source, a genesis of change.

Beginning in the 1930's, Kurt Lewin and Ronald Lippett conducted a series of experimental researches in group leadership. These studies, showing the response of members to varying types of leaders, are classic accounts of social change introduced through stimulus-response sequences. In these studies, some of which are now widely reprinted, Lippett and Lewin found marked differences developing in the interpersonal relationships among children when exposed to differing kinds of leadership climates. Where adult supervision was authoritarian, communication was inhibited and resulting group structure was less complex than where supervision was democratic. Expressions of irritability and aggressiveness appeared less frequently under democratic supervision than under either apathetic or authoritarian leadership.

It is improbable that any enumeration of conditions leading to change through social interaction can be complete. None of these conditions operates in isolation from the others; classification and enumeration are, therefore, arbitrary. We may say that innovative behavior arises wherever latitude, ambiguity, or rejection occurs in culturally patterned behavior. Yet, in the last analysis, all social behavior is partly idiosyncratic if only because organisms possessing different capacities and subjected to differing socialization processes and interests are acting in accord with cultural patterns which they perceive differently.

THE FORMATION OF GROUPS

When aggregates of individuals are brought into a state of persisting interaction, organization or structure must arise if a humanly intolerable state of chaos is to be avoided. Under some conditions the model of structure may be borrowed in rather complete detail from already existing groups. For example, if a new school is introduced into an American community its design is pre-established in great detail in the laws, conventions, and customs of the American educational institution. Obviously, in any such replication informal and unique variations are imposed upon the diffused design. However, such previously invented designs are not always existent nor if existent, known or acceptable to aggregates which are thrown into a common social context. The norms, the differentiated role expectations, and the authority structure must often be worked out rather fully in the processes of interaction at this time and this place. The principle is a clear one, supported by an immense range of research inquiry and observations. "When individuals interact with one another toward common goals, *in time* a group structure emerges with definite hierarchical statuses and a set of norms to regulate activities within the group . . ." (Sherif, M. and C., p. 330).

In one of America's earliest textbooks in sociology, Small and Vincent (pp. 99–168) described this process of norm and role differentiation arising from the interaction within the pioneer family and in the pioneer community as each works out the structure for orderly pursuit of group interests in an alien frontier environment. An interesting parallel to their account is given by Sherif and Sherif (pp. 269–277). Following Walter Prescott Webb in *The Great Frontier*, the Sherifs show that in meeting immediate problems men work out solutions in interaction and subsequently get their new practices recognized and incorporated into law. Much of the same process occurs in regard to role differentiation, where new and varied tasks are to be done. Small and Vincent were graphic in showing how "definite form" grows out of early disorder, as the pioneer community achieves "general, unformulated agreement upon a fundamental code." There arises differentiation into status levels; informal relationships are firmed up as local farmers join the town associations," and differentiation in function yields new roles in occupation and in authority. Small and Vincent also recognized the significant principle which modern experimentalists have not always remembered, that organizational patterns representing possibly centuries of growth are directly and immediately transplanted in the new situation.

Only under most rigorous laboratory conditions does a new structure grow without carryover from the old (Sherif, M., 1952). Yet the specific rules which guided life in an old New England town could do little more than provide hunches as moral citizens of the Western frontier sought to deal with claim jumpers. With a potpourri of strange ethnic groups, migrants who rejected old class positions, and exotic religious sects all shaken together, new patterns of order were evolved. Old skills found new modes of fitting into a community which was in the throes of "becoming." In the environment of the frontier community, abilities once of little consequence had survival—and status—value. Traditional class positions were significant for the introduction of bias into the developing status order of the frontier. The interaction toward producing the innovations required of a strange population in a strange environment were precisely the qualities of American life which so appalled Charles Dickens and intrigued Edward Dicey (Commager). The former saw the degeneration of civilized society in these communities; the latter saw the rebirth of a social order. Both agreed that social change was very much in process.

Although novel definitions of roles and norms no doubt are most likely to appear in unstructured situations, they may also arise where norms or role specifications have been clear but given broad definition. Individuals here are not deviant nor are they creating structure out of unstructured chaotic situations. They are simply giving normatively idiosyncratic definitions to principles of conduct. Where individuals are enjoined to behave in regard to principle rather than precept, such idiosyncrasies are tolerable. Under these circumstances, novel patterns may arise which have the ultimate effect of shifting the "main stream" of normative conduct toward a particular idiosyncratic version of the norms. Thus, acting under the strong valuation of marriage without specificity as to age of betrothal, India moved toward "child marriage" as fathers sought to protect their familial interests. Slight novelty may become intensified through cumulative interaction and ultimately be institutionalized in extreme form.

DEVIANCE

Groups, with their structured behavior patterns and social control systems, invariably build mechanisms to inculcate socially approved norms and goals of conduct into their members. When members are impelled to violate the norms in the pursuit of accepted goals we may infer that either the socialization process was pathological or that pressures within the social structure have prevailed against the forces of conformity. Innovative behavior is always idiosyncratic. It is deviance when it involves the pursuit of socially approved ends through means that are outside the limits of culturally prescribed conduct. Deviants are not innovative insofar as they are simply socialized by sub-groups which transmit an a-normative pattern of behavior. They are innovative, however, when their responses to social pressures are novel. Such spontaneous actions may in turn set a design which is diffused and made into part of the cultural fabric. Or such unpatterned actions may set off equally unpatterned responses in others. A series of stimulus-response transactions may ensue (cumulative interaction) which culminate in a new structure of group relations unlike either the original or the deviation. Of course, in all likelihood the majority of truly deviant innovations wilt into oblivion in the face of the controls exerted in favor of the established order.

In his well known essay "Social Structure and Anomie" Robert K. Merton outlined a theory of deviant behavior, including innovative actions (Merton, 1957; Clinard). This theory rested upon the concept of anomic which was created by Emile Durkheim in his theory of suicide. Anomie is a state in which the norms and values of the group have lost their binding power upon the individual. Merton developed Durkheim's concept around the thesis that social structures exert pressures upon certain members toward non-conforming rather than conforming conduct. While Durkheim sought to explain suicide, in part, by this general conception, Merton extended its explanatory breadth to crime, delinquency, radicalism, and other non-conforming activities.

In this theory it is observed that conformity to both cultural goals and institutionalized means to their attainment is the most common mode through which individuals strive to achieve. Complete conformity to both prescribed means and goals would yield a condition of perfect equilibrium with no interactional stimulus to change. But conformity is only one adaptation. All others are deviant but not all are properly termed innovative. The deviant under certain circumstances may pursue a course of retreatism or withdrawal in which cultural goals as well as means of achieving them are rejected. Examples of this type of responses are the psychotics, tramps, and alcoholics. Another non-innovative adaptation may be that of ritualism wherein the actor abides scrupulously by behavioral norms but does not apply his action toward attainable goals, e.g., persons who play it safe, avoiding high ambition and consequent frustration. None of these adaptations to anomic pressures would appear to hold much significance for social change. Two other adaptations are described by Merton which are significant for social change. These are innovation and rebellion.

Innovative behavior is stimulated when society places high values upon certain goals and at the same time places undue restriction on approved means for reaching them. Merton concluded that in a society valuing affluence and social ascent, Al Capone represents the triumph of amoral intelligence over morally prescribed "failure" (1957a, p. 146).

Merton originally explored the implications of this idea largely in regard to the aspiration of affluence in relation to social class disability.

In subsequent studies it was applied to juvenile delinquency and other forms of deviation. Undoubtedly it can arise in reference to any highly valued aspiration in which the normative means for achievement are inadequate, especially when the group rejects the notion of such inadequacy as a fallacious one. For example the hard-pressed football coach in his contract renewal year faces the season with a "hard-luck team" and with more than a little pressure to win at any cost. The pressures by irrational alumni and fans place considerable strain on the coach's ethical choice of means. Under such conditions it becomes normal to "take advantage" of a chance situation in such a way that there is deviance from the norms of sportsmanship.

While not termed "innovative" in Merton's basic statements on deviance, rebellion is a form of deviance in which the individual turns away from the existing social structure seeking to establish a new or greatly modified one in its place. The rebel, unlike the "innovator," is seeking to institutionalize new goals and new procedures to be shared by his fellows. This form of deviance leads toward change *of*, rather than *within*, the social system (Parsons and Smelser, 1956, pp. 247–248).

Innovative deviance and rebellion both work toward undermining the norms of the society and contribute to the spread of anomic conditions through the social system. This is not a process of diffusion of a pattern of acting but is rather the "diffusion" of vulnerability to anomie. Merton recognized the significance of his theory of deviance for social change but developed it mainly for an understanding of social problems. In that context he observes that:

In the history of every society, one supposes, some of its culture heroes eventually come to be regarded as heroic in part because they are held to have had the courage and the vision to challenge the beliefs and routines of their society. The rebel, revolutionary, nonconformist, heretic, or renegade of an earlier day is often the culture hero of today. [Merton, 1961, p. 736.]

It should be emphasized that not all innovations arise out of the anomic circumstances posed by Merton in this theory, or if they do, the theory needs much greater qualifying development than it has received. Creative manipulation of ideas (inventing) has little relationship to normative deviance and rebellion. And while deviance is indeed at work in much interactional innovating, it is not the major explanatory theory in the various types of innovation discussed below. Each of these types arises through interactional pressures which are not, in large part, anomic ones.

Relation of Deviance to Socialization and Control Processes

Socialization serves to inculcate in the individual the abilities and disciplines required for effective participation in the group. Social control relates to all mechanisms or pressures exerted upon the individual by the group toward conformity with group expectations. Largely but with important qualifications these processes work toward the inhibition of deviance.

Since inadequate socialization produces individuals who have failed to internalize the norms and role expectations of their forefathers, it lays a groundwork for deviance in the personality of the newcomer to that society. The inadequately socialized person does not recognize conventional cues to action when they arise nor does he possess ingrained response patterns to recognized cues. He lacks commitment to the ways of his social heritage. Erickson has emphasized the implication for personality development when the child has no valued role models in his adult world with which he can identify. Merton (1957b) has shown the importance of professional "role models" as a stabilizing force in the education of medical students as to the patient relationships. Inadequate socialization is the implicit source of receptivity to innovation in the theory of Homer Barnett and others. Most theories which pose alienation or disaffection with the social order as the basis for innovative behavior are in effect designating inadequate or incomplete socialization as a source for this proneness to innovate. Where social control mechanisms are sufficiently strong such disaffection may, of course, be repressed.

There are important qualifications to the idea that socialization is geared toward perfect replication of the parental generation. Socialization processes themselves are responsive to a changing social order and may even instill motivations toward further change. In interpreting their research on American businessmen, John and Ruth Useem (pp. 74–91) suggest that businessmen are socialized to tolerate irrational authority through flexibility and independence. The individual is socialized toward flexibility in personality patterns rather than simple conformity. On the basis of research among Russians, Alex Inkeles has also supported the idea that socialization processes are not wholly directed toward conformity to the status quo. Inkeles observes that although parents are responsible for conveying tradition, they still *learn* under conditions of social change. This learning may influence them to deliberately rear their children in a manner befitting newly arising conditions rather than traditional ones. Parents anticipate the future and act out this in the anticipatory socialization of their children. Inkeles' views are particularly important since he has demonstrated precisely such preparation for change in the shifting patterns of socialization in the Soviet Union. In an analysis of Russian life history documents he found that while pre-revolution and post-revolution parents both carried forward a common Russian cultural tradition, marked differences occurred in their emphases. Post-revolution parents placed much less emphasis upon traditional values and much greater emphasis upon intellectuality and political awareness than did the earlier generation.

In many societies an "independent" personality type is at least nominally idealized. The relationship of such a type to socialization processes is not well demonstrated. Many years ago W. I. Thomas visualized socialization processes as tending to yield three different personality types—the Philistine, a conservator of tradition; the Bohemian, the flaunter of tradition; and the Creative man (Thomas and Znaniecki). More recently the problem of socialization and change has been broached in somewhat similar terms by David Riesman (1950). Riesman has pointed to the "tradition-directed person" as one produced through socialization by the community. Another but somewhat similar type, the "inner-directed person" is produced through strong parental socialization, while a third type, the "other-directed," is socialized by peers. It is evident that Riesman's "tradition-directed person" is a conservator of tradition and so is the "inner-directed." The "tradition-directed person" feels shame at violation of traditional standards while the "inner-directed person" suffers guilt for his transgressions. The "other-directed person," however, is more isolated from the inter-generational agencies of socialization and in this sense less wedded to the ways of the past. Elsewhere, Riesman (1949) has suggested that in this modern society, which is the homeland of the rather unstable "other-directed person," there emerges a fourth type, the "autonomous person." Whereas both inner- and other-directed individuals knuckle under to group standards, the "autonomous" is referred to by Riesman as the "saving remnant." The "autonomous person" converts helplessness into a condition of advance. Unfortunately we have little inductive evidence as to how socialization processes operate in the production of such idealized types, whether in the guise of the creative man or an "autonomous person." (For a review of some inductive studies of creative persons see Chap. 4.)

The relationship of social control to innovation is as complex as is the socialization process. Some societies rigidly control actions which other societies view as unworthy of control. No society attempts to enforce rigid conformity upon every aspect of life. It is probable that even the most tradition-valuing societies applaud individual variations in certain spheres, while establishing ultimate boundaries beyond which variations are forbidden. Social values ultimately determine the types of behavior upon which control is exerted. Deviant behavior may, however, be repressed by control mechanisms and still set social changes in motion. Although the deviant may be permitted to set no example to be taken up by others, the very process of repression can stimulate change. Thus, rigorous control measures may have a dynamic effect upon personality structure so that aggressive tendencies repressed at a given time are fueled for manifestation on subsequent occasions. At the group level the repression of deviance can stimulate more intense traditionalism, a process observable as the radical right movement in the United States responds to its perception of deviance in the political behavior of national leaders.

While we may conclude that effective socialization and control processes are generally oriented against change, the conclusion is a highly qualified one. Socialization may become anticipatory of social change while social control is not only qualified in its application, but under some circumstances it is latently productive of deviant innovation through its very repressiveness.

CONFLICT

Conflict theories of social change have a long history in sociological thought. Under the stimulation of Darwinian principles of struggle for survival, the conflict principle was central to the evolutionary view of society propounded by such scholars as Ludwig Gumplowicz and Gustave Ratzenhofer in the late nineteenth century. In the past generation of sociologists, conflict as a force for change was largely neglected. As indicated earlier (Chap. 2) its significance has been revived since 1950 particularly in the works of Lewis A. Coser and Ralf Dahrendorf. The meaning of "conflict" varies as some writers emphasize overt conflict, others competition, and still others broaden its meaning to make it almost synonymous with "social tension."

Conflict Within the Social System

No social group can long persist without the appearance of opposition of interests and viewpoints. No social order is so "perfect," no socialization system so complete, and no social control system so powerful as to insure perpetual harmony among members of a group as they interact in the achievement of their personal and their common goals. The very fact of organization denotes the coordination of individuals holding differing positions and hence differing viewpoints and concerns. However, all persisting groups build into their structure more or less effective mechanisms for conflict resolution. It is in the working out of conflicts through these mechanisms that "accommodative novelty" arises. (It is possible, of course, to resolve conflict without novelty through acceptance of traditional types of settlement.)

Ralf Dahrendorf has emphasized conflict as the central dynamic principle in social change. He has shown particularly how an inherent conflict of interests between the authorities and the subordinated leads to structural change in society. As interests diverge those in opposition organize toward the formulation and promulgation of ideologies and movements toward change in the traditionally legitimate group structure. This position is supported in the researches of S. N. Eisenstadt. Eisenstadt (1963; 1964b) has found that in the early empires the chief root of change lay in the development of differentiated classes which could generate political pressures to which the rulers were unable to make effective responses. Eisenstadt concludes that the very process of institutionalization of a political system creates the forces that act to overthrow it.

Ronald Cohen, in a study of the contemporary Kanuri Muslim emirate in Nigeria, has also found that conflict is built into the political system in such a way as to yield a pattern of long-range, continuous change (Cohen; Frank). Cohen points out that in any hierarchical structure there are differences among people which create ambiguity in group goals as well as conflicting ideas about behavioral standards. Selective enforcement of standards arises out of such differences, particularly as governmental authority rests now in the hands of persons having one vision of group goals and then in the hands of differently oriented persons. Cohen shows that among the Kanuri these processes have resulted in predictable conditions favorable for change. He finds that conflicting standards of behavior generate innovations which are tolerated through the established patterns of selective enforcement. Although it is generally believed that societies such as the Kanuri are conservative and anti-progressive, Cohen finds that in fact there is built into such societies the dynamism for change. Such societies, he concludes, will "modernize" without drastic, revolutionary movements through the "built-in" responsiveness of their system to continued and constant pressure in a given direction.

Contrary to the opinion that internal conflict is destructive of group solidarity, the conflict theorists insist that through conflict continuing equilibria are maintained in group relationships. This viewpoint assumes that mechanisms of accommodation are operative or that they can be established and accepted by the opposing parties. Given the channels of accommodation, internal conflicts become positive forces toward preserving social order in the midst of change. To be sure, conflict situations do not eventuate in precisely the same group structure that was known before, but the truth of this assertion does not imply that conflict is purely disorganizing. It may disorganize a group if accommodative channels are inoperative, but more typically it re-organizes or changes rather than disorganizes.

Robert Dubin, from his studies of labor and management relations expresses some of the innovations in group organization which arise as personal interests clash within it.

What happens when clear, sharp competition comes forth? Stakes are involved. Personal reputations merge with group reputation. Some members, who are better able to talk than others, or for whom the thought of victory carries particular relish, begin to exercise more weight than previously had been characteristic of them. In the extreme the result can be essentially a complete "taking over" by one or two persons. Others who are less able and aggressive and more dependent, fall in line. To avoid being responsible for defeat, still others "bite their tongues" and are less vocal.

What are the results? There definitely is group accomplishment. A more differentiated pecking order is established. . . . [Dubin, p. 99.]

Where conflict reaches stalemate, the possibility of group disorganization is an immediate potential. Dubin has also shown how this threat of serious disorganization stimulates the invention of new accommodative channels and designs. Some years ago labor-management conflicts in the United States developed a conflict policy which Dubin has termed the "win-lose design." This is to say that at some point in negotiations each side found a position from which it could not or would not retreat. Stalemate was inherent in the design. For the first time in the history of American labor relations, government now entered the arena with novel instruments of mediation and accommodation. A novel accommodative structure was created to support and if necessary supersede direct negotiation, the pattern of which had been so modified through interactive processes as to no longer fulfill its function (Dubin, p. 69; Kahn-Freund).

American Race Relations: A Case of Inter-Group Conflict Within a Social System. When conflict within a society assumes significance for the preservation of the social order, it may be assumed that it is inter-group and not merely inter-personal. This, of course, was the case in Dubin's report on the consequences of a "win-lose" design in labor-management disputes. In the United States, the most complex and socially significant conflict within the society today is that of the Negro civil rights movement. Here is dramatic evidence of the innovative consequences of conflict upon the structure of the contending groups themselves as well upon the encompassing super-system of the nation. The following account draws largely upon Joseph Himes' perceptive essay on the functions of racial conflict.

1. *Conflict Stimulates Internal Changes in Each Group.* As a conflict group American Negroes have found new solidarity and have clarified the boundaries of the group, e.g., replacing white leadership by Negroes in the movement. At the same time their struggle to articulate viable goals and means for attaining them has touched off power struggles, internal schisms in developing action organization, and massive collective excitement and unrest. In the early stages of the conflicts, broad collective aims were easily established and individuals could "find niches and become polarized around the collective enterprise" (Himes, p. 9). All participants were drawn closer together both for prosecution of the strug-

gle and for common defense. In the movement individuals were led to make new commitments, accept new roles, evidence new racial pride, accept new and even dangerous criteria of status achievement as in demonstrations. But unity induced through conflict is an uneasy state. As conflict produces new racial identity, the very lack of Negro sub-group structure induces variant definitions of goals, honest differences of opinion as to how they are to be reached, and hence factional schisms. These are enhanced through power rivalries among leaders, especially as they seek support from the large unrestful mass as yet uncommitted to any structured approach to some clear-cut set of goals. While the state of the Negro sub-society appears chaotic and disorganized from an organizational point of view, the conflict of the past decade has already made of it an exceedingly different group, if group it could be called, from that which existed in the 1940's. If it is disunited in organizations and in goals and methods, it has in a short time span created many of these organizations, brought goals to articulate discussion, generated and applied techniques toward the achievement of some of them, and placed intense pressures upon both white sub-society and the national state to accommodate in the issues of conflict. Negro sub-society is utterly unlike Negro sub-society in the pre-conflict days of two short decades ago.

Responses to Negro demands have brought substantial changes in the white sub-group, but these changes are of much more limited proportion. Although the Negro movement is oriented toward gaining rights denied or inhibited by the white majority, substantial numbers of the white sub-group are in sympathy with several of the Negro organizations and with the main core of objectives. The issues, however, have brought into new sharp focus the boundary between white sympathizers and white opponents, with a large inert sector between. Differentiation was enhanced among whites. The sharpest innovative reactions within the white sub-group occurred as active reactionaries became increasingly differentiated. Thus, a white Citizen Council leader in Mississippi repeatedly voiced the rallying cry, "Organized aggression must be met with organized resistance" (Himes, p. 5). And the reactionary element of the white sub-group did indeed organize what has been termed the "white back-lash." Movement begets counter-movement. Forces of structural re-orientation arose in various white communities and organizations as new anti- or pro-integration factions struggled for power and their leaders vied for followers and organizational dominance. Unlike the Negro movement, criteria of status based upon conflict achievement were generally acceptable only to whites who had lost out in the more meaningful status-evoking activities of modern society.

2. *Conflict Stimulates Change in Inter-Group Relationships.* Much of the Negro movement has been aimed at bringing the maximum power

resources of a weak minority to bear upon a status quo supported by a strongly powered complacent majority. Martin Luther King expressed this strategy as one seeking to create such a crisis that a community which has persistently refused to negotiate is forced to face the issue. The race issue becomes so dramatized that a complacent community has no choice but to deal with it (Himes, p. 4; King, p. 81). The consequences of this move for changing Negro-white relationships has been systematically assessed by Joseph S. Himes. He observes that the application of mobilized social power tends to reduce the power differential between actors, to restrict existing status differences, and to alter the directions of social interaction. Negroes and whites long in contact through stylized supplicant-ruler relationships now confront each other on a horizontal plane of power-based negotiation. In this new relationship, communication processes shift from conventionalized avoidance of basic understanding to the discussion of substantive issues and the calculated demands of Negroes. As Himes puts it:

The communicators infuse their exchanges of cognitive meanings with the feelings that, within the traditional structure, were required to be suppressed and avoided. Many white people thus were shocked to discover that the "happy" Negroes whom they "knew" so well were in fact discontented and angry people. [P. 6.]

3. *Conflict Stimulates Change in the Total Social System.* At first glance it might be concluded that racial conflicts must have disunifying consequences for the total community or society. In the almost goalless violences supported by the most radical advocates of "Black Power" this might be true. In the conflict as outlined by responsible organizations such as the NAACP the reverse has been the case. Responsible Negro leadership has carefully laid out objectives and chosen tactics with the closest regard for the most sacred values unifying American society. The campaign becomes a dynamic force in which Americans of both races are required to review and reaffirm their unifying values. It is precisely for this reason that the White Citizens Councils and Ku Klux Klan have been left in such precarious positions, for they must contend against a movement firmly rooted in the support—and extension—of the most fundamental tenets of Americanism. In the responsive actions of communities and the nation, the American creed is extended. Out of conflict interaction, governments are stimulated to invent legal and other devices toward the fuller achievement of societal objectives.

When sub-societies conflict within the terms established by societal values and goals, the function of conflict is ultimately "to sew" the society together.

In this sewing function, realistic racial conflict is interwoven with political, religious, regional, rural-urban, labor-management, class and other persistent threads of struggle that characterize the American social fabric. What is deci-sive is the fact that variously struggling factions are united in the consensus of the ultimate societal values. The conflicts are therefore non-radical, criss-crossing and tend to mitigate each other. . . . Conflict not only projects the combatants into the social consensus; it also acts to reaffirm the ultimate values around which the consensus is organized. Moreover, conflict joins opposing actors in meaningful interaction for ends, whose importance is a matter of further agreement. [Himes, p. 8.]

Stripped of the valuative and extremely complex permutations of the so-called Negro Revolution, the experimental conflict studies of Sherif and Sherif support this cautious optimism. Using boys' camps as a locale, the Sherifs stimulated sub-group formation and systematically varied the circumstances under which these groups interacted. They conclude that when two groups are brought into competitive and reciprocally frustrating situations, they develop negative attitudes and stereotypes toward one another. But when the groups are induced to interact in a situation wherein mutually desirable goals cannot be achieved by one group acting alone, they tend to cooperate. As this occurs, inter-group conflict dimin-ishes and unfavorable stereotypes are reduced. Internally, in-group soli-darities are intensified in rivalry and reduced with the reduction of out-group tension-evoking circumstances (Sherif and Sherif, 1956, pp. 293–331).

Revolution: The Ultimate Schism Within Social Systems. Revolution is a condition in which an existing order of society is rejected through violence by its members. In this context, the term excludes social changes which simply because of their massiveness have frequently been called "revolutionary." Accordingly the great transformation of England asso-ciated with the "industrial revolution" is not included within the bounds of the concept. The significance of violence for a meaningful definition of revolution has been stressed by Chalmers Johnson (1964; 1966, Chap. 1). If violence or the threat of violence does not occur, then there simply has not been revolution. True revolution implies the acceptance of vio-lence to cause change in a social system when all other devices to effect change have failed. In practical terms, it involves armed insurrection against the militant forces commanded by an incumbent political power.

Since revolutionary violence is not aimed at issues but at people, revolution is directed toward those elements of the social system which authorize and preserve the order which the active dissidents would dis-solve and replace. This is to say that the revolutionary attack is aimed upon the existing system's elite. Revolution is the acceptance of violence to bring about changes which are opposed by the legitimate authority and have presumably been incapable of achievement through established accommodative channels. As Johnson observes, violence occurs because other and legitimate means of bringing about change are blocked by the ruling elite (1964, p. 6). One party in every revolution is an elite supporting the status quo.

The roots of revolution like other innovative actions lie in tensions or disequilibria in the social system. Revolutionary actions are rarely if ever found until such tensions are multiple, involving a wide range of life situations. Johnson finds that there always exists some threshold of extensity in tensions (dysfunctions) below which revolution is not appropriate regardless of how intransigent the elite may be in opposing efforts toward relief (1964, pp. 12–13). For example, the great depression in the United States during the 1930's brought serious tensions and dissatisfactions because of the dysfunctional operation of the social system. Yet these maladjustments did not disrupt many important spheres of life. Many aspects of life were influenced but nonetheless proceeded with fair satisfactoriness. When the operation of the system creates intense dissatisfactions in a wide range of activities, there is a realistic potential for violence against the responsible elite. (For discussion of revolutionary movements see Chap. 6.)

Conflict Between Social Systems

Conflict between groups ranges from the simple boundary disputes among competing welfare agencies within a community to war between nations. In all instances there is to some degree an over-riding super system of values and norms with respect to such group conflicts. However under some circumstances, notably conquest and war, the system of values and norms which bind the conflicting groups may scarcely exist before the conflict arises. Conflict between such distinct groups ultimately leads to the formulation of encompassing social systems, much as inter-racial conflict within the American structure serves the ultimate function of extending and solidifying that structure per se. Also, like inter-racial conflict, it stimulates change within each party to the conflict. Conflict between social systems differs most from conflicts within a social system where the opposing groups have lacked previous affiliation with each other. The most extreme form of normlessness in conflict appears in the case of conquest and domination by alien and culturally distant forces. This situation may or may not involve war or even physical violence.

Peaceful Invasion. When alien peoples enter territory occupied by an indigenous society of differing culture and identity, account must be taken of the invaders regardless of their status. It is inevitable that peoples of differing cultures and interests thrown into juxtaposition will find points of conflict, howsoever peaceful may be mutual intents. Such circumstances have arisen in the influx of European immigrants to the United States in the early part of this century, in the migration and settlement of Chinese through South Asia, and even in the recent influx of Jewish immigrants into Israel. The Chinese migration differs from the others cited in that it involves the persistence of the invading group as a distinct social system uneasily accommodated to a culturally different indigenous one.

The Chinese dispersion through South Asia illustrates a situation in which peaceful migration into alien territory has been associated with perpetual conflict-accommodation processes between groups neither seeking nor achieving common identity nor common culture. Modern emigrations of Chinese toward South Asian countries have historic precedents throughout all recorded history and undoubtedly before (Fitzgerald). As European colonial powers extended commerce and industry through the region, it became the more attractive to Chinese migrants who entered as merchants and as labor force. By 1965 Chinese communities of substantial size were living in a dozen or more South Asian countries. Thailand, Malaya and Indonesia each had over three million Chinese. A third of the population of little Sarawak was Chinese. In none of these regions did the immigrants identify or assimilate with indigenous peoples. On the other hand, they were consistently peaceful and eager to accommodate as a distinct society. Since the great Chinese concentrations in South Asia occurred mainly under colonial administrations, neither they nor the indigenous peoples themselves had much political power or influence. The Chinese consistently retained their orientation toward mainland China, maintaining Chinese traditions as well as political connections with the homeland. In these circumstances colonial authorities felt some threat in their presence, particularly since they were frequently powerful in commerce. Native peoples resented a cultural minority of such cohesion and affluence in their midst. With the political independence and resurgent nationalism in many of these countries, communal rivalries were intensified. The Communist Revolution in China further increased tensions, since the large displaced Chinese communities had always maintained political identity with the homeland and now were to be viewed as a potential fifth-column. The present context of world relationships sets up in each of these countries a complex of tensions composed of economic, political, and cultural conflicts.

While the Chinese in South Asia have been accommodated as a social and cultural plural, i.e., as a social system perpetually distinct from that of the indigenous society, this is by no means the only process whereby the overt and latent conflicts of immigrant peoples with their hosts are resolved. The experience of the United States undergoing the peaceful invasion of Europeans and the more recent formation of Israel show a different pattern. There are many reasons for the appearance of assimilative, rather than the "plural society" accommodative route in these nations. Not least among these reasons was the intense democratic and nationalistic spirit of each country in the days of its formation and the fact that pluralistic accommodation is made difficult by rapid urbanization, high mobility, and rational economic organization. It is observable that Israelis are as interested in the question of "What is Jewishness?" as Americans have been with "the making of an American." In both Israel and the United States assimilative processes were valued and deliberately fostered. In both nations the conflict of cultures was a very real conflict with shattering potentials. Old world ways did not jibe with the norms of life in Chicago, and social solidarities around old country bonds sometimes brought overt violence between minority groups as yet unassimilated. The American Negro has remained the only substantial group in American life set apart to a distinct social system. Curiously enough, Negro distinctiveness in social life lacks corresponding distinctiveness in cultural norms or values. Conflict in culture there is not; conflict as between social plurals there is in plenty. The term "integration" is a special word for *assimilation* in this context; *acculturation* is not at issue. For European immigrants who lacked genetic marks of sub-group membership, the process of integration (assimilation) into American society was so closely associated with the acceptance of American culture that the two are scarcely separable.

A favorite jest among Israelis is that "America was the melting pot, and Israel the pressure cooker." The joke is a sound one. The Jewish community in Palestine, from its beginnings, was a community welded out of different waves of immigrants (Eisenstadt, 1953, 1955; Eisenstadt and Ben David). However, the pioneers who settled before Israel gained statehood, after World War II, included entire Jewish communities seeking security. These groups perpetuated their organized identity throughout the process of migration and preserved their particular types of Jewish identification. Their interests in Israel were chiefly toward finding social and political security, and not social change (Eisenstadt, 1953; p. 54).

But seek social change or not, many of the newcomers to Israel brought with them cultures which clashed with the Westernized rational values and modes of the new nation. In the flood of immigrants, united it is true by Jewry, were many whose life patterns had been forged in such contrasting cultures as of the central European cities, the traditional villages of Yemen, the remote Atlas Mountains of Morocco, and India (UNESCO; Shumsky). As Israel's population nearly doubled between 1948 and 1953 due to immigration, the values, role skills, and norms of vast numbers of individuals underwent strong pressures toward change. Cultural contrast became sources of inter-ethnic hostility, and newcomers showed resentment against old-timers not undergoing the physical and emotional hardships of resettlement. Magnifying the pressures toward the preservation of ethnic sub-societies and sub-cultures was a great diversity of languages in a state whose official tongue was modern Hebrew.

Israeli policy brooked no compromise with the goal of unity through oneness. Social change had to occur, and in Israel's design it had to occur through assimilative mechanisms. This approach to this relatively gigantic assimilation problem is a classic chapter of rational social planning based on mature political judgment and guided by scientific sociological research. In the battery of assimilative techniques was the utilization of the army as an instructional vehicle, quick transfer of children from immigrant camps to temporary foster homes, youth communities ("Youth Aliyah") encompassing a broad spectrum of ideological and general education, and of numerous more conventional agencies directly or indirectly involved, such as the public schools, and welfare agencies (Frankenstein). While ethnic identities and aspects of minority group status for oriental Jews has not been avoided, Israel is unquestionably resolving these ethnic conflicts rapidly via the assimilative route, the permanent method of intergroup conflict resolution.

Conquest and Domination. The conquest and domination of weaker peoples by stronger ones may be accomplished without war or other forms of physical violence. Frequently war has been subordinate to intrigue or to the show of such power that weaker peoples accepted a subordinate relationship with limited physical resistance. Conflict ensues as domination is exercised and acculturative changes are induced or imposed. Such situations were apparent with accompanying warfare as Europeans expanded in North America, but the direct effects of war were perhaps less significant for change among American Indians than the persisting conflicts arising through their domination and acculturation by whites. The impact of Europeans and their culture upon many non-Western peoples has entailed critical changes with little or no organized physical conflict, e.g., as Pacific Islands come under the mandate of a civilized power or as colonial powers insinuated their rule to supersede another power which had long since liquidated native potentials for violent opposition.

Conquest and domination establish conflict processes within the subordinate group as well as between it and the dominant. In the first place, insofar as the subordinated group perceives threat to its integrity by acculturative influences, counter-acting actions and movements will arise. Since social organization is built around traditional values and norms, it is evident that threats to these become threats to the individuals and the groups which function in reference to them. While long-range acculturative influence will be felt by the dominant group as well as by the subordinate one, the short-range impact for change falls differentially upon the subordinates. Power and prestige support the dominants' cultural integrity while the goals of conquest usually demand that overt, immediate accommodative changes are to be made mainly by the weaker party.

It is evident that power domination influences the subordinate group in two diametrically opposed ways. It induces schisms within the group in adaptation to the power system of the dominant party, and it establishes cohesions in support of threatened values. These cohesions may be parochial or nationalistic or both. Insofar as the group is split up by internal power struggles cohesions become parochially defined. Insofar as the group is capable of seeing threat to national or tribal values and solidarity, the effect is universally solidifying.

How Domination Introduces Schisms.   There are many instances of conquest in which a significant element within the subordinate society welcomed the conqueror. Aggressive but frustrated groups may well find hope of greater self expression and advancement under what they perceive to be the new order. In such situations, internal schism is built into the very fabric of conquest. A similar but more subtle schism is analyzed in detail by Roland Force in his study of changes in leadership in a Micronesian society.

The Palau islands became an American Trust following World War II, having been previously dominated most recently by the Japanese, earlier by Germany, and during the late nineteenth century, Spain. Long influenced by the emissaries of "civilized" societies, the Palauns are not unfavorable either to outsiders or acculturative change. Yet the imposition of American administration has created a covert conflict relationship with Palau generally and an overt conflict among Palauns.

Traditional leadership in Palau was recruited from a narrow range in the population. Hereditary chiefs were legitimated through sanctions of heredity, age, and the supernatural. They were supported through traditional means of acquiring wealth.   Under acculturative influences, prohibitions were placed upon traditional means of wealth acquisition: traditional concepts of the supernatural were denigrated as was the very validity of rule by a gerontocracy. The imposition of alien governmental concepts, religion, and economic policies placed traditional leaders in a position where they were ineffectual in dealing with the alien administrators and increasingly unable to support the loyalty of their followings. In this subtle conflict situation, there emerged a new leader type oriented toward alien policies and competing for popular support with the traditional leaders on new and, under modern conditions, more practical gounds.

The result is a precarious balance between two leadership-authority structures, one rooted in the traditional and moral order, the other in the Western oriented order—which now pays off. In this island schism, both traditional and emergent leaders are insecure and the residents are equally insecure as to whom they should look to for guidance. If one follows the leadership of the magistrate he will be able to pay his taxes but not perform his traditional civic responsibilities. If one performs his traditional responsibilities he will not be able to pay his taxes. On the one hand he faces the punishment of the management; on the other, the wrath of his chief.

As Roland Force recognizes, our view of Palau today is not so much the outcome of conflict as a stage in the cumulative process of change. Traditional and emergent leaders represent conflicting interests which continue to stimulate change in the community power structure and affect the processes of acculturation as well. In the long run, Force concludes, the competitive bid of the emerging leaders must prevail and a new equilibrium will arise oriented to the ways and the pressures of the dominating external power.

War.   War as a force for change is largely a phenomenon of civilization (Turney-High; Montross). Organized conflict between primitive, tribal societies was often part of the accommodated system of relationships understood and accepted by both. Among, for example, the Marquesas Islanders the function of war did not include annihilation, territorial conquest, political supremacy nor control of markets. Not even the termination of hostility was a purpose of fighting. War, if it may be termed that, followed conventionally understood patterns with conventionally accepted weapons and toward conventionally accepted ends. This was true to some degree among the warlike Plains Indians. The Cheyenne sent out "war parties" to capture horses from the Tetons; the Tetons sent out war parties to capture horses from the Cheyenne or to avenge a killing. The Marquesans of one valley fought those of another toward a victorious cannibal feast. In each instance, glory of the warrior, a basic function of the fighting, was served only through adherence to traditionally understood tactics. In such a setting neither an arms race nor establishment of an impersonal, professional military body could serve the functions of war. War was not much stimulus to change simply because its terms were traditionally stated and its goals so defined that violation of the traditional terms were without purpose. The event took place as one phase of a continuing accommodated system of relationships. An equilibrium existed through time in which "war" was an accepted part.

Modern warfare is different in its functions and its significance for equilibrated relationships. The purposes and methods of war among civilized societies make of it a dynamic force for innovation. Today in mainland China, and perhaps Russia, the legend of Western Imperialism is as forceful as is the comparable legend of "Communist enslavement" in the United States. With mutual perceptions of threat to group survival, both sides accelerate those realms of invention best calculated to win an ultimate total war. On the technological side this is evidenced in a national budget giving priority to ultimate weapons and space science. If the United States today can allocate billions to direct military purposes, we may be sure that potential enemies do not fail to reciprocate—in what has appeared to be an unending spiral in reciprocal interstimulations. It is no accident of science that expenditures on the control of atomic fission vastly exceed expenditures upon the control of floods and hurricanes. War and the threat of war focus inventive effort and resources upon those aspects of technology which are preparative to successful war.

That such developments are not restricted to use in some problematic future war is a crucial fact for social change. Nuclear fission was speeded by war, but the associated discoveries and inventions are having repercussions upon peaceful community life as well. Technological advances in drugs and insecticides during World War II have become household items around the world affecting death rates and agricultural production. However, it is unquestionable that the war focus in scientific effort yields large amounts of technical progress which is totally wasted from the standpoint of civilian use.

As the uneasy accommodations of one nation to another are modified by some unilateral action, responsive measures are taken by the potential enemy. As in an earlier century, when the idea of a conscripted army called forth reciprocal conscription in the enemy nation, a huge submarine fleet on one side is countered with electronic sensing devices by the other. The missile is responded to with an anti-missile and the anti-missile with an anti-anti-missile *ad infinitum*, until some wholly new technological base for extermination and potential victory renders this line obsolete and sets a new pattern for reciprocal developments. In organizational structures much the same process occurs. The arms race is paralleled by increasingly rational, specialized, and bureaucratic social structures adjusted to the new technologies and to increasingly rapid and efficient operations.

As a threat of war, or war itself, appears, the values and social structures associated with the military establishment achieve increasingly paramount roles in national policy and power decisions. Even in the early half-hearted days of the undeclared Vietnam action, cries of treason and of comforting the enemy were leveled by loyal Americans against equally loyal Americans who opposed the going U.S. foreign policy. Civil liberties received new challenges; new organizations arose to pursue war aims, new federal budget items appeared to meet new presumed threats to national integrity (Cf. Anderson and Ryan, p. 36). External relationships of the conflicting parties were extended and reshaped. War itself requires norms for the conduct of the opposing nations in reference to each other and to neutrals. It also disturbs the equilibria of each conflicting party to neutral ones. Alliances are tested, broken, and sought out. Conflicts with some stimulate bonds with others (Coser, p. 141).

These influences of war arise not out of the disasters and uprootings of communities, but out of responses to perceived shifts in the balanced relationships of one nation to another. It is clear that actual war in modern times, involving colonial rule, territorial conquests, and massive movements of population both military and civilian are strong forces for disruption of established community structure and for the diffusion of culture. The American occupation of Japan following World War II proved a two-way street for cultural exchange and set a base for new relationships between these nations as well. Some sixteen million citizens of United Nations countries were in the displaced labor force in Germany at the end of World War II. That such massive mixing of peoples had no significance for diffusion and acculturation would be difficult to believe. In the realm of disaster, modern war requires innovative patterns of community organization for meeting the threats of disaster. Although the flattened cities are re-built and the decimated populations gradually replenished, many of the organizational structures to cope with war and threat of war become an ongoing part of the cultural heritage (U.S. Strategic Bombing Survey; Wallace).

Schismogenesis: A Special Conflict Theory

The concept of *schismogenesis* was developed by Gregory Bateson (p. 175) some thirty years ago as he attempted to explain the origin of the contrasting ethos of men and women in a New Guinea tribal society. Bateson defined the concept as, "a process of differentiation in the norms of individual behavior resulting from cumulative interaction between individuals." Bateson recognized two types of processes, one "complementary" and the other "symmetrical" schismogenesis. "Complementary schismogenesis" arises when the person who is the object of an action reciprocates with complementing behavior. When an assertive act is directed toward the other, the other responds with submissive behavior. This is a potentially progressive state of affairs in which the first actor may become increasingly assertive as the second becomes increasingly submissive until other factors arise to restrain and limit the process. "Symmetrical schismogenesis" is found in relationships wherein the original action is picked up and intensified by the other. Thus, boasting is reciprocated with boasting, which in turn stimulates still greater efforts in the same direction by the initiator. Arms races between nations also illustrate this concept. Bateson cautions us, however, to think of schismogenesis not as a process which relentlessly continues, but rather as a process of change which is either controlled or counteracted by inverse processes. Orlando Fals-Borda has utilized the idea of symmetrical schismogenesis in explaining the rapid spread of a technological device introduced into an Andean Highland community. In a competitive situation adoption of the innovation by one person quickens the response of the next and both have a cumulative effect upon the third. A related schismogenic process is that reported by Harbison and Dubin in regard to labor management relations in the United States:

Bigness on the side of industry leads to bigness on the side of organized labor. The reverse case is also true. In the coal industry, for example, region-wide and later nation-wide pressure by the United Mine Workers made a strong employers' organization necessary for purposes of collective bargaining. [Harbison and Dubin, p. 184.]

Closely related to the idea of schismogenesis, but without its implicit dialectic, are the ideas of change through *perseveration* and through *drift*. The former concept was one used constructively by William Isaac Thomas in many contexts and the latter by Edward Sapir in the field of language and later by Melville J. Herskovits and Fred Eggan in broader contexts (Thomas, 1937; Sapir, 1921; Herskovits; Eggan, 1963; Kroeber, 1944; cf. Eisenstadt, 1964). Herskovits used the term *cultural focus* to denote the tendency of every society to concentrate its interests and innovative ideas upon certain limited areas of culture. In such areas the status quo is not "sacred" and receptivity to innovation is high. *Perseveration* emphasizes the tendency of a people having once set a course of action in regard to a "focus" to develop and elaborate it. *Drift* emphasizes the long-range directional changes in cultures arising through the slow accumulation of minor variations. The ideas of *focus, drift,* and *perseveration* are very similar. Each concept implies adumbration and elaboration of certain existing values or interests with strains toward consistency, and probable resistance to diffusion not in accord with "drift." Thomas was more inclined to limit his analysis of perseverative tendencies to single institutional structures or values, whereas anthropologists utilizing the "drift" concept have applied to it broad trends in social organization.

COLLECTIVE BEHAVIOR

The study of cumulative, although often transitory, change through interaction has been particularly developed in the literature on collective behavior. Collective behavior refers to that broad area of social interaction wherein persons express concern in a relatively unstructured situation. The "concern" may be a specific and well-understood grievance or issue, or it may be simply a vague disquiet or anxiety. Lack of explicit structure in the ensuing interaction offers latitude for emotional and uncritical behavior and actions which are spontaneous, out of the ordinary, and extreme (Turner & Killian, Chap. 1; Sherif and Sherif, 1956, Chap. 10; Broom and Selznick, Chap. 8; Smelser). Structure may grow out of the collective interaction, but the bonds uniting such collectivities are frequently too ephemeral to support developed organization.

Kurt and Gladys Lang have analyzed the relation of collective behavior to social change in their work *Collective Dynamics.* "To understand the dynamics of collective behavior, then," they write, "is to understand social action that cuts across social structure and has not yet crystallized into a structure of its own. Such an 'unorganized' collective pattern may arise within some group structure, or it may form in areas where there is no organization." Many of the transformations of social life arising out of collective behavior rest on rumors, waves of excitement, and "contagions." As the Langs observe, "unorganized and transient patterns develop spontaneously from some sort of 'contagion'" (p. 12).*

The major significance of collective behavior for social change is that out of unstructured, emotional inter-stimulation there emerges an organization associated with a novel program to ameliorate the causes of social unrest. Insofar as the rise of such social movements is out of unstructured interaction, collective behavior has great significance for social change (see Chap. 7). However, much collective behavior has little, or at best indirect, relationship to change. "Crowd," "mob," and "riot" do not so much denote change as they refer to situations within which interaction is conducive to deviation and possible collective action "to change something." While some crowd behavior, like anti-civil rights demonstrations, are emotional affirmations of status quo, those too set up circumstances conducive to normative deviance.

The processes which we tag with the terms "fad," "fashion," "panic," and "craze" not only imply change—they each suggest ephemeral duration as well as emotional contagion. Of these, panic implies less a social change than a disruption of organizational structure as persons interpret an emotionalized threat or a goal in individualistic rather than group terms. It connotes as well the cumulative heightening of egotistic concern and consequent rejection of group norms through a process of symmetrical schismogenesis. *Fashion* and its step-sister *fad*, are terms reflecting true innovation. They bring us to an interesting borderland in

---

* Kurt Lang and Gladys Engel Lang, *Collective Dynamics,* Copyright © 1961 by Thomas Y. Crowell Company.

which innovations take hold in a society but in such a circumscribed manner that social change is often extremely limited.

The classic statement of a theory of fashion and fad is that of the anthropologist Edward Sapir (1930–35, pp. 139–144). Sapir looked upon a fad as behavior which is truly deviant from custom whereas fashion is a variation or embroidery upon custom. When a purported fashion is sensed as conflicting with the historical continuity of style it is probably destined to be a short-lived fad. Fads carry with them an implication of the unexpected, the irresponsible, or the bizarre and are short-lived. They arise out of the weaknesses of fashion just as fashions arise out of the weaknesses of custom. The significance of fad for social change is almost entirely symbolic in that the spread of faddish behavior and the prevalence of fads reflects deeper unrests and anxieties in the society which have not been focused realistically in directions of change in social organization. Fashion, on the other hand, is historically rooted. It is valued in terms of its variation or fluctuation in an understood sequence, as departure from an immediately preceding mode, but it lacks significance for change in the structure of the social system.

While fashion is deeply involved in collective behavior, the more conventionalized and commercialized it becomes the better do we understand it as a matter of cultural inventing and diffusing (Richardson and Kroeber; Lynes; Lang and Lang, Chap. 15). Fashions in modern, Western society arise less out of the spontaneous interaction of a "collectivity" than out of the deliberate diffusion of inventions. Like many inventions, unorganized and emotional inter-stimulations and pressures stimulate and regulate the diffusion processes.

CONCLUSION

The ultimate sources of social change lie in the interactions of man as these are influenced by the conditions set forth in Chapter 3. The major innovative processes of interaction are (1) the formation of groups out of aggregates of individuals; (2) deviance, wherein individuals are led to reject the normative structure or elements of it; (3) conflict, a multifaceted process ranging from rivalry to revolution and war in which individuals or groups strive against each other; and (4) collective behavior, wherein people interact in unstructured relationships within social systems to give rise to such innovative phenomena as fad and fashion and set foundations for social movements.

1. *Group Formation.* Where aggregates of individuals persist through time and are directed toward common ends, social structure emerges. Norms, values, roles, and other elements of social structure arise through interaction. This process is well documented in historical studies of

frontier settlement and the growth of stable communities, and it is documented in experimental studies of contrived groups. In this sphere innovation refers to the production of structure in social relationships.

2. *Deviance.* When individuals or groups reject normative means for achieving socially approved objectives, they are deviant. When they reject socially approved objectives they are *rebellious,* a condition included here as a special form of deviance. Deviant behavior, unless it is learned as an already existing pattern, is innovative since it departs from established ways of acting. Conditions which commonly underlie it are inadequate socialization and ineffective social control mechanisms. Under some circumstances deviance from traditional patterns of action is induced through socialization processes which anticipate changes in the social order.

3. *Conflict.* Conflict is viewed by some theorists as the most fundamental process of social change inherent in all social systems. Through conflict and ultimate accommodation the equilibrium of social systems is maintained through time and the exigencies of adjustment to changed conditions of group life. The process of conflict induces innovation in the conflicting groups and in the encompassing social system of which they may be a part. Some innovative consequences of conflict are (a) the creation or revitalization of the framework of norms binding the contenders together, (b) the establishment of new structures to enforce the new framework, (c) stimulation of a search for allies and hence new associations of groups, and (d) within conflicting groups the stimulation of changes toward cohesion and centralization and at the same time the opening of new avenues for internal schisms and power struggles.

4. *Collective Behavior.* This term has long been applied to situations in which aggregates of individuals within social systems interact with a minimum of organization or structure, united more by common emotions than by group bonds or group objectives. In this vaguely structured group situation aberrant behavior arises which is frequently without significance for social change. Some forms of collective behavior having long-range significance are fashions and incipient social movements. As social movements take root they develop beyond the collective stage into organized structures which may have great significance for change in the social order.

6

Diffusion

THE SCOPE OF DIFFUSION IN CULTURAL CHANGE

Culture-building, and hence cultural change, depends as much upon the communication of novelty as it does upon its very creation. Probably no human society has ever lived without interchange with some others, and within a single society an invention which did not spread would usually have no significance for change. It is true that men in the primitive world lived in relative cultural isolation compared with modern societies caught up in their multiple and massive networks of communication. The fact that aboriginal Australians, numbering perhaps 200,000 persons, spoke no less than five hundred different languages indicates the relative isolation of Paleolithic societies (Childe, p. 20).

But such isolation means that the pace of diffusion was slow, not that it failed to occur. The time span of human culture is a million years and perhaps much more. We find that the stone-working techniques of Neanderthal man were widely spread through Europe, the Middle East, and possibly Asia. In Pre-Columbian America the invention of agriculture in Andean and Middle American centers was followed by wide diffusions through both North and South America. Nor can we conceive of the original migrants to the Americas as having left their various Asian homelands empty-handed and empty-minded. Agriculture as invented in the Middle East has been traced as it moves up the Danube Valley to new peoples. V. Gordon Childe (p. 50) speaks of diffusion when he describes the astonishing uniformity of Neolithic artifacts and ornaments over the vast territory of Central Europe.

The history of Old World civilizations is replete with interdependence as the Indus Valley is linked with Sumeria; as iron is spread through the old world by barbaric nomads; as an alphabet, invented only once, and in the Sinai Peninsula, fathers the written languages of Europe, the Middle East, and India. The ancient Greeks were synthesizers and organizers of ideas coming to them from Sumerians, Israelites, Egyptians, Minoans, Hindus, and many others. Romans, building upon Greek civilization felt the direct influences of Asian and African civilizations as well as those of Western and Northern Europe. Silken fabrics out of China became almost as familiar in Londinium as in Lo Yang (Hudson). We should remind ourselves that the great modernizing transformations that were to come in Western Europe involved the melding of different cultures, which themselves were fused out of infinitely diverse traditions. Hogden, for example, has documented the mergers of various local innovative traditions with crafts borne by migrating French, Flemish, German, and Italian workers as sources of the industrial revolution in England. Numerous ideas, crucial for commercial and industrial expansion, like printing, the compass, and arithmetic had earlier been borrowed from exotic, Asian civilizations.

The spread of novelty within the large and complex modern societies is not less sensational than these immense intercultural linkages. Even recognizing the effectiveness of modern mass media, the spread of the contraceptive pill in the United States from its introduction in 1960 to its use by seven million American women by 1967 is staggering. Little less impressive was the speed with which thousands of farmers shifted from the use of open-pollinated corn seed to costly hybrid seed during the decade of the nineteen thirties, or the more recent introduction of jet airliners in the airline passenger business or the computer in the worlds of business and of science. Of course these intra-societal diffusions do not necessarily stop short at the United States border. Some women in most countries of the world have adopted contraceptive pills; major airlines throughout the world use jet planes.

How much any culture owes to borrowing from others is a difficult question to answer—difficult to the point of impossibility. Ethnocentric members of most nations typically exaggerate the degree to which their own culture is home invented. In combating such evident bias, it is likely that even the actual scope of diffusion itself has been somewhat exaggerated by social scientists. Some years ago Ralph Linton (p. 325) suggested in a now widely reproduced passage, that at least 90 per cent of every culture is the result of borrowing. As a figure of speech, this properly emphasizes the significance of diffusion throughout all times and places. As a statistic, however, the statement is nonsense, since in borrowing, societies so modify and develop foreign traits that the analyst could never extricate the borrowed from the locally invented for a count. Linton's widely reprinted pages on the ethnocentric 100 per cent American who owes most of his good life to borrowed inventions, is a half truth. *The bed* we may well derive from the Chinese, but not the innerspring or foam mattress. The hen's *egg* is derived from Middle East domestication—but techniques of poultry raising, egg grading, and marketing were not. Linton's case of the world-dependent 100 per cent American may be good pedagogy, but it is poor science.

The study of the spread of cultural traits and influences has long been a branch of both sociology and cultural anthropology. As a field of study it has been so variously defined in these disciplines that students of the common field might not always recognize their colleagues. Howsoever defined, diffusion always involves the communication of a cultural trait or idea to someone previously unfamiliar with it. This communication process has been studied with varied purposes, as in attempts to reconstruct the history of civilizations and again to learn how better to sell new kinds of weed-spray to farmers. It is not surprising, then, that as a theoretical and research field it is extremely differentiated. In this chapter the range of diffusion theory will be presented, but emphasis will be placed upon current conceptions of diffusion theory, as it contributes to the contemporary sociology of change.

DIFFUSION THEORY IN CULTURAL ANTHROPOLOGY[1]

Anthropological theories of diffusion had their early rise in the period of that discipline's heroic efforts to reconstruct the historical origins of human culture and stages in the evolution of civilization. The later years of the nineteenth century were strong with evolutionary doctrines, some of which gave little heed to problems of "cultural borrowing" or diffusion as they posited natural, evolutionary stages appearing in identical sequences in every human society. Among these unilinear evolutionists, the possibility of diffusion to upset their neat schemes of cultural history was not denied, but it was evaded. Strong reaction to such theories of natural unfolding of civilization appeared from several directions, including those who stressed the significance of borrowing rather than independent inventing as a source of change.

The Heliolithic Complex

This is the name given a theory developed especially by G. Elliott Smith and W. J. Perry in the 1920's. It claimed, in essence, that all early civilizations throughout the world owed their rise to the diffusion

[1] For general treatments of diffusion theory and research in anthropology, see Lowie, Chapters 10 and 11; Herskovits, 1947, Chapters 30 and 31; Linton, 1936, Chapter 19; Kroeber, Volume 5, pp. 139–142. In these works are critical evaluations of the various theories also discussed here.

of culture out of Egypt. Elliott Smith virtually denied that any significant invention ever occurred outside the Nile region, even alleging that the complex totemism of aboriginal Australians was a degeneration of beliefs and practices having their origin in Egypt. The assumption that there is only one possible origin for all traits, i.e., that a trait cannot be twice invented, was sufficiently fallacious, but Smith and Perry surpassed even this in contending that the origin of everything civilized lay in Egypt and only in Egypt. As Lowie has suggested, if Smith, an eminent anatomist, had happened to have been stationed on the Euphrates instead of the Nile, he might as readily have developed an equally "good" theory of history which was pan-Babylonian instead of pan-Egyptian.

German-Austrian Culture—Historical School

Like the British diffusionists, Smith and Perry, the German and Austrian school sought to understand world culture history through historical reconstructions of diffusion patterns. These reconstructions, unfortunately, did not rest upon factual data so much as inferences drawn from living peoples regarding early historic growth sequences. Unlike the Egypt protagonists there is no assumption here of a common single origin for world civilizations. However, the tracings of world diffusion currents in antiquity frequently relied upon questionable evidence and shaky inferences. Nonetheless, Herskovits (1947, p. 511) has hailed this school and particularly its founder, Fritz Graebner, with having sharpened the criteria by which one is to infer that a given trait has been borrowed or has been invented independently within a society.

When similarities are found in the cultures of two separate groups, the probability that these derive from a single source increases with the greater complexity of the trait and the greater number of details in which correspondence is found. If a Gothic cathedral were found in the heart of the Australian desert, we would conclude that there had been European contact (Herskovits, 1947, p. 513). The chance of its creation in such an alien cultural milieu would be virtually nil. Unfortunately, not all conclusions are so clearly admissible and modern scholars are urgent in demanding evidence of actual historical linkings, as well as similarities in structural detail and meanings.

The general rejection of the main thesis of *Kon-Tiki*, i.e., that Polynesian culture derived from South America, was partly based on the fact that the details of similarity in culture were so small as to be explained by chance in independent invention (Heyerdahl). Evidence was given only that the voyage was possible, not that it was made or contemplated by the South Americans. Further, there is much stronger evidence of migrations from other sources. No one could conclude that Peruvians did *not* reach Polynesia, but there is not much evidence that they actually did so, and if they did, that they had very deep impact.

The Age-Area Theory

While the British and the German diffusionists hoped to reconstruct world cultural history, American ethnologists made their historical reconstructions on a more modest scale. Edward Sapir and Clark Wissler, outstanding diffusionists in the earlier years of this century, developed what came to be termed the age-area hypothesis or theory (cf. Herskovits, 1947, pp. 517–521). Essentially, this was a formulation designed to assist anthropologists in drawing orderly conclusions regarding sequences of change in the past. In societies without written history, the signs of the past become a confusing mass of data unless some system for determining their chronological status is devised. The age-area hypothesis presumed in a tentative manner to offer such a system. Sapir argued that the relative age of a culture trait is assessable on the basis of its complexity. The simpler the design the older the trait. Sapir was well aware that this need not always be true, but he believed it to be a general guide line if cautiously applied. Sapir next proposed the proposition that a culture trait is diffused continuously out from the culture center toward the border of the culture region. Hence a distribution or diffusion of narrow range may be suspected of being later than one of wider range. When this principle is coupled with that of simplicity in the earlier designs, bases are established to show chronology in the sequence of diffusion. Further, the point of origin for such diffusion can be estimated. This is done on the assumption that the most complex (latest) designs will have narrower distributions than the simpler (earlier) ones. Conversely it is in the remote parts of a cultural region that the older, simpler designs persist longest, giving rise to the concept of marginal survivals. Ralph Linton has illustrated this by the fact that dial telephones took over in the cities while the old fashioned sets survived in outlying areas most remote from the city—the source of innovation.

The age-area theory is likely to be true under some circumstances. The problem is to determine the degree of likelihood in any given set of circumstances. Roland Dixon (Chap. 5), himself an eminent student of diffusion, attacked the approach as dangerous and limited in validity. It applies only within a circumscribed cultural region and even then assumes concentric expansion from a center, a condition not always present. Sapir, who originated it, was well aware of its dangers but in an armory of weapons for historical reconstruction one must confess that among poor weapons it was less poor than most of its companions. It at least offers stimulating hypotheses and suggests potential reconstructions which here and there can be supported by documentary sources.[2] In the methodology of historical reconstruction it was superior to the major methodologies of the unilinear cultural evolutionists (Bock). However, the attention of anthropological diffusionists was to undergo an immense shift so that interest in historical reconstructions was largely abandoned and with it, its arsenal of questionable methods and propositions, in both evolutionary and diffusionist camps.

Acculturation Studies

The term "acculturation" is sometimes defined to apply to the special diffusion situation in which neighboring peoples influence each other over long periods of contiguity and contact (Redfield *et al.*, pp. 149–152). Herskovits came to reject this special circumstantial use of the term. Herskovits contended that "diffusion" applies to already achieved cultural transmissions, while acculturation is the study of the processes of cultural transmission (1938; 1947, Chap. 31). The main point is that acculturation is an integrative process which Herskovits wished to distinguish from simple "borrowing." The basic meaning implicit in acculturation is that one culture *influences* another. The connotations of "diffusion" emphasize communicative process and distribution through time. The connotations of "acculturation" have closer reference to the acceptance and integration of diffused novelty into the receiving culture. It does not matter whether this is a historical fact or a contemporary process. The integration of diffusing traits or ideas from one culture into another is essentially what most anthropologists view as acculturation. As Herskovits contended, this does not *require* contiguity between peoples, although the merging of cultures is probably *most complete* when long and contiguous residence is a fact.

The study of cultural borrowing in contemporary anthropology has now been directed toward acculturative or integrative processes far more than toward the use of diffusion as a method in historical reconstruction (Linton, 1940; Siegal and Wax). The diffusion tradition of anthropology has, in this transition, become closely affiliated with similar interests of sociologists in the study of "Western" influences upon non-Western and peasant peoples, especially since World War II. Acculturation in this sense is treated here under the more generalized heading of "integration" (see below, Chaps. 9 and 10). The communication focus of diffusion research is emphasized in the present chapter.

[2] In the history of the caste system in Ceylon, as it is derived from India, Ryan (1953, Chap. 1) uses age-area reasoning with documentary support to argue the case for marginal survivals in that island.

DIFFUSION THEORY AND RESEARCH IN SOCIOLOGY

Development of Diffusion Studies. The growth of diffusion study in sociology has a quite different history from those aspects developed by anthropologists. The first great sociological diffusionist was Gabriel Tarde whose *Les Lois de L'imitation* was published in Paris in 1890 and translated into English in 1903. Tarde's view of imitation was a broad one as he in reality set himself the task of finding the laws which govern the appearance of invention and its spread in society. Tarde from the vantage point of his central concept "imitation" had a limited view of processes which contemporary anthropologists would term acculturative. But Tarde made important observations in regard to the rapidity of diffusion and the circumstances favoring adoption and rejection of the new. For example, Tarde recognized clearly that diffusing invention is less likely to be adopted ("imitated") if it is logically incongruous with existing culture. In the realm of time sequence, he foreshadowed the theory that the adoption of an invention proceeds according to an S-shaped, or "growth," curve (see below, pp. 160–163). And also, more by logic than induction, he offered characterizations of innovative types and those resistant to innovation.

The next great contributor to the sociological tradition of diffusion was F. Stuart Chapin in his work *Cultural Change,* published in 1928. In this volume, Chapin outlined the theory of the S-shaped curve in technological diffusion and showed by a brilliant case study of the city-manager form of government how diffusion and developmental inventing moved hand-in-hand in their evolution. During the 1930's, sociologists in several specialties became concerned with diffusion processes. For the most part these concerns related to time factors in diffusion, communication media and their effectiveness, and to some extent the circumstances associated with adoption of novelties (Bowers, 1937, 1938; McVoy; Pemberton). While sociologists were also concerned with the problems arising in the integration of inventions into society, these interests, following the lead of W. F. Ogburn, were directed out of the realm of communication and diffusion to be absorbed in theories of social disorganization and social problems.[3]

Concern with diffusion over the past twenty-five years developed among rural sociologists and among public opinion analysts in almost

---

[3] It might be said that studies of the assimilation of immigrants into American urban life paralleled and preceded the anthropologists' shift toward integrative, accumulative studies. The works of William Isaac Thomas, Constantine Panunzio, Jesse Steiner, and many others on "assimilation" problems, in roughly the World War I period, faced directly the problems of cultural interpenetrations (acculturation) as well as social assimilation (mergers in group affiliations).

total isolation from each other (Katz, 1960; Katz *et al.;* Rogers, 1962). In general the rural sociologists were directing their researches toward ascertaining the relative effectiveness of, and interrelations among, various communication media in the transmission of new farm practices. Associated with this was interest in "decision making processes," i.e., how farmers came to make positive or negative decisions at any given time regarding a communicated device.

From a beginning marked by studies of the diffusion of new techniques among celery farmers and the diffusion of hybrid corn in Iowa, diffusion studies blossomed in rural sociology (Hoffer; Ryan and Gross, 1943, 1950). Everett Rogers reported in 1962 (p. 4) that since the hybrid seed corn final report published in 1950, rural sociologists had completed over 286 diffusion studies.

If rural sociologists were partly motivated by a desire to increase the rapidity with which farm educational material might be disseminated, mass communication scholars no doubt had similar interests in making more scientific the advertising campaigns of the mass media. They centered their studies around the processes whereby ideas, not necessarily technological ones, are communicated.

Beginning with a media focus, i.e., radio, the communication sociologists soon found what the rural sociologists already had learned, that the diffusion process was too complex to be analyzed through any single set of media and their influence (Katz *et al.*, 1963). The findings of Katz and Lazarsfeld in *Personal Choice: The Part Played by People in the Flow of Mass Communication* showed remarkable convergence with findings regarding the diffusion of hybrid corn. This convergence was fruitfully extended by Katz shortly after.

After 1950 significant contributions to the sociology of diffusion continued to be made in rural sociology and in communications research. To these were added comparable studies especially in fields of medical and health practice dissemination, and in the spread of new educational methods.

While comparison is frequently difficult among conclusions reached in various "research traditions," nonetheless, an impressive body of knowledge regarding diffusion process is accumulating. The remainder of this chapter is largely devoted to these findings, particularly as they relate to the dissemination rather than the adoption of novelty. Processes of acceptance and rejection of novelty and impact of innovative ideas upon social systems will be treated separately, so far as this is practicable, in subsequent chapters.

A Sociological Definition. Elihu Katz and associates have defined the process of diffusion as "1) *acceptance,* 2) over *time,* 3) of some specific *item*—an idea or practice, 4) by individuals, groups or other *adopting units*, linked, 5) to specific *channels* of communication, 6) to a social *structure*, and 7) to a given system of values, or *culture* (p. 240)." This definition covers the crucial processes and conditions which together constitute the total process. We would amend the definition here only insofar as a diffusing item may be accepted *or rejected*, a circumstance which is implied but not explicit in Katz's definition. No diffusion will be fully comprehended without reference to each of the constituent parts of this definition, although numerous research studies have been focused upon only one or two aspects of the complete process. Social and cultural factors influencing adoption or rejection of novelty will be treated in a separate chapter, i.e., we are here distinguishing "decision-making" processes from communicative ones insofar as practicable.

The Item and the Adopting Unit

It would be difficult to conceive of an innovation which would hold equal interest to all individuals at any given time. The appeal of a novelty arises in its particular function in reference to a particular social category or group. Most innovations are irrelevant to somebody. New style baby-bottles and bifocal glasses each by the nature of the item have appeal to limited social categories unless their functions are redefined by the recipients. Degree of relevance is hence a significant variable in all diffusion instances.

Attributes of the Diffusion "Item."   To achieve greater comparability and reliability in research generalizations, several analysts have attempted to provide sets of dimensions for measuring and classifying diffusing ideas or items. Mort and Cornell, studying the spread of new educational practices, have suggested classifying diffusing traits by an economic set of criteria, such as the extent of capital outlay required for adoption, anticipated profit, etc. These are of course, important factors for the *evaluation* of proposed innovations by the potential adopters— along with many non-economic considerations as well. They are not intrinsic qualities of the diffusion trait or idea which are relevant to its diffusion as a communication process. Homer Barnett (pp. 375–377) concluded that material culture traits diffuse more readily than non-material ones. He pointed out that this has been found true in a number of anthropological studies and that there are pressing reasons why it should be so. It is difficult, he says, to explain an idea but the more subject an idea is to overt presentation the less difficult it is to explain. The difference in material and non-material diffusion becomes especially marked where language barriers exist. Barnett also argues that the advantage of one idea over another is more readily shown when the advantage lies in demonstrable physical properties. The advantage of a new religious idea is more difficult to demonstrate than is the advantage of an iron over a stone knife. Finally, Barnett believes that when a physical object is accepted, the acceptor does not directly involve his associates by his action. Social pressures against adoption of material traits are less, since their immediate effects upon the group surrounding the adopter are less readily foreseen.

Somewhat similar to Barnett, Menzel has classified medical innovations in contemporary diffusion, in terms of (1) communicability, (2) risk, and (3) pervasiveness, or the generalized appeal of the innovation to a social category. Concerned also with the qualities of an item which render it readily diffusable, Ryan and Gross in their study of hybrid corn seed concluded that the seed's great *divisibility* was a strong factor in its rapid adoption (1943; 1948). Farmers adopted it "on the installment plan" making no major decision at any given point in the process of acceptance.

Everett Rogers (Chap. 5), summarizing the results of many diffusion studies, lists the following as characteristics of a trait which are significant for its diffusion: (1) relative advantage over that which it would supersede, (2) compatibility with existing values and experiences of the adopters, (3) lack of complexity, in terms of the trait's ready understanding and application by potential adopters, (4) divisibility or the degree to which the trait can be tried on a limited basis, and (5) communicability or ease with which the novelty can be observed and communicated. As in the case of Mort and Cornell, several of the criteria he suggests relate less to inherent qualities of the trait than to the social situation in which it is assessed by potential adopters. Further, practically all of the studies upon which Rogers, and for that matter, Mort and Cornell, based their conclusions were reports on the diffusion of scientifically supportable, technological ideas capable of clear material manifestation.

While a novelty must in the long run be considered in terms of the adopter's culture and wishes, most of these classifications mix the inherent properties of the trait with its culturally rooted desirability to adopters. The first question to be answered is how do intrinsic properties of a trait or "item" affect its *communication* to potential adopters. (The recipient's *assessment* of the trait is an *analytically* separate issue.) Barnett is most directly approaching the inherent communication capacity of a trait, while the others have been at least equally concerned with qualities affecting the dynamic assessment of the trait. From these various studies and analyses let us draw out those inherent qualities of a diffusing trait which are relevant to its effective communication. These are: (1) Simplicity in design—to the point that the item can be communicated in an intelligible fashion. (2) Capacity of the item to be given observable or tangible manifestation so providing it further sensory stimulating capacity to reinforce symbolic explanations of its meaning and function. (3) Divisibility of the item so that its adoption would require no major commitment, i.e., a risk-reducing element inherent in the trait itself. While all diffusing traits are ultimately communicated to recipients to be valued by them in terms of their own perceptions and values, conditions being equal, these factors specified above are conducive to adoption.

Most studies which have found "observability" and "physical manifestation" significant for successful diffusion have been influenced by the fact that the traits studied did not possess much moral or normative significance. Rather, they were items or ideas having almost a pure "instrumental" value. Continuing research will probably suggest grouping traits together in terms of common clusters of attributes significant for communication and ease of adoption. It is simpler, for example, to communicate the "meaning" of a steel knife in an undistorted fashion than it is to communicate the "meaning" of holy communion. This is due not entirely to the physical observability and simplicity of the one in comparison to the other but also to the fact that the meaning of communion is alien to all but Christian societies whereas the *meaning* of a cutting tool is universal. Some ideas are more universal than others in their constituent meanings. It is possible also that some are more universally exempt from moral and normative significances, i.e., cutting tools as contrasted with religious ideas. The study of diffusing innovations toward their more meaningful classification is a fertile field for further development in the sociology of change.

Different-Type Adoption Units for Different "Items." The social unit toward which diffusion is directed is not necessarily that of discrete individuals united only as social categories. As Katz (1962) has recalled, "It takes two to tango." In his article on units of adoption, Katz has distinguished three types of social units toward which diffusion may be directed. These are, respectively, *individuals, collectivities,* and *groups.*

In diffusions applicable to individuals, a person is the acceptor or rejector by his own decision. When a new farm technique is disseminated, the individual farmer makes up his mind regarding it. Needless to say, outside influences act upon him, but the decision is made by himself for himself. Other types of traits require adoption by a collectivity as the tango requires a partner and the telephone implies both a speaker and a listener. Somebody else must go along in adopting the innovation or it is meaningless. Group adoption takes place in regard to innovations requiring "corporate decisions." If a community decides to fluoridate its water, then even those who vote against the innovation become adopters of it. Many actions of families, communities, and nations involve such group decision-making.

Not only may the adoption unit vary with the nature of the diffusing trait, it also varies by the type of social structure and associated value system of the recipients. Some social systems prefer group adoption of innovations which elsewhere would be conceived in individual terms. Some Israeli kibbutzem, for example, have restrained their members from adopting electric refrigerators until such time as the entire community can enjoy such conveniences (Katz, 1962).

Channels of Diffusion

Prior to the invention of writing, all diffusion required some kind of physical contact among people. The most remote of these connections would have been when artifacts were found by later, or at least by different, peoples from those who had used and abandoned them. Most diffusion in early society must have occurred through migration, by contiguity in domain, and possibly by raids. With development of writing, communication no longer required physical contact to the same degree, but for many centuries this new symboling mechanism had limited influence on largely illiterate populations and between societies maintaining relative physical isolation from each other. Only after the fifteenth century with the development of the printing press and general increases in literacy through at least the Western world did the written word become as significant for diffusion as it had long been for the preservation of knowledge. Not until the nineteenth century were the steps visible which were to result in the revolutionary transformation of communication channels through the telegraph, the telephone, and ultimately through radio, television, and related inventions in communication technology.

The communications revolution of modern times would be difficult to over-stress as to its role in the rapidity of change found today not only in the West but in nations which even two decades ago were basically dependent upon physical contiguity for communication purposes. Modern devices do not even require literacy, and with television there is complementation of auditory stimuli with visual ones. Along with the sudden growth of mass media there has also been increasing mobility of people in the physical sense, and with no diminishment in the age-old power of personal contact as a diffusion channel.

The massive communications networks of North America and Europe are too ubiquitous to warrant further comment here. Less well known are the immense media developments in countries like India and China (Schramm, 1960, p. 667; 1964; cf. Amaya). India, with 465 daily newspapers in 1960 had also 59 radio transmitters and about 3000 motion picture theatres—and access to international radio broadcasts as well. Even the Congo Republic (Brazzaville) by 1960 had three daily newspapers, twelve radio transmitters, and 1.3 radio receivers per 100 population. Between 1950 and 1962 the number of radio transmitters increased 156 per cent for all Africa, 140 per cent for South America, and 180 per cent for Asia. Since 1960 the transistor has revolutionized listening in the most remote areas where electrical current or batteries are practically unavailable.

While it is true that much of the content of radio programs is not innovative, a great deal is innovative. This is probably truer in the developing countries than in the West, since many of their governments are dedicated to the rapid dissemination of new production methods as well as new ideologies. The fact that China's 233 radio transmitters are used for propaganda ends also means they are used to transmit revolutionary ideologies of family, government, and religion as well as novel achievement motivations and technological skills.

The study of diffusion in modern times requires us to attend to complicated inter-relationships among the normal established patterns of inter-personal relationship, movements of people, and the specialized organizations and media for diffusion. Some of these are inter-societal in their scope, others encompass single communities, and still more are intra-community organizational structures. Whether in a peasant village of Pakistan or in Brooklyn, New York, most individuals are intimate with fellow members of a residential family. In both locales this communication system has connections linking it to related units and individuals elsewhere. Such familiar groups, even in Brooklyn, are frequently linked into neighboring relations with similar families nearby and these with kin in other cities. In much of the world, families and extended kin groups are also linked with lineages, clans, castes, and other ascribed groups which frequently are intensely intra-communicative. At the periphery of familistic groups, most individuals participate in cliques and friendship circles. While each of these groups may be viewed as a distinct social system, they are overlapping among themselves, as a man has friendship with members of another family, kin, or caste. And neighborhoods cut across these and other lines.

Beyond the realm of partially linked and overlapping primary relationships, practically all communities have special interest groups whose boundaries form gerrymanders among kinsmen and neighbors and persons not otherwise attached to each other. The local church or temple, labor union, lodge, sports club, or rural development society establishes communication patterns which cross and re-cross various primary group patterns. As we move into the realm of these formal associations, link-ages with other communities become more systematic through regional, national, and even international organization. Many of these organizations use mass media as well as personal contact, trade journals, tracts, and newsletters. In daily life, also, there are numerous regular, though utterly informal, social relationships which may involve significant communication linkages: the barbershop, tavern, and teahouse. None of these activities and relationships avows cultural diffusion as a major purpose, yet all function in message transmission.

Overlaid upon this fabric of social contacts is the self-conscious, deliberately organized, communication system. News may travel by word of mouth through town criers. Drums may take messages between sister communities or runners stand by awaiting a leader's announcement. One of the salient features of modern society, however, is the growth of specialized communicative groups. These are in part additions to the community interest group fabric, e.g., adult book clubs and forums, etc. More obviously, they include institutionalized educational organizations such as schools and public libraries. Reaching around and through such groups are the overlaid networks of mass communication systems: the press, radio, and TV and their affiliated services.

While the mass media are renowned for inter-societal and inter-community communication, it should be remembered that they reach *individuals,* not just *communities.* Further, many specific mass media are community confined and oriented. These range from the small town weekly to some metropolitan dailies and local radio stations. Community-centered mass media are interlocked with national and in-ternational service networks which also interact with local organizations and cultural emissaries in various ways. A book enters a community from a distant publisher. It may be discussed on radio, reviewed in the newspaper, picked up by the local literary circle or censorship group whose members in turn write protesting or upholding letters to local and national journals and the school librarian (Head; Klapper, 1957, 1960; Lazarsfeld, 1940). A diffusion is very much in action. The impact of the mass media does not end once a message has been transmitted. Dis-semination continues as the diffusion process is taken up in the organiza-tional fabric of the community. S. A. Rahim's study of the diffusion of water pumps in Pakistan villages exemplifies a situation in which mass media apparently had virtually no part in diffusion (1961b). However, the transmission of pumping practices to Pakistan itself involved ex-tensive use of books, pamphlets, and possibly radio.

The Mass Media and Diffusion. Mass communication involves the professional use of technology for the dissemination of materials holding identical content to large and physically dispersed populations (Lang and Lang, p. 403; cf. Riley and Riley). What goes on in massive communication is largely a one-way flow of information. To a certain extent the content of the transmitted message is modified by the limitations and restraints upon the medium itself and to a similarly limited extent there is "feed back" from the audience, which influences future messages. However, the overall interaction balance is strongly weighted on the flow of information from the power source to ultimate "consumer."

In the early days of radio's rapid sweep into popularity, it was widely feared the mass media might exert almost magical powers upon their enormous audiences. By the late 1940's it was apparent to communication sociologists that the immense coverage of such media was not equalled by their capacity to sway their publics. Lazarsfeld has excellently described one process as it serves to reduce the innovative quality of a radio program which was presumably directed toward inducing change.

Some time ago there was a program on the air which showed in different installments how all the nationalities in this country have contributed to American culture. The purpose was to teach tolerance of other nationalities. The indications were, however, that the audience for each program consisted mainly of the national group which was currently being praised. There was little chance for the program to teach tolerance, because the self selection of each audience produced a body of listeners who heard only about the contributions of a country which each already approved. [1942, pp. 66–78.]

In addition to the "selective exposure" noted by Lazarsfeld numerous researches have shown additional limiting factors upon the capacity of mass media to change attitudes. Not only is there selective exposure to messages, there is selective perception of elements within the message, and there is selective retention of those ideas supporting previous biases (Klapper, 1960).

So limited is radio's impact upon social change, Paul Lazarsfeld and Robert K. Merton felt justified in concluding a 1948 essay with the observation that the same conditions that make for the great effectiveness of the mass media operate toward the maintenance of the status quo rather than toward change. Since those tempering words were written, many serious studies have been made of the processes through which conformity and change are in fact influenced or not influenced by the mass media. No doubt Lazarsfeld and Merton were thinking more of conversion by revolutionary and ideological propaganda than of novelties which are consistent with the established normative social order. Moreover, there is substantial evidence that where chaotic conditions exist in a society and social norms are already challenged, the mass media, including television, carry heavy weight (Larson, 1964). Such warnings should not lead to disregard for the demonstrable significance of the mass media in the introduction of novel instrumental ideas in stable societies and very likely for subtle effects upon ideologies and values.

Despite "self-selection," restriction policies by media owners, and the obvious catering to modal taste, the mass media produce substantial innovative impact. The "commercial," however much it pains, is frequently as significant for cultural diffusion as is the serious educational program. The introduction of new tooth pastes and underarm deodorants to persons previously unfamiliar with them is innovative. Although it is not innovative when a commercial influences the viewers to "Switch to Weeds and enjoy their full-bodied tobaccos," it is innovative when commercials spread the practice of cigarette smoking to a more youthful clientele. Lazarsfeld noted that one out of three listeners to a radio book program recalled having been stimulated to do further reading, while Suchman found that radio played an important role in the *development* of many listeners' interest in music (Klapper, 1949, pp. iv–10).

There is substantial evidence that the mass media can do relatively more in the dissemination of factual material than in the modification of attitudes (Klapper, 1949; 1960). Yet even TV westerns and comic books, while largely non-innovative, may carry subtle impacts and "sleeper effects" upon attitudes and value systems. In the heyday of the daytime radio serial, 41 per cent of a sample of women listeners claimed these programs helped them to solve their own problems. More obviously such media set off fads, fan clubs, and "quick draw" competitions. There is evidence that TV is gaining a prominent role in the socialization of children, a process with a change potential which is extremely difficult to measure. The average North American child, from age 3 to 16, watches television during one-sixth of his waking hours—as much time as he spends in school (Schramm and Parker). However, evidence as to the content of TV shows is better documented than are the processes through which this content is perceived and internalized by viewers. In a study of Negro and White adolescent youths, W. M. Gerson found that youths who were not well integrated with their family and school milieux were particularly susceptible to mass media suggestions in guiding their personalities and activities (Larson, 1964). The implication of this and other research is that where traditional socializing agencies are ineffective, the mass media tend to fill the vacuum. While there is presumptive evidence that socialization via mass media entails significant consequences for the social order, little solid ground exists as yet for verifying logical extrapolations.

In the realm of ideologies and attitudes, the power of the mass media is probably most pronounced in areas of social unrest. Melvin Tumin observes that in regard to such deep social changes as race relations in the South, increased exposure to mass media yields small but consistent increases in readiness to desegregate schools. Numerous other studies suggest that the simple fact of broad exposure to world currents of information, almost regardless of specific content, opens the way to acceptance of more rational and secular innovations in values as well as in technology (Lerner; Ryan, 1952, 1958, Chap. 12). Close associations were found in Ceylon between acceptance of modern (Western) social values and *knowledge* of the outside world (see Chap. 14 below). It is true in practically all researches on diffusion in developing countries, that the broader and more intensive the mass media participation, the greater the receptivity to new ideas of a rational and "modern" nature.

COMPLEXITY OF "EFFECT." The communication of novelty is not simply the passing of information from a source to a recipient who has only to reject or accept the message. The effectiveness of communicative processes is no simple dimension. Harold Mendelsohn has properly criticized much communication analysis for having confused the "learning" of a message with the "effect," i.e., the activating impact of the message. Even in tangible and unemotive diffusions such as hybrid corn seed, communicative effectiveness is not so simple to determine as one might think. In the first place the idea of hybrid corn and some knowledge of it is one phase of diffusion. In Iowa, farmers' knowledge of the new seed was more rapid and earlier than utilization of it. However, if one is concerned with "effective" diffusion we would not consider mere information as a full measure of "effect." (After all, if hybrid seed had any meaning at all its meaning was wrapped up in overt behavioral changes in reference to farm crops.) In this instance, then, we would dismiss the possibility of measuring effectiveness in diffusion simply by an attitudinal change on the part of the farmer favoring the new seed over older ones. Insisting now upon behavioral modification in farm operations as a measure of acceptance of diffusing novelty, do we consider the farmer an adopter when he simply tries out the novelty on howsoever small a scale? Or are we to insist that he reach 100 per cent adoption before we judge the diffusion to have been effective? In fact, all of these points are relevant to understanding the case. The point is that *effect* is not simple informing, nor is it always a simple matter of "yes" or "no." Even the most prosaic traits offer us difficulty in the operationalizing of "acceptance." How much more difficult is the situation when no clean-cut, ready-made units of adoption are provided, as in the spread of ideologies, values, and moral precepts.

It is also entirely plausible that the mass media are today evoking subtle value changes of which neither the sponsors, writers, producers, or other "agents" are really aware, and which social scientists are only beginning to pinpoint. Effect becomes a matter of multi-dimensional response patterns. J. T. Klapper (1960) has recognized the complexity of "effect" analysis in communications and has specified the following basic plan for approaching its complexities. Klapper suggests that in "persuasive" communications, a message must follow one or another of the following directions in respect to effect. It may: (1) create attitudes or opinions in persons who previously had no position on the matter, or (2) intensify or reinforce existing attitudes, or (3) produce a conversion to the point of view opposite that previously held, or (4) simply reduce the intensity of an already held attitude, or (5) have no effect whatever.

We must bear in mind, of course, that modifications of states of mind do not constitute social, or even cultural, change. As Mendelsohn indicated, it is not enough to be concerned with effect as a purely psychological state. Klapper's categories of response direction are purely prefatory stages from the standpoint of the introduction of change.

GENERAL EFFECTS ON MODERN SOCIETY. A general characterization of the effects of the mass media revolution of our time has been given by a long-time student of communication and diffusion problems, Otto N. Larsen. Professor Larsen has stated these generalizations very broadly, with full recognition that they merit qualification. His propositions, however, express clearly the staggering scope of the mass media toward influence for change in modern society. Larsen (1964, pp. 353–354) offers eight generalizations describing these effects that are paraphrased as follows:

1. The mass media have stimulated vast new complexes of activities centering on symbol manipulation, e.g., advertising, public relations, entertaining, market research.
2. By narrowing distances, mass communication has expanded the public that is to be taken into account on multifarious issues. Thus environment is today extended through mass communication.
3. New contents have been introduced into interpersonal relations, with increasing standardization of basic speech and language habits.
4. The mass media have become the major arbiter of social status through manipulating the degree of prestige and recognition assigned to persons, issues, and organizations.
5. New emphasis is given to personality as a factor in social life, not only in regard to real persons but by providing hero and villain role models that serve as socializing forces.

6. Family patterns have been changed at many points, especially through challenge to traditional authority systems, redefinitions of parental and children's roles, and by providing direct guidance on family problems, as well as by portrayal of values such as the idealization of romance.

7. In association with mass production, mass communication has magnified material and economic values.

8. The process of cultural diffusion has been speeded, and contrasts as between rural and urban have been diminished. Social change has been stimulated generally.

In his formulations, Larsen has been cautious but nonetheless impressive as to the scope of mass media in their impact on modern life. How, and how drastically, individuals are influenced would be a subject for volumes within each of the categories of influence Larsen has has laid out.

How Personal and Mass Media Relate.   The rise of mass communication media, impressive as it has been, did not bring an eclipse of personalized and "non-mass" media. The established social networks retain significance, and personal influences are of continuing importance in societies overlaid by massive impersonal communication systems.

In many diffusion circumstances the various mass media are utilized along with more personal communication networks created for the purpose. Thus the Agricultural Extension Service was created in the U.S. Department of Agriculture as an organizational structure to carry messages of better farming from the research laboratories to the individual farmer. Local groups of farmers were organized into a centralized farm organization, which in turn was linked to the state college of agriculture, which in turn participated in the federally supported research and extension organizations. Farmers were bombarded with technically sound methods of farming through the personal visits of the local county agricultural agent, a salaried professional within the organization, and by printed pamphlets provided by him through the federal and state extension service, especially through the state college of agriculture. The county agent also organized campaigns, lectures, fairs, and contests to further the diffusion of agricultural knowledge in his region. On top of all this, many state extension services acquired their own radio stations to disseminate identical information. Many of the same messages were also diffused over commercial channels of TV and radio and through privately owned farm magazines both as technical articles and as advertisements by commercial firms. All of these channels served as calculated diffusion agencies deliberately created. Some involved personal participation in small groups, others participation in large fairs and demonstrations, and still others participation at the level of dispersed publics.

But farmers do not live merely in these communicative networks. Agricultural messages are also spread, along with many other types, through church groups, lodges, bowling alleys, neighborhood parties, family reunions, and back-fence gossip. Diffusion may follow any line of communication whether created for the purpose of such diffusion or not. And the overwhelming evidence is that few instances of diffusion rely exclusively upon a single communication channel. A large amount of research has laid out in detail the nature of the complex relationships among these very different types of media in diffusion.

THE TWO-STEP PROCESS.[4] Evidence from several directions indicates that the impersonal mass media have a qualitatively different role in communication process from that of interpersonal relationships. Typically mass media are *informing* devices rather than *influencing* ones. However the various mass media do not serve identical informing functions. American farmers, for example, appear to gain more information via radio than non-farmers. Magazine, book, and newspaper reading habits in the U.S. population are related to variations in information gained (Nafziger *et al.*).

Obviously individuals cannot be led to adopt innovations of which they have not heard. At informing the community of what is afoot, the mass media have incomparable power; at influencing action, these media are surpassed by the more personalized ones. The complementing roles of personal and impersonal media have been demonstrated in researches conducted on the diffusion of farm practices, medical technology, and in mass communication analysis. Writing with apparent ignorance of findings in the field of technological diffusions, Lazarsfeld and Merton illustrated this years ago when they observed that neither the ideologies of Nazism nor Soviet communism gained their holds upon millions of people simply through mass media indoctrination (Lazarsfeld and Merton, 1948). While both Germany and the Soviet made impressive use of the mass media for propagandizing enormous populations, these media did not operate alone. Supporting the impersonal messages of radio were local centers for indoctrination. "Reading huts" and "listening stations" were meeting places where there could be group exposure to the mass media.

---

[4] The phrase "two-step process" seems to have emanated from the Columbia University Bureau of Applied Social Research in connection with the study of the 1940 presidential election (Lazarsfeld *et al.*). The phrase and the idea were subsequently developed in various publications by Elihu Katz and Lazarsfeld. In the tradition of rural diffusion research, the idea was developed about as early and as rapidly. Some well-known contributions are: Ryan and Gross, 1943; 1950; Beal and Rogers, 1959; 1960; Lionberger, 1960; Copp *et al.*, 1958; Deutschmann and Fals-Borda, 1962; Wilkening *et al.*, 1960.

Reading rooms and clubs were established so that the rank and file readers and radio listeners could discuss the messages with the local ideological elite. As Lazarsfeld and Merton observed, the scarcity of radios in private homes in those years contributed to group listening and hence discussion of ideas presented through the impersonal medium.

The interaction of mass media and personal communication systems becomes the "two-step process" as ideas flow from radio, television, and print to opinion leaders who then influence the rank and file of the population. Under many circumstances, professional technicians, salesmen, and outside educators, often termed *change agents,* replace or support the mass media as informing, and to a variable extent, influencing agents.

Studies in the diffusion of farm practices in various parts of the United States have been supported by public opinion research in attesting the validity of *at least* a "two-step process." In rural researches it has frequently been found that the mass media inform, but the peers, the neighbors along with local specialists, do most of the convincing. A local reference group is crucial for action. Visual evidence also is an important part of the conviction process among farmers, especially as the evidence is provided in their neighbors' fields and crops. Farmers watch what is done by the men they know well and whom they know to be good farmers.

In a Japanese village, Lindstrom observed that while "attitudes toward adopting practices were influenced by mass media . . . the chief influence causing adopting was the observation of good results obtained by other farmers and the urging of extension advisors and neighbors" (1958, p. 171).

LEADERSHIP IN DIFFUSION. Merton, following the lead of Carle C. Zimmerman, has suggested that local leaders or "influentials" are of two types, viz., "cosmopolitans" who are geared to messages from the broader society, and "locals" who are strategically located inside the sociometric system of the community (Merton, Chap. 10; Schramm, 1960, pp. 175–177). The cosmopolitan plays a critical role as "gatekeeper," i.e., to pass on or not pass on messages. In a village studied by Rahim in Pakistan it was a day laborer temporarily in another village who acted as "gatekeeper" and "cosmopolite" for his own people (1961b). His message was quickly channeled into the hands of "true" influentials within the community, i.e., persons having prestige, organizing ability, and sociometric centrality.

The role of the professional, or the "change agent," is intermediate to and supportive of both informing and influencing functions in diffusion (Beal and Rogers, 1959; Wilkening, 1956). In the spread of opinion and ideology, the professional may range from the pastor of the local church to a party precinct captain. In the realm of less valuative diffusions, the range is perhaps as great, to include the advertising copy writer, the agricultural extension agent, and on occasion the Fuller Brush man. Normally the idea of "change agent" is limited to one who personally bridges the organizational source of the diffusing item with the potential recipient, or at least, the local influentials. Rural research would seem to indicate that effective operation of the professional arises when he is jointly viewed as "scientist" *and* personal associate. His influence seems also to be most effective in personalizing the gap between the massive impersonal media and the opinion leaders.

Many researchers have found that persons of influence do not exert influence in a wide range of activities.[5] Leadership in unrelated special interest groups, for example, is not particularly related to "leadership" in the diffusion of technical practices. Persons of influence are those who are and who are known to be in touch with specialized bodies of knowledge and specialized diffusion media outside the community. Circumstances can qualify this and probably do so, particularly in authoritarian and highly paternalistic communities. However, it is notable that Rahim (1961a,b) also found in his Pakistan villages that in general a farmer chose another farmer for communication purposes because he was a friend or a good farmer capable of giving information and advice. Factors such as "kinship group" and "proximity of the residence" did not play an important part in such a choice. The pattern of communication on agriculture indicated that the formal leadership did not necessarily provide the leadership on agriculture. Leaders are more likely to play a number of roles in the promotion of a specific type of issue than to exert leadership on many different issues. Ryan (1942) studying midwest farm leaders found different leadership functions performed by identical individuals, but rarely was one of these persons viewed as a leader on several different issues. Similar specialization has been noted in many other research studies on a wide range of diffusing topics. The Rovere opinion study learned that persons of local influence on cosmopolitan issues differed from those who were influential on immediate local issues (Merton, Chap. 10). There are specialized gatekeepers for different spheres of interest and there are special community activators as well. A gatekeeper for one sphere is more likely to be also a sociometric leader in that sphere than he is to be a gatekeeper in another field of concern. Numerous other studies have borne this out in finding that persons holding leadership roles in unrelated local organizations are not necessarily leaders in innovation.

[5] Like the "two-step process," this finding seems to have been developed independently in rural and in mass communication research (Ryan, 1942; Katz and Lazarsfeld; Wilkening, 1952; Ryan and Gross, 1950; Merton, 1959, Chap. 10; Emery and Oeser; Rahim, 1961a,b).

The local influential or referent on technical diffusion matters is indeed a lay specialist who in turn is supported by individuals with high centrality in sociometric position, if he himself lacks this. These roles may be found in the same individual, or the individuals may be common members of local groups. Rahim's studies in Pakistan have evidenced the fine interplay between specialists, gatekeepers, centrality, and reference groups. None of these functions is sufficient in itself. In regard to referent functions, it appears that outside specialists can have significant roles, but rarely without the referent support of local primary group members.

In many spheres of diffusion, it has been found that local influentials keep in closer touch than others with outside sources of knowledge in their spheres of influence. Influential farmers have high participation in extra-community events, technical reading, radio listening, and associations with outside specialists (Rogers, 1962, pp. 237–253). These persons usually are themselves above average in "innovativeness" in the fields of their influence or "opinion leadership."

The impersonal sources of both information and influence appear to have differing significance in different stages of the community diffusion process. Generally speaking, institutionalized and mass media have both greater informational scope *and* greater activating influence upon early, rather than late, adopters. Everett Rogers (1962, pp. 178–186) has assessed the results of many studies of communication behavior in the adoption of diffusing inventions.[6] These studies include a wide range of technical traits undergoing diffusion in various types of population, e.g., various farm practices, medical technology, industrial ideas, and radios. Rogers' well-supported conclusions are that (1) "Impersonal sources of information are more important than personal media for earlier adopters of innovations than for later adopters." (2) "Cosmopolitan sources of information are more important than local community for earlier adopters than for later adopters." (3) "Early adopters utilize information sources that are in closer contact with the origin of the novelty than do later adopters." (4) "Early adopters utilize a large number of different information sources than do later adopters."

Where encroachment is made upon the free choice of the individual to decide, or where a power structure is authoritarian or patriarchal, we would expect less differentiation among influentials. Also, it seems likely that the qualities of the diffusing "trait" may be a significant variable. Where the traits or ideas under diffusion possess emotive and normative qualities, recipients may be swayed by charismatic leaders toward a social

[6] Some major studies supporting the conclusions cited here include: Bowers, 1938; Carter and Williams; Coughenour; Copp; Copp *et al.*; Emery and Oeser; Fliegel; Rogers and Beal; Marsh and Coleman; Rogers and Burdge; Wilkening, 1956; Ryan and Gross, 1950.

movement (see Chap. 6). The "halo" effect has also long been observed, wherein a person of recognized knowledge in one field is credited with knowledge in others. Once the words of the great scientist Luther Burbank on matters of religion were given greater credence than those of less known amateurs in that field, just as the current football and baseball idols "know" more about good tobacco and good shaving creams than do less eminent mortals. When innovations take the form of ideologies, or even mass unrests, rationally based communication channels are likely to fall before "circuit jumping" emotional contagion. When "true believers" find their leader, sources of influence are narrowed, and reference groups can become mere reflectors and justifiers of one's own conviction.

Corn and Drugs: A Comparison of Communication Processes. Perhaps the single most constructive piece of recent research on the communication process in diffusion is that based upon the work of Herbert Menzel, James Coleman, and Elihu Katz. This study of the diffusion of a new ethical drug among physicians fortuitously paralleled in design one of the early diffusion researches, the Iowa hybrid seed corn study. Whereas the corn seed study lacked precision in demonstrating the place of informal relations in diffusion, the drug study was notably strong in this. After Katz discovered the similarities of the drug study with the corn seed study, he proceeded to make a careful comparison of their designs and conclusions (1961). From this came constructive amplification of our knowledge of diffusion media processes.

In both studies adopters of the innovation cited impersonal media as the most common sources of information, but less frequently as the most influential sources. Similarly, comparable results appeared in the differences between the media for early adopters of the respective innovations and the late adopters. Understandably, surface differences arise in the two studies, but both support the conclusion that diffusion agencies are of two types, one informing and introducing, the other influencing and activating. In each study the commercial sources, salesmen, and mass media had much less influence than they had informational power. Many additional studies also support the conclusion.

Additionally, Katz's comparison of the two studies indicates that in both the later adopters of the innovation assigned more significant places to neighbors and colleagues than did early adopters. There is clear evidence in the case of hybrid corn, and some evidence in the case of the drug, that "early adopters" were relatively influenced as well as informed by the impersonal media whereas later adopters were more likely to pick up their knowledge from colleagues as well as react to the influence of their colleagues who had already accepted. The two-step process is borne out as influentials receive the message and mediate it via personalized and informal networks.

Perhaps the outstanding contribution of the drug study is its demonstration of the supporting power of a colleague reference group for the acceptance of innovation. This condition was not clear among the farmers but was particularly evident among physicians. Inter-personal relations appear to have operated among the doctors so that colleagues could support each other in accepting the "risk" of a new drug for their patients. Communication among colleagues served to spread and thus reduce the individual risk. Katz suggests that the data almost suggest that "group decisions" were made to adopt the drug, a circumstance which would not have been particularly useful in adopting hybrid corn but was sound "insurance" for the bolder physicians.

In both studies adoption of the innovation first occurred in small units. Both farmers and physicians seem to have been encouraged by the fact that no total commitment to the novelty was required. Farmers increased their plantings of hybrid corn season after season. Physicians increased their prescription use of the new drug as time went on. Divisibility along with results that were personally visible and demonstrable supported diffusion.

Patterns Through Time—The Diffusion Curve

Some innovations diffuse with almost immeasurable rapidity, but most continue through measurable time as different adopting units accept the innovation.[7] For numerous innovations, such as the use of drugs by physicians and seed by farmers, acceptance itself is a time-consuming process as the adopter gradually increases his use of the adopted item. For many years scholars have attempted to discover what, if any, formula applies to diffusion rates, and numerous theories of "the" diffusion curve have been advanced.

The earliest inductively based theory of the diffusion curve appeared in F. Stuart Chapin's pioneer work *Cultural Change*, published in 1928. Chapin concluded that innovations diffuse like the gathering sweep of a wave, slowly picking up momentum as early adopters accept in increasing numbers until a peak is reached. After the high point at which most

---

[7] Katz would apparently not consider the spread of an idea a "diffusion" if time lapse was not involved. Just how much time it takes to distinguish a "conversion" or a "campaign" from "diffusion" would be difficult to say. It is true that public opinion specialists are interested in the impact of a particular broadcast or leaflet— but they are becoming increasingly sensitized to the fact that immediate impact may be a phase of a longer term process. In a Ceylonese village, the writer attempted to study the diffusion of use of a novel rice hulling machine. When dates of first trial were collected it was found that analysis was simply not feasible since the entire 400 households of the village had accepted the innovation within a week or two. Thus, an error of a few days in recall would be a critical one. Furthermore, there really were no resistant families; practically all took up the new practice as soon as they heard of it.

who will accept have accepted, the curve drops sharply as the last strag-
glers join in. Chapin of course recognized this as a growth curve, commonly referred to as an S-shaped curve. Various scholars following
Chapin sought to refine this concept. In 1936 Earl Pemberton attempted
to demonstrate that diffusion follows a cumulative normal frequency distribution. A few years later there were efforts to apply Gompertz and
logistic curves to diffusion data (Davis).

The idea that any single mathematical formula will apply to each and
every instance of cultural diffusion is a false hope. Ryan and Gross
(1943), for example, tested Pemberton's hypothesis in regard to hybrid
seed corn and found that the actual curve differed with statistical significance from a normal frequency curve fitted to the data. Nonetheless, an
S-shaped curve *generally* does in fact describe numerous diffusions. This
has been remarked upon by Herbert Lionberger (1960) in his review of
many diffusion studies. Everett Rogers (1962, p. 158) has similarly reviewed the rural literature and concludes that past investigations generally show that adopter distributions follow a bell-shaped curve over
time and approach normality. That the curves for many technological
diffusions tend toward a "bell shape," or when the cases are accumulated
toward an S-shape, is indisputable. That they cluster around a single
mathematical formula for their proper statistical expression is questionable, and that the identical curve pattern will arise in other type diffusion
situations is extremely doubtful. The diffusion studies reviewed were
very similar in their locales and types of traits, and it should be recalled
that at least one of the diffusions (hybrid corn) was significantly different
from a normal curve although in a general way it was "bell-shaped" or
S-shaped.

In the field of simple message dissemination and rumor, Stuart C.
Dodd has employed various types of curves in attempts to develop formulae applicable to various diffusion circumstances (1955, 1959). Similar
efforts are found in medical researches, especially in epidemiology and
in economics (Katz *et al.*, 1963). There is recognition in most of these,
as was not always the case some years ago, that there is nothing "natural"
about the diffusion curve. While there are not as many different curves
as there are instances of diffusion, the problem of classification and effective model building is a difficult one. Although many diffusion scholars
might disagree, as does Rogers, heed should be paid Pitirim Sorokin's
warning that any given curve presumed to apply to all diffusion
situations in all cultures is a myth (p. 634). Diffusions occur in and
among social systems, and there is every reason to believe that the rate
at which diffusions occur is complicated by several sociological factors,
not least of which is the particular kind of social structures within which
or between which diffusion takes place.

Social Structure and the Diffusion Curve.   Diffusion curves are not of the order of natural phenomena. What we are speaking of when we refer to such curves is the fact that for some reason or reasons, different individuals adopt the same innovation at different points through time. The conditions which determine the point at which overt acceptance is made are to be expressed in some complex equation which includes the individual's relationships to various types of diffusion media and, no doubt, other numerous factors. To understand why many diffusions follow a growth curve patterning ultimately requires explanation in terms of factors and forces involved in decision making, a problem to be broached here only insofar as it relates to communication and social structure. Thanks to the mighty and pervasive communication channels of most communities, rarely have studies reported that ignorance of the trait in question retarded many acceptors. Farmers who adopted hybrid corn seed rather late heard about it almost as soon as the earliest adopters. Yet it took about ten years for hybrid to spread fully among Iowa farmers. In that study, as in practically all others involving rational, technological devices, the early adopters stood in different relationship to the social structure generally and the communication system in particular than did the later adopters.

The generalized growth-curve pattern is understandable as a type of chain-reaction situation where adoption grows as a function of the number of persons who have already adopted. This snowball effect presumes an intricate and encompassing network of personal relationships within the population, a condition actually implied by the significance assigned neighbors and colleagues by later adopters. There is more direct evidence for this as well. Torsten Hagerstrand, a geographer, demonstrated that the most probable adopter of a new farm practice is a farmer living nearby one who has just adopted it (Katz *et al.*, 1963). This finding is borne out in most rural studies which have shown the importance of demonstration plots and observation of neighbors' results. No doubt the visibility of measurable results enhances the snowball effect in such cases. Similar results have been reported by Robert L. Crain in the acceptance of water fluoridation by municipalities.

Social structuring in the community, and with it communication and influence patterns, was responsible for the more rapid acceptance of polio vaccine among rural Negroes than among whites (Belcher). Although results from a vast number of research studies would suggest that the high status and highly participating white group would be more rapid in their acceptance, this was not the case. Negroes were much faster in accepting the new vaccine. The author of this research, John Belcher, explained this "upset" in expectation as arising from the fact that Negroes and whites live in separate interactional systems and in this instance the Negro world was in closer touch with the sources of knowledge and influence, especially the U.S. Public Health Service. Negro influentials were in tune with Health Service "wave lengths" and utilized their distinctive local communication-influence network to spread this new immunization message.

A carefully detailed demonstration of the bearing of social structure upon rapidity of diffusion is found in the drug study by Menzel, Coleman, and Katz. What the hybrid corn research and to some extent the polio vaccine study had to infer, the drug diffusion demonstrated explicitly. Interpersonal networks of social relationship provide crucially important communicative patterns. Physicians who were most closely bound in personal friendships with colleagues moved into the new drug with a chain-reaction (growth) type curve of acceptance. Doctors who were socially isolated from colleagues accepted the drug slowly and steadily. Katz (1961) points out that the S curve applies only to those doctors who closely interact with each other. Among them there is indeed a snowball effect as laggards respond to the influences of increasing numbers of their close associates. The socially isolated doctors, i.e., with few associates, are also more isolated in their decision making. Consequently, there is no growth curve shown in their adoption patterning. Their adoption curve is more like a straight line than an S, reflecting a relative lack of influence on each other's behavior (cf. Crain). Although quite positive that diffusion can be predicted with mathematical precision, Stuart Dodd (1955) has also recognized the crucial significance of the social network for the proper determining formula to express a particular diffusion.

The next decade will probably see great advances in the measurement of time factors in diffusion. The plausibility of different curves for closely integrated versus relatively atomized populations will be explored further, as will the attributes of the diffusing item and the cultural perspective of the population as these influence adoption. In order to develop a reliable array of curve models for diffusion situations, we must have a fairly complete understanding of the significant variables involved in item attributes, in communication systems, and in the forces upon which dynamic assessments are based.

Innovators as Social Participants

Scores of researches have assessed the characteristics of persons who are prone to accept diffusing innovations, especially technological ones,

Cumulative Percentage of Doctors Accepting a New Drug over a 16-Month Period by Number of Friendship Choices Received *

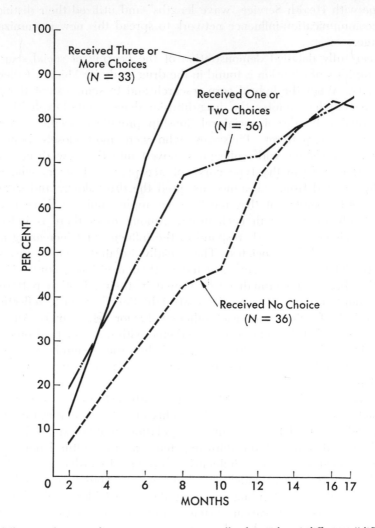

The diffusion of a new drug in a community really showed two different "diffusion curves." Doctors who were closely integrated with other doctors (3 or more friendship choices) accepted the drug on the "S-curve" model. Socially isolated doctors accepted on a more individualistic basis without the "snowball effect" evidently produced through personal interaction.

* Reprinted by permission from "The Social Itinerary of Technical Change: Two Studies on the Diffusion of Innovation," by Elihu Katz, *Human Organization*, Vol. 20, No. 2, Summer, 1961, p. 75.

as contrasted with those who are resistant or slow.[8] Typically the innovative early adopters are youthful, of high socioeconomic status, well educated and highly participatory in social affairs. The most consistent and sociologically significant finding of these studies is that persons most fully integrated in the community and inter-community social networks are most likely to be early adopters, while later adopters are low participants, perhaps semi-isolates.

Broad, extensive social contact, howsoever measured, is associated with receptivity to technical innovation. There is reason to believe that this relationship does not arise simply because highly participatory persons are enmeshed in communication networks. Evidence supports the view that participatory "innovators" in contrast with semi-isolated "traditionalists" or "laggards," view innovations in different ways. Although more research has been done on the diffusion of technological devices, the same conclusion is reached in the studies of the introduction of modern, secular values into traditional societies.

Many researches cited here have tested the hypothesis that laggards were late because they hadn't learned of the innovation before. Typically this has been found to be untrue. Broad social participation even when it is seemingly irrelevant to diffusion of ideas, yields a "way of thinking" in which the status quo can be manipulated in imagination. This is what Lerner termed the capacity for empathy in his study of modernization in the Middle East. These states may also bear some as yet undemonstrated relationship to creativity (see above, Chap. 4). People who have extensive contacts of diverse sorts appear to be more willing to make imaginative reconstructions of their situation.

In whatever manner extensive social contact is measured, it is almost invariably associated with receptivity to cultural innovation. Rahim's studies in Pakistan; Deutschmann and Fals-Borda, and others in Latin America; Bose and Dasgupta in India; Ryan's research in Ceylon and Forster's in Hawaii suggest that this is true in South Asia and Latin America as well as in the developed regions of the world. Correlates with ready adoption of innovative beliefs and practices typically include measures of travel outside the community, reading library books, membership

[8] Summary and analysis of a large number of researches may be found in Rogers (1962, Chap. 6) and in Havens. Conclusions are somewhat weighted by the large number of studies done in the field of American farm techniques. However, in general non-farm studies support the rural studies. A few of the basic researches in this field are: Hoffer and Stangland; Deasy; Pedersen: Larson, 1962; Carter and Williams; Coughenour, 1960; Copp, 1956; Van Den Ban, 1957; Bose; Lerner; Lindstrom; Fals-Borda. In general studies concerned with the psychological attributes of innovators and laggards have not been treated in this discussion although such matters are included as part of several of the researches cited. For a stimulating exploration in the relationship between psychological orientations and farm practice adoption, see Spaulding.

Characteristics of the Five Adopter Categories *

Characteristics	Innovators	Early Adopters	Early Majority	Late Majority	Laggards
1. Time of adoption	The first 2.5% to try out new farm ideas	The next 13.5% to adopt new farm ideas	The next 34% to adopt new farm ideas; they adopt just before the average farmer	The next 34% to adopt new ideas; they adopt just after the average farmer	The last 16% to adopt; they resist stubbornly new farm practices until whole community has adopted
2. Adoption leadership (or degree of personal influence)	Often not adoption leaders; they influence other innovators and possibly the early adopters	More adoption leadership than any other adopter category	Less adoption leadership than early adopters	Possess little adoption leadership	No adoption leadership
3. Specialization of farm enterprises	Most highly specialized	High	Medium	Medium	Least specialized
4. Income	Highest; innovators have risk capital	High	Medium	Medium	Lowest
5. Size of farm	Largest	Large	Medium	Medium	Smallest
6. Social Status	Highest	High	Medium	Medium	Lowest
7. Age	Youngest	Young (but older than innovators)	Slightly younger than average	Slightly older than average	Oldest
8. Education	Most have some college education	More education than average	Slightly above average	Slightly below average	Least education; seldom have any high school
9. Social contacts	Extra-community friendships and travel widely; they are cosmopolites	Leadership in formal organizations within community	Contacts largely within community limited to neighbors and friends	No contacts outside community; many with neighbors and friends	Very few contacts; semi-isolated
10. Personal sources of information	Agricultural scientists and other innovators	Extension agents, SCS workers, VoAg teachers	Agricultural agents, early adopters	Mainly neighbors and friends	Only neighbors and friends
11. Impersonal sources of information	Research bulletins and farm magazines	Farm magazines, Extension bulletins	Farm magazines, radio, and TV farm shows	Fewer magazines, mostly radio and TV farm shows	Very few magazines or radio farm shows, little impersonal information
12. Values and attitudes	Scientific and venturesome	Progressive	Slightly conservative	More conservative and traditional	Folk beliefs and tradition; agricultural magic; suspicious of change agents

* From *Social Change in Rural Society* by Everett Rogers, page 412. Copyright © 1960 by Meredith Corporation. Reproduced by permission of Appleton-Century-Crofts.

in special interest associations, listening to radio programs, watching television, etc. These various measures are highly inter-related and also reflect education and economic status, each of which is itself positively related to early adoption in nearly all research. Education, however, is in the broad sense, a measure of participation in the wider cultural world. When we rule out participation in the explicit organizations through which the innovation is diffused, it still seems that broad participation *per se* helps establish a frame of mind which is receptive. One of the few qualifications upon the relationship has been indicated by Duncan and Kreitlow who found *religious* participation negatively associated with early adoptions of innovation.

Since persons who adopt new technological practices are in this sense leaders in their community, it is interesting to note that leadership in technological improvement bears doubtful relationship to leadership in other community affairs. Individuals who "lead" technologically tend to be different from the leaders in the community organizations and affairs generally. Wilkening (1963) concludes that a position of leadership may actually lead to a conservative point of view when it is not specifically identified with the adoption of new programs or practices.

Numerous investigators have considered the question of neighborhood participation and family integration as factors which might stimulate greater receptivity to farm practices. The results are mixed, but on the whole would indicate that it is secondary rather than primary group affiliation which enhances receptivity (Rogers, 1961; Straus; Wilkening, 1954). This is qualified under conditions wherein the primary group offers immediate support to the recipient in covering risk or fear of censor which might arise through the adoption. Thus Wilkening found that membership in cliques influenced adoption but that family role structuring did not. The significance of clique membership is analogous to the finding that receptive physicians needed the support of intimates (Menzel *et al.*).

Various evidences would lead us to believe that where the primary group is a significant reference body, or where it is a risk reducing body, it will intervene in the diffusion process. Insofar as individuals are enmeshed within primary groups, those groups may retard *or* enhance the diffusion process. Insofar as the primary group is a risk reducing, buffer group for the individual decision maker, it becomes a positive force in diffusion, as evidenced in Katz (1961). Generally, however, it would appear that in diffusion of farm technology at least, the recipient who has non-primary referents and is accustomed to specialized groups and specialized services and breadth of social contact is the more probable acceptor. Where farmers accept the county agricultural agent as a major referent on technical matters, they understandably adopt recommended practices very early. An exception to this has been reported by Rogers and Burge among farmers in very highly specialized enterprises who consider their own technical knowledge superior to that of the more generalized knowledge of the county agent.

Generally, results show that the more impersonal influences such as those of the extension service and mass media are most important during the "trial" stage of diffusion into a community. "Other farmers" become the major influentials for the bulk of recipients, although not so important as secondary sources in the informing process. Accordingly, farmers who live in "conservative" neighborhoods and are oriented toward neighbors as referents for action are slow to adopt. Unless a neighborhood is very homogeneous in factors significant for adoption *and* has group referent significance, it probably has *little* influence *per se* in modern communities. People are not typically bound by their neighborhoods, nor even to intimate associates as sources of leadership in specialized enterprises. A "good" farmer will be recognized and consulted whether or not he is an intimate. Thus comparative studies of diffusion in neighborhoods having various ethnic composition find that where strong, homogeneous subcultural groups persist these are influential positively or negatively depending upon the kinds of values in this particular sub-culture. Most neighborhoods are less homogeneous culturally or at least do not represent cultural islands with strong sub-community bonds.

Inasmuch as many innovations are relevant to family groups and not merely to the "decisive" individual in the family, it has been suggested that family structure influences adoption of various traits. Larsen (1962) found significant correlations between the number of children in the family and early adoption of TV by Danish and German families. In Puerto Rico, investigators found that contraceptive devices were adopted more quickly by husbands and wives having closer communicative ties than by those who were more formal in their relationships (Hill *et al.*). However, apart from innovations which have direct functional bearing upon family matters, there is little evidence that family organization is significant for adoption. Straus found the wife's role was not significant for farm practice adoption and, as mentioned, Wilkening (1954) reports that family relationships have little direct influence on adopting farm practices. Specifically, the role of a farmer as husband-father has no consistent bearing upon his behavior in the role of farm operator.

Is There a General "Innovative" Type? There is limited evidence that individuals who readily adopt one technological improvement are likely to adopt others. Persons who resist a rational technical innovation are likely to be non-receptive to *similar* innovations. Research evidence in support of this view is flimsy, but positive (Gross and Taves; Rogers,

1962, pp. 186–187). The problem offers substantial research difficulties. Furthermore, statistical researches have been limited largely to U.S. farmers adopting agricultural techniques. It may be that similar conditions exist among businessmen generally. The producer who is alert to new developments is favorably exposed to many of them, while the rigid producer wedded to the status quo is unfavorably exposed to relatively few.

There is no reason to believe that there exists a *generally* "innovative" social type (also see below, pp. 202–207). Persons are susceptible to innovations depending upon their interests, motivations and values, and "personalities." The farmer or the businessman eager to increase productivity and profit is alert to techniques which will further these ends. There is no *a priori* reason to believe that the same farmer or businessman is eager for innovation in the mores or in the reorganization of local government, or in streamlining the Supreme Court. Nor is there any reason to believe he will be differentially susceptible to the lure of a new religious sect or extremist political movement. Suggestibility and persuadability are complex and are intricately influenced by knowledge, personal values, and psychological states such as *cognitive dissonance*—a "strain toward consistency" (Festinger; cf. Janis). There is limited and tenuous evidence that some individuals are more persuadable than others, but such psychological states are outside the range of our present interests.

It is probable that receptive and non-receptive individuals possess generalized reactions only within the range of their own particular orientations to the status quo. The technologically alert individual may or may not be equally alert to novel ideas relating to proposed social reform or acceptance of broad social trends. In Ceylon it was found that individuals who were "modern" in their status values were also "modern" in family and political attitudes (Ryan *et al.*, Chap. 12). They were also less enmeshed in traditional rituals and folk beliefs. However, insofar as evidence went, the persons who are receptive to a wide range of related secular value-attitude innovations showed no evidence of greater receptivity to technological innovations than their socially conservative neighbors. No doubt developing research will indicate that receptive and non-receptive social types exist within measurable limits. The probability is that such typologies will not form a simple dichotomy nor even be capable of rating upon some single overall generalized continuum from eager acceptors to adamant rejectors.

When we approach the problem of response to innovations borne up through social movements and charismatic leaders, the qualities of the ready acceptor are probably different from those described in this chapter. The "true believer" is no doubt a different social type from the technologically innovative. When innovations become associated with social movements, ideologies or emotional contagions, the quality of decision making is altered from that found in the rational evaluative situation. It is to be remarked that the diffusion researches covered in this chapter have been almost exclusively concerned with circumstances involving no collective behavior, no charismatic leadership, and no social movement formation.

CONCLUSION

In order that cultural items have impact upon social organization they must be communicated to and responded to by people. Diffusion is the process whereby innovative ideas and traits are communicated and presented to persons not previously familiar with them. Diffusion research has a long history in the field of cultural anthropology and a briefer but intensive one in sociology.

Early anthropological studies were generally oriented toward correcting the theories of cultural evolution which assumed that most change occurs spontaneously within societies. Some diffusionists substituted equally dogmatic theories regarding the sources of the world's cultures through diffusion processes. In modern times anthropological studies in this field have been either closely limited to the documentation of specific instances of diffusion or have concentrated on problems of the effects of diffusion on the receiving society, i.e., acculturative or cultural integration processes.

Sociological concern with diffusion in recent years has been developed largely within the fields of mass communication analysis and rural sociology. In general these diverse types of inquiry have supported each other in their findings. Distinctions between the informing and the influencing processes in the spread of innovation have been particularly fruitful. Typically the impersonal, mass media are more significant in creating awareness of novel ideas than they are in influencing persons to accept the ideas. In influencing acceptance or adoption, the individual's relationship to his social structure is crucial. The decision to accept the communicated idea depends upon its introduction through appropriate "influentials" or opinion leaders and the nature of reference group support for the innovative trait. Mass media and personalized diffusion channels complement each other, as recipients find support in local reference groups in their decision making.

The rapidity with which diffusion takes place within a social system is frequently expressed as an "S-shaped" or growth curve. However, the rapidity and time patterning of diffusion are complexly related to variables in social organization, values, and the nature of the diffusing trait itself.

While it is probable that individuals who are innovative in regard to one trait (i.e., early acceptors) are also innovative in regard to others as well, it is improbable that there are generalized innovative social types. Farmers receptive to one technological diffusion appear to be more receptive to additional diffusions of similar order. It is unlikely that such innovativeness is carried over into diffusions involving ideological or value innovations. The evidence regarding technological diffusion indicated that persons of broad and extensive social contacts are more receptive than those with narrower social worlds. It is improbable that this generalization is equally applicable where innovations carry heavy emotional and social value tones, a matter better approached through the study of social movements.

7

Social Movements

THE SCOPE OF SOCIAL MOVEMENTS

Throughout the ages people have joined in concerted action to gain collective goals. At times their actions have not gone beyond evidences of unrest or the expression of common fears or hopes. Under differing circumstances collective unrest has become focused and organizationally directed toward changes, or the prevention of changes, in the basic social fabric and values of the larger society. Collective actions are imminent wherever and whenever an existing social order so operates as to yield widespread anxiety and unrest. In the turmoil of thirteenth-century Europe the Fifth Crusade gained momentum as thousands of children went forth to conquer the Holy Land. In contemporary China the Red Guard youth shout their slogans and march toward Mao Tse-tung's conception of a new China. In medieval Europe villagers armed with pitchforks marched out to do battle with mythical brigands. In twentieth-century America, thousands of citizens joined behind a U.S. senator to drive out equally legendary villains from our public services. The period of World War I saw collective action germinate and blossom into movements for women's suffrage and prohibition. Contemporary decades witness the massive unrest of Negroes and the formation of action groups and programs toward significant changes in the structure of American society. In depressed regions of the world, concerted action is directed here toward national identity and there toward revolutionary overthrow of feudalistic or of colonial regimes. As C. Wendell King (p. 117) has observed, the field of social movements provides virtually a bottomless pit of materials useful for study in the field of social change.

The study of social movements has long been a branch of sociology.

At times it has merged with the field of "collective behavior" and at times with the study of social change. The direction of emphasis depends upon whether one approaches the subject with a major concern for interactional processes in social movement formation or with concern for the causes and consequences of movements in the changing social orders within which they arise. The very term "social movement" denotes a dynamic force arising out of interactional processes.

In sociology, the field of social movement analysis has been conventionally limited to a range of phenomena in which "collective behavior" is organized toward the achievement of socially significant goals. This core of meaning is shared in the formal definitions given by two current texts in the field. The Langs (p. 490) define a social movement as *"Large-scale, widespread, and continuing, elementary collective action in pursuit of an objective that affects and shapes the social order in some fundamental aspect."* * Turner and Killian (p. 308) define a social movement as "a collectivity acting with some continuity to promote a change or resist a change in the society or group of which it is a part."

It is unlikely that these authors could find much disagreement in their conceptions of social movements. Significantly, they both strongly underscore the relationship of collective behavior to ultimate change in the larger social order. Both would insist that such collective behavior is not sporadic, but continues toward goals related to shaping the social order. Both viewpoints would accept movements supporting or resisting change to be within the terms of the concept. However, certain types of movements are not deliberately focused on social change, whatever force for change they may actually exert. On the other hand, most social movements are consciously and deliberately aimed toward changing or preventing change.

Killian, in a more recent essay (1964), has observed that these and other current definitions all emphasize the efforts of men intervening upon the processes of social and cultural change. In social movements men are active, not passive. They work collectively toward affecting the social order. Less emphasized but present in these definitions is the idea that social movements are groups in "process of becoming." "Social movement" connotes a large, slightly structured, unorganized grouping which often becomes more clearly defined in objectives and in organization over time. Although social movements are typically associated with the diffusion of some new cultural design, their existence adds a new dimension to diffusion processes. Simple diffusion involves distributive change as individuals within a common communicative network make their individual decisions to adopt the novelty. When diffusion is asso-

* Kurt Lang and Gladys Engel Lang, *Collective Dynamics,* Copyright © 1961 by Thomas Y. Crowell Company.

ciated with a social movement, the spread and adoption of novelty becomes a concerted program of action toward a collective goal. Also implicit in the idea of social movement is a sense of emotional affiliation, the sharing of a mission, or joining a crusade. Social movements are not strictly rational pressure groups. As the Langs have observed, "spirit counts" (pp. 490–491). In many movements, adherents are less "joiners" than they are "converts."

GENERAL AND SPECIFIC MOVEMENTS

Blumer has characterized as *general social movements* the unorganized and uncoordinated mass behavior related to some cluster of socially significant but fairly vague issues, e.g., the "labor movement," the "peace movement," the "woman's movement." Backgrounds for such general movements are provided by gradual and pervasive shifts in the values of people. Blumer identifies a general social movement with the long-range directional tendencies of a society which the anthropologists term "cultural drift." The development of new values is reflected in new images which people come to have of themselves in reference to the social order, awakening them to the dissatisfactions and hopes which in turn can be crystallized into *specific* social movements toward more or less explicitly defined objectives. Following Blumer's distinction, the anti-slavery movement in the United States was a specific social movement having roots in the widespread general humanitarian movement of the nineteenth century. Out of drifts in the climate of mass sentiment arise *specific* movements in which, for example, the objectives of labor, or of women, or humanitarians are more clearly defined; and like-minded or susceptible people are drawn into a more or less organized concert.

The range in the types of issues and objectives of social movements is immense. Included in the scope of general social movements could be anti-Colonialism, African nationalism, Fascism, Protestantism, and Communism. Specific movements arising in association with these respective tides would include the "Free India Now" movement in England and America; the "Lumumba" movement, Nazism in Germany, and Methodism in Western Europe. In the broad sense, the movement for women's rights in Western nations at the turn of the last century was toward *general* civil liberties, while the "woman's suffrage movement" in the United States was a *specific* movement arising within the broad drift of feeling expressed in the more encompassing and vaguer "woman's movement." Communism may be seen as a general social movement, while the rise of communism in China is a specific manifestation of a generalized drift apparent in several countries. The civil rights movement of the 1950's and 1960's in the United States, is perhaps better conceived as an articulated specific movement than as a general one. While there is, indeed, a generalized movement toward the protection and enhancement of civil liberties in the United States, the contemporary Negro rights movement has provided the effective focus at this time.

The whole drift toward civil liberties in America has in most recent years been dominated by the Negro's quest for justice. The specific social movement toward the Negro's right to equal opportunity to participate in our society and culture is highly differentiated. Although some writers have viewed activities such as "freedom rides" as social movements in themselves, these campaigns, like lunch counter "sit-ins" and Negro mobilizations against slums in Chicago, are not "splinter" movements so much as articulated parts of a single movement having *more or less* the same leadership, the same organizational structure, the same affiliated pressure groups, the same public, and meeting opposition in the same counter-movements (Olds; Vander Zanden). Insofar as any special program with objectives within the field of Negro civil rights develops distinctive leadership and organizational structure, we are justified in referring to it as a separate specific social movement. The Black Muslims represent the present spine of such a distinct specific social movement in the general Negro rights movement (Laue). Ideology and objectives are differently defined by the Black Muslims on the one hand, and the NAACP and CORE on the other. Whereas there is overlapping in many phases of organization and relative synchronization by CORE and NAACP, the Black Muslims stand apart structurally, ideologically, and functionally.

SOCIAL MOVEMENTS AND RELATED GROUPS

Associations

Social movements do not have the organizational structure, the clear boundaries, crystallization, and stable functions that characterize associations. The ultimate design of many social movements is to end as formally structured, stable, and institutionalized associations. This was in fact the outcome of the Methodist movement, the "labor movement," and the communist movement in China. But it was not the case in the woman's suffrage movement in the United States, and may well not be true of the Negro civil rights movement. The goal may not be a new permanent association, but a serious modification of traditional and continuing associations. This is not the only way in which movements relate to associations. Social movements often encompass organized groups which may well have an existence dating to a time at which no one could really say that a movement was under way. This is to say that a movement can involve and sweep up whole groups as well as individuals.

Thus, a long established organization for the protection of the rights of women is gathered into the sweep of a "planned parenthood" program. The plausibility of such encompassment is attested by the number of Americans who erroneously believe that organizations like the Civil Liberties Union have been swallowed up by the communist movement in the United States.

Associated with all social movements which gain much headway and permanence are organized associations at both their centers and at the peripheries. Movements rarely gain much ground without closely organized "hard core" leadership. In Negro civil rights the NAACP and related associations including CORE represent such pressure groups. Actually, pressure groups had been active for years before the "sit-in" strikes and "non-violent force" caught on and a *real* civil rights *movement* was launched. At the periphery are civic improvement associations, associations for the protection of civil liberties generally, religious organizations, and many others drawn in to support the movement but with a life of their own outside it. So it was with the Nazi Party and various athletic associations, and with the Anti-Saloon League, working with church groups and sewing circles for support of the prohibition movement in the United States (Lang and Lang; Turner and Killian). Political parties and pressure groups are not social movements, nor are associations such as the Anti-Saloon League, the NAACP, and the AFL-CIO. But political parties and pressure groups alike may be closely involved with social movements in core, directive positions or in peripheral, affiliative roles.

Crowds

Since the roots of social movements are in collective unrest and the consolidation of widespread individual dissatisfactions or desires to do something about the social order, it is understandable that crowd behavior is prevalent during social movement formation. Sporadic crowds, panics, mobs, and riots are not social movements, but the prevalence of crowd behavior in any society symptomizes stresses in the social order which commonly call forth social movements. The crowd is a harbinger of a social movement and may be part of it. Social movements are bred in crowd excitements as direction and some structure is given the collectivity. Additionally, crowds become tactical weapons through which the message and objectives of a movement are furthered, as protest marches are held in Alabama, or as citizens are gathered to stone a government building. A pantie raid in an American university was not a social movement, but we may begin to suspect that it was related to some incipient gathering movement when student protests erupt on many campuses. Typically, issues are secondary to collective expression. By 1966, the unrests and frustrations symptomized in diverse sorts of campus crowd behavior showed signs of focus toward a politically colored youth movement (Schiff). This sign of coalescence has been registered by editorialists with terms such as the "new left" and various other political epithets. Since social movements savor of crusades and involve not merely affiliation but belief in a cause, emotionally significant symbols are used by them and also against them. In fact Rudolf Heberle in his great work on political movements distinguishes a political party from a political movement by the very presence of commotion in the latter and organization in the former (p. 529).

Publics

The public is a large and relatively unstructured group expressing concern over an issue, but not necessarily agreement as to its definition or resolution. With vague boundaries and transitory membership, publics arise wherever and whenever issues are contemplated by masses of people. Since publics are concerned with issues relating to the social order they are seed-beds for social movements. Turner and Killian observed this when they stated:

> . . . if members of a public who share a common position concerning the issue at hand supplement their informal person-to-person discussion with some organization to promote their convictions more effectively and insure more sustained activity, a social movement is incipient. [P. 307.]

Social movements are formed as a segment of a public becomes convinced that its viewpoint is correct and justifies collective action. Movements do not debate internally; they promote. While the movement is taking form, the larger public may well continue its deliberations, taking account of the formation of the movement. The participants of what is now a movement must continue to be concerned with the larger public since it is there that increasing followership may fruitfully be sought. The public becomes a further "recruitment base" and source of support for the movement which has sprung from within it. It is also the source of an opposition to be watched.

Counter Movements and Convergent Movements

If public issues receive activist definition in one direction, they are likely to receive similarly active response from some other, often conflicting, standpoint. Movements inspire counter-movements and in a state wherein issues and objectives are loosely formulated movements within movements.

There has probably been no period in American history in which movements for welfare and humanitarian reform have not been confronted by nativistic, individualistic social movements. Indeed it would be impossible to say which precedes the other. In modern times such confrontations have been dramatically evidenced in regard to the Negro civil rights movement on the one hand, and the Citizens Councils, Birchites, and a revived Ku Klux Klan on the other. In the strange war in Vietnam, "hawks" and "doves" utter the epithets of peace- and of war-mongering. The signs of incipient movement and counter-movement are evidenced in rallies, petitions, demonstrations, and hard-core organizing bodies. The peace movement was met by a war movement, not simply a governmental action, although The Establishment is central to the movement. Despite the fact that war was the apparent decision of the organized group directing American policy, a social movement in its support seems to have been stimulated to build up consensus in an uncommitted public.

It is perhaps inevitable that where authoritarian suppression does not intervene, any serious proposal that would affect drastically the social structure touches off at least one social movement and usually more. An area in which we do not usually think of the presence of social movements is that of "socialization" of medicine. Yet, many specific movements have converged toward support of this objective. Special examples are the almost forgotten Townsend movement and the Senior Citizens, Inc. More broadly, the general movement toward greater welfare responsibility in government has supported the Medicare action, centering itself around organized pressure groups like Americans for Democratic Action. On the other hand, the American Medical Association, despite an immense budget, able debaters, and writers, was unable to stimulate a real social movement in support of their pressure group.

More significant than well-financed propaganda is the fact that socialized medicine has been consistent with the drift of the times—i.e., changing social values, as well as an increasing publicly dependent, aged population.

Kurt and Gladys Lang, basing their report on the researches of Samuel Yellen and George Brooks, have given a superb account of convergent movements in the history of United States labor. This report is of the Haymarket Affair of 1886, which occurred in the midst of great labor unrest regarding working hours. For many reasons, including current work-days of 14 to 18 hours and serious unemployment, there was widespread dissatisfaction and agitation toward an eight-hour day.

Grand Eight-Hour Leagues were formed in the principal cities and manufacturing centers of the North. The new Federation of Organized Trades and Labor Unions (forerunner of the American Federation of Labor) called in 1884 for an eight-hour day by May 1, 1886. As a result of rank-and-file agitation, the Knights of Labor, notwithstanding the reluctance of their leadership, who considered the demand too radical, found themselves spearheading a movement they had neither created nor approved. Powderly, their Grand Master, called the demands premature. He insisted that public sentiment was not yet ready to support the demand and that a hostile press, feeding on general ignorance of the movement, was successfully tying the demand to socialism, anarchism, and revolution. Nevertheless, the popularity of the demand was reflected in the membership figures of the Knights of Labor. It rose from 104,066 in July, 1885, to 702,924 in July, 1886, with the bulk of the increase occurring in 1886 as the target day neared.

Optimism concerning the chances of success ran high, especially in the first days of May as a series of strikes gained momentum. According to one report, altogether three hundred thousand workers struck. Then on the night of May 4, 1886, a bomb thrown in Haymarket Square in Chicago exploded, killing seven policemen and wounding sixty more. With them was blown up any hope that the eight-hour demands would be realized. This unforeseen event had a certain shock effect. Mass agitation for an eight-hour day ceased abruptly, and the subsequent history of the American labor movement was certainly shaped by it. Several anarchists were tried and convicted for throwing the bomb. Whether they actually did or whether the bombing itself was a "frame-up" is for the historian to decide. The police, claiming to have discovered evidence of anarchist plots, broke up gatherings of strikers. A disordered surrender began. There was much confusion among the rank and file; workers enthusiastic about shortening working hours were not necessarily enthusiastic about bomb-throwing anarchists imported from abroad. Indeed, it was the following year that a revived nativist movement got under way. Meanwhile with the connection between eight-hourism and anarchism already planted in the public mind by the press, much of the just indignation against the bombing naturally turned against the strikes then in progress. In these circumstances, employers were able to retract even the promises they had already given.

What happened in Chicago was that two movements crossed paths. The revolutionary goals of the one adversely affected the possibility of the other's gaining its reform demands. As a mass movement, eight-hour agitation was stopped in its tracks. [Lang and Lang, pp. 514–516.] *

NATURAL HISTORY OF SOCIAL MOVEMENTS

Social movements proceed through patterned stages of development. These have long been recognized by students of collective behavior and were given early expression in Park and Burgess, *Introduction to Sociology.* These ideas received development and empirical support especially in the works of Herbert Blumer and Warner E. Gettys. Gettys, in an introductory sociology textbook with Carl Dawson, published in 1929, and in his courses at the University of Texas, offered a well-developed

* Kurt Lang and Gladys Engel Lang, *Collective Dynamics,* Copyright © 1961 by Thomas Y. Crowell Company.

sequence which he termed "the life history" of social movements. This formulation was rooted in Gettys' mainly unpublished studies of a large number of movements. Heberle's studies of political movements broadly supports the theory, as does Brinton's more specific analysis of revolutions.

While the life-cycle stages are idealized and hence not perfectly reproduced in any given movement, they stand as an important set of verified sociological generalizations regarding the change process in society. Needless to say, many social movements do not live out the idealized life cycle, and still others survive long enough to materially abet their objectives and die as victims of their own successes. Dawson and Gettys (Chap. 20) enumerated four recognizable phases through which a "successful movement" passes. These are (1) the preliminary stage of unrest, (2) the popular stage of excitement, (3) the formal stage, and (4) the stage of institutionalization.

The preliminary stage of unrest is frequently one of diffuse crowd behavior, local disorders, and agitation. At this stage, there is no organizational structure, except in the most rudimentary sense; there is no discipline, and there is no focus upon specific objectives to correct the ills at issue. There may be an almost random exploration of potential avenues of action in the general viewpoint expressed by individuals, bonded by little more than similar feelings. This is a period of collective excitement and uneasiness, and correlative with this, it is a time of rumor and collective illusions. Emotions and emotional symbols are evident as calls may be made for unification toward righteousness, justice, and God. This stage was manifest in the almost issueless student uprising on the Berkeley, California, campus in 1965; it was apparent in the bonus march on Washington by ex-soldiers following World War II and by the Coxey army march toward Washington, D.C., in 1894, neither of which lived beyond a state of popular excitement. It was seen in the sporadic riots and attempted organizations among the unemployed of the great depression of the 1930's.

Such an enumeration reminds us of how many incipient movements quickly lose out or do not get off the ground. Yet Coxey's army, the bonus marchers, and relief rioters were ominous warnings to the American political establishment and no doubt had covert effect toward the extension of welfare legislation at the national level. Out of the unrests engendered in the great depression of the 1930's, the Townsend movement at least temporarily thrived and matured to a formal stage (Green, Chap. 26). For a time a political-economic reform movement known as Technocracy attracted much attention and some adherents. Among farmers, the "Farm Holiday Movement" met threatened farm mortgage foreclosures with action close to collective violence. While this specific "movement," soon died, it furthered reform in the banking and credit system, much as the Townsend movement helped social security legislation.

In Nazism, where the full cycle was completed, we find classic expression of the preliminary stage of movement growth and the transition which followed. In the midst of economic distress following catastrophic blows to national pride, Germany by the late 1920's was undergoing collective expressions of mass unrest. The stonings of Jewish shops in those early days were manifestations of vaguely directed responses to frustration rather than part of an organized plot. Howard Becker has given us a detailed account of the growth of youth wanderings out of the towering confusion that was post-war Germany and, more significantly, how these slightly organized roamers were perverted to become elements in the Nazi super-movement.

The stage of unrest is one of floundering and thrusting as individuals and groups seek a plan and a set of objectives. Leadership is likely to be non-directive. The leader is more agitator and speaker of grievances than a guide to goals. With the focusing of discontent there is a sharpening of issues. The collective unrest emerges from amorphous roots into a more identifiable social movement (Stage 2). Frequently this occurs as some perhaps already organized group seizes upon the situation to formulate a program for action. Or formulation may occur through informal leadership, spontaneously arising from the collectivity. In the formulation of direction and of goals the charismatic leader rises with prophecies of the glorious future. Arnold Green has expressed this stage as follows:

. . . local groups, clubs, or debating societies are formed, with local leaders who have heard the master; if the others have not heard him, the local leaders will interpret his word to them. Exaggerated and often fictitious reports of the number of fellow joiners are circulated. A spirit of invincibility wells up. Nothing can stop them. They love their leader. They love their fellows. They are a mighty army which will destroy the forces of evil. They will usher in whatever millennium is the stuff of their dreams. [1956, pp. 536–537.]

With embryonic organization, but inspiring leadership and broadly formulated objectives, the group becomes increasingly self-conscious, especially as it meets the attacks of counter-movements and vested interests. The threat from within may be as great to the life of the movement as that from without, as prophetic leaders with minimal organizational structure battle for discipline and cohesion among a followership buoyed up through contagious emotions.

The transition to the stage of formal organization requires that the paradox of collective excitement plus disciplined cohesion be met. Slogans and catch-phrases are graduated into ideologies. Prophecy smacks more of prediction, and the organizational structure proliferates. These difficult and not wholly consistent processes must be carried out along with evidences of progress or at least such secure illusions of progress that mass enthusiasm and support can be preserved. To maintain support in the mass fringes, as well as devotion among the old guard, requires continuation of crusading spirit along with continuous growth of disciplined organization. In this period the nature of crowd behavior must be transformed from the undisciplined and sporadic excitements into more restrained and directed crowds. The distinction is often expressed in the terms *expressive crowd* in contrast to the *conventional crowd*. The conventional crowd is integrated with the larger social system, in this instance with the now formalized movement and its norms. The significance of the conventional crowd for the maintenance of the crusade spirit was well understood by Adolph Hitler. The annual Nuremberg Party Rally was such an extravagant and orgiastic demonstration to cement bonds of faith and love and loyalty between leaders and followers and to make an incredibly dramatic and intense center for political "regeneration" of both people and party.

Dawson and Gettys have further described the formal state emphasizing its transition into the stage of institutionalization:

The motives which inspire the group movement have become fixed and the aim definitely established. The movement is now organized around its leaders and a program. It has developed a structure and is supported by a body of traditions. As a reaction to criticism it has developed a set of norms which find their formal statement in . . . dogma and their formal expression in ritual.

The leaders of this stage are usually of the statesman type. They are the ones who formulate policies and attempt to develop social policy into an art. It is they who gauge the forces in the current mores and perceive and evaluate their tendencies. They are the ones who endeavor to understand and voice the convictions which have become established, and to propose measures which will realize the interest of which the group has become conscious. The agitator of the period of unrest and the prophet and the reformer of the stage of popular excitement may become the statesman of this more formal stage, but they do not commonly do so because they are unable, as a rule, to make the necessary adjustment to the changing order . . .

Under conditions favorable to a movement it may terminate in the form of a lasting organization, a labor union, a nation, a denomination, or similar organization. These emerge as the culminations of successful social movements; they become established; they are institutions. The movement dies out and the institution remains . . .

The successful leader in this [institutional] stage is the administrator. He is the one who translates the policy for the movement into action. Every institution has its functionaries and on certain ones of these rests the business of direction and the responsibility of getting the organization to operate effectively with respect to its policies. Administration may devolve upon individuals, as officers, or upon groups, as boards or cabinets, or upon both.

Suffice it to say that the agitator, the prophet, and the reformer have no place in this formal arrangement. Personal ascendency, however, is less essential to this stable and established order than the impersonal instruments it has forged for itself—its laws, disciplines, faiths, dogmas, and ideals. As Sighele has indicated: "The members of a stable and legitimate association are more cultured, more calm, more settled, more reflective, than are the members of a sect or, a crowd. Personal appeal has less grasp upon them; with them the centers of control are more active; reason directs and checks sentiment, and immediate and complete adherence to a single man is rare and difficult."

With the emergence of a social movement in an established institution, it has reached the concluding stage of its life cycle. Fundamental social change comes about through the progressive and unilateral transformations wrought by a social movement. Its termination in a new social order or a single institution indicates that the change is complete and relatively permanent and will remain so until the time when fresh social contacts and accelerated interaction result in a new state of unrest and an increase in social and personal disorganization. Then a new trend of social change in the form of a movement will occur. [Dawson and Gettys, pp. 787–804.] *

We are warned, however, by the great revolutionary socialist Georges Sorel that the professed beliefs of the incipient social movement may bear little resemblance to actual behavior. This in no way reduces the power of the movement to produce change—to the contrary. Sorel, devout syndicalist that he was, looked upon the *idea* of the general strike as a potent myth for stirring revolutionary action which would necessarily be determined in its detail by the circumstances of the future—not by some ideological concept of a general strike. Yet the labor movement was to be swung into action with the idea of the general strike as a crucial stage in achieving some ultimate goals. It is even more apparent today than in the days of Sorel that the movements inspired by the prophetic ideologies of Marx, Engels, and other nineteenth-century socialists set up change sequences which in ultimate effect bore indirect relationship to the predictive myths which so stirred the imagination of the times.

TYPES OF SOCIAL MOVEMENTS

The interests, methods, and objectives of social movements are so varied that classification and a construction of typologies are both necessary and exceedingly difficult to formulate meaningfully. Numerous classifying criteria have been used which range from simple descriptive specification of the area of activity, e.g., political, religious, economic, to classifications in terms of ideological content. Of most general use in sociology has been a classification originating with S. Sighele and

* Carl A. Dawson and Warner E. Gettys, *An Introduction to Sociology,* The Ronald Press Company, New York, 1929.

developed in varying ways by Park and Burgess, Herbert Blumer, and Turner and Killian. Rather than re-echo these related but not always consistent classification schemes, the classificatory criteria of these writers have been merged in the following typological distinctions among social movements.

Expressive Movements

Expressive movements are those which are oriented more toward individual goals to be attained through the movement than toward collective social objectives. Hence, expressive movements do not seek to change or reform the social order; nor do they seek to prevent change in it. In purest form such a movement defines the surrounding world as irrelevant to its goals.

Movements of this type were termed "inward" by Sighele to signify that they arise in circumstances wherein disturbed and upset people are unable to act overtly in reference to their frustrations. Behavior is turned "inward" as tensions are released through mere expressive behavior, rather than toward some change in the actual external social situation. Turner and Killian have referred to such movements as "participation oriented." Such movements typically arise out of collective frustrations, a need for status, and even black despair. Purely expressive movements are most significant for change in that they can be directed toward social action. The dancing manias of the Middle Ages were less *social* movements than they were *expressive collective* movements (Blumer). They were participation-oriented social contagions, undirected toward goals of either personal or social character. Here collective behavior is no more than at the threshold of social movement formation.

As a social movement forms around needs for expressive satisfactions, it necessarily takes on more conscious objectives. These objectives relate more to the satisfactions derived through participation than to goals of collective action. Reformation, if it is sought, is a reformation of soul and mind rather than of society and culture. The peyote cult among American Indians is a good example of an expressive social movement responding to a disintegrating cultural world through resigned acceptance (Voget; Linton). Expressive movements are germinated in situations wherein a collectivity find themselves overwhelmed by an unacceptable social order. These movements promise individual gratifications by virtue of participation. They may be "passive reform" programs. Passive reform does not involve active intervention in the social order but rather preparation for some ultimate forthcoming state of affairs to come about without intervention by people. Some Christian sects have grown around the proposition that a second coming of Christ is imminent and that they are preparing themselves for that day of days (Boisen).

A number of Christian sects have grown through the belief that participation offered personal salvation and the status of an elect group in the eyes of God. Such movements are not consciously seeking social reform. They may even deplore the efforts of alternative religious movements to achieve reforms in the social order. Nonetheless change may be introduced by such groups, either as a latent function of their collective actions or, as is frequently the case, the development of a set of social objectives as an awakening when the group seeks a place for itself in the organized community. For example, Methodism owed its roots as a sect to participation-oriented motives and expressive activities; but as the movement matured, external social reforms were also sought collectively (Brewer). The Langs (p. 499) observe that most reform and revolutionary movements aimed at institutional change have overtones of a moral crusade while many movements which at an early stage enlist members as a moral crusade, are later to stress concrete reforms consistent with furthering their moral convictions.

External, Goal-Oriented Movements

These encompass the extremely wide range of movements seeking change in the external status quo or seeking to prevent such modification. Frequently the latter are in fact counter-movements of reaction rather than movements for stasis. There is little agreement upon how these externally directed movements should best be grouped. Some of the commonly recognized types having prime significance for social change are: (1) "revitalizing" movements, (2) "value-oriented or reform movements," and (3) "revolutionary" and other power-directed movements. Like most social phenomena, the complex realities of life do not conform neatly to pigeon holes. We should think of these types as frequently existing in mixed patterns. The utility of such classification is chiefly to provide conceptual tools for the analysis of social movements from the standpoint of their bearing upon change. It is evident that the woman's suffrage movement in the United States was almost purely a value-reform movement, while Nazism had elements of all of the above specified types as well as expressive qualities. Many movements are characteristically of a single pattern although not perfectly limited to it.

Revitalistic Movements. This term has been used by Anthony F. C. Wallace, to refer to a broad class of social movements which would revivify and reassert traditions and solidarities and create or re-affirm unfulfilled group destinies. Wallace has used the term "revitalization" to cover various related sub-types of movements widely reported by sociologists and anthropologists and students of religious history. All such movements arise in a pre-existing group, or sub-group, frequently an ethnic or religious body in which individuals are feeling severe stress and anxiety at the apparent loss of meaningful life in the existing socio-cultural structure. In the depths of collective helplessness, the anxious and apathetic group is awakened, united, and enthused by a prophetic destiny which is to be theirs. Such movements practically require goals which are both "separatist" and expressive, unifying them and creating sharp demarcations between themselves and some other group, often the larger society itself. Expressive movements like the peyote cult are hardly revitalizing, although they involve traditional revivals. The peyote movement was more fully expressionistic in its apathetic acceptance of the "unacceptable" realities of white domination. Revitalization movements are the awakening of an existing depressed group in reference to some image of a glorious future state. Frequently this is a projection of the legends of a glorious past.

The major sub-types of revitalization movements, expressed by Wallace in terms commonly found in sociological and anthropological literature, are these:

1. Nativistic movements, wherein emphasis is upon the elimination of alien ideas and persons
2. Revivalistic movements which emphasize some aspect of culture or social organization believed to have existed in the past and either lost or currently endangered
3. "Cargo cults" which arise among indigenous people in response to dominating invaders and center upon symbolic expectations (cargo)
4. Vitalistic movements, which arise in reference to invaders but do not involve "cargo" expectation
5. Millenarian movements, emphasizing supernatural transformation of the world into some idealized state
6. Messianic movements in which the world is to be transformed by a savior with supernatural powers

It should be emphasized that the above typology represents dominant emphases rather than a set of exclusive categories. "Cargo cults," for example, are obviously "vitalistic," and probably many "messianic movements" are millenarian and nativistic, and even "vitalistic" as well. Further, each of these patterns may be associated with varying degrees of "expressionism" or "participation-orientation." Revitalizations are pursued through psychological and social mechanisms in varying proportions. The Black Muslim movement is an excellent vehicle for illustrating practically all of the sub-patterns laid out by Wallace in "revitalization."

A REVITALISTIC MOVEMENT: THE BLACK MUSLIMS (Laue). The Black Muslim movement probably includes fewer than 100,000 members organized around some 80 "Temples of Islam" scattered throughout the United States. It is a militant movement led by a Prophet, who has had mystical association with God himself, as have had other prophetic forerunners in the movement. Muslim values and ideology allege that the black man was created 66 trillion years ago and that the Genesis story of creation applies only to the white race creation a mere 6,000 years ago. Whites are albino creations originally produced by an evil black scientist. With a strange merger of cultural and racial concepts, the Black Muslims find their *real* language to be Arabic; their *real* religion Islam; their *real* homeland, the Upper Nile. Robbed of all, including self-identity, by the white man, the Black Muslims enjoin "middle-class virtues" and in the main appear to practice them. They strive toward a separate black nation to be cut out of the present United States. While there are expressionist elements in the movement, it is sharply contrasted with the reform movement among American Negroes such as centers about the NAACP. The Black Muslims are separatist in goal, rather than reformative in reference to American social structure.

James H. Laue, has superbly assessed the Black Muslims in terms of the various types of revitalistic movements as expressed by Wallace.

The Muslim movement is one of several alternative avenues of expression for the angry, sensitive, disillusioned Negro in America today. He is thoroughly Americanized at the value level, but frustrated at the personality level because of lack of institutionalized channels of cultural achievement. While the closed-system nature of the dominant white culture in the nineteenth century dictated clowning, self-hate, and neuroticism as adjustive techniques, the more aggressive channels of protest safely available today include enhanced striving, in-group aggression, prejudice against out-groups, and militancy. The particular cluster of mechanisms demonstrated in the Muslim movement involves all of these, plus denial of membership—substitution of identity as a "Muslim" for identity as a "Negro."

The psychological stances represented by these reactions are all part of the Black Muslims' unique mazeway. They have been translated into a coherent movement, which exhibits elements of five of the six types of revitalization movements Wallace suggests:

The "nativistic" phase of the movement emphasizes elimination of the white slave-master and his evil system, to be replaced by an all-black nation-within-a-nation—in which contact with the white's alien customs and values is neither desirable nor possible.

Consequently, in "revivalistic" fashion the Muslims hope to institute the patterns of ancient Islamic society as they idealize it—an example of the Golden Age approach of every people who have ever suffered cultural disorganization.

From our perspective on the "outside," we can also call the Muslim movement a "vitalistic" effort, stressing importation of foreign elements. But it is clear that the Muslims do not accept this "importation" terminology, for the germ of the core-values they espouse is inherent in every black man, they say; he is phylogenetically a Muslim, and automatically superior to his white counterpart.

The "millenarian" emphasis of the movement is very strong. Minister Malcolm and the Messenger state time and again that Allah will engineer a Babylon-type demise of the white man if he does not repent in time.

And, while Fard was the official incarnation and Muhammad only a shamanistic prophet, Muslim leaders know that many members do not make the distinction, and indeed view the Messenger as a "messianic" figure actually participating in the divine. [Laue; p. 319.]

PREVALENCE OF REVITALISTIC MOVEMENTS. Revitalization movements with messianic and millenarian emphasis are found in numerous religious systems especially during periods of their early growth. Judaism, Christianity, and Islam proper have strong messianic elements, and these have been periodically revived in the growth of novel sects, such as the Pentecostal Church in Christianity. The idea of millennium associated with the second coming of Christ is a closely associated theme which is magnified in several Christian sects.

Millenarianism and messianism are also prevalent in African, American Indian, and Oceanic societies. In Oceania such movements have emphasized the "cargo" theme. Among American Indians, millenarianism has been closely associated with nativism. African movements have frequently tended to become political and revolutionary movements.

Cargo cults and millenarianism have been particularly common in Melanesia (Worsely; Burridge). Protestant missionaries noted such cults in Papua as early as 1857. With the domination by alien whites, the depressed native recognizes that the white has valued imports associated with powers, i.e., cargo, to which the native lacks access. In the cult, the native makes an identification with the white man's culture, building his "myth-dream" of a precious cargo coming for him, the native importer. The cargo that is to come is symbolic of the native's search for meaning and dignity in life as he exists in the shambles of his traditional culture, wracked by the white man's domination and even enslavement. A messiah or prophets may actively promulgate the myth and the cult. Frequently, in course of time, such cults have developed in the direction of nativistic and incipient nationalistic movements of hostility toward the alien exploiter.

Common through North, South, and Middle America, were messianic and nativistic and revivalistic movements with strong religious content (Wallace; Linton). The Ghost Dance in the North American West involved practically all elements of revitalization noted by Wallace, as

Indian prophets merged Christian doctrines in native conceptions to build a dream which for a time revitalized the Indians in their hopeless fight to retain their culture and their lands (Mooney). In Middle America as well, messianic prophecy, Christian symbols, and native super-naturalism merged into movements which were more revolutionary than millenarian (Edmonson *et al.*). True millenarianism, as in cargo cults, are movements of hopelessness and failure, rather than of resurgency or even symbolic defiance. Nonetheless they have frequently set in motion strong collective feelings which have been fundamental to the growth of nationalistic social movements.

When revitalistic movements manifest political goals they become movements of nationalism. In the United States, the Ku Klux Klan and the John Birch Society are revitalistic movements which are strongly nativistic and revivalistic. The Ku Klux Klan is almost certainly revolutionary as well and possibly the John Birch Society is as well, i.e., using tactics which are extra-legal and illegal. Nonetheless, the Klan makes a great to-do about God, motherhood, and "the little red schoolhouse." Scarcely a page of their *Kloran* (the secret book of ritual and law) is without some attempt to identify with traditional and firm American values. Their *methods*, not their objectives, make them revolutionary, since their success would denote the disruption of lawful authority.

In many new nations nationalistic movements have been more revitalistic than they have been expressive, reformative, or revolutionary. Through Asia, recent decades have witnessed the rise of a *general* movement of this character as Asian nationalists in various countries have risen to power through movements which would reassert the dignity and autonomy of their specific ethnic groups (Geertz). In some instances entire political states have revitalized their cultural roots and solidarity through anti-Western, anti-colonial movements. More commonly, the newly created political states have been torn internally by nativistic movements and counter-movements among constituent ethnic groups. Before, and in the early years of independence, the new Dominion of Ceylon gained solidarity through the anti-colonial movement centering in a pressure group modeled on the Indian Congress (Wriggins). However, a decade later a nativistic, and nationalistic revivalist movement arose among the Buddhist Sinhalese majority and was skillfully ridden to political power by S. W. R. D. Bandaraneike and later his widow, who was to become the first woman prime minister in the world. Typical of such ethnic movements was the assertion of dominance of the Sinhalese tongue in the land and the revivification of the ancient, especially religious, heritage of this ethnic group, in counter-distinction to the cultural heritages and languages of other groups. While the nation floundered on the brink of economic disaster, large sums were being spent on

Buddhist universities and the reconstruction of ancient ruins, symbolic of the Sinhalese people's proud past. Typical of many such situations was the counter-movement of a major minority, the Ceylon Tamils, who acted to preserve their own cultural integrity and their status in national affairs. Their major organizational core for this movement loudly voiced demands for political separateness and relative autonomy politically and institutionally. On both sides great care was taken to avoid the reality or the semblance of revolution as both Sinhalese and Tamil leaders sought to use tactics which would not bring censure in world opinion and the Sinhalese attempted to reconcile their program to traditional religious teachings.

Value Oriented or Reform Movements. Reform movements are successful insofar as their objectives are promoted and legitimated in the larger society. In the value-oriented reform movement care is exercised that the program, i.e., the precise objectives and tactics, are consistent with the existing normative order. Ideologies are constructed to effect and dramatize such reconciliations. Only through maintaining its non-revolutionary status can the movement gain ready access to legitimate means of self-creation and growth. It is significant in this connection that the bitterest enemies of the Negro civil rights program have attempted to brand it as a revolutionary movement (e.g., a communist-subversive plot to overthrow American values, etc.) and so to deprive the movement of legitimate means of support and expression. Movements like the New Deal, which sought to legitimate social values which many Americans construed to be contradictory to our "free enterprise" tradition, paid close heed to the justification of their programs as a means of *preserving* the most basic of American values, including "free enterprise" as properly conceived. Tactics as well as objectives must remain consistent with the traditional order or at least appear to be consistent.

Value-reform movements are always manipulative of the social order. They seek its modification in some direction which in the movement's ideology is justified by the fuller definition of the society's own values. Outstanding and relatively pure examples of such reform in American life movements are in the Negro civil rights movement, woman's suffrage movement, prohibition movement, and the Townsend movement. It is noteworthy that of the examples cited, excepting the Negro civil rights movement, each made significant impact upon American society but failed to survive as a significant continuing force in American society. A fully successful civil rights movement would also virtually require that movement's ultimate dissipation. Where specific movements form out of general movements in reference to attainable objectives, the movement withers away with its relative success. It may, of course, decline for many other reasons, such as ineffective leadership, changing circumstances which make the objectives irrelevant or unattainable, or organizational failure as in setting goals all of which are too difficult or too far distant to maintain the enthusiasm required for perseverance. Reform movements, as has been noted, are also particularly susceptible to the attacks of counter-movements on the grounds that they are revolutionary. A most important function of reform movement ideology is to show that the values supported by the movement as well as its program of action, goals, and tactics, are legitimate and support the normative order.

Whether or not a reform movement culminates in a separate group which is institutionalized around movement objectives depends upon many factors of circumstances and programing. In the labor movement, a program of continuing objectives was laid out for an increasingly organized and institutionalized group structure. The goals of the labor movement were not a limited set of static objectives but rather were aimed at a continuing legitimate power to influence economic structure in reference to general goals. The strategy of successful institutionalization required a hierarchy of objectives in terms of immediacy of attainment and generality, as well as an ideology and the organizational structure to carry on the battle. Unions and federations of unions persist as formal organizations giving precision and permanence to the vague drift known as the "labor movement" and pressing the interests of the collectivity.

The "woman's movement," or "feminist movement," provides a curious contrast somewhat paralleling as it does the rise of organized labor in the nineteenth century. The vague drift known as the "woman's movement," especially in England and the United States, like the labor movement gave rise to specific movements which were more or less convergent (Green and Melnick). As with the labor movement, numerous pressure groups supported the feminists in various of their objectives—and countermovements rose to oppose them. Also like the labor movement the feminists were effective in achieving or at least promoting legislative changes. Woman's suffrage was achieved and the movement had a significant part in the legislative reforms related to such matters as employment of women and property rights in marriage. How much significance it had for the general equalitarian and civil rights value drift in Western democracies is difficult to assess but there was surely an impact. The movement at least added an articulate and forceful ideology to the drift.

Why did the vigorous, actionist, and propagandistic woman's suffrage movement fade away to be weakly evident in questionable essays on the feminine mystique and scholarly homilies on the "natural superiority of women"? The clue to this riddle lies in the fact that the "woman's movement" faded away, but specific feminist groups of many shapes and sorts have arisen from the movement's adherents. These are as varied as the Mothers' March for Peace, the League of Women Voters, Federated Women of American Clubs, University Women's Clubs, and the National Organization of Women. Specific movements of another generation withered as their legislative reforms were accomplished. The new self-conscious women's associations are less integrated with any general social movement. They arise as female organizational mechanisms partially to validate civic roles claimed by the early and true organizational feminists. The movement washed out, but it spawned many service associations oriented to the problems of women and their special civic interests.

There is no crusade by women for women today. The breakdown of the movement as a movement lay in many factors. The feminists claimed to seek overall equality with men, but the organized movements were often very specific. The intense and organized suffrage movement won its struggle and faded. Along with limited success also came a vague feeling among women that *full* equality with men was either meaningless or undesirable. There were counter-movements among women themselves reasserting the distinctive values of womanhood in homemaking and in child-bearing and socializing. Women were to be *different* from men, not female counterparts. Perhaps most telling of all was the fact that with men as their opponents the women's movement was in a dilemma insofar as it sought a separatist and institutionalized organizational goal. As J. A. and Olive Banks point out, socialists might dream of a world without bosses, but feminists never sought to create a world without men. What women wanted was comradeship *with* their oppressors, not victory *over* them. Women's special interest associations proliferated and women turned their energies toward campaigns for humanitarian causes, but the *woman's movement* was diverted and fractionated.

One of the most challenging research problems in the field of social change is in the separation of cause and effect as societies shift in the direction advocated by social movements. The problem is superficially simpler when the movement is institutionalized and, as with labor, the movement can be given credit for the achievements. But the fact is that the labor movement like the feminists was organizing in support of and in furtherance of a cultural drift. Perhaps the ultimate reason for the failure of the feminists to survive and press onward was the conviction by most women that "they had gone far enough." For whatever reason, limited objectives were realized and the supporting collectivity was none too sure that it really wanted more. It is clear that the success of a movement is not to be measured by its permanence. What is not clear is how to evaluate the significance of a movement in the actual modifications which ensue. In many instances, the movement is the quickening catalyst to drift. This was probably true in the woman's movement and it is clearly true in the American Negro civil rights movement. Hopefully it too can ultimately fade away like the woman's movement with its non-separatist goal of equality achieved in each of the spheres of contention.

Revolutionary Movements. Revolutionary movements bear resemblances to those of social reform since both aim at goals which are to affect the norms and values of existing social structure. Further, revolutionary movements sometimes support the objectives of reform movements when it suits their strategy to do so. Some movements which were begun simply to effect social reform have been transformed into revolutions. As has been observed, reform movements accept the basic social structure and move toward its reformation with tactics which conform to the normative principles and values of the society—or which are in some manner reconciled to the legitimate order through ideologies. Revolutions differ in several respects. They are sudden and violent changes of the official law of the group or of its institutions and values (Sorokin, p. 481). Revolutions gather momentum and "explode." Violence akin to civil war is implicit in the idea of revolution as the illegal movement usurps the power of physical force to overthrow an established legitimate order. Social reform movements accept the legitimacy of the established institutions; revolutions do not. Reform movements involve a limited number of areas in which change is sought. Revolutions are usually broad in their goals relating to the overthrow of entire institutional structures, including the political state. However, where reform movements are forbidden or suppressed, there is great pressure for the movement to turn from reform to revolution.

Sorokin has pointed out that objectives of a revolutionary movement may be toward a single institution or in reference to overthrow of the entire social structure (pp. 481–487). He would, then, speak of a *religious revolution,* as in the violent struggles of the Reformation, in contrast to a *political revolution* or a *family revolution,* when the aims of movements are directed toward drastic changes in these institutions. Transformations such as the Communist Revolution in Russia he would term a *total revolution* since it aimed at revolutionary change in all established institutions. Many scholars, however, have limited their use of the term to movements of violence in reference to the political state, i.e., political revolutions. In the long run all revolutionary movements have political implications if for no other reason than their challenge to the state's monopoly upon physical force and violence as an instrument of power. Revolutions, whatever may be their institutional objectives, are movements in which the first tactical concerns must be the achievement of power and control in the setting which their violent upheaval has unstructured.

It is questionable if many movements either of reform or revolution spring directly from the most oppressed and disadvantaged persons. The feminist movement, for example, was largely a middle-class phenomenon and the last labor groups to assert themselves organizationally are typically the most depressed. Crane Brinton in his analysis of four major political revolutions found that they occurred while the countries were on the economic up-grade and originated among reasonably prosperous people who felt restraint and annoyance rather than crushing oppression.

Revolutions have distinctive aspects in their life cycle. This must be true if for no other reason than that a legitimate order destroyed must be replaced—a task quite different from that of insinuating reform into a continuing social order. As revolutionaries gain control and attempt to refocus their power from the foe to the problems of ruling, tensions toward disunity appear (Sorokin, pp. 481–495). Moderates come to be replaced by radicals and extremists as in the overthrow of Menshiviks by Bolsheviks or in Castro's replacement of his first diversely representative and moderate cabinet by a rigorous leftist one. The accession of extremists is frequently associated with a reign of terror culminating in a new social order based upon the centralization of emergency power. Equilibrium is restored, social convalescence begins, and the revolution is over. It may mean reinstitution of an order little different from the pre-revolutionary one (as in "palace revolutions") or it may usher in a broad societal revision (as happened in the Soviet Union and in Castro's Cuba).

POWER-CONTROL AND REVOLUTIONARY MOVEMENTS. "Power-control movements" are those in which the major orientations are toward gaining ascendancy rather than gaining certain substantive objectives. In its most pure form, the power-control movement is exemplified in "palace revolutions" or the coup d'etat, which usually have little to do with real social movements. Classic manifestations of pure power-control shifts are found in the struggles between contending *caudillos* for political supremacy in the Latin American states. These contrast with the rise of dictators such as Mussolini and Hitler, through true social movements, first of all toward power but also to institute a new program (Newmann). Most power-control movements are also revolutionary movements. Pressure is intense to justify the tactics by success rather than by the societal norms.

Within any movement there is likely to be a fairly continuous struggle between reform and power orientations. In consequence, many movements which begin with value goals are transformed into power movements in which the substantive goals are subordinated or forgotten. It is improbable that any true movement which culminates in a power-oriented coup d'etat did not have some substantive value goals, at least among the rank and file and minor leaders. As Turner and Killian show, there are several ways in which the struggle between value orientations and power orientations swing to the side of power.

First, a strong belief in the unlimited worth of a movement's objectives tends to provoke the attitude that any means are justified by the ends to be gained. The acquisition of power seems to be a much easier way to accomplish the aims of the movement than the slow process of winning a favorable public and getting constituted authorities to accept the movement program. To some extent, an extreme dedication to the movement—an inability to understand how anyone could disagree with its aims except through ignorance or willfulness—is a natural product of highly developed *esprit de corps* and morale. Such an attitude makes the members and leaders impatient with value-toned discussions of what methods are proper and what are not. Even when leaders are inclined to search their consciences regarding strategy, the demands by members for immediate and tangible accomplishments may force decisions in terms of power, irrespective of their consistency with the movement's values. Such compromise of principle probably occurs in every movement to a degree, but frequently it extends far enough that the value-orientations sink into the background of movement decisions.

Second, a movement may be taken over or subverted to power considerations by outsiders who see its potential usefulness to themselves. A movement of any considerable strength immediately has to contend with many efforts to "capture" it for power purposes. But even movements that represent only small minority interests have nuisance value or a potentially crucial influence when major forces are balanced. Consequently opportunists seek to capture the movements and trade concessions of policy for personal gain. It has been noted that many of the small political movements in the United States have lost their distinctive ideologies in this manner. Starting with a fairly radical viewpoint and commanding a small but vigorous body of supporters, the movement becomes important enough to trouble the leaders of the major parties. As skilled opportunists work themselves into key positions, the sharp edge of the radical doctrine becomes blunted until eventually it becomes almost indistinguishable from that of more established groups.

Third, certain kinds of opposition so narrow the range of tactics available to a movement that it has no alternative other than to adopt effective means irrespective of their immediate consonance with the values of the movement. The movement that is regarded as revolutionary by the society in which it operates is in this position, as we have pointed out earlier. If a revolutionary movement is to achieve any appreciable measure of success in the face of restrictive practices, it must develop an extensive strategy and employ tactics that more value-oriented movements avoid. Adherence to a carefully defined strategy must not be weakened by internal division, questions of public acceptability, or matters of sentiment. It is for this reason that some of the clearest and most realistic statements of movement strategy are to be found in revolutionary literature. [Turner and Killian, pp. 372–373.] *

The clearest examples of power-control movements are in cases of the quasi-revolutionary coup d'etat. However, varied movements use force toward broad overthrow of an established order or toward governmental control. Illustrations abound of the relationship between the search for power and efforts to achieve substantive change. The writings of Sorel, indicate that in the communist revolution the attainment of power must take precedence over specific, although not general, goals in the movement. It is his assumption that mass support will be secured through a myth that may actually be greatly modified in the process of power acquisition. Yet, it cannot be said that Sorel would sacrifice the ultimate goals of the movement simply for the acquisition of power. It is probably in much the same sense that Lenin is reported to have said of the Bolshevik revolution: "Seizure of power is the point of the uprising. *Its political task will be clarified after the seizure*" (Turner and Killian, p. 373). Similar policies are reflected in the contemporary words and tactics of militant students at a number of American universities.

Latin American "revolutions," excepting that in Mexico and possibly the Castro movement in Cuba, have been of a different character (Blanksten; Davis). Latin American soil has bred a characteristic, although not unique, revolutionary pattern. Many conditions and forces are responsible, including the great social distance between a tiny elite and a mass of abjectly poor, uneducated and suppressed peons and Indians. Further, the traditional regional strong man pattern, *caudillismo,* is readily transformed into political dictatorships founded upon force. On these and numerous other bases unrest in the masses has often been bitter and intense, but they have been poor material for movement purposes. All but distinct from the largely inarticulate mass have been "reform movements" carried on among intellectuals, especially students, humanitarians, and others. Rarely have such movements had very well-developed reform programs, if for no other reason than their very hopelessness in the established governmental pattern of corrupt self-seeking maintained by intrigue and violence. In the milieu of authoritarianism and arbitrary justice, reform movements have been of little consequence.

Movements by those who would *seriously reform* their government have been necessarily concerned with the *first* reality of success, the seizure of power. Ideologies have been developed and enunciated and their programs consciously sought, but in most instances either the chaos

---

and intrigues of the overthrow have made a humanitarian democratic regime impossible to attain, or the reformers and their plans were subverted by a power-control clique at a crucial stage of the "revolution." It is possible that the first situation was manifest in the inability of Juan Bosch to retain his government in the Dominican Republic following the overthrow of the Trujillo dictatorship. The second pattern, that of subversion of a weakly programmed revolution by reformers is no doubt the more characteristic one. Both are particularly interesting for the study of social change since they, especially the second, represent something very close to "static revolution"—in which new personalities replace old personalities within the same old governmental structure in the same old social system.

Static and the Dynamic Revolutions: Cuba and Mexico. The subversion of reform in the social order is well illustrated in the rise of Fulgencio Batista in Cuba. There was indeed a social movement of protest during the preceding dictatorship of Gerardo Machado who had in 1928 retained the Presidency without an election and remained in power until August, 1933, when he was forced to resign and flee for his life (Casuso; Phillips). That the revolutionary movement against Machado had a strong core among the university students is unquestionable. Since 1923, the students had been active in protest both in reference to humanitarian issues and toward their acceptance as a political force in the country. Under Machado, in 1927, they organized the first Student Directorate for the orientation and guidance of Cuba's youth. Various other organized groups were more or less affiliated to approximate a popular mass revolutionary movement. Feminists were involved, and an underground group, Cuban Youth, became particularly active in the chaotic days following Machado's resignation. At times these core groups made efforts to stimulate and capitalize upon unrest in the mass of the poor. There is not much reason to think that constructive ideologies were very significant at any level. School teachers struck for higher wages; Negroes attempted to oust whites in a park facility and met gunfire resistance; university students made fiery protest speeches, called strikes, and probably threw bombs. An American observer, Ruby Hart Phillips (p. 139) noted that through the entire school system, children were political first, last, and always with studies incidental to politics and normal extra-curricular life zero. She was unable to discern much difference between opposing factions in the schools, "the Lefts being a little more Communistic and radical than the Rights, although the difference is very little." * The fact of the matter seems

---

* From *Cuba, Island of Paradox* © 1959 by Ruby Hart Phillips. Reprinted by permission of the author and Astor-Honor, Inc. New York, N. Y.

to be that the attainment of power was the immediate goal while ideology, and substantive goals were vague and easily pushed into the background.

To say that these associational, core groups were reformists would be inaccurate, but many of them believed in strong, humanitarian, and democratic goals of change which they recognized must come perforce through revolutionary devices. However, it is probably true that in the post-Machado chaos the only thing all factions could really agree upon was their hatred of the United States (and, throughout, the United States has had a most significant role in the Cuban turmoil). The vague goals of the anti-Machado revolutionaries, and the absence of a disciplined core group with an orderly program, was all too evident. There was no one to harden fine ideals into objectives, programs, and bureaucratic structure. It is evident, too, that as the "revolution" progressed, the idealistic students had power and control more firmly on their minds than they had a modified social structure. Mrs. Phillips wrote on September 8, 1933:

The Commissioners, Sergeant Batista and the Students, have spent the entire day on the Palace balcony addressing the crowd . . . This may be a revolutionary government supported by the entire nation, as the frenzied orators shout over the radio, but you never saw so many machine guns and rifles and revolvers in your life . . . [Pp. 195–196.]

The "Sergeant Batista," who was not a very status-worthy figure publicly at the time, was, however a crucially influential figure with the military, as well as a most persuasive speaker. Even Batista's adulating biographer, Edmund A. Chester, does not seem to claim any deep ideological commitment on the part of his hero and most observers would find him to have been simply and unqualifiedly concerned with power. In the post-Machado strife and fumblings, Batista emerges as the shrewd and amoral insurrectionist leader of the military and hence the key determining factor in the various successive reformulations of the government. His reformulations continued amid the violent opposition of the student groups, communists and other, particularly youth groups, which were now suppressed with blood curdling violence. To be sure, Batista's reformulations contained many welfare provisions directed toward consolidating a mass support, but he was fully alienated from the liberal groups of the revolution. Batista "stole" the revolution (Casuso, p. 87).

By the middle of 1940, the now Colonel Fulgencio Batista had so consolidated his position, first of power and then of mass support, that he was able to win the legal leadership of his country in an election. And so began anew the familiar stable military dictatorship, enforced by a shrewd mixture of indulgence and intrigue and incredible brutality. The movements which brought the downfall of Machado were now the movements, more disunited and poorly organized than before, toward the downfall of Batista. Batista and his government were little more than personnel replacements for the Machado regime. The forces for social change, such as they were, had been effectively shut out.

In another Latin American country, Mexico, the significance of revolution for social change has been utterly different (Blanksten, pp. 131–141). Mexico had a *real* revolution, not a dictatorial replacement.

Under the brutal dictatorial rule of General Porfirio Diaz, who held power from 1877 until 1911, unrest was general and mass organizational attempts were violently suppressed by the government. But organizational efforts were persistent and a revolutionary ideology was articulated. Diverse specific movements pursued their various facets of a program which in total—if unplanned—effect was anti-government, anti-church, anti-feudal, and anti-imperialist. Amid the quickened voices of protest and mass uprisings, the Diaz government was becoming senile both in the literal psychological sense as well as in a figurative sense of diminishing morale and effectiveness. As moderate leaders failed in their attempts to compromise between the old regime and the heterogeneous revolutionary forces, Diaz was forced to resign, and the revolutionary chaos with its reign of terror held sway. Revolutionists were against revolutionists in bloody battle; intellectuals were here visualizing the true revolution in anti-imperialist terms and there in anti-clerical or in land-reform terms. *La Tormenta*, the time of terror, did not break until 1920 with the strong-man Obregon and did not really end until the rise of General Cardenas in 1934. Yet each of the dictator presidents from 1920 brought certain phases of the revolutionary movement toward fruition. To be sure, power-control came first but with Obregon came a measure of land reform, with Calles came regulation of foreign capital and the Church, and with Cardenas came the end of terror and a compromised but nonetheless broad fruition of revolutionary ideology.

The case of Mexico approaches a true social total revolution in the same sense as that of Russia. To account for differences between an abortive "revolution of stasis" and the true revolution would require painstaking analysis. No doubt the accidents of leadership and of current international pressure are significant in these particular instances. However, it is also probable that important underlying differences existed in the breadth and depth of mass unrest and the capacity of the mass to articulate grievances. Also significant was the presence of a Mexican intelligentsia which provided a solid ideology for post-revolutionary actionists. The true revolution has its Marx, but it also must have its Lenin. Cuba, before Castro, lacked both. Mexico had stronger ideologists than it had ideologically rooted actionists, but following the period of revolutionary chaos there was at least an ideology still vigorously alive and supported by a collectively aroused mass.

LEADERSHIP IN SOCIAL MOVEMENTS

Leadership and followership in social movements is a quite different phenomenon from that found in the adoption of rational, technological items which lack ideological meaning. The early English manufacturer adopting new-fangled looms was neither a leader nor a follower in a social movement. He was a technological innovator in a series of distributive cultural changes. On the other hand, the weaver who worked up the bands to riot and to destroy the new looms which seemed to threaten the workers' secure world was leading in a collective action, an embryonic social movement. Machines have probably never been a rallying point for capitalists in a social reform movement. The Manchester industrialist did not buy his power loom in a fervor of crowd excitement nor hold it as a symbol and instrument of a new age. If the industrialist was a "revolutionary," it was unself-conscious. The "revolution" he initiated was no social movement; it was a latent consequence of various distributive and convergent changes, among them, the increasing adoption of more productive equipment.

The adopter of diffusing water pumps, weed killer, or television is no "joiner," no "convert," no adherent to a cause. He is not identifying with any we-group, nor with an ideological position. He is acting to change a status quo only in regard to his own private world. Of course it is possible, and indeed it frequently happens, that technological devices take on symbolic meaning and that ideologies are formed with reference to them, thus generating social movements. The Luddites formed such a movement against machines. The prohibition movement in the United States was centered around a widely used cultural trait which moralistis sought to destroy. The family planning movement relates to the diffusion of technological devices, but it is a true social movement with crusading fervor, ideology, and reform-valuative objectives.

Any discussion of leadership and followership in socio-cultural change must keep clearly in mind the distinction between distributive and collective changes, even though they may converge in actual events. At this point we are dealing with collective changes in which the leader-follower relationship is qualitatively different from that of "diffusion-adoption" leadership. The social movement leader is a man of personal symbolic value and a group decision maker and perhaps many other things besides. The diffusion-adoption leader is a personal decision maker who may or may not possess symbolic qualities and engender loyalty in a following. He often exercises the influence of example more than the influence of persuasion and personal power. The leader in adopting hybrid corn seed or television *may* convince. He does not convert.

Types of Movement Leaders

Dawson and Gettys, in connection with their natural history of social movements had much to say about leadership. The theory of stages subsumed a theory of leadership. According to this scheme, in the stage of unrest the leader is an *agitator*. He evokes dissatisfaction; he fans the coals of discontent and spreads them as well. The agitator does not focus on program, goals, or hopes. He arouses people whose condition of life or feelings make them susceptible to arousal.

Coming out of the stage of unrest into the popular stage, the leader becomes the "prophet," the inspired seer. This leader is of the charismatic type discussed by Max Weber (Weber, 1946, pp. 51–55; 1947, pp. 358–373). The charismatic leader is legitimated by inspiration, often of divine origin. His followers are disciples converted to a cause. He *calls* them in *his* name, and *his* name, in hundreds of movements, has been overtly or covertly identifiable with the name of God and his voice with the voice of God. He possesses *mana*. Charismatic leadership appears in any sphere of collective affairs. It is manifest in varying degrees in the Biblical prophets, in Elija Mohammed of the Black Muslims, in Adolf Hitler, Mohandas Gandhi, and in Fidel Castro and Franklin D. Roosevelt. Such leaders typically are contemptuous of routine orders of business and refuse to let the cause be fettered by confining rules and formal structures. Devotion to the leader as an embodiment of the movement's ideals is a major source of obedience and group morale.

The Dawson and Gettys formulation continues to follow Weber's analysis as they see a movement shifting from the popular to the formal stage. From the inspirational authority of the prophet, the leader role is transformed into that of the statesman. Leaders are those who can formulate organizational policy in this period of increasing formality in structure and articulate dreams into the solid facts of programs and policies. In Weber's terms, charismatic power has been "routinized." The prophetic leader cannot live forever to exercise his cohesive power. Though his charisma may to some extent "brush off" onto certain disciples, there are limitations to this, and furthermore dreams must ultimately be translated into programs and hard patterns for dealing with counter-movements which will be instituted. Charismatic movements are inherently unstable. They endure only as they become structured in, and in reference to, their community milieu. The "routinization of charisma," as Weber called it, may result in some crystallized, traditional organizational pattern or, as is usually the case, become bureaucratized into a legal authority structure for the movement which is now a formal organization.

With institutionalization, leadership shifts toward that of the states-man-executive. Now a stable part of the organized community structure, the movement has ceased to be a movement. Administration is the major leadership function in contrast to agitation, inspiration, and pro-gram development, respectively. In Weber's terms, the authority of law is now supreme. Obedience is to an impersonal principle rather than to a person. The government by men is ended and a government by law is administered by men.

It is obvious that the stylized and almost organismic conception of stages set up by Dawson and Gettys is too perfect to be fully true. It applies perfectly to certain movements and imperfectly to others. In formulating the theory, Methodism and its rise was an exemplary model. The theory applies most perfectly to movements which are separatist in nature, i.e., those in which there is visualized the establishment of a distinct sect or a distinct society or sub-society. The latter stages of the overall theory, and of its leadership facet, do not apply to reform move-ments which, like the Negro civil rights program, should ultimately vanish in accordance with their own concept of complete success. Where movements run the full institutional cycle the theory has found general support both in its general and its leadership phases.

Also it seems clear that some given individuals can perform a multi-plicity of leadership roles and that the leadership stages are not neces-sarily distinct from each other. Some leaders of great charismatic power also prove to be able statesmen and bureaucratic executives. It is ap-parent, too, that the popular leader who loses sight of the continuing value of charisma and of collective emotion may also lose his public—and his movement. Yet these qualifications do not seriously detract from the fundamental fact that the leadership types perform designated function in reference to distinct analytical phases of social movements. Edward A. Shils suggests that many depression-born radical movements failed be-cause they lacked organizing leadership toward a formal stage (Shils, 1954).

Leaders as Social Types

"Agitators," "prophets," and "messiahs" are not average run-of-the-mill persons, and there is some justified presumption that people who respond to their calls are not a perfect cross-section of the population. However, it does not follow that either leaders or followers in social movements generally represent some lunatic fringe or even a socially maladjusted sector of the population. We cannot begin with an assumption of ab-normality or pathology in directing our attention either to movement leaders or adherents. This highly controversial issue in change theory is particularly complicated by the difficulty in extricating motivational patterns from personality attributes and both of these from the question of the individual's relationship to the broader social order. In the present discussion we are primarily interested in the latter problem, but necessarily the matter of motive and of personality attributes must arise.

In recent years, some students of change, notably Homer Barnett, have suggested that persons who are peripheral to their own culture or disenchanted with it become ready subjects to innovative ideas. Barnett suggested that acceptors of innovation be grouped in four categories depending upon their attitudes toward the "novelty equivalents" traditional in their society. That is to say that the classification rests upon attitude toward that part of the traditional order which is to be supplanted by the proposed innovation. Use of the term "traditional" here implies that Barnett is thinking of innovations which touch the moral order—the valued social fabric of a people. In any event, Barnett's classification (Chap. 14) seems to hold particular relevance for situations giving rise to social movements. The advocates of change he specifies as:

1. *The Dissident,* or those who have consistently refused to identify themselves with certain conventions of their group
2. *The Indifferent,* or those who are apathetic or ambivalent toward the established order and are uncommitted
3. *The Disaffected,* or persons who start out as full participants in their culture but develop a negative attitude toward it due to personal experiences, e.g., disillusionment
4. *The Resentful,* or those who are negativistic toward their own place in the social order but enamored of the positions held by more favored individuals

Each of the conditions suggested by Barnett unquestionably contributes to the support of innovations and movements toward innovations which are disruptive to the normative status quo. Kornhauser also has cited many studies supporting the idea that persons who lack a sense of belonging, who are alienated, "marginal," or uprooted, are ready subjects for movements which promise them a place in the community and the larger society. Related to this is Hagen's thesis that persons who have undergone status deprivation are those who lead out in enterprise toward economic development. Ultimately leadership in change, in Hagen's view, can be traced to pathology in the individual's socialization. Even Rogers (Chap. 7), discussing technological and generally non-emotive cultural innovations, appears to feel that innovators are "in step with a different drummer" and, in a qualified sense, are "deviants."

There are several reasons for the "deviant-marginal-pathology" interpretation of advocacy in social change. One of these lies in the age-old confusion of *dissent* with social maladjustment. It goes without saying that persons who would reform the social order perceive certain unacceptable features in that order as it exists. Such individuals *may* be alienated or marginal or mal-socialized types, but these concepts lose their meaning when we apply them to Franklin D. Roosevelt the leader and advocate of New Deal changes in American government or when we apply them to Mohandas Gandhi, a charismatic type if there ever was one, who led the movement against orthodoxy in regard to caste in India, or to Washington, Jefferson, and Franklin who plotted and executed a revolution against constituted governmental authority. It is difficult to consider seriously the idea that these reform and revolutionary leaders were mixed-up, socially maladjusted crackpots or even alienated or "marginal" lost souls. They were dissenters with tenets of the status quo, and they possessed crucial though diverse qualities of leadership. To dissent and to lead is perhaps not characteristic of the mass of people, but it is certainly not pathological.

In Barnett's theory it is probable that his bias arises not from his analysis but from the selectivity of the types of change situations which he analyzed. Barnett's ideas were strongly influenced by his analysis of a religious movement among American Indians, Shakerism. The Shaker movement was a millenarian, messianic cult of despair. It was a movement whose function was to give meaning to those "who had been sensitized to the vapidity and emptiness of their lives" (p. 397). That Barnett's conclusions apply to Shakerism there is no doubt. There is no basis in Barnett's work to think that they justify extension much beyond such expressive and separatist movements.

Richard Adams has suggested that Barnett's theory of change should be limited to movements which are rapid and violent.[1] It seems reasonable that they have implications also for movements characterized by a high degree of expressionism and retreat, as in revitalization movements.

Social reform, whether radical or reactionary, appeals to persons who have emotional stakes in preserving their society. This frame of mind may be due to value conviction, pecuniary self-interest, or other bonding agents. It would, therefore, be ridiculous to suggest that participants in any movements which spread "reform" are necessarily disenchanted,

---

[1] Barnett's position has been criticized constructively by a number of writers. Perti J. Pelto believes that Barnett's hypothesis operates most clearly in societies which make the individual subservient to the group and applies least in societies stressing individual freedom. Herbert Menzel's criticism appears extreme when he discounts the "marginality" hypothesis on the basis of results in the study of drug diffusion among physicians. To find that marginality and related conditions are unrelated to the diffusion of rational technology does not mean that those conditions may not be associated with changes brought through collective excitement and social movements.

alienated, or "marginal" individuals. The WCTU, for example, as a social movement pressing for new legislation, was a movement in which emotion-laden social conformists and traditionalists were the ones showing greatest suggestibility. Disenchantment was present only in displeasure at the flaunting of certain traditional norms. Emotional identification with tradition is similarly significant in many nationalistic and/or revivalistic movements, often by persons resentful at acculturative changes in their valued order. This does not gainsay the fact that lost souls may find psychological supports as participants in a crusade, regardless of their value commitments. Even in nationalistic, revivalistic movements wherein leaders are in fact "marginals," followers need not be. Thus an English educated elite can lead a nationalistic and nativistic revival in a new Asian or an African nation. Here, perhaps, is the violent rejection of "marginalism" by culturally marginal leaders who, if they fully identify with either social world, must identify with the Asian or African; otherwise they would be lost in a Western world which they know intellectually and in which they share culturally but not socially. Lest we attach too much significance to this, it is to be recalled that the counter-leaders who seek social and cultural fusions with the West are also "marginal." In regard to South Asia, Cambridge and Oxford have produced both sorts of "marginals" with about equal facility.

Daniel Lerner in the *Passing of Traditional Society* suggests that persons who lead in the urbanization movement in peasant locales are marginals between the village and city ways of life. He finds in such persons a high development of the capacity to empathize—to mentally transport themselves outside the surrounding traditionalism and "feel" the way of modern living. Similarly, Leo Silberman, following a lead by Professor Schumpeter, has discussed the concept of "social entrepreneur," the folk society member who is not bound by his culture and, in his susceptibilities to more secular ways, acts as middle-man to his people. To be sure, the movement of urbanism into the peasant world is not necessarily a social movement in the sense that the term is used here. However, many aspects of secular change require conscious rejection of norms and symbols precious to the old ways. It seems a truism that those who lead out in individual or in collective movement toward a drastically changed social order are those least bound by the values of the traditional order. However, Lerner offers no indication that such individuals are anomic or alienated—in fact his "transitionals" seemed *happier* persons at least than those solidly within the traditional order. This was also evident in *Sinhalese Village* where it was found that the persons most westernized in their attitudes were poor ritualists and were not thought to be particularly *pious people*, but these individuals were not isolated in any sense and could not be thought of in terms of "disenchantment" or "status deprived" (Ryan *et al.*). They were highly participant, well-respected, and well-to-do peasant land holders.

In regard to value-oriented, reform movements, Seymour Lipset has demonstrated the inaccuracy of the social maladjustment theory of social change leadership with suggestive implications as to how the idea arises. Lipset studied the C.C.F., a radical social and economic reform movement which gained substantial political power in Saskatchewan Province, Canada, during the 1940's. As is often true with social movements, ground was laid for the C.C.F. in strong social class cleavages. Lipset observes that:

> The statistical data on the backgrounds of the C.C.F. leaders demonstrate that in Saskatchewan a radical movement for economic reform was led at the "grass roots" by the people with status within the farming and working classes. *The local leaders of the party were not the marginal or deviant members of the society, but rather were the "old" class leaders.* This process was highly visible in the rural communities of Saskatchewan, since the class and community leaders were largely the same people. A class or community will not accept the leadership of its deviant members. The C.C.F. was able to grow rapidly in Saskatchewan because the "normal" class leaders were the first to become C.C.F.-ers. [P. 360.]

Lipset concludes that it is entirely reasonable that Harold Lasswell found members and leaders of the Communist Party of Chicago to be disproportionately maladjusted socially. Such a circumstance can arise, but only where a small party is not a genuine expression of larger scale social pressures. In such instances *the group itself* is marginal to the society and may well have differential attraction to marginal social types. But if such a party stimulates a significant social movement, it will necessarily attract the normally integrated members of the community. The C.C.F. from the beginning was a large popularly based movement led by the "normal" integrated leaders of the concerned groups.

Lacking detailed information on personal backgrounds, it would be fairly safe to observe that what was true for the C.C.F. was probably true for the feminist movement, the temperance movement, and the Vietnam peace movement. Most leaders in these movements were not disenchanted with their social order nor alienated from it, counter-movement propaganda to the contrary notwithstanding. They were trying to save a social order and make it work more effectively. And in one way or another the leaders were integrated with and status-worthy within their respective "classes."

There is reasonable evidence that many movements are led initially by persons who are closely integrated in sub-societies which are imperfectly integrated with the overall social order. Lipset observes that, based on his data, it would appear that *"when a class's attitudes are in a process*

of flux because of changing social and economic pressure, those individ-
uals, who are most integrated in the class through formal organization are
the first to change" (p. 361). This general position has some support
in Rudolph Heberle's analysis of the rise of Nazism in Germany. The
Nazi movement crystallized the long-standing feeling of "national un-
belonging." Heberle concludes that the movement was of adjusted individuals within unadjusted groups.

THE FOLLOWERS

Max Weber's typology of motivations was used by Heberle (pp. 94–
100) to locate four types of individuals who find appeal in social movements. These are theoretic formulations, and a single individual may
embody more than a single type of motivation. First are those who
affiliate because of belief in the righteousness of the cause. Such motivation is termed *value-rational* inasmuch as it is based upon deliberate
assessment of the validity of the ideas of a movement in furthering a
"good goal." A second class of participants are those motivated by
emotions such as resentment or the charm of a leader. This type is called
emotional-affectual. The third motivational type is *traditional.* Here individuals subscribe to the movement through adherence to long-established views and practices of their community, family, class, or other
group with which they identify. Southern Democrats exemplified this as
they long deplored their party's activities, but until the 1964 presidential
election stood solidly behind it at the polls. (34.4% of those Democrats
interviewed in a Gallup Poll relating to the 1943 presidential election
stated, "I always vote for this party.") Finally Heberle identifies those
who join a movement in expectation of personal advantage. This is
purposive-rational motivation, such as that exhibited by a depression-hit
mid-western farmer joining a radical movement aimed at nullification
of debts or a moratorium on farm foreclosures. With the growth of
power in a movement this motivation becomes dominant as individuals
seek to protect their interests even in spite of personal opposition to the
movement. This Heberle refers to as the *band wagon effect.* It is apparent that the varied motivations indicated above will appeal to individuals of differing personality characteristics and differing relationships to the status quo.

Many writers suggest that personality factors influence participation in
social movements. It is variously asserted that the neurotics and psychotics, and other abnormal personality types are motivated toward participation. Heberle shows that the personality-defect approach to participation in social movements leaves much to be desired and is subject to
serious qualifications. It is no doubt true, as Barnett says, that supporters

of many movements come from among those who are, or expect to be, frustrated by the existing order. They hopefully see relief from anxiety in the success of the movement. Correspondingly, opposition to the movement, or collective support of a status quo, is an action in response to anxiety in the face of threatened change. This, however, is a far cry from inferring that personality maladjustments or pathologies exist in the leaders or participants in social movements. Possibly the emphasis upon the personality maladjustments in movement leaders is an Anglo-American bias. In a country with numerous institutionalized mechanisms for accomplishing social reform, or for resisting proposed changes, those who resort to the techniques of collective behavior may well be more marginal than would be the case in countries having few mechanisms for orderly change. In recent years psychoanalytic writers have developed the idea of movement participation arising from frustrations which are expressed in aggressive action toward persons not responsible for the frustrations, i.e., "displaced aggression." Interpretations of Nazi leadership and Nazi appeals to the masses have been offered in terms ranging from mass "psychosis" to multiple frustrations. To these points Heberle sagely writes:

Among the founders of militant social movements, political as well as religious, we find a fair proportion of abnormal personalities; especially of neurotic and paranoiac individuals. The same is true of the early adherents of such leaders, the first disciples or followers. Although no statistical information is available, it is safe to say that, for example, among the early followers and collaborators of Adolf Hitler the proportion of abnormal individuals was probably significantly greater than in any other political movement of the time. This writer has known quite a large number of men and a few women who joined the Nazi Party before 1933 or soon after the seizure of power. In most of these cases he finds strong indications of frustration—disappointments in their careers, conflicts or frictions in marriage, absence of or unsatisfactory nature of sexual relations, and so forth. But, he also remembers similar types among members of a middle-of-the-road liberal club in Germany. After 1933, when the "bandwagon effect" came into play, the proportion of frustrated individuals among the members of the N.S.D.A.P. (National Socialist German Workers' Party) must have decreased to approximately the average proportion in the nation. The more extreme cases of Hitler, Hess, Goebbels, Streicher, Ley, and many minor figures in the Nazi hierarchy are now well known. Hitler's notorious craziness and the large number of crackpots among the early Nazis were one reason why the movement in the beginning was not taken seriously by most of its opponents.

The psychoanalytic explanation of the personality of a man like Hitler is obviously a fascinating task, but a rather hopeless one for lack of reliable data. A great deal of significance has, for example, been ascribed to the childhood experiences of modern dictators. A stern and authoritarian father has become a standard feature in the biographies of revolutionary leaders and a welcome basis for psychoanalytic interpretation of the leader's personality. Unfortunately, and contrary to the conditions under which clinical psychoanalysis operates, there is usually no possibility of checking the accuracy of these more or less legendary childhood experiences of great men; it is even more difficult to ascertain how they were experienced by the budding dictator himself. However, it must be remembered that millions of men have had stern and strict fathers without becoming dictators or even minor figures in militant social movements. [Pp. 110–111.] *

Numerous frustrated individuals, and no doubt seriously defective personality types, were concerned with Nazism as they are with other movements . . . and non-movements. In the case of Germany, Heberle observes that their frustrations were the result of reaction to personal experiences, not to the Treaty of Versailles, or the depression (p. 108). And, even among the Nazis, frustrated individuals were probably a minority. Not all Germans became Nazis—the real Nazis remained a minority; further, not all Nazis were frustrated; furthermore, not all frustrated individuals became Nazis.

The realistic though perhaps unsatisfying conclusion is that persons who rebel against the status quo or rise to its support, are individuals who perceive threat or security to self or to cherished values. These may indeed include maladjusted individuals, but not necessarily so in any personality sense. As Heberle observes, the neurotic and maladjusted are probably attracted more because of their sense of isolation and helplessness rather than by the objectives of the movements. In any case, motivational study is a small part of movement analysis.

As social movements progress toward institutional status, leadership, and rank and file as well, become increasingly conservative. In the early stages of movements there is room for fanatics, extremists, and prophets. This is the time for charismatic leaders, extraordinary individuals who draw forth unity in the group through the magnetism of their personalities. Such power can be only temporary. For persistence of the movement, charisma must be routinized. There is also room in such movements for adherents who are intellectually and rationally concerned with the objectives as well as for the alienated who find social support in belonging to the cause. As emotional states of devotion and fervor cool off, leadership is subordinated to the authority of office. Prophecy gives way to development, plans, and blueprints. Order based upon emotional rapport is supplanted by rules of conduct and procedural law. The conversion of new members gives way to recruitment on the basis of purposive self-interest and the rational support of value premises. In this transition the social movement becomes part of the legitimate social order. Abnormal persons and maladjusted persons no doubt remain, but the group itself moves toward integration in a social order composed of groups which, like itself, hold members who are drawn by diverse motives and possess wide ranges in personality attributes.

CONCLUSION

Social movements manifest the deliberate and conscious efforts of human beings acting collectively toward social change or its prevention. Actually social movements to "prevent" change cannot be fully successful since the very rejection of change forces modification, if only in the protective mechanisms for the established order. Often counter-movements against proposed change are movements which also demand change in the sense of reaction. It is difficult to conceive of any social movement which is without significance for modification in the social order, and most movements are directly and deliberately concerned with bringing about changes.

Social movements induce innovation through the collective interaction of people rather than through inventing and diffusing of cultural novelties. Frequently, however, movements arise to promote or suppress cultural inventions. The contrast between the change processes of social movements and processes whereby cultural traits are invented and diffused is suggested in the subtly different terminology conventionally applied to each. Movements often spread as "crusades," but we do not usually think of them spreading by "diffusion." The innovative *message* of the movement is accepted by the recipient more as "conversion" than as "adoption." Similarly, cultural diffusion operates through *cosmopolitans* and *influentials*, whereas movements spread through *advocates* and *evangelists*. In the growth of a movement we speak of *leaders* and of *followers*, whereas in an instance of cultural diffusion we may more precisely speak in terms of *innovators* and *laggards*. Diffusion may or may not stir emotions; movements always do.

There are several ways in which social movements operate toward change. These are expressed to some extent in the typological terms of "reform movements," "revitalistic movements," "revolutionary movements," and "expressive movements." Of these, only expressive ones are manifestly without significance for social change. Expressive movements, despite their participation orientation rather than social goal orientation, nonetheless actually effect social changes. Expressive movements are practically by definition separatist ones. Insofar as a movement results in a new institutionalized group within the community, it has successfully introduced social change. The social order now possesses an added range in its sub-cultural and sub-societal units. New sub-cultural patterns have been institutionalized. Existing groups must create or accept new accommodative patterns in reference to the new organization that has entered the community's constellations of sub-groups. Also, expressive, inward-directed groups often undergo transformations as they proceed through their cycle of development. The sect or cult which is concerned strictly with the inner salvation of its members frequently becomes program oriented as it approaches institutionalization. Revitalistic cargo cults may originate in millenarian dreams but end as violent nativistic revolts against alien aggressors. Equally deep long-range changes may be inspired by the movements of failure, as native peoples lose the zest for life and literally withdraw from it (Rivers; O'Brien).

In reform movements, success comes presumably only as the social order is modified in accordance with stated objectives. These may be limited objectives after the attainment of which the movement collapses, or the movement may have achieved sufficient structure to continue pursuit of new objectives in keeping with its ideology. In any case, further changes are postulated as the society responds and adjusts to the achievement of every immediate reform. Additionally, since reform movements typically engender counter-movements, the failure of the original movement can result in *reactionary trends* if newly inspired counter-movements gain ascendency. In the battle of contending groups, an outcome can be quite different from that sought by either.

In revolutionary movements, whatever else may be true, it is certain that even immediate social change will not be limited to the manifest goals of the revolution. Reform movements operate within the legitimate framework of the social order. Revolutionary movements threaten the very social order or significant sectors of it. Unsuccessful revolutions of any significance do not merely fade away leaving the society as it was. Counter-movements of suppression are themselves modifications of the legitimate order, as in restriction of civil liberties following insurrection. And in most revolutionary situations of significance, the interplay of revolutionary factions as well as the actions of counter-revolutionaries during a time of terror can basically warp revolutionary objectives.

Social movements are typically vehicles of change when tensions come close to the moral fabric of the society or to the deeply emotionalized collective interests of groups or large categories of people. To attribute the growth of social movements to the influence of psychopathic or sociopathic leaders who exert their power upon the disenchanted and alienated mass is to overlook the very normality of social movements in a changing social order. While certain types of movements may be led by marginal and alienated persons, perhaps even with psychopathic qualities, these do not usually have much mass support or appeal. Leaders of movements are more typically persons who are closely integrated with their own sub-groups within the social order. However, these groups themselves frequently are not smoothly integrated with the overall social order. While anomic and alienated persons find participant satisfactions in a movement, successful movements do not go far without stable, integrated adherents who believe in its ideology and come to respect the discipline of a growing organization.

8

Acceptance or Rejection
of Innovation

Cultural change does not occur until an innovation has gained response. In the present chapter we are concerned with the forces which operate in the "responsive situation." The responsive act is not as simple as the terms "acceptance" or "rejection" imply (Barnett, pp. 388–389). Response may simply involve attitudinal acceptance or negation or it may be overt. The potential recipient may grab at the bait or he may merely nibble. Yet again he may be favorably disposed toward it, but not be hungry at the moment, or perhaps be physically restrained from following out his latent tendencies into overt behavior.

In this discussion we will not distinguish between attitude and overt behavior except where the distinction is particularly useful. The two are closely and positively correlated. Their distinction, however, is something to bear in mind. The nuclear bomb as an idea has been widely known and a little less widely approved by the American public, but this obviously does not mean that individual citizens buy or replicate nuclear bombs for themselves. The idea has been communicated. "Acceptance" implies support for bomb manufacture, and possibly its use, by the U.S. government (Katz). Also, men may be enthusiastic about bikinis or miniskirts, but this doesn't mean that they wear them themselves, nor even that they buy them for their wives. Attitudes held by persons for whom the innovation is personally irrelevant from the standpoint of overt action are important for the diffusion process. It is the idea of "bikini" which diffuses—the material is a manifestation of that idea—a very flimsy manifestation of a notable idea. We are here more explicitly concerned with the forces yielding favorable and unfavorable tendencies to act (attitudes) than with overt behavior. For simplicity's sake we will frequently engage in the fiction that attitude and overt action are perfectly correlated and refer simply to "response."

Response to innovation arises in a culminating decision as the potential recipient makes his judgment. This judgment is rooted in a number of different assessments. Just how many varieties of assessment are involved depends somewhat upon the individual and the innovation. Even seemingly simple acceptances like hoola hoops and bouffant hair-dos involve complex factors of which he or she may be only vaguely aware. Our problem, then, is to outline the variables in the response situation in a sociologically meaningful way. An effort will be made to show how these interact supportively and opposingly to determine an eventual judgment. In this analysis we must bear in mind that the various forces in the innovative situation can yield a stalemate. Under action circumstances, at least, indecision falls to the negative side of the balance, since acceptance means something more positive than the absence of rejection.

COMPONENTS OF THE RESPONSIVE SITUATION

We may conceive of every innovation as being presented to an actor for his evaluation. A human organism with a particular personality is faced with a concrete novelty. A decision of some sort must be reached if only by negation through shrugging the shoulders.

The novelty presents itself in a situation that is composed of six different elements or variables, two of which are, of course, the actor himself and the innovation. The remaining four dimensions of the situation are (1) The social position of the actor, e.g., his statuses and his social referents. (2) The intervening cultural factors such as the values and world view or ethos which color all perceptions of the actor. (3) The intervening facts which surround the advent of the innovation itself, e.g., the repute of the media through which it is diffused and other circumstantial and often accidental factors. (4) The qualities of the perceptive process, i.e., the criteria upon which the actor judges the innovation as a basis for conscious decision. We suggest here that these evaluative perceptions or criteria are of four different sorts: (a) his evaluation in terms of the innovation's consistency with sacred norms and undefilable truths and symbols; (b) evaluation of the novelty in terms of its efficacy and efficiency; (c) evaluation in regard to its desirability; (d) evaluation in terms of aesthetic standards, including style, fashion, and taste. How well will it work? Is it, or its imputed effects, good or at least not bad? Does it work toward goals with which the recipient is identified?, i.e., does it appear to do what he wants done? Is it aesthetically pleasing?

These criteria are essentially an adaptation of Max Weber's action theory (Parsons, 1937, Chap. 17). In his terms, evaluation of novelty proceeds by the tests of the "efficiency norms of rationality," "legitimacy norms," and "matters of taste." We have here accepted these, creating a fourth simply by abstracting from the actor himself the criterion of "desirability."

Each of the situational elements specified is a complex cluster of variables, some at the level of organic and psychological functioning, other relating to social structure, and still others to cultural norms and ethos. Pro or con decision is reached in the culmination of balances among these various forces and influences. In some instances a particular innovation may have zero value in regard to certain of the variables. For example, the introduction of a new cut of beef into a Christian home has no normative significance—in contrast, of course, to a similar innovation in a Hindu cultural setting. For most Westerners beef is normatively neutral. Not all innovations are so clear-cut. A normatively negative value of birth control, for example, is for some individuals countered against their recognition of its goal-achieving desirability.

Perhaps even more complicated is the evaluation of efficiency and efficacy. Here we must move into the realm of economic decisions in which comparative costs of alternative devices enter the decision situation. In the following pages, we hope to do little more than lay out some patterned features of the innovative decision situation. Little can be done at this stage in analyzing the actual interplay among them in the real world of change. At various points, however, illustrative cases will be used with but little more purpose than to alert us to the complexities of balance among variables. We will begin by considering the least social of the variables, the actor as a human being.

The Actor as a Human Being

Acceptance of a new pattern of thinking or of overt behavior requires an expenditure of energy greater than maintenance of the old pattern. The individual becomes habituated to patterns of thought and overt action. A stimulus which requires modification of these must be greater than a stimulus which can be responded to through habitual patterns. Howsoever slight compared with other factors, there is a real psychological barrier to the acceptance of innovation among all individuals. A person who has learned one way of solving a problem will likely continue solving similar problems by this method though a newcomer might see simpler solutions (Chaplin; Krawiec, pp. 284–295). Once committed to a groove—or once the pathways are established—there is a strain toward retention. More energy is required to change than to preserve the psychological status quo.

Evidence has long been available in support of this observation, and the folk saying "You can't teach an old dog new tricks" has close enough approximation to the idea to gain widespread acceptance. V. Stefansson, the Arctic explorer, reported that when he changed the diet of his sled dogs the old dogs showed great resistance (Barnett, p. 386). The proverb, however, is scarcely accurate. The *aging* process appears correlated with declining *willingness* to do new tricks, but this is not the same as declining capacity, or even ability, to learn new tricks. As Barnett shows, there is substantial evidence to support this observation in human behavior as well.

Participants in any given culture are familiar with tools of particular design and are habituated to motor skills associated with them. Foster reports, for example, an attempt to introduce a raised cooking stove in the Cook Islands. Such a stove would have the advantage of protecting food from animals and dirt while being cooked and also make needless the constant bending and squatting of women while doing their cooking. The new stoves were rejected because these women found it more tiring to stand up to the stove than to stoop and squat over a ground-level fire (Foster, p. 88).

The human organism itself, as well as its habituation to culturally derived patterns of thought and muscular action, sets limits to the acceptability of innovation. Motor habituation and the firmness of thought patterns described in the concept of *Einstsellung* are, however, more or less readily qualified when situational stimuli outweigh these stabilizing forces. This is frequent—and often very simple—else new ideas and new skills would not take hold. As regards the fundamental restrictions imposed by the organic limitations of man, the story is different. A bicycle which required a third leg for its efficient propulsion would not be a good bet as the invention of the year. Nor can we expect the speed and retentive capacity of electronic calculators in the human brain. It is within man's organic capacity to create electronic brains, but it is not within his capacity to utilize manpower with equal speed in precisely the same problems. Human brains just don't seem to work this way. While we rarely think much about the way man's organism limits new patterns of thought and action, it is apparent that the directions of inventive activity are partly bound by organic facts. Interestingly enough, the immense range of variability in man's cultures testifies to his organism's adaptive capacity. Space explorations have in considerable part been devoted to determining the limits of the human organism to withstand previously unknown strains. Associated inventive processes have been geared to the expanding knowledge of man's organic capacity.

Within any given society it is apparent that different actors of the same age and occupation show different susceptibilities to proposed innovations. Some seem to have "innovative" personalities, while others are "hold outs," "conservatives," "laggards," or skeptics of the new. Such differences probably have little to do with organic factors, except as organic factors interact with social ones in the determination of personality.

Position in the Social Structure

It is evident that one's social position influences what is to his self-interest. In other ways as well, social position, vertically and horizontally, bears upon the actor's view of an innovation. It is as if a man in Death Valley might look upon Mt. Whitney as unscalable while a person standing on a neighboring though lesser peak sees challenge and potential glory in its ascent. A proposed innovation may be feasible or infeasible, desirable or undesirable, depending upon the social position of the actor. Position in the social hierarchy with its associated prerogatives of power and authority may determinately intervene upon all other considerations. The man of wealth views an innovation from a different perspective from that of the poor man. The question is not one of economic rationality in accepting or rejecting but one of economic capacity to act. Such capacity is translated into ways of looking at the world in which the "financially impossible" can be thrust outside an individual's orbit of consideration.

Similarly the actor's position in the authority structure of his society may render him incapable of even giving consideration to an innovation. Response to innovation involves a decision. To form a decision mentally or overtly requires imaginary constructions, i.e., as to the state of affairs with the innovation added. Potential innovations may be passed by because the individual does not conceive himself as having authority to make the type of decision required. The innovation is deemed irrelevant to the individual for purposes of active acceptance or rejection, although clearly he might perceive that its acceptance (by one in authority to accept) would influence his own life. In a Nigerian province studied by Ronald Cohen, strong governmental authority was so much a fact of daily life that peasants were suspicious of a new fertilizer on the grounds that if it were worthwhile the government would have required its use and not merely recommended it (pp. 21–36).

This state of affairs is less apparent in Western civilization than in some others. Here a wide range of decision making is viewed as a part of individual responsibility. However, all people operate within authority hierarchies in recognition of which they refuse to act upon certain innovations because of weak authority position. A college professor, for instance, might find great attractiveness in a novel plan of dismissing classes in favor of concentrated library study. His position in a hierarchy of authority would probably preclude his acting upon this sentiment—if he considered it. The GI does not engage in innovative behavior in regard to his uniform design howsoever appealing some new fabric and tailoring. This is not because such change is irrelevant to him. Here is a realm of innovative decision making which is not his, as defined in the legitimate social order, and it is one which he usually does not think much about— accepting the realities of the formal decision-making system. Position in the authoritarian hierarchy defines the realms within which the actor is open to consider innovations.

In many societies a wide range of innovative decisions is not subject to individual action. Under some conditions this is true because of highly developed authority structures permeating most phases of life. Elsewhere it is true because most decisions are viewed as group responsibilities rather than individual ones. Today the novel idea of courtship and romantic marriage is entering countries like India and Ceylon, but it is finding very slow acceptance. This is not because young people are uninterested in the idea. Some of them will sigh longingly at the thought of a "romantic" rather than an arranged marriage. But, apart from other forces leading to rejection of this innovation, there is the fact that morally the choice of a marriage partner is not an individual decision. The new concept defies a moral tradition in decision making. Spouses are to be selected by family groups with parents as the major authority figures. The young person may sigh but at the same time push the decision from him as really not being his affair. And many youth will not even sigh for the innovation; they view it as a kind of unreal practice engaged in by others but for them a matter simply outside the realm of consideration— much as American youth used to feel about Samoan sex life when they read Margaret Mead's *Coming of Age in Samoa*. Few individuals beat their breasts and wail at their incapacity to act in reference to the innovation, though the idea makes a gradual impact.

In many non-Western societies an individual occupies relatively fixed positions in networks of reciprocities with kinsmen and others. Innovation may here be viewed not in terms of personal authority to decide, but from the vantage point of the actor's responsibilities and expectations in reference to various others. The idea of using wage labor on one's land may be rejected because it disrupts reciprocities which the owner values.

The individual special position in the social structure conditions and influences all manner of evaluations. Differences in social position are associated with differences in self-interest. They are also associated with different conceptions of feasibility, or efficacy, since persons in differing positions have different kinds of knowledge with which to test the innovation. In highly differentiated societies this is especially true. The perspective of the laboring man on the issue of socialized medicine contrasts with that of the physician. Their differing positions in society also yield different needs and different ideas of personal self-interest. Further, social position entails differing viewpoints as to what the moral order really is. The executive from his vantage point can interpret the innovation as a sacrifice of the best values of American individualism, while the laborer sees the same innovation as fulfillment of the charter of human rights. The influence of self-interest in this particular issue can be nullified if we take for our illustration the position of the professor of engineering as compared with the professor of social science. It is probable that significant differences exist in the ideological perspectives of engineers and social scientists.

The intervening character of social position upon reaction to the novel is also evident in the influences exerted by associates for or against acceptance. Portions of the individual's immediate social world provide him with reference functions in the formation of judgment. Assessments of the new are not made in personal isolation. The actor is influenced by the views and actions of others whose judgment is respected or whose support is protective in the risk required by innovative behavior. The crucial significance of social affiliations for innovative response has been seen earlier in the discussion of diffusion process. For present purposes we have assumed that the actor is aware of the innovation. Step 1 in the flow of diffusion. Step 2 is the process of conviction, and here the referent and supporting power of associates overlays their possible significance as simple informational sources. The study of the diffusion of a new drug (see pp. 163–164 above) demonstrates how such social support—or its absence—influences physicians in its adoption. This is an influence which intervenes upon the actor—making that process a truly social as well as psychological one. Even where opinion leaders are non-existent and trusted confidants are not consulted, the individual forms his judgment with some regard to its effect upon his continued standing in his personally significant social world.

World View or Ethos

Beyond the norms and techniques of a people, even beyond their conscious goals and values, societies develop characteristic ways of viewing and of relating man to nature, to the supernatural, and to other men. All this is the posture of a society, its "bent," its "genius." When viewed from the standpoint of norms this has often been dealt with in terms of themes and patterns. When the scheme of values is summed, the descriptive conclusions are frequently called the "ethos" of a people. And when conceptions of man and his place in the universe are assessed, we deal in what is often termed "world view." These various abstractions are closely related, and distinctions are not readily made between them. In this discussion the term "world view" will be used to include what some might deem to be the "culture pattern" and "ethos." We are concerned here with how men in differing cultures view society, nature, and super-nature and how these conceptions may affect the assessment of innovation. Relevance of these matters to the acceptance of change will be discussed in only two of many possible dimensions: (1) the concept of man's place in nature, and (2) the normative-valuative concept of man's relationship to man.

Robert Redfield has observed that it is the modern Western world which has come to look upon nature as simply the physical matter which man is to master to his greater material comfort. "I read that it is Descartes," says Redfield, "who enunciated the principle that the fullest exploitation of matter to *any* use is the whole duty of man" (p. 110). Western man has set himself apart from the realm of nature. Indeed so real has become this distinction that Western man sees no room to cavil with an assertion which assumes that man and animal are distinct. Man is made to rule the earth and that which is in it. God stands above all as the Master Designer. The lesser animals, with plants and mineral resources, are placed here for man, the unique and incomparable, to exploit. This viewpoint is far from universal. It is merely the view of a particular branch of human society which has in this world view proved itself mighty in the exploitation of that which God in nature provided. Our belief in a man-centered universe is so ingrained that we forget that it is an invention.

In many other cultures, perhaps virtually all except as they are influenced by the West, man's relationship with nature is different. Very widely the distinction is not drawn which makes man naturally pre-eminent among God's creations. The materials of nature are not viewed simply as instruments and materials to be unconcernedly exploited. Man's relationship to natural resources and to natural products has a sacredness. In much of South Asia, for example, rice and its production is more than a way of making a living. Rice and its production is almost a moral matter. The Ceylonese peasant ritualizes practically every aspect of rice growing; threshing takes place in an almost spiritual atmosphere. In earlier days, even while the finished rice was cooking, the household preserved silence. With such a view of a food crop, it is not surprising that farmers do not consider alternative crops in the manner of an Iowa farmer. Rice is not merely a means to the end of survival. It is hallowed in and of itself. So also is the earth and its products to a greater extent in primitive societies which emphasize the unity of man with nature and super-nature. Consider the problem of one who would spread agriculture among peoples who conceive the earth as an inviolate mother. Smohalla, a prophet of a revitalizing religious cult among the Yakima in the

1880's, observed in the course of an emotion-laden interview with Major MacMurray who was trying to calm the Indians by getting them to settle down to agriculture:

"You ask me to plow the ground! Shall I take a knife and tear my mother's bosom? Then when I die she will not take me to her bosom to rest.

"You ask me to dig for stone! Shall I dig under her skin for her bones? Then when I die I cannot enter her body to be born again.

"You ask me to cut grass and make hay and sell it, and be rich like white men! But how dare I cut off my mother's hair?"

And in reply to another officer who pointed out that even Indians had to work during the fishing season to store up food for winter, Smohalla answered:

"This work lasts only for a few weeks. Besides it is natural work and does them no harm. But the work of the white man hardens soul and body. Nor is it right to tear up and mutilate the earth as white men do."

And when another officer asserted that the Indians dug roots and other foods from the earth, he replied:

"We simply take the gifts that are freely offered. We no more harm the earth than would an infant's fingers harm its mother's breast. But the white man tears up large tracts of land, runs deep ditches, cuts down forests, and changes the whole face of the earth. You know very well this is not right. Every honest man," said he looking at me searchingly, "knows in his heart that this is all wrong. But the white men are so greedy that they do not consider these things." [Mooney, pp. 720–721, 724.]

Such basic conceptions of man's place in nature go beyond merely the valuation of tradition versus progress (Wax). They reflect wholly different modes of viewing the world—not simply differing moral conceptions, but differing perspectives which unquestionably relate to the acceptance of change. Western man, with his exploitative ethos borne up in values of "progress" and the virtues of fullest use of the resources which God has given, knows few restraints as he tears at the heart of his mother earth. In this competitive struggle to maximize exploitative returns, there is great stimulus to technological achievement. The benign atmosphere of man's relation to the natural world, and at times fatalistic composure before the awesome forces of nature, are not built into the "materialistic," pragmatic, and utilitarian ethos of the Western man.

These abstract and highly generalized differences have direct bearing on events. Clearly, man in one context may well face his raw materials with sympathy, awe, and reverence. In the other it is simply workable stuff. So also does he have compassion for a natural world to be torn apart by man's tools. If the life of a tree is as sacred as the life of a human neighbor, who then wishes a saw! Where instruments—means to ends—hold value in themselves they are removed from the sphere of manipulation and innovating.

As man views his society, he has also certain basic assumptions which vary widely from culture to culture. As some non-Western peoples see themselves in harmonious whole with natural phenomena generally, so also they may see the individual man in cooperative, rather than competitive, relations to other men. The doctrine of evolution did much to emphasize the competitive ethos of Western peoples, although this had earlier roots as well in the Reformation and other individualizing movements. Contrasting sharply with this is the ethos of the Pueblo Indians for example. As Ruth Bunzel and others have shown, among Zuni the view of life is non-self-assertive and cooperative (Benedict). The idea of "getting ahead," so prevalent in our own society, has no grounds for taking hold among Zuni except as a major transformation in social structure and perspective takes place.

As part of his world view, modern man views competitive and authoritarian relationships as part of human nature. Such a view testifies not to the "naturalness" in these relationships but to their deep-seated actual significance in our culture. For all their democratic features, Western peoples have organized themselves upon fairly rigid and bureaucratic lines. Without precise allocations of formal responsibility and authority, the highly differentiated urban societies could scarcely maintain ordered life. Although dyed-in-the-wool individualists rail at increasing regimentation, Westerners have through several hundred years become increasingly conditioned to the precision demands of a massive society. Lewis Mumford has told us dramatically of Western man's enslavement by the clock and Lyle Saunders tells with equal vividness the problems of the children of a timeless Latin culture adjusting to life in split-second modern America.

In this highly individuated, competitive, and formally structured milieu, group patterns which are cooperative, communal, and loosely structured find a difficult access. Although a new special interest association may be launched easily, the social climate is not conducive to loosely organized communal groups. Formality is thrust upon such groups through requirements of a charter, through qualification as a non-profit—and tax free group—if it indeed is, and by the necessity of having officers, if only to deal with other groups which themselves understand formally structured associations. It has been surmised that in America more Indian "chiefs" were created in order to deal with Europeans who demanded to see *the* chief than had ever appeared spontaneously in the hundred years before Columbus.

Many societies do not organize themselves bureaucratically and also fail to comprehend the "special interest group" as a lasting, programmed, and officered unit in the community. When Western men confront a large problem they immediately visualize its resolution through a formally structured, bureaucratized association. While this may be a highly efficient manner of meeting a problem, some peoples would place the values of equalitarian companionship in time of crisis above those of efficiency. Even in our society we do not go overboard in applying rules of efficiency to ways in which our family groups operate together. The culturally varying view of the "good social life" may intervene upon all manner of innovations. Employment for wages, for example, can violate basic convictions of personal dignity in economic relationships. Agricultural improvements diffused through organizations of farmers may be treated haphazardly not because the improvements are unwanted, but because bureaucratic structures are incompatible with the traditional social structure and world view.

G. Gordon Brown has illustrated such a problem in a religious context (Brown, pp. 11–14; Foster, pp. 118–119). Three different Christian churches have essayed missionary work in Samoa, the Roman Catholic, the Congregational, and the Methodist. Brown points out that superficially the Roman Catholic might be expected to have great appeal since its high ritualism generally appeals to tribal peoples. Yet in fact neither the Roman Catholics nor the Methodists have found much success. The Congregational church has been much more successful in establishing itself there than has either of the others. Brown believes that the differences are due to the compatibility of Congregational denominational structure with the Samoan concepts of political and social structuring. Villages are highly autonomous and even federations among them are short-lived. In this loosely organized non-authoritarian social climate, the rigid central centrol of the Methodists is out of step with local autonomy. Their more rigid hierarchy has hindered Roman Catholics in gaining much success here.

Circumstantial Variables

From the standpoint of the actor in a socio-cultural system, the presentation of an innovation occurs amid accidental or external features involving time, place, and persons. The diffusing agency may or may not be prestigious and respected. Unexpected happenings coincidental to the diffusion may determine adoption or rejection. Such external conditions intervene and affect the evaluations of the actor as he perceives the innovation.

There is substantial literature demonstrating that high prestige on the part of a diffusing agent works toward the innovation's easy acceptance. The significance of a high status position by the introducer has been well documented in many instances. Trousers were picked up as an item of dress among South Asians for no particular reason other than that they were associated with the colonial elite. Advertising agencies pay famous baseball players to speak well of a new brand of cigarettes though there is no evidence that their taste buds are any more—or any less—acute than those of garbage collectors. Yet the idea that the prestige of the innovator is invariably a forceful positive factor in innovating is a half truth. Under some circumstances it may actually retard acceptance.

Ozzie Simmons has described a situation in which the high prestige of a diffusing agent retarded acceptance of a new practice. In this instance physicians in a Chilean health program were frustrated by inability to get the common folk to confide in them and talk freely of their health problems. The people viewed the physicians as being above them and considered such talk with them to be bordering on impertinence. On the other hand, the clients were ready to tell their problems to the nurses whom they considered common people like themselves, only educated. The nurses had something which prestige could not buy. Marriott studying similar innovative problems in India notes that in the village a doctor is always classed as a "gentleman." While persons of this class are looked upon as being of high status, they are also viewed as people with whom the ordinary villager would not think of entering into a relationship of mutual trust or intimacy. People of the "gentleman class" are typically perceived as exploiters rather than as trustworthy advisers (Marriott; Singh).

Prestige operates straightforwardly as a factor in promoting acceptance of certain innovations. Generally, however, these are innovations which can be given symbolic prestige or status value. Where a diffusing item is a status symbol, the high prestige of the diffuser is significant. Where this is not the case, confidence and trust in the diffusing agent's concern, integrity, and judgment are more significant than his prestige. As has been so clear in successful radio and television campaigns, it does not matter for initial response whether the diffusing agent is *in fact* sincere. Rather, people associate the voice and manner with their *percept* of "sincerity" (Merton).

Other circumstantial factors arise which can be as varied as changes in weather, the flights of birds, soil conditions, and mood of a neighboring society. Magical and astrological beliefs are infinitely various among themselves in assigning auspiciousness or inauspiciousness to fortuitous signs or to zodiacal positions. Under the exigencies of war and other threats to survival, innovations may be perceived and responded to favorably which otherwise would pass unheeded. Nations valuing civil liberties accept censorship devices under threat of extinction by war. Hunting peoples reluctantly settle to agricultural pursuits when environmental conditions supporting hunting and gathering shift. The ripeness of the times for the spread of an innovation has, of course, to do with social forces within a society, but it has also to do with exterior forces which set the scene within which life goes on. Nomadic slash and burn cultivators and gatherers in the Eastern jungles of Ceylon disdain but reluctantly accept settled farming ways under the joint threats of government edict and changes in jungle ecology. Where survival values are at stake, perceptions of efficacy or of normative consistency come to be modified or rationalized as the new traits are adopted.

Under despotic governmental demands, as in a police state, we find the ultimate intervention upon the exercise of choice in acceptance or rejection of an innovation. Here behavioral acceptance of new norms and new technologies may have no support in positive attitudes. They are nonetheless adopted and acted out. Control of communication channels may repress innovative ideas or may throw a weight for or against acceptance that makes denial improbable. Propaganda also intervenes upon the individual's perception of an innovation and influences personal choice. Proscription or demand by a coercive power can virtually eliminate individual choice in decision making. Such ultimate intervention by force and fraud introduces conditions which are better studied through the analysis of social control and power structures than of socio-cultural change processes.

THE DYNAMIC ASSESSMENT

As has been indicated, every innovation is subject to assessment in reference to its efficacy, its personal desirability, its normative consistency, and its aesthetic charm. In situations providing for choice, the individual's response rests in his particular balance of these considerations. In the foregoing pages we have considered forces which come to affect the manner in which the recipient makes these evaluations. It now remains to treat the processes of evaluation themselves. It is in their balance—influenced by the external and intervening factors—that an innovation is accepted or rejected.

Nearly half a century ago, William Isaac Thomas (1923, p. 42) coined the phrase "definition of the situation." By this he meant that there is a preliminary stage of examination and evaluation before any self-determined act. Transporting Thomas' concept into the innovative situation, we may paraphrase by saying that before the individual may act in reference to a novelty he must "define" it. Objective reality may exist in some philosophers' notebooks, but no individual can fully comprehend it. We comprehend realities as percepts. As we perceive them so are they real to us. Such perceptual definitions are weighted and biased by both personal and culturally derived attitudes, "facts," and values. As Thomas pointed out, *from the standpoint of one's responsive actions, it doesn't matter what the "reality" really is.* What matters is what one thinks it is. We behave as if the innovation is and does what we believe it is and does. There may or may not be high community consensus on the matter. And very frequently there is a low degree of inter-cultural consensus.

Fermented mares' milk is an esteemed drink in parts of Asia, but if introduced into North America it would probably be defined as nauseating. In the diffusion of tobacco, some communities have defined it as a health-giving herb to be smoked in pipes; elsewhere it is defined as a weed to be smoked in paper rolls, if one lacks regard for health and longevity. Some communities have defined tobacco smoking as health-ful and immoral, others have given it no moral sanctions, but considered it harmful to health. In such complicated situations, the potential re-ceiver selects a line of action contrary to certain definitions, but con-sistent with certain others. Actually, all of these particular definitions may be ignored and smoking might be rejected because it leaves a dirty taste or accepted because it seems the sophisticated thing to do. Con-sider the dilemma of Manuel de Nóbrega who went to Brazil in 1549 to convert the heathen to Christianity; Nóbrega wrote:

> No one of our brothers uses it, nor does any other of the Christians, in order not to imitate the unbelievers who like it very much. I need it because of the dampness and my catarrh, but I abstain—not what is useful for myself, but what is good for many that they may be saved. [Heimann, p. 10.]

Preliminary to any self-determined action there is a stage of examina-tion and reflection. Transporting Thomas' concept into the innovative situation, we may say that the individual must "define the innovation," before he acts in reference to it. It is apparent that the perceived reality for one person may be different from that of another even as participants in the same culture. A rose is a rose is a rose to Gertrude Stein, but to some of us it is hayfever, to others nostalgia, and still others mourning. If a hunter defines a cow as a moose, his behavior is guided by this perception and not the objective facts of the case. It is the per-ception of an innovation to which individuals respond. This percep-tion is influenced by the inherent qualities of the innovation, but these are seen through glasses which have been colored by a variety of psy-chological and situational factors. The action element in the "definition of the situation" has been emphasized by MacIver when he refers to this process of evaluation as the "dynamic assessment" (see p. 13).

Perception of Efficacy

When an innovation is presented to a potential public, one of the more obvious tests applied to it is, "Will it work?" That is to say, will it do what the potential recipient expects it to do? Does he think that the innovation will do the job for which it is to be used? Many innovations have multiple functions, and it is always possible that the recipient sees in an invention a result which neither the diffusing agent nor the inventor intended. In the government-sponsored colonization schemes in the Ceylon jungle, for example, some resettled villagers value their well-constructed pit privies as excellent storage houses for grain and equipment. It is not necessary that an innovation be perceived as accomplishing the purpose for which the inventor or instigator intended it.

As anyone knows who deliberates over buying a new model car, or what one believes is a *new* model car, determination of efficacy is no simple matter. When individual car buyers within the same society differ so widely in their evaluations, it is not surprising that peoples having utterly different cultures test efficacy from different standpoints. The ultimate test is in application, but when trial acceptance occurs the recipient has admitted the plausibility of the innovation.

Assuming rationality, the most basic factor determining the perception of efficacy in an untried innovation is the background of knowledge upon which the actor assesses it. This may be personal knowledge or it may be the accepted judgments of referent advisors or groups. The engineering scientist can judge the innovative turbine drive automobile in terms of conformity to what he knows as sound propulsive principles. Most of us will turn to friendly mechanics, consumer guides, advertising media, or a trusted neighbor who has already made the leap. In the latter case we will have evaded the utilization of propulsive and mechanical knowledge by letting our neighbor run for us a test by experience. Some information on the matter quite possibly guided him in *his* choice, so the chances are that something more than pure trial and error observation is at work. Actually many features of modern gadgetry and machinery and all ethical drugs are pre-tested by surrogate groups according to our Western society's body of scientific knowledge and also by trial runs. In this highly specialized world, the individual recipient acts upon faith in the knowledge of his reference groups and control agencies.

Within our own society different systems of knowledge give rise to different assessments. For many years scientific medicine in the United States was divided into two branches, homeopathic and allopathic, each with different knowledgeable standards to apply. In recent years the "allopaths" have dominated. Similar but unresolved differences may be found in regard to every phase of technology, especially as new designs are presented. Innovations in social structure are even more drastically subject to varying assessment based upon differential acceptance of our body of knowledge. Some individuals who are in favor of the principle of socialized medicine, for example, reject the idea because their understanding of social organization and "human nature" convince them that it "won't work." The sciences of social organization and human motivations are even less homogeneous in their understandings than those of propulsion and chemistry, and fewer individuals are willing to trust some equivalent of a Bureau of Standards or *Consumer's Research* for judgment. Also, innovations in social structure are more involved in normative controversy—belief or disbelief in efficacy is swayed more by normative judgment and, possibly, self-interest.

So-called premature inventions are those which the body of existing knowledge is capable of producing, but for which the state of culture is unprepared for their useful application. The potential recipients fail to see efficacy in such an innovation either because their knowledge of its effects is incomplete or its use involves what seems an impossible rearrangement of the existing culture. The streamlined train patented in 1865 was rejected because its technical superiority to older models was not perceived as being significant enough to justify acceptance (Berle and DeCamp, pp. 177–179). Many other strategic inventions are retarded in acceptance because they are not usable until associated changes have been made in related parts of the culture. Automobiles may be diffused to a roadless country, their great efficiency being fully perceived; rejection will then be in terms of their lack of efficacy within this particular terrain and culture. Such an instance of diffusion stands alongside the "premature invention." Its acceptance as a useful device is dependent upon a configuration of related cultural traits which in this instance are non-existent.

As innovations diffuse cross-culturally, the tests of efficacy are drastically different. Western society is relatively homogeneous in its acceptance of scientific method as a device for gaining principles of knowledge and for testing many innovations. While we have emphasized the diversity of factual belief in our society, this should not cover up the deep and extensive agreements. Other peoples have sharply contrasting methods of evaluating efficacy and different storehouses of knowledge against which to test innovation. Technicians engaged in planned change in non-Western cultures sometimes conclude that their potential beneficiaries are disinterested in material comforts, longer life, and better health, or that they are too unintelligent or lazy to make the small acceptances proffered them with promise of such great returns. While the reasons for rejection of Western devices are many, an important one is that the technologist may be asking people to do something which in terms of local, tested knowledge is not a feasible way of gaining the promised result. The knowledge held by people in so-called backward regions of the world is often not scientifically accurate or even remotely "correct," but it is knowledge that has proved itself in survival. It is knowledge painstakingly gained through centuries, and by its use these societies have made their living, often in difficult environments, with at least sufficient good health to survive as a people. And generally they will have felt life to have been rich and satisfying. They test the innovative device by the standards of their knowledge, not those of the innovator!

The casebooks on technological change in underdeveloped countries are thick with illustrations of disparities. In matters of sickness and health it is easy for the Western scientist to forget that his whole conception of disease causation is built upon quite recent discoveries. In the thousand years before 1500, Europeans were at least as "indifferent" and "unintelligent" in medical matters as are the most isolated peoples of today. It was in the middle nineteenth century that Semmelweis succeeded in cutting the maternal (puerperal fever) mortality rate in romantic Vienna, despite the fact that "the authorities once went so far as to refuse to purchase new sheets on the ground that several accouchements could very well be performed without a change of sheets" (Stern, p. 376). Where germ theory has still not penetrated, alternative understandings of disease survive. In India there is a highly developed system of medicine, Ayurveda, with an extensive pharmacopeia, specialized medical schools, and trained practitioners. Ayurvedic medicine is grounded in physiological and diagnostic assumptions which are at variance from those of Western medicine. To complicate matters still further, traditional Indians do not accept the same kind of dichotomy of supernatural versus natural factors common to modern Westerns (Marriott). Small wonder that a newly introduced health practice is resisted when it fails to conform to established knowledge practiced by trusted local physicians. The resistant villager—or practitioner—is neither indifferent to health, nor is he uninformed. He is informed and dedicated, but to the validity of a different and conflicting body of knowledge.

Widely scattered through folk peoples of the world is the belief that things, especially foodstuffs, are divisable into those which are "hot" and those which are "cold" (Madsen; Stein, pp. 80–85). This view of nature is reminiscent of ideas common in Greek civilization and suggests th   he actual origin of the contemporary idea stems from the Greeks. At any rate, numerous cultures include the dichotomy, often with a middle ground for things which are neither "hot" nor "cold." Classification has, of course, nothing to do with heat in the caloric or thermal senses. To the outsider it is an arbitrary classification. However, this manner of viewing objects has ramifications for religion, agriculture, animal husbandry, and nutrition. If too many "cold" foods, e.g., fish or lentils, are served, the family will surely get stomach aches. Baths in some localities must be taken sparingly for water is "cold" and can produce chill and sickness. A rattlesnake bite is very "cold" and hence should be treated by eating very "hot" foods like garlic. This belief system is so pervasive that in the Valley of Mexico, Indians have forced modern medicine and even surgery into the hot-cold system (Madsen). Aspirin, alka-seltzer, and surgical operations have all been defined as either "hot" or "cold." Thus diffusing traits are "defined" by existing knowledge and given meaning in its terms. Obviously certain restrictions are imposed upon ready acceptance of many new practices, especially nutritional ones.

The question of "Will it work?" is rarely capable of a simple direct answer of "yes or no." Efficacy is normally qualified by the possibility of alternatives. In regard to technology it is difficult to imagine any assessment of efficacy except in relative terms. Instruments are also evaluated with regard to economic efficiency in achieving some end, an assessment which requires the calculation of comparative cost in the use of one means rather than another. A diffusing invention may be more efficacious in reaching an end than is an existing device, in the sense that its use accomplishes more fully or more consistently the desired goal. Yet its cost may be greater than is justified.

Once basic efficacy is established, it remains to determine relative cost or efficiency (Lesperance; Strassman). Using an electric typewriter, one can produce a manuscript more rapidly than with a standard machine. Yet standard typewriters are more prevalent among private users than electric. The efficacy of the innovation is unquestionably greater, but many of us balance cost into the equation and reject the newer machine. Furthermore, the introduction of rational, productive agricultural practices among folk peoples may be viewed in cost terms which are not characteristic of the American corn-belt. In Ceylon most peasant proprietors do not utilize the practice of transplanting rice although they know very well that their crops would be larger if they did. Generally they consider the additional family labor demanded for this to be a cost which over-rides the greater productivity of transplanted rice. It is questionable if such a conclusion truly reflects a rational economic judgment of cost or a cultural preference for minimal work on the land and a reluctance to expend more labor or capital on the problematic harvest (Ryan, 1958). In other practices relative cost assessments have brought rejection of modern technology on grounds which may well be economically rational. Metal mold-board plows have been introduced as more efficacious substitutes for the traditional wooden "scratching" plow. These have been widely rejected not because villagers disbelieve in their excellence, but because they believe their existing draft cattle are not capable of pulling them. Whether this is correct or incorrect in fact, so long as the evidence is so assessed, villagers would be subjecting themselves to excessive cost in accepting the excellent innovation. Similar circumstances militate against expensive labor-saving devices where labor costs are relatively low.

As part of an efficacy evaluation, the comparative risk encountered through the use of alternative techniques must be assessed. Risk is considerably more complex than ascertainment of operability and efficiency, e.g., uncertainties due to governmental restriction, unforeseen customer preferences, risk of "unlucky" timing, etc. (Strassman). In a calculating economy the rational adopter tends to select the alternative which yields maximum return at the lowest risk. Frequently where high returns are potential but with substantial risk, innovative devices are introduced to reduce risk, as with insurance, lobbying, and hedging. Tolerance to risk undoubtedly varies between different cultures.[1] A prosperous commercial farmer in the United States faces the uncertainties associated with a new technique from a different vantage point from that of the non-commercial, subsistence producer. This is an important factor for the introduction of technical change in economically depressed regions. The Midwestern U.S. farmer can afford a certain amount of risk in the acceptance of technical innovation. The subsistence peasant, living on the margins of bare survival, can afford no risk whatsoever. Under such primitive conditions the peasant must choose the minimum risk regardless of return. It is one thing for the Iowa farmer to "try out" a new seed on a part of his land, but the seemingly identical act has utterly different significance to a farmer for whom the loss of one measure of grain from the coming harvest could make the difference between life and death for a family member.

Instruments, whether they be plows or new plans for organizing a company, are always assessed in comparative terms. Other things being equal, that which produces the maximum result at the minimum cost is the winner. Other things, however, are seldom equal, and at best the determination of cost is a complicated matter. To show that a new seed or tool or arrangement of workers yields greater production is one thing. To show that it is *worth doing* is quite another. This calculation must take into account such complex assessments as relative fatigue, cost of physical rearrangements necessitated by the new trait, interest rates, calculation of risks, ability to take risks, and in situations demanding increased personal labor, wage scales in alternate employments.

---

[1] The writer is indebted to Dr. Eugene Havens, formerly coordinator of the University of Wisconsin Land Tenure Research Program in Colombia, for his observations on peasant risk-taking, based on unpublished research in rural Colombia.

Perception of Normative Consistency

All societies have moral precepts, sacred beliefs, and organizational patterns which are precious. Innovations are generally tested against this "moral order," to assess their consistency or inconsistency and their supportive or destructive consequences, for these aspects of life which are held dear and inviolable. Patently, misassessment of such congruity is common and it is evident too that people will compromise their moral judgments for the sake of material satisfactions. Yet no society is without some loyalty to fixed points of ultimate value, and the evident relationship of innovations to these matters of value can become a crucial determinant in acceptance or rejection.

In societies like our own we enjoy so many conflicting and incongruous values that there is often reasoned basis for disagreement as to the normative consistency of a given innovation. (Socialized medicine and birth control are obvious examples.) In regard to many innovations, however, we are practically homogeneous in our assessments. This is particularly true when the innovation is consistent with our high value of technical material progress and bears no *immediate, readily visible*, negative relationship to ethical or moral precepts and cherished group structures. While technological innovations actually hold complicated moral and valuative significance, this is usually subordinated in our society to the values of material prosperity, efficiency, and progress.

The simplest circumstance wherein innovation is tested for consistency arises in reference to proposed novel precepts of conduct. This situation may be brought about by a proposed change in mores or by the necessity of creating new norms applicable to some new situation. Innovations in mores are by definition tamperings with the normative, moral order. Such innovating may be viewed as a simple extension of traditional verities or it may be viewed as destructive of the very foundations of social order. Conservative theologians such as Billy Graham offer us continual reapplication of traditional moral precepts to the circumstances of modern life. Radical reformers propose basic modification of the mores themselves. Bertrand Russell's views on ethical sexual conduct will be viewed as socially destructive by those who place sacred valuation upon traditional standards of marriage.

One of the most subtle innovative campaigns of modern times occurred when cigarette manufacturers sought to open up the female market in America. Although pipe smoking and snuff dipping have long been normative for women in remote mountain communities, in modern communities this was deemed improper and the cigarette smoking woman was a hussy capable of any immorality. Virtuous women should not and did not smoke cigarettes. The diffusion campaign designed to implant this "vice" into the positive folkways of femininity began with bill-boards showing a proper lady urging her gentleman to "Blow some my way." Gradually ladies on billboards came to hold cigarettes in their hands and eventually to puff as ardently as any male. Had the cigarette interests launched a sudden campaign for feminine smoking they would likely have met organized opposition by the powers of traditional decency.

A more significant case of response to innovation on moral value bases was that associated with the idea of companionate marriage (Lindsey and Evans). As proposed by Judge Lindsey its purpose was to save the American family from a trend of increasing instability and divorce. To do this he proposed that engaged couples enter a prefatory stage of the "companionate," before accepting the parental and other long-range responsibilities associated with legal marriage. Judge Lindsey's logic was unassailable. His facts regarding the growth of unordered "trial sex," were substantially true. His indictment of it strong and moralistic. His plan was a rational instrument designed to fulfill a social need. Yet this renowned and socially minded jurist became a pariah among those most actively concerned with meeting social problems. He could describe a public debate in a Midwestern city as follows:

My opponent was a local minister . . . He opened fire by saying that his sainted mother had told him of "the greatness of Judge Lindsey," but that the Judge had changed; something terrible had happened to him. Here he pointed at me with a thick forefinger and shouted that he was sick with the shame of me; that the asylums were full of people like Lindsey, people who thought they had an idea; that fellow-ministers of his in Denver had written him that Lindsey had been driven from his court by the rotten doctrine of free love he called Companionate Marriage. [P. ix.]

One should not conclude that only innovations in social organization and in norms are judged by normative criteria. Mechanical invention, from the most complex and socially disruptive to the most trivial gadgets, at one time or another have been assessed in normative terms. William Isaac Thomas observed that:

Up to recent years in white society no important or trivial noticeable cultural trait or divergent view was introduced without strong and often violent resistance. This was true in the case of medicine (anesthetics, vaccination), railroads, new varieties of foods, illuminating gas, stoves in churches, chimneys, saw mills, iron plows, silk hats, umbrellas, etc., not to mention the "warfare of science with theology" over the relation of the earth to the sun and man's place in nature.

There was a bitter fight in Europe against the introduction of potatoes on the ground that they were "injurious to society." . . . In Berlin, street lighting was opposed . . . on theological grounds as being a presumptuous thwarting of Providence, which had appointed darkness for the hours of night. . . . [Thomas, 1937, pp. 726–727.]

In the sphere of contraception there has long been a curious and qualified resistance in Western countries (Fagley, 1960; Bailey). In this controversy it would seem that the particular technology of contraception which is utilized has become closely relevant to the practice's conformity with "natural law." While there is keen religious opposition to mechanical devices inhibiting conception, there is less adamant opposition to alternative techniques such as "rhythm." In this particular matter the social end to be achieved by the techniques seems less relevant to normative valuation than is the nature of the sex act and the control instrument itself. Like most issues debated upon normative grounds, opposers insist that the act itself is immoral by God-given standards of right and wrong, much as they could claim the same for dissection in the fourteenth century. Supporters likewise can refer to normative standards in pointing out that under conditions of excessive population growth the greater morality is humanely to limit that growth rather than permit the harsh Malthusian checks to operate.

As modern secular society has matured, normative valuations for innovations appear to become less strong and less widely applicable. Few voices are raised against nuclear fission as encroachment upon God's domain, although nuclear weapons are widely disapproved as a nonnormative innovation on the basis of their consequences. Generally in the realm of mechanical improvements, chemical discovery, and even space travel, traditionalists among us rarely object upon grounds of immorality, wrongness, and disruptions of valued social order. The secular value of "progress" has become so ingrained that technological achievement *per se* is morally good—and the social order must take care of itself. Failure to assign normative significance to technology, and continued assignment of it to the norms which guide its use, creates serious "lags" or maladjustments in the socio-cultural system. On the one hand standards of efficiency are applied, while on the other, traditional morality.

Perception of the Innovation's Desirability

The recipient may be readily convinced that an innovation is morally good, beautiful, workable, and efficient. But does it fit into his estimate of a future state of affairs? If he has no desire to have done what this innovation purports to do, such favorable views are not translated into behavior. Narrowly conceived, the desirability of innovations can be treated as "self-interest." To say that an innovation is responded to favorably out of self-interest may mean that it will produce more money, or it may mean that it will preserve one's friendships or provide greater prestige or heavenly salvation and a future life. Early pagans accepted baptism to assure eternal life, although it may well be that larger numbers of modern Hindus have accepted the rite because this was how they got rice from the missionaries. All responded favorably to an innovation in pursuit of self-interest, yet the *definitions* of self-interest were wholly different. When strongly entrenched powers repudiate an innovation which threatens their position they have been referred to as "vested interests." Actually the assessment of desirability of an innovation is more complex than such economically laden terms imply.

Self-Interest Is Broader than Self.   In no society do individuals stand apart from all others as they visualize personal gain or loss. "Self-interest" is calculated by an actor who identifies self and self-interest with the interests of at least certain others. Although much emphasis has been placed upon alienation in modern society, the fact remains that, at the very least, most individuals see themselves merged into the collective interests of a family group. This is not simply a matter of having interests in common with certain others, as in social class or corporate interests. In a family group, advantage to self is *qualified* by one's concern over the advantage to certain others. Such extension or qualification upon self-interest is implied in the concepts of the *we-group* and the *primary group.* When a householder contemplates an innovative household comfort, he thinks in terms of "we" rather than "I." Desirability judgment is, hence, desirability for the persons or groups with which one identifies with "we-ness." Even in individuated societies such as ours, these feelings and judgments are not infrequently made in regard to groups beyond the family or one's buddies. Eminent Negro entertainers refuse lucrative offers as protest against a management's racially segregative behavior. Members of the low castes of India modify their food patterns less for personal advantage than that their sub-caste as a whole may be known as one following orthodox Brahminic standards, and is hence a caste of clean standing. Low caste men of wealth in forming a business deal may well place their caste's welfare into the calculation. The route of simple egoistic economic advantage would be to cut one's self apart from caste—or race consciousness and perhaps from familial we-ness as well.

Desirability Ultimately Determined by Social Values.   Whether an innovation is or is not desirable from the standpoint of the actor's self-interest depends upon his valuations and, closely related, his personal aspirations. In the secular Western world we have been heir to a theory of human nature in which man is visualized as ever striving to maximize his pecuniary advantage. The very term "self-interest" has taken on economic and pecuniary connotations. While it is possible that men of

Western civilization meet more nearly this over-simple conception of human motivation than do others, they are far from simon pure materialists. Reasonable and informed men do *not* make unqualified decisions to maximize profit or other pecuniary return! Proffered inventions which rational men should accept are frequently rejected because the terms of self-interest are non-rationally defined. George Foster (pp. 96–97) gives a clear and simple example of this when he tells of the rejection of labor-saving washing machines because the housewives concerned had greater interest in social wash-days on the river bank than in time-saving isolation. The issue, however, is much broader than such incidents in technical aid programs might imply. In the dawning of capitalism, European colonizers frequently ran into head-on collisions with "natives" who steadfastly refused to accept innovations toward their personal gain. To European businessmen and bureaucrats such rejections of the power of profit, wages, and material goods seemed scarcely human.

A classic case in point arose when the British opened up the interior of Ceylon for coffee plantations. It was fully expected that the neighboring Sinhalese villagers would eagerly seek wage employment on the estates and enter into business stimulated by the large-scale plantation enterprises (Ryan). Knowing "human nature," as they believed it to be, it seemed obvious that poor natives would grasp this golden opportunity to improve their material condition. Colonial officers were astounded and aghast to find such "natural" self-interest not only lacking but actually deplored. Ultimately, they were forced to import plantation labor from India. Small businesses also grew, but from the enterprise of other outsiders. The Sinhalese despised working for hire. Normatively too, they had distaste for the regimentation that such labor demanded. But also in strict terms of personal self-interest, the Sinhalese did not value highly those goods and services to be had through money. The British found them energetic and eager to work for honors of state, but not for the honors of wealth. The traditional feudal system had not bred in these people the understanding that a successful search for wealth through labor and shop keeping was a meaningful goal. In the traditional value system prestige, power, and the services of others were to be gained through political advancement. The status which was prized was an honorable acclaim achieved not through economic action, but through feudal office. Personal ambition could lead these people into government service at low pay, but it could not entice them into profit-making and wage labor. Even today there are vast numbers of Sinhalese who would prefer penury in the prestigeful government service to substantially greater material rewards for identical employment in private industry.

Every society offers to its members the system of personal goals worthy of effort, and it offers routes wherein these efforts are to be channeled and exercised. At the individual level such values are translated into motivations and aspirations. To understand the variety of aspirations we must know what a culture defines as worth working for and by what routes. What is one man's meat is another man's stomachache.

There is no gainsaying, however, that throughout the world there are generalized types of aspiration values common to all, variously as they may be defined. Numerous attempts have been made to categorize these and perhaps the now all but forgotten "four wishes" of Thomas are as adequate as any (Thomas, 1923, Chap. 1). In Western society, notwithstanding the excessive assumptions of classical economics, material rewards mediated through money have assumed great significance. With the individualism and rationalism inherent in the capitalistic ethic and speed of technological inventing, an immense range of innovation has been assessed primarily in terms of efficiency and of personal pecuniary advantage. Effective inventions like the mechanical hat tipper might well have become prevalent had an industrialist visualized profit in its manufacture. Stranger devices have been associated with status interests by parts of the American public. In an immense range of equipment, effectiveness plus economic advantage have pushed aside quibbles over normative consistency or potential societal disruption.

Many innovations have different influences upon the economic position of different sectors of the population. Certain fairly rare innovations hold approximately equal utility to all members of a community. The addition of chlorine to a municipal water supply is about equal in benefit to all, except perhaps for the additional self-interest of the chemical suppliers. The same cannot be said for most innovative items, such as lawnmowers, power saws, oil refineries, safety pins, and television. Some of us simply do not feel a need for certain of these; others of us stand to gain pecuniarily (or otherways) by accepting them; still others may be adversely affected from their adoption by members of the community. Cinema owners have a different interest in television than do electronics repairmen. Neither may buy a set; but they may well clash over measures which spread or restrict diffusion of the innovation.

Vested Interests and the Assessment of Innovation.   The term "vested interest" denotes an individual or organized group which has economic interest in preserving the status quo. Often vested interests are manifest when innovations are proposed in the way the economy or society is organized. Modern trends in social legislation generally have emphasized social innovations favoring labor and reducing the power of ownership. In such a period ownership appears with vested interest in the status quo since each new phase serves to diminish its power. Ownership, acting through management, does not express equally adamant loyalty to the status quo in regard to *implements* of production. Under conditions of expanding markets and increasing labor costs, competitive self-interest drives toward technological innovation. This drive, however, is not unqualified. There is evidence that "technical progress" outruns actual practice (Stern, pp. 61–68). Especially when a few giant companies have controlled production, or outright monopoly prevails, there has tended to be technological rigidity. The suppression of technological changes that would encroach upon the vast investment in earlier processes, the purchase and suppression of potentially competitive patent rights, the controls exerted upon research and development personnel are not all legends, although they are exaggerated by "the left" and brushed aside by "the right."

It may well be that conservatism toward technological change has been greater in the ranks of labor than in management, especially in earlier decades. Because it is "capital" which exercises the deciding vote based upon profit, this is not particularly surprising. Since the earliest days of the industrial revolution, labor has felt itself threatened by technological unemployment. In 1812, the industrial skies were dark—for workers. Weaving machines were appearing which in cold, hard, immediate fact threatened the livelihood of thousands of the "industrious poor" (Stern, pp. 60–61).

Laborers had no reason at that time to foresee what a century would bring. Hence, they moved to support a status quo which, if not good, was better than starvation. In zeal and resentment they set out to destroy machines! In this movement a vested interest lay with labor and its attempt to preserve a system of handicraft production. Although opposition to machines was rooted in numerous objections, it was basically rooted in a perceived self-interest by laboring men and women. But these Luddites (named for "King" Lud, their leader) were struggling against historic trends of infinite power. Industrialism and the factory system was on its way, supported by religious, political, and intellectual movements—and the economic power deriving from new productivity. The Luddites, be it remembered, were not protesting against capitalism, but against industrialism, and it may well be that theirs was the last loud voice in that key west of Suez.

Since their time, theatre musicians loudly objected to "canned music" as the talkies displaced them, and other technically displaced workers have also complained. But in an expanding economy, technological unemployment is a problem of reasonable dimensions—and one which can be constantly coped with by a modern state. In recent years the unions have shown serious concern over the new threat of automation, as revolutionary in potential as were the weaving machines of the English Midlands. But the vested interests in a static technology have survived even less well than the vested interests in a system of static income distribution. Modern labor leaders do not even speak of outlawing cybernetics or of smashing evil contrivances. Instead, they invent novel income distribution systems adjusted to the new production media, e.g., guaranteed annual wage. The economics of chaos may yet win their point!

On the other side of the slate, in most Western societies, those with vested interests in preserving laissez-faire capitalism have enjoyed the support of traditional norms. Hardly less sanctified than the Divinity Himself was Property and Private Enterprise. Somehow these concepts were fitted into a scheme of nature and were hence God-ordained. Curiously enough, innovation in techniques for modifying a natural order of forests, rivers, flora, and fauna were good and righteous devices to carry out God's more devious plan, whereas the veriest innovations in a tax or wage system were attacks upon a harmonious order of nature and hence wrong and futile. Similarly all manner of insurance and other security devices were developed against the property hazards of fire, earthquake, and tornado; yet it was extremely difficult to develop effective insurance against the insecurities of chronic illness, old age, and unemployment. That these positions had something to do with vested interests is indicated by the decades of consistency with which the National Association of Manufacturers fought social legislation while labor and humanitarians sought restraints upon the exercise of the naked power of capital. For perhaps no group in America has blatant self-seeking been so sanctimoniously garbed as has been true during much of the long history of the National Association of Manufacturers (Taylor).

A significant form of self-interested obstructionism in change arises through professional solidarity and the conservatisms of safety. This has been particularly evident in the medical profession with its intense socialization processes, its ethical vows, and forced decisions involving life and death. Yet it is clear that such conservatism has also been associated with pecuniary and boundary-preserving interests, professional autonomy, desire for an image of omniscience, pride, and the need to do as the majority do as protection from a fickle public (Stern, pp. 345–385). No doubt the bitterest pill the profession ever swallowed was when Oliver Wendell Holmes discovered and preached the true mechanisms of transmission of puerperal fever, so branding the profession itself as the "carriers of death." Such open wounds in professional pride and self-imagery were not conducive to rational assessments of the discovery's efficacy. Pride was less reasonably wounded as the medics of

Liverpool fought against public health education and sanitation laws in the mid-nineteenth century. However, the root of opposition was not much different than it was a hundred years later in the United States as medical care was "threatened" to be brought under provisions of the Social Security Act. To interpret such perversities as due to pecuniary interest in the established institution would be to leave out the greater part of the story.

Aesthetic Perceptions

Aesthetic evaluations relate to judgments based on feeling and the capacity of the object to evoke emotive sensations. In this context we are not concerned with fine distinctions between the ideas of "beauty," "artistry," and "tastefulness," but with the general category of objects and ideas which in and of themselves yield sensory pleasure. It is not necessary to know what things are, what they denote, or what they do, in order to take up attitudes toward them (Ogden and Richards, Chap. 7). Objects are here valued not in terms of symbolic or utilitarian reference but in evocative terms of emotion, attitude, and mood.

Evaluations which can be described as matters of taste, beauty, or aesthetics are closely bound with values held in the cultural milieu. Like normative evaluations, judgments cannot be passed without recourse to culturally defined standards—in the one case, those of legitimacy, in the other, those of "taste" and "beauty." Some activities are subject to almost purely aesthetic evaluation. In others the aesthetic component approaches zero. That whole category of action commonly labelled "art" or, more accurately, artistic creation, is one in which the "taste" or aesthetic element is predominant: poetry, painting, sculpture, music. Much the same is true in many forms of recreational behavior which are accepted on the basis of pleasurable feeling. In sharpest contrast are implements, especially those used in privacy or closely confined technical circles. The plumber chooses his wrench almost strictly in terms of cost and efficacy. When he describes its virtue his terms are those of reference to its functioning, durability, weight, maneuverability. If he calls it a "little beauty" his reference is functional, not aesthetic. When the suburban householder buys a new pump, his aesthetic standards are very low indeed. On the other hand, when he buys a new car his sense of taste may counter-balance his "good judgment," that is to say, his instrumental evaluation.

Talcott Parsons has illustrated the role of "taste" in relation to standards of efficacy in an instance of ritual (1949, p. 679). He points out that the Catholic mass may be conducted with the pomp and luxury of a great cathedral or in the most primitive circumstances, with a wooden box for an altar and rude pots for vessels. Yet the ritual efficacy of the ceremony is precisely the same in both situations. If the primitive version of the ceremony is enhanced with rich vestments and vessels of gems and precious metals, it is done on the basis of aesthetic criteria, not on grounds of efficaciousness nor even closer consistency with normative principles.

CONCLUSION

There is no short-cut to the prediction of response to innovation. We can do little more than discover the right questions to ask, if at this stage of social science we would develop prognostic devices. The preceding pages have suggested some of the "right questions." Positive or negative response to proposed innovations depends upon the dynamic assessment given that innovation by the potential recipient. How he perceives or assesses the innovation is determined in a complex equation, the variables in which include (1) the particular qualities of the actor and of the innovation, (2) intervening variables including the social position of the actor, the cultural forces coloring his perceptions, and the circumstantial facts attending the diffusion, and (3) the perceptive judgments of the innovation by the actor in terms of the its usefulness, desirability, normative consistency, and aesthetic acceptability. The individual assesses the innovation in terms of one or more of these perceptive criteria. Frequently an innovation may be positively evaluated in terms of one criterion but negatively evaluated in terms of another. The actor ultimately must balance these various assessments and arrive at a response.

One thing that is not suggested here is how to assess the relative significance of the various answers when placed in the decision situation. Will clear-cut recognition of efficacy outweigh strong scruples as to moral consistency? Will a personally desirable novelty be accepted in spite of astrological inauspiciousness? How efficacious must an innovation be to outweigh a particular moral scruple? How strong must personal desire be before one flies in the face of the astrological order? These are equations which are to be resolved only through the study of specific situations. No one can assign values to the terms of the equation except by knowing through scientific inquiry the cultural systems and stresses of the people concerned. It is perhaps too obvious to mention, but such knowledge must be derived from deeper analysis than the acceptance of speech responses at face value. Even in a society such as ours, which so values individualistic self-interest, the moral cloak for non-moral conduct is not infrequently found. Having asked the questions, we must, to paraphrase Vilfredo Pareto, be sure that the answers we *use* are of the *residues* and not the *derivations*.

9

Stress, Strain, and Equilibration

When innovative ideas are incorporated into group life, readjustments occur to "make room" for them, to use them, and, perhaps, to make them harmonious with established beliefs and behavior patterns. Instances have been reported in which a single innovation precipitated chaotic repercussions upon practically every aspect of life (Sharpe). Such dire chain reactions are uncommon. Many novelties are incorporated by social systems with no serious wrenching of the social structure. Often when social and cultural transformations occur it is impossible to point to one particular novelty and assign it focal importance. To attribute the radical transformation of Western civilization to the introduction of the steam engine is no more accurate, and no less, than to attribute it to the introduction of the mechanical clock or the rise of individualistic value systems, the factory system, etc. One set of innovations serves to set a stage within which other innovations may be stimulated and then themselves set up forces for further change.

MANIFEST AND LATENT FUNCTIONS OF INNOVATIONS

We must be wary of single-factor emphasis in interpreting the origins of change in historical reconstruction. Nonetheless we can isolate to some extent the particular ways in which the clock and the steam engine and Protestant ethics each contributed to a social transformation in which they, and scores of other innovations, also played crucial parts. The consequences of an innovation are to be understood as an often insolubly complex equation of variables. These variables include the inherent functional potentials of the innovation, its definition by the recipients, and the centrality of its functional position in the integrated socio-cultural system. In the case of the steam engine, its functional potentials lay in the readjustments implied by steam as an alternative and presumably more efficient form of power. These potentials will be manifest insofar as, and in spheres where, the recipient elects to apply the power of steam. Insofar as steam power is applied to areas of group life which are central to the ongoingness of the group, its functional potentials are maximized. The power of steam applied by Hero in ancient Greece had limited consequences for change. Never defined as economically significant, it was applied to a sphere of ritualistic action having little connection with other phases of community life. The functional capacities of steam power for social changes may have been as great in Greece as in nineteenth-century England, but it was applied to a peripherally integrated complex and its consequences seem to have been limited to that self-contained complex. Steam power remained a useful toy, and no more than that, in the Greek milieu.

It is the latent functions of innovations which yield the most sensational stresses in societies, if only because they are less expected. In Sharpe's case of the Yir Yiront, an aboriginal Australian tribe, steel axes were introduced in place of stone ones. The manifest difference was that steel did a cutting job more quickly and was re-sharpened with more facility than the older axe. No doubt certain disequilibria were created as adjustment was made to these facts. If so, these were so minor that they did not capture Sharpe's attention. On the latent side, however, the *stone* axe held an integrated relationship with core complexes to which the steel axe did not succeed. It was a symbol of maleness, and further, it was a totemic symbol. Its commerce served to maintain inter-tribal relationship, etc. In none of these matters was the steel version an equivalent. Manifestly the new axe was a moderately significant potential source of change, i.e., a higher level of living or less expenditure of energy and more free time. The unreplaced latent functions of the stone axe made its absence stressful in an immense range of activities. Attempts at re-equilibration through innovative adjustment were almost random and notably unsuccessful. The Yir Yiront became disorganized in their relationships, in their normative world, and as individuals.

The consequences of an innovation's functions, manifest and latent, arise in the interplay of that innovation as defined and in the precise nature of the socio-cultural system within which it is being integrated. In extremely isolated, relatively static and relatively simple socio-cultural systems, analyses such as Sharpe's may conceivably be carried on with some validity. They are usually dangerous oversimplifications. Analysis of "what happened when X was introduced" and "what might have happened but didn't, when Y was introduced" are common and relatively simple after-the-fact constructions. However, modern social science has little to offer here beyond cautions and analytical tools applicable to particular instances. Only under those rare circumstances in which isolated societies or insulated sub-systems are influenced by a single variable may we approximate understanding of even the immediate impact of a single innovation.

We have many cases describing these processes in relatively self-contained communities and many other attempts to isolate analytically the consequences of particular innovations in complex social systems.[1] Generalizations from these varied researches are rarer. Perhaps their greatest general contribution has been to alert us to the wide range of consequences which can attend the introduction of even a seemingly simple novelty into a particular social system. Always it must be remembered that the adjustments and stimuli to change attendant to an adopted innovation are dependent not only upon the qualities and capacities of the innovation itself, but also upon how the innovation is defined by the recipients and the unique character of the social organism in which it is at work. The once defined innovation yields consequences arising from its reciprocal relationships with the particular socio-cultural system.

CHAIN REACTIONS IN INNOVATIVE IMPACT

The farther we move from the original innovative impact the more tenuous the chain of events becomes. As chain reaction proceeds step by step, consequences are determined by geometrically increasing numbers of variables. Greatest understanding of such linkages undoubtedly comes from the laboratory-like conditions of isolated "static" and small communities and eventually, perhaps, will come from true laboratory, controlled analysis (Holmberg). Let us not, however, pursue the fallacy that permits one to prove in one chapter all that is modern in modern society derives from the clock and in the next chapter to demonstrate

[1] Many studies seek to demonstrate societal transformation by recourse to the introduction of a single trait. Still others are more conservative in trying to trace only the ramifying significance for social life of a certain innovation, e.g., automobiles permit suburbanization, elevators permit high rise buildings, etc. A number of examples of such studies are to be found in Francis R. Allen and others. Of different calibre are efforts to synthesize changes around some prime mover. See particularly Fred Cottrell, Leslie White, Marshall D. Sahlins, and Elman R. Service. Perhaps the ablest and most convincing historical analysis of the consequences of a single innovation is a study of the introduction of money into Japan by Matsuyo Takizawa, 1927; equally sound is the anthropological account by Allan R. Holmberg (1954) of the effect of several innovations introduced by him in an untouched primitive band.

with equal virtuosity that it was the steam engine which set things off. If we cannot go far, let us beware of going too far.

The idea of the *chain reaction* is useful as a corrective to the tenuous tracing of consequences of an innovation through lengthy historical sequences of event. An adopted innovation (A) creates stress with an established element of structure (B). That element is modified in response to the felt strain. Trait B has now become innovatively changed with disequilibrating power in its own right insofar as it is functionally integrated with traits C, and D, or E, etc. To attribute the ultimate modification of trait E to the impact of trait A is to overlook the presence of innovating processes in each stage of the series. Each instance of stress has its own life history in creativity and manipulation of the culture base. When these are overlooked a spurious logic gives continuity to the sequence. It is for this reason that case books giving ex post facto accounts of chain effects are so "obvious" but nonetheless contribute little to the development of generalization on functional consequences of innovation. Such cases may be pedagogically significant in impressing students with the integrated wholeness of cultures, but they are analytically ungeneralizable and of limited predictive value. Given a knowledge of a sociocultural system, one may indeed predict the directions of stress which arise from a given innovation defined in a given way. To go beyond such first-degree response is progressively difficult with each successive step. Such sequences make magnificent history but add no more to our predictive knowledge than knowing that "for want of a nail the shoe was lost and for want of a shoe . . ."

Even substantive generalizations regarding first-degree impact are difficult because of the immense range of variables surrounding every instance of integration. For example, hybrid corn seed diffusing in the Midwestern cornbelt might be identical in attributes and inherent capacities to that diffusing in the American Southwest, but the role of corn in the economy of the cornbelt so differs from that of the Southwest that the integrative readjustments of one area are foreign to those of the other. The full range of consequences arising from innovation can be understood only in the response of a particular *type* of receiving system to a particular *type* of innovation. In a sense this is what is done when we turn to the question of directional change wherein traditionalistic societies feel the impact of innovations which require impersonalization and segmentalization of social relationships and stresses toward individual achievement and higher living levels. Few studies have attempted systematically to comprehend the full implications of modernizing innovations since it requires a rare degree of control plus a possibly even rarer combination of professional talents. One such instance, and a notable success in the realm of planned community change, is that of the Hacienda Vicos Project in Peru.[2]

The Principle of Cumulation

This conception of equilibrium and change was posited by Gunnar Myrdal (p. 1065) as an explanatory "chain reaction" type principle in American race relations. Manifestations of Negro "inferiority" such as poverty, slum living, superstition, and criminality cumulatively support the prejudiced attitudes of whites. In a static condition of race relations, there would be just sufficient prejudice generated among whites to prevent the Negro from changing his plane of living. We would then find a theoretic equilibrium in which low plane of living supports prejudiced treatment, which is turn enforces the low plane of living. This phenomenon has been referred to by Merton (pp. 421–436) as the "self-fulfilling prophecy." Such a state of affairs would, according to Myrdal, result in a static equilibrium, a state of no change. Change in this situation would require disruption of the "perpetual" balance. The principle of *cumulation* suggests that any change in any aspect of the Negro's plane of living will have cumulative effect beyond its own significance. Myrdal recognized that he was posing a general sociological principle of change and one not limited to race relations, although this was his immediate concern.

If now, in this hypothetically balanced state, for some reason or other, the Negro plane of living should be lowered, this would—other things being equal—in turn increase white prejudice. Such an increase in white prejudice has the effect of pressing down still further the Negro plane of living, which again will increase prejudice, and so on, by way of mutual interaction between the two variables, *ad infinitum*. The push might even be withdrawn after a time, and still a permanent change will remain or even the process of change will continue without a new balance in sight. If, instead, the initial change had been such a thing as a gift from a philanthropist to raise the Negro plane of living, a cumulative movement would have started in the other direction, having exactly the same causal mechanism. The vicious circle works both ways. [Myrdal, p. 1066.]

It is to be observed that although Myrdal expressed his idea of *cumulation* in the concrete field of racial conflict, his principle is a broader one than is that of *schismogenesis*, resting as it does upon the theory of func-

[2] The Hacienda Vicos Project, initiated and directed for many years by Allan Holmberg of Cornell University, is a classic instance of the productive integration of research, planning, and social action toward community development. Many reports, studies, and popular accounts have been written regarding this project. For one important series of papers contributed respectively by Professor Holmberg, Harold D. Lasswell, Carlos Monge M., and Mario C. Vasquez, see *Human Organization*, Vol. 21, No. 2, Summer, 1962, pp. 107–121.

tional integration rather than the dialectic. Change through cumulation is analogous to the effects of driving a cue ball into the mass of balls on a billiard table. A single dynamic variable (the cue ball) has impact not only from its own immediate course but additionally sets off chains of dependent impacts. The directions in which the massed balls are driven will, as in Myrdal's theory, bear a *generally* positive relationship to the direction of the initial drive.

The "theory of cumulation" may be criticized in having contributed to over-optimistic expectations in regard to the simplicity with which racial prejudice might be broken down. However, as a theoretic statement it served to reawaken social scientists to the sociological, in contrast to the psychological, roots of prejudice. As a principle of social change, *cumulation* contributed to, and has become assimilated into, the body of modern functional sociology.

THE SOCIAL SYSTEM AS THE LOCALE OF INTEGRATION

Not only is every socio-cultural system internally integrated at least partially, it is normally integrated to some degree with other systems and to the natural environment. Thus we may treat a family group as a social system, but it is a social system closely integrated with a religious system, the church, an economic system, the factory or firm, and an educational system or the school. There is the potential that an innovation in any one of these implies, suggests, or requires response or readjustment within the affiliated social system.

Most immediately, an innovation requires adjustment within its own complex of associated behavior patterns and complementing traits. This kind of first-degree relationship is the easiest to visualize and the area of most accurate prediction of consequence. The mechanically related milieu must be adjusted somewhat just as the change in outline of a single piece in a jigsaw puzzle necessitates adjustive change in those pieces which touch it. Social systems, however, are more complexly integrated, and many innovations create strains beyond the adjacent traits. The literature of applied anthropology contains scores of cases of chain reaction linkages, as novelty, for example in economic technology, has profound effect upon family relationships or perhaps status systems.

In another sense also, social systems are inter-related. One may be a sub-system of another. So it is in the Hindu family institution where the nuclear unit may be treated as a system, but it is a system within the larger system of the patrilineal household. A caste may be treated as a social system, but it is a sub-system within the community or regional system as well as being integrated with the economic and religious systems. That which modifies the individual caste may call forth readjustments in the super-system of which it is a constituent part. This is not to say that any innovation within some sub-group of the caste structure will necessarily yield readjustments in political or religious life, or even in the life of other caste units, but such effects are potential. Potential effects arise insofar as the unit is integrated with other units, while chain reactions may be felt in areas remote from the original focus of innovation.

Innovations may also be directly and simultaneously diffused into many sub-groups of the society. The modern automobile has been diffused to the separate families of a community; to the various industries, business establishments, governing bodies, and service organizations. As the automobile has entered each individual group system it has had internal impact. That is, thinking of each group in isolation from each other, the automobile has required adjustive change within families, within business firms, etc. However, families are not in fact isolated from business firms and governing bodies from industries. In addition to internally stimulated readjustment, there has been inter-system impact, as when industrial trucking contributes to industrial decentralization and hence permits residential suburban living for a carless family. In actual situations it is often difficult to isolate inter-system linkages from internal stimulus-response adjustments to an innovation.

Qualities of the Social System as Relevant to Impact

It has been shown earlier that some social systems are more susceptible to innovating than are others. This is equally true for the acceptance of innovation. "Closedness" is sometimes said to arise when an existing system approaches complete equilibrium or "perfect" adjustment among its working parts. This is a questionable generalization. Resistance to innovation, in the first place, is a function of many complex features of social and cultural organization and especially the degree of sacredness attached to the existing order. Probably the most generally resistant societies have been isolated ones with a high degree of internal consistency, but their stability in the face of potential innovation has arisen through the concomitant characteristics of a sacred outlook and the strong institutionalization of all aspects of life (Ponsionen, p. 52).

On the other hand, it is surely true that the more fully and perfectly integrated the socio-cultural system is, the more permeating will be the chain of consequences and scope of adjustment responses as the new trait is made functional in the body of the system. Consistency among the norms and values of subordinate sub-systems tends to facilitate shifts all along the line. Parsons, following Max Weber, has pointed out the very integration of sub-systems within China, in contrast to India, facilitates social change. In this connection, Loomis (p. 82) observes that the remarkable adjustment of the Japanese to rapid urbanization and industrialization is to be explained by the ease in linking the Japanese family to the larger social system. In India, unlike Japan, the national governmental system did not reach the individual but stopped at the level of the caste, village, and other groups which retained a high degree of self government. In India, the individual has been insulated from the larger social system, whereas in Japan he was linked in and integrated with it.

Many other variables exist in social structure which affect the innovation's impact. One of these is the presence or lack of pre-patterned creative leadership within the group. Societies in isolation or with little experience in change usually lack groups dedicated to the creative thought necessary for innovative adjustments to innovation. When Sharpe's Yir Yiront were faced by the disorganization arising from steel axes they gave the impression of random response and even of quivering wonder as to just what had hit them. The response of the Japanese to the introduction of money was utterly different. With a literate and imaginative intelligentsia, the kingdom was deluged with schemes for dealing with the new state of affairs (Takizawa).

Another structural feature influencing adjustive processes lies in the degree of rigidity of existing norms and structure. Lack of rigidity does not signify poor integration or lack of equilibration in the existing order. It has rather to do with an ethos, in which principles of conduct are more valued than precise precepts of behavior, and both alternatives and specialities are easily countenanced in normative behavior (Ryan and Straus). A society that defines minutely the role of a husband in relation to his wife has less room for maneuvering in response to a new situation than does a society which merely sets up general standards or principles regarding this relationship. Where the letter of the law is sacred there is a smaller possibility of accommodating new behaviors and of adjusting to them without chaotic upheaval.

Still another feature affecting type of response has to do with the degree of the group's specialization. This is not to say that societies within which there is specialization have greater difficulty in adjusting to innovation. To the contrary, such societies are likely to have associated characteristics making them more familiar with adjustive techniques, e.g., patterned creativity, and more secular attitudes toward the social structure. But societies or social systems which are specialized *in their entirety* or in crucial areas of life have greater commitment to the status quo and less flexibility in meeting novel demands. V. Gordon Childe has used this hypothesis in explaining the slowness of the highly developed Paleolithic cultures of Western Europe to adapt to agricultural life upon glacial retreat, in contrast to the quickness with which agriculture formed a new ecological nexus of life in the technologically less developed Southwestern

Asian milieu. Similarly within societies where there has been a high perseveration and ritualization of an idea or practice, the social system so developed achieves inflexibility in meeting the new. Elman R. Service has expressed this idea in the context of broader evolutionary theory (Sahlins and Service, Chap. 5). What he terms "The Law of Evolutionary Potential" is, in his words, the principle that "The more specialized and adapted a form in a given evolutionary stage, the smaller is its potential for passing to the next stage" (p. 97).

VARIETIES OF DISEQUILIBRIA THROUGH INNOVATION

Additions and Substitutions of Functional Equivalents

The emphasis in social change literature has, quite understandably, been placed upon the analysis of innovations having substantial social significance. As has been observed, much attention has been given the study of chains of consequences as some innovation requires that adjustments be made so that it is effective and operable within the social order. The idea behind the concept of "culture lag," for example, was that serious maladjustments arise while the society works at digesting new technical devices. Such periods of disequilibrium or maladjustment are no doubt the more serious when the innovation has unforeseen effects upon the established order.

The simplest integrative situation is that in which the manifest and latent functions of an innovation correspond closely to those of a trait for which it substitutes. This we will call the condition of *functional equivalence*. Many innovations of significance for individual taste, fads, etc. are integrated with imperceptible effects upon at least some of the social systems within which they are used. The replacement of regular cigarettes by menthol ones involves no changes in the smoking complex itself. The same habit patterns, the same accoutrements, matches, lighters, and ash trays, suffice. Even the same lung cancer risk is inherent; the same commercials with the new magic word added bombard the householder. Much the same is true for "king size," although cigarette cases may be outmoded by the shift. Particularly familiar in this range of innovation are the annual changes in automobile models. While some of these imply new tools for mechanics and functional shifts in efficiency, the bulk of them involve little more than modifications more or less pleasing or displeasing to taste and, possibly, but not invariably, more or less costly in maintenance and repair.

It is questionable if even these minimal innovations are without consequence to certain social systems within the larger society, however. Functional equivalence is a relative matter. The new cigarette content may boost lagging sales and stimulate menthol manufacturing. The annual change in automobile styling has implications for community status systems, the demand for model designers, the use of new material, and probably higher insurance rates. Not all of these linked effects, however, are inherent in the innovation itself. Anything on earth or in space, a speck of dust or a worn-out shoe tongue, will have latent consequences *if* it assumes symbolic significance as well as instrumental functions.

Many innovations are additive and involve innovative additions to culture which singly considered are more symptomatic of change than manifestations of it. A multitude of items are added to households and other groups for which associated behavior patterns, implements, norms, etc. are already firmly established, and, for the integration of which, no modifications are either required or implied. If an American family is accustomed to sirloin steak and an innovative father returns with a porterhouse, then obviously the list of customary foods is lengthened. Impact upon the family structure is nil although personal tastes may be gratified. So it is within an immense range of additive items which have some qualitative difference from existing ones, but in reference to which the sociocultural system is already prepared. Since lack of consequence would be found if porterhouse steak were accepted into family diet in place of sirloin, we may reasonably presume that neither has functional significance much different from the other. Such conditions of "pre-digested" innovation can occur only when no special symbolic and normative significance is attached to the new item—or to one it replaces. (The introduction of shell fish into a fish-eating, orthodox Jewish household is quite different from adding bass or white-fish to the menu.) When quantitative variation in food behavior shifts from a narrow range to a broad range, somewhere along the line we would be justified in saying that a *qualitative* change is occurring in food behavior, i.e., a family of few alternatives has become one with many alternatives. Flexibility in accepting alternatives, even additive alternatives, is an important structural variable affecting the maintenance of group equilibrium under innovative impact.

At a higher level of integration, diffusion can introduce ready-made trait-complexes much as simple substitutive and additive traits are introduced into pre-existing contexts. In such a manner the hoola hoop, associated with its distinctive technique, may sweep a nation. If it replaces in popularity the yo-yo, one complex replaces the other without necessary implications for the further life of the group enduring it. Similarly bridge may be followed by cribbage or mah jong and canasta. Even though the central activity of the bridge club shifts, apart from the immediate game-complex the same organizational structure, the same norms, roles, and some material accoutrements stand. Further, this succession of games has little different impact upon the super-social system of which this club may be a segment or upon affiliated social systems such as family and church. (Needless to say, the original initiation of the game-club pattern involved greater readjustment with affiliated social systems.)

Countless innovations move in and move out of our lives as almost self-contained complexes, each functioning in practically every way as did the preceding one. These innovations provide uniqueness less in social function than in appeal to individual taste and relief from monotony.[3] We are not here dealing with substitutions which involve increased efficiency or less cost; these are of a different order and will be treated separately.

Innovations Yielding Mechanical Disequilibrium

Instruments and their use patterns must have an operational relationship to each other, according to the ends for which the instruments are utilized. This is in no sense "technological determinism." Under some circumstances pre-existing use patterns, not to mention norms, may inhibit or stimulate modifications in the innovative instruments themselves. In this context the term instrument is used in reference to all devices, social and cultural, which are introduced to achieve tangible ends. Thus the United States Supreme Court is an instrument to achieve tangible ends as well as being a sacred value in American life.

Instruments and Their Technologies. All social systems incorporate instruments which when used in particular contexts and by particular methods are expected to yield certain results. There is often a great range of possible use patterns or technologies for a specific instrument, although under conditions of high rationality and pressure toward efficiency, acceptable alternatives are diminished. There are "many ways of skinning a cat," but very few ways of operating a zipper.

Every group becomes somewhat habituated to certain modes of handling equipment, regardless of whether these are the most efficient means of achieving the given end with the given tool. New methods of handling a tool can stimulate individuals to "see" (innovate) modifications in the structure of the tool itself so that it may be used more effectively or

---

[3] This is not to say that substitutive traits and substitutive and additive trait-complexes may not have ulterior effects upon the social system and related social systems. If the skills required by a hoola hoop differ markedly from those required in yo-yoing, and symbolic meaning or latent function is attached to each, then linked changes are inevitable, e.g., if success in the sport yields status in various groups, then obviously new standards of success may upset the existing prestige hierarchy, etc. Once again, we must reiterate that where any trait has symbolic value, it automatically has latent functions, and we are not dealing with such complexes at this point.

meet some other criterion of desirability such as less effort. When new implements diffuse, they frequently carry with them associated use patterns. However, with the introduction of a device there is often a period of fumbling as old use patterns are revised or discarded to make the innovative implement effective.

It is apparent that every device must have associated use patterns which accomplish, more or less efficiently, the application of the instrument toward a goal. At the minimum level we can appreciate the absurdity of attempting to apply the motor skills associated with a button hook to the zipper on a sweater. Although no society is concerned exclusively with efficiency in the use of instruments, efficiency provides a yardstick for measuring operational or mechanical disequilibrium. Not infrequently "efficient" implements are tried and rejected by folk peoples simply because they do not fit a traditional context of use patterns. The inherently efficient tools would be less effective than the old ones if they were fitted into the traditional technological context: excellent mold board plows overstrain weak draft animals; tractors rust away when village blacksmiths do not know how to repair them. Every tool must be utilized in a patterned system of technology. Where new instruments require new use patterns at the motor level, or at the level of social control or role specialization and training, disequilibrium is present. It is solved as either tool or use pattern is modified toward mechanical congruity between device, skills, and associated technical equipment.

In practically all technologically simple societies there is at least some initial difficulty as workers come into the disciplined factory work room and are led to accept the "fetish of the machine." The worker previously free to determine the pace and rhythm of his work now must accept the unvarying motor pattern set by the machine. While resistance to such rigidification may be rapidly resolved, this is not always the case, especially where complex habit systems are involved. George M. Foster (pp. 86–89) has assembled many cases in which technical aid programs have failed because of, or have succeeded after the resolution of, disequilibrium between habitual and traditional technologies and new implements. Such incongruities are not limited to work situations. Commonly in the non-Western countries the sit-down type toilet or latrine has been greeted by traditional "squatters" with immediate scorn and subsequent disuse or modification.

Use patterns go far beyond motor habitations. Foster also recounts how the wheelbarrow introduced into a Mexican locale without its associated technological complex, was hoisted to the head in adaptation to a traditional pattern of earth-carrying with baskets. This is not particularly different from American Midwestern college students in the 1890's arriving fresh from the farm and amusing the sophisticated sophomores by washing themselves in the toilet bowl. It may be noted here that the manifest function of this piece of equipment was twisted into an old use pattern toward an equally old but a quite different end. In an instance cited by Foster, Bolivian farmers also modified the function of an innovation which was accepted but was found not to fit into existing use patterns.

In 1951 a yellow Cuban maize was introduced into the eastern lowlands of Bolivia in the Santa Cruz and Yungas regions. It had many apparent advantages: it grew well in the tropics, matured more rapidly, had more fat content than local varieties, was less subject to insect attack, and produced a higher yield per unit of land. The new maize seemed to be an excellent device to improve the diet of both people and animals, and it was for this reason that it was introduced. It has proved very popular, but not for the reasons anticipated. Its very hardness, desirable from the stand point of storage, makes it difficult to grind, and people are unwilling to take the time and trouble to haul it to commercial mills in towns. But it makes an excellent commercial alcohol and prices are high. Thus, a seemingly desirable innovation has promoted alcoholism instead of improved diet. [Foster, p. 85.]

Under some circumstances a tool which can do a job in one technological environment simply cannot be used for the identical job within another. This may be due to ecological forces surrounding use and/or technical behavior patterns. A mold-board plow is a "better" device (more productive per unit of expenditure) than a soil-scratching wooden one *provided* soil conditions are appropriate, work patterns are appropriate, and associated instruments such as draft animals are also appropriate. Here the word "appropriate" denotes a state of functional integration at a mechanical level. At times such integration reaches an absolute imperative unless modification is made in the device itself in adaptation to the mechanical milieu. In Afghanistan and Southeast India the practice of castration of draft animals had the effect of reducing the shoulder hump of bulls (Foster, pp. 82–83). Since bull power is harnessed in these localities by a shoulder yoke, the animals while stronger as a result of their operation could no longer be harnessed effectively. Here was an imperative disequilibration but one in which a new equilibrium might be sought by further innovation along several lines. In other locales bulls are harnessed by a yoke attaching to the horns rather than by one resting on the forward part of the shoulder.

Instruments and Related Group Structures.   Where use patterning involves integrated role relationships and specializations, the technological disequilibrium may be more far reaching, and it is difficult to draw any clear line between the adjustments in the technological milieu and the linked effects upon various social systems.

This is particularly apparent when innovative devices shift from those associated with individual craftsmanship to those requiring coordinate specialization and the restructuring of social relationships in production. In part the impact of factory production upon family relationships can be seen as technologically rooted adjustments. With the industrial revolution the work milieu was shifted from home and family to factory and firm. While the ultimate impact of the wage-job outside the home upon family and community life involves many secondary integrative processes, even the readjustments immediate to the utilization of new instruments were profound. On the negative side, family structure was perforce reoriented to the absence of economically productive activity and the adult male worker himself. On the positive side, the new milieu of production which was adapted to the new technology required the introduction of new skills, new work norms, new organizational patterns, etc. To say that such new patterns were required is not to say that the particular ones emerging in the industrial revolution were the only possible ones suited to the new devices. Nonetheless the new devices required new limits to the technical milieu within which they were operable.

The particular patterns which emerged were due to complex forces and sequences of innovation which were often remote from the machine and the factory, i.e., philosophy of government, growth of welfare values, the invention of the corporation, new emphases on individual achievement, and a host of other conditions and innovations which colored responses to the new technology. But the fact remains, mechanization of production in industry *required* the growth of special social systems which were distinctively associated with the new implements. Smelser has documented in great detail the differentiating effects of technological change in the textile industry upon English life, especially family organization, in the early nineteenth century.

More immediately we see, in the Industrial Revolution, the resetting of work relationships around the use of new tools, especially power looms. Moving further into the consequences of the factory wage-job we find a much more complex field of disequilibria and readjustments associated not only with the new work situation but with a great complex of change in which no single thread can be pointed to as prior to another, nor determinative of it. We may not, for example, construe the development of labor unions as a primary direct response to disequilibria created by the new machines. Union development rested upon scores of additional assumptions regarding values and social structure. That such distinctions are matters of degree is clear.

The development of safety regulations and devices (whether union stimulated or not) is more clearly part of the technological complex under adjustment to the new instruments. Like every other innovation these did not come automatically as "culture" sought to regain an equilibrium. While safety devices were infrequently imperatives, in the same sense that

new motor skills were imperatives, the new technological milieu associated with machinery provided its participants with ample evidence
that the situation was improvable. Innovations arise in dissatisfaction
with an existing configuration and industrial accidents soon suggested
to concerned workers that new protective norms and new devices should
be introduced into the technological milieu. New worker organizations
were essential for gaining these and other objectives. The movement
toward safety did not increase the operability or efficiency of the machine
but rather served to provide a needed equilibrium with humane values.

Disequilibrium is frequently not at the level of basic operability of a
device. In the case of safety, disequilibrium had already become a process
of social tension rather than mechanistic disequilibrium. Such social tensions inspire the recognition of normative disequilibria in the sense of non-
conformity or inadequate congruence of the emerging technological complex with certain values or goals which are believed to be applicable to
the situation. In consequence, workers and some employers and statesmen defined industrial accidents as a normative incongruity: a felt strain
and dissatisfaction with the emerging operational milieu.

The new machines also continually generated further tensions conducive to further adjustment (innovative responses) as employers and
their technicians visualized ways of increasing efficiency and profit. But
each new adjustive innovation was made with regard to constantly changing variables which intervened upon the simple stress-adjustment pattern.
Reorganization of work relations could not be innovated on a maximum
profit formula if for no other reason than that labor unions had arisen
and had to be taken into account. Some of this creative thought was
directed toward mechanical innovations and other was directed toward
skill improvement and social relationships in the technological milieu.
The new field of scientific management eventually showed the application
of organized inventive effort toward changing work skills and social relationships in reference to instruments as they existed at a given time and
place. With a goal of maximizing efficiency, the management specialist
sees each work situation as an imperfect and improvable equilibrium of
tool, skills, norms, and social organization of work.

The following anecdote from the father of scientific management, F.
W. Taylor, illustrates one early application of time and motion study to
unskilled manual labor in the hope of improving the equilibrium.

There were about 600 shovelers and laborers of this general class in the
yard of the Bethlehem Steel Company at this time. These men were scattered in their work over a yard which was, roughly, about two miles long
and half a mile wide. In order that each workman should be given his proper
implement and his proper instructions for doing each new job, it was necessary to establish a detailed system for directing men in their work, in place of

the old plan of handling them in large groups, or gangs, under a few yard foremen. As each workman came into the works in the morning, he took out of his own special pigeonhole, with his number on the outside, two pieces of paper, one of which stated just what implements he was to get from the tool room and where he was to start work, and the second of which gave the history of his previous day's work; that is, a statement of the work which he had done, how much he had earned the day before, etc. Many of these men were foreigners and unable to read and write, but they all knew at a glance the essence of this report, because yellow paper showed the man that he had failed to do his full task the day before, and informed him that he had not earned as much as $1.85 a day, and that none but high-priced men would be allowed to stay permanently with this gang. The hope was further expressed that he would earn his full wages on the following day. So that whenever the men received white slips they knew that everything was all right, and whenever they received yellow slips they realized that they must do better or they would be shifted to some other class of work.

Dealing with every workman as a separate individual in this way involved the building of a labor office for the superintendent and clerks who were in charge of this section of the work. In this office every laborer's work was planned out well in advance, and the workmen were all moved from place to place by the clerks with elaborate diagrams or maps of the yard before them, very much as chessmen are moved on a chess-board, a telephone and messenger system having been installed for this purpose. In this way a large amount of the time lost through having too many men in one place and too few in another, and through waiting between jobs, was entirely eliminated. Under the old system the workmen were kept day after day in comparatively large gangs, each under a single foreman, and the gang was apt to remain of pretty nearly the same size whether there was much or little of the particular kind of work on hand which this foreman had under his charge, since each gang had to be kept large enough to handle whatever work in its special line was likely to come along. [Taylor, pp. 68–69.]

The complex relationships among machines, technologies, and work groups in the pursuit of rational production make inane any theory which singles out "material culture" or even technological invention as *the* root of social change. If such a conception is faulty when applied to the determination of work group relationships, how more strained it is as we move farther afield in family, church, and school relationships. It is clear that certain organizational forms are mechanically inappropriate for certain tools, but human imagination shows immense ingenuity in finding various systems by which given tools may be used with more or less effectiveness. However, just as some tools cannot be utilized without new skills neither can they be utilized under the organizational plans previously integrated with alternative tools. The factory as an organized system of relationships was not a result merely of technological change, but it is certain that the new machines made imperative a form of productive organization other than the existing household work. However, during the past 150 years the factory has come to encompass such a widely varying set of organizational patterns as to make the term "factory" almost meaningless. This differentiation has been due only in part to changes in machines.

The subtlety with which technical change influences the organizational structure of a factory has been brilliantly analyzed by a group of social scientists studying the English steel industry (Scott *et al.*). They found that technological advances in a mill resulted in increasing occupational differentiation, with some pressure to recruit new persons possessing the novel specialized skills required by the improved machines. Related changes occurred also in the administrative structure since the increasing complexity of production stimulated expansion of administrative, technical, and managerial personnel. Important effects on the informal structure of the plant were also observed as innovative work relationships stimulated new personal affiliations among workers. Bureaucratic developments, in response to the new operational complexities, brought an end to the familistic values with reference to which a previously small and stabilized firm had operated.

Modern managers have been recognizing the need for innovating in social relationships as well as in equipment in order to maximize efficiency. And of almost equal significance has been the recognition of functional linkages within the organizational structure itself. This, for example, has been a major concern of the Foundation for Research on Human Behavior at the University of Michigan. A central concern in the industrial studies has been that of preserving organizational stability during the process of directed change in internal role definitions as well as the adjustment of personnel responsibilities and work norms to technological innovations. Contemporary industrialists are not sufficiently materialistic as to think that change is a simple process of mechanical congruity of work patterns and tools.

The introduction of modern technology into undeveloped agricultural countries carries with it not only new tools and skills but new relationships in reference to production. Some of these are directly dependent upon the technology itself, others are responses to the complex changes associated with economic rationality, urban living, and individualistic values. Looking narrowly at immediate responses to technical innovation, many of the consequences of the industrialization of the West are found similarly associated with it in Asia and elsewhere. The work group is shifted from a familistic one to an associational one. Under pressures toward efficiency, bureaucratic systems with line and staff distinctions are enhanced; new groups are stimulated to form as novel servicing requirements and new market relationships are required.

Even where new, efficient production techniques are not associated with urban industrialism, new relationships are inevitable. Tractor agriculture introduced to a community familiar with the wooden plow and ox reduces labor requirements in reference to the land and requires service and supply agencies to integrate with these new consumers of their services and goods. Changes in the rhythm and organization of community and of household are probable—depending upon how these are previously established. Thus plowing may be traditionally defined as a distinctively male role, but no such carryover is implied in the transition to tractoring. If cooperative community work groups customarily work in the harvest together, mechanized harvesting will reduce the significance of such groups.

Whenever new devices enter a situation, *potentials* are created for change along with imperatives for change in technical usage. In the steel mills described by Scott it is doubtful if he would choose to call *imperative* any of the innovations discovered by him and his colleagues. Under the strong and omnipresent pressure of rationality, steel mill management watches closely for the innovative potentials. Disequilibrium may exist only in the sense that new equilibria can be found which are more profitable. In many situations persons less keenly stimulated by efficiency leave unresolved and unarticulated the "tensions" which additional innovative effort could resolve.

When father continues to shave in the bathroom despite his shift to an electric razor, family members may or may not recognize that this new device sets the stage for getting shaving out of the bathroom and so reduce the rush hour traffic. Under dry shave conditions the need for running water as part of the technological milieu is dissipated. Disequilibrium has not developed due to the introduction of a new implement, but dissatisfaction with the established pattern can now result in the realistic perception of a more satisfactory new pattern in which only the matter of locale need be modified.

Innovations Yielding Free-floating Responses

The distinctive function of an innovation is irrelevant in certain classes of adjustive responses. This is particularly true of innovations which substitute for earlier ones in such a way that either time or money or both is released for new types of expenditure. The ways in which such freed time or freed money are spent has nothing to do with the particular functions (manifest or latent) of the innovation, nor with its technical complex. Time and money are in a sense "free floating," to be used in manners which bear no necessary relationship to the innovation itself. How these expenditures are made depends strictly upon unrelated circumstantial factors, e.g., value systems, etc.

This type of adjustment potential is found in a great variety of labor-saving and cost-cutting procedures and devices. When the rubber garden hose wears out, it may be replaced by a synthetic type of hose. Such innovation entails no shift in the complex of garden watering and certainly none in family structure and functioning. However, if the new hose outlasts rubber and costs no more, household funds have been augmented by the shift and presumably this sum will be spent or saved in accordance with the dictates of circumstances and familial values. Precisely how such a tiny and isolated "disequilibrium" is resolved might well be undiscoverable since these few extra cents per day have an effect which may be imperceptible even in the most careful budget study. However, in the multiplication of expenditure saving innovations, effects on the family living can be substantial.

Much the same kind of free floating consequence arises from time-saving devices. In certain types of productive situations we may be fairly sure that the saving of time will simply allow for additional repetitions of the performance, but this depends upon circumstance and values and is not dictated or implied by the nature of the innovation itself.

Some years ago the writer sought to study the introduction of rice hulling machines in a Sinhalese village (Ryan *et al.*, pp. 177–178). Traditionally rice is hulled in this community by the housewife pounding it in a wooden mortar with a staff-like pestle. When an entrepreneur introduced a machine which would hull the day's rice for a penny or two, the women eagerly took up this means of relief from the quite arduous and time-consuming task of pounding the rice.

In this innovation it is apparent that the traditional family trait-complex surrounding rice preparation has been replaced by a specialized contractual relationship. An activity formerly within the home has been removed. These innovations have significance in the long-range social changes of village life. But the problem *here* is how did the *families* respond to (1) increased money costs and (2) greatly increased time available for women of the household. The anecdote is strictly anticlimactic. If detailed time and money budget studies had been conducted prior to the event, the effects could have been seen. Though the time saved was substantial, and cost slight, we were unable to put our finger on any effects this had on other specific activities. Probably the time was dissipated among the multitude of tasks facing the peasant housewife and was hence difficult to trace. Yet mathematically we know that adjustive shifts in the use of time and money occurred. In the long range, with added innovating of a household labor saving type, patterns of adjustment will become apparent. Whether the time is freed by a rice hulling machine or by a sewing machine is irrelevant for adjustments of this order. To comprehend them we must turn directly to the socio-cultural milieu.

Tensions Created by Normative Incongruity

No doubt all tensions associated with norms ultimately appear in the challenge of traditional norms by innovative ones. But the forces which produce normative conflicts which are upsetting to group functioning are varied and complex.

At the simplest level, normative tensions are created when a technological innovation is accepted but cannot be operated by the established "rules of the game." This situation is evident when automobiles are introduced in an era possessing traffic laws designed for the horse and buggy, or as television is adopted while governmental communication controls are still adjusted to radio. This, of course, is the classic condition of "cultural lag" as described by William F. Ogburn. Often such situations have much in common with mechanical disequilibria, as treated earlier. They are disequilibria arising from inefficient, problem inducing lacunae or maladjustments in the regulatory norms. When such norms have but little base in the moral and valuative feelings of people, the problem of adjustment is relatively simple. The distinctive aspects of normative tension are called into play when the threatened norms are sacred ones, mattering to people in an emotional and moral way.

As norms take on more intense moral or sacred significance, the problems of adjustment shift from largely mechanical, technological ones rooted in tests of mechanical efficiency to questions of right and wrong. Although the traditional norms may not be mechanically suited to the conditions imposed by new situations, nonetheless they may continue to regulate behavior in the new situation. Tension exists, first, between norm and seemingly appropriate novel behavior and, second, as new normative standards appear which reconcile this new behavior but conflict with traditional norms.

In this complex disequilibrium lie some of the hottest and most bitterly debated public issues of our time. How do we reconcile the new modes of behavior which arise in response to new conditions of life but which appear to violate traditional truths? "New conditions" may be created by innovations in technology, or in social values, or simply in the actual deviant behavior of people. They can even arise without any innovations except as a free thinker challenges the rightness of a traditional norm. When any of these circumstances arise, the established normative order is made subject to revision toward a new equilibrium in which norms are functionally and logically reconciled to the novel state of affairs. The seriousness of normative disequilibrium is compounded by the tendency to treat moral norms as absolutes rather than as precepts which are "good" relative to a particular state of affairs.

Some norms which have been given moral flavor just won't work in a given situation, and something has to give. For example, specific norms of traditional respect for parental authority in occupational matters are directly undermined by the removal of economic production from the home. The father simply cannot remain the same kind of power figure in an urban, wage-dominated society than he can in certain agrarian ones. New authority norms compete with old ones. In this case there would have been a real functional value in the traditional norm, supporting the integrity of the familial producing unit. When the agrarian order declined, the traditional norm become dysfunctional and new patterns of authority and of filial relationship are imminent. It seems clear that a good many norms functionally adapted to the peasant social order do not work under industrial conditions. New patterns *must* be established. Human beings are uncomfortable when they perceive that their actions are inconsistent with their beliefs. Yet they may hold strongly to these beliefs in the face of challenge by alternatives more congruent with the pressures on actual behavior.

One of the most burning issues in the realm of normative tension and change is that posed by the contemporary "population explosion." In this case it is difficult now to find *functional* support for traditional norms which define birth control as wrong. (It is easy to find functional supports for the innovational norms which define birth control as good.) The traditionalist has a problem in logical consistency between doctrine and the acceptance of a practice which most people today would agree works toward socially desirable goals. No one, for example, would argue that *uncontrolled* child bearing supports some sacred aspect of family or social structure which is threatened by the use of contraceptives. The act of overtly preventing conception is simply contrary to a particular set of absolute moral precepts or doctrines. The tensions for change arise in man's desire for consistency: First of all, consistency between behavior and certain "good" social goals, and second, a consistency between the moral evaluation of that behavior and its evident consequences for "good."

There are usually alternative pathways toward the resolution of every state of tension. Possibly the clock could be turned back to a pre-existing situation of high death rates and slow population growth. This is hardly to be considered seriously as a deliberate move toward demographic equilibrium. On the strictly behavioral side it is evident that family planning is spreading, but it is also evident that its spread is inhibited by various ideologies and norms which appear to oppose it. There are several patterns whereby this behavior toward good ends can be reconciled with a tradition which says the behavior is wrong.

Perhaps the least satisfactory and most unstable equilibrium is to be reached through strictly psychological mechanisms. At the level of the practitioner, many individuals whose religious faith told them that birth control was wrong, long ago found psychologically satisfactory means of reconciling the conflict between belief and personal action. Processes of rationalization and compartmentalization are familiar to us all. Yet it is evident that doctrine actually is not fully consistent with such practice and psychological devices do not resolve the social tensions which can only be overcome by change either in doctrine (norms) or in practice. In fact both of these pathways seem now to be potential in the remaining powerful religious body, the Roman Catholic Church, which has retained reluctance to modify doctrine.

From a historic position in which any interruption in the conception process was defined as wrongful, the Church moralists came, more or less, to single out particular methods which were wrong and others which might possibly be consistent with doctrine. The rhythm method so offered an avenue of escape from an absolute position for some—in a period when it was clear that most Roman Catholics in Western urban countries were in fact practicing the control of birth by one means or another. The traditionalist position has also probably stimulated the search for new techniques which might be defined as consistent with moral precepts. So something gives on each side. Doctrine is re-interpreted. Birth control practices are developed which might fit more readily into modest redefinitions of doctrine.

The process of finding a new and viable equilibrium between norms and new conditions is no simple one. However one is reminded that one religious body accomplished a major adjustive feat rather quickly. When polygamous marriage was denied the Latter Day Saints, a new truth was revealed which corresponded to the new state of legal affairs. This revaluation was truly functional since it preserved the broader value system as well as the organization of that church from an inconsistency which might have been fatal.

In a different cultural context from that of North America the introduction of birth control could have dysfunctional repercussions for social structure and role behavior. In Ceylon, Buddhist religious values and precepts are logically irrelevant to birth control, but folk values, kinship, and family roles are functionally bound up with the "large family" ideal (Ryan, 1952; 1954). Furthermore, this structural consistency is a matter of conscious recognition. In such a context, the practice of family planning, if introduced, could have far-reaching consequences for family and community organization. Adult male and female status and economic security in the community are supported by a large number of children. While small family practices might well be rationalized and accepted, they would create stress and strain in existing social organization through mechanical functional linkages. Needless to say, however, the dysfunctional consequences of continued *uncontrolled* fertility are predictably disastrous for this island of limited resources.

A highly complex re-equilibration is exemplified in India as innovative relationships between castes are taking place. Equalitarian relations between traditionally unequal castes have been introduced in worship, education, and public affairs generally. By traditional Brahminic Hindu norms such relations are spiritually defiling. Since the new order is strongly supported by government and by other powerful forces, the conservative high caste Hindu has faced a seemingly irreconcilable dilemma. Yet the dilemma is in fact reconciled and the innovative relationships accepted. At the psychological level, this occurred through various mechanisms of "compartmentalization" and rationalization. Ideological innovations made such processes easier through reinterpretation of religious standards. Today many conservative Hindus are no longer "conservative," having joined in religious movements which reinterpret Hindu doctrines in a manner consistent with equalitarian behavior. For those who remain conservatives in their convictions, the expedience of adapting to the new situation has required more strictly psychological adjustment. To be sure some conservatives try to avoid situations in which the equalitarian relationships are enforced, as in avoiding train travel, but there are limits to the feasibility of this. And so the orthodox conservative Brahmin who sends his child to the caste-free public school shrugs and says, "It is wrong, but what can I do? Times are changing and this is beyond my control." Moral systems come to terms with established orders, if not by compromising with them or defeating them, then by reconciliation, ideologically or psychologically or both.

With the profitable actuality of Negro disenfranchisement and segregation, the white Christian American could cherish the ideal of the golden rule and the brotherhood of man and at the same time consider his norms of race relations consistent with ethical belief. In some pulpits today the innovation of integrated schools is attacked upon the grounds of its incongruity with those peculiar moral doctrines of Dixiecrat Christianity. In this particular state of tension, the Southern traditionalist is in much the same position as the orthodox Brahmin. In each case the untenable morality is being shifted by a process of conventionalization which exempts the school situation or, as for many more honest soul-searching Christians, by doctrinal reappraisal in terms of its inconsistency to broader teachings of the Church. Ideological leadership is not lacking either in India or in the United States to assist the traditionalist in his normative redefinitions.

Tensions Between Innovation and the System of Knowledge

Every society recognizes systems for the determination of truth and retains a large body of knowledge which explains that which is felt to require explanation. In Western civilization we have come to emphasize the scientific method, particularly sensory experience, as the foundation of truth. Elsewhere in time and place, revelations from God have been sound bases for knowledge, as have been ordeals, visions, and other phenomena which are here less popular. While Western peoples commonly accept certain truths which are unverifiable by sensory experience, e.g., belief in God or faith in salvation, such empirically unsupported beliefs have a narrow range of application. In most cultures the empirically unsupported has a wider range of application, while truths resting upon inductive bases are less extensive and less exact. Folk medicine, for example, may have nothing at all to do with the supernatural and rest purely in the secular healing experience of the ages, but no such system can attain a high degree of exactness without systematic scientific investigations. The body of knowledge of the Western world, whatever it may not be, is the most exact and precise and the largest the world has yet known. Science has furthermore idelibly branded the way we think as layman. As one anthropologist put it, the Hindu wants his science to sound like magic and the American wants his magic to sound like science (Marriott). At any rate the scientific world view differs radically from the magical world view. Bodies of knowledge not resting upon science differ vastly from the body of knowledge shared by those societies which have the scientific outlook. Innovations which are explicable and intelligible in the one context may not be so in another. An innovation resting upon principles of scientific knowledge challenges the age-old truths and age-old systems for deriving truth within an alien society. When the nonliterate, isolated peasant society is confronted with cultural devices inexplicable and even incapable of existence within his body of knowledge, reconciliation between truth and event is inevitable. Either such monstrosities will be erroneously explained by resort to established verities, or those verities, the system of truth upon which they rely, and the wise men who have taught them, must undergo transformation. Such significant shifts in knowledge and its sources are not limited in consequences to effects upon traditional truths, but have wide impact upon many phases of the socio-cultural system. The present discussion will leave these as implicit and make no particular point of associated secondary adjustments in other aspects of group life.

The dissemination of modern technology offers implicit challenges to ways of determining truth other than those of science. Every supernaturally oriented culture also has established systems for determining truth through sensory experience. Though the hunter may attribute his bad luck for the day to the ill will of supernatural entities, he is nonetheless quick to notice that his arrow was improperly feathered and requires replacement for successful hunting. Belief in supernatural interventions is never an exclusive route to truth. The primitive as well as the civilized devout does not forsake empirically grounded knowledge simply because he assumes the presence and force of supernatural powers. Because such universal dual systems exist in long conventionalized relationship, truth through science is rarely totally opposed as a principle.

Probably no body of knowledge and the system for determining it has established greater tension than did the rise of science in Western Europe. The norms of science were patently incompatible with the norms of revelation, and the traditional verities were part of a powerful, organized system. The disparity of truth through one, compared to truth through the other, was obvious. Copernicus' method and his truth were correctly assessed as infections which could eat into the keystone of an equilibrated order. No less acutely have Christian missionaries been assessed as they introduced beliefs which threatened to disrupt primitive societies. But in both the rise of science and in the conflict of Christianity with pagan systems the stresses have ultimately yielded as further innovations arose either to fuse or accommodate the seemingly irreconcilable. In a few cases, it may be that a new equilibrium was never reached as from the stress of competing value systems there came only the fulfillment of chaos (Rivers; O'Brien).

CONCLUSION

Innovative designs normally require further adjustive innovations to "fit them into" the functioning social system. The degree to which the established social system will be modified in response to the introduction of the innovation depends most basically upon the functional dissimilarities between the new trait and those traits which it may replace. Some innovations have minimal functional consequence, differing so slightly from established traits that virtually no adjustive modifications arise from their adoption. Others, insofar as they release time or money for other uses, yield unpredictable adjustive responses. However, many innovations also require substantial modification in the social system if a functioning equilibrium is to be re-achieved with the novelty added. Such adjustive processes arise in response to either the manifest or the latent functions of the innovation, or both.

Tracing the chain of effects of a particular innovation is methodologically hazardous. Chain-reactions or "cumulation effects" arise which are set in motion by an original innovation but whose precise nature is not explicable by knowledge of that innovation alone. Adjustive responses toward a new equilibrium arise as individuals dynamically assess the tensions arising from the novelty within the social order, and act toward a presumed satisfying resolution of the sources of unrest. Tensions or disequilibria are of two different types: (1) functional disequilibria involving mechanical or operational incongruity between the innovation and related parts of the social system and, (2) logical and meaningful tensions in which individuals perceive disharmonious meanings between established elements of the social system and the novelty. Functional disequilibria require modifications in the social "machinery," e.g., technology, role specifications, artifacts, group structures. Logical-meaningful disequilibria may also stimulate changes in the socio-technical structure but they particularly involve ideological and psychological mechanisms to yield seeming harmony between previously unreconciled beliefs.

Since innovation in the instruments (material culture) has been so emphasized in Western society, it is an area of disequilibrium worth special scrutiny. The group structures adapted to modern technology are unquestionably of a different order from those adapted to handicraft or hand-powered agricultural technology. However, it does not appear that any given set of machines or technological system possesses some single or optimal social adjustment. Technical innovation stands in complex reciprocity with innovations in work group norms and structures. The strain toward some optimal efficiency in adaptation to a given set of artifacts is always mediated by a multitude of additional variables. There is nothing special about the disequilibrating effects of "material" innovations in contrast to innovations in norms, skills, and social relationships.

10

Integrative Patterns

The presence of innovation virtually requires some adjustive innovative behavior. Such responsive innovating may be directed along one or more of several pathways through which perceived stresses are resolved and re-equilibration achieved. The various integrative patterns discussed here are probably not exhaustive. Moreover, frequently two or more of these processes operate to fit an innovation into the living social system. Four differing patterns of integration are distinguished. Their brief listing will be followed by more detailed discussion of each with illustrative material to show how they operate in concrete instances.

1. Perseverative or elaborative additions to established complexes
2. Incorporation of the novelty as an accommodated specialty
3. Incorporation of the novelty as an alternative to established traits
4. Syncretism, or the fusion of the novelty with the meaningful and functioning structure of an existing complex

INNOVATIONS WHICH ARE PERSEVERATIVE OR ELABORATIVE ADDITIONS

As Ralph Linton observed many years ago, man is the only animal capable of boredom. He is an eternal elaborator. Human beings do not "let well enough alone"; at least many such human beings turn up in every society from time to time. If we may again boldly presume upon our knowledge of the animal kingdom, man gets pleasure out of what would seem to other animals utterly useless activity. Man makes a tool—and then he decorates it. He draws an outline, and then he colors it, and then frames it, and then carves designs in the frame and finally inlays the designs. As with Tom Sawyer, the challenge in doing a job is not only in getting it done but doing it with style. Axe handles are carved, pots are embellished, actions are supported by ideologies. As elaborative extensions and variations these are not necessarily competitive with any established trait. And if they introduce new functions, these are presumably—if not in fact—supportive of traits in the status quo. Thus the introduction of decorating axe handles in a society in which axe handles were never so carved is aesthetic elaboration. While competition could ensue over carved versus uncarved handles, this is not intrinsic to the situation. Nor is carving necessarily functional or dysfunctional in an active sense in regard to the axe complex generally—it might be either or neither.

Simple elaboration is most clear in aesthetic and ritual matters as a new element is added to enhance the meaning of an established complex. When a church choir dons robes while in other ways continuing their ceremonies and singing as usual, there is simple perseveration. Ceremony is more extended and formalized toward the same old ends without modifying the traditional complex except in covering street clothes by a formal garb. Even such elemental substitution is lacking when the choir introduces a doxology for the service's end. The service ritual has simply been elaborated. Similarly does St. Christopher, long the patron saint of travelers, find a place over the instrument panel of the latest sports car. While any of these extended practices might find opposition as people call up norms with which inconsistency can be claimed, none of them competes with, replaces, or curtails in any way an existing structured activity. Rather, the traditional activity is extended, more highly developed, or pushed into newly opening circumstances.

In regard to norms, we are prone to think in terms of change in the sense of definitions of behavioral expectations and consequent shifting standards of conduct. Norms also change by elaboration as circumstances seem to require that the norms be spelled out in greater detail or that they be extended to cover newly created situations. While such elaborations often involve shifts in meaning, this is not necessarily the case. Old norms are frequently adapted to new circumstances. In many Eastern societies which traditionally held sharp status gradations, the etiquette due a person of high position was extended to European conquerors. In some instances it would appear that the Europeans demanded the old practices in more elaborate form than had the indigenous despots who preceded them.

In the realm of ideology, elaborations appear in support of action, and actions arise to bear out ideologies. Insofar as consistency is found between such theories and such actions by members of the social system, we are justified in speaking of elaborative innovations. As Pareto observed, man, unlike a cat, is unwilling to eat the mouse without spinning a theory as to why it was in the mouse's best interest to be eaten. Further, only man elaborates upon the etiquette of mouse-eating. More seriously, etiquette provides interesting elaborations upon general principles taken as starting points. Note the elaboration of behavior based upon the principle that food should not be handled with the fingers at the table. Not all changes in etiquette, by any means, are simply elaborative, but many are elaborative and still more begin as elaborations and end as "alternatives" and "replacements."

In utilitarian, or instrumental, traits, simple perseveration is less common, since tools are usually measured by efficiency and hence the more efficient novelty replaces the older less efficient device. However, this is not invariably true. Long-established tools may be applied in novel circumstances, as distance markers are shifted from horse and buggy utilization to modern highway use, with variation rather than replacement. Highway numbering itself was an innovation arising with the motorcar which simply elaborated a long-established system of directional devices. The extensive use of chromium on automobiles in the 1930's and 1940's particularly was a stylistic elaborative pattern.

Elaboration exists in its pure form only when a novelty fits into an existing complex without alteration in the meaning of the complex and without displacement, reduction, or modification of traditional traits. A sense of this continuity has been almost systematically disrupted by the overemphasis upon Marxian theories of change and the emphasis among culture lag adherents upon the adaptive—and hence, rootless—character of "non-material" culture. Social structures, norms, and values, as well as instruments, have their traditional antecedents as well as their adaptive and revolutionary aspects. Old patterns may be perseverated beyond recognition—or they may be junked and replaced by "new" ones —a non-elaborative change.

Although novelties frequently (no doubt usually) compete with, merge with, or perhaps displace established modes, such processes are at times *set in motion* as perseverations of the old. This principle is essentially that developed by W. I. Thomas in his great comparative sociology, *Primitive Behavior*. It is similar in idea to that of E. Sapir in his concept of "language drift," which ultimately gave rise to the more general concept of "cultural drift" (Herskovits, Chap. 34).

Sapir pointed out that a language has a historical "slope," in the sense of rather obscure tendencies which foreshadow and set the direction of future changes. The changes of languages are not accidental nor discontinuous. They persevere along continuous avenues which "prefigure" the kinds of innovations which will occur through succeeding centuries (Sapir, p. 165).

Thomas (pp. 8 ff.) uses the phrase "perseverative pattern" to express the point of view that a trivial situation may initiate a pattern which expands and ramifies and is stepped up to a position of emotional and social importance. (Thus a society having defined the birth of twins as an awesome but positive phenomenon sets out upon a path of perseveration or elaboration of practices and beliefs consistent with the basic definition.) In developing his own application of "drift" in cultural change, Thomas, as did Sapir, also uses linguistic developments as examples of the process he denotes as "perseverative." For example, the various words for "camel" were proliferated among Arabs as this animal's significance expanded. The following extract from *Primitive Behavior* was based upon an earlier account by Hammer-Purgstall.

Names of classes of camels according to the function to which they were devoted—milk camel, riding camel, freight camel, marriage camel, slaughter camel, sacrifice camel, etc.

Names of breeds, of different degrees of nobility of lineage, derivation from different lands, etc.

Names of camels in groups, as several, a considerable number, many, innumerable, etc., and with reference to their objectives—grazing, conveying a caravan, a war expedition, etc.

As many as 50 words for pregnant camels, stages of pregnancy, and pregnant behavior, including names for each month of pregnancy, for the stage at which movement of the fetus is first felt, for mothers who suckle and do not suckle their young during pregnancy, for those near delivery, those delivering prematurely, those bearing only once or twice, those bearing foals always living and always dead, those whose foals develop hair in the womb, those feigning or seeming to feign pregnancy, etc.

Names for young camels by years up to the age of ten, for those in various stages of dentition, for those beginning to walk.

Names for physically and mentally peculiar camels—those with large, small, slit, or hanging ears; those differently gaited; those persistently eating thorny or other injurious food; those not drinking until others leave, and those repeatedly returning to drink; those caressing the young with the nose but refusing such, and reserving their milk for some outsider for whom they have preference.

Names transferred to the camel and its trappings from other objects. *Hilal*, for example, means 1) full moon, 2) a thin camel, 3) a camel with the brand of a new moon, 4) the moon-shaped iron connecting the two sides of the camel saddle. [Thomas, pp. 68–69.]

While it is evident that the perseverative tendencies and drift constitute situational forces influencing innovation, innovations of this sort minimize the drama of integration processes. When novelty is functionally and logically congruent with an established complex it is in a sense pre-digested. It fills out or extends an established configuration. The innovation may arise as a product of diffusion as well as of intrinsic invention, as the society latches onto those novelties which add meaning to traditional modes and eschews those which show inconsistency or competitiveness. Erwin H. Johnson has reported an instance of "orderly change" in which the traditional governmental unit in Japan has gradually subtracted the tasks it performed while a new level of organization has consistently added tasks. Johnson views this process as perseverative in that one unit has as consistently added tasks as the other has subtracted them without competitive or other complicating processes. Of course, appearances are not always accurate, and apparent perseverative tendencies may have actual latent consequences undreamed of by those who would simply amplify the status quo.

INNOVATIONS INTEGRATED AS SPECIALTIES

The terms "specialties" and "alternatives" were introduced into the language of the social sciences by Ralph Linton. By a specialty he meant those sub-cultural traits and techniques known to particular groups within the larger social system, i.e., as their specialized knowledge. By an alternative he meant different normative modes of acting in the same situation, e.g., permissive monogamy and polygyny in the same society. The useful extension of these ideas to the field of cultural change was recognized by Linton, and his usage forms the basis for this discussion.

Innovations which enter social systems as specialties require the existence of a sub-group around them. Specialties involve parts of the body of knowledge or segments of the culture not understood or practiced by all members. This is to say that they are not "universals" fully applicable to all members, nor are they alternatives or patterned routes open to the choice of all individuals. Specialties belong to sub-cultures or parts of a culture known to sub-groups. Linton noted that specific age groups within our society accept innovations which have no relevance or interest for other age levels. Games of marbles, yo-yo tops, hoola-hoops, and skate-boards have, at one time or another, been innovations in the culture of American juveniles. Adults are rarely the means through which the skills associated with these items are transmitted. Similarly, the romantic techniques of adolescents are specialties belonging to an age group. They are transmitted from older to younger teen-agers without penetrating either the adult or juvenile levels of society (Linton, p. 278).

The clearest instances of significant specialties entering a social system are in occupational fields, especially with the proliferation of occupations in the nineteenth and twentieth centuries. It is improbable that any man in any society has really known the whole culture, but in modern times any given person knows an infinitesimal part of his cultural heritage and he keeps up with only a small proportion of the innovations bombarding it. Individuals keep up with new knowledge and new techniques mainly as these fit their special interests and their vocational specialties. It is not an accident that when textbooks in one academic discipline have reason to refer to material developed in other disciplines, the observations are all too likely to be out of date. (Unilinear evolutionary theories, for example, were to be found in some textbooks many years after those ideas were rejected by virtually all textbooks in sociology and anthropology.)

In the instance of space exploration, we have the addition of a new socio-cultural sub-system formed around a new set of objectives. Specialized implements are used by specialized persons toward specialized ends. All of these are newly introduced to the society. We cannot here speak of *an* innovation. Rather that which is novel is an entire complex of integrated knowledge, values, norms, techniques, and devices operated by, and also guiding the operations of, a distinctive group. The "distinctive group" becomes highly differentiated in minutely specialized sub-groups each with its own "sub-sub-culture."

Similar specialty integrations occur on much less complicated levels. As the potter's wheel appeared, very commonly the forming of the clay upon the wheel came to be a specialty craft of men. As innovations developed in the art of pot designing, these were perseverations of a specialty. As such they further built a sub-cultural craft among a community sub-group, e.g., the pot-making families. The process of the new design's absorption into the social system is through its acceptance by a specially defined sub-group alerted to this field of activity. Immediate integration of the innovation is socially limited, demarcated by the limits of sub-group culture.

If we continue with potting as an illustration we may see how abstract the distinction between specialty and alternative can become. The new complex of potting is indeed a specialty in its appeal to a limited group, but it is not a *pure* specialty (like space exploration) unless the function it fulfills is entirely new. If potting competes, say, with an already established basketry, we must conclude that it as accepted as a "specialized-alternative." An old trait (basketry) now shares its former broad function with a new specialized trait (pottery). Indeed, the old trait may be completely lost in favor of various diversified alternatives which replace it. If we now look back on the matter of language drift, the development of specialized words for "camel" actually involves perseveration plus specialization and possibly even the displacement of older generalized terms for camel.

"Specialized alternatives" have one clear difference from pure specializations. "Specialized alternatives" do not center around sub-groups with sub-cultures. They may be universally used within the social system in reference to limited functions rather than limited groups. What makes a "specialized alternative" *special* is not that it applies to a particular sub-group but that it applies to differentiation in function. If a subsistence community is using a particular type of small pot for all purposes and a new technique is discovered whereby a new style large pot can be formed, the innovation may indeed be accepted as a "specialized alternative." The large pot is used for storage and the small pot for transporting from the well and in cookery. The function of the first pot has been curtailed by the rise of the innovative specialty. What was once a general function served by a single traditional implement has now become divided between two. The two pots are not full alternatives: they are accommodated by limited use of each. The concept of specialty has to do with *who* takes up the novelty. The concept of alternative depends upon the *function* of the novelty.

INNOVATIONS INTEGRATED AS ALTERNATIVES

When a new trait or complex is introduced into a culture to fulfill a function already served by an established trait or complex, it is an alternative. Novel alternatives are by definition competitive or potentially competitive with established cultural traits.

Vast numbers of alternatives exist in our culture and no doubt in most others. They range from such obvious items as the rotory lawn mower being introduced competitively with the reel type mower to the alternative pathways to salvation offered by different religious groups. In our earlier discussion of societies having loose structure (see Chap. 3), one phase of loose structure was the provision of many alternative modes of acting. For example, in Western society we are rather rigid in our requirements regarding marriage. Some societies provide many normative alternatives, i.e., permitting polygyny, polyandry, and monogamy in the same community at the same time. Linton described alternatives in the following way:

There are in every culture a considerable number of traits which are shared by certain individuals but which are not common to all the members of the society or even to all the members of any one of the socially recognized categories. We will call these *Alternatives*. The elements of culture which may be included in this class have a very wide range, varying from the special and often quite atypical ideas and habits of a particular family to such things as different schools of painting or sculpture. Aside from the nature of the participation in them, all these Alternatives have this in common: they represent different reactions to the same situations or different techniques for achieving the same ends. The cultures of small societies living under primitive conditions usually include only a moderate number of such Alternatives, while in such a culture as our own they are very plentiful. Examples of such Alternatives for ourselves would be such things as the use of horses, bicycles, rail-roads, automobiles, and airplanes for the single purpose of transportation over-land; our variety of teaching techniques; or our wide range of beliefs and attitudes toward the supernatural . . .

The ability of all cultures to incorporate numerous Alternatives without serious interferences with their functioning is of vital importance to the processes of cultural growth and change. . . . Suffice it to say that in spite of the occasional realization of brand-new needs by a society, with the consequent introduction into the culture of elements with new functions, the bulk of all cultural changes are in the nature of replacements. The newly introduced element takes over the uses or functions of a preexisting element. Its general acceptance by the members of a society will depend very largely on whether it performs these functions more efficiently. Thus men had cutting tools long before they had metal, and the introduction of the new material was by a process of gradual replacement. Stone knife and metal knife were, for a time, used side by side. Even the forms of the older tools were carried over and copied in the new medium. Again, our own need for transportation was al-ready met by a variety of appliances at the time the automobile was invented. The new appliance was accepted because it was superior in one way or an-other to each of the preexisting ones, but it still has not replaced any of them completely. [Linton, pp. 273–280.] *

Linton argued that in serious matters, alternatives tend to be transitory, in movement toward either extinction or toward universal acceptance. No doubt this is often true but Linton was probably defining the idea of "alternative" narrowly. Porterhouse steak does not drive sirloin from the home nor from the market, nor does the Methodist route to salvation drive out the Presbyterian or the Roman Catholic. On the other hand, as was mentioned, organic American medicine was once composed of two competing systems, the allopathic and homeopathic. In this in-stance tests of efficiency in meeting desired ends were indeed significant in the virtual extinction of the method which did not stand up best to scientific scrutiny. Yet osteopathy, chiropractic, and orthodox medicine have areas in which they act as alternatives (and still others as special-ties) and none seems to be in process of extinction at this time. Also, in regard to illness or injury often treated through any of these methods, prayer is accepted by some persons as the correct alternative to all of them. In America, no doubt, the long-range trend in medicine supports Linton, in that a body of scientific medicine with its various specialties *tends* toward universality in the achievement of health. Prayer is not usually viewed as an alternative but as a complementing adjunct to applied science. For many Westerners prayer and science stand in a stable accommodated relationship—not as alternatives but as complement-ing systems.

* Adapted from *The Study of Man* by Ralph Linton. Copyright 1936, by Mere-dith Corporation. Reprinted by permission of Appleton-Century-Crofts.

There is no firm line to the distinction between alternative traits and systems and complementing ones. As a novel trait moves into a society it can remain in stable competition with an established trait. Or one or the other may be driven out. Linton is right in inferring that such a circumstance is stressful. But its stresses can be accommodated just as Methodism is accommodated to Presbyterianism or scientific medicine to prayerful therapy. Frequently the invading novelty gains status in part as an alternative and in part as a specialty. New and peripheral functions may be attributed to the device which at first seemed irreconcilable with the traditional trait serving the same general function. Or both traits may be redefined so that each of the alternatives serves distinctive roles in its achievement; or the function may be redefined so that it becomes two separate functions each served by an appropriate mechanism. Thus some modern chiropractors might attempt to set apart one phase of healing in which they would be in accommodative relationship to general medicine. If this were accomplished we would no longer be dealing with alternatives but with specialties. Here the alternatives are presumed to have differing and complementing roles in the achievement of the end.

Innovative ideas and contrivances do not necessarily drive out earlier ones which may have served identical functions. They may be accommodated as (1) stable alternatives, (2) adjunctive specialties, or (3) a little of both. They may, of course, exist side by side for long periods in an unaccommodated relationship with open conflict or rivalry between their respective adherents. If the issue is not one crucial for group survival, this may long remain an unresolved matter of personal taste or preference.

A Case of Integration Through Specialties and Alternatives

Modern medicine moves into different societies through widely varying integrational patterns. Dr. John Cassel has described his productive partnership with a Zula witch doctor in terms of virtual syncretic fusion as he contrived a partnership of specialists. (Dr. Cassel gave the patient the needed injection while the witch doctor performed the traditionally appropriate rituals.) [1] In Ceylon, a more sophisticated locale and one possessing literate civilizations dating back several thousand years, the accommodative patterns in medicine have been complex but neither syncretic nor fully describable as alternatives or as specialties. The integration of various systems of health in this locale, especially among the

[1] Personal communication. See also Cassel's chapter in Benjamin Paul (ed.) *Health, Culture and Community*, New York, Russell Sage Foundation, 1957.

Sinhalese, illustrates several accommodative processes operating simultaneously.

The preservation of good health and the return to normalcy when ill is to be achieved through any one or more of several patterns, each of which stands as an organized socio-cultural system in its own right, in something of the same way that in the United States recovery through prayer fits into a distinctively religious system while recovery through antibiotics fits a distinctively secular medical one. In Ceylon such systems are as highly developed but more various. The conventional relationships between them are perhaps less stably accommodated.

Prior to Western influence, the Sinhalese had, in addition to supernatural systems, a highly developed pharmacopoeia and a skilled body of medical practitioners, the *Ayurvedic* physicians. In addition to this Hindu-based system a similar type system called *Unani* was introduced by Muslims. These bodies of medicine are rooted in traditional uses of herbs and other "natural" materials (Opler; Marriott). Today colleges exist in Ceylon to train Ayurvedic physicians. Apart from this system of non-scientific but organic treatment, there are several supernatural and magical systems which may be used alternatively or concomitantly. Each of the latter has its own priesthood or set of practitioners. Unquestionably these various systems have points of origin in different historical epochs and no doubt from different geographical locales. Not only did any one fail to displace another but there has been surprisingly little fusion among them.

The major systems, which to a Western point of view are of magical or religious character, include demon exorcising, appeals to planetary gods, appeals to Hindu-like dieties, exorcising of various diverse supernatural entities like ghosts and poltergeists, and "cutting" sorcerers' spells. Beyond all these are the somewhat rarer appeals to the Buddha through established rituals of Buddhism and its monks. Each of these various plans is highly systematized within itself, except to some extent the diffuse charming used for ghosts, poltergeists, etc. Each has its separate "priesthood" with its distinctive rituals, ethics, and status. Disease demons are exorcised by professional devil dancers; the planet gods are served by astrologers who "divine" and by dancers who perform. A given ailment may be treated by an Ayurvedic physician or by a devil dancer, by a planetary dancer, or even by a magician using charms. To some extent the choice of a particular plan is a matter of chance and predilection of the patient, although it is known that some disorders have more to do with one set of factors than another and hence the more appropriate treatment will be sought. The different systems are *specialties* in one sense and *alternatives* in another. Often one is invoked after the failure of any other, including Ayurvedic and, today, Western type medicine. Planetary influence affects all aspects of life including health; demons are traditionally almost exclusively associated with diseases. The Hindu-type gods are appealed to because of their generalized power, and the Buddha because of his supreme power over all. In this reasoning some semblances of syncretism are apparent. Magical medicine is *rationalized* to Buddhism, and Hindu-type gods are viewed as being under the supreme intelligence of the Buddha. Organizationally each system is almost fully distinct.

Upon such an unstable yet institutionalized equilibrium modern Western type medical and health practice was introduced. It has had immense success as is attested by Ceylon's low death rate at the present time. Yet it has not driven out any of the more traditional practices nor has it fused with them. The opposition of Western scientific medicine to its predecessors, organizationally, conceptually, and methodologically, is and has been apparent from its very introduction which occurred in a substantial way at the end of the 18th century (Ceylon). British troops, then on the island, were being ravaged by dysentery and malnutrition, and epidemics of smallpox were feared. Both military and civil hospitals were established. Regional medical overseers were appointed and a vaccination campaign introduced. In 1805 it was reported that 33,000 persons had been vaccinated with surprisingly little objection in what must have been a mystified population. Although medical progress seems to have waned in the mid-part of the nineteenth century, Western medicine with its accoutrements became thoroughly established during this century. By 1880 a full-scale college of medicine was established, and in 1886 it is reported that there were 26 civil hospitals, 8 district hospitals, 6 immigration hospitals, 14 district dispensaries, and many more local dispensaries as well as "leper and lunatic asylums." Tea and rubber estates, in addition, maintained 96 hospitals and 670 dispensaries for their laborers. In the present century, medical and public health developments have given to Ceylon probably the most favorable health situation in South Asia. Western medical practice and hospitalization has been brought within the reach of virtually the total population. By 1949 there were 258 exceedingly busy hospitals which treated 651,939 indoor patients in a population then fewer than 8 million persons. During 1949 the number of patients treated in the Colombo General Hospital alone, the nation's largest, was nearly 54,000. This relates strictly to the practice of Western medicine. There is no doubt either from the mortality and health statistics or the data on the use of services that Ceylon has embraced Western medicine strongly indeed. What then is the fate of Ayurvedics, God-priests, demon dancers, astrologers, and assorted magicians?

No one is able to estimate very closely the number of demon dancers and God-priests and astrologers and other diviners and magical practitioners practicing their professions today in Ceylon, but they are certainly a very large number. Some hint is possible from the Ceylon census for 1946 which found 3,953 persons with their regular occupations in "astrology," "fortune telling," and "other arts not elsewhere classified." Demon dancing, planet God ceremonies, vowing to Hindu-type dieties, and, of course, Buddhist rituals, are possibly as widely performed in the interests of health as they were two hundred years ago. To be sure, these are often used as supernatural adjuncts to medical practice but never did such ceremonials stand alone without "organic" medicine in the form of Ayurveda. What, then, happened to this herbal medical system as Western medicine became universally accepted in the island?

Since Ceylon was for several centuries ruled by Western powers, it is understandable that Western style medicine was given precedence over "Eastern" in matters of state support. State aid to Ayurveda which had been practiced since ancient times was curtailed and eventually cut off altogether until recent years. Hospitals once supported by the Sinhalese kings were replaced by hospitals and dispensaries of Western medicine. Though bereft of state aid, the indigenous system continued to live—and even prosper. In most villages there was still the "native doctor," the "vederala," who knew the herbal pharmacopoeia, and even more importantly, knew and loved his village patients. No doubt the complex knowledge upon which the system is based was frequently transmitted informally from father to son and sometimes, no doubt, it was practiced with minimal knowledge and technical qualification according to the standards of the system. But it lived and prospered in the face of the seeming landslide support for a new and competitive system.

In 1928, a government-supported College of Indigenous (Ayurvedic) Medicine was opened, and an associated hospital was established in 1933 (Ceylon, pp. 90–92). In 1941, these services were greatly expanded. In 1949, the hospital treated over 3,000 patients and over 358,000 outpatients. From its inception to 1949, the College turned out over 500 practitioners adding them to the already established corps of less fully trained village doctors. In an effort to systematize the Ayurveda service, registration was pursued in the 1940's, and in 1949 over 5,000 applications for registration had been received. These figures give at least some hint of the pervasive significance of Ayurvedic medicine in Ceylon and there is no reason to think that it has suffered any major setbacks since 1949. In a survey conducted about 1950, villagers in a very progressive rural community were asked which they would miss most if taken away, "Western medicine" or Ayurvedic (Ryan *et al.*, Chap. 11). Two-thirds said they would prefer to lose Western medicine. None of them actually wanted to give up Western medicine however. In this same village, in which virtually everyone uses Ayurvedic physicians *and* Western physicians, about 10 per cent of all homes held a planet god or demon exorcising ceremony in the single year 1951.

There is every reason to think that all the different forms of treatment, herbal, magical, astrological, and Western will survive for many generations. First of all, there has been no syncretic fusion of any degree between Western medicine and its various traditional counterparts. Practitioners of each branch of the healing arts retain completely distinct identity. Western physicians who are, of course, strictly Ceylonese in personal origin but who are trained in modern scientific medicine are as intolerant of Ayurvedic practice as an American internist would be of Grandma's book of home remedies. It is a safe guess that the Western-type physician is more intolerant of Ayurveda than he is of astrology and demon dancing. (Like most Ceylonese, the educated doctor might attach validity to astrological "science," though he is not likely to petition the planet gods through ritual.) In any event, each system is distinctly organized and there is no hint of astrology in the practice of Western medicine nor is there acceptance of demonology or even Ayurvedic herban recipes. It is likely that Western medical science has had influence upon Ayurveda, but this has not served to blur the distinctiveness of the two systems. Demon dancing and the invocations of higher powers show no substantive change through contact with modern medical science.

To some degree every one of these separate systems is competitive with each other as an alternative, and in part each complements every other in the role of specialty. This can be illustrated by a minor village event in which a barefooted child stumbled over a rock and tore off a toenail. The writer was present with his car and was approached regarding taking the small boy to a Western dispensary for attention. Not heartlessly, but probingly, he asked the father why not go to the trusted "native doctor," practically next door. The response was, "In this, I fear there may be an infection." Had the injury been a bruise or general shaking up, the Ayurvedic would have been sought. The village man knows perfectly well that his valued herbalist is not the equal of the Western doctor in cases of infection—and in many other serious matters. This is much the same kind of distinction made by the average American when he decides whether to use a patent medicine on the advice of a knowledgeable friend or go to a medical specialist. Often the village man will try first one and then the other, using them as alternatives. More fundamentally, there tends to be specialization in the forms of illness and injuries which the Ayurvedics treat. If, as for the writer's village friend, the case looks serious and not a matter of comforting, assuring, and relief of temporary ills, the Western physician is likely to be sought. On the other hand, a patient may go directly to a Western-style physician, accept his treatment, and then go to his neighboring Ayurvedic physician just to be sure no stone is left unturned. Thus a young man with a broken arm had it set quite properly by a Western surgeon. He then had poultices applied to the arm by a "native doctor," to the disgust of the surgeon who was then called upon to undo the damage wrought by the Ayurvedic. At this level the practitioners' systems were brought into open conflict, with this surgeon practically ready to support an Ayurvedic extermination movement. Probably the more general attitude is "live and let live," with an understanding that the "native doctors" "do more good than harm."

The relationship of Western practice and demon dancing has become almost fully one of complementing specialties. As Western practice was introduced it cut down the range of illnesses ascribed to demon infestation. Although demon dancers complain that too many people are going to the Western doctors these days, the demon dancer is still in very active business and probably will long remain so. One area of healing is almost completely in his hands, that of psychogenic illness. Village people today believe in demons as factors in illness just as strongly as did their grandfathers, but they have restricted the scope of demons. Scarcely anyone would credit demons for an attack of malaria and call for the demon dancer. But it is different if the symptoms of patients are of the order of "persistent headaches," bad dreams, worriedness, persistent stomach upsets, sleeplessness, "madness," etc. In village surveys, village men practically always attributed symptoms of this nature to demons and practically none attributed the recognizable symptoms of organically rooted disorders to demons. In effect, demon dancers have become the psychiatrists of Ceylon—called in when organic foundation for the illness is not found or when chronic cases do not respond to treatment. For organic symptoms, demon dancing is a sort of last resort. For apparent psychogenic disorders, the dancer is a prime specialist.

Over the past century there has been a transition in demon dacing from the status of partial alternative to Western medicine to the status of complementing specialty. As evidence of the accommodative process, there is far less antagonism between Western medicine and demon dancer than between Western medic and Ayurvedic. These two systems have reached a fairly stable accommodation. This will probably last until Western-type medicine can introduce treatment for psychogenic disorders which is demonstrably more effective than demon dancing. If this should ever occur, we would see a shift from stable specialization into competitive alternatives. In the very long view, perhaps Linton's proposition will be borne out after all. Western medicine gradually reduces the spheres of alternative, specialized systems, ultimately, perhaps, to the point of extermination—but that is a long way off.

When we view the relationship of encroaching Western-style medicine upon the various God- and Buddha-oriented plans of treatment, there is little influence one way or another. Many ceremonies are held for protective purposes, e.g., planet god ceremonies to protect a pregnant woman. But a mid-wife in a Western-type hospital is likely to attend the delivery. Vows are made before the gods for the recovery of a loved one —who may be treated by any type of practitioner. Buddhist ceremonies may be held in the case of serious illness, much as the protective power of his God is sought by a Christian. These matters remain as complements to organic and other treatment systems.

The adoption of Western medicine in Ceylon exemplifies very little syncretism but a complex mixture of accommodative and competitive processes. The diffusing system of scientific medicine was given wholehearted recognition but not as a displacement of traditional ways. Nor is there any sign that total displacement is likely to occur.

INNOVATIONS INTEGRATED THROUGH FUSION (SYNCRETISM)

Innovations which provide new and alternative paths to ends achieved through traditional means do not necessarily replace or long continue to compete with their predecessors. They may fuse with them in a variety of ways so that the new is merged with the old to provide a single trait or idea, or even a unified single system for the accomplishment of the old goal. Goals and values themselves may be merged into a generalized whole. The term "syncretism" has been applied to such mergers, particularly where religious or supernatural systems have merged, as in the case of Christianity and paganism in aboriginal America. Syncretic processes are often accompanied by social conflict and ideological competition during the period under which syncretic fusion is taking place. Whether or not fusion occurs, rather than displacement or rejection, depends partly on the ability of the receiving people psychologically to reconcile the new with the old and, particularly, upon the degree of rigidity in the traditional system. When the traditional system is highly organized, with specialized functionaries, the syncretic process is less likely to take place than is some accommodative one. In the case of aboriginal America, the power and the coercive violence of the invader were significant factors.

Monro S. Edmonson has distinguished two varieties or levels of syncretic integration.

One of these, which may be called micro-syncretism, involves a relationship of logical implication. In this case the two patterns brought into spatiotemporal conjunction by diffusion are syncretistically combined by operations of elemental human logic in a more or less obvious fashion. It is essential for this purpose that the two patterns be rather simply related to one another, so that only a small step is needed for the synthesis. Application of a native weaving technique to a new and unfamiliar fiber is an obvious example. Rather more complex examples in which the element of logical implication is still strong would include such phenomena as stimulus diffusion. [P. 196.] *

What Edmonson is here terming "micro-syncretism" is no different from what has been earlier described in terms of mutation. It does not matter particularly that one element of the fusion is derived from diffusion and the other from internal sources. Micro-syncretism covers a vast range of innovations, becoming in fact a virtual minimum definition of invention itself, i.e., the establishment of a novel configuration of materials. Nonetheless, this is precisely the manner in which a multitude of new traits are in fact fused into a culture. Frequently the consequences of this fusion, i.e., the resultant innovation, may secondarily compete with or displace traditional devices within the culture. Thus when the old weaving technique is applied to the new fiber the result may be a process which is either an alternative or a specialty within the weaving milieu of the society. And the resultant fabric similarly may compete with, though not necessarily displace, the fabric derived from the traditional fiber.

Edmonson then recognizes the realm of "macro-syncretism" as an area of fusion in reference to which the term syncretic is more commonly applied. In macro-syncretism, the synthesis is achieved by analogy rather than by strict logic.

The equation of Aztec gods with the Christian devil, for example, upon which much of the syncretism of belief in Middle American folk Catholicism may be said to rest, is hardly to be derived by logic, yet many consequences follow logically from it. The analogy selects arbitrarily some elements of the previous patterns and makes possible an intercultural semantics with inevitably syncretistic results. While micro-syncretism proceeds in small leaps which most men's brains make similarly, macro-syncretism proceeds by larger leaps to which one must be specifically initiated. [Edmonson, p. 196.]

In the many studies of the confrontation of religious systems, it is apparent that macro-syncretism was in process—a process in which meanings are transmitted interculturally and a completely foreign system of ideas is found fusible with existing ideas at a sufficient number of points for the two separate religions to become one. The concept of syncretism has usually been used in regard to religious systems and at the level termed "macro-syncretism" by Edmonson. However, syncretic fusions can occur in the integration of a wide range of ideas and social structures, e.g., art styles, kinship systems, languages.

* Reprinted by permission of the Middle American Research Institute, Tulane University, from *Nativism and Syncretism* by Monro S. Edmonson and others, 1960.

Syncretism as here used will mean fusion in *meaning* and structure in contrast to mutation, i.e., the contrivance of separate ideas or devices into new working relationships. The distinction is tenuous, but we would not be inclined to view the merging of a vacuum tube with the wireless as an instance of syncretism. Syncretism involves reinterpretation as potentially alternative systems are brought to unity. Herskovits indicates how such fusion has occurred in the field of language as Africans in the new world took over the vocabulary of their masters recasting it into grammatical and phonetic structures of African origin.

When a Gulla Negro of South Carolina in a folk-tale, says "Rabbit tell Fox, said," for "Rabbit told Fox," he is expressing an African idiom with English words. When he says "Man, don' you see all dis fresh meat standing in dis lot?" or "Rabbit lie in de sun on he so' skin," . . . he is reinterpreting with English words the African expression of the following ideas: "Man, don't you see all these animals in this pasture?"; "Rabbit lay with the sun on his body . . ." [Herskovits, p. 555.]

The literature of syncretism is particularly rich in the areas of fusion in religious ideas and rituals. In theological discussions the term itself underwent a shift of meaning from the sense of "harmony" to the sense of fusion (Moffatt). No doubt every extant world religion has undergone some degree of syncretic fusion as it has come into contact with the other world religions and with local ones. The Buddhism of China is strikingly different from the Buddhism of Burma; the Christianity of Sicily different from that of Peru; the Judaism of the Atlas Mountains different from the Judaism of Miami Beach. In substantial part these differences reflect the varying sources of syncretic influence (Hoult, Chap. 3; Moss and Capinari).

In preceding contexts stresses between alternative religious systems and between science and supernatural systems have been cited. In both type situations syncretism has been a pattern of adjustment. Where beliefs in magical relationships are deep and systematized but the observable scientific systems clearly accomplish valued and evident ends, syncretism may well take place. As the Wilsons point out:

. . . the contradictions between dogma and observation may be resolved in the mind of the magician himself, in dreams. Among the Nyakyusa and Pondo new medicines for use in magical situations are dreamed of. The magician's ancestors, it may be, are held to "show them to him" in his dreams. The dream is a dogmatic revelation and so has authority within the magical situation. . . . In these dreams, and in the choice of magicians, there is an empirical element. Generations of such dreams, have, we suggest, introduced into magical operation actually effective factors, some of which may be still unknown to our science. [Wilson and Wilson, pp. 91–92.]

By a different process, these same tribal peoples have accommodated Western knowledge to their system of truth regarding some aspects of health.

Nyakysus who have been to school lay more stress on sorcery than on witchcraft, some teachers even insisting that they do not believe in witchcraft at all, but only in sorcery. Now sorcery (ubutege) includes poisoning, and these teachers are very vague in their own minds about the line between sorcery which involves putting poison in one's enemy's food, and sorcery which involves burying a charm under his doorway, or the thatch of his hut. They translate *Ubutege* to themselves as "poisoning," and find it quite compatible with their training of hygiene. [Wilson and Wilson, p. 154.]

Some of the better documented and clear-cut instances of religious syncretism have occurred with the introduction of Christianity, particularly into Middle and South America. Donald Thompson has analyzed the relationship between Mayan and the then contemporary Catholicism to show the conditions making for fusion and the points at which fusion occurred and culminated into an institutionalized religion in Yucatan. While his account does not purport to offer generalizations regarding syncretism, he has nevertheless put his finger upon many generalizable features.

By 1545 the Spaniards had subjected most of Middle America and were energetically converting Indians to Catholicism. Indians were generally reluctant to change their religion, and often their teachers were previously converted Indians who knew but little of the new religious thought (Edmonson *et al.*). The cult of the cross was singularly important to the Mayans as they were able to give it militant significance in their resurgence against the Spanish. The need for an Indian saviour exercising the powers of a Christ even led to a biblically ritualized crucifixation. In the realm of deities, pagan Gods persisted in the forests and fields as saints took over the functioning of local village gods, under the ultimate aegis of a remote Almighty. The gods of rain, or Chacs, were joined in a hierarchy under St. Michael Archangel, and were activated through chants invoking the Virgin. Communion was celebrated as a Chac rite but "in the name of God the Father, God the Son and God the Holy Ghost." The Virgin was fused with the Moon Goddess to become "beautiful lady, embracer of the maize." Traditional demons were degraded into hobgoblins and witches. The following extracts from Thompson's work emphasizes some of these points while obscuring somewhat his discussion of the nativistic movements associated with the new religion.*

---

* Reprinted by permission of the Middle American Research Institute, Tulane University, from *Nativism and Syncretism* (Publication 19) by Monro S. Edmonson *et al.*

The hybrid cult began early, and was almost surely a result of bewilderment and of confusion of the tenets of the two religions on which it drew. In Guatemala, for example, a dance representing the sacrifice of a prisoner of war was performed on the great festivals of the Christian church calendar. The participants, dressed as a jaguar, an eagle, a puma, and an unidentified animal, performed, in the dance, all the actions of a sacrifice except the actual killing of the victim. The dance was purely pagan, but was performed, as noted, on Christian holy days. It was finally prohibited in 1624, after lasting for a century of Christianity.

Referring again to the Landa material, it is evident that here also the two religions were combined and confused.[2] One witness, for instance, describes a midnight ceremony held (about 1557) by the cacique of Sotuta, in the local church, in which two small girls were tied to crosses.

The priest said, "Let these girls, placed on the cross, die as Jesus Christ died, who, they say, was our Lord, but we don't know if he was." After those words, they lowered and untied the girls from the crosses, and cut open and tore out their hearts, and offered them to the gods, as they were wont to do in ancient times. Later they threw the bodies of the sacrificed girls into a cenote. . . .

According to this witness, the crosses were kept specially for this ceremony which continued to be performed until a Catholic priest came to live in the town. The ceremony was not repeated during the priest's three-year stay, but was resumed shortly after he left. . . .

These ceremonies well illustrate the confusion of the two religions: whereas the actual sacrifices are essentially pagan, the crucifixions . . . are obviously new elements. In some cases, in fact, the victims were actually named, ceremonially, children of God or Jesus Christ. The cross itself, as I have pointed out, is used in pre-Columbian religion and art, but, of course, in a different context. In the case of these ceremonies, then, it seems highly probable that the teachings of the friars were confused with the pre-Columbian aspects of the cross, and resulted in a heightening of the importance of the cross in the post-Conquest religion. . . .

A desire to keep the old religion, constant pressure from the friars to accept Christianity, and a general willingness to compromise increased as time went on the desirability of this hybrid religion. . . .

. . . As Landa pointed out, it was the pagan priesthood who usually took the initiative in ordering sacrifices. It was also the priesthood who would gain the most by the perpetuation of the old religion. The rest of the population, too, suffered under the dominance and ill-treatment by the Spaniards, and probably were only too willing to perpetuate their old customs, and to hope that some day the Spaniards would leave.

The Spaniards, however, did not leave; and, as time went on, the discontent and confusion grew and eventually gave rise to more violent nativistic movements. Let us consider as an example the War of the Castes in Yucatan.

In 1847, rallying to the cry, "perish the whites," the Indians broke into open warfare, killing every available Spaniard and very nearly capturing all

---

[2] Reference is made here to a sixteenth century account. The following paragraph based upon this, is credited by Edmonson to F. Scholes and E. G. Adams, "Don Diego Quijada, Alcalde Mayor de Yucatan, 1561–1565," *Biblioteca Histórica Mexicana de Obras Inéditas,* Mexico, D.F.

of Yucatan. Merida almost fell; but the forces of the whites reorganized, aid came from Mexico, and many Indians left their own army to return home for the rainy season planting. Forced back into the area which is now the territory of Quintana Roo, the Indians continued the struggle; but, disheartened by their losses and disappointed in the rejection of their demands for autonomy, they despaired of their cause.

At this critical point, a time at which they were threatened not only by loss of self rule but also by the resultant humiliation and possible destruction of their culture as an entity, the Indians rallied to a new and magical source of hope.

At the town of Chan Santa Cruz, Quintana Roo, in 1850, a small cross began to get widespread fame for its ability to talk, its divine origin, and its power to help and protect the Indians. Although in fact the invention of a mestizo called José María Barrera and an accomplice with some ability at ventriloquism, the cross grew in fame; and Chan Santa Cruz shortly became the religious and political capital for the rebel Indians. The cross, which claimed to be the Trinity sent to earth by God the Father to help the Indians, encouraged the rebel natives to greater efforts, and at length became sufficiently powerful to warrant the whites' sending an expedition to destroy it and its supporters. In March of 1851 Chan Santa Cruz was secretly and successfully attacked, the cross was destroyed, and the ventriloquist killed.

Not so easily disheartened, the Indians reoccupied the town, and shortly thereafter appeared three new crosses which claimed to be the daughters of the cross. Barrera, who had escaped the attack, now proceeded to elaborate the cult and solve the problem of his lost ventriloquist. . . .

The cult of the cross formed not only the backbone of the continued resistance in the Chan Santa Cruz area, but also the basis for an elaborate system of labor levies, a standing army, and a theocratic government based on the attendant priests of the cross. . . .

The crosses were obviously out of the basic Christian context. The fact that they talked and were dressed in native costume indicates that they were more than just symbols; they were God Himself, alive on earth to help the Indians. Talking idols were known in pre-Conquest times so the concept was not a new one and its application to the cross can be accounted for by the pre- and post-Conquest use of the symbol. Possibly the image of Christ on the cross in pictures and on altars helped initiate or strengthen the idea of the cross as a being, but since pre-Columbian vegetal crosses, to judge by the Palenque example, were personified, it is more probable that the present personification of the cross derives from paganism.

Another important fact is that it was this particular cross or group of crosses, not crosses in general, which had this especially great power. Attempts were made elsewhere to establish a similar cult, but none of the new crosses had the power of those of Chan Santa Cruz. This concept exists today and is particularly important in the relative powers of different images of the same saint, as we shall see later.

This isolation of the Quintana Roo area resulting from the continued struggle kept alive the mixed Maya-Christian elements there, allowing neither one to dominate the other. Had it not been for the war, missionary work would in all probability have continued to the present. As it was, however, the amalgamated religion was isolated for over fifty years, and when Quintana Roo again became safe for whites in 1901, the proselytizing urge had lessened, and the use of force in religious teaching had ceased. [Thompson, pp. 16–18.]

Today as educated Maryknoll Fathers replace the older priesthood, perhaps purer Catholicism will emerge. But as Thompson observes, ". . . in any case perverted ceremonies, costumes, and dances will probably remain as an attraction for tourists to the economic advantage of the natives. It is a sad thought that a unique religion of four centuries' growth may end as a tourist attraction" (p. 32).

CONCLUSION

Innovations are integrated into functioning social systems through various pathways. Four integrative processes are examined, viz., (1) perseverative addition of the innovation to an already established complex or pattern within the society, (2) incorporation of a novelty as a specialized activity for some particular sub-group within the society, (3) incorporation of the novelty as an alternative to some traditional activity or train, and (4) the syncretic fusion of the novelty, structurally and meaningfully, with some existing complex or activity.

Where purely *perseverative* changes occur, societies are not seriously upset or wrenched in their integration of the novelty. Such introductions arise notably in linguistic drifts, ritualization, and artistic elaborations. Functional consequences are relatively slight for perseverative innovations. Where innovations are established as *specialties,* there is the implication of social differentiation concurrent with the integrative process. Specialties imply specialized sub-groups within the larger society which may or may not be newly created in response to the innovation. Where innovations enter a society as *alternatives* they enter as activities or traits competing with established ones which have served the same ends. While there is some tendency for one of the alternatives to ultimately drive out the other, many situations exist in which stable accommodations are reached between traditional patterns and novel alternative ones. Under some circumstances an alternative may be preserved by becoming an activity of a special sub-group, i.e., being translated into a specialty. *Syncretic* integration leaves neither the traditional pattern nor the innovative one intact. The two are fused to become a single trait or to form a single institution. Research in syncreticism has been most active in regard to religious institutions and concepts, wherein fusions are clearly evidenced. Examples are in the merger of early Buddhism with Tibetan supernaturalism to form Llamism, and the merger of Christianity with pagan cults in earlier centuries in Europe and in the Spanish conquest of America.

III

SOCIAL EVOLUTION
Directions of Change

11

Theories of Direction of Change

Social science in the nineteenth century was largely directed toward making science out of history. Sociology, at its foundations, was to be a science of social change. More precisely, it was to be the science that delineates the bases of social order upon which an evolving social structure could rest. As Kenneth E. Bock has said:

The task of sociology was more broadly conceived to involve the scientific demonstration of the basic conditions of social order, and above all, of the processes through which these conditions gradually developed. Social change through time thus became the main focus of interest and the objective was not simply to advocate a program of directed change but to discover natural laws of change that would serve as guides in social reorganization. Sociology was to be a *historical* science. [P. 5.]

Indeed it is difficult to explain to non-sociologists how the study of change can be anything other than that which its founders conceived it to be—a theory of historical sweep; knowledge of the directions of history and the forces moving "history" through its paces, the "laws of societal growth." Yet the impetus of the past half century in both sociology and anthropology has been toward structural and functional analyses, when it has not been toward descriptive empiricism. Scholars who insisted upon seeking generalizations through sequential historical data have run the risk of being branded "social philosophers," an opprobrious term in an era of empiricism. The eclipse of Social Darwinism for good and solid reasons also extended discredits to others who sought gen-

291

eralizations from data of the past. And even the immense stature of men like E. B. Tylor and Lewis H. Morgan could not prevail against the factual insufficiencies of their conceptions of universal stages in cultural growth. Strange how few have sought to reformulate evolutionary ideas and how many have rejected with vehemence the whole orientation.

Yet the *study* of history, in distinction to its recounting, has never ceased to stir the imaginations of a few scholars. Bold thinkers in various humanities and social sciences have been unable to resist the lure of seeking meaning and direction in the course of human history. Here interest has centered on finding a driving force upon which human progress rests. There the quest has been for the discovery of common stages through which all societies pass, or again, a formula which expresses the thread or patterning of human progress. Some scholars, like Arnold Toynbee and Karl Marx have attempted all of those objectives.

Contemporary ideas about the direction of change can be viewed as belonging to two different orientations: the cyclical and the linear. Cyclical theories no doubt have a longer and more distinguished lineage than do the linear ones, since the tempting analogy between the life cycle of the organism and the rise and fall of "civilizations" (or at least national states) has long been apparent. On the other hand, although speculative theories of evolution appealed to ancient philosophers, modern evolutionary interpretations have their roots in the early and mid-nineteenth century. Modern evolutionary thought is older than Charles Darwin, but evolution in the social sciences was hardly systematized prior to Auguste Comte. With the rejection of certain evolutionary theories in social science a half century ago, seekers after a universal thread in man's struggle have been singularly unpopular among sociologists and anthropologists. Cyclical theorists have had no easier going, since they have been beset with a multitude of basic methodological problems upon which they, let alone their detractors, can find only disagreement.[1] It is a real question if any human mind can so control the data of many civilizations, and even stone age man, that objective assessment of alternate hypotheses can be made. How can the student of history fail to perceive the infinite data of the *past* without selective perception rooted in the very nature of his theory?

The two approaches, i.e., cyclical and linear, differ somewhat in the problems to be solved. Hence it is not impossible for one writer to be both a cyclist and an evolutionist. Generally the students who think in terms of cycles are concerned with linear changes up to a point. This

---

[1] For example, Arnold Toynbee has been taken to task by supporters and critics alike for his identification of particular civilizations as distinct units. See F. Ashley Montagu (ed.) *Toynbee and History*, especially the chapter by Pieter Geyl, "Toynbee's System of Civilization."

"point" is the end of a particular defined "society," "political state," or "civilization." The ultimate objective is not to predict the long-range direction of human struggle but rather to predict the course of any given society, state, or civilization. Historical societies may not be viewed in lineal relationships to each other, but studied comparatively, to find generalizations regarding the stages of growth and decline. This is much as the physiologist might study the aging process in man regardless of the century in which the particular subject lived. Most evolutionists on the other hand, are keen to link up historic—and prehistoric— cultures in time sequences. The seemingly sharp distinction between cyclists and evolutionists is blurred as scholars like Sorokin and Toynbee seek out the roots of the new cycle in the collapse of its predecessor while *unilinear* evolutionists sought identical stages of progression in separate cultures. It is oversimplification to group together as cyclical such diverse views as those of Spengler and Sorokin, and as "evolutionists" such diverse writers as Karl Marx and Herbert Spencer. For the moment, however, evolution is being broadly conceived to encompass all theories which tend to show history in terms of lineal change, emphasizing sequence among historic societies rather than their comparative internal processes. (This contrast is sometimes described as that of *general* evolution versus *specific* evolution.)

It is interesting to note that most of the cyclists are "pessimists"—seeing and forecasting the demise of every particular civilization. Indeed if one chooses to identify and make discrete any civilizational or political unit of the past, it, even as all organisms, has perished. On the other hand, evolutionists have more often been relatively jolly people seeing man as an ever striving and an ever more efficient striver on the long rough road into the challenging future.

Not all lineal nor all cyclical theories of change deal with total societies, nations, or civilizations in their entirety. There are numerous middle-range theories which are linear and many which are cyclical. Actually, practically all attempts at productive generalization in the social sciences imply either lineal or cyclical assumptions or qualified expressions of one or the other. The entire literature of the trade cycle and its correlates is obviously reared upon evidences of cyclical change in societies. Vilfredo Pareto's theory of leadership in government and in economic affairs is forthrightly cyclical. Theories of urban ecology, when they chart the future of residential areas under invasion by commercial and industrial enterprises, are sometimes viewed as being cyclical, but in reality have usually predicted linear movements with emphasis upon stages of "invasion" and "succession." If such theories of land use were extrapolated toward reinitiation of the entire series, they would become truly cyclical. On the side of linear change, in a sense virtually every simple linear correlation expressed in predictive terms implies linear change. The extrapolations of divorce rates or increasing attendance of students in universities usually represent qualified linear predictions. Of course they may be turned into cyclical predictions by being hitched to causal phenomena which themselves are deemed cyclical, i.e., as university enrollments might be associated with the trade cycle, which intervenes upon an ever-increasing valuation of higher education.[2]

These are matters of importance but they are matters which call for methodological analysis beyond the scope of this book. Here we shall limit our discussion to the main ideas in "grand sweep" theories of societal or civilizational dimensions.

CYCLICAL THEORIES

Cyclical interpretations of history have an exceedingly long genealogy. They have become relatively unpopular in modern times. Sorokin attributes this as response to the type of sociocultural system bred in Western civilization. He points out that cyclical interpretations were accepted as a matter of course in ancient Babylon, India, China, Greece, Rome, Persia, and medieval Europe. As with Ecclesiastes, "The thing that hath been, it is that which shall be; and that which is done is that which shall be done" (Sorokin, 1947, p. 676).

Ibn Khaldun

The father of modern cyclical interpretations of social change was Ibn Khaldun, a fourteenth-century Arab historian, whose ideas were to be rekindled five centuries later by Oswald Spengler (Chambliss, Chap. 12; Issawi). Ibn Khaldun explicitly viewed history as a generalizing science, and to some modern historically minded sociologists he is viewed as a true founder of sociology. His aim was to discover in social phenomena "the transformations that succeed each other." Unlike some modern followers, he was not led into theological or metaphysical interpretations of historic processes, but found a life cycle in civilizations which needed no mystique in its explanations.

Ibn Khaldun saw the rise and fall of political states (or civilizations) as a movement paralleling the life cycle of the individual from vigorous youth through maturity into the withering of old age. He understood

---

[2] Sorokin advances the "principle of limits" which would qualify the infinite extrapolation of linear trends and hence tend to support the theory that societal change is ultimately cyclical (Sorokin, 1947, pp. 699–706).

history as a series of cycles, in which vigorous barbarians conquer their soft living urban predecessors and in turn become civilized, luxury-loving urbanites, who in their own eventual love of soft living are themselves destroyed by new barbarians. In his study of many early political states, Ibn Khaldun concluded that the life cycle was not long and that the time required for a state to move through the stages of emergence into maturity and on to decay was usually not more than three generations. These sequences did not rest on any crude transposed analogy. Ibn Khaldun found them understandable in terms of the roots of social solidarity which are destroyed in the civilizing process.

Ibn Khaldun probably had little influence upon Western European social science until this century. His *Prolegomena to Universal History* was first translated into a European language, French, between 1863 and 1868. It is certain, however, that he has contributed to the development of such contemporary cyclical theorists as Toynbee and Sorokin. Sorokin and Zimmerman had an instrumental role in introducing Ibn Khaldun's ideas to American sociologists prior to Sorokin's own personal concern with a "theory of history" (Sorokin *et al.*, Vol. I, pp. 53–68).

Giambattista Vico

Three centuries after Ibn Khaldun, another landmark in cyclical interpretations appeared. Giambattista Vico, a prolific philosophic and humanistic writer, produced *The New Science,* in 1725. (Fisch and Bergin; Chambliss, Chap. 15). His theory of change was derived mainly from his close study of Greco-Roman history, or at least it is those civilizations which he chose to support his theory. Out of social science, he believed, man gains a vision of what lies ahead. Although Vico believed in no crude and simple repetitiveness of cultural sequences, he felt that grand laws could be formulated through which scientific understanding and prediction of cultural growth was possible. As part of this "New Science," Vico elaborated his theory of universal historical stages. The generalizations deriving from his historical studies he termed the "Law of the Three Ages"—a phrase not to be confused with Comte's century later evolutionary concept termed "Law of the Three Stages." Vico's three ages are comparable to those posited by Ibn Khaldun (youth, maturity, and old age) albeit more sophisticated and set in a more explicit conceptual framework relating to cultural integration, human nature, and scientific methodology.

Vico saw, through national histories, the gradual transition from the "Age of Gods" to the "Age of Heroes" and thence to the "Age of Men." The time of gods is the original state of man in which superstition guides daily lives even as theocracy holds formal authority. (Reminding one of Comte's earliest stage, this view of primitive man contrasts sharply with the state of nature posited by Rousseau.) Out of superstition and social order through fear and force, the "Age of Heroes" reflects the application of reason to men's problems, the idealization of the hero, and the enstatement of blooded aristocrats to rule over serfs and plebeians. Here is the rise of a "society of status," a feudal order with its urban counterpart, emerging from the relative chaos of primitive times. The Age of Heroes ends as masses strive for, and gain, "natural rights." Patricians and epic heroes fall before the sovereignty of the people and the new demands of equity and requirements of civic duty (Chambliss, p. 378). And then, prophetic of many modern essayists, Vico posits a final period in which the unchecked liberty of the people leads into tyranny and thence chaos. Liberty becomes license, laws so multiply that none is respected, and, as Chambliss puts it, "people are stunned by their inability to govern themselves." Unless some strong leader rises, perhaps in conquest by another rising state, the nation sinks back into barbarism.

Oswald Spengler

The nineteenth century was a time of faith in progress and firm dedication to evolutionary process. Historiography was conceived as faithful reporting. Nonetheless, cyclical generalizing theories of history did not go into total eclipse. H. Stuart Hughes has suggested that the very aridity of historical writing, combined with revulsion from the faith in man's eternal progress, led several historians to attempt to restore in history "its essential qualities of universality and imagination . . ." (pp. 34 ff.). As part of movements in opposition to the dominant "positivism," cyclical theories of change thrived in the latter nineteenth century. Brooks Adams' work *The Law of Civilization and Decay* argued uncompromisingly the thesis that Western civilization was on the way out. With the accumulation of what he called surplus energy within a society, Brooks Adams predicted that internal pressure would reach a point of explosive tension (Hughes, pp. 43–46). Brooks' brother, Henry Adams, sought then to make mathematically precise the general stages of growth and decline posited by Brooks.

While Spengler was preceded by the Adams brothers, he was undoubtedly influenced by the ideas of Nikolai Danilevsky (Sorokin, 1950, p. 60; Hughes, p. 46). In a sense Spengler chiefly revived and brought into Western currency the ideas of Danilevsky, first published in 1869. Perhaps the major differences which Spengler brought to the laws of cyclical decline applied to the West was higher mysticism and a bleak pessimism which replaced Danilevsky's final renewal of civilization through the rise of the Slavic peoples.

The basic idea of Spengler's historical cycle is, as Barnes and Becker observe, "a sort of Hegelian idea of an 'oversoul' of historical entities, complicated by crude organismic notions" (Vol. I, p. 793). Spengler isolated each of the world's great civilizations and contended that the history of each demonstrates—or will eventually demonstrate—passage through a cycle of birth, vigorous maturity, and senility. The cycle is the same for all, whether ancient Egyptian, or contemporary Western civilization. Nothing can alter this immutable organic law and furthermore nothing can be done to accelerate or retard the process of ripening, withering, and decay. Hence Spengler is certain of "The Decline of the West." Spengler was frankly non-scientific in his reconstructions, and when his writings are judged as prophecy rather than prediction, he offers us, as H. Stuart Hughes has observed (p. 165), a dramatic exposition of the state of mind of an old society approaching its death.

Arnold Toynbee

The similarities between Spengler and Arnold Toynbee are deeper than their common organic life cycle of civilizations. If Toynbee is less crude in his organicism, he is at least as non-scientific in the basic convictions which permeate his work. Both are mystics seeking in history the expressions of their faith. The historical determinism of Toynbee is qualified by that remote hope that the West may yet turn to Jesus Christ and be born again. Toynbee has given us encyclopedic documentation of the view that the history of civilizations proceeds through an organismic cycle of birth, growth, decay, and death. In Toynbee, however, the analogy is covered in a complicated set of sub-theories having no foundation in the organic analogy. In the many years through which Toynbee toiled on his work, his ideas underwent some serious change. His basic debt to Spengler lies in the organic analogy but his chief criticism of Spengler, and the aspect of Spengler's position that he sought to remedy, was its excessively deterministic view derived from this analogy, i.e., ultimate decay and death as natural law in the life cycle of nations (1948, p. 10). Toynbee seems to have objected to this less for its content than because it derived from the German a priori method rather than from empiricism. He sought to test this law of cycles by means of a detailed assessment of all the world's civilizations. No doubt Toynbee's equivocal standing with many professional historians derives partly from his essential rejection of history and his treatment of civilizations throughout the ages on a strictly comparative basis, almost but not quite as if they were contemporary each with the other. Toynbee's painstaking search into the life and death of all world civilizations (except that the Western one is not quite dead) leads him to posit an old idea of progress in a new garb.

He observes that civilizations arise in response to some challenge. If the challenge is insufficient, or if it is too difficult to be met, there will be no effective drive toward the accomplishment of the cultural heights commonly called civilization. Toynbee shows how the right amount of challenge existed to drive twenty-one peoples at one time or another to the heights of civilization.

Each of them except Western civilization has run its course, and Western civilization is probably past salvation. The term "salvation" is not entirely figurative in this context since Toynbee believes that "our" only hope lies in the divinity of Jesus and an inspired Christendom. Toynbee's stages of cyclical growth and decay of civilizations have been expressed by Harry Elmer Barnes in a perceptive review of the former's major work:

> In the earlier and growing period of civilization—when mankind is responding to the first great pattern of challenges from the physical and social environment—the historic process is guided by what he calls a "Creative Minority," among whom great religious leaders are the most important and influential element. The masses follow this creative minority willingly and unquestioningly because of spontaneous admiration and trust. Toynbee espouses the "Great Man" theory of history with gusto and consistency.
>
> When the creative minority is supplanted by the dominant minority, as a result of the loss of spiritual creativity on the part of the leaders, what Toynbee calls the "Time of Troubles" arrives in the civilization . . .
>
> Despite the 'troubles,' there still is a chance to save the civilization through what Toynbee denominates the withdrawal-and-return and the resulting 'Etherialization' of leaders. There still remain creative geniuses and they withdraw from the masses to gain spiritual regeneration through communion with God, the contemplation of the Absolute, and the searching of their own souls . . .
>
> Yet, this regenerated leadership has never been able to save a civilization from ultimate decline and extinction—unless we of the Western World accept Christ's message before it is too late . . . [Barnes, pp. 483–484.]

Pitirim Sorokin

In Pitirim Sorokin's theories of the grand historical sweeps there are many similarities to the ideas of Toynbee but less mysticism and far closer adherence to rules of scientific method (1937; 1947). Sorokin, partly through quantitative techniques, has studied the pathway of civilization in the West, i.e., from classical Greece. He has sought to define historic periods on the basis of logically integrated cultural attributes and, having defined such periods in Western history, demonstrate the fluctuations among them and the processes of such flux. It is significant that Sorokin's most basic criticism of Toynbee relates to the latter's arbitrary delimitation of what he chooses to consider a civilization. Sorokin insists that historic cultural units must be demonstrably set apart from other epochs by their unique and integrated socio-cultural systems. Sorokin is thus alert to the methodological problems, which Toynbee was not, of reliable operational tools in defining and bounding historical periods. He seeks in history to find the appearance of logically integrated social systems having fundamental differences from each other.

In Western history, Sorokin discerns three fundamentally different socio-cultural systems each of which appears here and there through time and space in European history. Sorokin has been concerned with defining each of these systems in terms of its consistency to one or the other of three basic patterns. He effectively distinguishes between the life of an integrated cultural system and the more incidental attributes such as a language group or a political unit, which he contends are frequently mistaken for cultural entities. Striking at Toynbee's weakest point in a conceptual sense, he observes:

What really died out of the total Egyptian civilization was *language, the independent Egyptian state,* and some other systems and congeries. As the Egyptian "civilization" in the theories of Danilevsky, Spengler, and Toynbee is the total culture of the Egyptian language, territorial, and state group (Egyptian nation), the disappearance of the Egyptian language and state led these authors to the conclusion that the total Egyptian culture and civilization had died. Baselessly making the total Egyptian culture one system, they no less baselessly concluded that with the death of some of many systems and congeries of this civilization, the total Egyptian civilization died. Still clearer is the situation with the newer Graeco-Roman civilization, which is also much nearer to our own. An enormous part of this "civilization" has never died and is still very much alive. Greek and Latin language systems; Greek and Roman art as a living art imitated by and influencing the contemporary architecture and sculpture, painting, and drama; and Roman and Greek philosophical and ethical systems; Roman law, especially the *Corpus Juris Civilis;* Greek and Roman political and military organization, and many other vast cultural systems and subsystems are living and functioning, both in their Greek and Roman forms and as the formative elements of many western culture systems. The creations of Phidias and Praxiteles, Homer, Sophocles, Aristophanes, Thucydides, Herodotus, Socrates, Plato, Aristotle; of Cicero, Horace, Virgil, Lucretius, their creations and hundreds of other Graeco-Roman cultural systems are carrying on a very vigorous life. The notion of the death of the total Graeco-Roman "civilization" is derived mainly from the disappearance of the Greek and Roman state systems as living realities and from the relegation of Latin to the Christian clergy, scholars, and classically educated groups. But the death of these groups does not mean the death of a civilization. On the contrary, almost all of the great Graeco-Roman cultural systems are very vigorously alive. They make up a very large part of the western "civilization." * [Sorokin, 1947, p. 642.]

Although Sorokin's statistical techniques have often been criticized, he is upon sound methodological grounds in demanding that "civilizations"

* From *Society, Culture, and Personality,* by Pitirim Sorokin. Copyright 1947 by Pitirim A. Sorokin. Reprinted by permission of Harper & Row, Publishers.

be defined in time and space—a definition which is virtually impossible in concrete terms. Instead of viewing the unit of historic time in the equivocal concept of "a civilization," Sorokin chooses a higher level of abstraction. His epochal units are defined as integrated socio-cultural systems embodying characteristic and contrasting conceptions of the nature of reality and value. His view of historical periodicity is thence as fluctuation among three types of socio-cultural systems, the "sensate," the "ideational," and the "idealistic."

Ontologically there are no more all-embracing concepts than the three following definitions of the ultimate nature of reality and value: (a) True reality and true value are sensory—the major premise of the sensate super-systems. (b) True reality and value consist in a supersensory, superrational God, Brahman, Atman, Tao, or its equivalent—the major premise of the idea-tional supersystem. (c) True reality and value are an infinite manifold, partly supersensory and superrational, partly rational, and partly sensory—the premise of the idealistic supersystem. Implicit within each of these major premises is the definition of the kind of science, philosophy, fine arts, ethics, politics, economics, mentality, and way of life that must be created to make them consistent with itself and with one another. [Pp. 590–591.] *

The historical undulations of sensate, ideational, and idealistic periods are shown by Sorokin through series of correlations in changing cultural values, art forms, modes of determining truth, ethics, and personality attributes. Sorokin, more fully than any of the other cyclical historians, recognizes the linear cultural dependence of "civilizations" upon their predecessors, although value-meanings may be undergoing major trans-formation. Like some others, however, he posits growth, maturity, and decline in his systems but without rigorous demands of periodicity or sequence. His charges that contemporary society clings to the remains of an "over-ripe sensate culture" are well known. Sorokin is perhaps more prolific in dealing with the declines of the social systems than with their rise and climax. He views the growth of these "super" social systems as being in their progressively greater and more encompassing integration and consistency. The greatness of a culture he tends to equate with the degree of internal consistency reached in its various departments around the "theme" of sensate, ideational, or idealistic values-meanings. De-cline occurs as the integration of the super social system is lessened. In a section titled "Under what conditions systems grow and blossom to-gether," Sorokin pursues his basic thesis of logico-meaningful integration as the foundation of the rising socio-cultural system:

If a given culture is integrated into one of three supersystems then the following systems will grow and blossom in togetherness.

* From *Society, Culture, and Personality*, by Pitirim A. Sorokin. Copyright 1947 by Pitirim A. Sorokin. Reprinted by permission of Harper & Row, Publishers.

(a) When the *ideational* supersystem is rising we can expect: a creative blossoming of religion and theology; of idealistic and mystical philosophy, with its ontological idealism, eternalism, mysticism, religious or transcendental rationalism; ideational fine arts in all main fields; deep and real psychology of human mind and soul; ideational-absolutistic ethics and sacred law; theocratic, political, and social organization; developed familistic social groups, and other systems and subsystems of the ideational character, mentioned above. All these systems will be growing and blossoming together, though not all necessarily will be equally great creative systems. Likewise they will be growing together even if all systems remain only rudimentary. The dominant rudimentary ideational supersystem of such cultures as that of Tibet, or of the Zuni, and Hopi Indians are examples. On the other hand, science, natural science, technology, and economic empires; materialistic and empiricist philosophy, relativism, singularism, nominalism; sensate fine arts, sensate-relativistic, utilitarian, hedonistic, and sceptical ethics and law; these and all other sensate systems and subsystems will develop little in such a culture and at such periods. They will show little creativeness and little growth.

(b) When the *sensate* supersystem is rising, all sensate systems will be growing together, though not necessarily with equal creative splendor and magnificence. When the sensate supersystem begins to decline, all its systems and subsystems begin to decline also.

(c) When the *idealistic* supersystem emerges—usually as a passage between the declining ideational and emerging sensate systems—idealistic systems of religion and philosophy, science and arts, ethics and law, politics and economics emerge and grow. When the idealistic supersystem declines, all its systems and subsystems decline also.

Such is the change when a given culture is integrated into one of the supersystems. This answer takes into consideration the content and character of each of the systems. It is more precise than the answer given in Chapter 35 when the content and nature of each system was not considered and when the criteria of growth and blossoming were rather arbitrary, based upon the mainly sensate estimates of historians. For them there was no great medieval literature or music, no great medieval sculpture or philosophy, no development of psychology or social science. Consciously or unconsciously imbued with sensate standards they do not see any greatness in ideational forms of religion, philosophy, fine arts, law or ethics, politics or economics.

When we divest ourselves of these perfectly subjective and arbitrary standards, we clearly see that ideational systems in their supersystems are great in their own way, and are very consistently integrated with their major premises and with one another. As such they are great creations, emerging, growing, and declining in togetherness. [Pp. 645–650.] *

Sorokin has written prolifically on the "crisis of our decaying sensate age." Yet he implies the redevelopment of an ideational phase in our civilization, which, due to its inheritance from sensate technology, could know more rapid change than have the previous rather static ideational cultures (p. 695). Perhaps Sorokin is not so far from some linear theo-

* From *Society, Culture, and Personality,* by Pitirim A. Sorokin. Copyright 1947 by Pitirim A. Sorokin. Reprinted by permission of Harper & Row, Publishers.

rists as may appear to be the case. Unlike Spengler, who foresaw civilizational senility and a new era of primitive life, or Toynbee, who sees in the breakdown of Christian faith a disintegration of Western civilization in favor of some as yet exotic culture, Sorokin foresees a shift in values and meanings within Western civilization which will carry it on with new integrative principles. It is not inconceivable that Sorokin, in a curious way like Marx, might accept the possibility of some ultimate balance through which the coming idealistic epoch might preserve itself to infinity.

To assess the contributions of cyclical theory to the contemporary sociology of change is not an easy task. Superficially the contributions appear to be few. Even Sorokin, who is clearly in the forefront of sociological theorists, has made little impression upon his colleagues with his theories of grand historical sweeps. Like Toynbee he has been especially unappreciated by his colleagues. Both ascribe this unpopularity to the fact that cyclical concepts and "super-theory" are not of the present intellectual fashion, whereas their immense erudition cannot fail to impress the non-professional. Needless to say the faults found in the works of each range from basic conceptual issues to the weighing of evidence. Where Toynbee accepts truth in high mysticism, Sorokin offers statistical analysis of questionable data. Untrammelled if brilliant imagination is not likely to be popular when it counters the most basic orientations of historians on one hand and sociologists on the other. But without regard to the correctness or the falsity of any cycle theories (and it is probable that Sorokin and Toynbee could be reconciled in some major synthesis) (Geyl *et al.*), the plain fact remains that neither is particularly helpful to contemporary sociology in solving the kinds of problems to which it is generally addressed. Where one chooses to place the blame for this state of affairs depends mainly on what questions he thinks the science of social change should ask. Few contemporary sociologists think they should be along the grand pattern laid out by Sorokin. In consequence, research, and hence expanding generalized knowledge, on change has little relevance to such theory. Mainly sociological and anthropological research on change is on a much lower level of abstraction. It is rarely even done at the level of long-range directions and vast sweeps, for the very reason that modern social science is structural and functional in orientation rather than historical. And when it is historical, it is dominated by short-range linear conceptions. It is even possible that in the present mood of change research, Sorokin's theories are most useful in regard to their refinements of the concept of cultural integration, rather than the analysis of "trend." When contemporary sociologists deal with "trend," it is usually short range, within a given cultural context, or it relates to one or another of the linear change theories.

LINEAR THEORIES

The nineteenth century was an age of evolution. Concepts of linear progress dominated most areas of social, humanistic, and natural science investigation. (Sorokin has observed that such linear concepts are characteristic of "sensate" cultures.) The aura of science and "progress" permeated the nineteenth-century atmosphere. "The whole historical process was thought of as a kind of well-ordered college curriculum with primitive man or society as a freshman, subsequently passing through the stage of sophomore, junior, senior (or others when the classification contained more than four stages), and then graduating either in the class of 'positivism' or 'freedom for all' or any other final stage suggested by the fancy and taste of the scholar" (Sorokin, 1947, p. 680). Some writers chose to emphasize the formula of advancement while others emphasized the class levels through which the "student" progressed. Although few social scientists in the twentieth century did not come to repudiate the particular evolutionisms of the nineteenth, the impact of that orientation is still crucial to understanding modern thought on directions of social change. Even scholars who aligned themselves against the nineteenth-century ideas of social evolution built their concepts out of the materials provided by the writers they deplored. We cannot approach any understanding of the modern linear concepts such as *Gemeinschaft-Gesellschaft* and the folk-urban continuum, except through the nineteenth-century evolutionary orientations which were their thought-fathers. Substantial parts of Spencer are not only built in the methodological models of contemporary functional analysis but the basic Spencerian theorem of evolutionary process is deeply written in a host of works, some of which jeer at their toppled predecessor. Linear change (as in studies of "developing societies" today) is frequently approached through a conceptual marriage of seemingly incompatible strains associated with Spencer on one hand and Marx on the other.[3]

---

[3] It is popular to credit the modes of production, particularly technology, with determinative power for change in the developing nations. At the same time the sequential patterns of development are commonly interpreted in a manner reminiscent of Spencer's formula regarding increasing heterogeneity. See below, Chapter 14. It might be noted that there is really nothing incompatible between the idea of functional integration around the modes of production, as in Marx, and the Spencerian formula regarding increasing heterogeneity. Spencer was a good functionalist as well as an evolutionist. It is interesting that Lewis A. Coser and Bernard Rosenberg in their edited work, *Sociological Theory*, open the section on "Social Structure and Social Function" with an apt adaptation from Spencer's *Principles of Sociology*.

Nineteenth-Century Foundations
(Bock; Lowie, Chaps. 5, 6, 7; Barnes, 1948)

The nineteenth-century orientation to change was set by Auguste Comte, and from his foundation "evolutionism" took forms as it matured in the various theories of "stage" seeking anthropologists, and formula seeking sociologists. The century was one in which the recently developed powers of science were hailed with almost religious awe and fervor. There seemed no reason in heaven or on earth why science should not be used toward the eternal progress of mankind. Just what it was that science was to show us about human progress and just how it was to be applied remained a bone of contention. Few doubted the ultimate perfectibility of society—the very imperfections of man were, through science, to yield something approaching perfection in social order. Such faith was no less evident in the impassioned individualism of Herbert Spencer than in the equally impassioned collectivism of Karl Marx.

If Comte lay foundations for evolutionary thought in sociology, it was more as a prophet than as a delineator. Comte saw human progress in terms of three stages of growth, i.e., first the Theological state, then the Metaphysical, and finally, the Positive or the Scientific. In the first stage man seeks absolute knowledge through supernatural explanations. From this he passes to an age in which the supernatural is given animistic form and abstract concepts are viewed as real forces. Finally man emerges into an age in which the quest for certainty is abandoned and truth is achieved through the formulation of scientifically derived laws. Comte was free to admit that advancement is more rapid in some areas of life than others and that the social ideas in his day were rooted in a theological stage, whereas studies of nature had become truly scientific. While this broad schema is scarcely the plan upon which later evolutionary thought developed, it is to be noted that Comte, like later anthropologists, saw progressive stages yielding different institutional structures. Thus religion was believed to have advanced from a stage of primitive fetishism in which all objects are given animate reality to polytheism and thence to monotheism.

Spencer and Social Darwinism

Although Comte opened up the nineteenth century to potentials in social science and set the stage for almost a century of evolutionary orientation, it was Herbert Spencer in sociology and Bachofen, McLennan, and Tylor in anthropology who established the patterns that were to sweep across these disciplines. In the van of Spencer came Benjamin Kidd, William Graham Sumner, and others who in more recent times have come to bear the label "Social Darwinists." Although the anthropologists per se had no single system builder such as Spencer, the orientation which was to become known as "unilinear evolution," included such eminent figures, beyond those mentioned, as Lewis Henry Morgan and Jules Lippert. Strangely, while sociological evolution became the scientific foundation of political conservatism and even reaction, unilinear evolution out of anthropology was often keyed into Marxist philosophy (Stern, p. 168).

Spencer's most basic theorem has survived close to the core of sociological theory for a half century or more since his general evolutionary system collapsed. This is the formula of evolutionary progress—that change has persistently moved society from homogeneous and simple units toward increasingly articulated, heterogeneous units of size. As a statement of historic direction, Herbert Spencer's fundamental view of evolution lived on in Durkheim, in Tönnies, and in Redfield. As a premise upon which a theory of *progress* was built its significance was discredited and lost (Hofstadter).

Spencerian evolution insisted upon much more than this direction of history. Its most basic postulate was the idea of "struggle for existence" as a natural law, both organically and socially. Among few writers was "struggle" viewed as conflict to the extent that war itself was considered essential to human progress. In Spencer, and particularly in his ardent follower, William Graham Sumner, the struggle for survival was equated with "free competition." Sumner warned that the law of competition can no more be done away with than gravitation, "and men ignore it to their sorrow." Sumner and Spencer saw history as an unfolding of natural law. This is the meaning of progress, i.e., when the natural processes of struggle and survival are left unhindered.

Unrestrained, except for basic laws of property and life, man strives to better himself. He who succeeds is "fit" and he who fails is "unfit." The law of nature decrees that evolution or progress comes through the survival of the fit and the elimination of the unfit. Social Darwinists saw only social degeneration in welfare legislation which would "artificially preserve" the unfit, and in laws which might restrict the fit in their inheritance of the earth. Here was the full intellectual rationalization of individualistic, laissez-faire capitalism. Even some of the poor and disenfranchised came firmly to believe that they were God's natural casualties as God worked out His great design of the universe—progress through survival of those who prospered and the elimination of those who didn't.

Marx and Evolution

Karl Marx and his friend Engels had a high regard for Darwin's conception of evolution, but unlike Spencer they believed that the law of struggle and survival applied to the jungle rather than to human society.

They applied the concept of struggle to human society only in the idea of "class struggle," not as the struggle of all against all. In another respect Marxian evolutionary thought differed from both Darwin and Spencer. Marx was both an evolutionist and a believer in a "golden age" to be reached as a culmination of class struggle. This is, of course, the Communist State. In Marxian theory communism represents a final stage since it would presumably be in perfect integration with modern modes of production and yet conducive to continuing technological achievement (Bober).

Anthropology and Unilinear Evolution

Linear change theories among anthropologists were cut out of the same cloth as Spencerianism, but their general pattern left them outside the laissez-faire–humanitarian controversy. Although Marxists clutched at some of their theories, these marriages were usually a little forced. Only in one train of unilinear evolutionary thought, developed by L. H. Morgan, was there much consistency and even this really involved no greater compatibility with Marxism than has, say, "culture lag" or other theories implying simple technological dynamism in change. Morgan's theory of cultural growth, as noted earlier, held that cultures have shifted through time dependent upon the nature of the technological base upon which they rested and with which they were necessarily integrated. It should be noted that such a theory takes on political significance only in regard to its theory of dynamics. Actually most anthropological scholars were more concerned with historical reconstructions and sequences than with formulas of dynamics.

Although the political and ideological implications of evolutionary thought are of immense social significance, our concern here lies in these theories as they laid conceptual foundations for modern viewpoints of lineal change. Unilinear evolution (universal cultural epochs) is now of largely antiquarian interest although incidental to the main theories many of its writers made lasting contributions. Thus, McLennan, whose sequence of cultural stages in family life would be acceptable to possibly no Western scholar today, introduced the ideas of "endogamy" and "exogamy" to anthropology. The general design of cultural evolutionism was to deduce from the study of contemporary primitives what must have been the sequences in the growth of various social institutions. The "stages" of growth in marriage and family, government, economic systems, and religion were not neglected. Morgan found changes in each institution correlated with successive technological advances, a theory called the "geological" argument implying that historical culture change is to be visualized as layer upon layer of contrasting strata each of which is internally consistent.

Perhaps more than any other institution, the unilinear evolutionists attempted to reconstruct the successive stages of family life from the beginning of man. Sir Robert Filmer offered one of the earliest "evolutionary" doctrines regarding both the family and state in his work *Patriarchia,* published in 1680. Filmer attempted to support the divine right of kings as an authority handed by God to Adam and thence to the patriarchs from whom kings derived an absolute and divinely ordained authority. The unpopularity of Filmer's political argument in the late seventeenth century was sufficient to bring his view of an original patriarchy under scrutiny along with his argumentation. Others like Bernard Mandeville saw a patriarchal family as the original cell from which orderly communities evolved.

As evolutionary thought was spurred on by the discovery of exotic peoples with exotic family systems and sex and marriage practices, evolutionists sought to make some orderly sequential arrangement of these customs. The foundation stone of nineteenth-century anthropological evolutionism was in Bachofen's work *Das Mutterrecht,* in 1861. This was a decade after Herbert Spencer's earliest evolutionary writing—and still more removed from Darwin's first essays—but practically coinciding with *The Origin of Species.* Bachofen presented a plan of institutional evolution which in part was fantastic but nonetheless held much reason. Bachofen, no doubt more than any other person, set the stage for unilinear patterns which were to dominate anthropological thought for half a century (Lowie, Chap. 5). One root of particular importance lay in Bachofen's reasoned proposition that the origins of marriage lay in conditions of sexual promiscuity and uncertainty of paternity. From this primeval base the elemental development of matrilineally organized family life seemed incontrovertible. Later writers in legion developed refinements from this premise of early maternal authority and centricity with transitions toward patriarchy and paternally oriented family systems. While some writers emphasized the stages of familial organization, others emphasized the forms of marriage suitable to the various stages, and still others concerned themselves more with stages in descent reckoning. At the time, the logic of some of these constructions seemed inassailable. What was more reasonable than that rules of exogamy arose out of bride capture or that a shift from polyandry to polygyny paralleled shifts from matrilineal to patrilineal descent reckoning. Unfortunately logic seemed eventually to support various and often contradictory conclusions (Howard). Where Bachofen was able to "prove" that the origins of marriage lay in promiscuity, for example, Westermarck applied equally cogent logic to demonstrate that its primeval character was really monogamous.

There are few episodes in the history of sociological ideas more thrilling than that of the rise and fall of unilinear evolution. Only those writers who went beyond the deduction of universal stages made lasting contributions. These were sometimes unrelated to the heroic historical reconstructions which were at the center of their attention, but occurred as sort of peripheral insights by great minds wedded to erroneous assumptions. Under the withering attacks of pragmatic anthropologists such as Franz Boas and the scorn of historians for a theory of history based upon comparison and logic rather than historic data, the orientation of anthropology shifted from evolution to functionalism (Bock).

One of the basic flaws in nineteenth-century evolution as conceived by the anthropologists lay in a confusion of *general* and *specific* evolution (White, 1960). On the one hand they attempted to reconstruct the rise of civilization in general terms and on the other they sought stages of development characteristic of every specific culture. Although the assumption of universally valid stages in all cultures was unsupportable, there was much that was sound, particularly in Morgan's views, on the general evolution of civilization. Barnes and Becker have credited Morgan's *Ancient Society* as probably having "done more both to stimulate and distort historical sociology than any other work" (Barnes and Becker, Vol. I, p. 750).

In modern times the distinction between general and specific evolutions has been more clearly drawn. Research in specific evolution has proceeded under the leadership of Julian Steward (1955) who, rejecting unilinear stages, believes that comparative analysis will reveal parallel developments in cultures responding to similar ecological conditions. General evolution has also enjoyed renewed interest in anthropology under the leadership of such scholars as Robert Redfield, Leslie White, and V. Gordon Childe. In the mid-twentieth century, Redfield consolidated a general evolutionary theory built upon the concepts of Morgan from the side of anthropology and the many sociologists and others who from the time of Herbert Spencer have concerned themselves with the field of historical sociology.

Toward Contemporary Theory in Linear Change

In 1937 Talcott Parsons began *The Structure of Social Action* with a rhetorical question, "Who now reads Spencer?" The answer was, and had long been, "practically no one." Yet, if Spencer as an Evolutionist with a capital "E," was as dead as the protagonists of a flat earth, some of his ideas lived and evolved, even in the thinking of his sternest critics.

Spencer's faith in Progress as a natural law with its postulates of natural selection and laissez faire fell before new evidence, new theologies, new political values, and new conceptions of what sociology was to be. Yet Spencer's emphasis upon the organic unity of society offered stimulus to those who were to substitute functional approaches for historical ones. Spencer too was a "functionalist"—he simply subordinated his functional view to the "laws" of linear progression. Additionally, Spencer and other avowed evolutionists, notably Lewis Henry Morgan, have lived on in their assessment of the direction taken by historical trends. Even the bitterest antagonists of evolutionism viewed the contrasting nature of "early" and "modern" society in terms which bore close kinship to Spencer's main theorem of evolution, i.e., progression from the simple to the complex, or from the homogeneous to the heterogeneous. Spencer's assessment of this trend in human society was not the point on which his ideas fell. His failure lay in his theory to explain the observations. Much contemporary sociological and anthropological theory on the direction of lineal change is a sort of de-fanged and evolved Spencerianism.

Related theories were developed by the historically minded jurist Henry Sumner Maine, and much later, in seeming flight from Spencerian evolution, in the sociological writings of Ferdinand Tönnies, Emile Durkheim, and numerous others (see p. 311). Each of these scholars sought to articulate the contrasts between the social worlds of either primitives or peasants and that of the modern nineteenth- or twentieth-century European community or state. Each with his own emphasis contributed to a conceptual dichotomy which is manifest in the recent work of Robert Redfield, Sorokin and Zimmerman, Howard Becker, Charles P. Loomis, and perhaps most modern sociologists and social anthropologists who attempt to articulate the patterns of change associated with the rise of modern, urban life. These ideas have tended to be fused into the now popular studies in sociology and in economics of the consequences of various aspects of modernization for "under-developed" societies.

The concepts which have been useful in the analyses of linear change were frequently not aimed at being evolutionary. A number of scholars sought rather to articulate the foundations of social order in contrasting societies or groups. Priority in time of one of these conceptual types was either unintended or an afterthought. Thus, Howard Becker was not avowedly concerned with "change" throughout the development of his ideas of the "Sacred" and the "Secular." [4] Even more distant from

---

[4] Becker seems to have begun by viewing "secularization" as "the total historical process," but moved toward a non-historical orientation as his ideas developed. (Cf. his "Normative Reactions to Normlessness.") In one essay, however, he points out that Nazi Germany interrupted the trend toward secularization by retreat into a type of "sacred society."

conscious evolutionary contribution was Charles Horton Cooley when he perceived the crucial group differences in social relationships which he chose to call "primary" in contrast to "secondary" (Chap. 3). However, his distinction is consistent with that which Spencer or Redfield or Morgan or Maine drew in contrasting early with late forms of social organization. Sorokin and Zimmerman, while dealing with historic change were not doing so in the context of evolution so much as in analytical contrasts between rural and urban life. When Redfield appropriates this tradition of thought introduced to the United States particularly by Sorokin and Zimmerman, he deliberately replaces it in the evolutionary context.

If in the following pages, Redfield's ideas are treated more explicitly than those of Cooley or Sorokin and Zimmerman or Becker or even more recent sociologists in this tradition, such as Charles P. Loomis, the reason is that Redfield has been deliberately engaged in building a theory of general linear evolution while the others usually have not. All have attempted to construct ideal types or models of functionally integrated parts. Each writer has emphasized somewhat different aspects of what are fundamentally the same types of groups, or more accurately he has stressed types of relationships which are maximized in certain group structures. A society which is to Spencer a "military" (homogeneous-monolithic) one would be to Maine almost certainly one of "status" (non-contractualism) and to Morgan, "Societas" (ordered on kinship), etc. Inconsistencies largely arise as one author thought of "primitives" and another of peasants—making in effect the righthand column of the table on p. 311 more consistent throughout than the lefthand column. In the "modern" phase all have been trying to articulate the salient feature of a social structure which can scarcely be well described except in terms made famous by one or another of these writers. Very broadly they are all emphasizing societal differences which can be summed up in three dimensions: homogeneity-heterogeneity, primariness-secondariness, and sacredness-secularity. Spencer, Durkheim, and Tönnies have chosen to use terms which emphasize the homogeneity-heterogeneity dimension (or degree of differentiation) although they (especially the latter two) recognized full well the presence of the other conditions. The dimension of "primariness-secondariness" is explicit, of course, in Cooley, but is also the key to Morgan's thesis as well as that of Henry Sumner Maine. "Sacredness-secularity" is similarly explicit in Becker but is also central to Redfield's concepts and indeed to Levi-Bruhl's more questionable thesis regarding primitive mentality. Sorokin and Zimmerman's typological concepts emphasize no single aspect of the contrast, systematically comparing the farmer-peasant with the urbanite upon a wide range of characteristics including the three dimensions cited here.

The Related Concepts of Various Scholars

	Typologies	
	"Early"	"Modern"
H. Spencer	Military	Industrial
H. S. Maine	Status	Contract
T. Tönnies	Gemeinschaft	Gesellschaft
E. Durkheim	Mechanical	Organic
	(Segmented)	(Organized)
L. H. Morgan	Societas	Civitas
Lévi-Bruhl	Pre-logical	Logical
C. H. Cooley	Primary	Secondary
Sorokin and	Rural	Urban
Zimmerman		
H. Becker	Sacred	Secular
R. Redfield	Folk	Urban

Loomis, in following this up, rested his analysis heavily on Tönnies, whose major work he translated.

The dimension of "relative homogeneity" was crucial to the theories of both Durkheim and Tönnies. Durkheim's classic work, translated as *The Division of Labor in Society* expresses the significance he placed on the homogeneity variable. Labor, in this title, is a poorly rendered word, since his book is actually based upon the broad issue of social differentiation, its significance to social organization, and the forces which affect its degree. Durkheim had a heavy debt to Spencer both in the latter's recognition of the significance of increasing heterogeneity and in the specification of forces driving society toward increasing heterogeneity. Though Durkheim made a detailed critique of Spencer's theory of "order" in the heterogeneous (industrial) society, he did not really question Spencer's observation of the significant facts in history. With the increasing division of labor, Durkheim saw a transformation of society from the "segmental" type to an "organized" type. Tribal societies, he says, are built of repetitions of family-like groups rather than from variously constituted groups having different and interlocking functions. Early societies were built like earthworms, i.e., a series of organically united rings each a replica of the other. Modern societies are built of differentiated parts each with its special function and each organized with each other into functioning wholes. In accounting for the shift from "early" to "modern" society, Durkheim verged close to Spencer when he argued that increasing differentiation arises through increasing density and the struggle for survival (see above, pp. 40–41).

Durkheim's most studious contributions toward a theory of change arose when he traced the consequences of increasing social differentiation for group life and the relation of the individual to his society. With increasing "division of labor," Durkheim noted that law shifts from repressive to restitutive emphases. This is to say that in the early society law is aimed at the protection of the common interest, which is normal to people possessing a common life and unanimity in values. On the other hand with division of labor there is an absence of a "collective conscience," and law is aimed at preserving cooperative relations among persons having differing interests. The state becomes an organ engaged in mediating, regulating, and integrating groups having different but interdependent functions within the society.

Ferdinand Tönnies approached the same distinctions under the terms *Gemeinschaft* and *Gesellschaft*. Systematically he analyzed the nature of social relationships in three types of undifferentiated groups, family, village-neighborhood, and guild-town and in three types of highly differentiated ones, the city, the national state, and the metropolis. In the *Gemeinschaft,* obligations between persons are diffuse and unlimited; means and ends are not clearly distinguished. For example, with the peasant farming is an end in itself as well as a means of economic livelihood. Ascribed positions are prevalent, and social controls lie in the deep internalized attitudes of respect and love and in the informal social controls. From such a system of social relations we get concord in regard to the norms, and behavior is guided by custom, faith, and creed. With the rise of an industrial capitalistic civilization centered in the modern city, occupation ceases to be an end in itself as every person strives toward the rational pursuit of self-interest. Other parties are viewed as means to ends in limited contractual relationships. Impersonality and segmental relationship replace "primary," all-encompassing ones. Social control shifts from internalized attitudes and informal mechanisms toward institutionalized authority with external rules enforced through the state. Morality rooted in the concord of faith and creed becomes a morality geared to public opinion.

From utterly different points of interest, the convergence of Lewis Henry Morgan and Henry Sumner Maine is particularly interesting. The convergence is less startling of course, when we remember that Maine wrote his famous work *Ancient Law* in 1861, many years before Morgan or Durkheim or Tönnies, all of whom were probably influenced by the great jurist's studies. Maine, as a student of historical jurisprudence, was, like avowed sociologists, concerned with the problem of social order and its bases in widely differing types of communities. In the growth of law, he found a transformation akin to that sensed by Durkheim and by Tönnies. Maine found the nature of legal obligations shifting through time from diffuse obligation to limited contractual arrangements. The former he chose to call relationships of "status"—or relationships deriving from social position, in contrast to relationships based on specific agreement or "contract." In this shift, Maine found the essence of historical change and the key to a new basis for social order—an idea that both Durkheim and Tönnies were to build centrally into their own theories.

Morgan was one of the rather few social evolutionists who was a field worker as well as a scholarly archivist. In his personal studies of primitive societies and literary study of early civilizations he concluded that the crucial difference lay in the latter's diminution of kinship as a basis for organization and the substitution of its order for one based upon territoriality, i.e., the political state. While neither Morgan nor Maine chose to pursue the logical and historical consequences of the great transition, as did Durkheim and Tönnies, they were pointing in much the same direction. Tönnies is quite explicit in describing the *Gemeinschaft* in terms of "familism," although he recognized that localism was also a *gemeinschaftlich* bond for the feudal (early) village. However, both are speaking of bonds of status—of reciprocities borne of position and enforced by custom in contrast to the bonds of complementation enforced through formal mechanism. Of them all, Morgan and Maine were perhaps the only ones who had direct personal knowledge of something other than modern Western civilization. (Maine in later years became an authority on Indian communities and Indian law.) Some saw the contrast as between "primitive and civilized" and others between "peasant and urban," a difference which Robert Redfield was to seize upon and expand in his writings. Yet each of these men was attempting to articulate the contrast between sophisticated urban civilizations and either unsophisticated peasant communities or "primitives."

In the context of European sociology these contrasts were also contributed to by scholars not at all concerned with evolutionary formulae or sequences. Weber and Simmel, for example, paid little attention to these constructs, but contributed immensely to the understanding of social order in the city, so contributing to this general frame of thought (Weber; Wolff). Weber particularly emphasized the growth of rationality and bureaucracy while Simmel brilliantly analyzed the roots and consequences of the depersonalization associated with urban life.

It seems safe to say that on one hand the impersonality and contractualism of the modern city was exaggerated almost as much as the homogeneity and traditionalism of rural and tribal peoples. But though factual distortions appeared, these at least served to sharpen ultimately the theoretical concepts which were derived. The directions of the distortions were consistent with the directions of actual contrast of "early" and "modern" societies. Whether named *Gemeinschaft*, "Folk," "Status," or "Rural," the concept became a type of model, with "modern society," in its various guises, the opposite pole.

The Folk-Urban Continuum. In recent years Robert Redfield took the lead in developing these concepts in the context of linear change. Howard Becker elaborated them mainly through logical systematizing rather than furthering them in historical context. Although Redfield "found" his "folk" society in Yucatan, he was, in fact, describing a peasant village in conceptual terms laid out by Durkheim, Tönnies, Maine, Morgan, and Becker and given early currency in the United States through the rural-urban sociology of Sorokin and Zimmerman. Although Redfield never gave much attention to the "urban end" of his continuum, we may infer that it was a type conception resulting from the writings of Louis Wirth and others who in turn depended upon the group of scholars already discussed, including particularly, Simmel.

Redfield moves from his characterization of the folk community to a full-fledged linear evolutionary scheme which ultimately follows human society and culture from the Paleolithic to the Metropolis. Throughout, he prefers to deal with the folk end of his schema rather than the urban. However, there is no doubt that his concept of the urban is to be epito-mized in the terms of Durkheim, Maine, Tönnies, and Becker (or as these are epitomized by Wirth), i.e., the conceptual extreme of heterogenetic solidarity, contractual, impersonal, and secular, etc. Since the urban is that which the folk is not—as the *Gesellschaft* is the polar counterpart of the *Gemeinschaft*—we may know what Redfield had in mind, although he left it to others to demonstrate the empirical existence of communities approaching such an urban type.

The folk society, says Redfield, is

. . . small, isolated, non-literate, and homogeneous, with a strong sense of group solidarity. The ways of living are conventionalized into that coherent system which we call a "culture." Behavior is traditional, spontaneous, un-critical and personal; there is no legislation of habit or experiment and reflec-tion for intellectual ends. Kinship, in its relationships and institutions, are the type categories of experience and the familial group is the unit of action. The sacred prevails over the secular, the economy is one of status rather than of the market. [1947.]

At other times and in other places, Redfield added further traits, as his evolutionary thought developed. One of these added features comes finally to be his most critical analytical feature distinguishing folk from urban. In *The Primitive World and Its Transformations,* Redfield dis-tinguishes the folk from the urban on the relative significance of what he terms the "moral order" over the "technical order." The distinction is not significantly different from Becker's "sacred" and "secular." By the moral order is meant those aspects of life and culture which are sacred, normatively impermeable, true and right simply by the fact of their being. The technical order, in contrast, relates to those aspects of culture which are instrumental in valuation, those ways and things which are valued not for the traditional rightness but for their efficacy in accomplishing some end. Folk societies, says Redfield, have a pervasive "moral order." As a society moves along the continuum, more and more of its culture is to be found in the technical order. Civilization, and especially modern, Western-type civilization, values much of its culture and many social relationships in rational, instrumental terms.

Although Redfield began by assigning the term "folk" to both primitive and peasant village peoples, his later work offers some implicit and explicit distinctions between these (Redfield, 1953; Redfield and Singer). Possibly this was in view of the constructive criticisms of other anthropologists. Folk-peasant culture is a way of life arising with the Neolithic urban revolution. And, as Foster notes, contemporary primitive peoples are not becoming "folk" or peasant peoples but are assimilating directly to the industrializing, national, secular cultures.

Redfield saw all of these features not as a trait list but as functionally related ingredients, much as Durkheim recognized that with division of labor there is a related shift in norms, values, and personal relationships. It follows, then, that change—toward urbanism—in any one characteristic sets in motion changes along the same dimension in the remaining characteristics. It is, for example, contrary to the logic of the continuum that a community might vary *at random* along the folk-urban continuum in regard to these various attributes. Redfield affirms in effect that Maine, Durkheim, Tönnies, *et al.* were talking about different aspects of a single construct generally consistent with "early" communities as contrasted with "modern" communities. Further it is implied in Redfield and explicit in many other writers, including essayists like Aldous Huxley, that the "modern community" will move further toward the ultimate of secularity, or "urbanity" as Redfield conceives it.

Redfield's writing is particularly pertinent as an expression of linear change theory since he has deliberately synthesized concepts in such a way that his analytical framework encompasses significant changes in modern, Western societies and at the same time applies to many changes occurring in the developing regions of the world. From an early confusion over the comparative place of primitive and peasant peoples in his scheme, Redfield, particularly in collaboration with Milton Singer, ultimately produced not only a descriptive statement of the polar types but also the dynamic forces pushing communities along the continuum. Redfield's mature orientation is nowhere expressed by him in a finished and entirely consistent form. It may however be derived particularly from his collaborative work with Singer and a series of his lectures published in 1953, a few years before his death.

The course of man's life on earth has gone through three, rather than two significant stages, according to the more developed theory. The folk-urban continuum really becomes the "Primitive"—"Peasant"—"Secular-urban" continuum. Prior to the Neolithic revolution, which brought agriculture and settled communities, all peoples were primitive in the sense of being pre-literate, nomadic hunters, fishers, and collectors. Such communities meet Redfield's definition of the "folk community" but they are folk in a very special sense quite unlike the folkness of rural peoples. With the settling of tribal peoples in agricultural life in the Middle East, there developed written language with an associated literature and territorial states with cities as their organizational and ideological centers. But these are not the cities as posited at the end of the folk-urban continuum. These were folk capitols, not truly "urban" in the sense of being secularizing centers. The central city for the peasant folk is termed by Redfield and Singer an "orthogenetic" city, a city of a homogeneous cultural origin, a city that epitomizes and codifies the folk culture of its region. The city of Benares in India was such a city and continues so into contemporary times. It is a focal point for traditionalism and the preservation of Hindu folk culture. Early cities generally were religious and political capitols. The peasant is a countryman integrated with the life of such cities.

Particularly after the commercial and industrial expansion of Europe, the "new" city arose bearing the well-known tradition-shattering consequences. In contrast to the orthogenetic city, Redfield and Singer call this the city of heterogenetic origins. This is the city built upon rationality, world-wide interests, and varied ways of life. This is the city at the "urban" end of the continuum. This is the city which is an empirical referent for Tönnies' *Gesellschaft* or Becker's secular society. This is the city described by Simmel, by Sorokin and Zimmerman, and by Wirth. It is the focal point from which the transforming influences spread through a folk-peasant hinterland.

This conceptual city, which stands at the polar extreme from the "folk," has been described from many differing points of view. Its essential character as it emerges from the analyses of these many writers yields the following epitomization. It is a massive and mobile form of community life in which social values are rational and instrumental. Pragmatic truths are valued above traditional verities. Individual achievement is valued over group solidarity and social securities. Social relationships here are disproportionately specialized, instrumental, and limited in content and duration. New groups arise to serve community functions.

These are highly structured and rest upon the coordination of specialized parts in accordance with formal rules of organization. Interpersonal relationships, including communication channels are frequently depersonalized through the mediation of intricate exchange systems, money, and technological communication networks. Community members, by specialization, become increasingly dependent upon their fellows and upon increasingly remote communities and individuals brought into the expanding hinterland of reciprocities and mutual dependencies. In values, emphasis is placed upon efficiency and quantity of material goods and amenities of life. Time, too, is of the essence.

Functional Theory and the Direction of Change.   Reacting to criticisms that the structural-functional approach to change was static in its methodological assumptions and without regard to temporal processes and directions, several attempts have been made to extend the theory to include directional analysis. Talcott Parsons and Neil Smelser have attempted to graft the process of social differentiation into an approach which in Parson's original formulations dealt only with change in the sense of equilibrium-disequilibrium processes within a temporally limited social system (Parsons, 1960; 1964; Smelser). While neither writer assumes that differentiation is the only significant process which social systems undergo through time, following most social evolutionists they posit it as a very pervasive structural trend. Smelser's work on the industrial revolution offers magnificent documentation of certain of the permutations of this process and demonstrates that a functionalist can tangibly contribute to evolutionary analysis.

Amitai Etzioni has extended the functional theory of direction in change to include not only differentiation but a process something like its converse, which he terms *epigenesis*. *Epigenesis* is the process through which a social system originally serving a single function adds new functions. This process may, of course, be associated with increasing internal differentiation of the original social system. Etzioni's contributions, while not extensively developed, offer a potential pathway to improved understanding of the complex trends in modern society wherein, for example, governments and large corporations increasingly expand their functions and concomitantly differentiate their structures. The dual processes of epigenesis and differentiation give rise to more extensive and more centralized control within a society or an organization.

CONCLUSION

The nineteenth-century foundations of sociology were dominated by evolutionary concepts. The task of sociology was widely conceived as that of making a science out of history—the establishment of laws of social progress. Most of these efforts to establish a science of history understood history to be a linear process of growth more or less analogous with biological evolution. Some scholars of historical direction, however, took a differing organic analogy and have visualized historic directions in terms of cycles, analogous to youth, maturity, and old age. Among the classical linear evolutionary theories is that of Herbert Spencer, emphasizing the evolutionary principle of increasing differentiation, and that of Lewis Henry Morgan, emphasizing the "historic" stages in cultural growth. Although Marx saw history moving through a dialectic process, he too was an evolutionist, predicting from his analyses a utopian state to emerge through the natural outworkings of historic process.

Contrasting with the evolutionists, cyclists such as Sorokin and Toynbee have found recurrent cycles in history. Both have been at pains to warn that contemporary Western civilization stands at the brink of cyclical collapse. Cyclical theories have been particularly uninfluential in sociology, while evolutionary theories have been generally eclipsed by non-historic orientations during recent decades. Howsoever, the heritage of nineteenth-century evolution has lived on in the notable theories of Ferdinand Tönnies, Emile Durkheim, Robert Redfield, and others.

In their introductory sociology textbook, Broom and Selznick have referred to the linear pattern described here as the "Master Trend" (pp. 38–48). Their discussion epitomizes the integrated pattern, different facets of which have been described in as many different concepts. Also describing it in terms of declining ties of kinship, and fealty and fixed statuses, with increasing contractualism, bureaucratization, specialization, and rationalism, they hopefully point to counter-trends. While counter-trends such as new community solidarities may intervene, the weight has been on the side of the "Master Trend," differing facets of which have been emphasized in the writings of Durkheim, Tönnies, Spencer, Redfield, and others.

It is when we re-approach individual, living societies and attempt to understand their transitions that we run into difficulties. Criticisms of the continuum with its polar constructs are drawn from several kinds of pragmatists. The schema is criticized because it covers too much and because it covers too little. This seeming paradox arises on the one hand as we find peasant societies which are inconsistent with specific features of the ideal type (Tax). The other criticism arises as the continuum does not cover the full range of change within concrete societies (Lewis, 1951; 1955). It is, for example, quite evident that these concepts do not well express what has become a crucial issue in contemporary change, differences between totalitarian and non-totalitarian routes along which change may be effected. Likely, too, there has been a tendency to underestimate the significance of increasing bureaucratization. The conceptual models or polar types arising from linear evolutionary theory are nonetheless valuable as we attempt the difficult task of assessing trend data in contemporary societies as to their meaning and consistency in historical direction.

It remains to be seen how successful are present efforts to expand structural-functional theory to include the temporal and directional processes of change. The process of differentiation is demonstrably a central trend of most known societies and one which functionalists believe can be conceptually integrated with their approach to society. The converse of differentiation, i.e., *epigenesis* (centralization) is also such a trend. These processes deal strictly with changing structure of groups, and it remains to be seen whether or not structural-functional theory can encompass a broad range of substantive social trends in societies generally.

12

Technological Change in Contemporary Society

One need not be a Marxist nor a technological determinist to find that the growth of technology intervenes critically upon relationships among men. While this has always been true, the contemporary transformations of technology are infinitely more rapid and more immediately insistent than in perhaps equally drastic shifts in past centuries. While technology does not determine the direction of social change nor the specific qualities of the particular social structures which men create, it is a self-imposed variable requiring multiple, and frequently, radically new societal adjustments. How societies respond to their novel devices depends upon the "dynamic assessment," but assessment there must be and, barring technological stasis, a dynamic equilibrium to be maintained. In some instances technological novelty can be integrated through group structures and norms already understood. In other instances such change poses adjustive issues of revolutionary proportions. Thus, the introduction of agriculture into Neolithic society precluded by its inherent functional properties the retention of norms of nomadic savagery.

In modern, almost immediately recent times, the nature of technological change itself has been modified. We see this manifested in the form of suddenly accelerated change in various applied fields. The recent acceleration is not a simple intensification of technological dynamics of earlier centuries. Technological thrust has a different character. Never before has the systematic pursuit of *knowledge* been so bound to the systematic production of *technical* achievement. Also novel in current technological achievement is the creation and extension of technological manipulative knowledge to the organization of groups and the motivations of their members. While brilliant sociological "cook books" like Machiavelli's *The Prince* have long been written, today social science is giving support to practical group planning and control.

THE MARRIAGE OF SCIENCE AND TECHNOLOGY

The economist Kenneth Boulding has observed that the founding of the Royal Society in England, in the seventeenth century, is a crucially symbolic date. It signals the emergence of science as an organized subculture, which even at that time served to stimulate "an attitude of mind" toward invention. Emerging from the status of folk knowledge, science was here on its way toward institutionalization in the hands of prestigious specialists. This was to culminate in the mid-twentieth century in what has been appropriately described as "The Age of Acceleration."

Abstractly conceived, science is a method for the pursuit and extension of verified knowledge. Various societies have dignified the pursuit of knowledge but none other than Western civilization has pursued it with such skill, tenacity, and cold-blooded rationality. This has been possible through the emergence of scientific induction as a tool, and it has been supported in the sustained hope that such knowledge would pay off in application to advancing technology. Technology itself is not a pursuit of knowledge. It is the pursuit of control, the devisement of instruments and plans which serve purposes deemed useful to man. These two pursuits have not always been closely associated as wise men observed, speculated, and reasoned, while others, removed from the world of wisdom, improved technology.

While it seems to us that science is the parent of technology, until the sixteenth century the reverse was more accurate. The historian of technology L. T. C. Rolt observes:

That this evolutionary path, trodden by "rude mechanicals," many of whom were doubtless unable to sign their names, should have been completely misunderstood and misinterpreted by the scientific "philosopher" is a classic illustration of a failure in communication between science and technology that has persisted all through history.

The scientist still enjoys something of that superstitious awe and veneration that he inherited from the alchemist and wizard; whereas the technician is but the humble acolyte of this omniscient priesthood. Hence in the history of the invention the former commonly receive too much and the latter too little credit. [Pp. 116–117.]

Werner Sombart, the great economic historian, has argued that even the rising technology of the seventeenth century was almost divorced

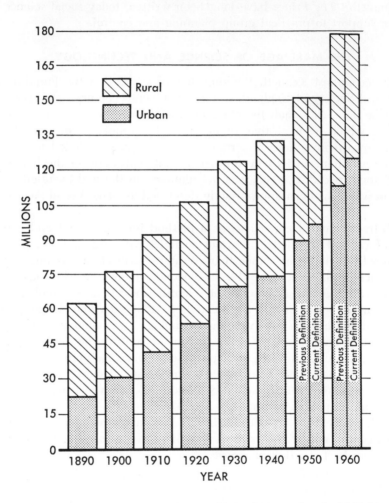

Technological Change Has Accelerated Urbanization
United States Population, Urban and Rural *

In 1900 the labor of one farm worker could feed 7 people. In 1965 his work fed 33 people. Plant genetics, scientific husbandry, and mechanization of agriculture have combined with industrial expansion to permit the transformation of American community life.

* From U. S. Department of Commerce, Bureau of the Census, *Statistical Abstract of the United States*, 1964, p. 4.

from the contemporary science and that the scientist and the inventor had gone their separate ways from Leonardo da Vinci to the eighteenth century (Merton). Still others contend that technology contributed more to the growth of modern science than did the growing sciences to technology. It may well be that the microscope owed less to scientific optics than it contributed to science through opening up a sub-visual world to the eyes of man.

However, by the seventeenth century, the split of science and technology was healing, contrary to Sombart's contention. Robert K. Merton's analysis of scientific development of that century shows Sombart guilty of gross exaggeration. Although scientists of the period were not interested in the development of industrial machinery, there was indeed contribution to technology in the realm of commerce, mining, and the military. It is also a historical bias that treats the early inventors simply as ignorant tinkerers. James Watt's contribution to the steam engine has been viewed in both lights. Watt, an instrument maker not a scholar, achieved a notable synthesis of mechanical ideas. But Watt the instrument maker was close in his daily life to the most eminent physicists of his time. To say his engine contributed vastly to the further growth of science does not mitigate his dependence upon a branch of science which had been developing since the days of de Caus, or before. By the eighteenth century fewer and fewer creative tinkerers and "rude mechanicals" were isolated from the expanding world of scientific knowledge.

N. A. Figurovsky (p. 701) credits Russia with a self-conscious and persisting unification of science and technology by the middle of the eighteenth century. He quotes Lomonósov, the great mid-eighteenth century chemist, "The sciences show the way to industries while the latter accelerate the progress of the former." Similar realizations were ripe in Western Europe and particularly England. The controversy as to science versus technology is well summed up by Figurovsky who observes that it is the *historians* of science and technology, not the scientists and the technologists, who have failed in recognizing the eternal reciprocity of the two. The establishment of the British Royal Society like that of the St. Petersburg Academy of Sciences in Russia and similar associations elsewhere testified to a broad early recognition that the path of progress lay in the deliberate reciprocity of the two.

It is of more than passing interest that beginning about 1820 Auguste Comte laid down his grandiose design for the science of sociology as the base of a monumental system of technology in social planning, organization, and control. Mercantilist economists too had had visages of a science in which nations might prosper through application of their knowledge. Although social sciences lost much of this during the rise of laissez faire and individualistic values and policies in the nineteenth and early twentieth century, the social sciences are more recently rejoined in the same fruitful marriage.

The merger of science and technology is one of the most basic changes in modern society. In it lies the secret of our distinctive acceleration of change. How complete is the marriage of science and technology is a moot question. Both C. P. Snow and Jacques Ellul argue that we have passed the point of useful distinction between the two—they are as one. In theory, science has an option of remaining free and pure; in practice the option has been closed. Ellul contends that science is becoming more and more subordinate to the search for technical application and that in decades to come technique will become stronger and its pace will be accelerated through the agency of the state. Is this indeed a marriage in which technology swallows up or enslaves its partner? The issue is a fearful one.

THE KNOWLEDGE EXPLOSION

The explosive acceleration in scientific knowledge since World War II has pervading significance throughout the social structure. In the new firm alliance of science and technology, the thrust of institutionalized science toward practical achievement is incredibly great. The repercussions of this acceleration in technology and their consequences in turn for social institutions and community are vast. Even the establishment of institutionalized science is, in and of itself, a change in social structure of considerable significance. But the *impact* of this emerging institution is truly profound. The almost sudden emergence of "Big Science" is close to the heart of "the knowledge explosion" and its direct and accelerative effects upon innovation.

The rapidity and scope of this growth is indicated in its budgetary and occupational significance in our economy. Expenditures on research and development in the United States increased almost five-fold between 1953 and 1967—from about $5 billion in 1953 to $24 billion in 1967 (National Science Foundation). In addition monies have been poured into basic scientific investigation at a still more rapid rate. The Director of the Ford Foundation, an institution largely devoted to the expansion of knowledge, complained in 1966 that the $3.3 billion assets of his organization were far too small for the work they were to do. In the United States, persons engaged in scientific activities numbered about 140,000 shortly after World War II compared with 1.4 million by 1960 (Kaplan). Ph.D.'s working in scientific fields increased from 25,000 to 87,000. In the Soviet Union the number of Doctors and Candidates of Science increased by one-third between 1955 and about 1960. The Soviet claimed about 4 million scientific workers by the late 1950's (Figurovsky).

The scope of the knowledge explosion is vividly illustrated in statistics on the so-called "publications explosion." It has been estimated that over 2 million scientific papers were published in the early 1960's. In addition, for the United States alone, some 100,000 informal reports are published annually (Kaplan, p. 857). Publications in the field of chemistry offer some insight into the scope of the explosion. *Chemical Abstracts* contained 54,000 abstracts of papers in 1930. By 1962 it was publishing 165,000 abstracts annually. Although it may be reasonably said that publications are not tantamount to scientific advance, the communication of scientific knowledge and the extent of scientific communication is closely correlated with rapidity of discovery and invention (Hagstrom).

Science and its all but indistinguishable incarnation, technology, has become an institutionalized establishment intimately affecting society and in turn affected by it. While, as Robert K. Merton has observed, the impact of science on society has been greater than that of society on science, science and society are today so closely linked that it is difficult to speak of greater or less effect of one upon the other (Kaplan). Scientists may, of course, choose to isolate themselves from the practical problems and the practical world, but it is increasingly clear that few will have the resources to do so even if they have the inclination. The knowledge explosion is one of direct significance for pursuit of ends and policies of organized groups, nations, industries, and schools.

As Norman Kaplan says, up to World War II, science continued to expand mainly through series of individual decisions made in universities and other laboratories by professionals who were attracted to the pursuit of scientific research. The growth of science was a better example of a true laissez-faire system than our economic structure ever provided. Kaplan appears to attribute, in part, the sudden and recent increase in American residents who are Noble prize winners to our departure from the laissez-faire policy in individualistic scientific achievement (Kaplan, p. 869).

The immense strides of the Soviet since World War II is testimony in considerable part to the rich proceeds of Big Science closely organized and directed. The competitive relationship of the United States with the Soviet has been a substantial stimulus to the kinds of scientific advance which require huge organization, huge financing, and huge bureaucracy. Vast federal expenditure for science through universities, government experiment stations, and industry cannot be effectively utilized except through highly developed coordination. As the federal government subsidizes Big Science it inevitably exerts policy direction upon the directions of scientific growth. In 1960 Hubert Humphrey, then a U.S. Senator, suggested the creation of a new Department of Science. Objection was voiced by many educators and scientists socialized in a time when values of independence in scholarship were inculcated along with fear of encroachment upon the free publication of truth. American scholars are suspicious of Big Science in something of the same way that Americans generally have been suspicious of Big Business and Big Government. Big grants for big production are desirable, but the bureaucratic structures and governmental controls that must accompany them are viewed with some concern. However, at this point there are numerous lines of research which are so costly that even smaller governments and major corporations are unable to afford them independently. International organizations for cooperative research ventures are arising in the fields of nuclear and space research (Kaplan, p. 873).

The increasingly close integration of scientific growth with national policies has brought closer participation of scientists in policy formation. The atomic scientists particularly have blossomed into discussions of foreign policy and strategy. The immense status which has accrued to the physical scientist in recent years coupled with the willingness of many to shuttle from laboratory to policy discussions gives meaning to the sub-title of R. C. Woods recent essay *Scientists and Politics: The Rise of an Apolitical Elite.*

THE TECHNOLOGICAL SOCIETY?

Ellul, in his pessimistic and provocative work, *The Technological Society,* has brilliantly contended that science is increasingly subordinated to technology and in this lies societal changes reminiscent of Orwell's *Nineteen Eighty-Four.* Through this fusion of science with technology, says Ellul, man is losing control of his own destiny by the increasingly determinative conditions set by this child of his own creation, technology. Ellul's is no Marxian with materialism revised. Nor is his, in reality, a technological theory of history. Ellul would not contend that what he writes has applicability for any other civilization or period. His views, and the counter-views, are worth exploration.

The conception of technology found in Ellul is more inclusive than the usual definition. However, it is consistent with contemporary sociological theory. Technology embraces the entire realm of the "instrumental." Knowledge, practices, and devices which are to accomplish some tangible end are all technology, a conception consistent with Redfield's "technical order" in contrast to the "moral order." Technology is measured by standards of efficiency rather than by inherent qualities. Knowledge through which human beings are manipulated or controlled is technology as much as knowledge through which inanimate forces are manipulated or controlled.

The issue as to whether or not man is to be dominated by his machines has been argued for many years. The question re-arose in the 1920's to receive mainly optimistic assurances that it is man, who controls, not his fabricated monster from which so much good can flow. Other definitions of the issue have asked if science offers man the keys to the control of his destiny. To this sociologist George Lundberg wrote *Can Science Save Us?* and seemed therein to find an affirmative response, while his adversary, Howard Becker, insisted that we must move *Through Values to Social Interpretation.*

This issue of Frankenstein versus his monster burns in controversy today and is more crucially important simply by virtue of the enhanced power we have provided for technological achievement in ever-expanding spheres.

In Ellul's view our civilization has become concerned with the development of ever more efficient means to ends and decreasingly concerned with the assessment of ends themselves and decreasingly capable of defining them. We are preoccupied with technology, including the technology of adapting our lives to technology. This he observes to be true not only in our interest in mechanical devices but in the formation of plans which make the economy function more *efficiently,* the creation of *efficient* organizational structures through the gamut of institutions which range from the courts of law to modern army organization, the *efficient* reformulation of the urban church, and finally the realm of technology relating to the *effective* manipulation of individuals per se as in propaganda and vocational guidance on the social side and medicine on the physical. In the latter phase man himself is the immediate objective of technique. Nothing, says Ellul, escapes technique today.

Technique has progressively mastered *all* the elements of civilization . . . man himself is overpowered by technique and becomes its object. The technique which takes man for its object thus becomes the center of society; this extraordinary event (which seems to surprise no one) is often designated as *technical civilization.* The terminology is exact and we must fully grasp its importance. *Technical civilization* means that our civilization is constructed *by* technique (makes a part of civilization only what belongs to technique), *for* technique (in that everything in this civilization must serve a technical end), and *is* exclusively technique (in that it excludes whatever is not technique or reduces it to technical form). [Pp. 127–128.]

If Ellul's statement appears extreme it is perhaps no less so than the observations of a number of eminent theologians of our time. Ellul's meaning is not far from that of Harvey Cox in his work *The Secular City.* Nor is it inconsistent with the ideas expressed in the "God is Dead" theological movement. The theme taken by Ellul is remarkably supported in a perceptive report on contemporary trends as viewed by a number of eminent theologians (*Time Magazine,* April 8, 1966, pp. 82–

87). These religious scholars express deep concern with our virtual sanctification of verified knowledge and retreat from unseen abstractions and the very wonders of existence.

Techniques are no longer simple machines substituting for human labor; they have intervened into the total fabric of life with a dominating force. What is distinctive about the present power of technology is that instead of being part of civilization, it seemingly "has taken over the whole of civilization" (Ellul, p. 128).

The subtle determinativeness of technology in modern society is demonstrated in practically every sphere, not simply as we respond to technological conditions but as a new and permeating value substitute. Ellul shows how modern art reflects technique as he quotes Stravinsky saying that "My work is architectonic and not anecdotal; objective construction and not descriptive." In prosaic affairs of life like bread and butter the demands of efficiency have yielded new tastes in the standards of what is good bread and what is a good spread for it. Human values were deliberately modified to suit the needs of bakery mechanization. From the technical standpoint, man is a brake on progress, a useless appendage (Ellul, p. 137). If man cannot live with nothing sacred, technology, the very force which has destroyed the sacred, becomes man's essential mystery as the awe of magic is redirected to the recurrent miracles of science (Ellul, p. 143).

According to Ellul the requirements of efficient operation push all economic systems and governments the same directions in their patterning and structure. Concentration of capital is evident in the "free enterprise" countries as it is evident in "socialistic" ones. Computerization is not cheap and its efficiency is for the large, more than the small, operators. Further, the planning now required in economic matters of the firm is transposed into government in reference not to the individual enterprise but to all enterprises. The state becomes the coordinating center for the administration in control of, and for, the stimulation of technology. This new political state must then be determined in its policies and in its structure by technological considerations. As the British statesman Bevan is quoted, "The techniques of modern war have destroyed democracy," and Ardant that "Good methods bring about good structure" (Ellul, pp. 277–278). "Technique puts the question," continues Ellul, "not whether a given state form is more just, but whether it permits more efficient utilization of techniques."

Human beings are directly influenced by technology at work, at play, and at rest. In all spheres there has been a profound shift from behavior that was rooted in art. Medicine has persistently left less room for artistic flair and "feeling"; teaching has become highly self-conscious as to method and procedure, and even artists gain acclaim through the practical psychology of public relations; the insights of the scholar are supported, and at times even displaced, by computer programming and technical virtuosity. Public entertainment is created with an actor's eye to "method" and a producer's knowledge of that which has got the ratings in previous shows. Manipulative techniques derived from social psychology are practiced not only on the enemy but upon one's own, for morale, profit, or a winning candidate. On all sides social relationships are persistently "improved" by standards of technical efficiency in functioning. Man has less and less time in which to be "conscious of his own living presence" (Ellul, p. 397).

The technical society is one in which efficiency is a universal standard. Increasingly man's life is dominated by devices selected over others because of their efficiency. The man who is adjusted to his society is the one who adjusts his living to the requirements of the new device. This is as true of adaptions to mechanical techniques as it is to techniques which manipulate other persons. Just as the communication structure of an army unit is modified to fit the new technology of wars, the organization of school classes shifts with the technology of teaching; industrial relations are made adaptive to automated offices and assembly systems. Man must make the efficient decisions whether he wants to or not. He continues to steer the ship, but his course is set in technology rather than in will. He steers but, for Ellul, he steers a programmed course.

Economist Kenneth Boulding, no technological determinist, has suggested that the model for the world which we are building is that of a space capsule; a world in which nothing is left to chance, a world in which rational decisions are the only decisions, a world of total conservation. Mass-man is hybridized with economic man. Even the ardent exponent of cybernetics, Norbert Weiner, appears to have been prescient of Ellul's thesis when he wrote, "We are the slaves of our technical improvement. . . . We have modified an environment so radically that we must now modify ourselves in order to exist in this new environment" (p. 46).

These long views of the meaning of technology for social change are not shared by other scholars, but the gravity of the issue is not at question. The distinguished historical sociologist Robert Nisbet has addressed himself to this trend for many years (1953; 1956; cf. Falk). His responses are hopeful that the space capsule is not our model for an emerging social order. Nisbet and others believe that we are not at the mercy of our techniques, that man is still the creative force in molding not only his instruments but organizational structures within which they are utilized and the norms through which their utilization is controlled. Technology is a pre-eminent example of man's self-domestication. He is capable, if he chooses, of controlling his normative environment more surely than he controls natural forces. Ultimate values can persist as the stars by which man steers his technological society. Nisbet has expressed his idealism as follows:

It was the fate of the modern world that its technological revolution had to occur during a time of massive social upheaval that left old communities lifeless and, for a long time at least, failed to create any new communities in their place.

Because of a social vacuum caused, as I have elsewhere argued, in very large part by centralization of power, leading to the development of masses of human beings divorced from both culture and community, the machine itself was given, for a period of time, an apparent autonomy which could not help but invite indictment. To say this is in no sense to underestimate the residual influence of the machine and its ways. It is to emphasize, rather, that even the most massive pieces of technology can in themselves exert no influence upon human behavior except insofar as they are caught up in sets of human purposes.

I am no more fearful of technology overpowering man by its physical immensity than I am of peoples being overpowered morally by the vastness of ranges of mountains or expanses of desert. There was a time, let us remember, when historians and geographers seriously argued the determinism of physical nature upon the mind of man, seeing in whole systems of belief and worship mere reflections of topography and climate. Now we know that such determinism is naive. I am equally convinced that technological determinism is unacceptable. I do not believe that either super-calculator, the high-speed railway, the jet plane, or the Golden Gate bridge has in itself the power to crush man's spirit any more than I believe that the spirit of man has ever been crushed by the natural elements around him, formidable as these may be.

It is not technology, but the patterns of function and power within which it has developed that seem to me central in any analysis of the problem of individuality. . . . Our problem . . . is to develop forms of human relationship large enough to contain our technical needs and objectives, but small enough for human beings to feel a creative sense of membership. [Nisbet, 1956, pp. 23 ff.]

There are those who accept an increasing alienation and disengagement of modern man as an inevitable trend for which technology itself may provide a satisfying answer. Donovan Bess in a provocative essay has argued that the new drug LSD-25 (d-lysergic acid diethylamide tartrate) now provides modern man with an inner peace and social warmth which can supersede the effects of the increasingly mechanized and anomic social world. According to Bess:

Viable people really want out, this time. They are willing to risk something. Some of them find revolutionary opportunities outside: they sit in, lie in, sleep in, teach in, think in. Others find the scene inside; that is the radical way, for it breaks with our tradition of looking for salvation in deeds alone . . . [Pp. 42–50.]

From induced psychic aloneness, it is argued that there is to be found the base of a warm and abundant man. Bess continues, "You die grown up." "If you can hang onto that, afterward, you can offer society some adult values."

Such viewpoints as those expressed by Donovan Bess are not widely held, and LSD along with numerous other drugs having similar effect are widely viewed as immoral, and probably physically dangerous. Whatever the effects of modern psychedelic drugs they are effects on individuals not upon social structures. The cult of LSD probably has no more significance for social change than other modern mystery "religions" in which solace has been found by transportation to another and more wonderful world. The issue of their use for the development of serenity in the technological society will not, however, depend upon such transitory evaluations as those now being made.

THE TECHNOLOGICAL PRESENT

The issue of man's ultimate enslavement by his own technological progress is one having the broadest significance for society in terms of linear, evolutionary change. Its discussion bypasses questions of the middle range relating to the immediate, verifiable impact of developments in technology. These are matters relating to the functional meaning of specific technological trends, the types of stresses they evoke in the social order, and the patterns of adjustive response to these stresses.

Technological trends are not social trends except insofar as the society itself becomes a network of manipulative technical devices. While the delineation of contemporary technological history is beyond the scope of this book, some outstanding transitions are so imperative in their requirements for social response that they are given summary presentation. To treat new technology as ingredients in the study of social trends is not to endow it with a deterministic role. New techniques open new potentials in social relations (see Chap. 9 above). Although no technique carries with it some single and precise institutional structure fitted to its nature, social structures may be mechanically adapted to one technology and not to another. It takes two to tango but one may frug; a competitive work group can function efficiently in one technical setting whereas in another, complementing relationships are essential for production.

These novel potentials associated with techniques arise in reference to their immediate utilization, as labor is released or regrouped in a particular production enterprise. They also arise in the manifest and latent consequences upon groups and institutions which are in some degree of integration with the operation. We may not say, for example, that the

Rapidly Growing and Declining Industries in the United States,*
1957–60 to 1960–65

Rapidly Growing Industries	Growth Rate	Declining Industries	Growth Rate
Plastics materials	17.8	Shoes and slippers	−0.3
Magnesium	12.5	Lumber	−0.5
Seamless hosiery	12.4	Farm tractors	−0.6
Man-made fibers	12.4	Wood containers	−0.7
Auto radios	10.2	Coke	−1.0
Light trucks	9.9	Home freezers	−1.1
Basic organic chemicals	9.7	Cattlehide leather	−1.2
Softwood plywood	9.5	Millwork	−1.2
Table television	9.3	Lead	−1.4
Electric housewares	9.3	Railroad cars	−1.4
		Home furnaces	−1.5
Man-made fibers	9.0	Console television	−1.5
Aluminum mill shapes	8.8	Skin leather	−2.0
Kerosene	8.7	Men's outercoats	−2.8
Asphalt, waxes, etc.	8.3	Aviation fuel	−4.5
Misc. rubber and plastics	8.3		
		Residual fuel oil	−5.3
Metalworking machinery	8.3	Full-fashioned hosiery	−19.1
Autos	8.0	Medium trucks	−24.1

Trends in industrial growth and decline reflect changing technology but they also reflect changing values, changing fashions, and changing recreational patterns.

* Based on Table 6, Part II, of *Long Term Economic Growth, 1860–1965*, U. S. Department of Commerce, Bureau of the Census, 1966, p. 87.

new machines of the industrial revolution *caused* the differentiation of traditional family functions. But we can say that as the new machines *were organized* for use, the stresses placed upon traditional family functioning were unbearable. The new machines were precipitants in a dynamic complex of variables which led to reassessment of family structure and the quest for new institutional and community structures to provide for education, financial security, and protection. New norms of family life were created fitting the milieu of industrial wage employment.

Contemporary technological achievement sets deep the stresses and hence issues for the social organization of the future.[1] The 1960's grope

[1] Although published too late for consideration in this chapter, the reader is referred to Herman Kahn and Anthony J. Wiener, *The Year 2000: A Framework for Speculation on the Next Thirty-Three Years*, The Macmillan Company, New York, 1967. This work is particularly useful for its extrapolations of technological developments.

for resolutions to the demographic crises evoked in Asia by the innovative application of pesticides and miracle drugs in the 1940's and 1950's. The 1970's must create the social innovations in adjustment to stresses evoked by the technological innovations of the 1960's. The technological present is a dynamic present. Discoveries and inventions, as we have observed in Chapter 4, are rarely presented for use as full-blown, unimprovable designs. The technological present includes evolutionary changes in long-established systems of events, like the automobile. It also includes innovative mutations whose functional consequences were practically unknown a decade or so earlier, e.g., nuclear power production. Additionally there are the technological thresholds crossed only yesterday and still more that give almost certain promise of being crossed tomorrow or the day after. Some, like contraceptive pills, are over the threshold of impact. Others like certain recent bio-chemical discoveries have potentials which may not be significantly realized for a number of years, but which have staggering implications for our eventual society.

Emphasis here is placed upon the technology which has crossed the threshold of application in the past decade or so, or is upon the verge of doing so. There is a wide range in the degree to which social assessments have already been formulated and response patterns established for the various techniques described.

Energy and Power

Significance of Sources of Power. The nature and efficiency of the sources of power utilized by a society are critical technological variables. There is a school of social scientists which argues that energy is the ultimate determining force in cultural evolution. Culture may be viewed in part as a mechanism for harnessing the available energy sources (White). Natural forces are invariably taken hold of by man and put to work in the fulfillment of his needs. Early and "undeveloped" societies relied fully upon human energy and progressed materially through improvement of devices whereby this particular form of energy could be harnessed. Human energy is weak in the power resources it makes available. Leslie White contends, and with reason, that early societies with complete reliance upon this relatively weak energy source could not but be meager and crude in the fulfillment of material needs. There are also drastic limits upon the efficiency of technological devices which can be geared to this source. If human life is not to be mean in the material and welfare sense, new energy forms must be found and new devices created for harnessing them. To some extent primitive societies have utilized fire, water, and wind, but as White (p. 370) points out, these were relatively insignificant during the first hundreds of thousands of years of culture history. Actually primitive man depended more upon solar energy "harnessed" for him naturally through the processes of photosynthesis.

With the Neolithic achievement of agriculture and animal domestication, there was a revolutionary control of photosynthesis. It cannot be denied that agricultural surpluses were one of the fundamental prerequisites for the rise of civilizations. With new energy sources added to human power, new technologies were stimulated for their increasingly efficient utilization. New potentials were laid open for changes in institutional structure, and settled community life was indicated where nomadic hunting bands had once roamed.

A second transformation of energy sources occurred at the start of the nineteenth century by the tapping of new fuel sources, coal, and subsequently oil and gas. Production and transportational technology was revolutionized in the engines capable of producing power through steam. New forms of community organization were stimulated; vast power for vast population increase occurred in Western Europe. Technological hand-springs occurred as inventors, increasingly abetted by scientists, sought more efficient utilization of these energy sources in engines, machines, and tools. New technological stimulus occurred as these energy sources were transmitted in the form of electricity permitting the ready transport of inanimate power into factories and homes. As with other transformations in energy sources and their technological accompaniments, shifts in social organization were made in reference to new production technology suited to new energy forms.

Through the middle years of the twentieth century, ominous warnings were sounded persistently by conservationists impressed by the dependence of our civilization upon the fuel energy sources undergoing rapid depletion. "Our plundered planet," coupled with world population growth, caused serious concern among many thoughtful scholars. Inevitably, it was said, depleted reserves meant utilization of increasingly scarce and expensive sources of energy for the increasing demands of more and more people. Excessive rises in the cost of power would occur through reversion to increasingly inefficient resources. As Sir George Thomson observed, this would at least "take the zest out of our technology." Against well-nigh Malthusian gloom, there were but vague hopes that the sun's energy might someday be more fully controlled or that tides might be fruitfully harnessed.

Advent of Nuclear Energy. The technological events of 1945 utterly changed the dimensions of the power resource controversy. At Hiroshima on August 6, 1945, there was triggered the first "practical" application of "atomic energy." Whether or not this most recent energy source stimulates technological revolutions as significant for social life as those triggered by agriculture and then by steam and electricity is improbable. That its consequences are to be substantial is unquestionable. However, unlike electricity or even the introduction of steam, nuclear power will not result in qualitatively new capabilities (Mullenback).

The bomb dropped on Hiroshima derived its energy from U-235, the only naturally occurring substance in which chain reaction is possible (Thomson, p. 28). While the presence of other substance prevents ordinary Uranium from exploding, it is possible to give a chain reaction by mixing it with pure graphite or heavy water. The process of fission produces energy which as heat offers power, and, in the case of the bomb, immense explosive force. Since the original bomb, the power in nuclear reaction has been expanded manyfold. The original A-Bomb damaged an area of 7 square miles, the improved A-Bomb an area of 25 square miles, and the H-Bomb perhaps 250 square miles (Hart, pp. 41–43). The sensational character of nuclear fission was not even fully expressed in the awesome toll of death and destruction from a single "small" bomb. But the energy released by this device made of it a truly revolutionary achievement in the history of man's search for power. Hornell Hart, who has studied the accelerating increase in explosive power through the past centuries, points out that the A-Bomb represented a "shift in gears." Over the past 600 years the chemical bomb showed a 22-fold increase in explosive power, whereas in the nine years following the first A-Bomb, there was a 500-fold increase in explosive power. Further, even the primitive Hiroshima A-Bomb had an explosive blast rating of over 10,000 compared to 25 for cyclamite bombs of the same year.

The bomb is a "fast reactor." Industrial uses of nuclear energy require slow reactors as well as protection from radiation. Devices are required to carry away heat without absorbing the neutrons which are the lifeblood of the material. All must be worked automatically due to radiation. Construction materials must not absorb neutrons as most metals do. These are all problems in the process of resolution toward the wide utilization of nuclear power in industrial life. Many of the problems have been tentatively resolved as evidenced in nuclear power stations and nuclear-powered submarines and ships. The first commercial use of nuclear power from a civilian reactor took place in California in 1959. Others are now operative, and many more are in various stages of planning or construction. Sir George Thomson (p. 33) could predict, even in 1957, that we will be able to continue to produce electrical energy in almost any quantity at prices no higher, and perhaps even lower, than are current today.

Social Effects of Nuclear Power. In 1950, Vincent Heath Whitney pointed out that the peacetime uses of nuclear power would neither develop automatically nor produce immediate short-run revolutionary consequences. This prediction is proving to be accurate. This is partly due to the scientific, technological problems involved in re-developing and re-harnessing fission in a manner suitable for industrial and commercial uses. There are, however, other reasons to expect nuclear power to enter our community life with some subtlety. In the first place, there are many points at which fission and fusion are not immediately congruent with our existing or foreseeable technical equipment. Automobiles will continue for some time to run on internal combustion engines, and when these become obsolete it is unlikely that nuclear reactors will be their replacement. The heating of houses is not likely to be shifted from immediate sources now in use. Nuclear power is entering the house, but it enters in the self-same form, electricity, to do the same old jobs a little more cheaply in some regions. The climatic control of entire cities through nuclear power is not "way out," but it is not immediate. This indeed would have consequences for the cycles of human behavior organized in reference to climatic factors, as well as for amenities of seasonal significance.

The replacement of conventional fuels by nuclear energy also should bring alleviation of smoke and smog troubles in our cities (Mullenback). In this sense nuclear wastes are "clean"; and their greater use will be welcome to the red-eyed and wheezing citizens of our major cities. This is a particularly important factor when we consider the probable needs for greatly increased power production in the years to come. On the other hand, nuclear wastes present a special problem. The very fact that radiation is a life and death matter offers reasonable insurance that disposal will be handled in a centrally controlled manner. Assuming successful solution of this waste problem, and its solution seems assured, air pollution will be abated by the change.

Whitney pointed out that the major limiting factor on nuclear power in the United States was the matter of relative cost. By 1964, however, it was claimed that nuclear power could be competitively priced (Mullenback). In power production generally we may expect nuclear sources to be introduced particularly in regions of high cost for traditional sources of electrical generation. Fissionable material is readily transportable and unlike coal and oil has slight bulk per unit of energy produced. One pound of fissionable material releases energy roughly equal to that of 1,500 tons of coal (Miller, p. 261). Extensive plans for nuclear source electricity are being made for Southern Florida. In this region electric power has been produced through oil shipped in and gas pipelined from Texas. In a region of rapidly expanding population and industry and high conventional fuel costs nuclear power offers an economically feasible alternative. The Atomic Energy Commission foresees that fuel cost will become equal throughout the country as nuclear sources enter the now high-cost areas.

Conditions are quite different in other countries. It is improbable that nuclear power will have impact for many years in nations like India, where necessary skills must first be developed, capital is lacking, and the problem of efficiency in power source is dwarfed by more immediate economic considerations including the great use of human energy.

In 1962 the Atomic Energy Commission reported that it was a reasonable expectation that nuclear power in the United States would by the end of the century be assuming the total increase in national electric energy requirements and would be providing half the energy generated (Mullenback, p. 11). This estimate was made on the assumption of a *tenfold* increase in our total use of electrical energy during the period.

The ultimate impacts of nuclear power upon world society in general and Western society in particular for the foreseeable future are more significant in the realm of military threat than in substantial differences made in peoples' lives through its peacetime uses. (Perhaps its very threat may intimate constructive social innovations for our culture.) However, such a forecast does not do justice to the facts. Minus nuclear power most significant stresses would be in store for us, assuming population growth and the demand for an ever more abundant material culture. To a substantial extent the social functions of nuclear power are not vastly different from those of alternative but now diminishing power sources. If we could not look forward to this new power resource, very sharp account would be taken of the scarcity and rising costs of energy through more traditional sources. While experiments and explorations are also underway in the utilization of tides and of solar power, for the immediate future these have limited potentials.

The development of nuclear power has, in addition to its manifest consequences, also served to expand the role of the federal government in the economy. As explained by the Atomic Energy Commission, industry could not have afforded to develop civilian atomic power because of the high investment toward returns which are small in the early years (Mullenback, p. 27). Under the economic conditions of its introduction, governmental support was indicated. The merger of government and private enterprise is not entirely new, but it represents here a fairly large step beyond even earlier retrenchments from "free enterprise." At the same time, the power vested in the federal government in regard to the development and utilization of nuclear energy far surpasses the controls exercised upon petroleum and coal fuels in either their production or in their use. Control of radiation is itself a sizable function which inevitably must reside with the federal government. Not only from the standpoint of its destructive potentials but from various economic angles as well, the transition to nuclear power contributes to further governmental bureaucratization, control, and centralization.

Cybernetics and Automation

Cybernetics is the science of communication and control mechanisms. The word derives from the Greek and in its literal meaning refers to a "governor" or "steersman." The mathematician Norbert Weiner popularized the term in his effort to create a general system of communication theory which would serve as a nexus for many disciplines, including physics, psychology, and sociology. The concept had earlier been used by André Marie Ampère (1775–1836) in regard to feedback in government (Veillette; Diebold). Reared upon the science of cybernetics, with its concepts of communication, memory, and feedback, is the technology of automation. Automation refers to machines which are self-regulating and which are integrated into action systems with other machines. As with all inventions, the constituent ideas which compose these complex machine systems have long histories. A primary step was the pressure cooker invented by Denis Papin around 1680, with a steam control mechanism capable of acting automatically. Progress gradually came in the automatic control of pressures in steam engines and (in 1868) the idea was applied to large ships, i.e., a cable mechanism connecting rudder, steersman wheel, and throttle wherein movement of the rudder feeds back self-correcting impulses to wheel and to engine. Other elements of automation have an equally long history. The integrating of machines in continuous production lines, i.e., automatic material handling, rests upon Whitney's development of interchangeable parts and the equally early assembly line systems such as Oliver Evans' fully automatic flour mill in 1784.

During the 1820's, the mathematician Charles Babbage worked assiduously but unsuccessfully to perfect the design of a computing machine (Rosenbloom). A few years later, Andrew Ure, like Babbage in his recognition of the technological trends of the time, foresaw that "the most perfect manufacture is that which dispenses entirely with manual labor. . . . The philosophy of manufactures is therefore an exposition of the general principles, on which productive industry should be conducted by self-acting machines" (Rosenbloom, p. 496). To find evolutionary roots for automation does not justify the conclusion that contemporary industrial devices are no more than a simple extrapolation of the assembly line system, a point of view sometimes elaborated by management representatives. While we have in a true sense been involved in an industrial revolution relating to specialization and mass production, the present phase of this trend suggests disequilibrating potentials perhaps as great as occurred with the introduction of weaving and spinning machines a century and a half ago. There is the vast difference in that we have today a relatively rational, controlled, and prosperous society basically adjusted to industrial production as well as the rights of labor and somewhat geared to requirements of perpetual change in a dynamic society.

Utterly incomparable with the industrial revolution of the early nineteenth century, however, is the application of cybernetic principles to office work and data processing. Nonetheless, attempts to speed and make more accurate the handling of information have a history perhaps longer than that of automation in production. The adding machine was invented in 1642 and a few years later a multiplying device was built into it. Dr. Herman Hollerith devised the now famous "punch card" in 1897, and in 1910 it was utilized for the U.S. census. His invention was probably based on the punch card "programming" developed by Jacquard in 1801 to activate an automatic weaving loom in respect to the pattern punched into the card. However, in recent years electronics has introduced fantastic speed into data processing machines such as the digital computer, which is capable of handling a multiplicity of functions. Recently James T. Culbertson has argued a thesis which far extends the theoretical potentials of automation. Culbertson contends that consciousness itself can be produced in artificially constructed devices. If Culbertson's as yet unproven assumptions are found valid, his theory could support greater capacity and speed in mechanisms than have yet been contemplated (Culbertson; Reiss).

How Automation Works. Norbert Weiner stressed the analogy of machines and human organisms. Although his popular book was titled *The Human Use of Human Beings,* it pertains more to the "human use of non-human beings"—machines. Information is fed into the machine and recorded in *memory.* The machine is directed as to how input data are to be transformed into the desired output. The special mode of conduct for the informed machine to follow in combining its accumulated data is given it through a special sort of input, which due to frequent use of punched or magnetic tape is called *taping* or *programming.* Central to automated machines are mechanisms of *internal control* based upon *actual* performance rather than expected performance. This is accomplished through *monitors* to indicate actual performance and then actuate elements of the machine toward control of mechanical tendency toward disorganization, i.e., to reverse the normal tendency toward *entropy.* The message relayed through the monitors is *feedback* or corrective communications based upon performance error. Weiner has used the elevator as a simple example of the processes.

> For example, if we are running an elevator, it is not enough to open the outside door because the orders we have given should make the elevator be at that door at the time we open it. It is important that the release for opening the door be dependent on the fact that the elevator is actually at the door; otherwise something might have detained it, and the passenger might step into the empty shaft. [Weiner, pp. 24–25.]

Weiner's concern was not merely with computers and automation but with a broad theory of communicative behavior that he was at pains to find supported in human behavior. It is clear that in driving a car the human being does not follow out a series of directions or commands dependent simply upon a previous reading of the map and his image of the task at hand. Constant monitoring and feedback occurs as the driver visually checks the road, checks his gauges, feels the drag of the wheel, and responds correctively.

Weiner's theory emphasizes the communicative processes including feedback (or "servo-mechanisms") through which deviations from purpose are electronically controlled. How these concepts are enlarged upon in working devices depends upon the nature of the job at hand. Basically there are two major directions in which cybernetics are technologically applied. These are, respectively, the industrial handling of materials or the application of cybernetics to the performance of "manual" tasks, and the application of cybernetic principles to office or "white collar" and clerical tasks, including so-called "computer technology" (Rose, pp. 443 ff.).

Automation in the industrial plant has as its object continuous production with a minimum of human labor. Automatic material handling replaces human dexterity and muscle. Ralph J. Cordiner of General Electric has defined automation as "continuous automatic production," largely in the sense of *linking together* already highly mechanized individual operations (p. 19). Automation is a way of work based on the concept of production as a continuous flow rather than processing by intermittent batches of work. The flow mechanisms have been more readily adapted to processing such as occurs in chemical and electrical utility plants than to plants producing discrete products as in metal goods. Recent estimates suggest that we may expect perhaps 80 per cent of the equipment in American industrial plants to be automated eventually (Rose, p. 445). Costs are likely to be too great for total automatization in most plants. It is evident too that the inelastic nature of the capital placed in automated equipment acts against its use in circumstances where capacity utilization is unlikely.

Office automation has been focused on data processing rather than machine integration. While it is an overstatement to say that computers "think," they do "read," "write," compare, and do basic arithmetic. A modern electronic computer has a memory device in which to store and retrieve specific instructions to itself along with the data to be manipulated. Analog computers reconstruct an actual situation under study as a basis for prediction. Digital computers make comparisons by means of series of yes-no answers to questions which can be introduced to the machine in such a program that the entire problem is covered. "Total system" computation is today possible in which a computer can design an entire problem or an industrial plant, taking into account costs of materials, use of space, and local zoning regulations. In the large continuous process plants, e.g., chemicals and power generation, there is hardly a distinction between office electric brain and automated "plant." All are within a single computer design system. Frequently, however, only limited and specialized activities are computerized as in bookkeeping, sales analysis, payroll or filing, and data storage and retrieval.

Social Effects of Automation and "Computerization." Automation is manifestly a set of techniques to accelerate production while reducing dependence upon immediate human labor or thought. Additionally, as human error is reduced, quality is controlled, production rejects diminished, and products are fully standardized. The machines are unaffected in any literal sense by family troubles and grievances.

Computerization and automatic factories have been greeted with fear, anxiety, and controversy. Spokesmen from the side of management and production tend to hail automation as the answer to the population explosion amid enhanced living levels, while labor leaders view it as an ultimate challenge to jobs and collective bargaining and hence income.

Automation involves the substitution of capital for labor in the automated sections of a plant. As this occurs there is pressure toward maximal use of the expensive equipment and hence pressure toward a greater total plant production. This may involve the extreme position such as that requiring no labor whatsoever as in some utility power stations, or more commonly it means a readjustment of the labor force in the plant, with probable overall reductions. New demands are felt for programmers, electronic technicians, and repairmen, as assemblymen and clerks are replaced by a few "console operators." Different sectors of the plant may expand in manual labor force at least temporarily, as in the need for men in a shipping department due to increased production (Faunce).

Psychologically the introduction of automation is associated with worker anxiety. A radio poll in Detroit several years ago indicated that listeners, when confronted with a list of fears, feared Russia most and automation second (Barton, p. 245). Scores of speeches have been made by top management officers attempting to assure American labor that, like atoms, "automation will be good for you." In immediate psychological effects in the individual plant there is some evidence of increased tension under automated conditions and dissatisfaction from reduced interaction with fellow workers as well as from increased supervision and a feeling of uselessness. But on the whole workers appear to prefer to be associated with automation since the work is easier (Faunce). Crafts decline as skill and dexterity are removed from the human body and made a function of the machine.

The argument that automation furthers the job alienation process which the assembly line and mass production methods began is disputed by Robert Blauner. Blauner believes that automation may return a dignity and enrichment to the worker which the assembly line took from him. Blauner reasons that with automation the worker will "supervise" a sequence of integrated operations rather than have responsibility for a meaninglessly limited segment of the production process. The new tasks will require training and scientific skills, particularly among maintenance technicians. Faunce's research cited above suggests that these expectations may be over-optimistic, and other scholars suggest that the automated worker so far from feeling the joys of craftsmanship becomes little more than a monitor and gauge watcher (Walker, Part 2).

The immediate structural adjustments attendant to automation are reasonably well known, and tensions associated with the transformation of individual plants have been much reduced through careful planning and frank bargaining and agreement between labor and management (French). But the latent consequences permeate many institutions and raise issues of public policy and directions of social change generally. Perhaps, the most succinct summing up of basic issues was that of Walter Reuther in a bit of repartee,

Several years ago, when I went through the Ford-Cleveland engine plant where they had fully automated the production of engines, and I looked over the acres and acres of automated machinery, I was asked by a management person how I liked the situation, and I told him I was very much impressed, and he says, "Well, you won't be able to collect dues from all of these automated machines," and I said, "You know, that is not what is bothering me. What is bothering me is, how are you going to sell cars to all of these machines?" [Murrow and Friendly, p. 225.]

Automation denotes increased production in plants which are paying for fewer workers. The potential of unemployment must be faced. But in the last quarter of the nineteenth century it is not being faced by Luddite mobs nor by "iron laws" of wages. It is apparent that in part the work force is shifted into new kinds of jobs through automation. The demand for precision skills and for assembly line and clerical workers may well diminish, but the increased demand for highly skilled technicians, engineers, and programmers will partly offset this. So far automation has also stimulated employment in new industries and the expansion of old ones as new electronic equipment is produced and existing corporation boundaries are extended. Further, it is evident that many occupations cannot for the foreseeable future be fully automated. The impetus is toward upgrading the labor force and at the same requiring less labor time to produce an even larger national product.

To say that the unions are concerned about the matter is a vast understatement, and well they may be. A shift in the quality and allocation of the labor force of this revolutionary dimension is a major challenge to the organizations which protect and extend the rights of labor. Transition to new production techniques raises a multiplicity of problems not answered by "up-grading of workers" or greater productivity. The job may be upgraded, whereas the individual worker is not. The adjustment process requires substantial innovating relative to workers' education, unemployment benefits, and facilitating labor mobility in regard both to job and to location (Buckingham). James Stern has pointed directly to a potential loss in power by organized labor and vastly increased power accruing to corporate management. In the automated plants, strikes will be more difficult since operations can be maintained more easily by a few non-bargaining personnel. In Stern's judgment also the increased proportion of technical jobs outside traditional spheres and units of union organization will erode the union's power to bargain. While automation enables a corporation to extend its boundaries across industry lines, unions are prevented by political considerations from raising their own organizational structure to match corporation power. With automation, unions must find new bases of solidarity and new program orientations such as job re-training. If, as Stern believes, the strike will decline in effectiveness as a prime weapon of labor, labor's ends will be increasingly sought through political and through governmental means.

The ultimate question relates more to income maintenance than to full employment, although American values are still such that payments to labor for work not performed will be odious. Basic questions to be resolved involve the manner in which individuals will share in the national product, e.g., the four day work week, early retirement, a guaranteed annual wage, socialization of goods and services, etc. In addition, issues are forced upon us in regard to planned re-training and compensation programs for the technologically unemployed workers.

In 1959 Charles Frankel gave an evaluation of the significance of automation for social change. In his assessment, published in the *New York Times* Magazine, he foresaw immediate consequences arising from the increased ratio of skilled to unskilled workers and the impact of the automatic factory on the way the working day might be arranged due to the economic need of employing high cost machines around the clock. He pointed also to more subtle effects—the changing attitudes of workers as they become more oriented to leisure. In the long run, Frankel observed, the most profound shifts would simply lie in the rapidly increased tempo at which we do things. This change of gears, he, like many others, attributed to the new application of theoretical science to technology.

While it is true that what has been termed the "threat of leisure" becomes an increasing reality, it is also probable that workers will come under closer managerial scrutiny during the work period itself. And, while technology has been spurred by its virtual merger with theoretical science, computerization in turn vastly increases the rapidity and magnitude of both theoretical and "practical" problem solving. Gendell and Zetterberg have observed that the electronic calculator may do to intellectual work what the steam engine once did for manual labor.

More philosophic writers are concerned that man is increasingly alienated from his work, increasingly computerized in his personal actions, and de-individuated in a society that places efficiency before art, peace, self-expression, and the thrill evoked by participating in nature (Ellul). Whatever the precise formulation of pathways for meeting the stresses and strains evoked by automation, the resolutions will rely strongly upon the role of the political state. The political forces in modern society, coupled with the magnification of welfare values, guarantees that unlike the factory revolution of the nineteenth century, government programs will intervene through the extension of educational and retraining programs, unemployment subsidies, and, if collective bargaining should fail, ultimately control much more fully the allocation of our national product. And we may be sure that this controlling state will be a fully computerized one.

Transportation and Mass Media Communication

As in many spheres of technology, acceleration is the dominant pattern of innovative change in transport and communication. Expanding scope is also significant, in the sense of drawing more participants into utilization of transport and of communication facilities. Speed is related to expanded utilization as is evident, for example, in increased passenger flights which can be made by a jet plane introduced as replacement for propeller craft on the same run.

Contemporary aircraft designs contemplate services in which several hundred passengers will be moved at sub- and at supersonic speed. Among tangible developments is the contracted delivery by Boeing of their 747 jet planes capable of carrying 490 passengers at a cruising speed of 625 miles per hour (*Time Magazine,* April 22, 1966, p. 69). Britain and Soviet Russia will have corresponding planes shortly, the Soviet version with a 724 passenger capacity. Supersonic commercial flights will soon be available also at substantially higher costs than those of the jet behemoths.

Such designs have little to do with speeding up short distance movements. Sir George Thomson suggests that we seem to pay a great attention to speed when our real problem is the midcity "rush hour"—a matter which he feels will be solved not in transportation technology but in social and other inventions, i.e., in community organization. The general acceleration of long distance movement no doubt facilitates a general increase in physical mobility, widening social contacts, and overall "keying up" of time-consciousness.

It is improbable that devices now available will in the foreseeable future eliminate familiar transportation equipment, although of course changes in their power plants and other elements are fairly certain. Automobiles, buses, trains, surface ships, and even bicycles will long remain as alternatives since advance in speed increases costs and such increases are economically infeasible for some purposes. Further, speedier devices do not always function in a way suited to particular circumstances and tastes which will long remain. We are in a period of proliferating alternatives in which greater specialization of design is creating a much wider range of adaptations to diverse needs. There are apparently no current developments likely to interject such radical trends as those associated with the automobile, with its dispersive potential for urban population and industry.

The most spectacular of all "transport" changes has been that occurring in the realm of rocketing and orbital and space travel. While this involves a knowledge thrust as sensational as that of nuclear fission and fusion, its development at this point has closely limited empirical implications, apart from warfare, and the furthering of knowledge mainly of meteorological significance. Although there will be a man on the moon shortly, there will not be many men on many moons in the foreseeable future. Tickets will cost more than the average millionaire will care to pay, and it is unclear just what will be transported as paying cargo (insofar as cargo can be carried) in interplanetary devices. As for visiting the stars, Thomson observes sardonically that "we may well be nearer to it in time than we are to Pekin Man" (p. 90). Needless to say the introduction of equipment satellites into orbit has already had significance for rapidity in communications and for meteorological research.

Most major recent developments in mass communication technology are now substantially diffused, and researches upon their social impact have been going on for some years. The use of transistors is currently having social consequences in expanding the range of radio listening in remote regions and in satellite transmissions.

A variety of minor advances in communications are occurring through the invention of the germanium transistor. This tiny transistor can be made to both rectify and amplify and may make short-range walkie-talkies feasible for common use. Chiefly this would serve as a specialized alternative to contacts now going through telephone circuits (Thomson, pp. 54–61). Although difficulties are substantial, there is a likehood that "meetings" will be held through the use of coaxial cables or other wave-guides. This suggests one technological response to the mid-city traffic jam.

The overall implications of technological trends in the realm of transport and communication are toward increased physical mobility and broadening of scale in social participation. Accelerated transport implies the greater availability of costly and perishable amenities and an enhancement of interregional and international economic dependencies. Speed is a factor whereby interdependent regions may assure greater mutual protection from the forces and catastrophes of nature, i.e., through shifting of population, famine relief, etc. Or, if the situational variables are otherwise, such technology can by man's volition be turned toward catastrophic destruction. If history is extrapolated in this regard, accelerated transport will further both increasing human welfare as well as destruction and pain.

Communication technology cannot fail to increase impersonal, secondary contacts, although in limited ways it may facilitate "personalized" contact via "photo-telephonic" means. Generally the mass communications media are simply extending their effects relative to diffusion, public formation, socialization, and horizon broadening into regions of the world as yet slightly touched by them. Their position is being strengthened by diversification and by saturated coverage in regions already habituated to certain of them. All will serve the end of accelerating the flow of ideas, if not on a world-wide basis then through the networks of vast politically defined world regions.

Environmental Knowledge and Technology: Climate and Food

In neither food production nor climatic control have such sensational achievements occurred in recent years as has been true for technologies rooted more closely in physics and mathematics. Agricultural productivity has been multiplied in the past twenty-five years through the chemistry of fertilizers, controlled plant breeding, and the application of engineering skills to automated equipment, irrigation programs, etc. All these and other types of achievement have resulted in great absolute increases in world food production.

It is significant, however, that few new foods have been added to the list developed by various Neolithic peoples. No revolution has overturned the cereals and tubers first discovered by them. And no domesticated animals have been added to those bequeathed to Western civilization by earlier or non-Western peoples. Nonetheless the application of science to meat and other food production has yielded revolutionary change in quantity if relatively little change in basic type of product. Hydroponic farming offers potential development, and advancing technology consistently makes possible bringing additional lands into cultivation. Present research points to the sea as the probable major food resource development area. Sea algae with high yield and high protein value will shortly appear as feasible diet supplements. There is good reason to believe that solar energy will continue to be utilized in the foreseeable future as it occurs through photosynthesis rather than in power generation (Idyll; Thomson, p. 112).

The technology of climate control is in elemental stages. "Substitute climates" for limited areas as in heated and air conditioned buildings are current. The actual control of weather through direct intervention is now slight. The technology of cloud-seeding and hurricane control are embryonic at this point. The application of cheap, transportable nuclear energy to water pumping and the continued development of the desalination plants toward greater economic feasibility are perhaps the most serious climatic control programs at this time. Agricultural and forest development of what is now desert and wasteland would moderate arid climates as well as affect world population distribution. Technology has persistently expanded the areas available to man's settlement. The remaining deserts will probably yield before the tropical rain forests.

Biological and Medical Technology

Controls on Death and on Birth. Some of the most socially satisfying and at once tension-evoking technological changes in recent decades have been precipitated through discoveries bearing upon health, longevity, and birth control. The contemporary population explosion of Latin America and Asia has been stimulated by the use of modern chemicals such as DDT and the diffusion, after World War II, of the "miracle drugs" (Wrong). Thus the use of DDT in malaria control contributed to a 40 per cent drop in the Ceylon death rate between 1945 and 1948. Nutritional improvement has also been credited in accounting for the sudden boom in population following 1945.[2] Equally spectacular drops in the death rate are not to be expected in these regions in the future, but the extension of public health and nutritional programs to additional areas of early death can extend these gains further.

The technological present is becoming more closely keyed to the invention and diffusion of devices which will serve to resolve stresses induced by rapid population growth through death reduction (Zimmerman; Nimkoff; Stycos; Segal). In some countries, older technologies have been adapted to large-scale utilization. Japan cut its birth rate in half in ten years largely by abortion. Sterilization is somewhat widely used in India, Korea, and elsewhere. Technical advance has recently been made in simplifying male sterilization or vasectomy. However, abortion is widely viewed in moral terms while sterilization, simple as it may be, requires surgical procedures. The quest for morally suitable and extremely simple birth control technology adapted to massive diffusion in poor regions has been rapidly extended in recent decades and with substantial success and with much more to come. Needless to say, these devices are more widely available in developed countries where birth control is more fully institutionalized than in the critical regions of rapid population growth. The modern birth control movement has now involved "big science, big business, and big effort" (Zimmerman).

Recent trends in birth control technology have focused upon the rhythm of ovulation. Some are directed toward synthetic hormone production. These are referred to as anti-ovulants. Others act to prevent the egg from becoming fertilized. Oral contraceptives have already become so widely used that *Time* reported sales in 1965 amounting to $65 million and expected them to reach $90 million in 1966. The over-seas market is said to have been but barely tapped. Of 700 million women of child-bearing age in the world only a small fraction have used "the pill" and even in the United States only about one-fifth had done so by 1967 (Zimmerman; *Time Magazine*, April 17, 1967, p. 78). Success has also been claimed for a small plastic intra-uterine device which seems effective in preventing conception, although no one quite understands why. This cheap and simple device is proving to be adapted to use in rapidly growing underdeveloped countries. The present diffusion curve shows rapid increase in adoptions in such countries as South Korea, Taiwan, and Pakistan. However, it is estimated that by 1967 there were only about 3 million adopters in all Asia and some 150,000 in Latin America (Popu-

---

[2] Until recently it has been generally accepted that the dramatic drop in the death rate for Ceylon after 1945 was due almost entirely to malaria control, through DDT spraying (Cullumbine). This theory has recently been disputed by Harold Fredericksen (1961) whose evidence points to the greater influence of generally rising levels of living.

lation Council). The significant diffusion of oral or intra-uterine devices on a world-wide basis has just begun.

Consequences of Death Control. The demographic consequences of life-saving chemicals and drugs upon peoples everywhere have been the subject of an immense and controversial literature. Alternative and complementing solutions to pressure upon potential food supplies are extremely varied, but few if any persons today hold with the laissez-faire and Malthusian resolutions wherein ultimate reliance is placed upon the positive checks of famine, war, and disease. Few if any serious demographers can visualize economic productivity keeping up with current world growth trends. A few emphasize the possibility that developed nations can feed the world while the underdeveloped regions gain necessary time to build up their own economies and resource utilization. More general, however, is the conviction that underdeveloped nations must fight a losing battle to establish viable economies amid the insistent pressures of population which are to double their size in some twenty-five years and to then redouble in somewhat fewer years. Long-range optimists recognize that reduction of family size accompanies urbanization. However, the resistance to family planning will be greater in some underdeveloped regions than it was in the West and such optimism does not cover the dilemmas of the next fifty years.

The technology of life preservation must be met not only by the technology and organization of economic production; it must be met by the technology of birth control or abortion. This conviction is shared by practically all population analysts and indeed by the statesmen and planners of most major Asian nations. There are nations, especially the more conservative Roman Catholic ones of Latin America, where the issues are less squarely faced. In Western nations such as the United States, the population explosion, while raising problems of some seriousness, is of a different order. Rational family planning is almost universal in the urbanized nations and the moral and institutional consequences create no critical tensions and relatively few problems of attitudinal change. In the West, birth as well as death is under control. Accordingly, birth rates respond to changing economic conditions and to shifting social values and expectations. The past decade has witnessed substantial reduction in the crude birth rate for the United States since the surge following World War II.

The technology of death control raises impelling problems of functional adjustment in many populous countries if the positive Malthusian checks are to be circumvented. On the one hand is the potential application of greater efficiency and modern technology in agricultural practice and the development of new areas of food resource such as deserts and seas. This must take place hand in hand with increasing industrialization and with increasing proportions of present agricultural labor forces brought into industry. Although these transformations are "economic" ones, they are equally sociological in their implications for urban growth, restructuring of work groups, alienation, etc. Even more immediately sociological are the transitions to planned parenthood. In the first place the control of birth is widely but not universally viewed in moral and religious terms. Even where this is not true in a philosophical sense, uneducated people widely believe that tampering with birth is vaguely "wrong" (Lorimer *et al.*). Much of the world undergoing the most serious population expansion upholds family values and familial organization systems different from those of the Western nuclear family. A doctrine and practice that reduces the size of family may be beneficial in the personally remote sense of national welfare, but the peasant knows that through his large family he gains status, security, dignity, and personal regard. Such facts preclude easy, rapid acceptance of family planning in many regions, short of governmental controls which are inconsistent with established rights of individuals in decision making. The reduction of family size also entails revolutionary changes in the functions of familial groups and in family values (Lorimer *et al.*, Chap. 5).

In Western societies the sociological implications of a more aged population are possibly as profound as the increased numbers of population. Many basic patterns for handling numerical increases among the youthful are perseverations of long-established practices, e.g., industrial development, expanded communication and transport facilities, additional schools, etc. The increase in aged persons, made possible in part through improved medical technology, is perhaps more clearly associated with changing institutions than is a moderate increase in our gross numbers.

Discoveries of Potential Significance. Most of the hundreds of improvements in drugs, vaccines, surgical techniques, etc., which occur each year have significance for the extension or preservation of life. In the low death rate countries, the demographic impact of even the most sensational of these innovations is at present relatively small. In the United States in the last decade it is questionable if infant mortality has declined as much through current innovative advances as through the broader application of known techniques to the high mortality sectors of the society. Nonetheless, significant life-saving discoveries are continuing to help more babies live and more adults live to old age. Some of the more critical research areas of immediate promise are in the application of nuclear science to medicine and particularly in discoveries relating to life processes, genetics, and heredity.

Of far-reaching ultimate sociological concern are the biochemical discoveries in the 1950's of DNA and RNA (Science Newsletter, April 30, 1960; Dec. 17, 1960; *Life,* Sept. 4, 1963; Beadle). As yet having little applied significance, these advances in knowledge intimate immense strides in the control of heredity, prevention of hereditary diseases, and even suggest the plausibility of the extension of the life-span of man. DNA is the substance that controls life activity in all living cells. RNA is the substance which transmits the DNA "instructions" to cells. The DNA molecule is truly the carrier of life itself, holding as it does the capacity through which the cell reproduces, as well as other functions. With cell reproduction each new cell in turn carries a complete set of the "instructions" for its future. In this molecule exists the exact point at which mutations occur. If something goes wrong in the "coding" of the instructions or in their transmission, the organism may be vitally affected. An error, for example, in a parent's DNA might result in sickle cell anemia or congenital feeblemindedness.

Research in this field is pushing close toward an understanding of the sources of life and leads to the introduction of life into non-living substances such as viruses. In the longer future there is the possibility for control of the structure and processes of congenital and inherited diseases and weaknesses. This raises potentials for the control of heredity not only in animal breeding but in man himself. It suggests that the aging process and perhaps even death are unnecessary aspects of human life except as death occurs by accident or choice. Never before has even the potential arisen for the extension of man's life span, let alone his eternal youth. The implications of such potentials are as yet more suited to science fiction than to sociological extrapolation, but the actualities may be closer than is interstellar travel.

Social Technology

The marriage of science and technology in the social sciences is no less and probably more apparent than in the natural and physical spheres. Sociology has enjoyed its phenomenal growth in recent years due to its practical significance in giving answers to problems in inter-personal relations and group structuring. Conceptual sociology has been widely applied, and some would say subordinated, to the search for practical solutions. Sociology as science has become of vast importance for urban renewal, minority group relations, rational industrial organization, mental health, the welfare of the aged, and many more spheres. While much of this research will have theoretical value, most of it is directly designed to assist somebody somewhere in carrying out action programs more effectively.

The technological knowledge of the social scientists does not impress the public as much as the electronic and mechanical devices of industrial plants, armies, and space probes. Nonetheless social technology is prerequisite for the utilization of those electronic and mechanical devices by organized teams, and it is crucial also to planned responses to strains precipitated by these mechanical and electronic novelties.

Not all organizational planning in regard to the productive groups is done by professional social scientists—just as not all mechanical inventing is done by professional engineers or scientists. But a great deal of it is so done. Part of this arises directly when program analysts and other social scientists participate in governmental programs and decisions. Part of it is deliberately done as analysts connected with industry study interpersonal relations within the plant and public relations and advertising outside it. Much more of it is done through the multitude of research projects designed independently by research teams in scores of universities, with results disseminated through professional meetings, journals, books, extension services, and consultancies. Texts in industrial sociology, minority groups, city planning, criminology, collective behavior, population policy, and group dynamics all demonstrate contemporary technological achievements in sociology. All engage the subject of how interpersonal relations operate under varying conditions and how they are effectively guided, influenced, and controlled. The anthropologist George M. Foster in his book *Traditional Cultures and Impact of Technological Change* has integrated a collection of sociological or anthropological techniques (or devices) whereby efficient economic and health practices are to be introduced smoothly into undeveloped societies. Works cited in earlier chapters on the methodology of diffusion and integration of mechanical implements into industrial plant social structures are as surely "technology" as those implements are themselves. Recently, Arthur B. Shostak has compiled a book deliberately directing sociological knowledge toward handling the problems of social change (Shostak, 1966; cf. Bennett *et al.*).

At this stage of social science technology it is difficult to single out particular innovative developments to vie with those discussed here in regard to bio-chemical and electronic ones. However, on an extremely broad and varied front social science is rationalizing the reformulation of group structures and motivations. In an age of mechanical, electronic, and bio-chemical acceleration, society must have an equally accelerated social science technology.

CONCLUSION

The significance of contemporary technological change for social change is to be viewed in two perspectives: (1) the consequences of the accelerating growth of technology in general upon modern life, and (2) the direct and indirect strains precipitated by specific technical inventions, and their resolutions. The first orientation is concerned with the effect of increasing instrumentalism in human affairs upon man's ability to guide social evolution in such a way that life holds meaning, warmth, and security in the sense of group belonging. The specific impacts of specific technologies are more directly analyzable by induction and are reasonably predictable through the logic and methods of functionalism. The functional potentials of specific techniques are assessable, and within broad limits we may suggest reasonable patterns of expected social adjustments to be made in response to the probable tensions precipitated by these novelties. Broadly it appears justified to view the accelerating expansion of technology as furthering trends toward a society in which decisions are increasingly made on grounds of efficiency and decreasingly made on grounds of ethics, justice, and ultimate value. Big technology both in its production and in its consequences establishes further pressures toward increasing governmental size, scope, and control.

In this chapter a brief review has been given of a few striking technological developments, particularly nuclear fission, cybernetics, and automation, and the technology of life preservation and birth prevention. Nuclear fission, cybernetics, and automation, particularly the last two, are close to the core of what has been termed our transition into an age of acceleration. Social tensions are to be expected out of automatic technology to a much greater extent than from the peaceful use of nuclear energy.

These by no means exhaust the ways in which an acceleration of pace is characteristic of this age. It is evidenced in communication, supersonic transportation, and even the greater demands upon school children toward rapid achievement. At the same time there is a striking increase in productivity and consumption, related in part to industrial and commercial acceleration. This has been furthered by international tensions, fears of "over population," and new values and policies regarding rights of all citizens to participate in the abundant life made possible by accelerated production. Perhaps most of all, the increasing abundance of goods and accelerated production is furthered by the high valuations attached to science and technology and the fusion of these two into an accelerative partnership.

In the realms of natural science and health, the past technological generation has bequeathed to the present a "population explosion" precipitated by various death-reducing devices. The resolution of this disturbing strain will lie in the rapid development, diffusion, and integration of productive food technology and in the enlarging field of contraceptive and related technologies. The introduction of these innovations in turn establishes stresses in surrounding institutions and community organization. The technological society must remain one of continuous innovation, continuous stress, strain, and disequilibration as well as equally continuous application of the ameliorative technologies of re-equilibration. The social sciences, similarly accelerated, are beginning to play a critical role in rationalizing social structures and forecasting points of stress. None of this is new, but its speed has now been electrified, and the terms under which change occurs seem inevitably to include increasing centralization of power and increasing control through the political state.

In the long run, it is an open question as to whether serenity and belongingness will be found through rational action programs in a "quest for community," through secular religions and meaningful group participation, or through psychological technologies as are currently suggested in regard to LSD.

13

Trends in Social
Organization

Social trends are the linear patterns of change which characterize a society. As such they are based upon an almost infinite number of specific innovations evidenced in social relationships, institutions, and values. It is only from the evidence for specific changes in specific groups and institutions that we are justified in finding generalizations denoting the direction or directions in which life in society seems to be moving. Understandably the evidence for linear patterns rarely conforms completely to theoretical expectations (see above, Chap. 11). Great caution is required lest we be swayed by some particular set of theoretical expectations and so overlook or discount the significance of specific changes which fail to fit the apparent pattern or indeed run counter to a pattern which has been evident in preceding years.

The future of society cannot be viewed as a simple extrapolation of dominant historical sequences. Every successive change whether in culture or in society rearranges the circumstances under which the assessment of additional novelty is made. For this and other reasons, the analysis of patterns in change can denote direction of movement but cannot delineate the qualities predicted for society by some specific future date. For example, if we find that increasing impersonality in social relationships is a patterned change in American society, the very fact of this trend and its recognition may serve to stimulate counter innovations in a concerned society. Such tapering off in trends as they reach an extreme position has been given general expression by Sorokin as "The Principle of Limits" (1947, pp. 699–701).

In this chapter an attempt is made to give brief summary description and assessment of sociologically relevant trends which appear to be major ones in the midst of twentieth-century America. Most of these are generally characteristic of other urban and developed societies. Counter currents inconsistent with, or retarding, many of these trends are also noted. There is no assumption, as for example there seems to be in Ellul's *Technological Society* (see above Chap. 12) that present trends must continue inexorably toward some ultimate theoretic extremity.

THE URBAN TREND

The Dominance of Urbanism and Eclipse of Rurality

Sociologically, no understanding of our times is possible apart from the rise of modern urbanism. The city, and the changing city, provides the community organization form within which changes in all manner of group relationships are generated. The distinctive qualities of modern civilization are so enmeshed with urban living that it is difficult to extricate them from the general concept of urbanization. Urban sociologists frequently distinguish conceptually "the city" in a physical sense from the distinctive pattern of life generated by modern cities (Queen and Carpenter, Chap. 3; Bergel, pp. 9–11). Redfield and Singer have argued that the qualities of life which we consider urban in the modern sense are not altogether "natural" to city living but rather were generated by the peculiar commercial and industrial qualities which have been characteristic of cities particularly in Western Europe since medieval times (cf. Sjoberg).

The modern city of the West stands in sharp contrast to the community organization form universal in Western Europe during the tenth century. The startling contrast with the social structure of the medieval village, as indeed with the contemporary Asian peasant community, have stimulated some of sociology's most important and significant work on the bases of social order and social evolution. Ferdinand Tönnies, for example, largely built his monumental theory of *Gemeinschaft* and *Gesellschaft* on the contrasting foundations of the manorial village and nineteenth- and early twentieth-century metropolis. Although historic excursions are not part of the substance of contemporary trends, these are so enmeshed with contemporary trends as to require their persistent recognition.

From the tenth century in Western Europe there began to appear new congestions of population associated with the revival of commerce, improved agricultural practice, and manufacturing. The rising cities owed their population growth to migrants, many of whom were fleeing from serfdom. In the new environment there developed systems of social values and social relationships bearing almost antithetical qualities to those of ascription, fealty, and familism, characteristic of the medieval village community. New power structures dominated by a rising bourgeoisie competed with and surpassed the rural powers. For many reasons this new community form was to hold the institutional structures and values which not only dominated the city itself but which eventually extended to dominate the patterns of life of those who remained rural.

The culmination of dominance for the city and its way of life occurred during the nineteenth century in response to revolutionary transformations in power and technology, particularly in industry, agriculture, and health (Weber, Adna). It was stimulated by aspirations of achievement, freedom, and a richer physical life. The most fundamental patterns of urban living were fully established in the nineteenth century. These included the industrial factory as a system of production relationships; the corporation as a structure of ownership, control, and organization; the differentiation in social life, most particularly as employment lost its association with the family group. Apart from these basic innovations, distinctive qualities of city life were established through the diversity and cultural heterogeneity of the urban immigrants, congestion in living, and the requirements of specialized roles in industrial, clerical, entrepreneurial, and professional activities.

M. Lee Taylor and Arthur R. Jones, Jr., have observed that in the United States during the middle of the nineteenth century, major differences between rural and city life reached their highest point of prominence. A generation earlier we had known little of city life, and rural values were an essential part of the American value system (Taylor and Jones, pp. 72–75). Even in 1830, over 90 per cent of the American population was rural and over 70 per cent of all employed persons were directly engaged in agricultural work. Taylor and Jones suggest that through the first half of the nineteenth century, American cities were strongly influenced by rural values and norms, a process which was soon to undergo rather basic reversal. The determination of whether rural or urban values would hold dominance throughout the land was a central aspect of the Civil War (Taylor and Jones, p. 56). The United States emerged definitely and strongly committed to the urban way of life, and the dominance of the city was to reduce the rural-urban contrast through its influence on the values and social patterns of those who continued to be country men. Supported by an internal rural exodus and the rising tides of European immigration, ex-ruralites thronged to rapidly industrializing cities. In these burgeoning and congested centers, rural norms and rural values and rural institutions found infertile fields. The new city was developing its new ethic. It was one forged less from a colonial heritage than from the hard contemporary fact of city living, congestion, polyglot population, industrial wage employment, and faith in capitalism to yield progress and personal achievement. If colonial values of Americans were rather directly derived from European sources, the same is hardly true for the new urban style of life. While European city life presented many of the same qualities as American city life, the similarities arose more as common response to common conditions and common forces than through diffusion. European cities were revolutionized in the industrial revolution, but American cities were created by it. Both had basically similar social adjustments to find. That the nineteenth-century city rose to dominance in a period of laissez-faire ideology and immense faith in progress is as crucial for the formation of the modern city as were the new sources of power and the technologies which made it possible (Mumford).

Current Trends in Urban Ecology

Up to about World War I, the trend of urban ecology and social organization perseverated trends set in the last half of the nineteenth century. However, from the 1920's, trends were becoming apparent which a generation later have resulted in major transformations of the city. The theory of urban ecological structure developed by Park and Burgess and others just after World War I, which laid out the city in terms of concentric zones surrounding a central business district, has long since ceased to apply very fully to many cities it once reasonably well described (Gist and Fava). Cities are no longer areas of congested population centering upon a main central business district. Nor are they understandable as circumscribed social, ecological, and legal entities exerting dominance over surrounding rural hinterlands. Cities in the nineteenth century sense are rapidly ceasing to exist. They are being supplanted by metropolitan regions which, as Boskoff observes, bear closer resemblance to political empires than to their recent ancestral form. Kenneth Boulding insists that the city is becoming a thing of the past—whatever the community form is in which we will live, it is not a *city* in any historic meaning of the word (1964). Others have suggested that the modern community be called Megalopolis, a pejorative term popularized by Lewis Mumford in his *The Culture of Cities,* while others speak of "metropolitan regions," and still others of "conurbations" or simply, "sprawl."

The new urban trend was stimulated by new social forces and made possible by new technologies. These social forces and techniques were long in developing, but their impact was seen fairly suddenly especially during and after World War II. The deterioration and congestion of central cities reached its climax in the 1940's. At the same time, a car in every garage, the extension of bus and truck lines, and the extension of electrification along with telephonic communication made technologically feasible the movement of people and some industries and businesses away from the city hub. Many of the efficiencies of central location were greatly reduced by the trackless auto and easily transportable electric power. A certain amount of decentralization may also have been stimulated by the government during the war with the possibility of city bombings. In the 1940's it became apparent that something was happening to the boundaries of cities in the social and ecological, if not in the legal, senses. And further, along with this expansion was a weakening of the centripetal force of the central downtown area. A multifaceted process of city de-centralization, deconcentration, and sprawl was occurring which by the 1960's has set off innumerable new adjustive reactions and subordinate trends in American community life.

Suburbanization and Conurbation. The suburban movement is not new. In metropolitan areas since 1920 population has increased more rapidly outside the central cities than within them (Bogue). However the suburban trend of growth became pronounced in the 40's and overwhelming in the 50's. Between 1950 and 1960, central cities grew by 10.8 percent whereas their suburban areas almost doubled (48.5%). The difference was even more striking for our largest cities and their suburbs. Movement of population to dormitory suburbia has been associated with considerable suburbanization of industry and striking decentralization in commercial establishments. The great suburban shopping center has become a familiar part of American life mainly since World War II. Suburban office buildings housing professional specialists, along with major department stores and specialty shops, have made an immense change in the life of cities that once centered most consumption activities "downtown." The suburbanization movement in total has offered some relief from mounting traffic congestion but has also been associated with serious strains not only for downtown merchandising and building maintenance but to the central municipality which must maintain increasingly costly governmental services with a decreasing tax base. Dilapidation of inner cities appeared most dramatically at a time when these cities were least prepared financially to deal with it.

The suburban movement is actually but one phase of the broad ecological trend toward the replacement of "the city" by the new "metropolitan region." Suburbanism has extended the urban area and introduced new trade and even industrial centers within the metropolitan area. Associated with this expansion has been the stimulation of old municipalities and the creation of new ones outside the legal limit of the central city. Satellite cities are stimulated in growth and even come to be partially surrounded by suburbanites escaping the family-living congestion of the central city. As suburbs of a central city meet those of a satellite city and then press toward the encirclement of what was once a typical American small town, we have in creation a wholly new concept of an urban community. Ultimately linked together by express-ways and commercial strip development are major cities, smaller, often industrially specialized, satellite cities, great suburban shopping and service complexes, and suburban housing developments of all shades, shapes, and prices. This is sprawl, or as it is more elegantly termed, "conurbation." Small wonder that Boskoff (p. 30) has observed that urban regions are becoming gigantic *functional* empires within the vague boundaries of national societies, upon which they are more or less dependent. This, the new urbanism, is not limited to a single country or region. It is one of the ubiquitous trends in Western civilization.

Not only has the urban reach been extended, but urban occupations, urban life orientation, and concomitant disaffiliation with rural life has continued unabated in its centuries-long course. Never before in most Western countries have so many people lived within the urban orbit. Today about 70 per cent of the U. S. population is urban. The proportions are even higher in a number of Western European countries. Such populations are not merely urban in a census classification sense. They are urban in that they are dissociated with rural life. Just a century ago the proportions were reversed. Since 1850, we have shifted from a basically agricultural society with a few small cities to a society in which perhaps a tenth of the population is agricultural and most of the remainder live in one of several massive conurbations.

Rural-urban migration must of course diminish as the vast bulk of our population establishes itself in urban areas. The trend of increasing urbanism will give way to trends which occur within an almost fully urban society. Even farming operations, a last stronghold of the economic family unit, have shifted from the family farm to "agribusiness" and "factories in the fields" (Taylor and Jones, Chaps. 6, 10). Our society is today a society of urbanized life even for most of the surviving rural remnant. The trend of urbanism and of urbanization are virtually complete, and the new trends which will represent our adjustments to life in conurbated metropolitan regions are being initiated.

The Inner City and Its Rejuvenation. Whether or not the search for neighborhood identity in the suburban movement bears fruit for the individual family, the growth of metropolitan regions has colored the old problems of city living and set the circumstances for new ones (Boskoff,

Part IV). The most basic stresses relate to the decline of central cities and a concomitant dilapidation in housing and other facilities, and the novel problems of intra-regional integration posed by non-conformity of the new metropolitan region with traditional legal, political, policing, and taxing jurisdictions. Associated with each of these basic issues has been a host of special adjustive problems. For a number of these, the nature of trends can be detected. (Cf. *U.S. News and World Report.*)

The plight of the Central City and its rehabilitation has set in motion three trends of major significance in American life. These are (1) the acceptance of stringent modification in the concept of real property rights, as city and regional governmental agencies place restrictions upon property owners in the interests of preserving real estate values and rehabilitating areas of housing blight. Such programs call for planning and control by government agencies to an extent which a few years ago would have been viewed as blatant interference with the rights of property owners and downright anti-capitalistic. Here is supported also a trend observed in other aspects of American life toward the subordination of property rights to human welfare rights. (2) A second and more manifest trend associated with inner city reconstruction lies in the reduction of congestion in housing and in traffic, as downtown businesses join their city governments in efforts toward inner city preservation and, frequently, resurrection. High rise apartments are appearing on land razed of slums; expressways slice through congested areas to invite the suburbanite back in—on new terms. Pittsburgh is one of the classic success stories in American inner city rejuvenation. Chicago by the 1950's was marshalling over $100 million to fight back the spread of slums near the University of Chicago. New partnerships have been forged between governmental, philanthropic, and business interests to turn back the trends established in the union of nineteenth-century urbanism with laissez-faire capitalism. (3) A third trend established in this now nation-wide program is that of federal government assistance, financial support, and partial control over urban renewal.

The immensity of inner city rehabilitation and the battle for fluid transportation staggers the imagination—and the financial capacities of local communities. The costs of urban renewal are close to incredible. A single neighborhood rejuvenation project in New Haven, Wooster Square, was effected at the cost of $19.3 million. *Time Magazine* estimates that if the per capita cost of this project ($130 per city resident) were projected on a national scale, it would cost $13 billion simply to create a Wooster Square in every U.S. metropolitan area (*Time Magazine*, March 4, 1966). And "Wooster Squares" in each American metropolis would all but pass unnoticed in the midst of blight. The vast costs of urban renewal have given rise to a trend toward federal intervention which is as important as trends in the redefinition of property rights and in land use planning and zoning.

City governments have long been dominated by those who had greatest gain from the very processes which lead to city blight. Never did the profits and gains associated with urban congestion, growth, and bad housing pile up in the coffers of municipal governments against the day of reckoning. Nor have state governments developed the financing required for major urban renewal. Into this vacuum the federal government has entered with its immense resources. Between 1949 and 1966, the federal government subsidized urban renewal in the United States to the extent of $4.7 billion (*Time Magazine*, March 4, 1966). In 1966, there was created a new federal agency, The Department of Housing and Urban Development, which will give cabinet representation to metropolitan Americans. An initial six-year project calls for $3 billion. The trend toward federal intervention, albeit at the strong behest of the cities, ushers in a broad extension of federal participation in local affairs, a trend which Lyndon B. Johnson has characterized as "creative federalism." This trend has counterparts in many spheres of American affairs as evidenced in federal welfare programs such as Medicare and the heavy subsidization of university research programs, public school systems, etc.

Intra-regional Integration.   Even where central cities are not plagued by border disputes with other local government authorities, spatial expansion has given rise to jurisdictional problems (Lepawsky). Where the typical conurbated complex of cities and suburbs has grown, especially in the United States, the problems of jurisdiction and integrated planning have been even worse. Traditional government units of municipality and county bear no relationship to the actual ecological patterns which have emerged. Distinct governmental areas have become functionally united as a common metropolitan sprawl extends itself. The new problems of transportation, equitable taxation, as well as equitable and efficient policing, sanitation services, and schools and a host of other normal municipal or county functions have required new concepts of local and regional governance. Until recently such broad regional governing bodies had either little power or closely limited functions (Zimmerman, 1966). Most planning in the United States has been at the local rather than regional level. The chaos of local governing has stimulated inventions in metropolitan government to federalize or to replace municipal and county units. Outstanding examples of this trend are found in St. Louis, Cleveland, and Miami (Greer; Sofen). The city of Miami, for example, is actually one municipality in a county holding a total of 27 municipalities and extensive unincorporated suburbs, all functionally fused in a single conurbation. In the 1950's a metropolitan county government was initiated to assume certain functions previously administered by separate municipalities and to establish county-wide zoning standards for local governments, etc. The new super-government was in part toward centralization of power and in part toward coordination of existing local governmental units. It is one of several experiments in a direction which must inevitably be pursued broadly in American metropolitan regions. Actually the South Florida conurbation does not stop at the boundary of the county in question. Eventually the question of metropolitan regional government must be faced for a coastal sprawl extending from Key Largo to Palm Beach and beyond.

In some European countries where urban sprawl is equally great, there is at least the absence of strong traditional attitudes favoring decentralization in governmental units. In several Latin American nations, however, there has been an almost total incapability of controlling the chaotic proliferation of vast suburban slums created in this new era of city growth. Social trends toward the amelioration of these are scarcely visible (Lewis, p. 325).

TRENDS IN SOCIAL RELATIONSHIPS

Many new qualities of modern life arise from the very fact of massive populations living in dense communities; others arise more directly from the innovative patterns created in adjustment to the peculiar stresses imposed by modern technology; still others reflect shifting value orientations and responses to conflicting concepts of civil rights, democracy, and the meaning of "the good life."

Broom and Selznick, in their introductory textbook in sociology, have referred to the "Master Trend" in modern society (pp. 38–51). The core of the Master Trend lies in increasing specialization and in increasing secularism and rationality. These linear patterns have many facets. They reflect increasing specialization of roles and relationships generally and the rise of specialized formal, associational type groups. Specialization implies segmental participation as one finds his social satisfactions in a round of different groups. Impersonality arises within a massive and highly differentiated social order. These conditions also denote trends toward contractual, limited relationships as the functions once performed by primary groups are parceled out among special and impersonal agencies. Secularism and rationality mean increasing instrumental valuation in personal relationships (the valuation of persons as means to ends); the building of social systems on bases of adaptive efficiency, as deplored by Ellul; the rise of bureaucratic structures and professionalism; and "standardization" or rise of "mass" culture. Most of these have been subsumed in classical sociological concepts such as Howard Becker's contrasts of "Sacred" and "Secular" societies, Redfield's concepts associated with his theory of the "Folk-Urban Continuum," Sorokin and Zimmerman's conceptual definitions of "Rural vs. Urban," Tönnies' *Gemeinschaft* and *Gesellschaft*, and Durkheim in "Mechanical" and "Organic" solidarities (see above, Chap. 11).

The Theory of Mass Society and Culture: Social Trend or Nostalgia?

That modern societies are massive in a literal sense is unquestionable. Never before have so many people been brought into affiliation in common political states and even into common community living. While this very massiveness requires changes in the scale and quality of many human relationships, the connotations of *mass society* and *mass culture* are more precise and often pejorative (MacDonald; Bensman and Rosenberg). Daniel Bell, a sturdy critic of the validity of the concept, has given a succinct statement of the ideas the terms connote.

The conception of the "mass society" can be summarized as follows: The revolutions in transport and communications have brought men into closer contact with each other and bound them in new ways; the division of labor has made them more interdependent; tremors in one part of society affect all others. Despite this greater interdependence, however, . . . group ties of family and local community have been shattered; ancient parochial faiths are questioned; few unifying values have taken their place. Most important, the critical standards of an educated elite no longer shape opinion or taste. As a result, mores and morals are in constant flux, relations between individuals are tangential or compartmentalized, rather than organic. At the same time, greater mobility, spatial and social, intensifies concern over status. Instead of a fixed or known status, symbolized by dress or title, each person assumes a multiplicity of roles and constantly has to prove himself in a succession of new situations. Because of all this, the individual loses a coherent sense of self. His anxieties increase. There ensues a search for new faiths. The stage is thus set for the charismatic leader, the secular messiah, who, by bestowing upon each person the semblance of necessary grace and of fullness of personality, supplies a substitute for the older unifying belief that the mass society has destroyed. [Bell, pp. 21–22.] *

The idea of the rise of "mass society" as laid out by Bell, is implicitly accepted by many scholars who insist that modern man is "lost" in his impersonal social world. Riesman has dramatized this in his title *The Lonely Crowd*. Bensman and Rosenberg express their view of contemporary trends in the title of their text *Mass, Class and Bureaucracy: The Evolution of Contemporary Society*. Neo-psychoanalytic interpretations of social phenomena, such as those by Erich Fromm find fascism appealing as an *Escape from Freedom* by modern mass-man. In the re-

* Reprinted with the permission of The Macmillan Company. From *The End of Ideology* by Daniel Bell, Copyright © 1960 by the Free Press, A Corporation.

lated concept of mass culture, there is stressed uniformity and conformity in an age of mass-man. Among some writers *mass culture* connotes the dulling of individuality in a society characterized by mass production and mass consumption conveyed through mass media. Among others, it is a concept emphasizing the deterioration of the "culture" of the elite; the cheapening of "high" culture; the dragging down of refined tastes to the level of hoi polloi.

The standardization of mass culture has been well expressed by Max Lerner in a statement which he recognized to be a caricature of reality but none the less one bearing "a frightening validity." *

Most American babies . . . are born in standardized hospitals, with a standardized tag put around them to keep them from getting confused with other standardized products of the hospital. Many of them grow up either in uniform rows of tenements or of small-town or suburban houses. They are wheeled about in standard perambulators, shiny or shabby as may be, fed from standardized bottles with standardized nipples according to standardized formulas, and tied up with standardized diapers. In childhood they are fed standardized breakfast foods out of standardized boxes with pictures of standardized heros on them. They are sent to monotonously similar schoolhouses, where almost uniformly standardized teachers ladle out to them standardized information out of standardized textbooks. They pick up the routine wisdom of the streets in standard slang and learn the routine terms which constrict the range of their language within dishearteningly narrow limits. They wear out standardized shoes playing standardized games, or as passive observers they follow through standardized newspaper accounts or standardized radio and TV programs the highly ritualized antics of grown-up professionals playing the same games. They devour in millions of uniform pulp comic books the prowess of standardized supermen.

As they grow older they dance to canned music from canned juke boxes, millions of them putting standard coins into standard slots to get standardized tunes sung by voices with standardized inflections of emotion. They date with standardized girls in standardized cars. They see automatons thrown on millions of the same movie and TV screens, watching stereotyped love scenes adapted from made-to-order stories in standardized magazines.

They spend the days of their years with monotonous regularity in factory, office, and shop, performing routinized operations at regular intervals. They take time out for standardized "coffee breaks" and later a quick standardized lunch, come home at night to eat processed or canned food, and read syndicated columns and comic strips. Dressed in standardized clothes they attend standardized club meetings, church services, and socials. They have standardized fun at standardized big-city conventions. They are drafted into standardized armies, and if they escape the death of mechanized warfare they die of highly uniform diseases, and to the accompaniment of routine platitudes they are buried in standardized graves and celebrated by standardized obituary notices. [Lerner, Vol. I, pp. 260–261.]

* From *America As A Civilization,* Vol. 1: *The Basic Frame,* copyright © 1957 by Max Lerner, published by Simon and Schuster, Inc.

It is cheapening of "high culture" through catering to crude mass tastes that Dwight MacDonald finds frightening. "For about a century," writes MacDonald, "Western culture has really been two cultures: the traditional kind—let us call it 'High Culture'—that is chronicled in the textbooks, and a 'Mass Culture' manufactured wholesale for the market . . . its distinctive mark is that it is solely and directly an article for mass consumption, like chewing gum. . . ."

"It is a debased, trivial culture that voids both the deep realities (sex, death, failure, tragedy) and also the simple spontaneous pleasures . . . (MacDonald, pp. 1, 16)." In his indictment of the debasement of a culture once produced by a creative elite and judged by the standards of that elite's creative taste and discrimination, MacDonald chooses phrases as, "nerveless routine," "spreading ooze of Mass Culture," and "collective monstrosity." A similar viewpoint, but toward a different argument, was expressed by T. S. Eliot in his prose essay *Notes Toward the Definition of Culture*. Mr. Eliot, like MacDonald, chose to find the "culture" of the intelligentsia "high" and that of the masses "low" or even absent. His view is the observation that *respect* for learning is more important for a society than is an actual high level of general education. To Eliot, the masses are incapable of culture building. He sees the necessity of a class-structured society of almost feudal rigidity to protect the creative elite from the depravity of the common man. Like Ortega y Gasset, he finds the common man a vulgar creator of mediocrity and virtually incapable of improvement.

The theory of trend which sees industrial, urban mass man alienated, disengaged, standardized, and debased in return for his material comforts is not shared by many scholars. Max Lerner well realized the partial truth in the theory. Daniel Bell and Edward Shils have each responded vigorously and critically to claims such as those reflected above as they seek accurately to interpret the master trend of our times.

Bell has argued that these views are riddled with value judgments, romanticism, and nostalgia for a vanished aristocracy. He correctly observes that the master trend exists which such writers interpret as debasing. But these same trends have an obverse side which they overlook:

If it is granted that mass society is compartmentalized, superficial in personal relations, anonymous, transitory, specialized, utilitarian, competitive, acquisitive, mobile and status-hungry, the obverse side of the coin must be shown, too—the right to privacy, to free choice of friends and occupation, status on the basis of achievement rather than . . . the exclusive and monopolistic social controls of a single dominant group. [Bell, p. 29.] *

---

* Reprinted with the permission of The Macmillan Company. From *The End of Ideology* by Daniel Bell, Copyright © 1960 by the Free Press, A Corporation.

To this Shils adds a response to the charge by adherents of the "mass culture theory" that modern industry has impoverished life and individuality. He observes that:

The contrary is true. Hunger and imminence of death, work such as we in the West would now regard as too burdensome even for beasts, over very long hours, prevented the development of individuality, or sensitivity or refinement in any except those very few in the lower classes who were either extremely strong personalities or extremely talented or extremely fortunate in forming a connection with the aristocratic or mercantile classes, or all three together. [Shils, 1957, p. 604.] *

In sum, no one may deny the fact of basic trends in modern society toward standardization, massive segmental participation, and impersonalization in many relationships. But the *theory* of "mass society" and "mass culture" has been victimized by value judgment and selective reporting. As Shils writes, "the sociological study of mass culture is the victim of the culture of sociological intellectuals" (1957, p. 338). Since the concepts "mass society" and "mass culture" have been so tinged by valuative and pejorative meanings, it is perhaps better that we use them sparingly in our conceptual vocabulary. There is much evidence supporting the trends of massiveness but not a "mass" *theory* which homogenizes these trends into a tearful farewell to a structure that never was more than a half truth and today is past any resurrection. Our significant trends are not toward restoration of *unmass society* but to innovate satisfying adjustments in our continuing massive society with its segmented relationship. Joseph Axelrod, an eminent college dean, asserts that the basic and most significant trend on American campuses at the present time is the deconforming of students while the second most significant trend is the deconforming of curricula. Mass society we have, but the implications of this fact are less simple and less disheartening that the romanticists contend.

Increasing Scale and Social Differentiation

The theory of "scale" is a useful extension of Durkheim's theories relating to the effects of increasing social differentiation. It has been developed and applied by Godfrey and Monica Wilson particularly in reference to social change in Africa, but the importance of the theory is not limited to undeveloped or "transitional" societies. By scale, the Wilsons mean the number of people in relationships to each other and the intensity of their relations. They point out that the members of all societies are equally dependent upon one another. The resident of an

---

* From Edward Shils, "Daydreams and Nightmares," *Sewanee Review,* Vol. 65, No. 4, Autumn, 1957. Copyright by The University of the South.

African village or of an American small town is as dependent upon his fellows as the metropolis dweller. But the scale of relationships is more spread out for the metropolitan. As the degree of dependence upon one's primary group diminishes, the range of interaction is broadened and becomes more specialized. This is the process denoted in the diminution of functions performed by primary groups in modern society and the increasing segmentalization of social life.

Differentiation and "Instrumental" Relationships. In the diminution of primary group functioning in favor of specialized associations and specialized role relationships, the quality of group ties changes. Ties to one's associates become "instrumental" and contractual ones.[1] This is inherent in the nature of associational, massive society. No one can emotionally identify with the full life and personality of more than a rather small number of persons. Increasing scale forces more relationships, more limited relationships, and more rationally calculated relationships. By contractualism is meant the specification of a relationship as to its duration and scope along with what is expected in return. Since relationship to the other party is valued only for so long as a contractual obligation is performed the relationship is "instrumental." If mother is a bad cook, we are sorry about it but she is still mother. If the housekeeper-cook is a bad cook, she is fired. Mother is valued as a unique, particular person; the housekeeper as an instrument, and hence substitutable. Modern life has tremendously increased the number of social contacts with specialized role performing persons who are valued instrumentally, contractually—and often—fleetingly. Similarly in the bonding of individuals to their social groups, membership in the special interest association is supported by its continued provision of that special interest. This too is of an instrumental and contractual nature unlike the multiple and emotionally laden bonds of the primary group and the identifying of self-interest with group interests, which it engenders.

Associational Groups. A classic documentation of the roots of social differentiation in the emerging modern city is found in Smelser's *Social Change in the Industrial Revolution*. Here is an account of the manner

[1] The classic work distinguishing relationships by the emphasis on "status" and "contract" is that of Henry Sumner Maine, first published in 1861. The term "instrumental" is one given currency by Talcott Parsons in relationship to his patterned variables. Many of the trends associated with urbanity were given encyclopedic documentation some forty years ago by Pitirim Sorokin and Carle C. Zimmerman in their *Principles of Rural-Urban Sociology*. A classic expression of the essence of urban life was that of Louis Wirth in an essay, "Urbanism as a Way of Life," first published in 1938. Wirth particularly emphasized the significance of special interest groups and undoubtedly drew heavily from Simmel regarding the impersonality of city life. See above, Chapter 11.

in which functions once performed in primary groups were parceled out into the specialized group structures of urban society. The lack of neighborhood and kinship solidarities in a mobile, money mediated, urban environment means reliance upon formal and specialized means of protection and security. However, even more significant than the weakening of such primary groups and their specialized, impersonal replacements was the transformation of the nuclear (conjugal-natal) family.

When the nuclear family ceased to be a producing economic unit, the movement toward an "associational" and differentiated community structure was firmly set. This trend has apparently continued in the United States for the past century and a half (Williams, Robin, pp. 494–501; Brunner et al.; Warner and Lunt). It is, perhaps, erroneous to think of this as a contemporary trend so much as a structural reality of modern life. However, there is evidence that the increasing size of metropolitan communities is in fact associated with increasing associational structure and segmentalization (Wright and Hyman, p. 290). The traditional family functions of production, socialization, protection, and recreation have been partly (almost totally, in the case of production) parceled out to differentiated agencies. Accompanying this has come the confusing differentiation in the role patterns of wives, husbands, mothers, fathers, and children.

DIFFERENTIATION WITHIN ASSOCIATIONS. The trend toward functional specialization of groups in urban life has not been unmitigated. Department stores still flourish, churches and temples are multifunctional, industrial firms produce multiple products, and universities are increasingly "universal" in their intellectual concerns. Functional differentiation has occurred in part through the establishment of distinct and independent social systems, but fully as persistent has been the process of differentiation *within* associational type groups. This is manifest in the familiar pattern of industrial organization into various divisions and divisions within divisions, the formalization of various church functions into special programs, the differentiation of academic specialities into departments within universities, and the creative addition of institutes and service branches within the established institution. The proliferation of specialized agencies within governments and of specialized branches in the military are well-known trends. Many of these proliferations are far from new. In American universities, however, truly innovative trends are currently being initiated in this direction.

The American university came into the era of the "knowledge explosion" and suddenly increased enrollments with a rather rigid and traditional structure. Within the framework of academic fields, specialization served to fractionalize the curriculum. The traditional structure did not provide for needed integration and could not cope with rapidly increasing functions along with greatly increased enrollments. In this situation, the university is undergoing increased differentiation, in part to absorb new functions, in part to handle the vastly increased student services and instructional and research demand, and in part to create new agencies which will integrate traditional as well as new departments. Long-established institutions are pursuing several well-defined innovative patterns in coping with their new stresses. Two of these are outstanding. New colleges within universities are being created and institutes with inter-disciplinary functions are proliferating. Experimental new colleges have been created in such established institutions as Wayne State University, University of California, University of Michigan, and Hofstra University (Axelrod, Joseph). Others are scheduled, such as "Small College" created on the California State College campus at Palos Verdes, an institution which itself came into existence in 1965. Institutes are growing like mushrooms throughout the nation's universities, in part to revitalize a moribund structure, in part to gain financing more effectively. These semi-autonomous "centers" would be difficult to count on a national scale. It is reported that one institution by 1965 had 80 such institutes within itself and that another had 25 in the international area alone (Wilson, L., p. 31). These may be exceptional cases but the university without a number of such newly introduced institutes would be exceptional in the extreme.

The Trend Toward Differentiation Qualified. When it is shown that associational type groups have taken on previously undifferentiated functions and that these groups are themselves characterized by internal, structural differentiation, it does not follow that individuals are bereft of primary, non-segmental relationships. Nor does the existence of a differentiation trend imply ever-increasing differentiation. If the industrial-urban transformation of life removed a large number of activities from the home, it in no way destroyed the home itself as a center of diffuse companionship and non-instrumental relationships. There has been no decline of family living in modern society. Marriage, and family living, is becoming increasingly popular rather than the reverse (Landis, pp. 619–622). Even in cases of family dissolution through divorce, the remarriage rates for divorcees are higher than for single persons of the same age.

Within associational type groups the condition of segmentalization and specialization is qualified also. Individuals are not simple cogs in the social machinery; they persistently engage in personalized and informal relationships with fellow association members. Extensive research has demonstrated how informal, primary social systems arise and function within the context of the formal and contractually based association

(Roethlisberger and Dickson; Shils and Janowitz). At the same time, there are evidences that specialization and group differentiation in function can reach points beyond which efficiency is reduced. This can be illustrated in such varied reverse trends as those toward "job enlargement" in industry and the movement in medical circles to up-date and revitalize the concept of the "family physician." Not only do individuals persist in complementing segmental relationships by non-segmental ones, the very process of segmentalization is subject to the "principle of limits" (Miller and Form, pp. 630–632.)

Centralization of Powers

Although associations have proliferated generally in modern society, certain of them have grown far more rapidly than others. In some spheres a few internally differentiated associations have achieved dominance. Power has been concentrated while new functions have been added, or competing associations swallowed up. In the case of government, the modern trend has been toward increasing centralization of power along with extension of functions and, of course, internal differentiation. In industry and business the trend has been toward oligopoly. In many spheres separate associations retain independence while participating in federations over which directorates exercise specific powers. We live in an age not simply of much industry, much business, much government, and much education, but one of big industries, big businesses, big governments, and big educational systems. The rise of vast congeries of affiliated associational type groups and sub-groups appears to be one of the major trends of our times in virtually all institutions except the family.

Centralization in Government. This century has seen immense expansion of functions and power in national governments throughout the world. The trend has been most apparent in totalitarian states and, among modernized nations, perhaps least apparent in the United States with its all but unique demands for the recognition of "states' rights" and demands for laissez faire among a still vocal minority. However, in spite of opposition, the course of the United States toward an increasingly strong and encompassing federal government is clear. Much of this trend has occurred by the assumption of formerly non-governmental functions by the political state rather than in displacement of local and state governmental prerogatives.

The ideological mood of the late nineteenth century was expressed in the slogan "That government is best which governs least." In the United States this philosophy was associated with continuing regional and local interests which had left residual powers to the individual states.

The insufficiency of laissez faire became increasingly evident by the growth of industrial monopolies and in problems arising from the growth and in the complexity of the new urban life. Primary groups were increasingly incapable of performing traditional functions such as the provision of security and welfare. Informal groups generally could no longer support welfare functions in an increasingly interdependent and differentiated group life. Local governments were increasingly unable to cope with growing regional and interregional dependencies. As has been observed earlier, the insufficiency of local and state governments in coping with urban renewal needs is adding strength to federalization of power, as are innumerable other exigencies of modern life such as scientific and educational financing. The process has been furthered also by shifting emphasis in American values, including increased concern for science, popular education, economic security, and the achievement of civil rights on a national scale.

The increased functional scope and power of the federal government is not a new trend in American life, but particularly since the great depression of the 1930's it has been extended. In his *The Changing Community,* published in 1938, Carle C. Zimmerman observed that the root problem of the modern community lay in the future of localism within the context of rapidly increasing standardization and centralization of government and business. Zimmerman's assessment was and is very much to the point. In the past half century, each decade has demonstrated increasing governmental (and probably business) centralization, the only qualifications arising due to the cut-back of temporarily extended federal activities after World War II (Fabricant). By the 1950's, federal government expenditures accounted for two-thirds of all government expenditures in the United States. In 1913, the federal government had accounted for about one-fourth of all government expenditures. The number of laws passed by successive Congresses has almost unfailingly increased throughout our national history. In general the greatest extensions of federal functions today are occurring in the areas of social welfare, including housing, social security, and medicare; and in scientific and technological development and education, the latter fields having been greatly stimulated by war both hot and cold. In 1965, the 89th Congress passed ten major bills relating to health; nine relating to education, including the $1.33 billion Primary and Secondary Education Act; and eleven relating to economic and social opportunity, including the extensive Housing and Urban Development Act and "Medicare" (U.S.H.E.W.). In addition U.S. Supreme Court decisions continued to support extensions of federal functioning in civil rights.

The question as to the extent to which federal concentration usurps traditional states' rights is a difficult one, but it is clear that the federal government is intervening in local affairs to an unprecedented extent. It should also be recognized that the functions of local governments have been increasing as well. This is due not only to local responses to the increasing complexity of urban areas, but also through the stimulation of, and major collaboration with, federal agencies in the administration of federally supported programs.

In relationship to business and industry both subsidy and control by federal government have long histories. There is scant evidence that government is increasingly taking over the productive and distributive functions from private ownership. Government agencies have, of course, proliferated in the control and the stimulation of new industrial developments and relationships. Of immediate significance has been a trend to go beyond subsidy into the establishment of joint working relationships with private industry. Telstar, the communication satellite, represents such a venture as does the TVA, rural electrification, and the development of nuclear power. Similar trends are more advanced in some other nations, which while eschewing totalitarianism have found it expedient to build extensive partnerships between government and private capital.

Centralization in Business and Industry. The evidence regarding concentration of economic power in the United States is controversial. On the one hand are the contentions supporting high concentration in government and business such as that of C. Wright Mills in his book *The Power Elite.* On the other side are those like Daniel Bell who read the evidence differently (Bell, Chap. 3; Anderson and Gracey). But whether or not we believe that our economic and political destinies are controlled by a clique of power-men, the growth of mighty industrial and business corporations is a fact of our times. The concentration of power is further enhanced by interlocking directorships, intercorporate stock holding, and various forms of participating agreements.

Tendencies toward such concentration are, of course, controlled through anti-trust legislation and other legislations. Nonetheless, oligopoly has become a fact of contemporary social structure. Whether or not it represents a continuing trend toward ever-greater concentration in ever-increasing spheres of industry is questionable.

In manufacturing enterprises the largest concerns, those having 1000 or more employees, employ about 40 per cent of all workers (Williams, Robin, pp. 162–187). Small firms having 20 or fewer employees provided about one-fourth of the jobs. General Motors alone employs over half a million persons. In automobiles, aluminum, cigarettes, etc. each field is dominated almost fully by three or four giant corporations. In other products such as petroleum, aircraft, and steel, from 50 to 96 per cent of production is in the hands of no more than twenty large corporations. While there are numerous lines of economic activity in which there are no dominating firms, such as in women's clothing manufacture, concentration is widely enhanced through various techniques of inter-corporation cooperation. As Robin Williams says, there is nothing new about corporations and there are still fields in which they are not the main form of economic organization. However, as he also points out, in modern times there has been an enormous extension of the corporate system and its emergence in fields once thought unadapted to its development (p. 168).

It is doubtful if areas already concentrated are undergoing truly monopolistic tendencies. Oligopoly is an established part of the American economic scene and its present trend is probably more toward extension into new economic spheres. In agriculture the concentration of production is recent and current. Somewhat like the small businessman

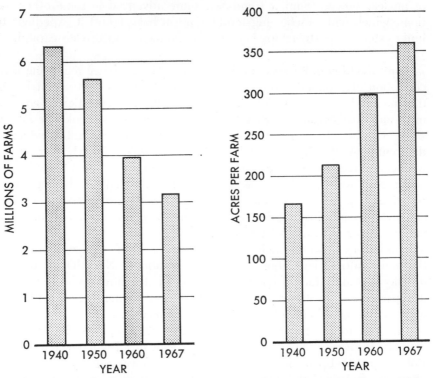

Trends in the Number of Farms and the Size of Farms in the United States, 1940 to 1967 *

Increasing technological efficiency associated with the rise of "Agribusiness" has meant rapid decline in the number of farms and also rapid increase in the size of farms. Modern technology and rational organization make it possible for one farm worker to feed almost 40 persons. In 1935 he could feed about 10.

* Based on charts in *200 Million Americans*, U. S. Department of Commerce, Bureau of the Census, 1957, page 46.

in urban affairs, "the family farm" is the "traditional" unit for most sectors of American agriculture. While the family farm is still current, the trend has been toward consolidation of farming into large units. Farm units over 1000 acres in extent have been growing in number, and the total production of small-size farms has a persistently decreasing share of national production (Taylor and Jones, p. 213). By the late 1950's there were about 4 million farm units in the United States, some 60 per cent of which were extremely small and contributed less than 10 per cent of the nation's total marketed food and fiber products. On the other hand the 150,000 large farms in the nation produced over one-fourth of marketed products. Trends toward concentration have been associated with technological developments, government programs differentially benefiting large units, and the transition from farming as a way of life to "agribusiness." No doubt increasing concentration will occur, especially through the vertical integration of agriculture with processing and distributive operations.

Centralization in Higher Education. The recent and rapid differentiation within higher educational institutions is only one part of a structural transformation occurring in our educational system. While there is no decline in the number of autonomous institutions of higher education, several centralizing patterns are emerging. The most spectacular of these is in the rise of the "multiversity" as several previously autonomous as well as newly created institutions are fused into a single state university system. Additionally, particularly among autonomous private schools, new associational congeries are forming and many coordinating bodies are being established. Fully autonomous and unaffiliated institutions now seem in transition toward either legal submergence in a larger institutional framework or voluntary membership in planning and financing associations. Accrediting associations are not new, and in these practically all institutions of higher learning have already submitted to some loss of sovereignty in favor of standards and acceptance in the academic world.

The American trends have not been realized in other Western countries, partly because higher education generally has not become so popularized and massive. In Britain, problems of coordination are almost sure to bring greater centralization under governmental organization. However, over the past decade Britain has mainly added additional autonomous universities to meet demand rather than having made major structural modifications in the system of higher education (McConnell).

The massive demands for higher education in recent decades have stimulated a variety of evolutionary patterns in centralization and growth. In the fall of 1930 there were 1,189,000 students enrolled in U.S. colleges and universities (King). In the fall of 1964 more than 5 million students were enrolled. In response to changed demands, as well as expanding functions, already large universities became huge; teachers colleges evolved into full-scale universities, and junior colleges sprang up to relieve pressures on four-year institutions. Many of these trends have reached their limits as some massive institutions declare that they will become no larger in enrollments and the upgrading of teachers colleges nears completion. With an immense growth in size and number of state institutions, there has inevitably been a movement toward coordination, often with central administration for planning and financing. State colleges are developed into networks of regional, and to some extent, specialized, institutions, bound within a single administrative framework. The state university system of California offered the prototype for a trend widely developed in various states (Brown). The California "Master Plan" was to achieve coordination while preserving institutional competition. Under this plan one governing board is responsible for the University of California in its many locations. The scope of this system with its quasi-autonomous units was shown in the following statement by Edmund G. Brown, former Governor of California:

We do not claim that our growing pains have subsided or that our plan has created an educational Utopia. But we have achieved a sizable measure of progress. For example, nine new campuses have been established for the University of California and the state colleges; seven additional sites are being studied and will be authorized as soon as practicable. The junior college system has expanded to seventy-four colleges and the state has given local districts new financial support. [Brown, pp. 106–107.]

Although not of the scope of the California trend, similar state congeries of institutions are found widely, notable examples being in New York and New Jersey. Pennsylvania has pioneered in drawing private institutions into voluntary cooperation with the public network through state financial aid (Gladfelter). It is rapidly becoming so that students can no longer designate their alma mater by some term such as "State College" or "The State University." New conglomerations of initials are evolving to distinguish the State University of New York at Buffalo from the State University of New York at some other location. All enjoy the prefix SUNY. All are ultimately administered through the State Board of Regents. Rutgers University, once a small private men's college, today shares its name with other institutions such as the University of Newark. Both as entities are sub-units in an encompassing legal and administrative structure of state higher education. Such networks of related institutions with limited autonomy are now an established and growing pattern for public higher education.

For private colleges and universities the solutions have been more through coordination than through centralized authorities. Many of the coordinating groups include state university representatives as well. Others like the six Claremont privately endowed colleges in California are oriented to one central institution in accord with an "Articles of Affiliation" (Benezet; Wilson, Logan [ed.], Pt. 5). In addition to such patterns in coordination there are scores of regional or national associations of colleges for collective effort, financing or planning, and accreditation.

Bureaucratization and Professionalization

Bureaucratization refers to the development of administrative structure in organizations involving the delegation of authority within a hierarchy of specialized functionaries (Weber; Marx; Merton *et al.*). Bureaucratic organization operates through a web of rules and standardized procedures governing decision making at all levels. It is peopled by officeholders having specialized roles in the performance of which they are expected to view their problem range with rationality and emotional detachment. Elemental features of bureaucratic organization have been present since the early city states and empires, but with the rise of modern urban society they have been elaborately refined and the pattern extended into spheres of life which previously were subject to informal, paternalistic, or consensual systems of administration and control. As Bensman and Rosenberg contend, it is not bureaucracy, but the bureaucratization of society that is unique to modern times. Unlike many early authority systems, modern bureaucracy gives fundamental precedence to "principles of sound management."

As functioning social groups increase in size there is necessarily an increase in their internal complexity. Kenneth Boulding (1953) has related this observation to his "principle of non-proportional change." Since the various parts of an organization grow at differing rates of speed there is inevitably readjustment and change within the overall group structure. The administrative apparatus becomes larger and more complex. C. Northcote Parkinson has satirized this in his law stating that the less work done by a group the greater its administrative staff. Other and non-satirical writers who are impressed by increasing bureaucratization argue that the seat of economic power in modern society is shifting from capitalists to bureaucrats (Burnham). While such extreme statements as Parkinson's and those in regard to the "managerial revolution" are not supportable, it must be concluded that "The larger the organization and the more specialized its subunits and individuals, the larger the number of intermediaries between the center of authority and the mass of its members" (Williams, Robin, p. 502). However, this does not mean that increasing the size of an organization necessarily produces an ever-increasing proliferation in administrative officers. Among some types of associations the proportion of administrative personnel is proportionately smaller among large as compared with small organizations (Blau and Scott, pp. 226–227). Increasing size and complexity of the administrative hierarchy is evidenced in the various levels and branches of burgeoning government and is stimulated in the continued growth of corporations, universities, labor unions, and churches.

Bureaucracy is frequently alleged to stifle social change through its own insistent growth and trend toward routinization and restriction of initiative. Rigid bureaucratic structures can indeed inhibit change in the adaptive processes of the group, but they need not necessarily do so. Virgil Williams has pointed out that the creation of new bureaucracies within an organization alleviates the previous rigidity in structure. Proliferation of bureaucratic sub-units gives impulse to organizational modifications somewhat as deviant sub-cultures stimulate changes in society.

The rise of high bureaucracy in business, industry, and government are trends long in evidence. The increasing size and differentiation of federal government in the United States has been associated with a perpetual acquisition of new functions. The rise of big government at the local level has furthered the new complexity of urban community organization. In industry the growth of giant corporations, stimulated in part by technological changes, has brought sharp increases in the proportion of gainfully employed who are in the managerial and bureaucratic professional levels. Increased professionalization is evident not only in professional classifications but in the growing movement toward professionalization in the sub-specialities of administration.

In some organizational spheres, we appear to be crossing a threshold of bureaucratization. Increasing size of urban churches and expansion of functions has been associated with bureaucratic tendencies (Schaller, 1963, 1965; Sanderson). These will inevitably be expanded especially with the success of various consolidational and ecumenical movements with their requisite super-structures. Already, single denominations once composed of loosely affiliated churches have been pushed toward creating encompassing administrative structures by the requirements of an increasingly complex society.

In the realm of universities and academicians, such trends are more advanced. There is probably no observer of the changing American university who is not impressed or offended by the rapid expansion of non-academic personnel. By 1950, the University of Minnesota was employing 4,000 non-academic workers of one sort or another such as clerks, statisticians, dietitians, truck drivers, and the like (Brubacher and Rudy, p. 353). The table of organization of the modern state university system competes in complexity with General Motors Corporation.

Although the University of Minnesota may have been particularly precocious, the new bureaucratic surge in American university structure has occurred mainly since 1950. Between 1957 and 1963, administrative staff in American institutions of higher education increased 159 per cent, whereas instructional staff increased 137 per cent.[2] Understandably, organizations so functionally differentiated have always required a fairly elaborate administrative structure. However, since 1950, functions have expanded as well as enrollments. Interdisciplinary institutes have blossomed and fund raising has been placed at a new level of professionalization as, indeed, has record keeping and processing, testing and counseling. All of these facts serve to require bureaucratic expansion and greater formality in structure. George W. Bonham (p. 67) observes that "Significant new faces have joined in helping the president bring his institution to confront twentieth century realities. Foremost among these is the chief development officer, who, under various euphemisms, may rank just behind the President and Vice President for Academic Affairs as a leading administrative spokesman." Stanford University has a staff of thirty-five in fund raising, fifteen in "university relations," and seven in alumni relations. The University of Michigan has a "professional communications" staff exceeding seventy. Bonham asserts that "a good many universities today carry on their payrolls development-public relations staffs which are larger than all but three of this country's corporate public relations firms." Other specialists and bureaucrats have blossomed too. Boston University's Vice President for University Affairs presides over an office staff of more than fifty people, many of them specialists in a variety of fields.

Like centralization, this trend of bureaucratic proliferation has been stimulated by increasing enrollments; the development of super-university systems as various state institutions are brought within a common structure; the new complexities in financing, such as through government research grants; and the increasing specialization of faculty members. There has been an expansion in services, and hence in administrators, professionals, and clerks in reference both to internal services and relationship to the outside community. New demands for student services are placed upon student personnel offices when residence halls cease to hold the student body. New concepts of student personnel service yield guidance clinics, extra-curricular advisors, "career planners," etc. As the university requires new financing so must its relationships and services to the community expand. What was once a simple "evening

[2] I am indebted to Dr. Abbott L. Ferriss, National Science Foundation, for providing these and other data from U.S. Office of Education Surveys. See Ferriss' "Data About Teachers, Faculty and Professional Staff," 1964. Cf. references to the respective works of Theodore Caplow; John S. Diekhoff; Charles V. Kidd; Lloyd S. Woodburne; and Samuel P. Capen.

school" operation becomes a multifaceted "continuing education division." The Dean for Research and likely the Vice President for Development, and others as well, require offices in Washington, D.C., to keep abreast of the latest potentials for funding.

There are limits to the trend toward bureaucratization just as there are limits to the extent that associational groups themselves can fulfill all social functions. Within developed organizational structure, trends toward de-bureaucratization have been noted (Blau and Scott, pp. 232–234). There is such a condition as "over specialization" and, of course, the excesses of "red tape" are proverbial in most large organizations. To assume that there are no limits to increased bureaucratization would be to infer that rational bureaucrats are more concerned with their organizational "game" than with rational efficiency and achievement of group objectives. It is true that the means whereby objectives are achieved can become goals in place of the original ones. However, the game playing and protection of the bureaucrats' vested interests is subject to review by patrons, clients, taxpayers, or stockholders as well as the consultants called in by top management.

Rapid growth in the officialdom of an organization has been shown to be characteristic only for the early stages of organizational development (Blau and Scott, p. 226). Contrary to Parkinson, bureaucracy does not necessarily proliferate itself—although short-run tendencies toward this are common. Nor is there, contrary to Michels, an "iron law" of perpetuation of power by those who hold office—although short-run tendencies toward this are also common. While there is an element of truth in the precept that bureaucracies persistently act to preserve and proliferate themselves, the dictates of rationality lead ultimately to limits in these trends and even toward de-bureaucratization in some circumstances. There have been tendencies toward relaxation in some of the greater rigidities of U.S. military bureaucracy, and studies indicate reductions in the hierarchical arrangements of several already highly organized industrial and governmental units. While there is no reason to think that the bureaucratic trend means an ever-increasing proliferation of administrative levels and procedural rules, many associations like universities are today on the up-swing in bureaucratism and its attendant growth of formalism, red-tape, and impersonalization.

Alienation, Anomie, and Disengagement

A persistent theme in writings related to the segmentalization of modern life relates to individuals who are "lost" in an atomized, impersonal, and confused society. The sociological conditions giving rise to this personal state are variously analyzed in terms of the sociologically related concepts of *alienation, anomie,* and *disengagement.* Although each of these concepts has somewhat different meanings, all relate to conditions under which many individuals are, or feel, deprived of meaningful relationships, with a consequent loss of a sense of self-identity. There is substantial reason to believe that such processes are characteristic of modern society and that they were less frequent in earlier periods when most people lived in more traditional communities possessing cohesive and internally consistent systems of norms and values.

Alienation. Alienation is a concept having its roots in nineteenth-century philosophic discussions which were given clear-cut sociological relevance by Karl Marx in his early writings (Bell, Chap. 10). Initially Marx conceived of alienation as the process whereby an individual lost his capacity to express himself in his work. He found the roots of alienation lying in the very nature of capitalistic industrialism. Here the worker is deprived of his own tools and his creative initiative through no sense of task completion. He is left without personal identification with his product, since it belongs to the employer rather than to him. Marx engaged in rather "close reasoning" to fix the blame for this state of affairs on capitalistic exploitation rather than on the industrial system *per se*—a source which seems at least as plausible to the non-Marxist.

Since the time of Marx an immense literature has grown around the theme of man's psychically meaningless work activities, particularly on assembly lines. The concept of alienation has been further extended in other spheres of life actions in which men have lost a sense of identification or meaning. Long ago, Georg Simmel was deeply influenced by this idea in his essays on the anonymity of city life.[3] More recently the concept has been explicitly and fruitfully applied to the citizen's attitude toward his political state. Gabriel Almond and Sidney Verba made an explicit attempt to measure "civic alienation" of citizens in several countries. Their findings fail to support any conclusion that political alienation is positively related to modernity and size of social structure. To the contrary they found much greater political alienation in Mexico and Italy than in Germany, Britain, or the United States. While actual governmental structure and functioning is important for the citizen's feeling of attachment to his political state, the crucial variable was that of education. In each country, it was the uneducated who expressed greatest

---

[3] See *The Sociology of Georg Simmel,* translated and edited by Kurt H. Wolff; also Daniel Bell, *The End of Ideology.* It is difficult to draw clear distinctions between "alienation," "anomie," the condition of "egoist," and "disengagement." The present distinctions would give a *psychological* emphasis to *alienation,* i.e., the *feeling* of non-identification, whereas *anomie* is *cultural* rootlessness, and a state of *egoist* or *disengagement* refers to social non-affiliation. One stimulating analysis of American city life practically equates *alienation* in its literal Marxian sense with *anomie.* Cf. Elwin H. Powell, *The American City and Anomie.*

feelings of alienation. While this research is highly suggestive, it is of course not definitive. However, political alienation is probably most acute in nations which are in process of emerging as viable democratic states and least among those having more fully ordered governments and more highly educated populaces. A developed modern state has built-in mechanisms, including those of "civic socialization," which provide for a participatory and meaningful relationship of the citizen to the state regardless of massiveness and bureaucratization.

Nor is the theory of alienation in work as devastatingly associated with industrial capitalism as might appear to be the case. While it is true that assembly lines and specialization have segmented the worker's relationship to the product, the trend in some industries has been reversed. "Job enlargement" and "job rotation," among other trends, are being extended as antidotes to the deleterious effects of over-specialization (Miller and Form, pp. 630–639). Further, persistent reduction is occurring especially as associated with automation in the proportion of workers who must be assigned to monotonous and repetitive tasks.

An even more telling condition which has intervened upon the presumed dehumanizing forces of industrialism lies in the capacity of human beings to find other areas of life in which to gain participatory and creative satisfactions. As Max Lerner puts it: "The catch is in the failure to see that men uprooted from one kind of social and institutional soil can become rooted in another. . . .

While the American has been alienated by the machine from his old role as independent farmer-artisan-entrepreneur, his culture still has a strong hold on him. The loss of a sense of independence in the productive processes has been replaced by a feeling of well-being in consumption and living standards. The pull of property, no longer in tools or productive land but in consumers' goods; the sense of power and pleasure in the means of sight and sound and movement placed at his disposal by the communications revolution; the glorying in what makes the world of drama and entertainment accessible; the whole range of popular culture; the feeling of access to new gradients of income and experience; there form the new soil in which the American has found new roots. [Lerner, p. 233.]

No one would deny that modern society has produced real problems in the matter of monotonous, uncreative, industrial work. On the other hand there is no reason to believe that the trend is continuing toward the future and there is considerable reason to believe that alternative and substitutive satisfactions are being seized upon. Productive employment is simply taking a different functional and psychic role in the life satisfactions of individuals. In regard to political alienation, it is similarly true that modern men miss the full participation of the town meeting.

But the town meeting has faded, as it must in a massive society, to be replaced by substitutive forms of participation in which civic identification is adjusted to modern community life. While it may well be that civic satisfactions are less intense and less widely shared, there is no reason to think that the secularization of society is yielding increasing numbers of increasingly alienated persons either politically or occupationally. Adjustive trends move in the direction of new equilibria.

Anomie. Every society develops a system of norms, values, and goals which establishes patterns for individuals in regard to conduct and their legitimate aspirations and expectations. When members of a society are loosed from this normative system, they are *anomic*, or victims of the sociological condition of *anomie*.[4] Anomic persons are not bound by their cultures. While this state may arise from psycho-social isolation, it is distinct from it. Numerous forces distinctive to modern non-totalitarian societies give rise to conditions in which people do not know, or do not care, what is expected of them by society. Conditions of anomie are distinctively associated with the rise of modern, urban societies. "Marginal men" with a foot in each of two cultural systems become confused or embittered as do migrants and the displaced torn loose from their traditionally familiar cues and responses. Rapid shifts in the norms, or in the organizational structure within which the individual is identified, yield confusion and disillusioning assessments of legitimate standards. Conflicting role expectations confuse as to priorities among seemingly inconsistent demands. The bitter paradoxes which appear in a complicated and imperfectly integrated socio-cultural order yield disillusionment with normative procedures and even bitterness toward a society which does not fairly reward legitimate effort. All of these conditions are conducive to the loosening of the individual from his cultural bonds.

The existence of anomie in American life has been documented for immigrant groups, urban Negroes, and others. Thus American society teaches Negroes to accept high personal aspirations but inhibits their equal access to these legitimate and valued goals. Caught in this bitter paradox the anomic rejection of legitimate means to the goals is imminent, with the potential substitution of illegitimate means to their attainment. This aspect of anomie has been developed particularly in regard to delinquent conduct in modern society (Merton, 1964; cf. Cloward and Ohlin).

---

[4] The term *anomie* is here understood essentially as Emile Durkheim developed its meaning in *Le Suicide*, and as exposited by Talcott Parsons in *The Structure of Social Action*, Chap. VIII. Robert K. Merton's extrapolation of the concept (1949) has tended to emphasize *normlessness* in the achievement of legitimate goals. In the present context, "goallessness" is considered part of *anomie*.

Contemporary associational, culturally heterogeneous, and rapidly changing society is the natural habitat of anomie. It is in the modern heterogeneous city that one finds conflicting norms and even lack of consensus on proper aspirations. It is here that persons are placed in situations requiring role behavior logically inconsistent with other roles placed upon them. It is here too that conflicting demands are placed upon the acting individuals in the complexity of a single role relationship. And it is in the modern city that individuals must be prepared to make rapid and often stressful shifts in normative evaluations of all types.

There is no doubt but that the Western type urban society has generated the conditions of anomie. Like *alienation* it is a concomitant of "our" type of social world. That it is *increasingly* characteristic of our society is a matter of opinion since the evidence is subject to different assessments. Scholars like Ellul who stress the trend toward a "valueless" social order of efficiency, or like David Riesman in his concept of the other-directed personality, or Erich Fromm in *Escape from Freedom* would probably emphasize a trend toward increasing anomie. On the other hand, there is reason to think that many culturally confused and frustrated individuals find meaning and self-identity in groups which are themselves marginal to the larger society or in protest against its structure. Many anomic Negroes, for example, find both social identification and cultural regeneration within the civil rights movement.

There are innumerable research questions to be studied before one concludes that anomie is a trend rather than a now-established characteristic condition of modern society. With a strong and vigorous movement to achieve personal identification with the state, its programs and ideology, many conditions conducive to anomie may be overcome. Fromm has argued that this was true in fascist totalitarian countries but at a price that was far too dear. While we are not likely to dissolve all the forces giving rise to anomie, some of them demonstrably are being reduced. For example, many youth find disillusionment with the established normative order, but it is apparent that some of them are finding or building effective mechanisms in changing the norms of that order through responsible action (Eisenstadt). The *youth culture* of America insofar as it exists is a sub-culture, not a chaotic jumble of behaviors in which anomic deviants choose up as to their particular patterns of deviance. The sub-culture of youth reflects the cultural values and the changing norms of American life as surely as does the civil rights movement or the Peace Corps. Participants have rejected certain societal norms, but they are far from being normless or goalless. The trends of our time probably lie in the patterning of constructive innovative responses to the conditions creating anomie rather than in the further growth of that condition.

Social Isolation and Disengagement. Disengagement is a concept recently introduced in sociological literature to express the decreased interaction of an individual in the social system to which he belongs (Cumming and Henry). The idea is closely related to that of Emile Durkheim's concept "egoist" which he used in reference to suicide among persons who have lost meaningful group ties. Modern society with its high degree of differentiation and its necessary preponderance of impersonal relations yields circumstances in which many individuals are cut apart from the social and emotional responses of meaningful others. While the concept of personal disengagement has been particularly applied to the narrowing social world of the aged, similar conditions arise for other age categories as well. The idea of disengagement may also be applied to groups, in what will be termed here "group disengagement." In "group disengagement" individuals have social ties and identity in groups or sub-societies which are themselves cut apart from the broader society and its institutions.

In American society, the proportion of people who have attained age 65 has risen from 3.4 per cent to about 9 per cent since 1880 (Drake). This significant demographic change has accompanied the diminishing capacity of the family to care for its own and a concomitant rise of formal structures for the security of the aged as individuals rather than as family members. As increasing numbers of the aging are financially able to retire from occupational roles, and frequently forced to do so, they are cut apart from activities and frequently from the social groups which formerly made life rich and meaningful. This is particularly true for the widowed and for those who migrate seeking a peaceful old age in the sun. But under the most optimal conditions, old age almost certainly brings reduction in the "life space" of the individual whether through withdrawal by virtue of infirmity, widowhood, or the decimation of those who were one's peers. Not infrequently all of these conditions apply. Such disengagement from meaningful social life is probably a significant factor underlying the onslaught of senility symptoms (Lipman and Smith). Elaine Cumming and William E. Henry write of this process as a normal transition into the status of death. They appear to consider progressive disengagement as a necessary process for the continuation of society. Other scholars, however, have shown that it is an adverse one, at least from the standpoint of the well-being of the individual (Lipman and Smith).

While disengagement may be associated with aging in every society, the circumstances and consequences are unique in the modern urban world. In peasant and primitive societies the aged person may circumscribe his social relations more closely than before, but he is bound, as a functioning and often resident member, into a family group and a small, personalized community. In many societies the claim of parents upon their children stands at all times pre-eminent over the claims even of a spouse (Stephens). Such obligations to the elders have only partial substitution in the impersonal systems of Medicare and pensions. Research on the social affiliations and identifications of the elderly in American society yields impressive documentation of the ubiquity of their withdrawal from meaningful group attachments (Tibbitts and Donahue).

An earlier generation of sociologists paid close attention to the city as a place of anonymity (Wolfe; Zorbaugh). Few of these studies dealt with the aged. Of particular interest was the "area of furnished rooms" in the city's "zone of transition." Those persons who inhabited the world of furnished rooms also lacked roots in meaningful social groups, but for them such a state was usually one of transition ultimately to culminate in marriage and "settling down" to community membership. For many immigrant groups in our cities, old world clubs and religious groups were transplanted into the new setting to provide social support during early stages in the assimilation process.

Apart from the aged in contemporary American society, disengagement is evidenced by urban youth and by urban Negroes. Both of these categories contain many individuals seeking a self-identity which can be found only in meaningful relationships with others. Youth have been cut off from adult society more than ever before. Negroes, crammed into the transitional areas of blight in our great cities, respond to the stimuli of "self-hate" and frustration. High mobility as well contributes to disengagement from even the segregated sub-society. Although the specific problems of the aged, youth, and Negroes are quite different, contemporary America is undergoing important structural changes as each of these categories struggles toward the creation of group life in which re-engagement is feasible and satisfying for the individual.

PROCESSES OF RE-ENGAGEMENT. Perhaps the bulk of contemporary social research and planning in reference to the aged bears some relationship to the processes through which a satisfying social life can be reinstituted for the later years of life. While the problem relates to developing new goals and replacement interests suitable to the urban elderly, the creation of new groups and stimulation of participation interests are crucial needs. Identification with meaningful groups is demonstrably associated with high personal morale among the aged (Wilensky; Lipman and Smith). While many aged persons apparently do not recognize this need and others are unable for a variety of reasons to reengage, new groupings by the score have arisen to fill this vacuum in modern, age-differentiated social structure.

The Townsend Movement of the 1930's brought a sense of affiliation, purpose, and personal identification to hundreds of thousands of aged.

Although the Townsend Movement declined, many of its functions have been taken up by proliferating groups of varying degrees of organization and scope (Rosow). The Senior Citizens of America is a national, formally organized association composed of rather folksy local units for recreation, service, and even vocational participation. Associations in many cities are devoted to breaking down employer resistance to hiring the retired. Perhaps no city in America is without scores of clubs and associations formed under the auspices of city recreation departments, welfare agencies, and churches which draw the aged into peer groups for varieties of activities. Every great retirement center has its special programs stimulative to the formation of group attachments and social concern (Harlan; Tartler).

The City of Miami Beach, for example, fills to capacity its beach-side lecture hall night after night with audiences in which the minimum age is about 60, all paying close attention to lectures on an immense range of public issues. In addition, facilities are provided for "sings" and other events on the public beach in which retired individuals are transformed into joyous and continuing groups, which, if nostalgic, are emotionally satisfying and give a renewed identification with one's own generation and cultural roots. Almost in the shadow of the ornate resort hotels which epitomize the nervous transiency of mass society, a folk society has been recreated for the elderly.

Another trend toward re-engagement of the aged is in the form of community and neighborhood settlements for the retired. Hotels in many cities have been taken over in the heart of the city which give accommodations at low prices and insure an immediate social world as perhaps the most important part of the bargain. Some of these are institutionally operated by Jewish or by Christian religious organizations. Increasingly too, organizations such as labor unions and religious groups are establishing residential colonies which not only provide community living among age-peers but systematically engage the residents in participation in broader community activities as well.

The social isolation of youth in the modern city has been less apparent because it has been partial and quickly responded to by youth themselves. Unlike the aged, youthful persons have not disengaged from the subsociety of youth. They have been disengaged from the world of adults. This has been a "group disengagement." As James S. Coleman observes: *

. . . in a rapidly changing, highly rationalized society, the "natural processes" of education in the family are no longer adequate. They have been

* Reprinted with the permission of The Macmillan Company. From *The Adolescent Society: The Social Life of the Teenager and its Impact on Education* by James S. Coleman, with the assistance of John W. C. Johnstone and Kurt Jonassohn. Copyright © 1961 by The Free Press, A Corporation.

replaced by a more formalized institution that is set apart from the rest of society and that covers an even longer span of time. As an unintended consequence, society is confronted no longer with a set of *individuals* to be trained toward adulthood, but with distinct *social systems,* which offer a united front to the overtures made by adult society.

Thus, the very changes that society is undergoing have spawned something more than was bargained for. They have taken not only job-training out of the parents' hands, but have quite effectively taken away the whole adolescent himself. The adolescent is dumped into a society of his peers, a society whose habitats are the halls and classrooms of the school, the teen-age canteens, the corner drugstore, the automobile, and numerous other gathering places. [Coleman, p. 4.]

In regard to youth the disengagement is less individual than collective. Research studies by Coleman and by others suggest strongly that the sub-society of youth is seriously disengaged from the broader socio-cultural system dominated by adults. In this new, partly disengaged sub-society it is not surprising that young people demonstrate and rebel against the domination of an "outside" agency like university administration; and it is understandable that individuals search for their personal identity within the youth world that means so much. The seriousness of this present trend toward individual re-engagement in a socially disengaged sub-society is evident in the words attributed to a Berkeley, California, student leader, "You just can't trust anybody over thirty."

The great migration of Negroes from the rural south into the urban slum has brought many of the same adjustment problems as for European immigrants, intensified by color visibility and historic and institutionalized discrimination systems. The "Black Metropolis" is a place of rootlessness, atomism, high mobility, and considerable anonymity (Cayton and Drake). Unlike many ethnic minorities, this new body in the urban milieu has few cultural roots to cling to. According to Broadus N. Butler, Negroes are so individualistic that they neither wish to be identified as a group nor to band together on collective projects except under conditions of specific and temporary provocation. An exaggeration no doubt, but it points up the Negroes' essential loss of social identity in the city and the foundations for its retrieval in race movements.

The circumstances surrounding the urbanization of the American Negro have offered almost consistent pressures toward marginality, anomie, and disengagement. The urban Negro is subject to frustration in seeking approved goals through legitimate means; he is torn between identifying with the group in which he is placed categorically by prejudice and that group which sets his standards of aspired position and conduct; and he is the psychological victim of apprehension, fear, violence, and self-hate (Simpson and Yinger). The largely atomized life of the "Black Metropolis" is partly structured into group participation patterns responding to persecution. Historically, and in the metropolis as well, the most significant form of organized participation was the church (Cayton and Drake; Simpson and Yinger, Chaps. 18, 23). Apart from familistic groups, here was found the emotional expression denied by a restrictive world. More significantly, the Negro church enabled the participant to gain a self-identity. It has been almost the only place in which its participants could become *somebody* among meaningful others.

If the urban Negro church carried over the tradition of the rural Southern church into the city, it was not to remain limited to such functions in the metropolis. The religious themes of an oppressed people once emphasized the paradise across the river with undertones of symbolic aggression toward whites. However, in the 1960's many church leaders are self-conscious "race men" not only exhorting but organizing movements to apply Christian principles in the quite specific and practical realms of suffrage, school, and housing blight.

While the Southern Christian Leadership Conference under Rev. Martin Luther King's leadership has dominated the race movement in the 1960's there should be no implication that religious groups have exclusive claim to spearheading the Negro revolt. Secular organizations like NAACP, the Urban League, and the Congress on Racial Equality (CORE) have been and are continuing to be tremendous sources of organizational thrust. However, it is significant for the historic and now transposed role of the church and its professionals that clergymen remain the most important and powerful of Negro leaders. The Negro religious institutions are without peer for reaching and organizing large bodies of people into action movements. Preaching is the oldest, most honored, and the most liberal profession available to Negroes.

In the protest movements oppressed and mainly urban Negroes are finding personal re-engagement with their social world. The development of race pride and self-sacrifice for the cause among even rank and file are symptoms of a regeneration of social affiliation and intense social participation. Nor are the major Negro protest movements leading the participant into a sub-society which is itself disengaged from the larger social order. The NAACP, the Urban League, CORE, the Southern Christian Leadership Conference, most of the effective protest organizations, are studiedly integrated with the larger "society of whites" and abide scrupulously by the norms of the larger society. The Negro who gains a personal re-engagement in meaningful social life through these movements is "engaged" in the life of total American society, not a segregated and cut-off sector of American life.

On the borders of the race movement there are, of course, the actions of those either who are anomic or disengaged or both. The Watts riots may be understood in terms of both anomie and disengagement but not as direct action within the rule of norms or toward re-engagement and identity. There is also an increasingly vocal revolutionary leadership which breeds an anomia and rejects "engagement" except in a deviant sub-society of rebellion. Additionally there are organizations like the Black Muslims which offer personal re-engagement in a legitimate sub-society which is itself disengaged from the broader social order. However the more significant organized movements among Negroes are fully concerned with the engagement of Negroes with whites in a national, universalistic social order. In the process of such action they are offering anomic and disengaged Negroes the social and emotional satisfactions of a new, prideful group identity, and through this a sense of social belonging.

Rationality, Universalism, and Achievement

The trend toward rationality has been evidenced in every aspect of life in which men have chosen criteria of efficiency over those of tradition. It is this trend rather than some other aspect of modern life which Jacques Ellul fears above all. Yet, associated with the broadening sphere of rational, secular orientation have been significant shifts in social values and relationships which few critics of the "technological society" could find threatening. With increasing rationality in social relationships have come new value orientations to make more equitable the criteria for establishing many social relationships, i.e., civil rights in the broadest sense. (Discrimination on arbitrary grounds is not the course of rationality and efficiency.) This shift involves greater *universalism* as individuals are judged by a common yardstick rather than by personal or *particularistic* qualities, especially ascribed ones. *Universalism* denotes the application of universal ethical and legal principles rather than specially differentiated ones limited to special categories of persons. Rights, duties, and life chances have increasingly become matters of *achievement* rather than matters determined by ascribed statuses such as in those accorded castes or feudal estates.

Generally speaking, the trend has been toward the opening of participation and achievement on a basis of equality to all who possess attributes which are relevant to the accomplishment of the objectives set forth by the group. Race differences have nothing to do with educational capacity or creative potential. On the other hand feebleminded children are *rationally* excluded from a public school due to inherent incapacity to participate effectively (Anderson and Foster).

That universalistic and achievement orientations have not been fulfilled completely is evident in the confusion regarding the role of women in American life and struggles of racial groups, particularly in South

Africa but also in the United States. In some other spheres as in the prerogatives associated with both old age and youth there is also current confusion. It seems likely, however, that society must always find a substantial basis for the categorical exclusion of children from certain rights and duties. Nor do the values of modern society prescribe that a man shall treat all women in precisely the same way. Wives would object. Primary relationships are particularistic ones. No trend of modern times has changed this in regard to family members or buddies. Rather, less of life today is organized around particularistic relationships and more of life is lived in relationships wherein rational, instrumental, and hence, universal, criteria apply. The rational employer does not care to know the race or the caste of a prospective employee. He wants to know how efficient a producer he will be.

Characteristic of traditionalistic particularistic-ascription oriented social orders is the concept of "station in life" or "knowing one's place." The Indian caste system demonstrates the highest development of this idea. In the rigidly birth-ascribed groupings of caste, the individual pursued his "way," his obligations, and his "proper occupation." With these duties he held occupational rights and group privileges. Historically, in South Asia even concepts of justice and punishment for offense depended upon the caste of the offender. The idea of "one's place in society" was further supported in orthodox Brahminical interpretations of Hinduism. Even today in very remote areas one may find individuals who cannot conceive of an orderly society on any other basis than ascribed rights and duties in a "society of status." Ascribed position was less rigid and somewhat less firmly supported in the institutions of medieval Europe, but the principles were similar (Weber, Max). This order was shattered by the rational standards of urban businessmen and ultimately by the individualistic and achievement orientations inherent in Calvinism. In fifteenth-century Europe, as in twentieth-century India, the power of ascriptive particularism was challenged by the new idealists and those who placed efficiency and profit above traditionalism and the security of a static, agrarian order. Where the individual bears no physical stigma of his birth, ascribed restrictions and prescriptions lose out in the massive and segmentalized community.

Despite social mobility in the cities, birth status groups did not fade away rapidly even in matters of economic and political participation and achievement. The constriction of achievement aspirations to those deemed appropriate to one's social class was not fully dead in the Western democracies even by the twentieth century. Nor were women able to participate and achieve upon an open and competitive basis with the men. In nations like America the Negro was typically constrained from participating and achieving by virtue of that caste-like, biological irrelevancy, race. Even toward the middle of the twentieth century some American Negroes could yet be found who professed to believe that the Negro's "place" was properly an inferior one and that a "good Negro" did not aspire to the "white" style of life. For whites, the idea of "station" or "place" by virtue of birth shifted rapidly from an organizing principle of society to a philosophy of failure for those who had failed to achieve.

Social Classes and Social Mobility.   Given the relative openness and complexity of status structure in modern society, it is hazardous to point to trends toward the increase or decrease of class rigidity and vertical social mobility. Throughout the history of Western nations, the recruitment of the elite has been disproportionately from families already possessing high status (Sorokin, 1927; Svalastoga). Whatever its professions and shibboleths, no nation has achieved full equality of opportunity for achievement. This has often been due to the inadequacy of the mechanisms of social mobility rather than ascribed restriction in regard to equally qualified individuals. This is to say that restrictionism relating to social class has usually operated at the level of entrance to vertical mobility channels. Unlike a successful Negro achiever, the white Protestant achiever from low class beginnings usually has not found that the high rungs on the ladder of success have been removed. Although restriction on access to education as a mobility channel has often been a serious class disability, mobility via business acumen or other routes has been possible. The Horatio Alger hero circa 1900 did not work his way through college; he made it through personal heroism, business acumen, hard work, and thrift. Nor was this "American dream" exclusively American although it was possibly more blatantly asserted as part of the national creed. There is no solid evidence that vertical mobility was much greater in nineteenth-century America than twentieth-century. Mobility then and now is in considerable part a function of economic growth. J. A. Kahl (pp. 254–256) has estimated that about one-third of all cases of inter-generational mobility can be attributed directly to technological change. He and other scholars have observed that the surest safeguard of high mobility is a high rate of social change generally.

S. M. Lipset and R. Bendix have tested a number of current hypotheses regarding vertical social mobility trends against research findings. In regard to the frequent assumption that the United States is more "open" in its vertical mobility than other modern nations they find no supporting evidence. Recruitment of elites seems to be about as "open" in Sweden, Britain, and the Netherlands. Nor is there evidence that the "openness" or "closedness" of the high status levels is undergoing much change in the industrialized nations. Studies fail to support the hypothesis that the maturation of industrial society is associated with decreased social mobility. Mobility is an integral and continuing aspect of the general process of urbanization, industrialization, and bureaucratization in modern society.

Although there is no rapid change going on in the prevalence of social mobility in modern nations, the channels of mobility are undoubtedly shifting. In part this would be true if for no other reason than the enormous changes which have occurred in occupational structures with increasing specialization and professionalization. Formal education is moving toward greater monopolization of mobility channels or at least toward the provision of a basic platform upon which mobility aspirations are potentially attainable. Kaare Svalastoga observes in this connection that knowledge as measured by formal education seems slated to achieve a gradually more dominant position in the stratification system of industrial society. The increasing stress on tested knowledge and training has already led to a general lifting of the educational floor through the demand for proofs of proficiency with the result that school diplomas are the main entry tickets to an increasing number of positions, thereby increasing the handicaps of those who lack an advanced education.

Possible shifts in the nature of "class structures" in the industrialized societies are more difficult to assess due to the very inexactness of social class realities in terms of boundaries, consciousness of affiliation, etc. The existence of social classes in modern nations depends upon how one conceives the concept. It is demonstrable that hierarchies of status exist, but that we are divided into hierarchical compartments is questionable.

Contemporary sociologists are shifting from a view of society as composed of separable social class levels to the acceptance of a stratification model assuming a continuous distribution of status levels from top to bottom. Lenski and Cuber and Kenkel have argued that the older conception of discrete social levels, as advanced notably by Warner and Lunt twenty-five years ago, is unjustified. Rather, they contend, there are several status ranges, more or less continuous from top to bottom, with no clear lines of demarcation. Such controversy in the interpretation of evidence probably relates more to methodological and conceptual assumptions than to social changes which have gone on during the past few decades. The moot character of the evidence is testimony to the probability of no rapid trends toward either crystallization or dissipation of social class lines, insofar as they have indeed existed in this century. There is some reason to believe that earlier studies tended to exaggerate the discontinuities associated with status gradations. Recently Kurt B. Mayer has suggested that for the United States an intermediate position may be near the truth. He argues that clear social classes still exist at the top and at the bottom of the social hierarchy, but for the bulk of the population, in the middle ranges of status, class lines have become quite blurred.

Civil Rights and Racial Integration in the United States. Since World War II, the most dramatic social movement in America has been that associated with the rights of Negroes to participate fully and equally in American institutions and community life. Particularistic discriminations have typically been applied to each new ethnic group entering American community life grasping for an integrated life of achievement. In the case of the Negro this process has been complicated, amplified, and extended by special factors (Young; Kahl). Chief among these are the existence of a crystallized discriminatory tradition rooted partly in the institutions of slavery and the fact that the Negro is more readily discernable than are ethnic minorities for whom prejudiced behavior patterns could be dissipated by acculturation and assimilation.

The incongruity of Negro discrimination in American life has been multi-faceted. The American creed of universalism and equality in opportunity was and is blatantly violated. Sharp as were the horns of this ethical dilemma, the paradox of ascription in a massive, rational social and economic order was even more clear. Here no rationalizing myth could dull the stresses. Yet the fact stubbornly remained that carried over into a rational, efficient, contractual, urban social order was this institutionalized pattern consistent with a static, agrarian "society of status." The documentation and examination of this monumental dilemma has been carried out more voluminously and more minutely than perhaps any other single aspect of American life (Simpson and Yinger).

At no period since colonial times have stresses been absent in respect to the race paradox. Frequently these have been responded to through ideological and psychological mechanisms which were directed toward the elimination of a social change potential in the ever-present stresses. Concepts of biological inferiority and of "separate creations" were stress-reducing formulae which would leave the social and ethical incongruities untouched. Frequently their preservation was enforced through legal and extra-legal devices. Yet at all times there have been white consciences awake to the ethical dilemma as at all times a substantial number of Negroes were much more keenly aware of it ethically and in personal frustration as well. For whites generally, following the Civil War, it was not too difficult to live with the paradox so long as it was confined to the surviving plantation system and its environs in the rural South, and its victims were too weak to make effective protest. During World War I there began the large-scale Negro migrations toward industrial centers which were not emancipated from the particularism coherent with a society of ascription and status. Under urban conditions, inherent stresses blossomed into conscious strains which were multiply increased in the new migrations of World War II and furthered by the Nazi racism —a bitter reminder of our own national sins.

The importance of the re-distribution of the Negro population for social trends in race relations would be difficult to overestimate (Dorsey). Two related demographic shifts have occurred; the first of these was the out-migration of Negroes from rural southern communities and the second is in-migration of Negroes to cities both North and South but especially North. Even in the South, Negroes are now more urbanized than are whites, and over 80 per cent of non-Southern Negroes are congregated in the large cities. Both North and South, the urban Negro has been forced to find a new life in an impersonal social system which in regard to him persists in compromising universalistic-achievement orientations.

In the 1950's and 1960's Negroes have had about twice the unemployment rates of whites; they were largely engaged in inferior status jobs; they had average incomes a little more than half that of whites, and an infant mortality rate 1.8 times that of whites (Miller and Form, pp. 446–450). Political equality in suffrage had been widely gained in the North but was less secure in many southern cities and widely abrogated in rural communities. Despite the integration pressure on the armed forces in World War II, by 1962 Negroes constituted 12.2 per cent of Army enlisted personnel but only 3.2 per cent of commissioned ranks; the comparable figures for the Air Force were 9.1 and 1.2 per cent (Coates *et al.*). Inequities in educational opportunity in the South, while reduced from preceding decades, continued to be substantial by practically all conceivable measurements.

Urban Negroes are nearly all cramped into densely populated inner city ghettos. Few churches are truly integrated. These observations are not intended to review the race relations pattern as its exists. They are cited because they are outstanding and tangible areas of stress underlying the contemporary anti-discrimination and civil rights movements.

A "mass society" theory of race relations does not provide total understanding of either discrimination or the movement away from it. However, the Master Trend has set the stage wherein particularistic-ascriptive racial policies are *functionally* inappropriate, in addition to being ethically inappropriate. Lohman and Reitzes (1952; 1954) have applied the Master Trend theory, or in their terms "mass society" theory, to the broad range of race relations in the urban milieu. They find that in modern society individual racial prejudices are no longer effective sources for discriminatory behavior, simply because individual attitudes are subordinated and mobilized by the organized associations and interest groups to which the individual relates. It is more important in predicting behavior to know the *association's* position on race than to know the *personal* feelings of the individual. While it is improbable that most scholars would agree that personal prejudices are of no significance whatever, the importance of associational definitions of race has much to do with the inconsistencies found in the white urbanite's race behavior as he moves from church to school to work and to country club.

In the present stressful period with increasing national prosperity, associated with an intense desire to burnish the U.S. democratic image abroad, the nation is pursuing trends toward institutionalizing the humane values we have long professed. All of these forces, internal and external, work to stimulate innovative movements toward rationality and racial equality. At the same time that the new urban Negro finds emancipation from the traditional controls of the rural South, a half century of slow gains in economic and educational strength is bringing forth able leadership as well as general support for movements of race identity and solidarity. The trends of race relations in the 1960's are perhaps guided and supported by the most revolutionary movement this nation has known in the twentieth century, and it is the more sensational for being largely within the framework of law. If the present trends continue, Negroes will first approach the white position in their educational status, next in occupational status, and much later in income (Glenn). Although legislation and social movements are powerful forces, these changes will be given significant facilitation by national economic growth generally and the continued expansion of medium status jobs and contraction in unskilled labor demands.

Changing Status of Women. As the roles of women have become more differentiated there has been marked reduction in the particularistic and ascribed nature of their position in society. It is tempting to draw analogies between the emancipation of women from their traditional "station" and the growth of universalistic-achievement orientations for Negroes. In some respects both represent minority groups associated with vigorous social movements toward voluntary and equal participation in society. But the analogy should not be pressed far since women possess distinctive biological functions such as child birth which render ascription of certain roles a cultural imperative (Zimmerman and Cervantes). Further the inequality of women in respect to men has been more legalistic and formal, tempered by her informal power and prestige within the family circle, both as wife and as mother. However with the rise of cities and the removal of production functions from the home as well as removal of a multitude of home-making functions from the home, there arose insistent pressures toward new roles in community life and a movement toward women's participation on the basis of their individual capabilities rather than their "station" as women.

In the industrial revolution, wage employment drew men outside the home which had traditionally been an economic partnership of husband and wife (Baker). With demand for women in the labor force, and other incentives to participate economically and socially outside the home, women were confronted by the stereotype of "woman the home-maker" and the myth of their intellectual and moral incapability to cope with a man's world. Discriminations of many types were imposed upon women who sought to participate and to achieve in the open society. The differentiation of woman's roles was associated with a persistent battle against restriction and discrimination, which, as for the Negro, had backing in rationalizing myths and concepts of God-ordained function. The "woman's" movement swelled in Western nations, often toward the achievement of unrealistic and doubtful equalities, but among its goals were the achievement of political suffrage, access to educational opportunity, equal property rights, and the right to work on the basis of capability on a par with men (Green and Melnick).

It has been said that the feminist movement in the United States began when Thomas Jefferson thought it best to exclude women from politics to "prevent deprivation of morals and ambiguity of issues." In 1848 the Woman's Rights Convention at Seneca, New York, demanded equal property rights, the franchise, equitable divorce laws, the end of occupational limitations, and the opening of educational opportunities for women. From that time the feminist movement in America continued. It achieved considerable success by linking itself to various welfare and humane causes in which men too were interested. By 1900 the main theme of the feminist movement was equal suffrage, a program which culminated in the constitutional amendment granting this right in 1920. Throughout this period increasing numbers of educational institutions were opening their doors to women, and emancipation from traditional stereotypes were showing in expansion of occupational roles, increasing participation in civic affairs, and in symbolic matters of dress, etc.

In the mid-twentieth century the woman's movement has lost much of its momentum. Women have not gained full emancipation from their traditionally ascribed roles, but as greater equality and achievement opportunity has come about, confusion has arisen as to how far the issues should be pressed. In educational participation, recreation, courtship, and symbolic behavior, ascription of status has been virtually eliminated in Western societies. In legal rights, substantial changes have been made toward equality, but there are still states which forbid jury duty by women and impose legal handicaps on them in reference to property rights. Occupationally women have moved strongly into the labor market but not on terms of full economic equality with men. Women are widely discriminated against in wages—while differentially protected against health and other hazards. They are very under-represented in the professions and in governmental office in most countries.

This is partly because of their continuing role dilemmas and in part because of outright discrimination, i.e., male preference. The open participation of women in economic life is probably most advanced in the socialist countries where deliberate efforts have been made to integrate the female roles associated with child bearing with the demands of wage employment. In a number of countries, perhaps notably the United States, confusion is intensified by the desire of women to be treated in accord with the standards of chivalry as they practice open competition with males who are understandably confused by these incongruities. Some cynics insist that women simply want *greater* equality than men. The more sober fact is that women today want the *rights* of free competitive participation, but they want to retain the status associated with their traditional and distinctive biological functions as in child bearing and rearing (Williams, Robin, pp. 59–67). The integration of these two types of roles is not impossible, but it is one involving numerous stresses which stimulate innovative thrusts and social experimentation in role integration.

Outside the Soviet Union and a few other nations there is no evidence that women will press toward full competition with males in a wide gamut of occupations. Women are highly concentrated in the occupational fields wherein they seek achievement, some of these being dominated by them, i.e., nursing and social work. Most women appear loath to enter the engineering and other technological professions. Relatively few American women enter medicine and those who do are likely to specialize in diseases of women and children. (In contrast medicine in the Soviet Union has now become virtually a woman's profession—75% of all physicians are female.) Female technicians tend to specialize in some phase of home economics or design. Robin Williams has remarked that in regard to American society even the political issues in which women are most active relate to "traditional" feminine functions of nurturance and protection, e.g., schools, delinquency, mental health, aud child labor.

As Williams points out, if women were indeed to compete with men for jobs on a fully equal basis, it would require drastic changes in either the family system or the occupational structure, or both. The pressures which act to retain the traditional roles of homemaker and mother in the hands of women are more than simple prejudice or inertia.

VIVE LA DIFFERENCE. It is inconceivable that in the foreseeable future men and women will participate on a completely open, competitive achievement basis. On the other hand there are unquestionable trends toward the establishment of conventionalized spheres and patterns within which universalism and achievement values will be applied. Today well over one-third (36%) of all U.S. married women are employed. Most of these are also child bearers and homemakers. In some European countries the proportions of wage earning homemakers are higher. The female child bearing function is increasingly integrated with the universalistic ethic through various social devices ranging from state supported nursery schools to legal job protection during pregnancy. Frequently, too, accommodation of the different role patterns arises as these are accepted sequentially rather than concomitantly. Some young women enter an occupation upon graduation from high school or college, resigning from it for the duration of the early stage in the family cycle. As the most time-consuming demands of child rearing are passed on to the specialized agencies, limited return to professional activities follows. No doubt many middle-aged and elderly women are today entering the labor market for the first time. Of all women 35 to 44, nearly half were at work or seeking work by 1966.

For increasing numbers of wives the "empty nest" is a signal for them to return to college and thence into the occupational world, now with minimal conflict between the outer world of open-achievement and familial milieu. There is no sign that Western women are giving up marriage and family for total emancipation. The evidence is that they will continue to explore innovative patterns toward their integration of these separate roles.

CONCLUSION

Practically all long-range directional trends in modern society are inextricably bound up with the rise of the modern city as the dominant form of community living. In the United States, the Civil War period marked the point at which distinctively urban values and social structures were to gain predominating significance. This transformation occurred both in the rising size and significance of cities in national affairs and also in reference to their influence exerted upon rural dwellers. In the past half century, new directions of city growth have appeared. The nineteenth-century urban structure with its centralized business core has shifted toward the more decentralized, sprawling metropolitan region in which former cities are linked through industrial and residential suburbs into huge conurbations. The transition from the single-city pattern of urban ecology to the regional metropolitan pattern has given rise to distinctive adjustive trends in governmental structure to meet the problems of new interdependencies of established communities, new suburban developments, and shifts in population and in property values.

The modern city has been associated with the rise of a secular, specialized, and rational way of life. There are many facets to this trend. While family life continues to be a vital force, specialized associational type groups have come to complement, and at some points supplant, primary groups in performance of many functions. The individual lives in the social world of broadened scale of relationship, and with this, increasing segmentalization of his social life. Within associational groups, there have been trends toward increasing centralization of power associated with greater internal differentiation in regard to functions. This is evident in the increasing power and increasing functional complexity of national governments and in the trends of oligopoly in business and industrial life—and in some countries monolithic and monopolistic economic systems as branches of the political state. With the increasing complexity of large associational groups, bureaucracy and professionalism is enhanced. While these trends are all unmistakable, it is probable that there are limits beyond which rationally organized groups cannot go in the centralization of power, functional complexity, and bureaucratic differentiation. There is no reason to think that many complex groups are becoming more simplified and informal, but there is evidence that a point of "diminishing returns" occurs, beyond which such growth fails to serve a rational purpose. Complex organizational structure is not increasing in complexity within already large organizations so much as it is being extended into spheres of life traditionally organized through less formal, impersonal, and bureaucratic patterns. An outstanding example of the innovative extension of complex organizational structure is in the present trend toward the "multiversity" in higher education.

Some social scientists and others have frequently argued that modern life is characterized by "mass culture" and "mass society." These concepts imply dull standardization in consumption interests and tastes in a society dominated by shallowness in values and weak group affiliations. It is frequently argued that in this modern society men get lost in the lonely crowd, alienated, anomic, or disengaged from meaningful group life. While it is certain that the modern style of life breeds conditions in which anomie, feelings of alienation, and social disengagement are prevalent, there is no indication that this is a trend to be infinitely extrapolated. The state of Orwell's *Nineteen Eighty-four* is something less than a human potential. Numerous counter-trends oppose and limit the growth of "mass society" in this sense. Conditions expressed by such concepts as anomie and alienation are facts of modern life rather than secular trends. So called "mass culture" is balanced by trends of literacy, increased general welfare, and wider interests and social participation for "the masses."

One of the persistent struggles in the development of Western civilization has been to insure the broader applications of universalistic criteria in the quest for status and the good things of life. The significance of social class position at birth has been notably reduced in its influence upon the life chances of the individual, but it is doubtful if social class mobility is becoming greater than in earlier times. However, new criteria for mobility are arising, especially formal education. Nonetheless as a social value the concept of "station in life" is vanishing in the face of spreading universalistic-achievement orientations. Ascribed status still holds significance for Negroes and for women, although for the former it is almost completely rejected as a viable value. Considerable confusion still exists in the reconciliation of women's biological roles and their equal participation in the open, competitive society. In the area of American race relations, we are witnessing perhaps the last major campaign in this country's struggle toward the general principle of universalistic criteria in the judgment of individuals in civil and economic affairs, with more equitable and rational utilization of human capacities and aspirations.

14

Change in the Developing Societies

The preceding chapter has described social trends in the urbanized, developed nations. Such changes have ultimate roots in the institutions and technology which have arisen in the West since the collapse of an agrarian feudal order. It has been this pattern which evolutionary theorists have attempted to express in several of the conceptual dichotomies and continua presented in Chapter 11 and which has been characterized as the "Master Trend." The new Western world of urbanism, with its expanding material culture and amenities based upon mass production, technology, and science, was not exported to most of Africa, Asia, and Latin America. Although four centuries of colonialism and imperialistic domination made some impact upon indigenous social structures, transformations similar to those of Western Europe and North America occurred in rare instances prior to World War II.

UNREST IN TRADITIONAL REGIONS

At the time of World War II the fires of nationalism were burning in many colonial lands. Frequently these burned hotter for ethnic nationalism than for support of an encompassing political state, but they were nonetheless strong for self-determination and sovereignty. The value revolution which had stoked the transition in the West was also in motion. Ralph Turner, the world historian, touring Asia and Africa in 1950, reported that these peoples already seethed with a new-found realization of worth and dignity. Increased market involvements and the war itself brought comprehension of world inter-dependencies. Mass communications were offering viaducts for the emancipating ideologies of both the American and British brand, as well as the Soviet. And, at this point, a new, educated elite oriented to the revolutionary doctrines of the West was emerging. In much of the undeveloped world, these conditions were ripe for the catalytic effects of the cold war in which

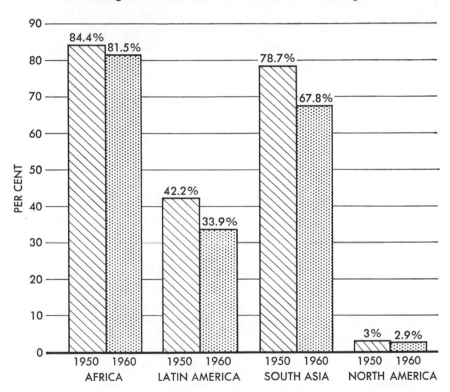

Percentages of Illiterates in Various World Regions *

Literacy is both a sign of development and a means to its further attainment. Despite strong efforts since 1950, the great majority of all Africans and South Asians are still illiterate. Illiteracy in Northern Europe and in Japan is even less than in North America.

* UNESCO, *Statistical Yearbook, 1965*, New York, 1966, pp. 32–33.

technical aid and associated programs stimulated the impoverished economies, reduced death rates, and stirred aspirations.

Immediately following World War II, India freed herself of colonial rule, followed by Ceylon, Burma, Indonesia, and others. In China, a reactionary and pro-Western regime was liquidated, and a new era of self-determination and modernization was pressed through a Communist revolution. In all Africa as of 1945, there existed only four independent states (Melady). By the end of 1964, there were 37 independent African states. Through most of South America, there was massive unrest against traditional authoritarian and feudal type elites and the ascriptive social structures they stood for. There was also massive escape to presumed opportunities in the cities. The stresses of rapid urbanization and the very fact of urban development, particularly in Africa and in Latin America, served notice to alert leaders that rapid industrialization was crucial to the attainment of what the restive masses demanded in this "revolution of rising expectations."

By 1950, the "revolution of rising expectations" had been transported into the far reaches of the Andes, the Congo, and the Indian Deccan. Political and governmental leaders throughout the world were put on notice to innovate both in design and implementation social and economic orders consistent with rising mass expectations, or be liquidated through ballots or bullets.

THE DEVELOPMENTAL CONTINUUM AND THE THREE-STAGE MODEL

Based upon the generalized tendency of societies to follow the trend laid out in theoretical statements of the great transition, students of social development have frequently categorized societies in three groupings, dependent upon their stage in the developmental process. The initial phase includes societies which are termed "undeveloped," "premodern," or "traditional." These terms denote characteristics implied in Redfield's "folk" community or in Tönnies' *Gemeinschaft* (see above, pp. 308–316). The second stage is that of "the developing" or "transitional society" denoting that change along the expected lines of the continuum is in progress. The third stage is that of the "developed society," or "modern," or "industrial" society conforming generally to Redfield's concept of the "urban" pole or to Tönnies' *Gesellschaft*.

The use of a three-stage model does not imply any sharp demarcations between "stages." The shifts of social development are like tentative and irregular thrusts at various points along a long and rugged frontier. They are not to be understood as a shift across a boundary marker separating the "traditional" from the "transitional" and the "transitional" from the "modern." Dichotomies such as folk-urban and *Gemein-*

Total Energy Consumed (Solid Fuels, Liquid Fuels, Natural and Imported Gas, and Hydro-, Nuclear, and Imported Electricity) in Various World Regions (in kilograms per capita, coal equivalent) *

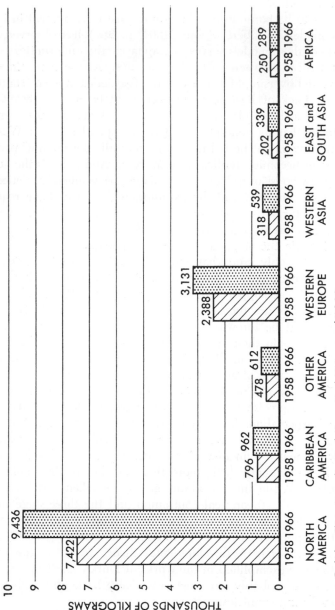

Excluding China, Mongolia, North Korea, North Vietnam, and U.S.S.R.

Increasing consumption of energy is crucial for economic development and the amenities of modern life. Although crude consumption data do not tell us how effectively energy is used, they provide one significant measure of economic development. The underdeveloped regions are increasing their energy consumption but are very far below levels which will support a high level of living. As these regions get underway industrially, energy production and consumption may increase rapidly. For example, energy consumption in Japan increased by 70% between 1930 and 1939.

* *Statistical Yearbook, 1967,* United Nations, New York, 1968, Table 11, pp. 62–65.

schaft-Gesellschaft are useful, but they become misleading when not understood as theoretical models serving as polar extremities on a multi-faceted continuum.

Cautions are to be borne in mind as we discuss development in terms of stages or models. Wilbert Moore (1964, p. 884) has observed that the utilization of these models serves to emphasize the uniformities rather than the differences between particular societies. At the same time the three-stage model oversimplifies the nature of societies at each "stage" in the sequence. Lack of historical perspective blots out significant differences among societies classified in the same stage. Another danger of the model is that its general theory is so dependent upon Western experience that we might be led to assume that all "developing" peoples are in process of becoming replicas of ourselves. And there is the added question of just who is "ourselves" since existing "developed" societies are variable in many qualities and the assumption that "we" have reached a particular structural pinnacle would be a deceptive one. Some writers have suggested in reference to this last problem that we extend our model building to include the stage of "overdevelopment."

It is unquestionably true that most theoretic concepts basic to a sociological approach to evolution or social development have had their main empirical supports in the experience of Western Europe. When these theories are focused on the realities of the late twentieth century, we should be forewarned that the cultural bases from which the new nations begin their transition have certain striking differences from the cultural base of medieval Europe as it emerged from a traditionalistic, "sacred" type of agrarian order toward the "urban," "secular," and rational society of "modern" type. Furthermore, the evidence is not clear as to the precise conformity of transitional changes today with certain of the expectations logically derived from the theory. No doubt a growing body of comparative research in urbanization and development will yield many refinements and qualifications in developmental theory which are presently little more than hunches in the thinking of critical scholars. While these cautions are to be taken seriously, they do not mean that the theoretical continuum and the three-stage model should be discarded. As Moore observes, "what is interesting and instructive about this approach is not its crudity but its utility" (Moore, 1964, pp. 883–884; Marcson). A developmental theory based in the evolutionary continua as exemplified in the works of Durkheim, Tönnies, Redfield, and others is probably our most satisfactory basic approach to the presently developing countries.

A Note on the Semantics of Development. Since the issues of transformation in the non-Western world have become matters of wide concern, the search for terminology has been persistent and somewhat confusing. Economists and technical aid personnel appear early to have popularized the term "underdeveloped" as an improvement over the hopelessness denoted in the term "undeveloped." Anthropologist George Foster thinks "newly developed" is still nicer. The same countries have been designated "pre-industrial" to emphasize their economic status. As social scientists realized that problems of economic development were intricately involved in concurrent value and relationship systems, phrases like "social aspects of development" and "secularization" appeared frequently in the literature. Sociologist Wilbert Moore, whose concern with the issues has taken at times a somewhat economic direction, prefers simply to discuss the problems of "modernization."

The question of what to call the process of transformation is perhaps less difficult than what to call the countries undergoing or about to undergo the transformation. As the broad social implications of development became clearer, societies which were not "modern" came to be termed "traditional" or "pre-modern." While it is rather easy to hit upon "transitional" as a designation for societies in process of modernization or development, it is less clear what positive descriptive term applies to the preceding state. The theoretic concepts of evolutionary sociology have too many qualifications and implications to be well used. The term "traditional" has come into currency as an unobjectionable and more sociologically meaningful term than "pre-modern," "pre-industrial," "underdeveloped," "undeveloped," and perish the thought, "primitive," "static," and "backward."

TRADITIONAL SOCIETIES

The Underdevelopment Syndrome

After World War II, the term "underdeveloped" became the popular euphemism applied to the poverty stricken regions of the world participating slightly or not at all in the material amenities associated with modern science. Economically, these regions lacked the efficient organization and the capacity to engage in self-generating economic growth (Rostow; Jacobs, 1966). A virtual corollary of underdevelopment is a low level of living for the bulk of a population. While the nations of the world, even in 1940, might have been arrayed upon a continuum of "development" or underdevelopment, the fact remained that a very substantial proportion of the world's population lived in regions which contrasted sharply with Western Europe and North America as a whole in their level of living (Linton, 1949; Berry; Sjoberg). In 1940, the death rate in India was about double that for either the United Kingdom or the United States and her infant mortality was over three times that for the United States. The death rate in Egypt was even higher than in India, and Chile's was not much better. Over 50 per cent of the world had daily caloric intakes of less than 2250. Practically all of these countries were in Africa, Asia, and Latin America. With the exception of a few nations like Japan and the white population of the Union of South Africa, the "underdeveloped" included virtually all of Asia, Africa, the Middle East, South and Middle America, and parts of South Eastern Europe. Very few of the countries or regions involved were undergoing rapid changes before World War II in the directions so long manifest in the already urban, industrial nations.

Notwithstanding the great cultural differences among the various undeveloped regions, a common syndrome was present (Spengler). These characteristics include a composite of economic, technological, political, demographic, and community organizational features. They involved some basic value sets as well as attitudinal and social participational patterns. From the economic standpoint, agriculture was the backbone of life. Furthermore it was technologically inefficient agriculture. Per capita income was low; capital equipment and capital formation were low; natural resources were badly exploited. Politically, these regions suffered from a "lack of civic culture" (Almond and Verba). For multiple reasons the rank and file citizens have widely been non-participants in governing, and sense of membership in a political state had generally been weak or absent. Demographically these regions had relatively high death rates. The age composition was generally unfavorable to productivity. Community and other group structures were basically oriented to security and survival rather than risk and change. Middle classes were lacking or formed small groups between large and impoverished peasantries and small but exalted traditional elites—except in much of Africa where these concepts were scarcely applicable. Social values and supporting attitudes and norms have been typically ascriptive, particularistic, and conserving rather than enterprising and achievement oriented, in any significant sense. Economic activities were generally embedded in a traditional system of obligations and reciprocities often rooted in family and kinship systems and, in some regions, caste or feudal statuses.

Whatever benefits may have occurred to "native peoples" under several centuries of colonialism, the stimulus to urban and industrial development was rarely strong. Where European colonialism did not penetrate, or in Latin America, where it was ousted, feudalistic social structures were widely enforced either by the descendants of the white conqueror or by indigenous lords. In some regions, as in parts of South Asia, colonial rulers deliberately utilized indigenous caste and feudal systems for purposes of profit and tranquility. At best, enlightened colonial policies maintained such regions in agrarian dependence upon European industrialization. In Africa south of the Sahara, it was tribal structure which offered the organizational base for "colonial" rule and exploitation. Whether colonial or independent, these regions were all generally without the kind of rational value system which had proved so dynamic in Western Europe. Many of them had social institutions closely geared to stability and security. Their economic activities were embedded in conditions described in Chapter 3 as inconducive to social change.

Traditional Societies vs. Traditionalistic Ones

The term "traditional" is accepted and utilized here; however certain cautions are in order. That these societies are rooted in norms resting upon the moral, sacred past rather than upon criteria of rationality is basically true. However, to view tradition as simply the dead hand of the past and hence the arch-enemy of modernization is unjustified. Edward Shils has made this point when he writes:

Tradition is not the dead hand of the past but rather the hand of the gardener, which nourishes and elicits tendencies of judgement which would otherwise not be strong enough to emerge on their own. In this respect tradition is an encouragement to incipient individuality rather than its enemy. It is a stimulant to moral judgement and self-discipline rather than an opiate. It establishes contact between the recipient and the sacred values of his life in society. [Shils, 1958, p. 156.]

Buddhism, for example, may well prove to be a positive force for modernization in South Asia rather than the reverse (Niehoff). Looked at in this fashion, tradition *may* become a powerful impediment to social and technical change, but may also perform important stabilizing functions in society in throes of development. Tradition can become a nexus around which change is rationalized and integrated. It all depends upon just what the tradition is and how it is assessed in the innovative context. *Traditionalism* as the cult of the past is indeed a barrier to all change; *traditions* as the *ways* of the past which have been found good may be neutral or of positive value in regard to change.

"Traditional societies" are those which, without developed science, have built a stable set of norms and techniques to cope with relatively unchanging conditions. They are different from "modern societies" in that broader ranges of behavior are subject to traditional criteria, not that the nature of tradition is different or inherently more impermeable by innovative thought.

Qualitative Differences Among Traditional Societies

It is important that we do not let the concept "traditional society" homogenize significantly different societies into a single pattern. While all of these societies approach the generalized concepts described in

Chapter 11, each makes its approaches in its own distinctive manner. Among the traditionals there are to be found several variables significant for developmental change. Several of these more important differences are described below.

1. *Tribal Peoples and the Ancient Civilizations.* Broadly speaking, the traditional societies are divisible into the civilized, who have prior development of literacy and of city life, and the societies without literate traditions and without cities. The developed institutions of tribal Africa are, for example, of a different order from those which emerged from the ancient civilizations of the Middle East, India, and China. The latter populations are predominately composed of peasants; the former are commonly referred to as "primitive" or tribal.[1] The peasant societies have been anciently oriented to literate traditions developed by their intelligentsia in orthogenetic city centers. Many of these societies, howsoever diverse their subcultures, have at least the unifying bonds of a common "great tradition" (Redfield).

In countries long civilized there also appears a phenomenon which has been termed "the dual society" in which a modernized sector of life exists side-by-side with a much larger traditional one (Erasmus). This contrast is sharp in amenities and material culture as modern hotels rise among thatch hovels and Rolls Royces contend with oxcarts and barefooted pedestrians. Frequently these contrasts in style of life are associated with highly differentiated social class structures possessing degrees of rigidity unfamiliar to "Western" urban society. While the monied classes enjoy the amenities of the industrialized world, it does not follow necessarily that they subscribe to its value system or participate in a system of social and economic organization consistent with modernizing trends. The "dual" societies have contrasts in status, power, and privilege practically unknown among tribal peoples. In many regions, notably Latin America, the "dual society" of the city has a hinterland further complicated by the presence of unintegrated tribal peoples as well as peasants integrated with the dominant social structure and its traditions.

These complexities involve something more than the accommodation of ethnic groups and minorities in national developmental programs. The presence of an urban "dual society" means at the very least a recognition by the urban majority that relative deprivation is institutionalized in the existing social order. However, it is probable that several thousand years' experience with literate, urban-centered civilization offers a more subtantial cultural base for the rapid integration of modernizing trends than is to be found where tribal structures, nomadism, and preliterate languages have persisted to the present time.

---

[1] The sharpness of this distinction is disputed by Lloyd Fallers (1961; 1963).

2. *Feudalistic and Non-Feudalistic Societies.* While most traditional societies emphasize ascribed statuses, the particular types of ascription are of key importance for the nature of developmental change. In a large number of peasant regions, the most encompassing power system protecting tradition, social structures, and values is that of the landed aristocracy. Even in countries like Colombia which lack feudalism in a literal and legal sense the landed proprietors are powerful forces of conservatism (Havens). In vast regions of Asia and Latin America, agrarian, especially land tenure, reform is widely viewed as a first and foremost objective toward economic and social modernization. This is particularly true where landed classes have extended their power into the functioning of the political state.

Different policy toward transition can arise where feudal and quasi-feudal structures are absent or of relatively small scope. The immediate focus of developmental objectives for the Congolese is not as "land" oriented as for the Colombians or as in the initial phases of the Chinese revolution. Also some predominantly peasant countries such as Ceylon have not been faced with a crucially important overthrow of a landed aristocracy.

3. *Ethnic Homogeneity and Cultural Pluralism.* Modernization takes place mainly within territories possessing political sovereignty. Where the political state is to be composed of strongly rooted and diverse ethnic groups, the approach to development is significantly complicated and requires different approaches from those in states built upon ethnic solidarity, or where competitive ethnic groups have weak solidarities (Furnival; Geertz (ed.)). The problems of ethnic nationalism are particularly acute in new states composed of tribal units and where historical antagonisms have existed among cultural plurals now unified only by the exigencies of statehood.

The problem of cultural pluralism is an exceedingly widespread one in South Asia and Africa. The failure of Ceylon, for example, to meet rapidly the economic demands of modernization stems in part from the ethnic nationalism within groups required to formulate strategies of collaborative effort. Approaches can be quite different in Pakistan, which at least is unified by its intense, nationalistic spirit centering upon Islamic traditions. To be sure, a theocratic state raises still different issues relevant to modernization.

Differences in "Ethos" and Social Integration. The traditional societies of the world differ markedly among themselves in their "world views," "social values," group structures, modes of dealing with deviance, and scores of matters all of which are relevant to their unique assessments of innovation. One of the most basic structural variables for change is that of the rigidity or looseness of social structure and culture. This was recognized by Ralph Linton in 1952 as a significant but rather intangible distinguishing feature among societies then approaching economic development. Linton observed that:

> There are some cultures which seem to be built like finely adjusted clock movements. At the other end of the scale there are cultures which are so loosely organized that one wonders how they are able to function at all. . . . In closely integrated cultures the introduction of any new culture element immediately starts in train a series of obvious dislocations . . . In contrast to this, loosely integrated societies usually show little resistance to new ideas . . . [Linton, 1952, pp. 86–87.]

In a different context Ryan and Straus have argued that the loose structuring of social groups and relationships in Theravada Buddhist countries is significant for easy change, in contrast to societies possessing rigid social structures (see above, pp. 56–57). Societies differ in the precision of the norms and group organization patterns and in the strictness of their demands for adherence to moral and organizational norms. In some communities of puritan type background the straight and narrow way is pressed strongly upon the citizenry. Elsewhere, as in southern Buddhist countries, moral leaders speak in terms of the "middle way." Here norms are broadly defined: there are many alternative patterns which are normative, and deviants are not harshly repressed. Modernization in Ceylon villages is rather smooth, as the new creeps in almost unnoticed upon the old (Ryan et al.). Hoselitz also has shown for the Maori how modern economic life was grafted onto a social structure utterly dissimilar from Western community life, and Manning Nash similarly tells how industry enters a Guatemalan community without traumatic effects on its social structures (Hoselitz, 1960, pp. 73–80; Nash). We may hypothesize that loose-structured societies avoid head-on collisions between traditional modes and secular innovation, finding routes for syncretism and accommodation which tide them over a transitional period which in a rigidly structured social system might reasonably yield disorganization and conflict.

It is also evident that specific traditional value emphases have much to do with incentives to achieve modernization and with the aspirations of individuals which are relevant to development. In many of the long civilized societies possessing landed gentry and a literate intelligentsia such achievement patterns as existed denigrated the very activities basic to economic development (Smith, T. Lynn; Ryan, 1961). Widespread among these societies is an ethos in which hand-dirtying toil is demeaning and business enterprise unfit for gentlemen. Correspondingly, the traditional goals for personal achievement are dysfunctional from the standpoint of modernization.

THE TRANSITIONAL SOCIETIES

Except for tiny and extremely remote tribal peoples, the traditional societies of yesterday are transitional societies today. By the 1950's, dozens of "transitional" societies had each spawned its "five-year plan" or "six-year plan" or "Great Leap Forward." To term a people "transitional" is to say simply that a change in pace has occurred in orienting their society toward rationality and other aspects of modernization. Although we base our concept of modernization upon the transition which first occurred in the West, it is, as has been observed, inaccurate to view the transitional societies as moving toward "Westernization." If there is one fundamental truth regarding traditionals beginning their thrusts toward modernization, it is that with few exceptions they do not wish to become *Westernized.* As Ralph Turner pointed out, "The Chinese intend to remain Chinese, the Indians, Indian, and the Moslems, Moslem." As Cambodians, Bantus, and Aleuts move into the "master trend," they will become secularized Cambodians, Bantus, and Aleuts not a socially nor a culturally indistinguishable mass. Although nationalistic fervor in most transitional countries insists upon this, it would be true in any case.

The Models for Transition

If most traditional societies reject "Westernization" it is a rejection of de-nationalization, not a rejection of the material achievements attainable through emulation of the West. However, it is misleading to speak of *The West* as if it were a homogeneous model upon which the new nations might plan their own transitions. It is true that all modern nations have a great deal in common, but there are notable divergences among them, especially in the routes and methods toward achieving modernity. Two major alternative pathways are epitomized in the routes followed by the United States and by Soviet Russia. Additionally several of the presently transitional societies, particularly China, are themselves serving as tentative models for still others.

Recently Irving Louis Horowitz has emphasized the significance of the differing Soviet and United States models for the transitional processes of the developing societies. While the United States represents the fuller attainment of efficiency and industrialization, it is impressive to the weak new nations that the Soviet has attained its own immensely developed status so recently and relatively rapidly. Furthermore, centuries of domination by the Western European nations, and in this century by the United States as well, has not warmed many transitional nations to the United States example. Most critical perhaps for their choice of models is the fact that the new nations recognize the greater significance of the political state for their own growth than was true in the nineteenth century. Here the Soviet offers a viable model for transition which the United States does not, and furthermore United States spokesmen have often voiced ideological rejection of such strong, central governments. Also, to the dark-skinned peoples of most of the world, United States race relations are widely construed as sum and substance of capitalism and precisely the kind of structure these new nations seek most to avoid. The capitalistic, imperialistic image of the United States is additionally burnished by the deliberate extension of United States "defensive" military action into the countryside and the cities of Vietnam. On top of all this, the salesmen of the United States model seem frequently to cling to the ethnocentric view that "what's good for Uncle Sam is good for you"—a proposition widely disputed both as a basis for political alignment and for economic growth as well.

Although ideologically and politically, the United States is no doubt the most significant model for efficient industrial operations, it is not for the means of achieving them. The Colombian peasant, for example, can understand the desirability of making Colombia an economic replica of the United States, but he is likely to find such a goal inconceivable without revolutionary changes in the economic and political power structure *supported* there by ·the United States. It is the United States which offers the clearest economic goal. It is the Soviet which more commonly supports seemingly effective means for attaining it under the given conditions.

Not only do the presently developed nations serve as models, they act also to support those transitional nations which will pursue courses acceptable to them. Under some circumstances the "model" nations intervene forcefully to determine certain aspects of transitional change. More commonly, the technique of influence is in various forms of carrot dangling, i.e., economic aid, trade agreements, etc. There is no firm evidence based upon examination of contemporary transitional nations as to which affiliation and which ideological route is the more effective in achieving the complicated set of goals which every developed nation must establish (Malenbaum and Stolper).

Whatever model, or ingredients of several models, a transitional nation chooses, there are inevitably many phases of development which are not according to plan. In part this is due to the practical difficulties in effecting complex plans. However, it is also due to the fact that achievements carry side effects which are unplanned and frequently unwanted. People plan for greater health and longevity, and when their plan succeeds they have also an excessively rapid population growth. Some South Asian traditionalists want to achieve the good life known to the West—but avoid "Western" materialism. Still others want political democracy—and the retention of caste privileges. Many of the trends in social organization were in the West—and will be in the East—latent functional consequences of industrialization and urban life. The new nations hope to borrow from the West and by planning avoid the mistakes and the disequilibria arising in the development of the West, a reasonable desire which offers serious difficulties in practical application.

Some Significant Differences from Modernization in Europe

Institutional Bases. Since all innovative proposals are assessed in part on the basis of pre-existing values and ethos, it follows that no two societies will respond to identical innovations in precisely the same manner (Eisenstadt). If India, for example, were faced with precisely the same innovative forces occurring in medieval Europe, the outcome would be different. Hinduism gives a different coloring to innovative perceptions from those engendered by medieval Roman Catholicism or, for that matter, Protestantism. Cultures are not chunks of putty upon which innovations make standard impressions. While many of the differences between the West and the recently traditional societies are matters of degree, some are of such substantial degree as to be qualitatively different.

An outstanding difference between *most* twentieth-century traditional societies and pre-modern Europe lies in the relative importance of extended families and kinship and quasi-kinship organization. A most pervasive organizing principle in Asian and in African societies is that of blood kinship. Frequently it is supported by ancestor worship or veneration. No comparable emphasis existed in Western Europe after the rise of feudalism. In Asian society, the descent groups and extended families were effectively accommodated to feudal structures where these arose. The demographer Frank Lorimer (pp. 154 ff.) has emphasized this contrast in referring to Western Europe as having been radically different in both values and social structure from the contemporary traditional societies. Unlike most of the present traditional world, Europe valued the nuclear family and, within the feudal estate, it was the major functional group.

Nuclear family groups are capable of greater mobility than are extended families. They are more individuated in the sense that members do not have the deep sense of personal commitment to larger stabilizing kin groups. Most crucial of all is the fact that the nuclear family, fortuitously perhaps, was closely congruent with the demands imposed by urban industrial life. As a residential unit particularly, extended and linear family organization is notably maladapted to modern urban life. The fact that such family groups are so multi-functional in many non-urban societies makes this a difference of fundamental importance in the contemporary transition. Adherence to large-family values in rural areas intensifies certain other problems, notably the resistance to family planning and restriction of birth.

Role of Government. A significant shift from earlier centuries is the role which the political state is expected to fulfill in the transition. While the Soviet model demonstrates the introduction of centralized state authority into the transition process, the creation of increasingly strong and multi-functional central governments is a major world-wide phenomenon of the twentieth century. The now transitional nations have avidly seized upon the new ideology and new concepts of governmental power and function.

Whereas the West embarked on the great transformation with faith in a guiding hand which directed the pursuit of self-interests toward the common good, no such naive naturalism is found among the new elites of the new nations. Bureaucrats and politicians are more powerful and prestigeful and entrepreneurs less so in these nations (Fallers, 1963). Almost universally the transitional peoples are looking for stimulation and control of development through governing systems that range from moderate socialism to totalitarian versions of Marxism. Faith in laissez faire and Spencerian evolutionary dynamics is utterly and absolutely dead.

In the twentieth century, socialism has replaced Protestantism as the basis of disciplined developmental drive, giving ethical and ideological motive power as well as structure to the transition (Apter; Fallers, 1963; Kerr; Cumper). Socialism and nationalism combine to yield tremendous drive toward change in the new, emerging leadership. Frequently a single political party arises and epitomizes these aspirations as it offers god-like features of leadership, a phenomenon which Horowitz has referred to as "party charisma." In this new concept of the state, the formation of capital and its allocation to the various sectors of development is planned and centrally controlled, partially or completely. The new centralized bureaucratic elites know greater power than did the "economic royalists" or "robber barons" of another age. Hiatuses and vacuums in institutional functioning, such as the breakdown of the urban family's capacity to educate its young or care for its aged are, theoretically at least, adjusted to through direct state action. Whereas the growth of the public sector of services was long delayed in the United States, the new ideology brooks no similar delay. The often shocking evidences of insecurity in the new urban life intensify support of the principles of the welfare state.

Demographic Transition. In the modernization of Western Europe, death rates were reduced as the result of greater food production, improvements in nutrition, better sanitation, and other innovations in the conservation of life (Wrong; Davis). As death rates were brought under control, following 1650, Europe had its "population explosion." However, while the net increase in population was rapid, there was also being set in motion a long-range trend of declining fertility. The conditions of life and the social values arising in the rapidly growing cities were unfavorable to the preservation of large family values. Paralleling almost three centuries of gradually declining death rates were similar though lagging trends in the birth rates. Over this long period European populations grew immensely but at gradually declining rates of growth and were hence moving toward eventual stabilization. It was also during these centuries that vast frontiers such as those of North America were opened to settlement and economic exploitation.

The phrase "demographic transition" has come into currency in reference to the transition of Western Europe from the demographic condition of high death rates associated with high birth rates to that position reached by the 1930's when death rates and birth rates were both low. Before the mid-nineteenth century, most modern nations were bringing population growth under fairly strict control and under circumstances favorable to good health and long life.

There are significant differences in the demographic transition of the contemporary developing nations. These societies, like Western ones, begin their process of modernization with high death rates and high birth rates. They, too, value long life and good health and have seized avidly upon modern drugs and pesticides toward these ends. In this they have succeeded with an effectiveness and rapidity far beyond the earlier European experience. Dramatic public health programs have reduced death in some transitional countries in a few years to points that took two and a half centuries to reach in the European experience. On the other hand, there has been no comparable rapidity in the decline of fertility. The result is, of course, sudden and consequential rises in the rate of natural increase. At current rates some of these countries will double their populations in one fourth the time this took European nations. The seriousness of this sudden growth is compounded since the new population explosions are from base populations of already staggering sizes. Nor do the present modernizing nations have extensive unexploited frontiers or colonies to serve both as quick sources of capital formation and as a safety valve through migration and settlement.

Given their present rates of natural increase, many transitional peoples have literally no place to go—except toward their own industrial development at incredible rates of speed. While urbanization seems likely ultimately to have depressing effects on fertility as it had in the West, these countries with their suddenly depressed death rates cannot afford the centuries that it took Europe to bring birth rates under control.[2] There are also cultural factors such as the power of extended families which could have a retarding effect on birth limitations not felt in Europe. Few if any reputable social scientists can conceive of successful economic development programs in these countries unless they are associated with crash programs to restrict population growth. Continuation of present growth rates in India for thirty years, for example, would require utterly fantastic growth in that economy simply to maintain the presently depressed level of living. It is understandable that many students of development view the demographic issue as the most crucial one of all for the success of the transitional nations in raising their levels of living. It is generally conceded that, however vigorously nations such as India pursue industrialization, births must be quickly restricted or the level of living will decline, health will suffer, and death rates rise again, a resolution which is universally unacceptable.

But there are additional demographic features of the latter twentieth century which suggest that birth rates may indeed be brought under control more rapidly than was true for the West. These differences include the changed state of technology in contraception and the greater rational planning and control exercised by modern states and the extremely effective modern agencies of diffusion available today throughout the world. For the first time in history simple and effective contraceptive devices are in production which are adapted to mass use in underdeveloped countries. Promoted through vigorous, governmentally supported organizations and using a wide range of communication media, small-family values along with contraceptive technology may be diffused with remarkable rapidity.

New International Relationships.   The twentieth century provides an utterly different context of political alignments and market arrangements from those ever known in the past. Western Europe, excluding the Soviet, developed industrially through exploitation of precisely those lands now seeking development. The new nations' spurt toward development arises through collaborative and reciprocal international understandings rather than through colonialism or economic imperialism. Significant for developmental funding is the political ability to manipulate the world power blocs, particularly those associated with the United States and with the Soviet.

---

[2] There are some developing nations wherein small but significant declines in fertility are taking place (Freedman et al., 1964). Even small declines in fertility are important for economic development. Ansley Coale and Edgar M. Hoover (cf. Dennis Wrong, 1964) have estimated that at present rates of economic growth, India's per-capita income would increase by nearly 40 per cent if the birth rate fell by one-half in one generation.

Estimated Population for Selected World Regions *

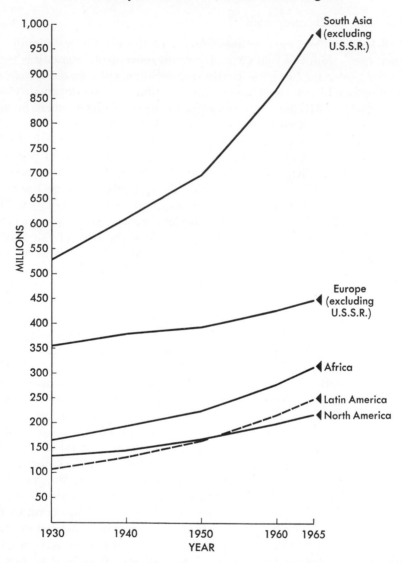

Until almost recent times populations in undeveloped regions had grown slowly, due to high death rates. Particularly since the 1940's, death rates in these regions have declined sharply but birth rates have not. By 1965, the population of Asia, excluding the Soviet, had reached 1,830,000,000. The annual rate of increase in South Asia was 2.5% between 1960–65. For Latin America it was 2.8%. These rates contrast with 1.5% annual increase in North America in the same years. Present rates of natural increase suggest astronomical population growth for Latin America, Africa, and Asia in the immediate future.

* Based on *Statistical Yearbook, 1966,* United Nations, New York, 1967, Table 2, p. 26.

Leadership in Development

The Role of the City. Although many of the disquietive stimuli for change come from rural unrest and peasant movements, the city is typically the center for formal leadership in development and the source or mediating point from which innovations are diffused. Heterogenetic cities (see pages 316–317 above) inherently are modernizing in their impact both upon their own populations and upon their hinterlands.

The transitional nations and regions are predominately rural. India, for example, with its one fifth of the human race has over 80 per cent of its population living in rural areas. While an important aspect of modernization is industrialization with attendant urban growth, the secular impact of the modern city does not require its subjects to live within the city confines. The heterogenetic or "generative" city is a focal point from which the country side is stimulated along the path of the Master Trend (Hoselitz, 1960, pp. 185–215; Davis). Much as this was true in the dissemination of the secular pattern in the West, it is true today in Africa, Asia, and Latin America. In most locales, the urban influences first are felt through the migrants themselves, but everywhere the channels of impact on the countryside are multiple and include a flow of urban workers back to their villages. From the "new" city goes direction and coordination of educational institutions in the hinterland; from urban-centered educational centers flow the teachers themselves. In the city is the radio station with news of the political and scientific worlds given in regional dialects along with advice to farmers and housewives and health counsel. Newspapers circulate outward as do the orders of governments. The regional metropolis does not create all of this knowledge, but for the peasant it originates interest and mediates the knowledge coming from the world beyond. International wire services, air freight lines, consulates, embassies, technical aid experts, politicians, and professors are all engaged in diffusing news of the world in the broadest possible sense. Many of these agencies are also engaged in coordinating, sifting, interpreting, and digesting the various informations before they are disseminated by the regional media. Even the boundary-jumping media like the BBC and the Voice of America are interpreted against an intellectual background influenced by the regional city-centered media and organization.

As once remote villages are brought into the orbit of national political and economic programs they perforce participate in urban type and urban-centered social structures. The market is organized through regional or national entrepôts. Rural extension or development programs are of secular type, oriented toward city-based planners and politicians. The political ties and organizations have focal points in the city. Even political revivalists of tradition paradoxically rely upon the secularizing means of radio and special interest groups and publics to gain and hold their power.

There are signs in some transitional countries that urban growth has run ahead of industrialization and that the drift to the city has been only in part due to the economic opportunity there. Rural people have migrated to escape the violence and the multiple insecurities and oppressions in the bush and countryside. Although the masses of unemployed and partially employed people in these cities are a source of unrest, this unrest stimulates change as it produces political and social instability.

The Roles of Entrepreneurs and Intellectuals. Leadership in the modernization of traditional countries appears to be centered in two categories, the "entrepreneurs" and the "intellectuals." From the entrepreneurial group has come the dynamics and guidance for development in the business and industrial sectors. From the intellectuals has come the political and ideological leadership to unify new states, blue-print their hopes, maintain solidarity, and hopefully to manipulate the entrepreneurs and the international power blocks. Everett Hagen and David C. McClelland, respectively, find the entrepreneur the leader and driving power behind modernization processes (see above, Chap. 2). Edward Shils (1960) and some other sociologically oriented social scientists have viewed the intellectual as the broader leader in innovation and development, at least for Asia and Africa. Shils argues convincingly that the conception, birth, and continuing life of the new states of Asia and Africa are in large measure the work of intellectuals. In no national formations in all of human history, he believes, have intellectuals played such a role as they have in the events of the present century.

Shils finds that so long as the intellectuals of the underdeveloped countries pursued paths of constitutional reform, their actions conformed to interests of traditional elites and power structures within these countries. However, for various reasons, socialist ideas fired the rising intelligentsia after World War I. Shils suggests that the socialism of intellectuals in the underdeveloped nations arises from their pained awakening to the misery of their own people (p. 347). This new awareness was epitomized in the title Jawaharlal Nehru gave his autobiography, *The Discovery of India*. The widespread unemployment of young Asian intellectuals no doubt furthered their disillusionment with the traditional social structure.

Shils' observations apply less well to Latin America. Latin American governments are more frequently dominated by landowning aristocracies who favor modernization enthusiastically up to the point that it does not interfere with their own economic and political dynasties. For Latin

America there is more to be said for Hagen's or McClelland's view of the significance of entrepreneurs in initiating the developmental processes. Needless to say, the conflict of power between traditionalized vested interests and the newer socialistic nationalism is present to some extent in all transitional countries.

A governing elite, whether it be carried over from earlier times or is a rising nationalistic and socialistic "charismatic party," must perforce take a stand in reference to the entrepreneurs. In some developing nations the entrepreneurs become a managerial class in a socialistic government. Elsewhere they emerge as independent operators seeking and sometimes gaining ascendency in economic, if not in political, spheres. In parts of the Middle East and Latin America, governments resist *economic* development as dangerous to themselves but may seek development in less threatening spheres (Blanksten; Jacobs). Elsewhere enterprisers, either as free agents or as government bureaucrats, are integrated into a design given broader direction and leadership by the new intellectual elite. This, perhaps outside of Latin America, is the more familiar structure of developmental leadership (cf. Eisenstadt, 1961, pp. 30 ff.; Lipman; Silvert).

The Master Trend in Developing Societies

There is substantial evidence that trends in the social organization of developing societies follow in broad outline those patterns earlier observed in the Western nations. Some of these patterns are virtual corollaries of urban, industrial community life. No doubt other features of the Western transition are responses which, but for accident of circumstances, might well not have appeared and may not appear elsewhere. For example, it is difficult to conceive of modernization anywhere without increasing scale in social relationships. On the other hand, it is plausible that the anomie found in rising Western cities would not be reproduced under conditions of nationalistic or other ideological fervor and organization.

It is probable that the half-truths involved in the alleged rise of "mass culture" and "mass society" in the West are about equally half-true of the developing societies. For most members of the transitional societies, the introduction of standardized machine products is, for example, inescapable and to the detriment of certain of the traditional arts and crafts. But the fact remains that these mass products fill a vacuum created by the scarcity and the cost of hand-tooled items—making them inaccessible to most citizens. The diffusion of mass culture is the diffusion of new horizons in the amenities of life. As for "mass society," there is no question but that the rationalization of economic life creates pressures toward increased differentiation, instrumentalism, contractualism, and mobility. In Redfield's terms the "technological order" is extended and in Tönnies' the shift is in the direction of the *Gesellschaft* (see above, Chap. 11). Erstwhile primitives and peasants move toward participation in a segmental and depersonalized social world, sometimes referred to as "mass society." However, the semantics of "mass culture" and "mass society" are such that the terms will be avoided in this discussion (see above, Chap. 13).

Increasing Scale in Social Relationships. As Godfrey and Monica Wilson have emphasized, a fundamental feature of change in developing nations is the increased range in relationships and interdependencies among people. This process is central for an understanding of many derivative changes such as segmentalization of social contacts, increased scope of instrumental relationships, and the rise of associational type special interest groups.

The extent of the breakdown in space- and time-limited social relations is dramatized as the Wilsons remark that the scope of Nyakyusa society a short time ago included perhaps 250,000 souls and ten past generations but today the modern Central African community takes into account nearly the whole population of the world and perhaps 7,000 generations. In the context of traditional communities in the peasant Middle East, Daniel Lerner has expressed this phase of "expanding scale" in a different manner. He refers to the traditional society as being "non-participant" in contrast with modern industrial, urban, literate society which he dubs "participant society." He writes that:

. . . among the marks of this historic achievement in social organization, which we call Participant Society, are that most people go through school, read newspapers, receive cash payments in jobs they are legally free to change, buy goods for cash in an open market, vote in elections . . . and express opinions on many matters which are not their personal business.

Especially important for the Participant Style is the enormous proportion of people who are expected to "have opinions" on public matters. . . . "How can you ask me such a question?" [What he would do if he were head of the government?] gasped the Balgat shepherd. His gasp resounded often in our interviews around the Middle East. [Lerner, pp. 50–51.] *

The increasing scale of participation through secondary and primary means has counterparts in subjective realities. Lerner found that the most fundamental change in persons in transitional societies is their development of the ability to empathize. This he would place as the basic socio-psychological difference between traditional man and modern secular man. Traditional man becomes modern man as he learns to par-

* Reprinted with the permission of The Macmillan Company. From *The Passing of Traditional Society: Modernizing The Middle East* by Daniel Lerner with the collaboration of Lucille W. Pevsner and an introduction by David Riesman. Copyright 1958 by the Free Press, A Corporation.

ticipate vicariously in the broader world and place himself imaginatively in a situation far different from the one that he is in. In this shift the bases for an individual's dynamic assessment of further novelty have been charged.

Nowhere has this broadening involvement been better documented than in regard to expanding economic relationships. With recognition of dependence upon world markets comes the quest for information on the forces which affect them—and on the techniques of controlling or of adjusting to them. In the Sinhalese village of Pelpola the introduction of rubber stirred village folk to such recognition as they discovered that the prices they received fluctuated in response to far-off events. These events, ranging from newly competitive synthetics to the consequences of war, brought price shifts which the villager could, if well informed, turn to his own advantage (Ryan *et al.*, 1958). General literacy, daily newspapers, radios, and geography classes in school developed and expanded the economically stimulated interests. Pius Ikigho has shown how increasing efficiency in palm oil production enlarged the exchange economy of the villager in West Africa, eroded the subsistence sector of village economy, and yielded broader and more depersonalized interdependencies.

Of no less importance than expanding economic ties are the newly developed political and cultural identities beyond the confines of locality and even region. As village folk are brought out of their isolation there is frequently a conflict among the larger units with which they are to identify. In Africa, emancipation from both localism and colonial rule yielded conflict as tribes bid for power in the new "national states." Expanding scale for the new African city dweller is evidenced in a broadening of national identity. In reference to a Johannesburg slum, E. Hellman (pp. 179–190) has argued that common persecution, suffering, and disillusionment have been supported by intertribal marriage to make the African a Bantu citizen and not merely a tribesman with parochial loyalties.

In South Asia, as the emancipated villager learns to identify with the nation frequently he is torn between the nationalistic movements of his ethnic group and the newer nationalism of his political state, which presumably subsumes parochial loyalties. While political scale is indeed broadening, it would seem that in some regions the jump to a culturally heterogeneous political state is asking too much too quickly of peoples bred to seek their security in primary groups and communities with a homogeneous heritage.

Differentiated Relationships and Group Structures. The specialization of occupational life is paralleled by the specialization of groups serving individuals and in which social wants are satisfied. One of the most profound aspects of increasing differentiation is in its effect upon traditional family organization with its multi-functional encompassment of the individual.

THE URBAN BREAKDOWN OF EXTENDED FAMILIES. The reordering of group structures has been most obvious in those regions which traditionally held strong and extended families. This is especially true where urbanward migration and industrialization have been rapid. Modern society with its non-agricultural, wage-earning, impersonally organized work groups is a direct threat to traditional familial structures which involve large residential units structured upon descent principles. The new work groups are especially tension-evoking when such extended or joint families have been producing as well as consuming groups. Ralph Linton expressed the matter succinctly when he observed that modernizing economic change is always destructive to a joint family system. He suggested an important motivational link in accounting for the disorganization of such units.

It can be stated as a theorem, valid in a very high percentage of cases, that the greater the opportunity for individual economic profit, provided by the social-cultural situation, the weaker the ties of extended kinship will become. [Linton, 1952, pp. 82–83.]

The diminishment of extended family functioning is associated as much with social value changes as with industrial organization and mobility (Moore, 1961, pp. 76–77; Nash). The modern concept of the "good life" simply does not include the submergence of individuals into a strong decision-making extended family group. The emancipation of the individual in Western social transition included his emancipation from patriarchalism and "groupism" as a basis for personal decision making. It probably is similarly interpreted in many strong family, strong kinship societies now undergoing the similar transformation. While the evidence is not firm, it is reasonable to believe, for example, that the arrangement of marriage by kinsmen will suffer in India as individuals increasingly seek security in a competitive, impersonal world, rather than in the primary, familistic one.

Jean L. Comhaire has found that under some local circumstances the survival of extended households is remarkable. However, where *residential* kin groups do not largely disappear in the urban setting, this is likely to be mainly an evidence of economic distress as poverty stricken newcomers seek refuge in the households of their slightly more established city dwelling kinsmen (Ryan and Fernando).

INCREASES IN ASSOCIATIONAL AND MASS PARTICIPATION. The modification of the extended family is associated with the relatively increased significance of the conjugal or nuclear group and also with the parceling out of former primary group functions among special interest associations and bureaucratic agencies of the state. As we have seen, one must keep in touch with the activities of many diverse persons and groups, personally unfamiliar to him, in order to protect his interests in the wide-scale dependencies of modern life. Even in the rural areas, as villagers seek social and economic efficiency and its bonuses in better health and amenities, they are brought into this new differentiated life. The villager must orient his life to some extent in reference to businesses in the commercial town or city, the new health service, the secondary school, and the various governmentally inspired programs and special interest groups which may aid him in satisfying these newly satisfiable wants associated with a longer, easier—albeit more complicated—life. Robert R. Smithers, a field worker in community development programs, has found that the growth of secondary groups is a crucial stage in carrying forward economic programs.

In the city itself the process of formal and special interest group formation is heightened for many reasons. These include the very massiveness of the community and the necessary impersonality in many relationships, industrial employment and hence wage earning and mobility, and the fact that more people live outside such multi-purpose groups as the family. Manning Nash has shown how industrialization is associated with the rise of voluntary organizations increasing in the wake of industrialization, particularly as these are directly connected with wage work, e.g., labor unions, and with the creation of political interest. K. Busia and E. Hellman (pp. 724–743) respectively, report that in African cities, there are flourishing occupational associations, trade unions, and recreational and political organizations. The performance of funeral rites and benefits for members are common among these groups. It should not be implied that migrating peasants rapidly become joiners in the sense of "Mainstreet" or "Middletown." Very widely participation and security are found by new city immigrants through less formal and more traditional group mechanisms. Some scholars are more impressed by the lack of impersonal special interest group affiliation in the "new" cities than by its presence (Abu-Lughod; Hauser). But new directions are evidenced nonetheless.

Familiarity with bureaucratic structuring is essential for participation in the local branch of the national credit association, in gaining admission to a government hospital, or in making a report to the police. These are all phases of both urban and rural modernization which require a transition from the usually informal, personalized devices through which these needs were once satisfied. To be sure, credit with the traditional landlord or money lender was not always "personalized," but it was scarcely an introduction to bureaucratic organization. Villages which understand little of formal organizational structure must now create and maintain these innovative types of group structures. Where traditional communities had, as some did have, organized special interest groups, no doubt the transition to new group forms is more rapid and fraught with less fumbling, corruption, and cross purposes.

With increasing interest in the outside world and participation in money economy, new audience and mass communication participation habits are acquired which serve to further entrench the modernizing process. One must journey far into remote areas today to find peasants who have not seen moving picture shows, a new form of group participation. Mass participation situations have always occurred in peasant recreational and religious life, but now there is a more typically urban audience in which participation is with unknown others of diverse origin. And here too the informational impact, unlike the traditional audience situation, does not serve to reinforce traditional interests and values— quite the contrary if the source of a movie has been Hollywood or of a radio program the BBC, Voice of America, or Moscow.

TRADITIONAL TYPE GROUPS ARISE OR CONTINUE TO FUNCTION. Under conditions of chaotic migration as has been true in certain of the burgeoning African cities, the nuclear family and surrounding closely bonded groups seem always to reassert themselves and to offer at least some replacement for the emotional and personal securities of the traditional kin and village. Janet Abu-Lughod has observed that in Cairo with one third of its population village migrants, newcomers quickly form benevolent associations and protective ghettos reminiscent of the responses of European peasant migrants to American cities at the turn of the century. Similar responses occur in West African cities based on bonds of tribal affiliation (Busia, p. 84). It should be remembered too that in such rapidly changing environments, individuals may live in what superficially seems like primary group chaos while actually retaining strong ties to spouse and kin in the village. Continuous physical association is not essential for the preservation of strong affective and economic ties. The continued existence of village groups, although weakened perhaps by emigration of members, provides an orderly route of transition from the traditional pattern of group structure to the typically urban. "My village," is a phrase and concept which many urban workers hold dear as a constant reminder of their emotional ties with their personal past and, if necessary, their insurance policy against some future crisis.

Just as the kin and the home village may long provide emotional securities, even with diminishing overt functions, traditional village recreational and work groups do not dissolve before the town bazaar and the cinema. In some relationship spheres, reciprocities stand alongside money-mediated relationships for many years. The Hindu jajmani system of reciprocity in services between castes has remarkable tenacity (Wiser). Erosion of the old relationships is taking place unevenly, but few services are lost without marketed ones to replace them. It would be hazardous to say whether monetary relationships arise when vacuums occur in village reciprocities or that contractualism drives out status reciprocation. Money, no doubt, opens the road to "contamination" of fixed status obligations. As a jungle village headman said: "Once money passes between us [fellow villagers] we can never be the same again."

Despite the strain, there is no reason to think that cooperative groups and reciprocities must all melt rapidly away as villagers come into contact with cities. Our experience in the distinctive patterns of Western Europe and North America probably leads us to exaggerate the degree to which modernizing nations must conform to the Western pattern. Abegglen, among others, has described in detail how traditional, noncontractual relationships survive even in the highly developed industrial setting of modern Japan. Even less evidence is there to support the view that the commercial and impersonal recreations of city life displace the traditional neighboring, gossiping, and gaming. Much of the new is additional to much of the old.

Where traditional bonds fail to form a realistic basis for primary, mutual-aid groups in the city, traditional concepts of cooperation are built into groups united by new types of bonds. In the African cities groups of neighboring couples eat together; persons bearing the same Christian name join in mutual-aid groups as do persons of the same sex within some neighborhoods (Busia; Hellman, pp. 724–743). Spontaneous groups of endless variety and varying degrees of formality cut across traditional bonds of tribe and kin, representing innovative adaptations of folk experience in adjustment to the conditions of urban living.

Even in matters of folklore, traditional dances, etc., the evidence of threat from the Westernized city has been strong motive power behind revivalistic social movements to preserve the old ways at almost any cost. The organizational devices of the new order are aroused to preserve certain aspects of the old, as village schools teach world geography at the nine o'clock hour and traditional lore at the ten o'clock—and the government radio blares traditional music, as well as jazz, in the lunch hour. Where traditional garb and traditional symbols and customs are not demoted by a new set of status values of urban origin, there is room for the integration of much of the traditional with the modern.

Achieved Positions Emphasized.   Not all traditional societies have had rigidly ascribed status systems. Probably the ascription of prestige and power positions is more common in traditional agricultural societies than in primitive ones. Nonetheless when we consider all positions, i.e., all statuses with attached roles in the broad senses of these words, there is unquestionably greater dependence upon birth and the automatic allocation of expectations and duties in traditional than in modern societies. The rationalism of modern society in the allocation of function on the basis of demonstrable ability presses toward the valuation of individual achievement along with individual rewards for so achieving. Additionally, equality of opportunity to rise in the social order has become an almost universal value sought on ethical grounds as well as rational ones. In the present connection we are concerned primarily with the ideas of status in its prestigeful, and power-and-rank connotations. Loosely, we may say that our concern is with shifts in social class and with the disintegration of estate and caste systems as societies enter the modernizing transition.

The ultimate test of the affects of modernization on an ascribed status system is that of India. Practically all students of the Indian caste system recognize the disruptive effects of modern urban influences (both way of life and associated social values) upon the traditional status structure. The various transitions described under other headings as aspects of modernization make virtually impossible the retention of discriminations and rituals rooted in birth, especially as birth status is not reflected in physical stigmata. This is only a little less true in village life than city, when it is oriented to the expanding, rationally differentiated urban world. The righteousness of birth position falls before the new righteousness of position through individual action. The economically impersonal, rational, contractual, and segmental relations of modern life set an environment in which the old values would in any case perish. As David Morris points out, in spite of the almost proverbial strength of the caste system, the industrialization of India is proceeding with almost total disregard for it.

Modernization requires functional conformity between achievement aspirations and the motivational requirements for economic development. Prestigious occupational roles in traditional societies have often had little relationship to the prerequisites of economic rationality, even when achieved. Nonetheless they are supported by various institutions, especially the educational. For example, regardless of monetary reward and economic requirements of the society, upwardly mobile persons in many transitional societies carry over a traditional disvaluation of work with the hands or even business enterprise. The particular nature of this value syndrome varies from place to place, but achievement channels in many transitional societies are almost monopolized by a tiny educated elite who achieve through soft-handed and often not very productive clerical work. In some places entrepreneurial activities, like toil, are still tarred by the traditionalist brush as beyond the pale of decent society. Barring perhaps revolutions as in China, such prestige achievement systems will probably compete with alternative ones for many years in many countries.

Tumin has outlined the main features of the transition in stratification in a work emphasizing its industrial aspects. Some of his generalizations are (1) there is an increasing division of labor with correlative complexity in social status, (2) status tends to be allocated on the basis of achievement rather than ascription, (3) traditional rewards for work which derived from the social relations enjoyed in work itself are replaced by pecuniary rewards, (4) as industrialization increases the gross product, there are increasing total rewards to be distributed among those who effectively achieve, and (5) there is also a general tendency toward greater equality of rewards among various sectors and levels of society. It is also suggested by Alex Inkeles that with modernization there is a trend toward greater homogeneity in any given person's social status, that is, his standing on any one stratification scale tends to be the same as his standing on any of all other scales of stratification. Finally, the gap between the upper and the lower sectors of society narrows in regard to "life chances" and the economic welfare indices.

The least problematic and most certain trend in status associated with modernization is the narrowing of spheres within which ascribed positions are significant. Thus the modern Indian still belongs to his caste and marries within his caste, but this ascription is rapidly becoming insignificant for any form of discrimination and has increasingly little to do with any form of prestige ranking which matters. The routes to high status are through the achievement complex with its familiar pattern of educational and occupational mobility. Although social class formation in dynamic societies is difficult to study and to assess, there is substantial evidence of the formulation of social classes in something of the sense that these are manifest in Western, industrial communities. The evidence from Africa shows clear signs of social cohesion along status lines which often cut across tribal and kinship solidarities (Parker). Similarly in South Asia social classes coalesce in the urban community cutting across the boundaries of caste and creating new loyalties and new interactional patterns centered upon position in the urban occupational-educational-economic world of achievement (Ryan, 1953, Pt. 4).

Anomie, Alienation, and Disengagement. As village folk flood into the burgeoning slums of the new cities, they must adjust to an utterly new way of life with the dubious supports of poverty, economic insecurity, and illiteracy. Under such conditions, it would be easy to assume that widespread normative confusion reigns, that individuals feel bereft of satisfying relationships with both work and with meaningful others. While the social and psychological shocks of serious re-adjustment undoubtedly exist in these circumstances, evidence that the migrants are generally anomic, alienated, and disengaged is mixed and unsensational in degree (Mangin; Abu-Lughod; Erasmus).

Studies of many mushrooming cities in Africa south of the Sahara indicate serious and widespread overcrowding, malnutrition, crime, and disease (UNESCO). But they also find preservation of tribal identities and strong and active ties to the home village and kin. Studies among migrants to rapidly developing industrial centers elsewhere in the world also suggest that, whatever the real pathologies in urban living, the newcomers do not generally suffer from conditions of anomie and psycho-social isolation. In fact, Erasmus has discovered in the current status of Yucatan that anomie is more evident in the villages than in the city. Quite possibly the lessened opportunity and hopelessness of peasant life as contrasted with the buoyant opportunities of the city contribute to a sense of goallessness and personal ineffectiveness. In Egypt, Janet Abu-Lughod reports that migrants to the city exhibit little evidence of anonymity and social isolation in view of the variety of institutions they have built which protect them from the shock of anomie. Studying poor migrants in Lima, Peru, William Mangin similarly observes:

> Some current (and ancient) writings in social science would lead us to expect that the low-status migrants whose culture differs most from that of the dominant group will suffer severe stress and exhibit disorganized and mal-adaptive behavior supposedly characteristic of people in the trans-culturation situation. The problem is enormously complex and has been studied minimally, but my own four-year study in Peru does not support this expectation. The important factors in the adjustment of migrants to Lima seem to have relatively little to do with migration as such. Many are faced with the necessity of learning new patterns in a short time, but my data indicate that they do so in a manner characteristic of their response to problems in the mountains. Drastic changes in personality were not found among the respondents, and changes in the degree and nature of social participation seemed to be largely within the control of the individual; that is, a man who desires either more or less contact with kinsmen and/or *paisanos* can usually arrange it either way . . . [Mangin, p. 547.]

It is probable that crime rates in the "new" cities are relatively high and may reflect some rejection of normative standards in the pursuit of reasonable goals of economic security and advancement. However, any way the evidence is read, there is little or no support for belief in extensive social disengagement or the psycho-social isolation of individuals. Associated with this is a lack of evidence that mental disorders are particularly prevalent among urban migrants and some tentative evidence in some developing locales that urban mental disorders are no higher than for the rural population.

Changes in Material Culture. It is perhaps obvious that material culture changes toward "Western" type goods in the modernization process. Indeed, a driving force behind the whole movement toward modernization lies in achieving these material fruits of a secular, industrial society. Even more rapid than mechanization of productive equipment in many regions is the importation of drugs, pesticides, canned milk, bicycles, jack knives, and sewing machines—the consumer goods and scientific procedures which make life longer and physically easier. Closely associated with these prosaic devices and sometimes preceding them are goods which are gratifying stylistically or evoke and symbolize status in the secularizing order of status. Fountain pen clip-caps are reported to stick out of coat pockets of African illiterates; elsewhere "store" haircuts are demanded by the modern sons of proudly long-haired fathers (cf. Erasmus).

Typically the expensive household and family equipment of the West moves into the urban centers of developing countries. In most of these cities, whether Bogotá, Calcutta, Bangkok, or Durban, discrepancies in income are associated with great class distinctions, with the majority of the population living fairly close to the survival level. Western-type equipment becomes both an amenity of the wealthy and a symbol of wealth and high position. In a well-to-do home of Colombo an electric refrigerator, holding mainly cold drinks and ice, may be alongside art objects in dining room or living room. A luxury and a symbol, it has little to do with cookery. In very many regions, a substantial proportion of the urban population live more like peasants in their material culture than they do like their wealthy urban countrymen. Industrial goods are "cheap" and plentiful, but they are not cheap to a laborer living in the kind of squalor the pay scale of Bogotá, Calcutta, or Durban requires. If trinkets often precede more substantial purchases, price is a significant factor (Hoyt).

Aspiration for the products of industry is another story. As old orthogenetic cities are transformed into industrial ones and new cities are created, the production of equipment for the secular society competes with and gradually replaces traditional crafts and traditional consumer goods as well.

Some new nations, for various reasons, have more decentralized industrial development than characterized youthful North America. Here village people are directed into industrial occupations without migration to cities as places of residence (Nash). Handicrafts diminish as the new machines require human specialization so that their efficiency may be utilized. The worker is increasingly surrounded by power tools, often brought into curious transitional arrangement with persisting crafts and traditional power sources. In a rural veneer manufacturing plant in

Southern Ceylon, a modern electric-powered log-peeling machine is served by an elephant dragging the logs to the "ready" position. But, nonetheless, power equipment, specialized machine operation, and assembly line organization are coming into the experience world of the village.

There is some legitimate evidence and a large mythology regarding the resistances of folk peoples to rational economic productive devices. This is a matter discussed more fully in earlier chapters, but let it be repeated that there is often a solid reason for such resistance. Frequently these assessments are completely logical and sometimes based upon sounder perceptions than those of the "salesman" of the devices. In general, traditional peoples are probably much as Sol Tax and Ralph Beals, respectively, described the Guatemalan and the Mexican Indian. Beals says:

> . . . the Indian is not averse to change which will improve his economic situation.
>
> In the main the Mexican Indian then does not have sharp rejection patterns to those things which have "practical" value. . . . I have tried to follow up the negative reaction toward steel plows, radios, etc., and invariably I found that the Indian gave his initial reaction, not because he did not want these things, but because he did not wish to admit that he either could not afford them or did not know how to go about getting them. Perhaps the strongest argument in Mexico is the almost universal presence of the sewing machine and mechanical corn grinders, including power-driven machines. In the case of the sewing machine, its wide distribution is related to a credit and sales policy which has been adapted to the Indian economy . . . [Tax, p. 231.] *

One should not conclude that the entire world is moving toward the replication of some "average" between the United States and Western European countries. However, increasing quantities of machine-made, mass-produced, efficient consumer goods flow from similarly constructed factories in many parts of the world. Those who decry the trend toward uniformity and the decline of handicrafts must at least confess world-wide increases in levels of physical comfort, leisure, and health. The game of deploring the introduction of "Western materialism" is played by well-fed nationalists, who support traditional "spiritual values" and peasant life from the vantage point of a well-staffed villa with a Bentley or Mercedes in the garage. If all regions are becoming more similar in their material goods, as in their social values, they are surely becoming so in their own distinctive fashions. No amount of mass-produced consumer goods can obliterate the differences between the complexly traditioned polyglot

Hindu workers of Bengal and the newly Americanized, polyglot sons of Europe and Africa in the U.S. industrial city. Change proceeds by functional adjustments, some of which are necessarily similar to those made in the West, but syncretic processes are also at work reconciling and fusing these responses to the local ethos.

The Scientific Viewpoint. Not only does the body of functional knowledge and equipment become broader with modernization, its roots grow in different soils. All societies have a large amount of empirically tested, pragmatically derived knowledge as well as magical techniques. However, Western civilization has brought to a peak refined methods of knowledge acquisition and especially its verification. It is generally true that wherever man's empirically grounded controls over natural forces are weak, his utilization of supernatural controls tends to be high. Furthermore, when empirically derived knowledge can change very slowly, greater emphasis is placed upon the retention of workable knowledge and techniques than upon their extension. Practical technology tends to be ritualized and may even be given sacred standing. The limited technical truths of traditional societies have supported them through all time, and this indeed is one critical test of validity. Where refined means have not been developed for discovering and verifying seemingly improved knowledge, what surer safeguard is there than the test of time? And where time is the crucial test, the authority for truth lies with those who most perfectly preserve tradition.

Modern rationalism and scientific method cut into both supernaturalism and traditionalism to upset old truths, old authorities, and the very way of looking at the nature of truth itself. Knowledge of electricity has no roots in peasant constructs of lightning storms; insecticides are not to be understood through traditional knowledge either worldly or sacred. While the new theories are not necessarily in contradiction to the old, the bulk of them have limited consistency with traditional ideas and require new concepts of authority in knowledge and new tests of validity. Schools oriented to the relativity of knowledge and the scientific method must introduce either rejections or circumscriptions of the traditional truths. In the secular world that which is true is that which verifiably works. The ethos of modernization, like that of science, is pragmatic and systematically experimental. The mastery of nature toward the satisfaction of man's material wants is an unrealistic goal for societies which have not grounded their truths in science.

The transformation implied here is not a matter readily subject to direct measurement. (One is reminded of the anthropology student who began his interview by asking the aboriginal, "And what is your world view?") We are dealing with a transformation in modes of viewing reality, nature, supernature, time, and truth. Perhaps the best evidence of transition must lie in concrete behavior: the new valuations are manifest in scientific laboratories; the growth of clientele in Western-type medical clinics; the use of savings for gadgets and productive equipment—in contrast to religious uses; the use of clocks; etc. And, while attitudinal evidence is not substantial, it is probable that feelings of dependence upon supernatural powers diminish, as does faith in the ancestors to provide the guide-lines of the future.[3] Such changes need not be revolutionary ones. Like other phases of the transition, scientific truths can be integrated as accommodated specialties or alternatives or through syncretic integration with magical and folk beliefs (see above, Chap. 10).

In Asia, Africa, and Latin America men are demanding emancipation from the grasp of natural forces and the equally tenacious power of traditional authorities. The transition involves greater personal freedom through a technology that liberates man from the excesses of drought and flood just as it involves freedom to move within a more flexible social hierarchy. In these senses we add a final dimension to the direction of change found in recently traditional societies. The first traditions which the masses of men move to destroy are those of traditionalistic authority and the traditions of poverty in their technology, health, and life chances. "We are people too."

Lags and Leads in Development

Changes which arise in social development occur neither simultaneously nor in any universal sequential pattern. As Louis Horowitz (p. 335) has put it, "sectors develop rather than societies." And the order of their precedence in change varies from society to society. It is perhaps partly for this reason that some social scientists have expressed dissatisfaction with "master trend," evolutionary theory (Hauser, 1961; Lewis, 1951). They have observed developing countries in which certain theoretically expected qualities of transition have not been clearly evidenced, at least at the moment of observation. While it is the function of a social science of development constantly to qualify theory with reference to new observations, it is probable that this lack of conformity between theory and observation is more the product of differential rates of sector development than evidence of the gross insufficiency of the theory itself. Obviously the theory of the "master trend" is at best valid only in broad patterns. The task remains of determining conditions under

[3] It is precisely because the requirements of development threaten ethnic identities and traditional truths that we find such vigorous movements of nationalist and cultural revivalism in the midst of pressures toward modernization. This seeming paradox is extremely widespread. For examples see various chapters in Clifford Geertz, (ed.), 1963; Wriggins, 1960.

which variations within these patterns arise and the conditions under which certain sectors of the society advance more rapidly than others.

Traditional Societies with Developed Sectors. A paradox of colonialism is that certain limited sectors of life in generally undeveloped contemporary societies have already been very highly developed. While this is less true of Africa, it is not uncommon in Latin America and in Asia. Such development has occurred particularly in the realm of governmental organization and specific economic affairs of concern to colonial powers. While these discrepancies may be thought of as "lags and leads," in the developmental process some of them are far from new in origin and come into the twentieth century firmly established in the social structures of the societies concerned.

Although the search for national political identity is an acute element of development practically everywhere, many colonies were left by their former rulers with viable governments of modern design. The structure of government in British India, for example, had many aspects of modern bureaucracy. Ceylon, Jamaica, and other of the small colonies entered the modern transition with well-developed parliamentary systems and fairly well-developed ministries and attendant services relating to roads, communications, health, and finance. The roots of modern government were superimposed upon peasant economies which were anything but modern. Such structures had at least provided experience to an elite in problems of governing and offered elemental blueprints for self-determined political development.

Considerable variation also has long existed within some of the traditional societies in regard to various social values and institutions. For example, a certain amount of erosion in caste relationships occurred under British influence in India—and considerably more in Ceylon. In India such early transition was particularly marked in regions of industrial concentration. The significant fact is that traditional values had been modified due largely but not exclusively to long-range changes which preceded the recent thrust toward national modernization.

In a strictly economic sense certain sectors of some generally undeveloped countries were highly developed, particularly through colonial enterprise. A case in point is development of commercial plantations in Indonesia and in Ceylon, the former under Dutch governance and the latter under British. The Ceylon tea industry is highly efficient, modern in soil conservation and other scientific agricultural practices, and rationally oriented toward world markets (International Bank, pp. 227–235). The problems of economic development relate to practically every other phase of the economy, but this sector has long been truly developed. To some extent similar observations might apply to certain latifundian systems in Latin America, as for example the enterprises of the Grace Lines and the United Fruit Company. In such circumstances the immediate developmental problems relate to realigning these sectors toward national development generally rather than toward the profits of "Western" shareholders. Discrepancies such as these are relatively less significant in India and China but may well be of importance in some African regions which have been minerally exploited by European powers.

Differences in Continuing Development. The various developing nations started from different points in regard to sectors of greatest traditionalism, and they also differ in the priority they give to various aspects of the transition. Some, for example, must first of all engage in nation building, whereas others may reasonably attach primacy to land reform and agricultural development, and still others to immediate industrialization. There is no fixed sequence of steps through which nations become modern, although there are certain principles of order which are more rational than others under given conditions. As for the priority given specific aspects of the transition, it is relevant that what "hurts most" is the economic privation of consumers. Consequently, improvement of the level of living is inherently a central goal in modernization. However, a rising level of living through economic growth is a complex matter and achievable through very complex means. Usually these include immediate restriction of consumer goods for the sake of capital accumulation along with numerous expensive non-economic programs basic to economic efficiency.

Wilbert Moore (1964) has likened the position of the new nation in its choice of steps to that of a shopper in a well-stocked supermarket who can select goods without regard to the time they were placed on the market's inventory. This is not, of course, literally true, but transitional countries are varied in their lags and their leads in developmental processes. Priorities are never based exclusively upon wholly rational grounds. Internal political pressures, ideologies of government officials, sensitivities to the feelings of an electorate, as well as straightforward mythology regarding the prerequisites of economic growth are all factors in determining which programs are given precedence.[4]

It is also apparent that the goals of development within a given country are not entirely self-consistent in other than a utopian sense. The immediate attainment of improved material amenities, for example, is inconsistent with the creation of capital for long-range industrialization.

[4] The problem of determining priorities in the allocation of effort and capital is an extremely difficult one and one for which there is no single answer. For evidence on a few of the varied complications, see references below to Norman Jacobs; Edgar A. and Kathryn R. Schuler; Mary Jean Bowman and C. Arnold Anderson; Joseph S. Vandiver; and Bert Hoselitz (1961).

The appeasement of militant minorities is frequently inconsistent with the rational regional allocation of limited capital resources or even the achievement of an efficient governing bureaucracy. All sectors cannot move uniformly since many goals are competitive with others and at least temporarily retard their achievement. Even more disordered is the transition when we consider trends which arise inadvertently in social organization as unplanned, and in some instances, undesired responses to the pursuit of conscious goals, e.g., shifts in family values and organization.

Generalizations as to priority patterns in developing countries are difficult to draw from the available literature. Illustrative, however, is the widespread tendency of governments to foster elaborate educational programs to the immediate detriment of capital allocation to other spheres. Bowman and Anderson have expressed strong qualifications as to the rationality of the extensive priority given formal educational programs in the developing countries. While they have found positive relationship between the level or spread of education and economic levels in developing nations the connections are very loose.

Although statistical comparisons in other spheres are generally lacking, it is apparent that governmental structure is highly developed in some countries which are notably retarded in their industrial development and may long continue to be. Political stability does not correlate closely with either economic growth or economic prosperity (Hoselitz and Weiner).

When we turn to the social organizational phases of modernization the evidence shows great disparity among the various sectors of the Master Trend. Tambiah and Ryan, for example, found that in Ceylon traditional family values remained more intact than did status and political values although all have shifted toward the modern "urban" pole. In an associated study, it was found that peasants in one area were highly modernized in their status values and aspirations and political attitudes but were traditional in their agricultural attitudes and technology (Ryan et al.). In many other countries as well, sharp contrasts are evident among the sectors of development.[5]

CONCLUSION

The broad currents of change which produced the urban and secular society of the West did not penetrate most of Asia, Africa, and Latin

[5] It is probable that few students of modernization fail to find lags and leads in the various phases and sectors of development. For a review of many studies see Robert J. Smith (1951). Cf. *Journal of Social Issues*, Vol. XIV, No. 4, 1958; papers in that issue by William W. Stein, Tom. J. Sasaki, and Charles C. Hughes are particularly pertinent.

America until almost the mid-twentieth century. Most of the people of the earth continued to live in societies more closely approximating the *folk* or *Gemeinschaft* type than the *urban* or *Gesellschaft* type. These predominately peasant peoples continued in this century to live in rural communities under the conditions of undeveloped resources, meager amenities of life, and uncontrolled birth and death rates. Sociologically the scale of life was limited, statuses frequently ascribed, and primary groups, especially familial, were strong and multi-functional. Such societies have commonly been termed "underdeveloped," "pre-industrial," and "traditional." Variations upon the general pattern were, of course, evident. Some were tribally organized while others lived within the great traditions of ancient civilizations; some were feudally structured, others largely composed of freeholding farmers or herders; some had colonial histories, and others did not. In many, certain limited sectors of the society and economy were modernized. Outside the tribal areas, social class gradations were typically sharp and class lines rigidly drawn.

Especially after World War II, these economically underdeveloped and traditional societies moved rapidly into the type of transition which had characterized the West. Political aspirations for national sovereignty were associated with vigorous demands for higher levels of living and freer avenues of vertical social mobility and achievement. The transition was rapidly manifest in the attainment of political sovereignty by numerous colonial societies and by the rapid introduction of dramatic public health and medical techniques. Industrialization was spurred as a means to greater national product and greater material welfare, and with it, urbanward migration and city life.

Guidance and overt assistance has been widely offered the transitional societies by both the United States and the Soviet Union. Both of these nations serve as models to the developing nations as they plan their own courses toward modernization. While the levels of living and industrial achievement of the United States are impressive, the rapidity and recency of the Soviet Union's growth is at least equally impressive. The contemporary transitional nations typically reject the nineteenth-century ideology of progress represented by the United States. Most demand that their governments take an active role in economic planning and development and in the provision of economic security and welfare.

The modernization process in the twentieth century holds different as well as similar developmental problems as were faced earlier in the West. In the present century many techniques of change are diffused rather than hammered out in trial and error processes. There is today little opportunity for developing nations to build upon colonial territories, or even frontier expansion, and world markets generally are utterly different than in preceding centuries.

Even amid political discordances, widespread illiteracy, inadequate capital formation and allocation, and a host of other major problems, the most potentially devastating is found in the demographic transition. Almost universally among developing nations death rates have been sharply cut while birth rates remain high. Natural increase in many of them is now so rapid as to more than cancel out their reasonable economic gains. While the long-range effects of urbanization will, as in the West, be associated with declining fertility, the next few decades impose the requirement of stringent controls on fertility if continued low death rates are to be maintained and effective economic growth achieved.

The modernization of the formerly traditional societies is much more complex than the achievement of health, longevity, and higher levels of living. With urbanization, traditional extended family systems are affected, giving way to nuclear forms of family life; impersonal relationships are increased, and segmental, special-interest associations arise to fulfill new functions or old ones once performed by primary groups. Even in social values such as individualism in achievement and in decision making, the modernizing societies approach the model of the secular West. However, despite general conformity to the functional requirements of an urban, economically rational social order, the new nations will not become replicas of any of the Western models. Not only does each begin its modernization process from its own distinctive cultural base, but within the broad patterns of development, alternative designs in growth must differ today from those which arose in the earlier developing Western nations.

References

CHAPTER 1

BOSKOFF, ALVIN. "Social Change: Major Problems in the Emergence of Theoretical and Research Foci," in Howard Becker and Alvin Boskoff, *Modern Sociological Theory in Continuity and Change*. New York: Holt, Rinehart & Winston, Inc., 1957. Chap. 9.

JOHNSON, HARRY M. *Sociology: A Systematic Introduction*. New York: Harcourt, Brace and World, Inc., 1960.

LOOMIS, CHARLES P. *Social Systems: Essays on Their Persistence and Change*. Princeton, N. J.: D. Van Nostrand Co., Inc., 1960.

LYNES, RUSSELL. *A Surfeit of Honey*. New York: Harper & Row, 1957.

MACIVER, ROBERT M. *Social Causation*. Boston: Ginn & Co., 1942.

MARTINDALE, DON. *Social Life and Cultural Change*. Princeton, N. J.: D. Van Nostrand Co., Inc., 1961.

PARSONS, TALCOTT. *The Social System*. New York: The Free Press of Glencoe, Inc., 1951.

SMELSER, NEIL J. *Social Change in the Industrial Revolution: An Application of Theory to the British Cotton Industry*. Chicago: University of Chicago Press, 1959.

CHAPTER 2

AAAS COMMITTEE. "The Integrity of Science," *American Scientist*, Vol. 53, No. 2 (June, 1965), pp. 174–98.

ALLEN, FRANCIS R., and others. *Technology and Social Change*. New York: Appleton-Century-Crofts, Inc., 1957.

BARNES, HARRY ELMER. *Historical Sociology, Its Origins and Development: Theories of Social Evolution from Cave Life to Atomic Bombing*. New York: Philosophical Library Inc., 1948.

————, and BECKER, HOWARD. *Social Thought from Lore to Science*. Boston: D. C. Heath & Co., 1938.

BARNETT, HOMER. *Innovation: The Basis of Cultural Change*. New York: McGraw-Hill Book Co., Inc., 1953.

BECKER, HOWARD W. *Man in Reciprocity: Introductory Lectures on Culture, Society and Personality*. New York: Frederick A. Praeger Inc., 1956.

BELLAH, ROBERT N. "Durkheim and History," in Werner J. Cahnman and Alvin Boskoff (eds.), *Sociology and History*. New York: The Free Press of Glencoe, Inc., 1964. Pp. 85–103.

BERNARD, LUTHER LEE. *Instinct: A Study in Social Psychology*. New York: Henry Holt & Co., 1924.

BERTRAND, ALVIN L. "The Stress-Strain Element of Social Systems: A Micro Theory of Conflict and Change," *Social Forces,* Vol. 42, No. 1 (October, 1963), pp. 1–10.

BIDNEY, DAVID. *Theoretical Anthropology.* New York: Columbia University Press, 1953.

BOBER, MANDELL M. *Karl Marx's Interpretation of History.* Cambridge, Mass.: Harvard University Press, 1948.

BODIN, JEAN. *The Six Bookes of a Commonweale: A Facsimile reprint of the English translation of 1606, corrected and supplemented in the light of a new comparison with the French and Latin Texts.* Introduction by Kenneth Douglas MacRae. Cambridge, Mass.: Harvard University Press, 1962.

BOSKOFF, ALVIN. "Recent Theories of Social Change," in Werner J. Cahnman and Alvin Boskoff (eds.), *Sociology and History.* New York: Holt, Rinehart & Winston, 1964. Pp. 140–58.

BOULDING, KENNETH E. *The Image: Knowledge in Life and Society.* Ann Arbor, Mich.: University of Michigan Press, 1956.

CAHNMAN, WERNER J. and BOSKOFF, ALVIN (eds.). *Sociology and History.* New York: The Free Press of Glencoe, Inc., 1964.

COON, CARLETON. *The Story of Man: From the First Human to Primitive Culture and Beyond.* 2nd rev. ed. New York: Alfred A. Knopf, Inc., 1962.

COSER, LEWIS A. *The Functions of Social Conflict.* New York: The Free Press of Glencoe, Inc., 1956.

————. "Social Conflict and the Theory of Social Change," *British Journal of Sociology,* Vol. 8 (September, 1957), pp. 197–207.

COTTRELL, W. FREDERICK. *Energy and Society.* New York: McGraw-Hill Book Co., Inc., 1955.

DAHRENDORF, RALF. "Toward a Theory of Social Conflict," *Journal of Conflict Resolution,* Vol. 2, No. 2 (1958), pp. 170–83.

DAVIS, KINGSLEY. "The Myth of Functional Analysis as a Special Method in Sociology and Anthropology," *American Sociological Review,* Vol. 24, No. 6 (December, 1959), pp. 757–72.

DE GOBINEAU, ARTHUR JOSEPH. *Essai sur l'inegalite des races humaines.* Paris: Firmin-Didot, 1853–1855. 4 Volumes.

DURKHEIM, ÉMILE. *The Division of Labor in Society.* Trans. by George Simpson. New York: The Free Press of Glencoe, Inc., 1947 (first published 1893).

FEUER, LEWIS S. *The Scientific Intellectual: The Psychological and Sociological Origins of Modern Science.* New York: Basic Books, Inc., 1963.

FROMM, ERICH. *Escape from Freedom.* New York: Holt, Rinehart & Winston, Inc., 1941.

GILFILLAN, S. C. "The Coldward Course of Progress," *Political Science Quarterly,* Vol. 35 (1920), pp. 393–410.

————. *The Sociology of Invention.* Chicago: Follett Publishing Co., 1935.

GRAY, J. K. "Karl Marx and Social Philosophy," in Fossey John Cobb Hearnshaw (ed.), *The Social and Political Ideas of Some Representative Thinkers of the Victorian Age.* New York: Barnes & Noble, Inc., 1950. Pp. 116–50.

GREEN, ROBERT W. (ed.). *Protestantism and Capitalism: The Weber Thesis and Its Critics.* Boston: D. C. Heath & Co., 1959.

HAGEN, EVERETT F. *On the Theory of Social Change, How Economic Growth Begins.* Homewood, Ill.: The Dorsey Press, Inc., 1962.

————. "How Economic Growth Begins, A Theory of Social Change," *Journal of Social Issues,* Vol. 19, No. 1 (January, 1963), pp. 20–34.

HANKINS, FRANK. *The Racial Basis of Civilization: A Critique of the Nordic Doctrine.* New York: Alfred A. Knopf, Inc., 1926.

HART, HORNELL. *The Technique of Social Progress.* New York: Henry Holt and Co., 1931.

——. "Acceleration in Social Change," in Francis Allen and others, *Technology and Social Change.* New York: Appleton-Century-Crofts, Inc., 1959(a).

——. "Social Theory and Social Change," in Llewellyn Gross (ed.), *Symposium on Sociological Theory.* New York: Harper & Row, 1959(b). Pp. 196–238.

HIELD, WAYNE. "The Study of Change in Social Science," *British Journal of Sociology,* Vol. 5, No. 1 (March, 1954), pp. 1–11.

HOFSTADTER, RICHARD. *Social Darwinism.* Rev. ed. New York: George Braziller, Inc., 1959.

HOMANS, GEORGE. "Bringing Men Back In," *American Sociological Review,* Vol. 29, No. 6 (December, 1964), pp. 809–18.

HUNTINGTON, ELLSWORTH. *Civilization and Climate.* New Haven, Conn.: Yale University Press, 1924.

——. *Mainsprings of Civilization.* New York: John Wiley & Sons, Inc., 1945.

KLINEBERG, OTTO. *Race Differences.* New York: Harper & Row, 1935.

KLUCKHOHN, CLYDE. *Navaho Witchcraft.* Boston: Beacon Press, 1944.

KROPOTKIN, PETER. *Mutual Aid: A Factor in Evolution.* New York: McClure, 1907.

LOMBROSO, CESARE. *Man of Genius.* New York: Charles Scribner and Sons, 1891.

LOOMIS, CHARLES P. *Social Systems: Essays on Their Persistence and Change.* Princeton, N. J.: D. Van Nostrand Co., Inc., 1960.

LOWIE, ROBERT HARRY. *History of Ethnological Theory.* New York: Holt, Rinehart & Winston, Inc., 1937.

MALINOWSKI, BRONISLAW. *A Scientific Theory of Culture and Other Essays.* Chapel Hill, N. C.: University of North Carolina Press, 1944.

McCLELLAND, DAVID C. *The Achieving Society.* Princeton, N. J.: D. Van Nostrand Co., Inc., 1961.

——. "Business Drive and National Achievement," *Harvard Business Review,* Vol. 40, No. 4 (1962), pp. 99–112.

MacIVER, ROBERT M. *Social Causation.* Boston: Ginn & Co., 1942.

MERTON, ROBERT K. *Science, Technology and Society in Seventeenth Century England. Osiris,* Vol. 4, Bruges, 1938.

——. *Social Theory and Social Structure: Toward the Codification of Theory and Research.* Rev. ed. New York: The Free Press of Glencoe, Inc., 1957.

MICHELS, ROBERT. *Political Parties: A Sociological Study of the Oligarchial Tendencies of Modern Democracy.* New York: The Free Press of Glencoe, Inc., 1949.

MILLS, C. WRIGHT. "The Power Elite: Military, Economic and Political," in Arthur W. Kornhauser (ed.), *Problems of Power in American Democracy.* Detroit, Mich.: Wayne State University Press, 1957. Chap. 15.

——. *The Power Elite.* New York: Oxford University Press, 1959.

MOORE, WILBERT E. "A Reconsideration of Theories of Social Change," *American Sociological Review,* Vol. 25, No. 6 (December, 1960), pp. 810–17.

——. Review of Everett F. Hagen's *On the Theory of Social Change: How Economic Growth Begins,* in the *American Sociological Review,* Vol. 28, No. 2 (April, 1963), p. 296.

——, and FELDMAN, ARNOLD S. *Labor Commitment and Social Change in Developing Areas.* New York: Social Science Research Council, 1960.

MOSCA, GAETANO. *The Ruling Class.* New York: McGraw-Hill Book Co., 1938.

MUMFORD, LEWIS. *Technics and Civilization.* New York: Harcourt, Brace and

World, Inc., 1934.

OGBURN, WILLIAM F. *Social Change with Respect to Culture and Original Nature.* New York: B. W. Huebsch, Inc., 1922.

PARETO, VILFREDO. *The Mind and Society: A Treatise on General Sociology.* Trans. by Andrew Bongiorno and Arthur Livingstone. New York: Dover Publications, Inc., 1963.

PARK, ROBERT E. "Human Migration and the Marginal Man," *American Journal of Sociology,* Vol. 33 (1928), pp. 881–93.

PARSONS, TALCOTT. *The Structure of Social Action.* New York: McGraw-Hill Book Co., 1937.

———. *The Social System.* New York: The Free Press of Glencoe, Inc., 1951.

———, and others (eds.). *Theories of Society: Foundations of Modern Sociological Theory.* New York: The Free Press of Glencoe, Inc., 1961. Vol. 1.

POLAK, F. L. *The Image of the Future: Enlightening the Past, Orientating the Present, Forecasting the Future.* Trans. by Elise Boulding. Dobbs Ferry, N. Y.: Oceana Publications, Inc., 1961. 2 volumes.

PONSIONEN, J. A. *The Analysis of Social Change Reconsidered.* The Hague, Netherlands: Mouton & Co., 1962.

RADCLIFFE-BROWN, ALFRED REGINALD. *Structure and Function in Primitive Society: Essays and Addresses.* New York: The Free Press of Glencoe, Inc., 1952.

RAUSCHENBUSCH, WALTER. *Christianity and the Social Crisis.* London: Macmillan and Co., Ltd., 1907.

———. *A Rauschenbush Reader: The Kingdom of God and the Social Gospel.* New York: Harper & Row, 1957.

SAMUELSSON, KURT. *Religion and Economic Action.* Trans. by E. Geoffrey French, edited by D. C. Coleman. New York: Basic Books, Inc., 1961.

SIMKOVITCH, V. G. "Hay and History," *Political Science Quarterly,* Vol. 28 (1913), pp. 385–403.

SMELSER, NEIL. *Social Change in the Industrial Revolution: An Application of Theory to the British Cotton Industry.* Chicago: University of Chicago Press, 1959.

SOREL, GEORGES. *Reflections on Violence.* Trans. by T. E. Hulme. New York: Collier Books, 1950.

SOROKIN, PITIRIM A. *Contemporary Sociological Theories.* New York: Harper & Row, 1928.

STREIDER, JACOB. "Origin and Evolution of Early European Capitalism," *Journal of Economic and Business History,* Vol. 2, No. 1 (November, 1929).

TÖNNIES, FERDINAND. *Community and Society–Gemeinschaft und Gesellschaft.* Trans. and introduced by Charles P. Loomis. East Lansing, Mich.: Michigan State University Press, 1957.

TOYNBEE, ARNOLD. *A Study of History.* Abridgement of Volumes 1–10 by D. C. Somervell. First American ed. New York: Oxford University Press, 1947–1957.

TOZZER, ALFRED M. "Biography and Biology," in Clyde Kluckhohn and Henry A. Murray (eds.), *Personality in Nature, Society and Culture,* 2nd ed. New York: Alfred A. Knopf, Inc., 1948. Pp. 144–60.

TURNER, RALPH E. "Asia's Multiple Revolution—The Nature of the Crisis," *Saturday Review,* Vol. 32 (April, 1951), pp. 16ff.

USHER, ABBOTT PAYSON. *A History of Mechanical Inventions.* Cambridge, Mass.: Harvard University Press, 1954.

VANDER KROEF, JUSTUS M. "Population Pressure and Economic Development in Indonesia," *American Journal of Economic Sociology,* Vol. 12 (1953), pp. 355–71.

VEBLEN, THORSTEIN. *Imperial Germany and the Industrial Revolution.* New York: B. W. Huebsch, 1915.

————. *The Place of Science in Modern Civilization.* New York: B. W. Huebsch, 1919.

————. *The Engineers and the Price System.* New York: B. W. Huebsch, 1921.

WARD, LESTER F. *Pure Sociology: A Treatise on the Origin and Spontaneous Development of Society.* New York: The Macmillan Co., 1903.

WEBER, MAX. *The Protestant Ethic and the Spirit of Capitalism.* Trans. by Talcott Parsons. London: George Allen and Unwin, 1930.

WHITE, LESLIE A. *The Evolution of Culture, The Development of Civilization to the Fall of Rome.* New York: McGraw-Hill Book Co., 1959.

WILSON, GODFREY and WILSON, MONICA. *The Analysis of Social Change: Based on Observations in Central Africa.* Cambridge, England: Cambridge University Press, 1945.

CHAPTER 3

ANGELL, ROBERT COOLEY. *Free Society and Moral Crisis.* Ann Arbor, Mich.: University of Michigan Press, 1958.

BALES, ROBERT F., and BORGATTA, EDGAR F. "Size of Group as a Factor in the Interaction Profile," in A. Paul Hare, Edgar F. Borgatta, and Robert F. Bales, *Small Groups: Studies in Social Interaction.* New York: Alfred A. Knopf, Inc., 1955. Pp. 396–413.

BATES, F. L., FOGLEMAN, C. W., PARENTON, V. J., PITTMAN, R. H., and TRACY, G. S. *The Social and Psychological Consequences of a Natural Disaster: A Longitudinal Study of Hurricane Audrey.* Disaster Research Group Study No. 18. Washington, D.C.: National Academy of Science, National Research Council Publication 1081, 1963.

CAPLOW, THEODORE. *Principles of Organization.* New York: Harcourt, Brace and World, Inc., 1964.

CARR, L. J. "Disaster and the Sequence-Pattern Concept of Social Change," *American Journal of Sociology,* Vol. 38 (September, 1932), pp. 207–18.

COTTRELL, W. FREDERICK. *Energy and Society.* New York: McGraw-Hill Book Co., 1955.

DURKHEIM, ÉMILE. *The Division of Labor in Society.* Trans. by George Simpson. New York: The Free Press of Glencoe, 1947 (first published 1893).

EMBREE, JOHN. "Thailand—A Loosely Structured Social System," *American Anthropologist,* Vol. 52 (1950), pp. 181–93.

FIRTH, RAYMOND. *Social Change in Tikopia, Re-study of a Polynesian Community after a Generation.* London: George Allen and Unwin, 1959.

GOLDENWEISER, ALEXANDER. *Anthropology: An Introduction to Primitive Culture.* New York: Appleton-Century-Crofts, Inc., 1937.

GOULDNER, ALVIN WARD. "The Problem of Succession and Bureaucracy," in Alvin W. Gouldner (ed.), *Studies in Leadership: Leadership and Democratic Action.* New York: Harper & Row, 1950. Pp. 644–59.

————. *Patterns of Industrial Bureaucracy.* New York: The Free Press of Glencoe, Inc., 1954.

HAUSER, PHILIP (ed.). *The Population Dilemma.* Englewood Cliffs, N. J.: Prentice-Hall, Inc., 1963.

HERMAN, ABBOTT P. *An Approach to Social Problems.* Boston: Ginn & Co., 1949.

HOLMBERG, ALLAN R. *Nomads of the Long Bow: The Siriono of Eastern Bolivia.* Publication No. 10. Washington, D.C.: Smithsonian Institution, Institute of Social Anthropology, 1950.

INDIK, BERNARD P. "Some Effects of Organization Size on Member's Attitudes and Behavior," *Human Relations,* Vol. 16, No. 4 (November, 1963), pp. 369–84.

ISARD, WALTER, and WHITNEY, VINCENT. *Atomic Power: An Economic and Social Analysis.* New York: McGraw-Hill Book Co., 1952.

JEWKES, JOHN, SAWERS, DAVID, and STILLERMAN, RICHARD. *The Sources of Invention.* London: Macmillan and Co. Ltd., 1958.

KLUCKHOHN, FLORENCE, and STRODTBECK, FRED L. *Variations in Value Orientations.* New York: Harper & Row, 1961.

LANDSDELL, NORMAN. *The Atom and the Energy Revolution.* New York: Philosophical Library, Inc., 1958.

LEE, DOROTHY D. *Religious Perspectives of College Teaching.* New Haven, Conn.: Edward Hazen Foundation, 1951.

LEIGHTON, ALEXANDER H. *The Governing of Men.* Princeton, N. J.: Princeton University Press, 1945.

LINDSEY, JUDGE BENJAMIN BARR, and EVANS, WAINWRIGHT. *The Companionate Marriage.* Garden City, N. Y.: Garden City Books, 1927, 1929.

LINTON, RALPH. *The Study of Man: An Introduction.* New York, Copyright 1936 Appleton-Century-Crofts, Inc., 1936.

LOOMIS, CHARLES P. *Social Systems: Essays on Their Persistence and Change.* Princeton, N. J.: D. Van Nostrand Co., Inc., 1960.

McCLEARY, RICHARD H. "The Governmental Process and Informal Social Control," in Donald Ray Cressey, *The Prison: Studies in Institutional Organization and Change.* New York: Holt, Rinehart & Winston, Inc., 1961.

MILLS, THEODORE M. "Power Relations in Three-Person Groups," *American Sociological Review,* Vol. 19, No. 1 (February, 1954), pp. 23–28.

MOORE, WILBERT E. *Industrialization and Labor: Social Aspects of Economic Development.* Ithaca, N. Y.: Cornell University Press, 1951.

MORCELL, BEN. *Our Nation's Water Resources.* Chicago: University of Chicago Press, 1956.

NATIONAL SCIENCE FOUNDATION. *National Patterns of R & D Resources: Funds & Manpower in the United States 1953–1968.* Washington, D.C.: National Science Foundation, 1967.

NISBET, ROBERT H. "Man and Technics," Riecker Memorial Lecture No. 2, *University of Arizona Bulletin,* Vol. 27, No. 1 (January, 1956).

OGBURN, WILLIAM FIELDING. *Social Change with Respect to Culture and Original Nature.* New York: B. W. Huebsch, Inc., 1922.

PARETO, VILFREDO. *The Mind and Society: A Treatise on General Sociology.* Trans. by Andrew Bongiorno and Arthur Livingston; edited by Arthur Livingston. New York: Dover Publications, Inc., 1963.

PIGGOTT, STUART. *Prehistoric India.* Middlesex, England: Penguin Books, Ltd., 1950.

REDFIELD, ROBERT. *The Primitive World and Its Transformations.* Ithaca, N. Y.: Cornell University Press, 1953.

RYAN, BRYCE. "Status, Achievement and Education in Ceylon," *Journal of Asian Studies,* Vol. 20, No. 4 (August, 1961), pp. 463–76.

———, and STRAUS, MURRAY. *The Integration of Sinhalese Society.* Research Studies, Washington State College, Vol. 22 (1954).

———, ARULPRAGASUM, CHANDRA, and BIBILE, CUDA. "The Agricultural System of a Jungle Village," *Eastern Anthropologist,* Vol. 8 (1955), pp. 151–60.

———, JAYASENA, L. D., and WICKREMESINGHE, D. C. R. *Sinhalese Village.* Coral Gables, Fla.: University of Miami Press, 1958.

SAUNDERS, LYLE. *Cultural Difference and Medical Care.* New York: Russell Sage Foundation, 1954.

SHARPE, LAURISTAN. "Steel Axes for Stone Age Australians," in Edward Spicer (ed.), *Human Problems in Technological Change: A Casebook.* New York: Russell Sage Foundation, 1952.

SOROKIN, PITIRIM A. *Social and Cultural Dynamics.* New York: American Book Co., 1937. Vol. 1.

STERN, BERNHARD JOSEPH. *Historical Sociology: The Selected Papers of Bernhard J. Stern.* New York: Citadel Press, 1959.

THOMPSON, HOLLAND. *The Age of Invention.* New Haven, Conn.: Yale University Press, 1921.

VOGT, WILLIAM. *Road to Survival.* New York: William Sloane Associates, Inc., 1948.

WARNER, W. KEITH, and HILANDER, JAMES S. "The Relationship Between Size of Organization and Membership Participation," *Rural Sociology,* Vol. 29, No. 1 (March, 1964), pp. 30–39.

WASHBURNE, NORMAN F. *Interpreting Social Change in America.* Garden City, N. Y.: Doubleday & Co., Inc., 1954.

WHITNEY, VINCENT HEATH. "Resistance to Innovation: The Case of Atomic Power," *American Journal of Sociology,* Vol. 56, No. 2 (September, 1950), pp. 247–54.

WOLFF, KURT H. *The Sociology of Georg Simmel.* New York: The Free Press of Glencoe, Inc., 1950.

CHAPTER 4

BARNETT, HOMER G. *Innovation: The Basis of Cultural Change.* New York: McGraw-Hill Book Co., 1953.

BERLE, A. K., and DeCAMP, L. S. *Inventions and Their Management.* Scranton, Pa.: International Textbook Co., 1947.

BOSKOFF, ALVIN. "Social Change: Major Problems in the Emergence of Theoretical and Research Foci," in Howard W. Becker and Alvin Boskoff, *Modern Sociological Theory in Continuity and Change.* New York: Holt, Rinehart & Winston, Inc., 1957.

BUTLER, RAYMOND RENARD. *Scientific Discovery.* London: English University Press, Ltd., 1947.

CARTER, THOMAS F. *The Invention of Printing in China and Its Spread Westward.* New York: Columbia University Press, 1955.

CHAPIN, F. S. *Cultural Change.* New York: The Century Co., 1928.

CHILDE, V. GORDON. *What Happened in History.* Middlesex, England: Penguin Books, Ltd., 1942.

DREVDAHL, J. E. "Factors of Importance for Creativity," *Journal of Clinical Psychology,* Vol. 12, No. 1 (January, 1956), pp. 21–26.

———, and CATTELL, R. B. "Personality and Creativity in Artists and Writers," *Journal of Clinical Psychology,* Vol. 14, No. 2 (April, 1958), pp. 107–11.

FULLER, FREDERICK L. *My Half Century as an Inventor.* New York: Mail and Express Printing Co., 1938 (privately published).

GETZELS, JACOB W., and JACKSON, PHILIP W. *Creativity and Intelligence: Explorations with Gifted Students.* New York: John Wiley & Sons, Inc., 1962.

GILFILLAN, S. C. *The Sociology of Invention.* Chicago: Follett Publishing Co., 1935(a).

———. *Inventing the Ship.* Chicago: Follett Publishing Co., 1935(b).

———. "The Prediction of Inventions," *Technological Trends and National Policy.* Washington, D.C.: National Resources Committee, June, 1937, pp. 15–23.

GOUGH, H. G. *California Psychological Inventory Manual.* Palo Alto, Calif.: Consulting Psychologists Press, 1957.

GREENLEAF, WILLIAM. *Monopoly on Wheels: Henry Ford and the Selden Automobile Patents.* Detroit, Mich.: Wayne State University Press, 1961.

HADAMARD, JACQUES. *An Essay on the Psychology of Invention in the Mathematical Field.* Princeton, N. J.: Princeton University Press, 1945.

HALL, JEROME. *Theft, Law and Society.* Indianapolis, Ind.: Bobbs-Merrill Co., Inc., 1952.

HARRISON, H. S. "Discovery, Invention and Diffusion," in Charles Singer and others (eds.), *History of Technology.* Oxford: Clarendon Press, 1954–1958. Chapter 3, Vol. 1.

HART, HORNELL NORRIS. *The Technique of Social Progress.* New York: Holt, Rinehart & Winston, Inc., 1931.

———. "Technological Acceleration and the Atomic Bomb," *American Sociological Review,* Vol. 11 (June, 1946), pp. 277–93.

———. "Acceleration in Social Change," in Francis R. Allen, Hornell Hart, Delbert C. Miller, William F. Ogburn, and Meyer F. Nimkoff, *Technology and Social Change.* New York: Appleton-Century-Crofts, Inc., 1957. Chap. 3.

HERING, DANIEL W. *Foibles and Fallacies of Science: An Account of Celebrated Scientific Vagaries.* Princeton, N. J.: D. Van Nostrand Co., Inc., 1924.

JAPP, FRANCIS R. "Kekulé Memorial Lecture," *Journal of the Chemical Society Transactions,* Vol. 73 (1898). Part I, pp. 97–138.

JEWKES, JOHN, SAWERS, DAVID, and STILLERMAN, RICHARD. *The Sources of Invention.* London: Macmillan and Co., Ltd., 1958.

KETTERING, CHARLES FRANKLIN. "Motor Car," *The Encyclopedia Britannica,* 14th Ed., Vol. 14 (1929), p. 80ff.

KNEALE, W. C. "The Idea of Invention," *Proceedings of the British Academy,* Vol. 41 (1955).

KÖHLER, WOLFGANG. *The Mentality of Apes.* Trans. by Ella Winter. London: Routledge & Kegan Paul, Ltd.; New York: Harcourt, Brace and World, Inc., 1926.

KROEBER, ALFRED L. "The Superorganic," *American Anthropologist,* New Series, Vol. 19, No. 2 (1917), pp. 163–213.

KROEBER, A. L. "On the Principle of Order in Civilization as Exemplified by Changes of Fashion," *American Anthropologist,* Vol. 21 (1919), pp. 235–63.

KUBIE, LAWRENCE S. *Neurotic Distortion of the Creative Process.* Lawrence, Kansas: University of Kansas Press, 1958.

LINDSEY, JUDGE BEN, and EVANS, WAINWRIGHT. *The Companionate Marriage.* Garden City, New York: Garden City Publishing Co., 1929.

LINTON, RALPH. *The Study of Man: An Introduction.* New York: Appleton-Century-Crofts, Inc., 1936.

LOMBROSO, C. *L'homme Criminel: Étude Anthropologique et Medico-Legale.* Paris: F. Alcan, 1887.

LOWENFELD, VIKTOR. *Creative and Mental Growth.* 3rd ed. New York: The Macmillan Co., 1957.

LUCHINS, A. S. "On Some Aspects of the Creativity Problem in Thinking," *Annals of the New York Academy of Sciences,* Vol. 91 (December 23), 1960, pp. 128–40.

MACKINNON, DONALD W. "The Nature and Nurture of Creative Talent," *American Psychologist,* Vol. 7 (1962), pp. 484–98. (a)

———. "The Personality Correlates of Creativity: A Study of American Architects," in G. S. Nielsen (ed.), *Proceedings of the XIV International Congress of Applied Psychology,* Copenhagen: Munksgaard, Vol. 2 (1962), pp. 11–38. (b)

MERTON, ROBERT KING. "Civilization and Culture," *Sociology and Social Research,* Vol. 21 (1936), pp. 103–13.

OGBURN, WILLIAM FIELDING. *Social Change with Respect to Culture and Original Nature.* New York: B. W. Huebsch, 1922.

————. "The Great Man Versus Social Forces," *Social Forces,* Vol. 5, No. 2 (December, 1926), pp. 225–31.

————, and THOMAS, DOROTHY. "Are Inventions Inevitable," *Political Science Quarterly,* Vol. 37 (March, 1922), pp. 83–98.

PARETO, VILFREDO. *The Mind and Society: A Treatise on General Sociology.* Trans. by Andrew Bongiorno and Arthur Livingstone. New York: Dover Publications, Inc., 1963.

POINCARÉ, H. *The Foundations of Science.* Trans. by George Bruce Halsted. Ephrata, Pa.: Science Press, Inc., 1946.

PORTERFIELD, AUSTIN L. *Creative Factors in Scientific Research: A Social Psychology of Scientific Knowledge, Studying the Interplay of Psychology and Cultural Factors in Science with Emphasis upon Imagination.* Durham, N. C.: Duke University Press, 1941.

ROE, JOSEPH WICKHAM. *Interchangeable Manufacture in American Industry, A Newcomen Regional Meeting Address.* Birmingham, Ala.: Birmingham Publishing Co., 1939.

SINGER, CHARLES, HOLMYARD, E. J., and HALL, A. R. (eds.). *A History of Technology.* London: Oxford University Press, 1954–1958. 5 volumes.

THOMPSON, HOLLAND. *The Age of Invention: A Chronicle of Mechanical Conquest.* New Haven, Conn.: Yale University Press, 1921.

THURSTON, ROBERT H. *A History of the Growth of the Steam-Engine.* Centennial Ed. Ithaca, N. Y.: Cornell University Press, 1939.

USHER, ABBOTT PAYSON. *A History of Mechanical Inventions.* Cambridge, Mass.: Harvard University Press, 1954.

VAN ZELST, R. A., and KEN, W. A. "Some Correlates of Technical and Scientific Productivity," *Journal of Abnormal and Social Psychology,* Vol. 46 (1951), pp. 470–75.

WALLACH, MICHAEL A., and KOGAN, NATHAN. "Creativity and Intelligence in Children's Thinking," *Trans-Action* (January–February, 1967), pp. 38–43.

WERTHEIMER, MAX. *Productive Thinking.* New York: Harper & Row, 1959.

CHAPTER 5

ANDERSON, C. ARNOLD, and RYAN, BRYCE. *War Came to the Iowa Community.* Ames, Iowa: Iowa State College, Agricultural Experiment Station Bulletin, 1942.

BATESON, GREGORY. *Naven: A Survey of the Problems Suggested by a Composite Picture of the Culture of a New Guinea Tribe Drawn From Three Points of View.* 2nd Ed. Stanford, Calif.: Stanford University Press, 1958.

BONNÉ, ALFRED. "The Adjustment of Oriental Immigrants to Industrial Employment in Israel," UNESCO, *International Social Science Bulletin,* Vol. 8, No. 1 (1956), pp. 6–12.

BROOM, LEONARD, and SELZNICK, PHILLIP. *Sociology: A Text With Adapted Readings.* 3rd ed. New York: Harper & Row, 1963.

CLINARD, MARSHALL BARRON (ed.). *Anomie and Deviant Behavior: A Discussion and Critique.* New York: The Free Press of Glencoe, Inc., 1964.

COHEN, RONALD. "Conflict and Change in a Northern Nigerian Emirate," in George K. Zollschan and Walter Hirsch (eds.), *Explorations in Social Change.* Boston: Houghton Mifflin Co., 1964. Chap. 19.

COMMAGER, HENRY STEELE. *America in Perspective: The United States Through Foreign Eyes.* New York: Random House, Inc., 1947.

COSER, LEWIS A. *The Functions of Social Conflict.* New York: The Free Press of Glencoe, Inc., 1956.

DAHRENDORF, RALF. "Toward a Theory of Social Conflict," *The Journal of Conflict Resolution,* Vol. 2, No. 2 (1958), pp. 170–83.

DUBIN, ROBERT. "Leadership in Union-Management Relations as an Intergroups System," in Muzafer Sherif (ed.), *Intergroup Relations and Leadership: Approaches and Research in Industrial, Ethnic, Cultural and Political Areas.* New York: John Wiley & Sons, Inc., 1962. P. 99.

EGGAN, FRED. "Cultural Drift and Social Change," *Current Anthropology,* Vol. 4, No. 4 (October, 1963), pp. 347–55.

EISENSTADT, SHMUEL NOAH. "The Process of Absorption of Immigrants in Israel," in Carl Frankenstein (ed.), *Between Past and Future: Essays and Studies on Aspects of Immigrant Absorption in Israel.* Jerusalem: Henrietta Szold Foundation for Child and Youth Welfare, 1953. Pp. 53–81.

———. *Palestine, Emigration and Immigration.* New York: The Free Press of Glencoe, Inc., 1955.

———. *The Political System of Empires.* New York: The Free Press of Glencoe, Inc., 1963.

———. "Institutionalization and Change," *American Sociological Review,* Vol. 29, No. 2 (April, 1964), pp. 235–47. (a)

———. "Processes of Change and Institutionalization of the Political Systems of Centralized Empires," in George K. Zollschan and Walter Hirsch (eds.), *Explorations in Social Change.* Boston: Houghton Mifflin Co., 1964. Chap. 17. (b)

———, and BEN-DAVID, J., "Inter-generation Tensions in Israel," UNESCO, *International Social Science Bulletin,* Vol. 8, No. 1 (1956), pp. 54–74.

ERICKSON, ERIK. *Childhood and Society.* New York: W. W. Norton & Co., Inc., 1950.

FALS BORDA, ORLANDO. *Facts and Theory of Sociocultural Change in a Rural Social System.* 2nd ed. Monografias Sociologicas, No. 2. Bogotá, Colombia: Bis, Universidad Nacional de Colombia, Facultad de Sociologia, 1962.

FITZGERALD, C. R. *The Third China: The Chinese Communities of Southeast Asia.* Vancouver: University of British Columbia, 1965.

FORCE, ROLAND W. *Leadership and Cultural Change in Palau.* Fieldiana: Anthropology, Vol. 50, Chicago Natural History Museum (February 19, 1960).

FRANK, A. G. "Goal Ambiguity and Conflicting Standards: An Approach to the Study of Organizations," *Human Organization,* Vol. 17, No. 4 (1959), pp. 8–13.

FRANKENSTEIN, CARL (ed.). *Between Past and Future: Essays and Studies on Aspects of Immigrant Absorption in Israel.* Jerusalem: Henrietta Szold Foundation for Child and Youth Welfare, 1953.

HARBISON, FREDERICK H., and DUBIN, ROBERT. *Patterns of Union—Management Relations: United Automobile Workers (CIO), General Motors, Studebaker.* Chicago, Ill.: Science Research Association, 1947.

HARE, A. PAUL, BORGOTTA, EDGAR F., and BALES, ROBERT. *Small Groups: Studies in Social Interaction.* New York: Alfred A. Knopf, Inc., 1955.

HERSKOVITZ, MELVILLE. *Man and His Works: The Science of Cultural Anthropology.* New York: Alfred A. Knopf, Inc., 1948.

HIMES, JOSEPH S. "The Functions of Racial Conflict," *Social Forces,* Vol. 45, No. 1 (September, 1966), pp. 1–10.

INKELES, ALEX. "Social Change and Social Character: The Role of Parental Mediation," *Journal of Social Issues,* Vol. 40, No. 2 (1955), pp. 12–23.

JOHNSON, CHALMERS. *Revolution and the Social System.* Stanford, Calif.: Stanford University Press, The Hoover Institution on War, 1964.

―――. *Revolutionary Change.* Boston: Little, Brown & Co., 1966.

KAHN-FREUND, O. "Intergroup Conflicts and Their Settlement," *British Journal of Sociology,* Vol. 5 (1954), pp. 193–227.

KING, MARTIN LUTHER, JR. *Why We Can't Wait.* New York: Harper & Row, 1964.

KROEBER, ALFRED LOUIS. *Configurations of Culture Growth.* Berkeley, Calif.: University of California Press, 1944.

LANG, KURT, and LANG, GLADYS ENGLE. *Collective Dynamics.* New York: Thomas Y. Crowell Co., 1961.

LEWIN, KURT, and LIPPITT, RONALD. "An Experimental Approach to the Study of Autocracy and Democracy: A Preliminary Note," *Sociometry,* Vol. 1 (1938), pp. 292–300.

―――, and WHITE, RALPH K. "Patterns of Aggressive Behavior in Experimentally Created 'Social Climates'," *Journal of Social Psychology,* Vol. 10 (May, 1939), pp. 271–99.

LIPPITT, RONALD. "An Experimental Study of Leadership and Group Life," in T. M. Newcomb, Guy E. Swanson, and E. L. Hartley (eds.), *Readings in Social Psychology.* Rev. ed. New York: Holt, Rinehart & Winston, Inc., 1952. Pp. 315–30.

LYNES, RUSSELL. *The Tastemakers.* New York: Harper & Row, 1954.

MAIMON, JACOB. "Teaching Immigrants in Ma Abarot," in Carl Frankenstein (ed.), *Between Past and Future: Essays and Studies on Aspects of Immigrant Absorption in Israel.* Jerusalem: Henrietta Szold Foundation for Child and Youth Welfare, 1953. Pp. 178–93.

MERTON, ROBERT. "Social Structure and Anomie: Revisions and Extensions," in Ruth Nanda Anshen, *The Family: Its Function and Destiny.* New York: Harper & Row, 1949. Pp. 275–312.

MERTON, ROBERT KING. *Social Theory and Social Structure.* Rev. ed. New York: The Free Press of Glencoe, Inc., 1957(a).

―――. "Social Problems and Sociological Theory," in Robert K. Merton and Robert A. Nisbet (ed.), *Contemporary Social Problems: An Introduction to the Sociology of Deviant Behavior and Social Disorganization.* New York: Harcourt, Brace and World, Inc., 1961.

―――, READER, G. G., and KENDALL, P. L. (eds.). *The Student-Physician: Introductory Studies in the Sociology of Medical Education.* Cambridge, Mass.: Harvard University Press, 1957(b).

MONTROSS, LYNN. *War Through The Ages.* New York: Harper & Row, 1944.

NEWCOMB, THEODORE M., SWANSON, GUY E., and HARTLEY, EUGENE L. *Readings in Social Psychology.* New York: Holt, Rinehart & Winston, Inc., 1952.

PARSONS, TALCOTT and SMELSER, NEIL J. *Economy and Society: A Study in the Integration of Economic and Social Theory.* New York: The Free Press of Glencoe, Inc., 1956.

REINHOLD, HANOKH. "Dynamics of Youth Aliyah Groups," in Carl Frankenstein (ed.), *Between Past and Future: Essays and Studies on Aspects of Immigrant Absorption in Israel.* Jerusalem: Henrietta Szold Foundation for Child and Youth Welfare, 1953. Pp. 215–47.

RICHARDSON, JANE, and KROEBER, ALFRED. *Three Centuries of Women's Dress Fashions.* Berkeley, Calif.: University of California Press, 1940.

RIEGER, HAGITH. "Some Aspects of the Acculturation of Yemenite Youth Immigrants," UNESCO, *International Social Science Bulletin,* Vol. 8, No. 1 (1956), pp. 82–108.

RIESMAN, DAVID. "The Saving Remnant, A Study of Character," in J. W. Chase (ed.), *The Years of the Modern*. New York: David McKay Co., Inc., 1949. Pp. 115–47.

RIESMAN, DAVID. *The Lonely Crowd*. New Haven: Yale University Press, 1950.

SAPIR, EDWARD. *Language: An Introduction to the Study of Speech*. New York: Harcourt, Brace and World, Inc., 1921.

———. "Fashion," in Edwin Robert Anderson Seligman (ed.), *Encyclopaedia of the Social Sciences*. New York: The Macmillan Co., 1930–1935. Vol. 6.

SHERIF, MUZAFER. "Group Influences Upon the Formation of Norms and Attitudes," in Theodore M. Newcomb and others, *Readings in Social Psychology*. New York: Holt, Rinehart & Winston, Inc., 1952. Pp. 77–90.

———, and SHERIF, CAROLYN W. *An Outline of Social Psychology*. New York: Harper & Row, 1956.

SHERMAN, ALEPH V. "Korath Gag: An Evaluation of a Temporary Foster-Placement Scheme for Immigrant Children," in Carl Frankenstein (ed.), *Between Past and Future: Essays and Studies on Aspects of Immigrant Absorption in Israel*. Jerusalem: Henrietta Szold Foundation for Child and Youth Welfare, 1953.

SHUMSKY, ABRAHAM. "Clash of Cultures in Israel," *Commentary*, Vol. 23 (May, 1957), pp. 490–92.

SHUVAL, JUDITH T. "Patterns of Inter-group Tension and Affinity," UNESCO, *International Social Science Bulletin*, Vol. 8, No. 1 (1956), pp. 55–123.

SMALL, ALBION W., and VINCENT, GEORGE E. *An Introduction to the Study of Society*. New York: American Book Co., 1894.

SMELSER, NEIL J. *Theory of Collective Behavior*. New York: The Free Press of Glencoe, Inc., 1963.

SOROKIN, PITIRIM A. *Society, Culture and Personality: Their Structure and Dynamics, A System of General Sociology*. New York: Harper & Row, 1947.

THOMAS, WILLIAM ISAAC. *Primitive Behavior*. New York: McGraw Hill Book Co., 1937

———, and ZANIECKI, FLORIAN. *The Polish Peasant in Europe and America*. New York: Alfred A. Knopf, Inc., 1927.

TURNER, RALPH H., and KILLIAN, LEWIS M. *Collective Behavior*. Englewood Cliffs, N. J.: Prentice-Hall, Inc., 1957.

TURNEY-HIGH, H. H. *The Practice of Primitive Warfare*. University of Montana, Publication in Social Science No. 2, 1942.

UNESCO. *International Social Science Bulletin*, Vol. 8, No. 1 (1956). (This issue contains papers on various aspects of the Israeli acculturation process by Alfred Bonné, S. N. Eisenstadt, and Judith T. Shuval.)

United States Strategic Bombing Survey, *The Effects of Strategic Bombing on German Morale*. Washington, D.C.: U. S. Government Printing Office, 1947.

USEEM, JOHN, and USEEM, RUTH. "Social Stresses and Resources Among Middle Management Men," in Egbert Gartley Jaco (ed.), *Patients, Physicians and Illness: Sourcebook in Behavioral Science and Medicine*. New York: The Free Press of Glencoe, Inc., 1958.

WALLACE, ANTHONY F. C. *Human Behavior in Extreme Situations: A Survey of the Literature and Suggestions for Further Research*. Washington, D.C.: Committee on Disaster Studies, National Academy of Sciences, National Research Council, 1956.

WEBB, WALTER PRESCOTT. *The Great Frontier*. Boston: Houghton Mifflin Co., 1952.

WHYTE, WILLIAM FOOTE. *Street Corner Society*. Chicago: University of Chicago Press, 1943.

ZOLLSCHAN, GEORGE K. and HIRSCH, WALTER (eds.). *Explorations in Social Change*. Boston: Houghton Mifflin Co., 1964.

CHAPTER 6

AMAYA, SUSANA. "Problems in Communicating Government Action Programs to Rural Masses," in D. T. Myren (ed.), *First Inter-American Symposium on the Role of Communications in Agricultural Development.* Mexico City, 1964.

BEAL, GEORGE M., and ROGERS, EVERETT M. "Adoption of Two Farm Practices in a Central Iowa Community," Iowa Agricultural Experiment Station, Ames, Iowa: Special Report No. 26, 1960.

————. "The Scientist as a Referent in the Communication of New Technology," *Public Opinion Quarterly,* Vol. 22, No. 4 (Winter, 1958–1959), pp. 555–63.

BELCHER, JOHN C. "Acceptance of Salk Polio Vaccine," *Rural Sociology,* Vol. 23 (1959), pp. 158–70.

BOCK, KENNETH E. *The Acceptance of Histories: Toward a Perspective for Social Science.* Berkeley, Calif.: University of California Press, 1956.

BOSE, SANTI PRIYA. "Characteristics of Farmers Who Adopt Agricultural Practices in Indian Villages," *Rural Sociology.* Vol. 26, No. 2 (1961), pp. 138–45.

BOWERS, RAYMOND V. "The Direction of Intra-Societal Diffusion," *American Sociological Review,* Vol. 2 (December, 1937), pp. 826–36.

————. "Differential Intensity of Intra-Societial Diffusion," *American Sociological Review,* Vol. 3 (1938), pp. 21–31.

CARTER, C. F., and WILLIAMS, B. R. "The Characteristics of Technically Progressive Firms," *Journal of Industrial Economics,* Vol. 7 (1959), pp. 87–104.

CHAPIN, F. STUART. *Cultural Change.* New York: The Century Co., 1928.

CHILDE, V. GORDON. *What Happened in History.* Middlesex, England: Penguin Books, Ltd., 1942.

COPP, JAMES H. *Personal and Social Factors Associated With Adoption of Recommended Farm Practices Among Cattlemen.* Manhattan, Kansas: Kansas Agricultural Experiment Station, Technical Bulletin No. 83, 1956.

————, STILL, MAURICE L., and BROWN, EMORY J. "The Function of Informational Sources in the Farm Practice Adoption Process," *Rural Sociology,* Vol. 23, No. 2 (1958), pp. 146–57.

COUGHENOUR, C. MILTON. "The Functioning of Farmers' Characteristics in Relation to Contact with Media and Practice Adoption," *Rural Sociology,* Vol. 25 (1960), pp. 183–297.

CRAIN, ROBERT L. "Fluoridation: The Diffusion of An Innovation Among Cities," *Social Forces,* Vol. 44, No. 4 (June, 1966), pp. 467–76.

DASGUPTA, S. "Innovations and Innovators in Indian Villages," *Man in India,* Vol. 43 (January–March, 1963), pp. 27–34.

DAVIS, ALICE. "Technicways in American Civilization," *Social Forces,* Vol. 8 (March, 1940), pp. 317–30.

DEASY, LEILA CALHOUN. "Socio-Economic Status and Participation in the Poliomyelitis Vaccine Trial," *American Sociological Review,* Volume 21 (1956), pp. 185–91.

DEUTSCHMANN, PAUL J. "Media in an Undeveloped Village," *Journalism Quarterly,* Vol. 40 (1963), pp. 27–35.

————, and FALS BORDA, ORLANDO. *La Comunicacion de las Ideas Entre Los Campesinos Colombianos.* Monografias Sociologicas, No. 14. Bogotá, Colombia, Universidad Nacional de Colombia, Facultad de Sociologia, 1962.

DIXON, ROLAND B. *The Building of Cultures.* New York: Charles Scribner's Sons, 1928.

DODD, STUART CARTER. "Diffusion is Predictable: Testing Probability Models for Laws of Interaction," *American Sociological Review,* Vol. 20, No. 4 (August, 1955), pp. 392–401.

DODD, STUART CARTER. "Formulas for Spreading Opinions," *Public Opinion Quarterly*, Vol. 22 (1958–1959), pp. 537–54.

DUNCAN, JAMES A., and KREITLOW, BURTON W. "Selected Cultural Characteristics and the Acceptance of Educational Program and Practices," *Rural Sociology*, Vol. 19 (December, 1954), pp. 349–57.

EMERY, FREDERICK EDMUND, and OESER, O. A. *Information, Decision and Action; A Study of the Psychological Determinants of Changes in Farming Techniques.* Victoria, Australia: Melbourne U. Press, 1958.

ERASMUS, CHARLES J. *Man Takes Control: Cultural Development and American Aid.* Minneapolis, Minn.: University of Minnesota Press, 1961.

FALS BORDA, ORLANDO. *Facts and Theory of Sociocultural Change in a Rural Social System.* Monografías Sociologicas, No. 2. Bogotá, Colombia: Bis, Universidad Nacional de Colombia, Facultad de Sociologia, 1960.

FESTINGER, LEON. *A Theory of Cognitive Dissonance.* Harper & Row, 1957.

FLIEGEL, FREDERICK C. "A Multiple Correlation Analysis of Factors Associated with Adoption of Farm Practices," *Rural Sociology*, Vol. 21 (1956), pp. 248–92.

FORSTER, JOHN. "Social Organization and Differential Social Change in Two Hawaiian Communities," *International Journal of Comparative Sociology*, Vol. 3 (December, 1962), pp. 200–20.

GRAHAM, SAXON. "Class and Conservatism in the Adoption of Innovations," *Human Relations*, Vol. 9 (1956), pp. 91–100.

GROSS, NEAL, and TAVES, MARVIN J. "Characteristics Associated with Acceptance of Recommended Farm Practices," *Rural Sociology*, Vol. 14 (1952), pp. 148–56.

HAVENS, A. EUGENE. "A Review of Factors Related to Innovativeness." Columbus, Ohio: Ohio Agricultural Experiment Station, 1962.

HEAD, SYDNEY. *Broadcasting in America: A Survey of Television and Radio.* Boston: Houghton Mifflin Co., 1956.

HERSKOVITS, MELVILLE J. *Acculturation: A Study of Culture Contact.* Locust Valley, New York: J. J. Augustin, Inc., 1938.

———. *Man and His Works.* New York: Alfred A. Knopf, Inc., 1947.

HEYERDAHL, THOR. *Kon-Tiki: Across the Pacific by Raft.* Trans. by F. H. Lyon. Chicago: Rand McNally & Co., 1950.

HILL, REUBEN, BACK, KURT, and STYCOS, J. MAYONE. "Intra-Family Communication and Fertility Planning in Puerto Rico," *Rural Sociology*, Vol. 20 (1955), pp. 258–71.

HOFFER, CHARLES R. *Acceptance of Approved Farming Practices Among Farmers of Dutch Descent.* Michigan Experiment Station Special Bulletin No. 316. East Lansing, Michigan, 1942.

HOFFER, CHARLES R., and STANGLAND, DALE. *Farmers' Reactions to New Practices.* East Lansing, Michigan: Michigan Agricultural Experiment Station, Technical Bulletin No. 264, 1958.

HOGDEN, MARGARET. *Change and History: A Study of the Dated Distribution of Technological Innovations in England.* New York: The Viking Press, Inc., 1952. (Publication in Anthropology No. 18.)

HUDSON, G. F. *Europe and China: A Survey of Their Relations From Earliest Times to 1800.* London: Edward Arnold, Ltd., 1931.

JANIS, IRVING L. "Personality as a Factor in Susceptibility to Persuasion," in Wilbur Schramm (ed.), *The Science of Human Communication.* New York: Basic Books, Inc., 1963. Chap. 5.

KATZ, ELIHU. "The Two-Step Flow of Communication: An Up-to-Date Report on an Hypothesis," *Public Opinion Quarterly*, Vol. 21 (1957), pp. 61–78.

————. "Communication Research and the Image of Society: Convergence of Two Traditions," *American Journal of Sociology*, Vol. 65 (1960), pp. 435–40.

————. "The Social Itinerary of Technical Change; Two Studies on the Diffusion of Innovation," *Human Organization*, Vol. 20, No. 2 (Summer, 1961), pp. 70–82.

————. "Notes on the Unit of Adoption in Diffusion Research," *Sociological Inquiry*, Vol. 32, No. 1 (Winter, 1962), pp. 3–9.

————. "The Diffusion of New Ideas and Practices," in Wilbur Schramm (ed.), *The Science of Human Communication*. New York: Basic Books, Inc., 1963. Chap. 7.

————, and LAZARSFELD, PAUL. *Personal Influence: The Part Played by People in the Flow of Mass Communications*. New York: The Free Press of Glencoe, Inc., 1955.

————, and LEVIN, MARTIN L., and HAMILTON, HERBERT. "Traditions of Research on the Diffusion of Innovation," *American Sociological Review*, Vol. 28 (April, 1963), pp. 237–52.

KLAPPER, JOSEPH T. *The Effects of Mass Media*. New York: Columbia University Bureau of Applied Social Research, 1949.

————. "What We Know About the Effects of Mass Communication," *Public Opinion Quarterly*, Vol. 21 (Winter, 1957), pp. 453–74.

————. *The Effects of Mass Communication*. New York: The Free Press of Glencoe, Inc., 1960.

KROEBER, A. L. "Diffusionism," in R. A. Seligman (ed.), *Encyclopedia of the Social Sciences*. New York: Macmillan Co., 1930–35. Vol. 5.

LANG, KURT, and LANG, GLADYS. *Collective Dynamics*. New York: Thomas Y. Crowell Co., 1961.

LARSEN, OTTO N. "Innovators and Early Adopters of Television," *Sociological Inquiry*, Vol. 32, No. 1 (Winter, 1962), pp. 16–33.

————. "Social Effects of Mass Communication," in Robert E. L. Faris (ed.), *Handbook of Modern Sociology*. Chicago; Rand McNally & Co., 1964. Chap. 10.

LAZARSFELD, PAUL. *Radio and the Printed Page*. New York: Duell, Sloan & Pearce, Inc., 1940.

————. "The Effects of Radio Upon Public Opinion," in Douglas Waples (ed.), *Print, Radio and Film in a Democracy*. Chicago: University of Chicago Press, 1942. Pp. 66–78.

————, and others. *The People's Choice*. New York: Duell, Sloan & Pearce, Inc., 1944.

————, and MERTON, ROBERT K. "Mass Communication, Popular Taste and Organized Social Action," in Lyman Bryson, *The Communication of Ideas*. New York: Harper & Row, 1948. Chap. 7.

LERNER, DANIEL. *The Passing of Traditional Society, Modernizing the Middle East*. New York: The Free Press of Glencoe, Inc., 1958.

LINDSTROM, DAVID E. "Diffusion of Agricultural and Home Economics Practices in a Japanese Rural Community," *Rural Sociology*, Vol. 23, No. 2 (1958), pp. 171–83.

LINTON, RALPH. *The Study of Man*. New York: Appleton-Century-Crofts, Inc., 1936.

———— (ed.). *Acculturation in Seven American Indian Tribes*. New York: Appleton-Century-Crofts, Inc., 1940.

LIONBERGER, HERBERT F. *Adoption of New Ideas and Practices*. Ames, Iowa: Iowa State University Press, 1960.

————. "Needed Research on the Structures of Inter-Personal Communication and Influence in Traditional Societies," in D. T. Myren (ed.), *First Inter-American Symposium on the Role of Communications in Agricultural Development*. Mexico City, 1964.

LIONBERGER, HERBERT F., and COUGHENOUR, C. MILTON. *Social Structure and Diffusion of Farm Information.* Missouri Agricultural Experiment Research Bulletin 631. Columbia, Mo.: 1957.

LOWIE, ROBERT H. *The History of Ethnological Theory.* New York: Holt, Rinehart & Winston, Inc., 1937.

MARSH, C. PAUL, and COLEMAN, A. LEE. "Differential Communication Among Farmers in a Kentucky County," *Rural Sociology,* Vol. 20 (1955), pp. 289–96.

McVOY, EDGAR C. "Patterns of Diffusion in the United States," *American Sociological Review,* Vol. 5 (April, 1940), pp. 219–27.

MENDLESOHN, HAROLD. "Measuring the Process of Communication Effect," *Public Opinion Quarterly,* Vol. 26 (1962), pp. 411–16.

MENZEL, HERBERT. "Innovation, Integration and Marginality," *American Sociological Review,* Vol. 25 (October, 1960), pp. 704–13.

————, COLEMAN, JAMES, and KATZ, ELIHU. "The Diffusion of an Innovation Among Physicians," *Sociometry,* Vol. 20 (December, 1957), pp. 253–70.

MERTON, ROBERT KING. *Social Theory and Social Structure.* Rev. ed. New York: The Free Press of Glencoe, Inc., 1957.

MYREN, D. T. (ed.). *First InterAmerican Research Symposium on the Role of Communications in Agricultural Development.* Mexico City, Mexico, 1964.

NAFZIGER, RALPH O., ENGSTROM, W. C., MACLEAN, JR., M. S. "The Mass Media and an Informed Public," *Public Opinion Quarterly,* Vol. 15 (Spring, 1951), pp. 105–14.

PEDERSON, HAROLD A. "Cultural Differences in the Acceptance of Recommended Practices," *Rural Sociology,* Vol. 16 (1955), pp. 37–49.

PEMBERTON, H. EARL. "The Curve of Culture Diffusion Rate," *American Sociological Review,* Vol. 1 (August, 1936), pp. 547–56. (a)

————. "Culture Diffusion Gradients," *American Journal of Sociology,* Vol. 42 (September, 1936), pp. 226–33. (b)

————. "The Effect of a Social Crisis on the Curve of Diffusion," *American Sociological Review,* Vol. 2 (February, 1937), pp. 55–61.

PERRY, W. J. *Children of the Sun.* London: Methuen & Co., Ltd., 1923.

POLGAR, STEVEN, DUNPHY, HOWARD, and COX, BRUCE. "Diffusion and Farming Devices: A Test of Some Current Notions," *Social Forces,* Vol. 42, No. 1 (October, 1963), pp. 104–11.

RAHIM, S. A. "Diffusion and Adoption of Agricultural Practices—A Study in a Village in East Pakistan," *Technical Publication,* No. 7. Comilla, Pakistan: Pakistan Academy for Village Development, 1961.

————. *The Diffusion and Adoption of Agricultural Practices in a Village in East Pakistan.* Comilla, Pakistan: Pakistan Academy for Village Development, 1961(a).

————. "Voluntary Group Adoption of Power Pump Irrigation in Five East Pakistan Villages," *Technical Publication,* No. 12. Comilla, Pakistan: Pakistan Academy for Village Development, 1961(b).

REDFIELD, ROBERT, LINTON, RALPH, and HERSKOVITS, M. J. "Memorandum on the Study of Acculturation," *American Anthropologist,* Vol. 38 (1936), pp. 149–52.

RILEY, JOHN W., JR., and RILEY, MATILDA WHITE. "Mass Communication and the Social System," in Robert K. Merton, Leonard Broom, Leonard S. Cottrell, Jr. (eds.). *Sociology Today.* New York: Basic Books, Inc., 1958. Chap. 24.

ROGERS, EVERETT M. *Characteristics of Agricultural Innovators and Other Adopter Categories.* Wooster, Ohio: Ohio Agricultural Experiment Station, Research Bulletin 882, 1961.

————. *Diffusion of Innovations.* New York: The Free Press of Glencoe, Inc., 1962.

————, and BEAL, GEORGE M. "The Importance of Personal Influences in the Adoption of Technological Changes," *Social Forces*, Vol. 36 (1958), pp. 329–35.

————, and BURDGE, RABEL J. "Community Norms, Opinion Leadership and Innovativeness Among Truck Growers." Wooster, Ohio: Ohio Agricultural Experiment Station Research Bulletin, 1962.

RYAN, BRYCE. *Social and Ecological Patterns in Farm Leadership of Four Iowa Townships*. Ames, Iowa: Iowa Agricultural Experiment Station, Bulletin 306, 1942.

————. "A Study in Technological Diffusion," *Rural Sociology*, Vol. 13 (1948), pp. 273–85.

————. "The Ceylonese Village and the New Value System," *Rural Sociology*, Vol. 17 (1952), pp. 9–28.

————. *Caste in Modern Ceylon: The Sinhalese System in Transition*. New Brunswick, N. J.: Rutgers University Press, 1953.

————, and GROSS, NEAL. "Diffusion of Hybrid Seed Corn in Two Iowa Communities," *Rural Sociology*, Vol. 8, No. 1 (March, 1943), pp. 15–24.

————. *Acceptance and Diffusion of Hybrid Corn Seed in Two Iowa Communities*. Ames, Iowa: Iowa Agricultural Experiment Station, Research Bulletin No. 372, 1950.

————, JAYASENA, L. D., and WICKREMESINGHE, D. C. R. *Sinhalese Village*. Coral Gables, Fla.: University of Miami Press, 1958.

SAPIR, EDWARD. *Language: An Introduction to the Study of Speech*. New York: Harcourt, Brace and World, Inc., 1921.

————. "Time Perspective in Aboriginal American Culture, A Study in Method," *Memoir*, Vol. 90, No. 13, Anthropological Series, Canadian Geological Survey (Ottawa).

SCHRAMM, WILBUR (ed.). *Mass Communications*. 2nd ed. Urbana, Ill.: University of Illinois Press, 1960.

————. *Mass Media and National Development*. Stanford, Calif.: Stanford University Press and UNESCO, 1964.

SIEGEL, BERNARD, and WAX, ROSE. *Acculturation: Critical Abstracts*. Stanford, Calif.: Stanford University Press, 1955.

SMITH, ELLIOTT. *The Diffusion Controversy*. New York: W. W. Norton & Co., 1927.

————. *In the Beginning: The Origin of Civilization*. London: G. Howe, Ltd., 1928.

SOROKIN, PITIRIM A. *Social and Cultural Mobility*. New York: The Free Press of Glencoe, Inc., 1959.

SPAULDING, IRVING. *Farmer Operator Time Space Orientations and the Adoption of Recommended Farming Practices*. University of Rhode Island, Agricultural Experiment Station Bulletin, 1955.

STRAUS, MURRAY A. "Family Role Differentiation and Technical Change In Farming," *Rural Sociology*, Vol. 25 (June, 1960), pp. 219–28.

TARDE, GABRIEL. *The Laws of Imitation*. Trans. by Elsia Clews Parsons. New York: H. Holt and Co., 1903.

THOMAS, W. I. *Primitive Behavior*. New York: McGraw-Hill Book Co., 1937.

TUMIN, MELVIN. "Exposure to Mass Media and Readiness for Desegregation," *Public Opinion Quarterly*, Vol. 21 (Summer, 1957), pp. 237–51.

VAN DEN BAN, A. W. "Some Characteristics of Progressive Farmers in the Netherlands," *Rural Sociology*, Vol. 22 (1957), pp. 205–12.

WILKENING, EUGENE A. *Acceptance of Improved Farm Practices*. Raleigh, N. C.: North Carolina Agricultural Experiment Station, Technical Bulletin 98, 1952.

————. "Change in Farm Technology as Related to Familism, Family Decision Making and Family Integration," *American Sociological Review*, Vol. 19 (February, 1954), pp. 29–37.

WILKENING, EUGENE A. "Roles of Communicating Agents in Technological Change in Agriculture," *Social Forces,* Vol. 34 (1956), pp. 361–67.

————. "Informal Leaders and Innovators in Farm Practices," *Rural Sociology,* Vol. 18 (1963), pp. 272–75.

————, TULLY, JOAN, and PRESSER, HARTLEY. "Use and Role of Information Sources Among Dairy Farmers of Northern Victoria," paper presented at Rural Sociological Society, August 25–27, 1960.

WISSLER, CLARK. *The Relation of Nature to Man in Aboriginal America.* New York: Oxford University Press, 1926.

CHAPTER 7

ADAMS, RICHARD. "Personnel in Culture Change: A Test of a Hypothesis," *Social Forces,* Vol. 30, No. 2 (December, 1951), pp. 185–89.

BANKS, J. A., and BANKS, OLIVE. "Feminism and Social Change—A Case Study of a Social Movement," in George K. Zollschan and Walter Hirsch (eds.), *Explorations in Social Change.* Boston: Houghton Mifflin Co., 1964. Pp. 547–69.

BARNETT, H. G. *Innovation: The Basis of Cultural Change.* New York: McGraw-Hill Book Co., 1953.

BECKER, HOWARD. *German Youth: Bond or Free.* London: Routledge & Kegan Paul, Ltd., 1946.

BLANKSTEN, GEORGE I. "Revolutions," in Harold Eugene Davis (ed.), *Government and Politics in Latin America.* New York: The Ronald Press Co., 1958. Pp. 119–46.

BLUMER, HERBERT. "Social Movements," in Alfred M. Lee (ed.), *Principles of Sociology.* New York: Barnes & Noble, Inc., College Outline Series, 1951. Chap. 22.

BOISEN, ANTON T. "Economic Distress and Religious Experience: A Study of the Holy Rollers," *Psychiatry,* Vol. 2 (1939), pp. 185–94.

BREWER, KARL D. C. "Sect and Church in Methodism," *Social Forces,* Vol. 30 (May 30, 1952), pp. 400–408.

BRINTON, CRANE. *The Anatomy of Revolution.* Englewood Cliffs, N. J.: Prentice-Hall, Inc., 1952.

BURRIDGE, KENELM. *Nambu: A Melanesian Millennium.* New York: Humanities Press, Inc., 1960.

CANTRILL, HADLEY. *The Psychology of Social Movements.* New York: John Wiley & Sons, Inc., 1941.

CASUSO, TERESA. *Cuba and Castro.* Trans. by Elmer Grossberg. New York: Random House, Inc. 1961.

CHESTER, EDMUND A. *A Sergeant Named Batista.* New York: Holt, Rinehart & Winston, Inc., 1954.

DAVIS, HAROLD E. "The Political Experience of Latin America," in Harold Eugene Davis (ed.), *Government and Politics in Latin America.* New York: The Ronald Press Co., 1958, Chap. 1, pp. 3–25.

DAWSON, CARL A., and GETTYS, WARNER E. *An Introduction to Sociology.* New York: The Ronald Press Co., 1929.

EDMONSON, MUNRO, THOMPSON, DONALD E., CORREA, GUSTAVO, and MADSEN, WILLIAM. *Nativism and Syncretism.* New Orleans, La.: Tulane University, Publication 19, Middle American Research Institute, 1960.

GEERTZ, CLIFFORD (ed.). *Old Societies and New States: The Quest for Modernity in Asia and Africa.* New York: The Free Press of Glencoe, Inc., 1963.

GREEN, ARNOLD. *Sociology: An Analysis of Life in Modern Society.* 2nd ed. New York: McGraw-Hill Book Co., 1956.

———, and MELNICK, ELEANOR. "What Has Happened to the Feminist Movement," in Alvin Ward Gouldner (ed.), *Studies in Leadership: Leadership and Democratic Action.* New York: Harper & Row, 1950. Pp. 277–302.

HAGEN, EVERETT E. *On the Theory of Social Change: How Economic Growth Begins.* Homewood, Ill.: The Dorsey Press, Inc., 1962.

HEBERLE, RUDOLF. *Social Movements: An Introduction to Political Sociology.* New York: Appleton-Century-Crofts, Inc., 1951.

KILLIAN, LEWIS M. "Social Movements," in Robert E. L. Faris (ed.), *Handbook of Modern Sociology.* Chicago: Rand McNally & Co., 1964. Chap. 12.

KING, C. WENDELL. *Social Movements in the United States.* New York: Random House, Inc., 1956.

KORNHAUSER, WILLIAM. *The Politics of Mass Society.* New York: The Free Press of Glencoe, 1959.

LANG, KURT, and LANG, GLADYS ENGEL. *Collective Dynamics.* New York: Thomas Y. Crowell Co., 1961.

LAUE, JAMES H. "A Contemporary Revitalization Movement in American Race Relations: The Black Muslims," *Social Forces,* Vol. 42, No. 3 (March, 1964), pp. 315–23.

LERNER, DANIEL. *The Passing of Traditional Society, Modernizing The Middle East.* New York: The Free Press of Glencoe, Inc., 1958.

LINTON, RALPH. "Nativistic Movements," *American Anthropologist,* Vol. 45 (1943), pp. 230–40.

LIPSET, SEYMOUR. "Leadership in New Social Movements," in Alvin W. Gouldner (ed.), *Studies in Leadership: Leadership and Democratic Action.* New York: Harper & Row, 1950.

MOONEY, JAMES. *The Ghost Dance Religion and the Sioux Outbreak of 1890,"* 14th Annual Report of the Bureau of American Ethnology, Pt. II, Washington, D.C.: Smithsonian Institution, 1892–93.

NEWMAN, FRANZ. *Behemoth: The Structure and Practice of National Socialism.* New York: Oxford University Press, 1942.

O'BRIEN, FREDERICK. *White Shadows in the South Seas.* New York: The Century Co., 1919.

OLDS, VICTORIA M. "Freedom Rides: A Social Movement as an Aspect of Social Change," *Social Work,* Vol. 8, No. 3 (July, 1964), pp. 16–23.

PELTO, PERTI J. "Innovation in an Individualistic Society," paper presented at 59th Meeting of American Anthropological Association. Minneapolis, Minn., November 18, 1960.

PHILLIPS, RUBY HART. *Cuba, Island of Paradox.* New York: Ivan Obolensky, Inc., 1959.

RIVERS, WILLIAM HALSE (ed.). *Essays on the Depopulation of Melanesia.* Cambridge, England: The University Press, 1922.

ROGERS, EVERETT. *Diffusion of Innovations.* New York: The Free Press of Glencoe, Inc., 1962.

RYAN, BRYCE, JAYASENA, L. D., WICKREMESINGHE, D. C. R. *Sinhalese Village.* Coral Gables, Fla.: University of Miami Press, 1958.

SCHIFF, LAWRENCE F. "Dynamic Young Fogies—Rebels on the Right," *Trans-Action* (November, 1966), pp. 31–36.

SHILS, EDWARD A. "Authoritarianism—Right and Left," in R. Christie and Marie Jahoda (eds.), *Studies in the Scope and Method of the Authoritarian Personality.* New York: The Free Press of Glencoe, Inc., 1954.

SILBERMAN, LEO. "Social Entrepreneurship: The Mauritian Case" (mimeo) Chicago: 1955.

SOREL, GEORGES. *Reflections on Violence*. Trans. by T. E. Hulme and J. Roth. New York: The Free Press of Glencoe, Inc., 1950.

SOROKIN, PITIRIM A. *Society, Culture and Personality: Their Structures and Dynamics, A System of General Sociology*. New York: Harper & Row, 1947.

TAYLOR, CARL C. *The Farmers' Movement*. New York: American Book Co., 1953.

TURNER, RALPH H., and KILLIAN, LEWIS M. *Collective Behavior*. Englewood Cliffs, N. J.: Prentice-Hall, Inc., 1957.

VANDER ZANDEN, JAMES. *Race Relation in Transition: The Segregation Crisis in the South*. New York: Random House, Inc., 1965.

VOGET, FRED W. "The American Indian in Transition, Reformation and Accommodation," *American Anthropologist*, Vol. 58 (1956), pp. 249–63.

WALLACE, ANTHONY F. C. "Revitalization Movements," *American Anthropologist*, Vol. 58 (1956), pp. 264–81.

WEBER, MAX. *From Max Weber: Essays in Sociology*. Trans. and edited by H. Gerth and C. Wright Mills. Cambridge, England: Oxford University Press, 1946.

———. *The Theory of Social and Economic Organization*. Trans. by Talcott Parsons. Cambridge, Mass.: Oxford University Press, 1947.

WORSELY, PETER. *The Trumpet Shall Sound: A Study of 'Cargo' Cults in Melanesia*. London, MacGibbon & Kee, 1957.

WRIGGINS, W. HOWARD. *Ceylon: Dilemmas of a New Nation*. Princeton, N. J.: Princeton University Press, 1960.

CHAPTER 8

BAILEY, SHERWIN. *Sexual Ethics: A Christian View*. New York: The Macmillan Co., 1963.

BARNETT, HOMER. *Innovation, The Basis of Cultural Change*. New York: McGraw-Hill Book Co., 1953.

BENEDICT, RUTH. *Patterns of Culture*. New York: Pelican Books, 1946.

BERLE, ALF KEYSER, and DE CAMP, L. SPRAGUE. *Inventions, Patents and their Management*. Princeton, N. J.: D. Van Nostrand Co., 1959.

BROWN, G. GORDON. "Some Problems of Culture Contact with Illustrations from East Africa and Samoa," *Human Organization*, Vol. 16, No. 3 (1957), pp. 11–14.

CHAPLIN, JAMES PATRICK, and KRAWIEC, T. S. *Systems and Theories of Psychology*. New York: Holt, Rinehart & Winston, Inc., 1960.

COHEN, RONALD. "The Success that Failed: An Experiment in Culture Change in Africa," *Anthropologica*, Vol. 3, No. 1 (1961), pp. 21–36.

FAGLEY, RICHARD M. *A Compendium of Statements of Parenthood and the Population Problem*. Geneva, Switzerland: World Council of Churches, 1960(a).

———. *The Population Explosion and Christian Responsibility*. New York: Oxford University Press, 1960(b).

FOSTER, GEORGE McCLELLAND. *Traditional Cultures and the Impact of Technological Change*. New York: Harper & Row, 1962.

HEIMANN, ROBERT K. *Tobacco and Americans*. New York: McGraw-Hill Book Co., 1960.

KATZ, ELIHU. "Note on the Unit of Adoption in Diffusion Research," *Sociological Inquiry*, Vol. 32, No. 1 (Winter, 1962), pp. 3–9.

LESPERANCE, J. P. "Work Study Under Private and Public Enterprise," *Time and Motion Study*, Vol. 11, No. 11 (November, 1962), pp. 22–25.

LINDSEY, JUDGE BENJAMIN, and EVANS, WAINWRIGHT. *The Companionate Marriage*. Garden City, N.Y.: Garden City Publishing Co., 1929.

MACIVER, ROBERT. *Social Causation*. Boston: Ginn & Co., 1942.

MADSEN, WILLIAM. "Hot and Cold in the Universe of San Francisco, Tecospa, Valley of Mexico," *Journal of American Folklore*, Vol. 68 (April–June, 1955), pp. 123–40.

MARRIOTT, McKIM. "Western Medicine in a Village of Northern India," in Benjamin Paul (ed.), *Health, Culture, and Community: Case Studies of Public Reactions to Health Programs*. New York: Russell Sage Foundation, 1957. Chap 9.

MERTON, ROBERT KING, and others. *Mass Persuasion: The Social Psychology of a War Bond Drive*. New York: Harper & Row, 1946.

MOONEY, J. "The Ghost-dance Religion and the Sioux Outbreak of 1890," 14th Annual Report of the *Bureau of American Ethnology*, Pt. II, Washington, D.C.: Smithsonian Institution, 1892–1893.

MUMFORD, LEWIS. *Technics and Civilization*. New York: Harcourt, Brace and World, Inc., 1934.

OGDEN, C. K., and RICHARDS, I. A. *The Meaning of Meaning: A Study of the Influence of Language upon Thought and Science of Symbolism*. 8th ed. New York: Harcourt, Brace and World, Inc., 1946.

PARETO, VILFREDO. *The Mind and Society: A Treatise on General Sociology*. Trans. by Andrew Bongiorno and Arthur Livingston. New York: Dover Publications, Inc., 1963.

PARSONS, TALCOTT. *The Structure of Social Action: A Study in Social Theory with Special Reference to a Group of Recent European Writers*. New York: McGraw-Hill Book Co., 1937.

REDFIELD, ROBERT. *The Primitive World and its Transformations*. Ithaca, New York: Cornell University Press, 1953.

RYAN, BRYCE. "Status, Achievement and Education in Ceylon," *Journal of Asian Studies*, Vol. 20, No. 4 (August, 1961), pp. 463–76.

————, JAYASENA, L. D., and WICKREMESINGHE, D. C. R. *Sinhalese Village*. Coral Gables, Fla.: University of Miami Press, 1958.

SAUNDERS, LYLE. *Cultural Difference and Medical Care: The Case of the Spanish-Speaking People of the Southwest*. New York: Russell Sage Foundation, 1952.

SIMMONS, OZZIE. "The Clinical Team in a Chilean Health Center," in Benjamin Paul (ed.), *Health, Culture and Community: Case Studies of Public Relations to Health Programs*. New York: Russell Sage Foundation, 1957.

SINGH, RUDRA DATT. "The Introduction of Green Manuring in Rural India," in Edward H. Spicer (ed.), *Human Problems in Technological Change: A Casebook*. New York: Russell Sage Foundation, 1952. Case 4.

SPICER, EDWARD H. (ed.). *Human Problems in Technological Change: A Casebook*. New York: Russell Sage Foundation, 1952.

STEIN, WILLIAM W. *Hualcan: Life in the Highlands of Peru*. Ithaca, N. Y.: Cornell University Press, 1961.

STERN, BERNHARD JOSEPH. *Historical Sociology: The Selected Papers of Bernhard J. Stern*. New York: Citadel Press, 1959.

STRAUSSMAN, WOLFGANG PAUL. *Risk and Technological Innovation: American Manufacturing Methods During the Nineteenth Century*. Ithaca, N. Y.: Cornell University Press, 1959.

TAYLOR, ALBION GUILFORD. *Labor Policies of the National Association of Manufacturers*. Urbana, Ill.: University of Illinois, 1928.

THOMAS, WILLIAM ISAAC. *Unadjusted Girl, with Cases and Standpoint for Behavior Analysis*. Boston: Little, Brown & Co., 1923.

THOMAS, WILLIAM ISAAC. *Primitive Behavior, an Introduction to the Social Sciences.* New York: McGraw-Hill Book Co., 1937.

WAX, ROSALIE, and WAX, MURRAY. "The Magical World View," *Journal for the Scientific Study of Religion*, Vol. 1 (April, 1962), pp. 179–88.

CHAPTER 9

ALLEN, FRANCIS R., HART, HORNELL, MILLER, DELBERT C., OGBURN, WILLIAM F., and NIMKOFF, MEYER F. *Technology and Social Change.* New York: Appleton-Century-Crofts, Inc., 1957.

CHILDE, V. GORDON. *What Happened in History.* Middlesex, England: Penguin Books, Ltd., 1942.

COTTRELL, W. FREDERICK. *Energy and Society: The Relation Between Energy, Social Change and Economic Development.* New York: McGraw-Hill Book Co., 1955.

FOSTER, GEORGE M. *Traditional Cultures and the Impact of Technological Change.* Harper & Row, 1962.

FOUNDATION FOR RESEARCH ON HUMAN BEHAVIOR. *Managing Major Change in Organizations.* Ann Arbor, Mich., 1961.

GILFILLAN, S. C. "The Prediction of Inventions," *Technological Trends and National Policy.* Washington, D.C.: National Resources Committee, June 1937, pp. 15–23.

HOLMBERG, ALLAN R. "Adventures in Culture Change," in Robert F. Spencer (ed.). *Method and Perspective in Anthropology.* Minneapolis, Minn.: University of Minnesota Press, 1954. Pp. 103–13.

LOOMIS, CHARLES P. *Social Systems: Essays on Their Persistence and Change.* Princeton, N. J.: D. Van Nostrand Co., 1960.

MARRIOTT, MCKIM. "Western Medicine in a Village of Northern India," in Benjamin Paul, *Health, Culture and Community: Case Studies of Public Reactions to Health Programs.* New York: Russell Sage Foundation, 1957. Chap. 9.

MERTON, ROBERT KING. *Social Theory and Social Structure.* Rev. ed. New York: The Free Press of Glencoe, Inc., 1957.

MYRDAL, GUNNAR, with the assistance of RICHARD STERNER and ARNOLD ROSE. *An American Dilemma.* New York: Harper & Row, 1944.

O'BRIEN, FREDERICK. *White Shadows in the South Seas.* New York: Century Books, Inc., 1920.

PARSONS, TALCOTT. *The Structure of Social Action.* New York: McGraw-Hill Book Co., 1937.

PONSIONEN, J. A. *The Analysis of Social Change Reconsidered: A Sociological Study.* The Hague, Netherlands: Mouton & Co., 1962.

RIVERS, W. H. R. *Essays on the Depopulation of Melanesia.* Cambridge, England: Cambridge University Press, 1922.

RYAN, BRYCE. "Institutional Factors in Sinhalese Fertility," *Milbank Memorial Fund Quarterly*, Vol. 30 (1952), pp. 359–81.

———. "Hinayana Buddhism and Family Planning in Ceylon," in *Interrelations of Demographic Economic and Social Problems in Selected Underdeveloped Areas.* New York: Milbank Memorial Fund, 1954.

———, and STRAUS, MURRAY. *The Integration of Sinhalese Society.* Research Studies of the State College of Washington, Vol. 22, pp. 179–227.

———, JAYASENA, L. D., and WICKREMESINGHE, D. C. R. *Sinhalese Village.* Coral Gables, Fla.: University of Miami Press, 1958.

SAHLINS, MARSHALL D., and SERVICE, ELMAN R. (eds.). *Evolution and Culture.* Ann Arbor, Mich.: University of Michigan Press, 1960.

SCOTT, W. H., HALSEY, A. H., BANKS, J. A., and LUPTON, T. *Technical Change and Industrial Relations: A Study of the Relations Between Technical Change and the Social Structure in a Large Steelworks.* Liverpool, England: Liverpool University Press, 1956.

SHARPE, LAURISTAN. "Steel Axes for Stone Age Australians," in Edward H. Spicer (ed.), *Human Problems in Technological Change: A Casebook.* New York: Russell Sage Foundation, 1952. Case 5.

SMELSER, NEIL H. *Social Change in the Industrial Revolution.* Chicago: University of Chicago Press, 1959.

TAKIZAWA, MATSUYO. *The Penetration of Money Economy in Japan, and Its Effects Upon Social and Political Institutions.* New York: Columbia University Press, 1927.

TAYLOR, FREDERICK WINSLOW. *The Principles of Scientific Management.* New York: Harper & Row, 1911.

WALKER, CHARLES R. *Modern Technology and Civilization: An Introduction to Human Problems in the Machine Age.* New York: McGraw-Hill Book Co., 1962.

WHITE, LESLIE. *The Evolution of Culture.* New York: McGraw-Hill Book Co., 1959.

CHAPTER 10

CEYLON DEPARTMENT OF INFORMATION. *The Health of the Nation.* Ceylon Government, Colombo.

EDMONSON, MONRO S., THOMPSON, DONALD E., CORREA, GUSTAVO, and MADSEN, WILLIAM. *Nativism and Syncretism.* Publication 19, Middle American Research Institute. New Orleans: Tulane University, 1960.

HAMMER-PURGSTALL, S., "Das Kamel," *Denschriften der Kaiser. Akad. der Wissensch. zu Wien (Philos.-Hist. Klasse),* Vol. 6, pp. 1–84. (See William Isaac Thomas, *Primitive Behavior.* New York: McGraw-Hill Book Co., Inc., 1937, pp. 68–69.)

HERSKOVITZ, MELVILLE J. *Man and His Works.* New York: Alfred A. Knopf, Inc., 1948.

HOULT, THOMAS F. *The Sociology of Religion.* New York: The Dryden Press, 1958. Chap. 3.

JOHNSON, ERWIN. "Perseverance Through Orderly Change," *Human Organization,* Vol. 22, No. 3 (1963), pp. 218–23.

LINTON, RALPH. *Study of Man.* New York: Appleton-Century-Crofts, Inc., 1936.

MARRIOTT, McKIM. "Western Medicine in a Village of Northern India," in Benjamin Paul (ed.), *Health, Culture, and Community, Case Studies of Public Reactions to Health Programs.* New York: Russell Sage Foundation, 1957. Chap. 9.

MOFFATT, JAMES. "Syncretism," in James Hastings (ed.). *Encyclopedia of Religion and Ethics.* New York: Charles Scribner's Sons, 1922. Pp. 155–57. Vol. 12.

MOSS, LEONARD, and CAPINARI, STEPHEN. "The Black Madonna: An Example of Cultural Borrowing," *The Scientific Monthly,* Vol. 76 (June, 1953), pp. 319–24.

OPLER, MORRIS E. "The Cultural Definition of Illness in Village India," *Human Organization,* Vol. 22, No. 1 (Spring, 1963), pp. 32–35.

RYAN, BRYCE, JAYASENA, L. D., and WICKREMESINGHE, D. C. R. *Sinhalese Village.* Coral Gables, Fla.: University of Miami Press, 1958.

SAPIR, E. *Language, An Introduction to the Study of Speech.* New York: Harcourt, Brace and World, Inc., 1921.

THOMAS, WILLIAM ISAAC. *Primitive Behavior.* New York: McGraw-Hill Book Co., Inc., 1937.

THOMPSON, DONALD E. "Maya Paganism and Christianity, a History of the Fusion of Two Religions," in Monro S. Edmonson, Donald E. Thompson, Gustavo Correa and William Madsen, *Nativism and Syncretism*. Publication 19, Middle American Research Institute. New Orleans: Tulane University, 1960.

WILSON, GODFREY and WILSON, MONICA. *The Analysis of Social Change Based on Observations in Central Africa*. Cambridge, England: Cambridge University Press, 1945.

CHAPTER 11

ADAMS, HENRY. *Degradation of Democratic Dogma*. Introduction by Brooks Adams. New York: The Macmillan Co., 1919.

BARNES, HARRY ELMER. Review of Arnold Toynbee's *A Study of History*, *American Sociological Review*, Vol. 12, No. 4 (August, 1947), pp. 483–84.

―――. *Historical Sociology, Its Origins and Development: Theories of Social Evolution from Cave Life to Atomic Bombing*. New York: Philosophical Library, Inc., 1948.

―――, and BECKER, HOWARD. *Social Thought from Lore to Science*. Boston: D. C. Heath & Co., 1938.

BECKER, HOWARD. "A Sacred-Secular Evaluation Continuum of Social Change." *Transactions of the Third World Congress of Sociology*. Amsterdam, Holland, 1956. Vol. 6. Pp. 19–41.

―――. "Current Sacred-Secular Theory and Its Development," in Howard Becker and Alvin Boskoff, *Modern Sociological Theory in Continuity and Change*. New York: Holt, Rinehart & Winston, Inc., 1957. Chap. 6.

―――. "Normative Reactions to Normlessness," *American Sociological Review*, Vol. 25, No. 6 (December, 1960), pp. 803–10.

BOBER, MANDELL M. *Karl Marx's Interpretation of History*. Cambridge, Mass.: Harvard University Press, 1948.

BOCK, KENNETH E. *The Acceptance of Histories: Toward a Perspective for Social Science*. Berkeley and Los Angeles, Calif.: University of California Publications in Sociology and Social Institutions, University of California Press, 1956.

BROOM, LEONARD, and SELZNICK, PHILIP. *Sociology: A Text With Adapted Readings*. 3rd Ed. New York: Harper & Row, 1963.

CHAMBLISS, ROLLIN. *Social Thought from Hammurabi to Comte*. New York: The Dryden Press, 1954.

CHILDE, V. GORDON. *Social Evolution*. London: Abelard-Schuman, Ltd., 1951.

COOLEY, CHARLES HORTON. *Social Organization*. New York: Scribner's, 1909.

COSER, LEWIS A., and ROSENBERG, BERNARD (eds.). *Sociological Theory*. New York: The Macmillan Co., 1957.

DURKHEIM, ÉMILE. *The Division of Labor in Society*. Trans. by George Simpson. New York: The Free Press of Glencoe, Inc., 1947 (first published 1893).

―――. *Suicide: A Study in Sociology*. Trans. by J. A. Spaulding and G. Simpson, edited by George Simpson. New York: The Free Press of Glencoe, Inc., 1951 (first published 1897).

ENGELS, FREDERIC. *The Origin of the Family, Private Property and the State*. New York: International Publications Service, 1942.

ETZIONI, AMITAI. *Studies in Social Change*. New York: Holt, Rinehart & Winston, Inc., 1966.

FOSTER, GEORGE. "What is Folk Culture." *American Anthropologist*, Vol. 55 (1953), pp. 159–73.

GEYL, PIETER, TOYNBEE, ARNOLD J., and SOROKIN, PITIRIM A. *The Pattern of the Past: Can We Determine It.* Boston: Beacon Press, Inc., 1949.

HOFSTADTER, RICHARD. *Social Darwinism in American Thought.* Boston: Beacon Press, Inc., 1955.

HOWARD, C. E. *History of Matrimonial Institutions.* Chicago: University of Chicago Press, 1904.

HUGHES, H. STUART. *Oswald Spengler, A Critical Estimate.* New York: Charles Scribner's Sons, 1952.

ISSAWI, CHARLES. *An Arab Philosophy of History: Selections from the Prolegomena of Ibn Khaldun of Tunis.* London: John Murray, Ltd., 1950.

LEVY-BRUHL, LUCIEN. *Primitive Mentality.* Trans. by Lillian A. Clare. London: Geo. Allen & Unwin; New York: The Macmillan Co., 1923.

LEWIS, OSCAR. *Life in a Mexican Village: Tepoztlán Restudied.* Urbana, Ill.: University of Illinois Press, 1951.

———. "Peasant Culture in India and Mexico: A Comparative Analysis," in McKim Marriott (ed.), *Village India: Studies in the Little Community.* American Anthropological Association, Comparative Studies of Culture and Civilization, Memoir no. 83 (June 1955), pp. 145–70.

LOOMIS, CHARLES P. *Rural Social Systems.* Englewood Cliffs, N. J.: Prentice-Hall, Inc., 1950.

LOWIE, ROBERT. *History of Ethnological Theory.* New York: Holt, Rinehart & Winston, Inc., 1937.

MAINE, SIR HENRY SUMNER. *Ancient Law.* London: Oxford University Press, 1931 (first published 1861).

MONTAGU, M. F. ASHLEY (ed.). *Toynbee and History: Critical Essays and Reviews.* Boston: Porter E. Sargent, Inc., 1956.

MORGAN, LEWIS HENRY. *Ancient Society, or Researches in the Lines of Human Progress from Savagery, Through Barbarism to Civilization.* New York: H. Holt and Co., 1877.

PARSONS, TALCOTT. "Evolutionary Universals in Society," *American Sociological Review,* Vol. 29, No. 3 (June, 1964), pp. 339–57.

———. "Some Considerations on the Theory of Social Change," *Rural Sociology,* Vol. 26 (1961), pp. 219–39.

PAUL, BENJAMIN. *Health Culture and Community: Case Studies of Public Reaction to Health Programs.* New York: Russell Sage Foundation, 1955.

REDFIELD, ROBERT. "The Folk Urban Continuum," *American Journal of Sociology,* Vol. 52 (January, 1947), pp. 292–308.

———. *Primitive World and Its Transformations.* Ithaca, N. Y.: Cornell University Press, 1953.

———, and SINGER, MILTON. "The Cultural Role of Cities," *Economic Development and Cultural Change,* Vol. 3 (October, 1954), pp. 53–73.

SMELSER, NEIL. *Social Change in the Industrial Revolution.* Chicago: University of Chicago Press, 1959.

SOROKIN, PITIRIM. *Contemporary Sociological Theories.* New York: Harper & Row, 1928.

———. *Social and Cultural Dynamics.* New York: American Book Co., 1937. 3 volumes.

———. *Society Culture and Personality: Their Structure and Dynamics.* New York: Harper & Row, 1947.

———. "Toynbee's Philosophy of History," in Pieter Geyl, Arnold J. Toynbee and Pitirim A. Sorokin. *The Pattern of the Past: Can We Determine It.* Boston: Beacon Press, Inc., 1949.

SOROKIN, PITIRIM, ZIMMERMAN, CARLE C., and GALPIN, CHARLES J. (eds.). *Systematic Source Book in Rural Sociology*. Minneapolis, Minn.: University of Minnesota Press, 1932. 3 volumes.

SPENCER, HERBERT. *The Principles of Sociology*. New York: Appleton, 1876–1897. 3 volumes.

——. *The Study of Sociology*. New York: Appleton, 1874.

SPENGLER, OSWALD. *The Decline of the West*. Trans. by Charles Francis Atkinson. New York: Alfred A. Knopf, Inc., 1926–1928.

STERN, BERNHARD J. *Historical Sociology: The Selected Papers of Bernhard J. Stern*. New York: Citadel Press, 1959.

STEWARD, JULIAN. "Cultural Causality and Law: A Trial Formulation of the Development of Early Civilizations," *American Anthropologist*, Vol. 52, No. 1 (1949).

——. *Theory of Culture Change: The Methodology of Multilinear Evolution*. Urbana, Ill.: University of Illinois Press, 1955.

TAX, SOL. *Penny Capitalism: A Guatemalan Indian Economy*. Publication of the Institute of Social Anthropology, Bureau of American Ethnology. Washington, D.C.: Smithsonian Institution, 1953.

TÖNNIES, FERDINAND. *Community and Society: Gemeinschaft und Gesellschaft*. Trans. and edited by Charles P. Loomis. East Lansing, Mich.: Michigan State University Press, 1957.

TOYNBEE, ARNOLD. *A Study of History*. Abridgement of Volumes 1–10 by D. C. Somervell. First American ed. New York: Oxford University Press, 1947–1957.

——. *Civilization on Trial*. New York: Oxford University Press, 1948.

VICO, GIAMBATTISTA. *New Science*. Trans. by M. H. Fisch and T. G. Bergin. Ithaca, N. Y.: Cornell University Press, 1948.

VON WIESE, LEOPOLD, and BECKER, HOWARD. *Systematic Sociology*. New York: John Wiley & Sons, Inc., 1932.

WEBER, MAX. *The City*. Trans. by Don Martindale and Gertrud Neuwirth. New York: Crowell-Collier Co., 1962. (Collier Book paperback.)

WESTERMARCK, EDWARD. *A Short History of Marriage*. New York: The Macmillan Co., 1926.

WHITE, LESLIE A. "Energy and the Evolution of Culture," *American Anthropologist*, Vol. 55 (1944), pp. 335–36.

——. *The Science of Culture*. New York: Farrar, Straus & Co., 1949.

——. *The Evolution of Culture*. New York: McGraw-Hill Book Co., 1959.

——, in Marshall D. Sahlins and Elman R. Service (eds.), *Evolution and Culture*. Ann Arbor, Michigan: University of Michigan Press, 1960.

WIRTH, LOUIS. "Urbanism as a Way of Life," *American Journal of Sociology*, Vol. 44, No. 1 (July, 1938).

WOLFF, KURT H. *The Sociology of Georg Simmel*. New York: The Free Press of Glencoe, Inc., 1950.

ZIMMERMAN, CARLE C. *The Changing Community*. New York: Harper & Row, 1938.

CHAPTER 12

BARTON, WILLIAM W. "Automation and Responsibility," in Howard Boone Jacobson and Joseph S. Roucek (eds.), *Automation and Society*. New York: Philosophical Library, Inc., 1959. Chap. 20.

BEADLE, GEORGE. "Genes, Culture and Man," *The Columbia University Forum*, Vol. 8, No. 3 (Fall, 1965), pp. 12–16.

BECKER, HOWARD. *Through Values to Social Interpretation: Essays On Social Contacts, Actions, Types and Prospects.* Durham, N. C.: Duke University Press, 1950.

BENNET, EDWARD, DEGAN, JAMES, and SPIEGEL, JOSEPH. *Human Factors in Technology.* New York: McGraw-Hill Book Co., 1963.

BESS, DONOVAN. "LSD: The Acid Test," *Ramparts,* Vol. 4, No. 12 (April, 1966), pp. 42–50.

BLAUNER, ROBERT. *Alienation and Freedom, The Factory Worker and His Industry.* Chicago: University of Chicago Press, 1964.

BOULDING, KENNETH E. *The Meaning of the Twentieth Century: The Great Transition.* New York: Harper & Row, 1964.

BUCKINGHAM, WALTER. *Automation: Its Impact on Business and People.* New York: Harper & Row, 1961.

CORDINER, RALPH J. "Automation in the Manufacturing Industries," in Howard Boone Jacobson and Joseph S. Roucek, *Automation and Society.* New York: Philosophical Library, Inc., 1959. Chap. 2.

COX, HARVEY. *The Secular City: Secularization and Urbanization in Theological Perspective.* New York: The Macmillan Co., 1965.

CULBERTSON, JAMES T. *The Minds of Robots: Sense Data, Memory Images and Behavior in Conscious Automata.* Urbana, Ill.: University of Illinois Press, 1963.

CULLUMBINE, HARRY. "An Analysis of the Vital Statistics of Ceylon," *The Ceylon Journal of Medical Science,* Vol. 2, Parts 3 & 4 (December, 1950), Colombo, University of Ceylon.

DIEBOLD, JOHN. *Automation: The Advent of the Automative Factory.* Princeton, N. J.: D. Van Nostrand Co., 1952.

ELLUL, JACQUES. *The Technological Society.* New York: Alfred A. Knopf, Inc., 1964.

FALK, HOWARD. Review of Ellul's *The Technological Society* in *Technology and Culture,* Vol. 6 (1965), pp. 534–35.

FAUNCE, WILLIAM A. "The Automobile Industry: A Case Study," in Howard Boone Jacobson and Joseph S. Roucek, *Automation and Society.* New York: Philosophical Library, Inc., 1959. Chap. 4.

FIGUROVSKY, N. A. "The Interaction Between Scientific Research and Technical Invention in the History of Russia," in A. C. Crombie (ed.), *Scientific Change: Historical Studies in the Intellectual, Social and Technical Conditions for Scientific Discovery and Technical Invention from Antiquity to the Present.* Symposium on the History of Science, University of Oxford, July 1961. New York: Basic Books, Inc., 1963.

FRANKEL, CHARLES. "The Third Great Revolution of Mankind," *The New York Times Magazine,* February 9, 1958.

FREDERICKSEN, HAROLD. "Determinants and Consequences of Mortality Trends in Ceylon," *U. S. Public Health Reports,* Vol. 76, No. 8 (1961), pp. 659–64.

FRENCH, J. R. P., Jr. "Employee Participation in a Program of Industrial Change," *Personnel,* Vol. 35, No. 6 (November–December, 1958), pp. 16–29.

GENDELL, MURRAY, and ZETTERBERG, HANS L. (eds.). *A Sociological Almanac for the United States.* New York: Charles Scribner's Sons, 1964.

HAGSTROM, WARREN O. *The Scientific Community.* New York: Basic Books, Inc., 1965.

HART, HORNELL. "Acceleration in Social Change," in Francis Allen, Hornell Hart, Delbert C. Miller, William F. Ogburn and Meyer F. Nimkoff, *Technology and Social Change.* New York: Appleton-Century-Crofts, Inc., 1957. Chap. 3.

IDYLL, CLARENCE P. *Abyss: The Deep Sea and the Creatures that Live in It.* New York: Crowell and Collier, Inc., 1964.

JACOBSON, HOWARD BOONE and ROUCEK, JOSEPH. *Automation and Society*. New York: Philosophical Library, Inc., 1959.

KAPLAN, NORMAN. "Sociology of Science," in Robert E. L. Faris (ed.), *Handbook of Modern Sociology*. Chicago: Rand McNally & Co., 1964. Chap. 22.

LEWIS, OSCAR. *Life in a Mexican Village; Tepoztlán Restudied*. Urbana, Ill.: University of Illinois Press, 1951.

LORIMER, FRANK, and others. *Culture and Human Fertility: A Study of the Relation of Cultural Conditions to Fertility in Non-Industrial and Transitional Societies*. Paris: UNESCO, 1954.

LUNDBERG, GEORGE. *Can Science Save Us*. London: Longmans, Green & Co., Ltd., 1947.

MERTON, ROBERT KING. *Science, Technology and Society in Seventeenth Century England*. *Osiris*, Vol. 4, Bruges, 1938.

MILLER, DELBERT C. "Influence of Technology on Industry," in Francis Allen and others, *Technology and Social Change*. New York: Appleton-Century-Crofts, Inc., 1957. Chap. 11.

MULLENBACK, PHILLIP. *Civilian Nuclear Power, A Report to the President*, U. S. Atomic Energy Commission, 1962.

MURROW, EDWARD R., and FRIENDLY, FRED W. "Automation-Weal or Woe," in Howard Boone Jacobson and Joseph S. Roucek, *Automation and Society*. New York: Philosophical Library, Inc., 1959. Chap. 18.

NATIONAL SCIENCE FOUNDATION. *National Patterns of R & D Resources: Funds and Manpower in the United States 1953–1968*. Washington, D.C., 1967.

NIMKOFF, MEYER. "Biological Discoveries and the Future of the Family: A Reappraisal," *Social Forces*, Vol. 41, No. 2 (December, 1962), pp. 121–26.

NISBET, ROBERT A. *The Quest for Community: A Study in the Ethics of Order and Freedom*. New York: Oxford University Press, 1953.

———. *Man and Technics*, Riecker Memorial Lecture No. 2, *University of Arizona Bulletin*, Vol. 27, No. 1 (January, 1956).

REISS, RICHARD W. Review of Culbertson's *The Minds of Robots* in *Technology and Culture*, Vol. 5, No. 4 (Fall, 1964), pp. 635–38.

POPULATION COUNCIL. "Retention of IUDs: An International Comparison," *Studies in Family Planning*, April, 1967.

ROLT, L. T. C. Review of H. W. Dickenson's *"A Short History of the Steam Engine,"* in *Technology and Culture*, Vol. 6 (Winter, 1965), pp. 115–18.

ROSE, ARNOLD M. *Sociology: The Study of Human Relations*. New York: Alfred A. Knopf, Inc., 1965.

ROSENBLOOM, RICHARD S. "Some 19th Century Analyses of Mechanization," *Technology and Culture*, Vol. 5, No. 4 (1964), pp. 489–511.

SEGAL, SHELDON J. "Report on Research Toward the Control of Fertility," in C. V. Kiser (ed.), *Research in Family Planning*. Princeton, N. J.: Princeton University Press, 1962. Pp. 337–69.

SHOSTAK, ARTHUR B. (ed.). *Sociology in Action: Case Studies in Social Problems and Directed Social Change*. Homewood, Ill.: The Dorsey Press, Inc., 1966.

SINGER, CHARLES J., and others. *A History of Technology*. Oxford, England: Clarendon Press, 1954–1958. 5 volumes.

SNOW, C. P. *The Two Cultures: and a Second Look*. London: Cambridge University Press, 1963.

STERN, JAMES L. "Automation—End or a New Day in Unionism," *The Annals of The American Academy of Poltiical and Social Sciences*, Vol. 350 (November, 1963), pp. 25–35.

STYCOS, J. MAYONE. "The Outlook for Population Growth," *Science,* Vol. 146 (1965), pp. 1435–40.

THOMSON, SIR GEORGE. *The Foreseeable Future.* London: Cambridge University Press, 1957.

VEILLETTE, PAUL T. "The Rise of the Concept of Automation," in Howard Boone Jacobson and Joseph S. Roucek, *Automation and Society.* New York: Philosophical Library, Inc., 1959. Chap. 1.

WALKER, CHARLES H. *Modern Technology and Civilization: An Introduction to Human Problems in the Machine Age.* New York: McGraw-Hill Book Co., 1962.

WHITE, LESLIE A. "Energy and the Evolution of Culture," from *The Science of Culture: A Study of Man and Civilization.* New York: Farrar, Straus & Co., Inc., 1949 (Bobbs Merrill Reprint A-235.)

WHITNEY, VINCENT. "Resistance to Innovation: The Case of Atomic Power," *American Journal of Sociology,* Vol. 56, No. 3 (November, 1950), pp. 247–54.

WIENER, NORBERT. *The Human Use of Human Beings: Cybernetics and Society.* Boston: Houghton Mifflin Co., 1954.

WOODS, R. C. "Scientists and Politics: The Rise of an Apolitical Elite." Columbia University Council for Atomic Age Studies, 1962 (mimeo).

WRONG, DENNIS H. *Population and Society.* 2nd ed. New York: Random House, Inc., 1961.

ZIMMERMAN, CARLE C. "The Population Explosion (Sociological and Ethical Problems)." Fargo, N. D.: Department of Sociology, North Dakota State University, 1967 (mimeo).

CHAPTER 13

ALMOND, GABRIEL A., and VERBA, SIDNEY. *The Civic Culture: Political Attitudes and Democracy in Five Nations.* Princeton, N. J.: Princeton University Press, 1963.

ANDERSON, C. ARNOLD and GRACEY, HARRY L. Review of C. Wright Mills' *The Power Elite, Kentucky Law Journal,* Vol. 46 (Winter, 1958), p. 301.

———, and FOSTER, PHILLIP J. "Discrimination and Inequality in Education," *Sociology of Education,* Vol. 38, No. 1 (Fall, 1964), pp. 1–18.

AXELROD, JOSEPH. "New Patterns of Internal Organization," in Logan Wilson (ed.), *Emerging Patterns in American Higher Education.* Washington, D.C.: American Council on Education, 1965. Pp. 40–61.

AXELROD, NORRIS. "Urban Structure and Social Participation," *American Sociological Review,* Vol. 21 (February, 1956), pp. 14–18.

BAKER, ELIZABETH FAULKNER. *Technology and Women's Work.* New York: Columbia University Press, 1964.

BELL, DANIEL. *The End of Ideology: On the Exhaustion of Political Ideas in the Fifties.* New York: The Free Press of Glencoe, Inc., 1960.

BENEZET, LOUIS T. "College Groups and the Claremont Example," in Logan Wilson (ed.), *Emerging Patterns in American Higher Education.* Washington, D.C.: American Council on Education, 1965. Pp. 199–203.

BENSMAN, JOSEPH, and ROSENBERG, BERNARD. *Mass, Class and Bureaucracy: The Evolution of Contemporary Society.* Englewood Cliffs, N. J.: Prentice-Hall, Inc., 1963.

BERGEL, EGON ERNEST. *Urban Sociology.* New York: McGraw-Hill Book Co., 1955.

BLAU, PETER M., and SCOTT, W. RICHARD. *Formal Organizations.* San Francisco, Calif.: Chandler Publishing Co., 1962.

BOGUE, DONALD J. *Population Growth in Standard Metropolitan Areas, 1900–1950.* Washington, D.C.: Housing and Home Finance Agency, 1953.

BONHAM, GEORGE W. "The Ivory Tower Crumbles," *Saturday Review,* May 21, 1966.

BOSKOFF, ALVIN. *The Sociology of Urban Regions.* New York: Appleton-Century-Crofts, Inc., 1962.

BOULDING, KENNETH E. "Toward a General Theory of Growth," *Canadian Journal of Economics and Political Science,* Vol. 19 (1953), pp. 326–40.

————. *The Meaning of the Twentieth Century: The Great Transition.* New York: Harper & Row, 1964.

BROWN, EDMUND G. "Public Education in California," in Logan Wilson (ed.), *Emerging Patterns in American Higher Education.* Washington, D.C.: American Council on Education, 1965. Pp. 199–203.

BRUBACHER, JOHN S. and RUDY, WILLIS. *Higher Education in Transition: An American History 1636–1956.* New York: Harper & Row, 1958. P. 353.

BRUNNER, EDMUND, HUGHES, GWENDOLYN S., and PATTEN, MARJORIE. *American Agricultural Villages.* Garden City, N. Y.: George H. Doran and Co., 1927.

BURNHAM, JAMES. *The Managerial Revolution: What Is Happening in the World.* New York: The John Day Co., 1961.

BUTLER, BROADUS N. "The Negro Self-Image," in Arnold M. Rose and Caroline B. Rose, *Minority Problems.* New York: Harper & Row, 1965. Pp. 354–60.

CAPEN, SAMUEL P. *The Management of Universities.* Buffalo, N. Y.: Henry Stewart, Inc., 1953.

CAPLOW, THEODORE. *The Academic Market Place.* New York: Basic Books, Inc., 1958.

CAYTON, HORACE R. and DRAKE, ST. CLAIR. *Black Metropolis: A Study of Negro Life in a Northern City.* New York: Harcourt, Brace and World, Inc., 1945.

CHAPIN, F. STUART. *Urban Land Use Planning.* New York: Harper & Row, 1957.

CLOWARD, RICHARD, and OHLIN, LLOYD. *Delinquency and Opportunity: A Theory of Delinquent Gangs.* New York: The Free Press of Glencoe, Inc., 1960.

COATES, CHARLES E., PELLEGRIN, ROLAND J., and HILMAR, NORMAN A. *Military Sociology: A Study of American Military Institutions and Military Life.* University Park, Md.: The Social Science Press, 1965.

COLEMAN, JAMES S. *The Adolescent Society: The Social Life of the Teenager and Its Impact on Education.* New York: The Free Press of Glencoe, Inc., 1961.

CUBER, J. F., and KENKEL, W. F. *Social Stratification in the United States.* New York: Appleton-Century-Crofts, Inc., 1954.

CUMMING, ELAINE, and HENRY, WILLIAM E. *Growing Old: The Process of Disengagement.* New York: Basic Books, Inc., 1961.

DIEKHOFF, JOHN S. *The Domain of the Faculty in Our Expanding Colleges.* New York: Harper & Row, 1956.

DORSEY, EMMETT E. "The American Negro and His Government," *Crisis,* Vol. 68 (October, 1961), pp. 469–78.

DRAKE, JOSEPH T. *The Aged in American Society.* New York: The Ronald Press Co., 1958.

DURKHEIM, ÉMILE. *Suicide: A Study in Sociology.* Trans. by J. A. Spaulding and George Simpson, edited by George Simpson. New York: The Free Press of Glencoe, Inc., 1951 (first published 1897).

EISENSTADT, S. N. *From Generation to Generation: Age Groups and Social Structure.* New York: The Free Press of Glencoe, Inc., 1956.

ELLIOT, T. S. *Notes Toward the Definition of Culture.* New York: Harcourt, Brace and World, Inc., 1949.

ELLUL, JACQUES. *The Technological Society.* New York: Alfred A. Knopf, Inc., 1964.

FABRICANT, SOLOMON. *The Rising Trend of Governmental Activity Since 1900.* New York: National Bureau of Economic Research, 1952.

FERRISS, ABBOTT L. "Data About Teachers, Faculty and Professional Staff," Washington, D.C., 1964 (mimeo). Presented at annual meeting of the ASA, September 3, 1964.

FROMM, ERICH. *Escape From Freedom.* New York: Holt, Rinehart & Winston, Inc., 1941.

GERTH, H. H., and MILLS, C. W. *From Max Weber, Essays in Sociology.* New York: Oxford University Press, 1946.

GIST, NOEL P., and FAVA, SYLVIA FLEIS. *Urban Society.* New York: Thomas Y. Crowell Co., 1966.

GLADFELTER, MILLARD E. "The Pennsylvania Way," in Logan Wilson (ed.), *Emerging Patterns in American Higher Education.* Washington, D.C.: American Council on Education, 1965. Pp. 159–64.

GLENN, NORVAL D. "Some Changes in the Relative Status of American Non-whites, 1940 to 1960," *Phylon,* Vol. 24 (Summer, 1963), pp. 109–22.

GREEN, ARNOLD W., and MELNICK, ELEANOR. "What has Happened to the Feminist Movement," in Alvin W. Gouldner (ed.), *Studies in Leadership: Leadership and Democratic Action.* New York: Harper & Row, 1950. Pp. 277–302.

GREER, SCOTT. *Governing the Metropolis.* New York: John Wiley & Sons, Inc., 1962.

HARLAN, W. H. "Community Adaptations to the Presence of Aged Persons: St. Petersburg, Florida," *American Journal of Sociology,* Vol. 59 (1953), pp. 332–39.

HATT, PAUL K., and REISS, ALBERT J., JR. (eds.). *Cities and Society: The Revised Reader in Urban Sociology.* New York: The Free Press of Glencoe, Inc., 1957.

HAVIGHURST, ROBERT J., and ALBRECHT, RUTH. *Older People.* London: Longmans, Green & Co., 1953.

KAHL, J. A. *The American Class Structure.* New York: Holt, Rinehart & Winston, Inc., 1957.

KERR, CLARK. *The Uses of the University.* Cambridge, Mass.: Harvard University Press, 1964.

KIDD, CHARLES. *American Universities and Federal Research.* Cambridge, Mass.: Harvard University Press, 1959.

KING, JOHN E. "Changes in the State College System," in Logan Wilson (ed.), *Emerging Patterns in American Higher Education.* Washington, D.C.: American Council on Education, 1965. Pp. 74–78.

LANDIS, PAUL. *Making the Most of Marriage.* New York: Appleton-Century-Crofts, Inc., 1960.

LENSKI, G. E. "American Social Classes: Statistical Strata or Social Groups," *American Journal of Sociology,* Vol. 58 (September, 1952), pp. 139–44.

LEPAWSKY, ALBERT. "The London Region: A Metropolitan Community in Crisis," *American Journal of Sociology,* Vol. 46 (May, 1941), pp. 826–34.

LERNER, MAX. *America as a Civilization: Life and Thought in the U.S. Today.* New York: Simon and Schuster, Inc., 1957. Vol. 1.

LEWIS, OSCAR. "Mexico Since Cardenas," in Richard N. Adams and others, *Social Change in Latin America Today.* New York: Random House, 1960. Chap. 6. (Vintage Books.)

LIPMAN, AARON, and SMITH, KENNETH J. "Structural Disengagement and Old-Age." Paper read at the Southern Sociological Society Meeting, Atlanta, Ga., April 1966.

LIPSET, SEYMOUR M., and BENDIX, REINHOLD. *Social Mobility in Industrial Society.* London: William Heinemann, Ltd., 1960.

LOHMAN, J. D., and REITZES, D. C. "Deliberately Organized Groups and Racial Behavior," *American Sociological Review*, Vol. 19 (June, 1954), pp. 342–44.

————. "Note on Race Relations in Mass Society," *American Journal of Sociology*, Vol. 58 (November, 1952), pp. 240–46.

McCONNELL, T. R. "The Coordination of State Systems of Higher Education," in Logan Wilson (ed.), *Emerging Patterns in American Higher Education.* Washingington, D.C.: American Council on Education, 1965.

MacDONALD, DWIGHT. "A Theory of Mass Culture," *Diogenes*, No. 3 (Summer, 1953), pp. 1–17.

MAYER, KURT B. "The Changing Shape of the American Class Structure," *Social Research*, Vol. 30, No. 4 (Winter, 1963), pp. 458–68.

MERTON, ROBERT KING. "Anomie, Anomia, and Social Interaction: Contexts of Deviant Behavior," in Marshall B. Clinard (ed.), *Anomie and Deviant Behavior: A Discussion and Critique.* New York: The Free Press of Glencoe, Inc., 1964. Pp. 213–42.

————. *Social Theory and Social Structure.* Rev. ed. New York: The Free Press of Glencoe, Inc., 1957.

————, GRAY, A. P., HOCKEY, B., and SELVIN, H. G. (eds.). *Reader in Bureaucracy.* New York: The Free Press of Glencoe, Inc., 1952.

MICHELS, ROBERT. *Political Parties.* Trans. by Eden Paul and Cedar Paul. New York: The Free Press of Glencoe, Inc., 1949.

MILLER, DELBERT C., and FORM, WILLIAM H. *Industrial Sociology: The Sociology of Work Organization.* New York: Harper & Row, 1964.

MILLS, C. WRIGHT. *The Power Elite.* New York: Oxford University Press, 1956.

MUMFORD, LEWIS. *The Culture of Cities.* New York: Harcourt, Brace and World, Inc., 1938.

ORTEGA Y GASSET, JOSÉ. *The Revolt of the Masses.* London: George Allen & Unwin, 1951.

PARK, ROBERT E., BURGESS, ERNEST W., and McKENZIE, RODERICK D. (eds.). *The City.* Chicago: University of Chicago Press, 1925.

PARKINSON, C. NORTHCOTE. *Parkinson's Law and Other Studies in Administration.* Boston: Houghton Mifflin Co., 1957.

PARSONS, TALCOTT. *The Structure of Social Action.* New York: McGraw-Hill Book Co., 1937.

————. *The Social System.* New York: The Free Press of Glencoe, Inc., 1951.

POWELL, ELWIN H. "The American City and Anomie," *British Journal of Sociology*, Vol. 13, No. 2 (June, 1962), pp. 156–66.

QUEEN, STUART A., and CARPENTER, DAVID B. *The American City.* New York: McGraw-Hill Book Co., 1953.

REDFIELD, ROBERT, and SINGER, MILTON. "The Cultural Role of Cities," *Journal of Economic Development and Cultural Change*, Vol. 3 (October, 1954), pp. 53–73.

RIESMAN, DAVID. "The Saving Remnant," in J. W. Chase (ed.), *The Years of the Modern.* New York: David McKay Co., 1949. Pp. 115–47.

————, with GLAZER, N., and DENNEY, R. *The Lonely Crowd: A Study of the Changing Character of American Society.* New York: Doubleday & Co., Inc., 1955.

ROETHLISBERGER, F. J., and DICKSON, W. J. *Management and the Worker.* Cambridge, Mass.: Harvard University Press, 1940.

ROSENBERG, BERNARD, and WHITE, DAVID (eds.). *Mass Culture: The Popular Arts in America*. New York: The Free Press of Glencoe, Inc., 1957.

ROSOW, IRVING. "Retirement Housing and Social Integration," in Clark Tibbitts and Wilma Donahue (eds.), *Social and Psychological Aspects of Aging*. New York: Columbia University Press, 1962.

SANDERSON, ROSS W. *The Church Serves the Changing City*. New York: Harper & Row, 1955.

SCHALLER, LYLE E. "Centralization-Decentralization in Formal Organization: A Case Study of American Protestant Denominations," *Review of Religious Research*, Vol. 5, No. 1 (Fall, 1963), pp. 5–11.

————. *Planning for Protestantism in Urban America*. Nashville, Tenn.: Abingdon Press, 1965.

SHILS, EDWARD. "Daydreams and Nightmares: Reflections on the Criticism of Mass Culture," *Sewanee Review*, Vol. 65 (Autumn, 1957), pp. 587–608.

————, and JANOWITZ, MORRIS. "Cohesion and Disintegration in the Wehrmacht in World War II," *Public Opinion Quarterly* (Summer, 1948), pp. 280–315.

SIMPSON, GEORGE EATON, and YINGER, J. MILTON. *Racial and Cultural Minorities: An Analysis of Prejudice and Discrimination*. New York: Harper & Row, 1965.

SJOBERG, GIDEON. *The Pre-Industrial City, Past and Present*. New York: The Free Press of Glencoe, Inc., 1960.

SOFEN, EDWARD. *The Miami Metropolitan Experiment*. Bloomington, Ind.: Indiana University Press, 1963.

SOROKIN, PITIRIM. *Social Mobility*. New York: Harper & Row, 1927.

————. *Society, Culture and Personality*. New York: Harper & Row, 1947.

————, and ZIMMERMAN, CARLE C. *Principles of Rural-Urban Sociology*. New York: Henry Holt & Co., 1929.

STEPHENS, WILLIAM N. *The Family in Cross-Cultural Perspective*. New York: Holt, Rinehart & Winston, Inc., 1963.

SVALSTOGA, KAARE. *Social Differentiation*. New York: David McKay Co., Inc., 1965. (McKay Social Science Series.)

TARTLER, RUDOLF. "The Older Person in Family, Community and Society," in Richard W. Williams, Clark Tibbitts, and Wilma Donahue (eds.), *Processes of Aging: Social and Psychological Perspectives*. New York: Atherton Press, 1963. Vol. 2, chap. 32.

TAYLOR, M. LEE, and JONES, JR., ARTHUR R. *Rural Life and Urbanized Society*. New York: Oxford University Press, 1964.

TIBBITTS, CLARK, and DONAHUE, WILMA (eds.). *Social and Psychological Aspects of Aging*. New York: Columbia University Press, 1962.

TÖNNIES, FERDINAND. *Community and Society–Gemeinschaft und Gesellschaft*. Trans. and introduced by Charles P. Loomis. East Lansing, Mich.: Michigan State University Press, 1957.

UNITED STATES CENSUS BUREAU. *Census of Population, 1960*. Vol. I, Part A. Washington, D.C.: U. S. Government Printing Office, 1961.

UNITED STATES DEPARTMENT OF HEALTH, EDUCATION AND WELFARE. *1965, Year of Legislative Achievement*. Washington, D.C.: U. S. Government Printing Office, 1966.

U. S. News and World Report, "Can the Big Cities Come Back," July 19, 1957, pp. 72–89.

WARNER, W. LLOYD. *The Status System of a Modern Community*. New Haven, Conn.: Yale University Press, 1942.

————, and LUNT, PAUL S. *The Social Life of a Modern Community*. New Haven, Conn.: Yale University Press, 1941.

WEBER, ADNA. *The Growth of Cities in the 19th Century: A Study in Statistics.* Ithaca, N. Y.: Cornell University Press. 1963.

WEBER, MAX. *The Theory of Social and Economic Organization.* Trans. by A. M. Henderson and Talcott Parsons, edited by Talcott Parsons. New York: Oxford University Press, 1947.

WILENSKY, HAROLD L. "Life Cycle, Work Situation and Participation in Formal Associations," in Clark Tibbitts and Wilma Donahue (eds.), *Social and Psychological Aspects of Aging.* New York: Columbia University Press, 1957. Pp. 919–30.

WILLIAMS, RICHARD, TIBBITTS, CLARK, and DONOHUE, WILMA (eds.). *Social Processes of Aging.* New York: Atherton Press, 1963. 2 volumes.

WILLIAMS, ROBIN M., JR. *American Society: A Sociological Interpretation.* New York: Alfred A. Knopf, Inc., 1963.

WILLIAMS, VIRGIL. "Bureaucratic Proliferation, A Theoretical Approach," *American Journal of Economics and Sociology,* Vol. 22, No. 3 (July, 1963), pp. 337–46.

WILSON, GODFREY and WILSON, MONICA. *The Analysis of Social Change Based On Observations in Central Africa.* Cambridge, England: Cambridge University Press, 1954.

WILSON, LOGAN. "Form and Function in American Higher Education," in Logan Wilson (ed.), *Emerging Patterns in American Higher Education.* Washington, D.C.: American Council on Education, 1965. Pp. 29–37.

WIRTH, LOUIS. "Urbanism as a Way of Life," *American Journal of Sociology,* Vol. 44, No. 2 (July, 1938), pp. 1–24.

WOLFF, KURT H. *The Sociology of Georg Simmel.* New York: The Free Press of Glencoe, Inc., 1950.

WRIGHT, CHARLES R. and HYMAN, HERBERT H. "Voluntary Association Memberships of American Adults: Evidence From National Sample Surveys," *American Sociological Review,* Vol. 23 (June, 1958), pp. 284–94.

YOUNG, DONALD. *Research Memorandum on Minority Groups in the Depression.* New York: Social Science Research Council, 1937.

ZIMMERMAN, CARLE C. *The Changing Community.* New York: Harper & Row, 1938.

———. "The County in the United States of America, Its Nature, Origin, Changes and Reform," Barcelona, Spain: Institute de Ciencias Sociales, 1966.

———, and CERVANTES, LUCIUS F. *Marriage and the Family: A Text for Moderns.* Chicago: The Henry Regnery Co., 1956.

ZORBAUGH, HARVEY (ed.). *The Gold Coast and the Slum.* Chicago: University of Chicago Press, 1929.

CHAPTER 14

ABEGGLEN, JAMES. *The Japanese Factory: Aspects of Its Social Organization.* New York: The Free Press of Glencoe, Inc., 1958.

ABU-LUGHOD, JANET. "Migrant Adjustment to City Life: The Egyptian Case," *American Journal of Sociology,* Vol. 67 (July, 1961), pp. 22–32.

ALMOND, GABRIEL A., and VERBA, SIDNEY. *The Civic Culture: Political Attitudes and Democracy in Five Nations.* Princeton, N. J.: Princeton University Press, 1963.

APTER, DAVID E. "Political Religion in the New Nations," in Clifford Geertz (ed.), *Old Societies and New States: The Quest for Modernity in Asia and Africa.* New York: The Free Press of Glencoe, Inc., 1963.

BERRY, BRIAN J. "An Inductive Approach to the Regionalization of Economic Development," in Norton Ginsburg (ed.), *Essays on Geography and Economic Development.* Chicago: University of Chicago Press, 1960.

BOWMAN, MARY JEAN, and ANDERSON, C. ARNOLD. "Concerning the Role of Education in Development," in Clifford Geertz (ed.), *Old Societies and New States: The Quest for Modernity in Asia and Africa.* New York: The Free Press of Glencoe, Inc., 1963.

BRAIBANTI, RALPH, and SPENGLER, JOSEPH J. (eds.). *Tradition, Values and Socio-Economic Development.* Durham, N. C.: Duke University Press, 1961.

BUSIA, K. A. "Social Survey of Sekondi-Takoradi," *Social Implications of Industrialization and Urbanization in Africa South of the Sahara.* Paris: UNESCO, 1956. Pp. 74–86.

COMPHAIRE, JEAN L. "Economic Change and the Extended Family," *Annals of American Academy of Political and Social Sciences,* Vol. 305 (May, 1956), pp. 45–52. (*Agrarian Societies in Transition,* edited by Bert F. Hoselitz).

CUMPER, G. E. "Commitment, Class and the Ex-Colonies," *Co-Existence,* Vol. 3 (May, 1965), pp. 33–39.

DAVIS, KINGSLEY. "Urbanization and Development of Pre-Industrial Areas," *Economic Development and Cultural Change,* Vol. 3, No. 1 (October 1954).

EISENSTADT, S. N. "Transformation of Social, Political and Cultural Orders in Modernization," *American Sociological Review,* Vol. 30, No. 5 (October, 1965), pp. 659–73.

ERASMUS, CHARLES J. *Man Takes Control: Cultural Development and American Aid.* Minneapolis, Minn.: University of Minnesota Press, 1961.

FALLERS, LLOYD. "Are African Cultivators to be Called Peasants," *Current Anthropology,* Vol. 12 (1961), pp. 108–10.

————. "Equality, Modernity and Democracy in the New States," in Clifford Geertz (ed.), *Old Societies and New States: The Quest for Modernity in Asia and Africa.* New York: The Free Press of Glencoe, Inc., 1963.

FARIS, ROBERT E. L. *Handbook of Modern Sociology.* Chicago: Rand McNally and Co., 1964.

FOSTER, GEORGE W. *Traditional Cultures and the Impact of Technological Change.* New York: Harper & Row, 1962.

FREEDMAN, RONALD, TAKESHITA, JOHN Y., and SUN, T. H. "Fertility and Family Planning in Taiwan: A Case Study of the Demographic Transition," *American Journal of Sociology,* Vol. 70, No. 1 (July, 1964), pp. 16–27.

FURNIVAL, J. S. *Netherlands India: A Study of Plural Economy.* Cambridge, England: Cambridge University Press, 1939.

GEERTZ, CLIFFORD (ed.). *Old Societies and New States: The Quest for Modernity in Asia and Africa.* New York: The Free Press of Glencoe, Inc., 1963.

HAUSER, PHILIP M. (ed.), "World Urbanization," *American Journal of Sociology,* Vol. 40, No. 5 (March, 1955).

————. "Observations on the Urban-Folk and Urban-Rural Dichotomies as Forms of Western Ethnocentrism," in Philip M. Hauser and Leo F. Schnore (eds.), *The Study of Urbanization.* New York: John Wiley & Sons, Inc., 1965. Pp. 503–17.

HAVENS, A. EUGENE. "The Relationship Between Two Land Tenure Systems and Agrarian Reform Programs in Latin America." Paper presented to the XV Annual Mexican Sociological Meeting, Tepec, Mexico, October, 1964.

HELLMAN, E. "Rooiyard: A Sociological Survey of an Urban Native Slum Yard," in *Social Implications of Industrialization and Urbanization in Africa South of the Sahara.* Paris: UNESCO, 1956. Pp. 179–90.

————. "The Development of Social Groupings Among Urban Africans in the

Union of South Africa," *Social Implications of Industrialization and Urbanization in Africa South of the Sahara*. Paris: UNESCO, 1956. Pp. 724–43.

HOROWITZ, IRVING LOUIS. *Three Worlds of Development: Theory and Practice of International Stratification*. New York: Oxford University Press, 1966.

HOSELITZ, BERT. *Sociological Aspects of Economic Growth*. New York: The Free Press of Glencoe, Inc., 1960.

————, and WEINER, MYRON. "Economic Development and Political Stability in India," *Dissent*, Spring, 1961. Reprint No. 12, University of Chicago, Committee on Southern Asian Studies.

HOYT, E. "The Impact of Money Economy on Consumption Patterns," *Annals of the American Academy of Political and Social Sciences*, Vol. 305 (May, 1956), pp. 12–22. (*Agrarian Societies in Transition*, edited by Bert Hoselitz)

INKELES, ALEX. "Summary and Review: Social Stratification in the Modernization of Russia," in Cyril E. Black (ed.), *The Transformation of Russian Society*. Cambridge, Mass.: Harvard University Press, 1960.

INTERNATIONAL BANK FOR FINANCE AND RECONSTRUCTION. *The Economic Development of Ceylon*. Baltimore, Md.: Johns Hopkins Press, 1953.

JACOBS, NORMAN. *Sociology of Development: Iran as an Asian Case Study*. New York: Frederick A. Praeger Inc., 1966.

KERR, CLARK. "Changing Social Structures," in Wilbert Moore and Arnold S. Feldman (eds.), *Labor Commitment and Social Change in Developing Areas*. New York: Social Science Research Council, 1960. Chap. 19.

LAMBERT, RICHARD D. *Workers, Factories, and Social Change in India*. Princeton, N. J.: Princeton University Press, 1963.

LERNER, DANIEL. *Passing of Traditional Society: Modernizing the Middle East*. New York: The Free Press of Glencoe, Inc., 1958.

LEWIS, OSCAR. *Life in a Mexican Village, Tepoztlán Restudied*. Urbana, Ill.: University of Illinois Press, 1951.

————. "Further Observations on the Folk-Urban Continuum and Urbanization with Special Reference to Mexico City," in Philip M. Hauser and Leo F. Schnore (eds.), *The Study of Urbanization*. New York: John Wiley & Sons, Inc., 1965. Pp. 491–502.

LINTON, RALPH. "Cultural and Personality Factors Affecting Economic Growth," in Bert F. Hoselitz, *The Progress of Underdeveloped Areas*. Chicago: University of Chicago Press, 1952.

———— (ed.). *Most of the World: The Peoples of Africa, Latin America and the East Today*. New York: Columbia University Press, 1949.

LIPMAN, AARON. *The Colombian Entrepreneur*. Coral Gables, Fla.: University of Miami Press, 1968.

LORIMER, FRANK, and others. *Culture and Human Fertility*. Paris: UNESCO, 1954.

MAINE, HENRY SUMNER. *Ancient Law*. London: Oxford University Press, 1931 (first published 1861).

MALENBAUM, WILFRED, and STOLPER, WOLFGANG. "Political Ideology and Economic Progress," *World Politics*, Vol. 12, No. 3 (April, 1960), pp. 413–21.

MANGIN, WILLIAM P. "Mental Health and Migration to Cities: A Peruvian Case," in Dwight B. Heath and Richard N. Adams (eds.), *Contemporary Cultures and Societies of Latin America*. New York: Random House, Inc., 1965. Pp. 546–55.

MARCSON, SIMON. "Social Change and Social Structure in Transitional Societies," *International Journal of Comparative Sociology*, Vol. 1, No. 2 (September, 1960), pp. 248–53.

MELADY, THOMAS PATRICK. "The Sweep of Nationalism in Africa," *The Annals of the American Academy of Political and Social Science*, Vol. 354 (July, 1964), pp. 91–96. (*Africa in Motion*, edited by James C. Charlesworth.)

MOORE, WILBERT. "The Social Framework of Economic Development," in Ralph Braibanti and Joseph J. Spengler (eds.), *Tradition, Values, and Socio-Economic Development*. Durham, N. C.: Duke University Press, 1961. Chap. 2.

———. *Social Change*. Englewood Cliffs, N. J.: Prentice-Hall, Inc., 1963.

———. "Social Aspects of Economic Development," in Robert E. L. Faris (ed.), *Handbook of Sociology*. Chicago: Rand McNally & Co., 1964. Chap. 23.

———, and FELDMAN, ARNOLD S. (eds.). *Labor Commitment and Social Change in Developing Areas*. New York: Social Science Research Council, 1960.

MORRIS, DAVID. "The Labor Market in India," in Wilbert E. Moore and Arnold S. Feldman (eds.), *Labor Commitment and Social Change in Developing Areas*. New York: Social Science Research Council, 1960. Chap. 10.

NASH, MANNING. "Kinship and Voluntary Associations," in Wilbert E. Moore and Arnold S. Feldman (eds.), *Labor Commitment and Social Change in Developing Areas*. New York: Social Science Research Council, 1960. Chap. 17.

NEALE, WALTER C. "Must Agriculture Come First," *Co-Existence*, Vol. 3 (May, 1965), pp. 40–48.

NIEHOFF, ARTHUR. "Theravada Buddhism: A Vehicle for Technical Change," *Human Organization*, Vol. 23, No. 2 (Summer, 1964), pp. 108–12.

OKIGHO, PIUS. "Social Consequences of Economic Development in West Africa," *The Annals of the American Academy of Political and Social Sciences*, Vol. 305 (May, 1956), pp. 125–33 (*Agrarian Societies in Transition*, edited by Bert F. Hoselitz).

OPLER, MORRIS E., and SINGH, RUDRA DATT, "Economic, Political and Social Change in a Village of North India," *Human Organization*, Vol. 11, No. 2 (Summer, 1952), pp. 5–12.

PARKER, M. "Political and Social Aspects of Municipal Government in Kenya," in *Social Implications of Industrialization and Urbanization in Africa South of the Sahara*. Paris: UNESCO, 1956. Pp. 127–31.

REDFIELD, ROBERT. *Folk Culture of Yucatan*. Chicago: University of Chicago Press, 1941.

———. *The Primitive World and Its Transformation*. Ithaca, N. Y.: Cornell University Press, 1953.

———. *Peasant Society and Culture*. Chicago: University of Chicago Press, 1956.

ROSTOW, WALT W. *The Stages of Economic Growth: A Non-Communist Manifesto*. Cambridge, England: Cambridge University Press, 1960.

RYAN, BRYCE. *Caste in Modern Ceylon*. New Brunswick, N. J.: Rutgers University Press, 1953.

———. "Primary and Secondary Contacts in a Ceylonese Peasant Community," *Rural Sociology*, Vol. 17 (1952), pp. 311–21.

———. "Status, Achievement, and Education in Ceylon: An Historical Perspective," *Journal of Asian Studies*, Vol. 20, No. 4 (August, 1961), pp. 463–76.

———, and FERNANDO, SYLVIA. "The Female Factory Worker in Colombo," *International Labor Review*, Vol. 64, Nos. 5–6 (November–December, 1951), pp. 438–61.

———, JAYASENA, L. D., and WICKREMESINGHE, D. C. R. *Sinhalese Village*. Coral Gables, Fla.: University of Miami Press, 1958.

SCHULER, EDGAR A., and SCHULER, KATHRYN R. *Public Opinion and Constitution Making in Pakistan, 1958–1962*. East Lansing, Mich.: Michigan State University Press, 1967.

SHILS, EDWARD. "Tradition and Liberty: Antinomy and Interdependence," *Ethics*, Vol. 68, No. 3 (1958), pp. 153–65.

———. "The Intellectuals in the Political Development of The New States," *World Politics*, Vol. 12 (October, 1959–July 1960), pp. 329–68.

SILVERT, H. P. "National Values, Development, and Leaders and Followers: A Summary Statement of Theory, Some Research, and Some Implications," *International Social Science Journal*, Vol. 15, No. 4 (1963), pp. 560–70.

SJOBERG, GIDEON. "The Rural-Urban Dimension in Pre-Industrial, Transitional and Industrial Societies," in Robert E. L. Faris (ed.), *Handbook of Modern Sociology*. Chicago: Rand McNally & Co., 1964. Chap. 4.

SMITH, ROBERT J. "Comparative Studies in Anthropology of the Interrelations between Social and Technological Change," *Human Organization*, Vol. 16, No. 1 (Spring, 1951), pp. 30–36.

SMITH, T. LYNN. "Values Held by People in Latin America which Affect Technical Cooperation," *Rural Sociology*, Vol. 21, No. 1 (March, 1956), pp. 68–76.

SMITHERS, ROBERT R. "Breaking Through the Traditional Village Society," *Community Development Review*, Vol. 2, No. 17 (June, 1963), pp. 55–60.

SPENGLER, J. "Economic Development: Political Preconditions and Political Consequences," *Journal of Politics*, Vol. 22 (August, 1960), pp. 387–416.

TAMBIAH, S. J., and RYAN, BRYCE. "The Secularization of Family Values in Ceylon," *American Sociological Review*, Vol. 22, No. 3 (June, 1957), pp. 292–99.

TAX, SOL (ed.). *Heritage of Conquest*. New York: The Free Press of Glencoe, Inc., 1952.

TUMIN, MELVIN. "Competing Status Systems," in Wilbert E. Moore and Arnold S. Feldman (eds.), *Labor Commitment and Social Change in Developing Areas*. New York: Social Science Research Council, 1960. Chap. 15.

TURNER, RALPH E. "The Nature of the Crisis," *Saturday Review of Literature*, Vol. 34, No. 31 (August 4, 1951), pp. 16ff.

VANDIVER, JOSEPH S. "Problems Encountered in the Planning and Development of an Educational Program in an Underdeveloped Country (Ethiopia)." Gainesville, Fla.: University of Florida, 1964 (mimeo).

UNESCO. *Implications of Industrialization and Urbanization in Africa South of the Sahara*. Paris: UNESCO, 1956.

WILSON, GODFREY, and WILSON, MONICA. *The Analysis of Social Change Based on Observations in Central Africa*. Cambridge, England: Cambridge University Press, 1954.

WISER, WILLIAM HENDRICKS. *Hindu Jajmani System: A Socio-economic System Interrelating Members of a Hindu Village Community in Services*. Lucknow, India: Lucknow Publishing House, 1936.

WRIGGINS, WILLIAM HOWARD. *Ceylon: Dilemmas of a New Nation*. Princeton, N. J.: Princeton University Press, 1960.

WRONG, DENNIS H. *Population and Society*. New York: Random House, Inc., 1961.

———. "Population Myths," *Commentary*, Vol. 38, No. 5 (November, 1964), pp. 61–64.

Name Index

Subject Index

Acceleration, age of, 353–354; *see also* Cultural acceleration, theory of
  in cybernetics and automation, 341–344
  in knowledge, 324–326
  in transport and communication, 344–346
Accommodation, as innovative process, 118–120, 125, 135; *see also* Integration, of innovation
Acculturation, 126, 128–129, 131
  and diffusion, 141, 142n
Achievement orientation, 35–36
  in developing societies, 428–429, 435
Adopters; *see* Innovators
Aesthetics, affecting response to innovation, 214, 240–241
Afghanistan, response to innovation, 254
Africa, 137, 148
  developmental processes in, 423–424, 426–427
Age-area theory, 140–141
Aging, and disengagement, 385–387
  as factor in social change, 58, 62–63, 350
Agribusiness, 360
  trends in number and size of farms, 374 (chart), 375
Alienation
  in developing societies, 431
  as force for change, 38–40
  in modern society, 381–383
  and social movements, 203–205, 212
Alternatives, cultural, 262; *see also* Functional equivalence in innovations; Integration, of innovation
  innovations integrated as, 276–282
  meaning of concept, 274–276
American Indians, 82, 105, 127
  economic aspirations (Middle American), 433
  ghost dance, 188–189
  syncretism among (Middle American), 285–288

world view, 220–222
  Middle American, 229–230
Anomie, in developing societies, 430
  as force for change, 38–39, 114, 115
  in modern society, 383–384
  in social movements, 212
Anthropology, and unilinear evolution, 306–308
Apollo program, and innovative stimuli, 25
Asia
  Chinese dispersion in, 125
  diffusion in, 148, 165, 254, 348
  mass media in, 148
  revitalistic movements in, 189, 205
  source of inventions, 82, 105, 106, 137, 249
Assembly line, invention of, 102
Assimilation, lack of by Chinese, 125
  in Israel, 125–127
  in U. S., 125–126, 142n
Associations, differentiation in, 369–370, 400
  growth in developing societies, 425–448
  growth in modern society, 368–369, 370–371, 400
  and social movements, 176
  in traditional societies, 222
Atom bomb, 65, 83, 334–335
Atomic energy; *see* Energy sources, significance for change
Authority; *see* Social power
Automation, 239; *see also* Cybernetics
  meaning, 338, 340
  operation of, 339–340
  social significance, 341–344
Automobile, 99, 101–102, 105
Autonomous person, 117
Ayurvedic medicine, 229
  as specialized alternative, 277, 279, 280, 281

Biological determinism, 24–27, 30, 49